Society, Culture, and the State
in Germany, 1870–1930

review: Wehler

Central Eur History

Social History, Popular Culture, and Politics in Germany
Geoff Eley, Series Editor

Society, Culture, and the State in Germany, 1870–1930

Geoff Eley, editor

Ann Arbor
THE UNIVERSITY OF MICHIGAN PRESS

First paperback edition 1997
Copyright © by the University of Michigan 1996
All rights reserved
Published in the United States of America by
The University of Michigan Press
Manufactured in the United States of America
♾ Printed on acid-free paper

2000   1999   1998   1997   4   3   2   1

A CIP catalog record for this book is available from the British Library.

Library of Congress Cataloging-in-Publication Data

Society, culture, and the state in Germany, 1870–1930 / Geoff Eley, editor.
    p. cm. — (Social history, popular culture, and politics in Germany)
    Includes bibliographical references and index.
    ISBN 0-472-10627-9 (alk. paper)
    1. Germany—Social life and customs. 2. Germany—Social
Conditions. 3. Germany—Intellectual life. 4. Women—Germany—
Social conditions. 5. Germany—Politics and
government—1871–1918. 6. Germany—Politics and
government—1918–1933. 7. Feminism—Germany—History. 8. Political
culture—Germany. I. Eley, Geoff, 1949– . II. Series.
DD228.3.S58   1996
043.08—dc20   95-42516
                                                            CIP

ISBN 0-472-08481-X (pbk. : alk. paper)

Contents

Preface

The purposes of this volume originated in a conference held at the University of Pennsylvania on 23–25 February 1990 on the theme "The *Kaiserreich* in the 1990s: New Research, New Directions, New Agendas." Most of the essays were originally delivered as papers on that occasion, with others added later to strengthen the coherence and round out the thematics of the volume. The conference was very much an effort at taking stock in light of controversies dating from the 1960s and 1970s and the subsequent research and perspectives they helped produce, with the intention of exploring some new directions. But despite some calls for a "new synthesis" (a familiar hankering when historians sit down amid the fallout from successful critiques), and a certain amount of nostalgia for lost grand narratives, the main tones stressed experiment and feeling the way. The boundaries of this collection, which exceed the conventional chronology of 1871–1918, with a number of essays exploring the coherence of developments between the 1890s and the end of the Weimar Republic, are a part of this indeterminacy. So while the volume's ambitions are certainly programmatic, there is no unifying editorial line and no common outlook of the contributors, whether theoretically, methodologically, or in relation to the arguments laid out in the two Introductions. Rather there is a common and more open-ended desire to see how a variety of new directions will run. Something of this open-endedness can be gleaned from the excellent report on the original conference by John Williams, Lora Wildenthal, Jennifer Jenkins, and Teresa Sanislo in *German History* (9, no. 2, 1991, pp. 200–207).

I would like to thank the Council for European Studies, the DAAD, and the University of Pennsylvania for supporting the original conference, and my co-organizer Thomas Childers for his efforts as the local host. Derek Linton and Wolfgang Natter (who decided not to contribute their papers to the volume), Ellen Kennedy and John Röhl (who provided closing comments), and Jane Caplan, Tom Childers, Konrad Jarausch, and Vernon Lidtke (who moderated the discussions) all deserve special thanks. I would like to thank my graduate students at the University of Michigan for the energy and intellectual stimulation the new directions presuppose; Julie Stubbs for help with the editorial work and preparing the index; Lorna Altstetter for endless help with the mechanics of the volume; the contributors for their patience; and the University of Michigan Press for its support both of the volume itself and the series in which it appears.

Introduction 1: Is There a History of the *Kaiserreich?*

Geoff Eley

The *Kaiserreich* and the *Sonderweg:* Where We Are Now

More so than in many national histories, perhaps, historians of modern Germany are conscious of themselves participating in an intellectual history of some import, in an engagement with a national past whose impact on the present seems permanently unfinished, forever tumbling into fresh dispute. This remains as true for those students currently entering the field as it was for those who helped lay the foundations in the 1950s, let alone the key groups of West German scholars who redefined the agenda through the passionately waged methodological, theoretical, and substantive controversies and febrile political atmosphere of the 1960s. Of course, this is all to do with the Third Reich. The Nazi past has simply refused to lie down and pass away. Throughout the 1970s and 1980s, in fact, one scandal or controversy after another kept it in the public eye, forcing an unusually intense connection between the scholarly debates of historians and a wider public domain. Though not an immediate focus of these debates since the 1960s, the *Kaiserreich* has held a special place in the longer view of German history in which the evaluation of the Third Reich has had to be set. Moreover, now that Germany is unified once again, and the Nazi time recedes ever further from the lived experience of most Germans, we can expect pressures to grow for a reopening of discussion around the earlier unification of the nineteenth century and the issue of continuity, presumably in ways every bit as intense as before.

The contributors to this volume form a particular generational cohort relative to the historiographical background mentioned above, joining those who were formed by the debates of the 1960s to those whose training already presupposes those critical gains. Our volume, which began in a conference at the University of Pennsylvania on 23–25 February 1990, attempts to see where we are now. It seeks both to explore current directions and emerging agendas of discussion about the *Kaiserreich* and to break the latter out of its immediate context to examine the continuities with the subsequent course of German history that it now makes sense to see.

The starting point for the intellectual history behind this volume is in one sense the earlier collection edited by Richard J. Evans in 1978, *Society and Politics in Wilhelmine Germany,* which in retrospect had the effect of initiating a particular framework of debate around the *Kaiserreich.* The overall unity and coherence of that volume can easily be exaggerated. The contributors were a heterogeneous group, by outlook and type of history, held together by nothing like a unifying perspective. At the same time, the editor's introduction and several of the individual essays did speak from within a distinctively British tradition of social history, one stressing locality, "people's history," everyday life, and "history from below." Moreover, this standpoint also challenged the main framework within which the West German revisionist historiography of the 1960s had tended to move, and several of the volume's authors went on to develop a full-scale critique of that new work.

To situate our present discussion, therefore, some account of this earlier historiographical moment—the West German revisionism, the British critique, and the debates they provoked—must be given. Without rehearsing that complete story, we can say that a combination of major departures—the famous Fischer controversy over Germany's responsibility for World War I, Hans-Ulrich Wehler's magisterial study of Bismarck's imperialism, and a range of monographic research on the dominant socioeconomic interests behind the foundation and governance of the Second Empire—had sustained a new consensus about the *Kaiserreich's* essential authoritarianism and its causal relationship to the weakness of the Weimar Republic and the rise of the Third Reich.[1]

---

1. There is a helpful summary of this historiographical context from within the West German revisionism by Hans-Ulrich Wehler, "Historiography in Germany Today," in *Observations on the Spiritual Situation of the Age,* ed. Jürgen Habermas (Cambridge, Mass., 1984), 221–59. For the British critique, see Richard J. Evans, ed., *Society and Politics in Wilhelmine Germany* (London, 1978); and David Blackbourn and Geoff Eley, *The Peculiarities of German History: Bourgeois Society and Politics in Nineteenth-Century Germany* (Oxford and New York, 1984). There are good introductions to the resultant debates in Robert Moeller, "The Kaiserreich Recast? Continuity and Change in Modern German Historiography," *Journal of Social History* 17 (1984): 655–83; James N. Retallack, "Social History with a Vengeance? Some Reactions to Hans-Ulrich Wehler's 'Das Deutsche Kaiserreich,'" *German Studies Review* 7 (1984): 423–50; Roger Fletcher, "Recent Developments in West German Historiography: The Bielefeld School and Its Critics," ibid., 451–80; Roger Fletcher, introduction to *From Kaiserreich to Third Reich: Elements of Continuity in German History, 1871–1945,* by Fritz Fischer (London, 1986), 1–32. See also Georg Iggers, Introduction to *The Social History of Politics: Critical Perspectives in West German Historical Writing since 1945,* ed. Georg Iggers (New York, 1985), 1–48. My own historiographical essays have been collected in Geoff Eley, *From Unification to Nazism: Reinterpreting the German Past* (London, 1986).

This 1960s revisionism produced a set of organizing ideas—some of them already anticipated in the Anglo-American scholarship of post-1945, some going back to older, pre-Nazi critical traditions of German political life—that rapidly acquired conventional status. They included the belief in direct continuities between Bismarck and Hitler; the idea of a fundamental contradiction between economic modernity and political backwardness leading to the empire's structural instability; the view that Germany lacked the emancipatory experience of a successful bourgeois revolution, falling prey instead to the continued dominance of old-style "preindustrial elites" in the political system; the notion that these elites exercised their power by repressive forms of social control and manipulative techniques of rule; and the belief that German history was the site of an exceptional "misdevelopment" by comparison to the healthier trajectories of the societies of "the West."

The power of this set of perspectives has been clear enough. Some form of a deep structural explanation for the origins of Nazism, as for any societal catastrophe of that kind, will be indispensable, and the best approaches have stressed the contradictions of Germany's accelerated capitalist transformation when compared with Britain, the Low Countries, and France; the importance of uneven and combined development; and the related idea of the "contemporaneity of the uncontemporary" (Ernst Bloch). In this sense, Germany was the classic land of contradiction, where the speed and scale of industrialization and the simultaneity of its national-state formation, in a global setting of heightened imperialist competition, created an extreme surplus of social and political tensions. Above all, a highly advanced capitalist economy coexisted with large "traditional" sectors (a small-holding peasantry and a small-business petite bourgeoisie) and faced the concurrent rise of a socialist working class. But the West German revisionist historians took this deep-structural argument much further, stressing how backward political interests—traditional elites and their preindustrial mentalities—prevented any democratic modernizing of the political system and allowed "authoritarian and antidemocratic structures in state and society" (Karl Dietrich Bracher) to persist. The resulting continuity of backwardness is then taken to be crucial for the development of Nazism. As such, the approach implies a teleological and extremely deterministic line of explanation in which Nazism's primary origins are placed somewhere in the middle of the nineteenth century, or even earlier, in the era of Napoléon and the French Revolution, when Germany failed to take a "Western" path of liberal-democratic evolution.

Against this teleology of German exceptionalism—in which the dramatic and undeniable difference of Nazism, the peculiarly violent resolution of the interwar crisis in Germany, are made the basis for a deeper-rooted historical pathology that made German history *in general* different from the history of the West—the Evans volume stressed the importance of trying to see German history between the 1860s and World War I in its own terms. This was certainly not an argument *against* comparison. Nor was it a naive form of nominalist historicism that sought to remove the criteria for judging the period before 1914 from the difficulties of what came after. It was more an attempt to rethink the appropriate contexts in which German history before 1914 should be compared. If this was done, German history in the nineteenth century might start to look less irredeemably wanting beside the histories of Britain and France, and what differences there were might look less deterministically aligned with the events of 1930–45. The sources of the interwar crisis might have to be disengaged from the history of the *Kaiserreich*—not absolutely but as the argument of first recourse—and the whole notion of the German *Sonderweg* (special path, a normatively understood deviant course) would be rethought.

A great deal of valuable and stimulating research has been done under the sign of this debate, with a rich array of results. For our purposes, the following five points might be picked out.

1. The narrative of the *Sonderweg* is constructed to a great extent as a story of liberalism's failure. Germany's "misdevelopment" is linked, in this view, to social bases of persisting authoritarianism that survived industrialization and that German liberalism proved inadequate to overcome. Through a series of compromises and defeats (1848, 1860s, 1878/79), German liberals either betrayed the true liberal heritage or were condemned to powerlessness and ineffectuality—to "liberalism in an illiberal society," in James Sheehan's view.[2] In a questionable conflation of categories, liberalism is also made the weakness of the bourgeoisie, so that the one (the deficiencies of liberalism) becomes causally attributed to the other (peculiarities of class formation and the bourgeoisie's willingness to accommodate to the given mores and power structures of a preindustrial society). Such an approach flies in the face of both liberalism's actual sociology (which was complex and heterogeneous rather than straightforwardly "bourgeois" to begin with) and the conceptual and methodological difficulties of attributing unitary ideologies to whole social classes. It elides the possibilities of a successful liberalism with the degree of realization of the class consciousness of the bourgeoisie, so that if the latter was problematic, the former was bound to run into trouble, too. In the words of one leading historian of this school, "Political liberalism emerged as the political outlook of the rising bourgeoisie."[3] And if the bourgeoisie did not "rise," ipso facto liberalism could not be a vital force.

---

2. This is the title of the introduction to *German Liberalism in the Nineteenth Century*, by James S. Sheehan (Chicago, 1978), 1–3.

3. Heinrich August Winkler, "Liberalismus: Zur historischen Bedeutung eines politischen Begriffs," in *Liberalismus und Antiliberalismus: Studien zur politischen Sozialgeschichte des 19. und 20. Jahrhunderts* (Göttingen, 1979), 15.

In the meantime this view of the German bourgeoisie was considerably rethought.[4] In particular, the older ideas of bourgeois weakness and self-abnegation, the so-called *Defizit an Bürgerlichkeit*, or lack of bourgeois virtues, have been called into doubt.[5] There is now a much greater willingness to see the extent to which bourgeois values were in the ascendant in the period after the 1860s—in everything from taste, fashion, and the everyday conduct of affairs to the main lines of the German Empire's public culture, including the ethos of local administration; the prevailing views of the law, morality, and the social order; the notions of private property and social obligation; and the general principles of public life. Moreover, a case can be made for seeing the

---

4. The debate was initiated in David Blackbourn and Geoff Eley, *Mythen deutscher Geschichtsschreibung: Die gescheiterte bürgerliche Revolution von 1848* (Frankfurt, 1980), which was the earlier, German version of Blackbourn and Eley, *The Peculiarities of German History*. The best general introduction to the wider literature is David Blackbourn, "The German Bourgeoisie: An Introduction," in *The German Bourgeoisie: Essays on the Social History of the German Middle Class from the Late Eighteenth to the Early Twentieth Century,* ed. David Blackbourn and Richard J. Evans (London and New York, 1991), 1–45. Compare also Jürgen Kocka's introductory survey, "Bürgertum und bürgerliche Gesellschaft im 19. Jahrhundert: Europäische Entwicklungen und deutsche Eigenarten," in *Bürgertum im 19. Jahrhundert: Deutschland im europäischen Vergleich,* ed. Jürgen Kocka, 3 vols. (Munich, 1988), 11–76, which unfortunately avoids any direct engagement with Blackbourn and Eley's argumentation. See also Jürgen Kocka, ed., *Bürger und Bürgerlichkeit im 19. Jahrhundert* (Göttingen, 1987); Jürgen Kocka, ed., *Arbeiter und Bürger im 19. Jahrhundert* (Munich, 1986); Ute Frevert, ed., *Bürgerinnen und Bürger: Geschlechterverhältnisse im 19. Jahrhundert* (Göttingen, 1988); Hannes Siegrist, ed., *Bürgerliche Berufe: Zur Sozialgeschichte der freien und akademischen Berufe im internationalen Vergleich* (Göttingen, 1988); Geoffrey Cocks and Konrad H. Jarausch, eds., *German Professions, 1800–1950* (New York, 1990); Werner Conze and Jürgen Kocka, eds., *Bildungsbürgertum im 19. Jahrhundert, part 1, Bildungssystem und Professionalisierung im internationalen Vergleich* (Stuttgart, 1985); Jürgen Kocka, ed., *Das Bildungsbürgertum in Gesellschaft und Politik* (Stuttgart, 1989); Konrad H. Jarausch, *The Unfree Professions: German Lawyers, Teachers, and Engineers between Democracy and National Socialism* (Oxford, 1989); Lothar Gall, *Bürgertum in Deutschland* (Berlin, 1989); Lothar Gall, ed., *Stadt und Bürgertum im 19. Jahrhundert* (Munich, 1990); Franz J. Bauer, *Bürgerwege und Bürgerwelten: Familienbiographische Untersuchungen zum deutschen Bürgertum im 19. Jahrhundert* (Göttingen, 1991); Rudolf Boch, *Grenzenloses Wachstum? Das rheinische Wirtschaftsbürgertum und seine Industrialisierungsdebatte, 1814–1857* (Göttingen, 1991); Marion A. Kaplan, *The Making of the Jewish Middle Class: Women, Family, and Identity in Imperial Germany* (New York, 1991); Lutz Niethammer et al., eds., *Bürgerliche Gesellschaft in Deutschland: Historische Einblicke, Fragen, Perspektiven* (Frankfurt, 1990); Hans-Jürgen Puhle, ed., *Bürger in der Gesellschaft der Neuzeit: Wirtschaft—Politik—Kultur* (Göttingen, 1991); Jürgen Kocka and Alan Mitchell, eds., *Bourgeois Society in Nineteenth-Century Europe* (Oxford and Providence, 1993).

5. In one of the stronger and extremely influential statements of this older, conventional view, Germany was described as lacking the characteristics of a bourgeois society in this full and strict sense. See Ralf Dahrendorf, *Society and Democracy in Germany* (London, 1968), 397: "neither in the sense of a society of citizens nor in that of one dominated by a confident bourgeoisie did a modern society emerge." This doubled meaning of *bürgerlich* is more central to the German etymology than to the anglicized use of "bourgeois" and is a particular difficulty of the German term *bürgerliche Gesellschaft,* with its varying inflections of "bourgeois society"/"civil society."

Kaiserreich institutionally as a classic embodiment of bourgeois values as they have usually been understood: that is, in the constitutionalizing of public authority via parliamentary institutions; in the recodifications of commercial and civil law; in the models of administrative efficiency, particularly at the level of the city; and in the growth and elaboration of public opinion. In the structures of the capitalist economy, of course, the strength of bourgeois achievements goes without saying.

Such discussions have shifted perceptions of the *Kaiserreich* quite strikingly during the past decade, but two major questions stay unresolved. On the one hand, if we ask, How "bourgeois" was the *Kaiserreich*? (in the title of one key reflection on the above discussion), we obviously need to clarify what the limits of this adjective (in its causal and explanatory connotations) really are.[6] On the other hand, what the revisions mentioned above still leave untouched is the central argument regarding the backwardness of the *Kaiserreich*'s political structure—the monarchy, the military, the bureaucracy—and the primacy of preindustrial interests and elites. Such backwardness has always been counterposed to the ideal of bourgeois modernity that for Germany *was not* attained. This volume cannot hope to resolve such matters by itself, but a number of the essays that follow below—notably those dealing with issues of the welfare state and those addressing issues of culture—try to clarify the issues and move the discussion further on.[7]

2. However we assess the character of the *Kaiserreich*'s political institutions in this respect, the uncoupling of the question of *Bürgerlichkeit* (in the sense of bourgeois values, or even bourgeois societal hegemony) from its assumed relationship to political liberalism makes it much easier also to take a fresh look at the specific character of German liberalism as a political tradition. The assumptions about bourgeois weakness have always been one factor impeding discussion of German liberalism's specific achievements. The normative critique of German liberalism by standards of liberalism in Britain and the United States, ones usually abstracted from the period since 1945 rather than the late nineteenth century, is another. But if we take a genuinely European view of liberalism's emergence and ascendancy as a political creed in the third quarter of the nineteenth century, focused in particular on the dramatic constitutional transformations of the 1860s, when German unification featured as one of the decade's key progressive changes, a much different picture of German liberalism's strengths will emerge. That is, the appropriate comparative context for considering German liberalism should be less the mature forms of liberal

---

6. See Hans-Ulrich Wehler, "Wie 'bürgerlich' war das Deutsche Kaiserreich?" in *Aus der Geschichte lernen? Essays*, by Hans-Ulrich Wehler (Munich, 1988), 191–217.

7. See especially the detailed discussion in my contribution to this volume below, "German History and the Contradictions of Modernity."

democracy in the post-1945 West than the trans-European conjuncture of constitutional change, nation forming, and state making in the 1860s, powerfully overdetermined by the global process of capitalist boom, spatial expansion, and social penetration, articulated through the patterns of uneven and combined development. *This* context, rather than the binary contrast with some misleading and idealized construct of liberalism in the English-speaking world, will allow the specific characteristics—in a sense, its national authenticity—of German liberalism between 1860 and 1914 to come into view. Again, this is no rejection of comparative inquiry per se, in favor of a nominalist or traditional historicist account (every history—or liberalism—is equal in its own terms). It is the advocacy of one context of comparison (Europe as a whole in the 1860s) as against another (Britain and the United States, defined more by the late twentieth century).

3. If we reconsider discretely both the degree of Imperial Germany's bourgeois reformation and the forms and effectiveness of German liberalism, we are also led to reevaluate the conventional view of the German polity's structural instability. In the new perspectives that emerged from the 1960s, that instability was linked to the authoritarian backwardness of the *Kaiserreich*'s political institutions and their failure to be "modernized" in accordance with the breakneck pace of Germany's industrial transformation: destabilizing contradictions arose between the modern economy and the backward state that could only be artificially bridged by manipulative techniques of "social imperialism" and "secondary integration" (so long as the "real" solution of "modernizing" democratic reform was not grasped, that is). However, if we break the causal associative chain that links authoritarianism (as opposed to liberal democracy), preindustrial elites (as against a triumphant bourgeoisie), and political backwardness (contrasted with the modernizing political change that Germany is thought to have lacked until after 1945), the issue of the imperial polity's stability and viability appears in a rather different light. Each of these terms requires the others in the conventional framework of interpretation, and if one of them changes, the others fall into doubt, too.

For instance, if bourgeois values were more powerful and tone setting in Bismarckian and Wilhelmine society than has been allowed, then authoritarianism might look less like the vehicle and expression of the traditional power of preindustrial elites and more like the specifically late-nineteenth- and early-twentieth-century context of bourgeois influence, in the sense of the specific conditions under which bourgeois interests could be constructed and secured. In that case, authoritarian forms might be quite functional and modern relative to the conditions and requirements of capitalist reproduction, societal cohesion, and state effectiveness of that time (I am speaking abstractly here), and not a sign of backwardness at all. If we shift the overall perspective in this way, moreover, a number of central questions appear in a quite different light. For example, the issue of "parliamentarization" has previously been presented in terms of the Reichstag's possible evolution toward a situation of full-scale parliamentary-democratic responsibility before 1914, a prospect that, on the whole, recent historians have been justified in thinking to be unrealistic. But once we dismantle the assumption that modernity—in the sense of a normalized pluralist polity and a well-functioning governmental stability—requires a parliamentary-democratic constitution in the post-1945 Western sense, then we are free to explore how less "pure" forms of parliamentary stabilizatin might occur. That is, we can explore the diversity of political arrangements adequate for the conduct of effective modern government, relative to the specificities of particular societies and times. Other questions would also benefit from that shift of perspective, including the bases of employer paternalism in industrial relations, the early forms of the welfare state, and the general question of German administrative efficiency. The essays in this volume by Steinmetz, Hong, Crew, and myself all engage this issue of perspective.

4. Existing paradigms of German historiography—whether the post-1960s stress on continuities between Bismarck and Hitler, the primacy of preindustrial traditions, and the overarching idea of the *Sonderweg,* or the more conservative versions of national history these perspectives succeeded—have been overwhelmingly Prussocentric. Whether in a positive light (the Bismarckian story of German unification under Prussian leadership) or a negative light (the authoritarian and antimodern consequences of aristocratic privilege and the Prussian bureaucratic and militarist traditions), German history has usually been composed around evidence and arguments drawn from Prussia as opposed to the other parts of Germany, usually on the peremptory grounds that Prussia was by far the largest and most powerful of the German states. Such Prussocentrism is reflected in the continued prevalence of deeply entrenched "statist" perspectives in the post-1960s revisionism, whose contributions have still focused to a striking degree on national policy-making processes conceived in relation both to Bismarck and his successors and to a wider sphere of interest articulation through a corporative structure of pressure groups and economic lobbies. Moreover, the richly proliferating field of social history (including labor history, social-science work on demography, family, and so on, women's history, and everyday-life history), which does take a local or regional perspective, has tended not to engage with the salient political history questions of the *Kaiserreich.* This also contrasts with the literature on Nazism, where one of the dominant approaches has been precisely to ground the rise of the NSDAP in a rich accumulation of local and regional studies.

Consequently, we know far less than we should about the nature of popular political involvement under the *Kaiserreich,* whether in relation to the parties and pressure groups (with the exception, of course, of the SPD) or to the implementation and effects of government policy. We remain rather ill informed about the political grass roots or the social dynamics of political mobilization; and we know much more about the "state" than we do about "civil society." In this respect, the work signaled by Evans's *Society and Politics in Wilhelmine Germany* strongly emphasized the value of non-Prussian perspectives, particularly that of David Blackbourn on Württemberg and Evans himself on Hamburg.[8] Such work has more than a simply "additive" importance (that is, completing the overall picture by including the smaller states and regions that the Prussocentric story leaves out); it has above all shown how the framing of national policy was actually far more contested and insecure than previously believed. The view from the province destabilizes and problematizes the view at the center, just as the view from "below" (to invoke the familiar social-history slogan of the 1960s) shifts and enriches the view at the "top." In a sense, this involves a further stage in the radical questioning of received assumptions that the post-1960s revisionism originally set in train, extending that critique to the bases of the historical "small-German" (or greater-Prussian) outcome of the nineteenth-century state-building project, which implicitly structures both the Prussocentrism and customary statism that, I have suggested, organizes so many existing accounts.[9]

In that case, we are drawn to the contingent and unfinished character of the new German nation-state of 1871 and to the indeterminacy of national consciousness in the period of unification itself. One of the insights that a non-Prussian stress on locality produces is, of course, the richer and more complex materials from which German national identity had to be constructed; and one of the outstanding issues for historians of the *Kaiserreich* concerns the making of German identity between the 1860s and World War I, from both a government-centered and a societal point of view. This question has become a crucial one in light of current political conflict in the Germany of the 1980s and 1990s and had major implications for the subsequent development of German history after 1918. A number of the papers in this volume struggle with it in their different ways, especially those dealing with culture as such. While not necessarily speaking from a localist or non-Prussian vantage point per se, the authors certainly reap the benefits allowed by those perspectives. The essays by

---

8. See David Blackbourn, *Class, Religion and Local Politics in Wilhelmine Germany: The Centre Party in Württemberg before 1914* (New Haven, 1980); Richard J. Evans, *Death in Hamburg: Society and Politics in the Cholera Years, 1830–1910* (Oxford, 1987). For an excellent example of such work in Germany, see Gert Zang, ed., *Provinzialisierung einer Region: Regionale Unterentwicklung und liberale Politik in der Stadt und im Kreis Konstanz im 19. Jahrhundert: Untersuchungen zur Entstehung der bürgerlichen Gesellschaft in der Provinz* (Frankfurt, 1978).

9. See Celia Applegate, *A Nation of Provincials: The German Idea of Heimat* (Berkeley, 1990). See also James Retallack's essay in this volume.

Blackbourn, James Retallack, and Rudy Koshar are particularly rich instances of such an engagement.

5. Finally, one of the strongest emphases of debate in the later 1970s and early 1980s concerned the importance of the 1890s as a major political watershed. In a certain sense, the post-1960s West German revisionism always recognized this, both because it signified the end of the Bismarckian era in the narrow biographical sense (Bismarck left office in 1890) and it reflected the socioeconomic periodization, whose sovereignty historians such as Jürgen Kocka and Wehler have made so primary for their understanding (namely, the end of the so-called great depression in 1895–96 and the transition to organized capitalism).[10] But such historians have also always seen the earlier watershed of 1878–79, which solidified the underlying coalition of industrial and agrarian interests that they believe to have been the main axis of politics under the *Kaiserreich* (the protectionist, antisocialist alliance of "iron and rye" in the "social refoundation of the Reich"), as the really crucial one in the sense that it established a pattern that endured until the demise of the empire in 1918, and that the changes of the 1890s therefore only confirmed. It was against this strong perspective of a highly structured political system, organized for the preservation of certain traditional and antidemocratic interests within a manipulative and authoritarian political repertoire, that a number of the essays in the Evans volume were also directed, stressing instead the elements of political flux and popular mobilization, through which the character of the Wilhelmine political system was strongly recast. In that immediate debate, these arguments became fixed into a dichotomous framework of "manipulation from above" versus "self-mobilization from below," which was perhaps not the best way of conceptualizing and continuing the discussion.[11]

---

10. See especially the contributions in Heinrich August Winkler, ed., *Organisierter Kapitalismus: Voraussetzungen und Anfänge* (Göttingen, 1974). The argument for the centrality of the Great Depression to the periodization is classically stated in Hans Rosenberg, *Grosse Depression und Bismarckzeit: Wirtschaftsablauf, Gesellschaft und Politik in Mitteleuropa* (Berlin, 1967). I have developed a critique in Geoff Eley, "Hans Rosenberg and the Great Depression of 1873–96: Politics and Economics in Recent German Historiography, 1960–80," in Eley, *From Unification to Nazism*, 23–41.

11. The idea of a refounding of the *Reich* via the settlement of 1878–79 goes back to Rosenberg, *Grosse Depression und Bismarckzeit;* and Helmut Bohme, *Deutschlands Weg zur Grossmacht: Studien zum Verhältnis von Wirtschaft und Staat während der Reichsgründungszeit, 1848–1881* (Cologne and Berlin, 1966). For the issue of manipulation/self-mobilization, see the following essays in Evans, *Society and Politics:* Geoff Eley, "The Wilhemine Right: How It Changed," 112–35; Ian Farr, "Populism in the Countryside: The Peasant Leagues in Bavaria in the 1890s," 136–59; and David Blackbourn, "The Problem of Democratization: German Catholics and the Role of the Centre Party," 160–85. See also Geoff Eley, *Reshaping the German Right: Radical Nationalism and Political Change after Bismarck* (New Haven, 1980); and Blackbourn, *Class, Religion and Local Politics.* More generally, see David Blackbourn, "The Politics of

How should we conceptualize the transition of the 1890s, then? So far, this has tended to be done in terms of either: (1) the reconstitution of the Bismarckian system of politics under the aegis of Bernhard von Bülow and Alfred von Tirpitz during the period 1897–1902, through the alliance of iron and rye, social imperialism, *Sammlungspolitik,* and parliamentary antisocialism, orchestrated via the tit-for-tat of Navy Law and tariffs, as laid out in Eckart Kehr's now famous analysis in *Schlachtflottenbau und Parteipolitik* and adopted by the post-Fischer West German revisionists as their own; or (2) the Blackbourn-Eley critique of this via the discussion of widespread popular mobilization.[12] Clearly, I find the latter much more persuasive—that is, the emphasis on the elements of fracture and change in the 1890s rather than on the elements of continuity and containment. But what can be said more specifically, now that we have more distance on the immediate polemics of more than a decade ago, with a view to constructive discussion in the future? Three areas of work strike me in particular.

We have to begin with the Bismarckian transition in the immediate sense—with the abolition of the Antisocialist Law in 1890, the expansion of the electorate, and the coming together of a public sphere that was far less subject to restriction and harassment and more directly based on the masses—or at least on the need to *address* the masses politically—and to a lesser extent on the ability of the masses themselves to participate in the political process. This was one of the common starting points from which Blackbourn and I have approached the specific history of the Wilhelmine time; and in *Reshaping the German Right* I discussed some of the ways in which a new structure of public communication reshaped the very terms on which political life took place. However, we need to do much more to explore the nature of this mass communication/public sphere/civil society complex of questions, and the concrete relations between change in this underlying social and cultural sense and the events of national politics remains one of the areas open to research and debate.[13]

Demagogy in Imperial Germany," *Past and Present* 113 (1986): 152–84, reprinted in Blackbourn, *Populists and Patricians: Essays in Modern German History* (London, 1987), 217–45; Wolfgang Mock, "'Manipulation von oben' oder Selbstorganisation an der Basis? Einige neuere Ansätze in der englischen Historiographie zur Geschichte des Deutschen Kaiserreichs," *Historische Zeitschrift* 232 (1981): 358–75. See also Stanley Suval, *Electoral Politics in Wilhelmine Germany* (Chapel Hill, 1985); and James Retallack, *Notables of the Right: The Conservative Party and Political Mobilization in Imperial Germany, 1876–1918* (London, 1988).

12. See Eckart Kehr, *Schlachtflottenbau und Parteipolitik, 1894–1901* (Berlin, 1930), translated as *Battleship Building and Party Politics in Germany, 1894–1901: A Cross Section of the Political, Social and Ideological Preconditions of German Imperialism* (Chicago, 1975).

13. There is little advance in current discussion over the works cited in note 10 above. I have returned to the issue in two further essays: "Notable Politics, the Crisis of German Liberalism, and the Electoral Transition of the 1890s," in *In Search of a Liberal Germany: Studies in the History of*

Second, I would argue that a distinctive configuration of politics did emerge from the 1890s to replace the Bismarckian configuration that had started to decompose with the beginning of the decade. This new structure of politics consisted of two main party-political or organizational features. The first is what I would call a limited stabilization of political life within the given constitutional forms and rules of parliamentary action. We can date this fairly accurately from the late 1890s, and it lasted until roughly 1909–12. It had a variety of features, including the coalescence of a relatively stable parliamentary majority, ordered around a National Liberal and Center core. A key negative symptom was the recession of the threat of *Staatsstreich* (coup d'état) in the thinking of governmental and right-wing party-political circles after 1897, together with the concomitant transition to a parliamentary and propagandist type of antisocialism instead. Rather than seeking a policy of confrontation with the Reichstag, to the point of repeated dissolutions, mobilizing the electorate against the parliamentary majority, suspending constitutional government, and procuring a more compliant legislature through a reactionary revision of the constitution, I would argue, the government and most of the Right now accepted that the Left needed to be fought on their own terms, within the framework of a liberal and constitutionalized public sphere. For a complex of reasons, this period of parliamentary normalization came to an end around 1911–12.[14]

And third, a key element in the breakdown of parliamentary stability after 1909—this is the second feature of the post-Bismarckian political configuration—was the availability of a powerful extraparliamentary radical-right public, which had gradually taken shape during the previous decade. One source of this was the campaigning nationalism associated with the Navy League, the Colonial Society, the Ostmarkenverein (an anti-Polish pressure group), and other so-called *nationale Verbände* (nationalist associations), for which the Pan-German League acted as a kind of ideological vanguard. Another source was the emerging protest movement of the *Mittelstand* (traditional petite bourgeoisie), originally on a local and regional basis, but linked to Anti-Semitic and other radical-right electoral formations and shortly to acquire its

German Liberalism from 1789 to the Present, ed. Konrad H. Jarausch and Larry Eugene Jones (New York, 1990), 187–216; and "Anti-Semitism, Agrarian Mobilization, and the Conservative Party: Radicalism and Containment in the Founding of the Agrarian League, 1890–93," in *Between Reform, Reaction, and Resistance: Studies in the History of German Conservatism from 1789 to 1945*, ed. Larry E. Jones and James Retallack (Providence, 1993), 187–228.

14. I have explored the political moment of 1897–98 in Geoff Eley, "*Sammlungspolitik*, Social Imperialism, and the Navy Law of 1898," in Eley, *From Unification to Nazism*, 110–53; and I have returned to the more general issue of parliamentary normalization in Geoff Eley, "The Social Construction of Democracy in Germany, 1871–1933," forthcoming in *The Social Construction of Germany*, ed. Reid Andrews and Herrick Chapman (New York, 1995) on this general theme.

own national lobby in the Imperial German *Mittelstand* Association in 1911. When the agrarians and their industrial allies moved into opposition to the government between 1909 and 1911, and their existing party-political representation, a loose front of Conservative and right-wing National Liberal parliamentarians, achieved minimal success in the 1912 elections, the conditions were ripe for the coalescence of a new extraparliamentary bloc directed against the government, capitalizing on the popular potential mobilized by the nationalist pressure groups and the incipient *Mittelstand* movement. This so-called national opposition materialized in the *Kartell der schaffenden Stände* (cartel of the productive estates) in autumn 1913, which became the rallying point for a new antiparliamentary authoritarianism, no longer accommodating to the given constitutional norms but aspiring to replace them.[15]

Each of these questions—the restructuring of the public sphere in and after the 1890s, the relative stabilization of public life within the given constitutional and parliamentary frame, and the sources of the latter's breakdown after 1909 through the emergence of a new extraparliamentary Right—remains open. They were placed on the agenda by the debates of the 1970s, but there has been, perhaps remarkably, little further discussion during the last decade. To that extent, the fixing of the argument into the "manipulation" versus "self-mobilization" dichotomy during the early 1980s has rather prevented new questions from being fruitfully generated and pursued.

These are some of the areas of active research and discussion (and doubtless others could be added) that, broadly speaking, have defined the *Kaiserreich* as a historical field during the last two decades. Of course, much interesting work that falls within the chronological boundaries of the period is not

---

15. There has been little added by way of scholarly research to this theme beyond the arguments laid out in my *Reshaping the German Right,* which in turn were grounded in the monographic research of the 1970s, especially the following: Dirk Stegmann, *Die Erben Bismarcks: Parteien und Verbände in der Spätphase des Wilhelminischen Deutschlands: Sammlungspolitik, 1897–1918* (Cologne, 1970); Peter-Christian Witt, *Die Finanzpolitik des Deutschen Reiches von 1903 bis 1913* (Lübeck, 1970); Klaus Saul, *Staat, Industrie, Arbeiterbewegung im Kaiserreich: Zur Innen- und Sozialpolitik des Wilhelminischen Deutschlands, 1903–1914* (Düsseldorf, 1974); Siegfried Mielke, *Der Hansa-Bund für Gewerbe, Handel und Industrie, 1909–1914: Der gescheiterte Versuch einer antifeudalen Sammlungspolitik* (Göttingen, 1976); Hans-Peter Ullmann, *Der Bund der Industriellen: Organisation, Einfluss und Politik klein- und mittelbetrieblicher Industrieller im Deutschen Kaiserreich, 1895–1914* (Göttingen, 1976). Three recent monographs, each valuable in its own way, adds little of substance to our understanding of the high-political process on the eve of World War I: Roger Chickering, *We Men Who Feel Most German: A Cultural Study of the Pan-German League, 1886–1914* (London, 1984); Marylin Shevin Coetzee, *The German Army League: Popular Nationalism in Wilhelmine Germany* (New York, 1990); and Stig Forster, *Der doppelte Militarismus: Die deutsche Heeresrüstungspolitik zwischen Status-quo-Sicherung und Aggression, 1890–1913* (Stuttgart, 1985). See also the new introduction to the second edition of Eley, *Reshaping the German Right* (Ann Arbor, 1991), xiii–xxvi.

encompassed by the five topics I have outlined above, particularly in areas of social history. But on the whole, it seems to me, such work in social history is not being harnessed to any overarching interpretation or reinterpretation distinct from the ones I have mentioned. The social history of the working class, in both its new social-science and everyday-life modes, is perhaps a good example of this. In general upswing since the mid-1970s, with a growing accumulation of monographic research and the major syntheses of Kocka, Gerhard A. Ritter, and Klaus Tenfelde at the forefront, the literature on working-class formation nonetheless bears an oblique and uncertain relationship to the central problematic of the *Sonderweg*. To the extent that it does engage directly with the latter, it is to reassert the backwardness and authoritarianism of the *Kaiserreich*'s political system, as in the Ritter-Tenfelde thesis concerning the origins of the German labor movement's "exceptional" radicalism (the labor history variant of the *Sonderweg* thesis) in its exclusionary and repressive mistreatment by a reactionary Prusso-German state. The primacy of preindustrial traditions, in other words, imposed a marginalized standing on the German labor movement (expressed through the rhetorical "othering" of its democratic aspirations via such terms as *Reichsfeinde* and *vaterlandslose Gesellen*) that prevented its admittance to the legitimate political system on the model of, for instance, the labor movements of Britain and Scandinavia (although where this leaves the comparison with other countries, such as France, Italy, and the United States, is less than clear).[16]

Moreover, the interest in *Alltagsgeschichte* (history of everyday life) has likewise seldom engaged with the prevailing interpretations directly, being more concerned with a set of methodological and theoretical issues internal to the concerns of social history, and in any case (because of the highlighting of oral history and popular memory) is drawn more to the later (Weimar, Third Reich, Federal Republic) periods.[17] In fact, this new social history is drawn to a rather different set of primary questions, which can certainly be related to the

---

16. The most recent and "authoritative" statement of this mainstream view can be found in the Dietz series, *Geschichte der Arbeiter und der Arbeiterbewegung in Deutschland seit dem Ende des 18. Jahrhunderts,* the relevant volume in which is Gerhard A. Ritter and Klaus Tenfelde, *Arbeiter im Deutschen Kaiserreich, 1871–1914* (Bonn, 1992). I have surveyed the literature on the labor movement and the social history of the working class in two essays: "Combining Two Histories: The SPD and the German Working Class before 1914," *Radical History Review* 28–30 (1984): 13–44, reprinted in *From Unification to Nazism,* 171–99; and "Labor History, Social History, *Alltagsgeschichte:* Experience, Culture, and the Politics of the Everyday—A New Direction for German Social History?" *Journal of Modern History* 61 (1989): 297–343.

17. In general, see Eley, "Labor History, Social History, *Alltagsgeschichte*"; and Alf Lüdtke, ed., *Alltagsgeschichte: Zur Rekonstruktion historischer Erfahrungen und Lebensweisen* (Frankfurt and New York, 1989). For the pioneering work on oral history and popular memory, see Lutz Niethammer and Alexander von Plato, eds., *Lebensgeschichte und Sozialstruktur im Ruhrgebiet, 1930–1960,* 2d ed., 3 vols. (Bonn, 1986).

Sonderweg complex, but which are not formally *about* the latter in its stronger sense (that is, the form outlined above). In the case of literature on the working class, it concerns such issues as the bases of reformism and radicalism in the labor movement before 1914, the character of the militancy and working-class radicalization during World War I and the German Revolution, the working-class response to Nazism, and so on.[18] One apparent exception to this generalization about the attenuated effects of the work in social history is the recent literature on *Bürgerlichkeit,* but even here the analysis has proceeded in a very contained way, abstracted from the *Kaiserreich*'s political system and for which the old framework of backwardness, authoritarianism, and the primacy of preindustrial traditions is felt to be largely intact.[19]

Reframing the Questions

The essays in this volume have much to say to these more obliquely positioned literatures of social history—both the social history of the working class and the broader analysis of everyday life—and in ways that challenge the given orientations of such existing work in the German field. Kathleen Canning and M. J. Maynes show the necessity of considering gender in framing the question of working-class formation, while Young Sun Hong, Belinda Davis, Lora Wildenthal, and Elisabeth Domansky all explore the consequences of thinking about the major questions of German history with a gendered perspective, and Jean H. Quataert provides an overarching view of the field from this point of view. Willfried Spohn and Blackbourn explore the importance of religion—an astonishing absence, in the given problematics of social history in the German field—in the making of the working class and the shaping of popular culture. All of the essays—but especially those of Retallack, Eley, George Steinmetz, Hong, Davis, and Domansky—bring the national political process under review and ask us to reconsider the ways in which the polity of the *Kaiserreich* has usually been understood. Koshar and Frank Trommler—and, in another dimension, Spohn and Blackbourn—show how the importance of culture in the formation of German national identity after 1871 might be critically rethought.

But the exciting new impulses may well be coming, in fact, from *outside* the established framework of debate altogether. On the evidence of the con-

---

18. One connection to the *Sonderweg* thesis is the tendency to explain the strength of the SPD and its unusually strong attachment to a formal revolutionary program and officially Marxist outlook in terms of the repressive political culture of the *Kaiserreich,* which prevented the labor movement from developing the "natural" reformist orientation that it would have acquired under "normal" liberal-democratic conditions.

19. See especially Wehler, "Wie 'bürgerlich' war das Deutsche Kaiserreich?" 206ff., 216–17. I have also addressed this question in my own contribution to this volume, Eley, "German History and the Contradictions of Modernity," below.

ference discussion from which this volume originally derives, there are three sources in particular: women's history and the study of gender; post-Foucauldian understandings of knowledge and disciplinary power; and the new cultural history and cultural studies.

Gender Studies

Women's history visibly entered discussions among German historians in the early 1980s but achieved its strongest impact not surprisingly in the United States, where recognition of women's history had made most progress in the profession at large, as opposed to West Germany, where the emergence was slower and less securely based. A number of benchmark collections were published.[20] A key source of ideas was the east-coast German Women's History Study Group, which began meeting in the late 1970s, and whose members sponsored the conference "The Meaning of Gender in German History" in April 1986 at Rutgers University, in which they challenged male German historians to use gender perspectives to recast their work. This initiative was extended a year later into a graduate student conference on the same theme.[21] At a certain point in this process, one strong tendency among women's historians in North America began theorizing their work via the category of gender, and while not uncontested in women's history, this shift from the separate study of women to the variable construction of sexual difference has begun to have a discernible impact on the German field.[22]

---

20. See especially Ruth-Ellen B. Joeres and Mary Jo Maynes, eds., *German Women in the Eighteenth and Nineteenth Centuries: A Social and Literary History* (Bloomington, 1986); John C. Fout, ed., *German Women in the Nineteenth Century* (New York, 1984); and Renate Bridenthal, Atina Grossmann, and Marion Kaplan, eds., *When Biology Became Destiny: Women in Weimar and Nazi Germany* (New York, 1984).

21. While neither conference issued a published volume, they marked a definite watershed in the entry of gender perspectives into the mainstream of discussion in the German field. For subsequently completed work, see Kaplan, *The Making of the Jewish Middle Class;* Robert G. Moeller, *Protecting Motherhood: Women and the Family in the Politics of Postwar Germany* (Berkeley, 1993); and Claudia Koonz, *Mothers in the Fatherland: Women, the Family and Nazi Politics* (New York, 1987). In the meantime, of course, several participants in the graduate student conference have since completed dissertations, taken up jobs, and begun significant publication, including Kathleen Canning, Belinda Davis, Dagmar Herzog, Young Sun Hong, and Nancy Reagin.

22. The key text here is Joan Scott, "Gender: A Useful Category of Historical Analysis," *American Historical Review* 91 (1986): 1053–75, reprinted in Joan Scott, *Gender and the Politics of History* (New York, 1988), 28–50. In the German field, see Kathleen Canning, "Gender and the Politics of Class Formation: Rethinking German Labor History," *American Historical Review* 97 (1992): 736–68, originally presented at the Philadelphia conference on the *Kaiserreich* and reprinted in this volume; and Eve Rosenhaft, "Women, Gender, and the Limits of Political History in the Age of 'Mass' Politics," in *Elections, Mass Politics, and Social Change in Modern Germany: New Perspectives,* ed. Larry Eugene Jones and James N. Retallack (Cambridge, 1992), 149–74.

In Germany itself progress has been much slower. The creation of a strong monographic literature focusing specifically on women has begun, and some major projects (notably Kocka's large-scale comparative and interdisciplinary project on the bourgeoisie and bourgeois culture) have explicitly admitted gender to their repertoire of themes, though not perhaps to the fundamental reframing of their agendas. A stronger presence of explicitly gendered analysis has been achieved for the Weimar and Nazi periods, where work has converged with the interest developing in the English-speaking world in the context of reproductive politics and the explanatory importance of what a recent volume of essays calls "a new eugenic paradigm for Nazi racism."[23] Some chairs of women's history have finally been created in German universities, although the ridiculous underproduction of fully qualified women historians (given the way the German academic career structure continues to militate against their emergence) will complicate their ability to be filled. Some recent programmatic volumes have also marked out the lines of existing advance.[24]

"Gender," of course, implicates not only the analysis of issues specifically affecting women but also the complex structuring of sexual differences as they bear upon the categories of both women and men, whose recognition consequently affects our perceptions of how the world in general is ordered. The consequences can be approached in the first instance at a general theoretical level. Feminist theory has shown just how fundamentally the terms of modern social and political identity—of class, citizenship, "race," nationhood, religion, the very category of the modern self—have been assembled from the continuously refigured and redeployed binarism, within meanings simultaneously contingent and entrenched, of what is entailed in being a woman or a man. Such assumptions were ordered during the nineteenth century into a pervasive dualism that has survived into the normalizing rhetorics of the present, aligning men with the worlds of work and the public domain of politics and women with the home and the private worlds of domesticity, the one a site of control, agency, and reason, the other a place of quiescence, passivity, and emotion. Inscribed in the language of identity have been definite notions of masculinity and femininity, which limited "women's access to knowledge,

---

23. Thomas Childers and Jane Caplan, introduction to *Reevaluating the Third Reich*, ed. Thomas Childers and Jane Caplan (New York, 1993), 3. This volume originated in a Philadelphia conference of spring 1988.

24. See Hanna Schissler, ed., *Geschlechterverhältnisse im historischen Wandel* (Frankfurt, 1993); Ute Frevert, "Männergeschichte oder die Suche nach dem 'ersten' Geschlecht," and Hanna Schissler, "Geschlechtergeschichte: Herausforderung und Chance für die Sozialgeschichte," both in *Was ist Gesellschaftsgeschichte? Positionen, Themen, Analysen*, ed. Manfred Hettling et al. (Munich, 1991), 31–43, 22–30; Dorothee Wierling, "Alltagsgeschichte und Geschichte der Geschlechterbeziehungen: über historische und historiographische Verhältnisse," in Lüdtke, *Alltagsgeschichte*, 169–90; Gisela Bock, "Challenging Dichotomies: Perspectives on Women's History," in *Writing Women's History*, ed. Karen Offen, Ruth Pierson, and Jane Rendall (Bloomington, 1991).

skill, and independent political subjectivity."[25] Indeed, the basic category of "civil society" (one inflection of the German *bürgerliche Gesellschaft*) itself presumed the exclusion of women via the construction and naturalizing of claims about sexual difference, and to argue for women's emancipation into fully recognized citizenship therefore makes it "necessary to deconstruct and reassemble our understanding of the body politic" in general.[26]

Similarly, this "gendering of the public sphere" was matched by the gendered construction of class identities. Thus in a British context Leonore Davidoff and Catherine Hall have stressed *both* the constitutive role of gender (the historically specific structuring of sexual difference) in the ordering of the bourgeois social world *and* the interactions between this private sphere and the public sphere of associational activity and politics. Whereas the one focuses on particular structures of family and domesticity and on particular styles of consumption, the other reflects and actively reproduces the gendered distinctions of class identity generated at home and at work.[27] Nor can the importance of gender, sexuality, and the family be bracketed from the processes of working-class formation, because notions of physical labor, skill, the wage, respectability, and political voice were all completely shot through with assumptions about masculinity. In the light of this accumulating authority of feminist scholarship, it seems naive to present the possibility of women's emancipation as being inscribed in "certain foundational principles of bourgeois society," so that the rise of women's rights appears as the logical but delayed accompaniment of progressive social development, "as a late consequence of the dynamic set into motion with the transition to bourgeois society."[28] Such Whiggishness takes no account of the feminist critiques mentioned above. Nineteenth-century conceptions of progress were, on the

---

25. Sally Alexander, "Women, Class, and Sexual Differences in the 1830s and 1840s: Some Reflections on the Writing of a Feminist History," *History Workshop* 17 (Spring 1984): 137.

26. Carole Pateman, "The Fraternal Social Contract," in *Civil Society and the State: New European Perspectives,* ed. John Keane (London, 1988), 123.

27. Leonore Davidoff and Catherine Hall, *Family Fortunes: Men and Women of the English Middle Class, 1780–1850* (London, 1987). For Germany, see Karin Hausen, "Family and Role-Divison: The Polarization of Sexual Stereotypes in the Nineteenth Century—An Aspect of the Dissociation of Work and Family Life," in *The German Family: Essays on the Social History of the Family in the Nineteenth and Twentieth Century,* ed. Richard J. Evans and W. R. Lee (London, 1981), 51–83; Ute Frevert, "Bürgerliche Familie und Geschlechterrollen: Modell und Wirklichkeit," in Niethammer et al., *Bürgerliche Gesellschaft in Deutschland,* 90–100; and Frevert, *Bürgerinnen und Bürger.*

28. Kocka, "Bürgertum und bürgerliche Gesellschaft," 46–47. Significantly—and in contrast with the rest of his generously footnoted essay—the bibliographical citations dry up at this point in Kocka's survey of research and discussion on the bourgeoisie (that is, there are no references to Davidoff and Hall, *Family Fortunes,* to the feminist literature in political theory and the history of political thought, or the extremely large literature in U.S. women's history in this area).

contrary, inscribed with extremely powerful assumptions that worked consistently *against* women's emancipation, assigning women to dependent positions and a disempowered subjectivity.

In addressing the challenge that this poses to historians of women—both the silence of the available record and the silencing that produced it—recent commentators have stressed the political and theoretical conundrum left by the main forms of theory currently being used, namely, the varying combinations of poststructuralist and deconstructive skepticism around issues of agency, experience, and the stability of meaning, and the resulting critiques of the coherence and sufficiency of available analytical categories. The radical critique of existing categories—the self-conscious destabilizing of the unitary meanings that our deployment of such concepts as "class," "culture," "women," "agency," and "experience," tends to presume, and of the fixity of binary oppositions such as the "private and the public"—seems to remove the solid ground of identity as the recognized basis for constituting collective political agency just at the point when previously silenced groups—such as women—are claiming their common voice. This is the tension of "gender history" and "women's history," on which is focused so much discussion among women's historians of late. The stress on destabilizing, fracturing, fragmenting, decentering, and so on is bound to worry the advocates of women's interests, the acceptance of whose legitimacy (whether in a political sphere or among historians) has barely begun. As Canning puts it, in one recent airing of this dilemma,

> It is clear that attempts to decenter a subject whose own subjectivity (in a historical sense) is still in the process of being constituted—the white western woman, women and men of color, the gay or lesbian subject—have been far more contested than the first wave of deconstructive history aimed at the white male subject-individual-citizen of western European history. This process of fragmenting, decentering, dissolving narratives and paradigms has created a number of dilemmas for feminist historians.[29]

Thus in doing women's history at the start of the 1990s, several different moves are being undertaken simultaneously. To begin with, there is still a crying need simply to put women back into the historical record, both empirically (making women visible) and historiographically (changing the blithely masculine language and terms of the existing historical accounts). Secondly, for the given historical questions and understandings the conse-

---

29. Kathleen Canning, comment to the forum "Women's History/Gender History: Is Feminist Scholarship Losing Its Critical Edge?" *Journal of Women's History* 5 (Spring 1993): 106. The forum was originally held at the Social Science History Association, New Orleans, Nov. 1991.

quences of taking women's history seriously have to be more than simply additive; rather, they need to change the bases on which those existing problematics are themselves put together. In this sense, calling on German historians to acknowledge and reflect upon the presence of women destabilizes and reconstitutes concepts and analyses hitherto centered around men (much as our understanding of the "center" can be transformed by including the "periphery," and the view from "above" by adding the one from "below," to cite the similar moves already discussed above), and for the purposes of theorizing this relationality the category of gender inevitably comes into play. But lastly, in thinking through the consequences of bringing women into the picture—in "gendering" our conceptions of German history—there is no need for the specific agency and subjectivity of women to be effaced. In other words, by theorizing the further implications of women's history via the category of gender, by making women's history into gender history, we are not removing the need for more work on women specifically to be done.

Frequently, however, it is the very absence of women from the easily available record—their displacement from the story, their removal from the terms in which the meanings of German history have been mainly understood, the silencing of a female voice—that exerts the greatest challenge. Taking the grandest view for the moment, it is precisely the biggest questions of German history—the ones that organize its place in general historical understanding and the comparative wisdom of the social sciences and continue to attract the most interest from both students and a general historical public—that prove the most resistant to any gendered transformations of meaning. I am thinking of such questions as the origins and conduct of World War II, the collapse of the Weimar Republic, the rise of Nazism, the German Revolution, the outbreak and origins of World War I, and the underlying paradigm of the German *Sonderweg*. The dominant practitioners in these "core" domains have a seemingly limitless desire to continue deflecting the challenge of gender to the "margins": women's history is all right, in this view, so long as it stays in its place—with the history of the family and domestic life, with the history of women's associations, with the history of women in the professions, and with the history of particular groups of women workers. But until German historians (whether they work immediately on women or not) explore the relationship of the mutually constitutive understandings of masculinity and femininity to the complex structures of public life (for instance) or the bearing of social-policy innovation around the family on the state-society field of relations in general or the relevance of women's work to the overall formation of the working class, the exciting—and necessary—potential of gender perspectives will not be tapped.[30]

---

30. The one area in which some general progress has been made in changing the terms of the former problematic is that of Nazism and the social history of the Third Reich, where work on

Recently Eve Rosenhaft has provided a brilliant conspectus of how such approaches might be used. Reflecting on the existing state of German historiography ("It is still possible to write a general account of German history that excludes women," she regrets), she points to the "impenetrably masculine" character of the history of politics or public affairs in the German field, which the two significant recent achievements in connecting women's activity to the formal world of politics ("the feminization of the public sector in the growth of the welfare state," and "the Nazi cooptation of the idea of female *Lebensraum*") have barely touched. As she says, in establishing the political relevance of these stories ("in order to find women in politics"), historians have had to expand the definition of what politics conventionally includes:

> The tendency of empirical research up to now has been to establish the role of women in politics as a positively charged absence; there was a women's politics, but it took place in spheres distinct from the one in which state power was directly assigned and exercised—in occupational and confessional organizations, the women's sections of political parties, the expanding field of public and private social work.[31]

Part of the problem, of course, is that contemporary consciousness itself marked these activities as different, as beyond the political sphere in the true sense. Rosenhaft cites two examples close to the argumentation earlier in this essay, and their differing valence in her context casts a salutary light on the limits of the historiographical advances that my discussion is meant to record. One concerns the making of the Civil Code (*Bürgerliches Gesetzbuch*), which was completed in 1896 and formed a centerpiece of the National Liberal–dominated parliamentary consolidation that I attribute to the period after 1897. Women's political mobilization around the family law provisions of the code, initially through the submission of evidence and then through mass meetings and petitions, was both a key part of the process and yet virtually written out of the main historical accounts. Likewise, "if we want to treat elections and political organizations as the motor and manifestation of political mobiliza-

the complex of questions about eugenics and motherhood, and more generally on the bases of Nazi racism, has significantly shifted the prevailing perspectives of the field in general. See Koonz, *Mothers in the Fatherland;* Gisela Bock, *Zwangssterilisation im Nationalsozialismus: Studien zur Rassenpolitik und Frauenpolitik* (Opladen, 1986); Bridenthal, Grossmann, and Kaplan, *When Biology Became Destiny;* Dagmar Reese, *"Straff aber nicht stramm—Herb, aber nicht derb": Zur Vergesellschaftung von Mädchen durch den Bund Deutscher Mädel im sozialkulturellen Vergleich zweier Milieus* (Basel, 1989); Carola Sachse, *Siemens, der Nationalsozialismus und die moderne Familie: Eine Untersuchung zur sozialen Rationalisierung in Deutschland im 20. Jahrhundert* (Hamburg, 1990); Lerke Gravenhorst and Carmen Tatschmurat, eds., *Tochterfragen: NS-Frauen Geschichte* (Freiburg i. Br., 1990); Atina Grossmann, "Feminist Debates about Women and National Socialism," *Gender and History* 3 (1991): 350–85.

31. Rosenhaft, "Women, Gender, and the Limits of Political History," 150. The preceding quotations may be found ibid., 151, 149.

tion" before 1914 (as I certainly do in my arguments above), then women, who "did not have the national franchise and were largely excluded from party-political activity until 1908," "pose a real problem."[32] Thus if we confine our thinking about the relationship of gender to politics to these examples, we will largely confirm the conventional wisdom about women's exclusion and irrelevance: "The world of politics in which parties and other organized groups seek to translate perceived interests into power and to exercise power in pursuit of interest remains largely untouched by these approaches."[33]

The answer, Rosenhaft argues, is to look elsewhere. We need to reread the languages of politics in order to recognize women through the mechanisms and structures of their exclusion, whether such silencings are the result of direct discriminatory or exclusionary policies or practice, or whether they eventuate through less consciously directed logics of social relations and cultural behavior. She invokes the work of Dorinda Outram on the meanings of the body in the French Revolution to suggest how "modern ideas of the body politic and of the bourgeois individual as citizen came to be realized in social practice and internalized as part of a civic identity that was defined as essentially masculine"; and she argues that the processes of continuous negotiation through which this gendering of social and political identity became articulated with relations of dominance and subordination during the nineteenth and twentieth centuries can bring us closer to the circumstances of women as the group whose access to public virtue and the formal attributes of citizenship was so expressly held at bay.[34] Rosenhaft provides a number of specific examples, including the need to rescrutinize the terms of conservative and acquiescent religiosity through which women's active involvement in the organized culture of Catholicism is usually devalued as "demobilizing" or "depoliticizing" rather than being seen as a distinctive form of women's political engagement. As she says, this is a particularly strong instance of "the 'private' politics that is not only implicit in the familiar masculine forms of politics but constitutes its premise."[35]

The most interesting point Rosenhaft makes in this respect concerns the discourse of the "mass" between the 1880s and 1930s, in which certain feminized constructions of the urban mass public "coincided" historically with the pressure of women for political rights, culminating during the Weimar Re-

---

32. Ibid., 153–54.

33. Ibid., 150.

34. Ibid., 159. See also Dorinda Outram, *The Body and the French Revolution: Sex, Class and Political Culture* (New Haven, 1989); Joan B. Landes, *Women and the Public Sphere in the Age of the French Revolution* (Ithaca, 1988); and Geoff Eley, "Nations, Publics, and Political Cultures: Placing Habermas in the Nineteenth Century," in *Habermas and the Public Sphere,* ed. Craig Calhoun (Cambridge, Mass., 1992), 307–19.

35. Rosenhaft, "Women, Gender, and the Limits of Political History," 158.

public in access to the franchise and large-scale recruitment into the new apparatus of the welfare state. In Rosenhaft's view, "mass," with its distinctive feminine coding, "appears almost as a deliberate circumlocution" on the part of male 1920s intellectuals for "this significant feminization of the political order."[36] The new public arena of commercially provided mass entertainment (film, radio, advertising, dance halls, spectator sports) thus provides a rich field of analysis for a gendered reading of political discourse. But whereas work in cultural studies, focusing on genre criticism and originating primarily within literary theory, has accumulated a large corpus of relevant work for such a project, particularly on film, historians have barely scratched the surface of these possibilities.[37] As Rosenhaft says,

> As a term that simultaneously insists on the femininity of the new public and obscures the presence of women within it, "the mass" has the advantage of directing us to the operation of gender discourses in the definition of politics (and the political subject) and to the issue of how the development of new media of mass communication affects the ways in which political opinion and participation are shaped.[38]

These perspectives are in the process of entering discussion among German historians in a major way. The beginnings of this process were already mentioned above (with the 1986 Rutgers conference and its follow-up), and by 1989–90 something resembling an organized exchange of ideas was beginning to take shape. At a small symposium in Chicago in October 1989 on interdisciplinary and new theoretical influences on German history, at the stock-taking conference on the *Kaiserreich* of February 1990 where the papers published in this volume began, and at another major conference in Toronto, "Elections, Mass Politics, and Social Change," in April 1990 (where Rosenhaft's paper was presented), "gender in German history" was a major

---

36. Ibid., 162.

37. The preliminary ground for such a history is marked out, but the pioneers are almost exclusively working from a literary, as against a historical background. See especially Patrice Petro, *Joyless Streets: Women and Melodramatic Representation in Weimar Germany* (Princeton, 1989); Thomas Elsaesser, "Film History and Visual Pleasure: Weimar Cinema," in *Cinema Histories, Cinema Practices,* ed. Patricia Mellencamp and Philip Rosen (Frederick, Md., 1984), 47–84; Thomas Elsaesser, "Social Mobility and the Fantastic: German Silent Cinema," *Wide Angle* 5 (1982): 14–25; Miriam Hansen, "Early Silent Cinema: Whose Public Sphere?" *New German Critique* 29 (1983): 147–84; Miriam Hansen, *Babel and Babylon: Spectatorship in American Silent Film* (Cambridge, Mass., 1991); Bruce Murray, *Film and the German Left in the Weimar Republic: From Caligari to Kuhle Wampe* (Austin, 1990); James Hay, *Popular Film Culture in Fascist Italy: The Passing of the Rex* (Bloomington, 1987); Annette Kuhn, *Cinema, Censorship and Sexuality, 1909–1925* (London, 1988).

38. Rosenhaft, "Women, Gender, and the Limits of Political History," 163–64.

theme.[39] The essays in this volume provide further evidence of the progress of these discussions.

Post-Foucauldian Analysis

Few names of social theorists can polarize—unequally—a roomful of historians quite as rapidly as Michel Foucault, particularly as it tends to function as a general sign for the so-called linguistic turn, or the inescapable contemporary influence of poststructuralist theory, linguistic analysis, deconstructionist literary theory, and related forms of theoretical address. The Philadelphia conference on the *Kaiserreich* was no exception to this generalization, and most of the open tension in the discussions flowed from a certain impatience with the characteristic language of post-Foucauldian analysis and the perceived absolutism of its claims. Such tension, of course, reflects wider conflicts within the profession—precipitated to a great extent by the mid-1980s interventions of Joan Scott—in which the practitioners of social history have felt called upon to defend the ground of a materialist analysis constructed so carefully and painfully during a previous era of methodological and theoretical duress (the 1960s and 1970s).[40] To this degree (though without quite the overt political charge) these conflicts parallel the debates within feminism alluded to above. The retreat from confident assumptions of social causality and materialist ideas of determination, combined with the playfulness of much of the so-called new cultural history, has led many social and political historians to see the recent turning to cultural analysis as a betrayal of the historian's groundedness in the archivally bounded investigation of an empirically knowable world, as a distressing symptom of the age, the slow seepage into historical discourse of a postmodernist sensibility.[41]

---

39. The proceedings of the Chicago symposium were published as a special issue of *Central European History* 22 (1989) under the title "German Histories: Challenges in Theory, Practice, Technique." The Toronto proceedings have appeared as Jones and Retallack, *Elections, Mass Politics, and Social Change.*

40. See Bryan Palmer's intemperate book-length polemic, *Descent into Discourse: The Reification of Language and the Writing of Social History* (Philadelphia, 1990). I have addressed this field of difficulty and debate in Geoff Eley, "Is All the World a Text? From Social History to the History of Society Two Decades Later," in *The Historic Turn in the Human Sciences* , ed. Terrence J. McDonald (Ann Arbor, forthcoming).

41. For the flavor of historians' anxieties, see the somewhat ridiculous call to arms published by Lawrence Stone and the carefully reasoned responses by Gabrielle Spiegel and by Patrick Joyce, together with Stone's subsequent rejoinder, all published in *Past and Present* under the rubric "History and Post-Modernism": Lawrence Stone, *Past and Present* 131 (May 1991): 217–18; Patrick Joyce, 133 (Nov. 1991): 204–9; Gabrielle M. Spiegel, 135 (May 1992): 194–208; Stone, 135 (May 1992): 189–94. The most substantial statement by a social historian hostile to the new culturalism is Palmer, *Descent into Discourse,* which reflects accurately both the legitimate scruples and the polemical over-the-topness of so much of the current response. For efforts at a

Discussion can easily become ensnared in ungenerous and ill-tempered disputes about Foucault's historical work as such. But the reception and working through of Foucault's insights have had an impact on contemporary social and cultural analysis that cannot simply be ignored. In particular, I would argue, his distinctive understanding of power has unmistakable bearing on how we are able to think about the state/society set of relationships today, and some laying out of these ideas can usefully clarify the way in which historians are now constructing their questions.

On the one hand, Foucault's influence has encouraged us to look for power and its operations away from the conventionally recognized sites of public political life. His ideas have fundamentally directed attention away from institutionally centered conceptions of government and the state, away from the allied sociological conceptions of class domination, and toward a dispersed and decentered notion of power and its "microphysics." Foucault's approach carries the analysis of power away from the core institutions of the state in the national, centralized sense and toward the emergence of new strategies of governance, regulation, and control focused on both individuals and larger social categories, whose operation depends as much on the very definition of the subject populations as it does on the more practical mechanics of coercive or regulative control. Such processes "function outside, below, and alongside the State apparatuses, on a much more minute and everyday level."[42] On the other hand, Foucault's ideas have also sensitized us to the subtle and complex interrelations between power and knowledge, particularly in the modes of disciplinary and administrative organization of knowledge in a society. This is where the concept of discourse becomes important as a way of theorizing the internal rules and regularities of particular fields of knowledge (their "regimes of truth") and as a term for the more general structures of ideas and assumptions that delimit what can and cannot be thought and said in particular contexts of place and time. Such an approach has radically challenged the historian's customary assumptions about individual and collective agency and their bases of interest and rationality, forcing us to see instead how subjectivities are constructed and produced within and through languages of identification that lie beyond the volition and control of individuals in the classical Enlightenment sense.

In these two senses, Foucault finds power at work in the basic categories of modern social understanding—in the visions and imaginings that project the transparency and coherence of society, in the programmatic descriptions of its

more considered discussion, see Jane Caplan, "Postmodernism, Poststructuralism, and Deconstruction: Notes for Historians," *Central European History* 22 (1989): 260–78; and Eley, "Is All the World a Text?"

42. Michel Foucault, "Body/Power," in *Power/Knowledge: Selected Interviews and Other Writings, 1972–1977 by Michel Foucault,* ed. Colin Gordon (Brighton, 1980), 60.

desirable organization, in the theories (practical and esoteric) that seek to order and alter its workings, and in the policies and practices that act on its actually existing forms. He calls into question the very categories of modern understanding, from the collective goods of society and citizenship to the individual values of rationalism and the self. He does so by historicizing them, by specifying the terms of their own social, political, and intellectual history and of their emergence and elaboration into the constitutive elements for ordering the material and mental world. We can do this for the foundational category of "society" itself by looking at the terms under which "the social" first became abstracted into thought and practice—as an object of theory-knowledge, a target of policy, and a site of practice—so that the material context in which "society" could be convincingly represented as an ultimately originating subject or causality became gradually composed.[43] This is not to deny society's "existence" in the realist sense, its materiality, or the structures and relations that "really" compose its shape and forms. But the latter can barely be engaged without simultaneously unraveling the discursive constructions that mediate their accessibility to our minds. In this sense, we are increasingly forced to step back from the more confident projects of analysis that social history had previously proposed—that is, from the immediate capturing of social realities—to a more cautious exploration of the discursive formations, the complex histories of meanings and representations, through which those realities have to be approached.

Concretely, we can focus on the ways in which "society" or "the social" themselves became recognized for nineteenth-century governments as the main object of science, surveillance, policy, and power. Population, economics, poverty, crime, education, and welfare became not only the main objects of government activity but also the measure of solidarity and cohesion in the emerging nineteenth-century social order. If we are to understand nineteenth-century politics, Foucault argues, we must look to the new knowledges "concerning society, its health and sickness, its conditions of life, housing and habits, which served as the basic core for the 'social economy' and sociology of the nineteenth century."[44] In the early twentieth century, of course, the range of power-producing knowledges then expands further—through psychology and psychiatry, social work, youth policy, industrial rela-

---

43. Whereas this approach derives strongly from Foucault himself, it also has affinities with the "keywords" method of Raymond Williams and with the work of Reinhart Kosselleck and the West German tradition of *Begriffsgeschichte*. See Raymond Williams, *Keywords: A Vocabulary of Culture and Society,* rev. ed. (New York, 1983); Otto Brunner, Werner Conze, and Reinhart Kosselleck, eds., *Geschichtliche Grundbegriffe,* 5 vols. (Stuttgart, 1972–89).

44. Michel Foucault, "The Politics of Health in the Eighteenth Century," in *Power/ Knowledge,* 176.

tions, public health, social hygiene, eugenics, and the general apparatus of the welfare state and its societal interventions.

At one level, this discursive move—the focusing of attention on the histories through which dominant forms of understanding (categories, assumptions, perspectives and policies and practices as well as theories, programs, and philosophies) have been shaped—involves a turning back to questions of ideology; and to understand why such a Foucauldian approach is proving attractive, some reflection on earlier treatments of ideology in German historical discussion will help. Basically, the terms and tone of this discussion were set for many years by works such as those by Fritz Stern and George Mosse, *The Politics of Cultural Despair* and *The Crisis of German Ideology.* Here ideology was approached as a set of false and malevolent beliefs, often distortions of older traditions of thought produced by the pathologies of the German historical context (the *Sonderweg* again), that could only take widespread hold in conditions of extremity, crisis, and disorientation and could be tracked visibly and unambiguously through policies, institutions, and decisions, assigned to individuals, and derived from precursors. An entire genre of works exists on the "ideological origins" of Nazism in this sense. To a great extent, the turning to social history in the 1960s and 1970s was a conscious rejection of this stress on ideology, an assertion that the peculiar dynamism of Nazism had an altogether more complicated relationship both to its own internal structures and to the larger social context than such an emphasis had allowed.[45]

For a while this turn encouraged a certain indifference, bordering on outright hostility, to ideological analysis as such, resulting in a dichotomized historiographical outlook privileging social history, which in many ways still defines the field. Yet given a different conception of ideology, one which is discursively founded and socially embedded in a line that runs through structuralist and poststructuralist approaches from Louis Althusser through Antonio Gramsci to contemporary feminist theories of subjectivity and the reception of Foucault, there is no reason for this to be so. I would argue that the recent interest in the racialist, gendered, and biomedical dimensions of Nazi policies has provided ideal ground for such a differently conceptualized discussion of ideology to begin, even if in most particular works this is happening in a mostly practical (as opposed to consciously theorized) way. The growth of research into the larger domain of "biological politics" as a unifying principle of Nazi practice, linking anti-Semitism and the racialist offensive of the war years to a complex of policies before 1939, including population planning, public health,

---

45. See Fritz Stern, *The Politics of Cultural Despair* (Berkeley, 1961); George L. Mosse, *The Crisis of German Ideology* (London, 1966). For critiques, see Geoff Eley, "The Wilhelmine Right: How It Changed," in Evans, *Society and Politics,* 112–35; and Eley, *Reshaping the German Right,* 160–205.

welfare policies directed at women, family policy, euthanasia, sterilization, and eugenics is the key here.

The best work on the Third Reich from this point of view has stressed the origins of this racialized social-policy complex in ideas and innovations that go back to the Weimar Republic and even further, to the period before 1914. Thus, without diminishing the centrality of the Nazis' anti-Jewish genocidal commitments, the effect of the new work has been to shift our attention increasingly to the larger racialist ambitions in which the logic of the Final Solution was inscribed. On the one hand, it is clear now that not only the Jews but also other ethnic groups (Sinti and Roma, Poles, other Slav peoples), entire social categories (homosexuals, the physically and mentally handicapped, the incurably ill, potentially the vagrant, the homeless, the permanently unemployed, the criminal), and political enemies (Polish intellectuals, Soviet prisoners of war, "political commissars," Communists and other subversives) were made the object of racist and eugenicist ambition. And on the other hand, this could only occur via the prior diffusion of eugenicist and related ideologies of social engineering, which to a great extent had permeated the thinking of social-policy and health-care professionals long before the Nazis themselves had arrived. In both respects, that is, the ground for the Final Solution was being discursively laid.[46]

If we take this argument about the conditions of possibility for the Final Solution seriously—both the preconceptions and embedded social practices with which the Nazi political project in the stricter sense could work, and the laying of this ground before 1933—then the importance of ideological analysis surely becomes clear, not as a return to the exegetical focus on Hitler's and other Nazi leaders' immediate ideas and their etymology but as an expanded cultural analysis of the production of meanings and values in pre-Nazi (and non-Nazi) society. In the immediate domain of biological politics and racial hygiene, for instance, there is now a general recognition that Nazi excesses only became possible through the "normal" achievements of respectable science, so that the Nazis' appalling schemes become less an eruption of "un-

---

46. The best general introduction to this literature is Michael Burleigh and Wolfgang Wippermann, *The Racial State: Germany, 1933–1945* (Cambridge, 1991); and Bridenthal, Grossmann, and Kaplan, *When Biology Became Destiny.* Work on Sinti and Roma and work on the euthanasia program (known as "T-4," after the address at Tiergartenstrasse 4) have been especially key in getting this broadened understanding of the "racial state" off the ground, as has Ulrich Herbert's pioneering work on forced foreign labor during World War II. See Ulrich Herbert, *Fremdarbeiter: Politik und Praxis des "Auslander-Einsatzes" in der Kriegswirtschaft des Dritten Reiches* (Bonn, 1985); Ulrich Herbert, *A History of Foreign Labor in Germany, 1880–1980: Seasonal Workers/Forced Laborers/Guest Workers* (Ann Arbor, 1990), 127–92; and Ulrich Herbert, "Labour and Extermination: Economic Interest and the Primacy of *Weltanschauung* in National Socialism," *Past and Present* 138 (Feb. 1993): 144–95. A broadly contextualized introductory discussion can also be had through Zygmunt Baumann, *Modernity and the Holocaust* (Ithaca, 1989).

science" and the irrational than the advent of technocratic reason and the ethical unboundedness of science, fully continuous with the logics of earlier ambitions. This amounts to a decisive shift of perspective, away from Nazism's immediate cadres to the broader, deeper, and less visible ideological consensus that they were able to use—to "the genesis of the 'Final Solution' from the spirit of science," in the words of Detlev Peukert.[47] Foucault could easily be the patron saint of this new turn, given the salience of arguments about discipline, knowledge, science, and domination.[48]

There are two key aspects to this reinstatement of the importance of ideology in the extended understanding of ideology *qua* discourse that I have briefly indicated above; and both have a vital relevance to the problematics within which historians of the *Kaiserreich* are now starting to work. One aspect concerns the nature and effectiveness of the Nazis' popular appeal. In keeping with the shift from ideological analysis in the older sense, the tendency for many years was to downplay the originality and power of the NSDAP's own ideological message during the electoral rise of 1928–33, emphasizing instead the chameleon-like nature of Nazi propaganda and its ability to capitalize manipulatively on the existing values of the German bourgeoisie and petite bourgeoisie. This approach as such is consistent with the post-Foucauldian notion of ideology (as widely diffused meanings, representations, ordering assumptions and practices) I have outlined above, although its main practitioners tended to see themselves as doing social history in contradistinction to studies of ideology.[49] However, far from revealing the unimportance of ideology to the Nazis' success or their character as a political formation, I would argue, both the history of the party's electoral rise and the bases of the regime's stability show the vital centrality of ideological analysis. The NSDAP was a phenomenon without precedent in the history of the Right in Germany in that it discovered the forms of unification among the hopelessly fractured parties and constituencies of the Right and simultaneously grounded itself in a remarkably

---

47. See Detlev Peukert, "The Genesis of the 'Final Solution' from the Spirit of Science," in Childers and Caplan, *Reevaluating the Third Reich,* 234–52.

48. In fact, Foucault is rarely referred to in these discussions.

49. See Edward N. Peterson, *The Limits of Hitler's Power* (Princeton, 1969); William Sheridan Allen, *The Nazi Seizure of Power: The Experience of a Single German Town, 1922–1945,* rev. ed. (New York, 1984); Ian Kershaw, "Ideology, Propaganda, and the Rise of the Nazi Party," in *The Nazi Machtergreifung,* ed. Peter D. Stachura (London, 1983), 162–81; Ian Kershaw, "How Effective Was Nazi Propaganda?" in *Nazi Propaganda: The Power and the Limitations,* ed. David Welch (London, 1983), 180–205; Richard Bessel, "The Rise of the NSDAP and the Myth of Nazi Propaganda," *Wiener Library Bulletin* 33 (1980): 20–29; and Richard Bessel, "Violence as Propaganda: The Role of the Stormtroopers in the Rise of National Socialism," in *The Formation of the Nazi Constituency, 1919–1933,* ed. Thomas Childers (London, 1966), 131–46. This last is a good example of an excellent collection of work on themes of political mobilization that devotes little attention to questions of ideology as such.

broad base of popular support in sociological terms. And it did so precisely by its ability to bring together and articulate a diverse and hitherto contradictory ensemble of ideological appeals. This was an achievement of remarkable power and baleful implications, and we really need to work hard at understanding how it came to occur. The question here is, What were the connotative principles (the integrative or unifying bases, the principles of articulation) that allowed so many diverse categories of people to recognize themselves in the Nazi celebration of the race/people, that allowed the Nazis to capture the popular imagination so powerfully before and after 1933? And if we formulate the question in this particular way, with its implied contrast with the political fragmentation of earlier right-wing formations, some tasks are identified for the research on the Weimar and Wilhelmine periods that came before. That is, how exactly were the politics of the Right constituted in this earlier time, and what were the conditions of possibility for change?[50]

The second task set by the shifts in the problematic of Nazism for the historians of the *Kaiserreich* is the need to ground the arguments about the more broadly diffused context of biomedical discourse in the 1930s in a densely textured history of such ideas in the earlier period after the turn of the century. This will mean much fuller and more imaginatively constructed investigations of the social-policy contexts of the *Kaiserreich,* investigations in which the production of new values, new mores, new social practices, new ideas about the good and efficient society—new "normativities"—and their forms of projected and achieved realization occupy pride of place. It will mean paying careful attention to the gendered meanings of such histories, as well as to the power-producing effects in Foucault's "microphysical" sense. Strategies of social policing and constructions of criminality, notions of the normal and the deviant, the production and regulation of sexuality, the definition of intelligence, and the understanding of the socially valued individual will all play a part in this analysis, as will the coalescence of racialized thinking about the desirable character of the people-nation and its social and political arrangements, about the character of the body politic. Some beginning has been made in these directions, as in Paul Weindling's major synthesis in *Health, Race and German Politics,* which extends across the whole period from 1871 to 1945; in Derek Linton's work on the youth question before 1914; and Peukert's work on the general issues of *Sozialdisziplinierung*.[51] One feature of the work I have

---

50. This became the conceptual starting point for my own work on the Wilhelmine Right, although I was able to formulate it more clearly at the end of my research than when it began. See Eley, *Reshaping the German Right;* and Geoff Eley, "Conservatives and Radical Nationalists in Germany: The Production of Fascist Potentials," in *Fascists and Conservatives: The Radical Right and the Establishment in Twentieth-Century Europe,* ed. Martin Blinkhorn (London, 1990), 50–70.

51. See Paul Weindling, *Health, Race and German Politics between National Unification and Nazism, 1870–1945* (Cambridge, 1989); Derek S. Linton, *"Who Has the Youth, Has the*

been describing is that it diminishes the importance of the old chronological markers of German history (1914–18, 1933), encouraging instead a re-periodizing of the late nineteenth and early twentieth centuries to stress the coherence of the years between the 1890s and 1930s as a unitary context in which definite themes of national efficiency, social hygiene, and racialized nationalism coalesced. Several of the essays in this volume explicitly take this view, especially those by Hong and David Crew, which focus specifically on the social-policy domain.

Cultural Studies

Integrally connected to the first two influences I have discussed is the rapidly emerging importance of the "new cultural history." There are various ways of narrating the latter's origins (in what serves as the flagship collection of essays, for instance, various periods and types of society are represented, among which early modern Europe has probably been the key).[52] But for our present purposes, I want to stress the gathering impact of the somewhat different field of contemporary cultural studies, which in its stronger versions has inspired relatively little historical work, but whose future influence promises to be great.

A still-emergent cross-disciplinary formation, cultural studies comprises a varying miscellany of influences—sociology, literary studies, and history in Britain (but, interestingly, rather little anthropology); mass communications, film studies, literary theory, reflexive anthropology in the United States, with a supportive institutional context in such programs as women's studies and American culture. So far, the main U.S. initiatives have come from the humanities, whereas the proliferating interdisciplinary programs and institutes in the social sciences have shown much less interest. In Britain the logic has tended perhaps in the other direction, although the greater strength of qualitative sociologies there has also blurred the sharpness of the social sciences/humanities divide. On the other hand, feminist theory has had a major role in both Britain and the United States, as has the post-Saidian critique of colonial and racist forms of thought in the Western cultural tradition. Again, individual influences vary (for instance, Gramsci and psychoanalytic approaches in Britain, and Clifford Geertz and subsequent anthropologies in the United States), but the so-called linguistic turn and the fascination with postmodernism have increasingly allowed the two national discussions to converge. Moreover, although most of the concrete research has focused strongly on the "long pres-

---

Future": The Campaign to Save Young Workers in Imperial Germany (Cambridge, 1991); Detlev Peukert, *Grenzen der Sozialdisziplinierung: Aufstieg und Krise der deutschen Jugendfürsorge 1878 bis 1932* (Cologne, 1986); and Detlev Peukert, *Jugend zwischen Krieg und Krise: Lebenswelten von Arbeiterjungen in der Weimarer Republik* (Cologne, 1987).

52. See Lynn Hunt, ed., *The New Cultural History* (Berkeley, 1989).

ent" of cultural studies since 1945, this in itself is a period badly in need of historians' attention, and transference of the interests concerned to earlier times is already under way. Simply enumerating some main areas of current activity will be enough to make the point: the visual technologies of film, photography, television, and video, and commercial media such as advertising, comic books, and magazines; the relationship of women in particular to popular reading genres (romances, gothic novels, family sagas), television (soap operas, detective series, situation comedies), and film (film noir, horror, science fiction, melodrama); the growth of new consumer economies, particularly in the mass entertainment industries but also affecting food, fashion and dress, domestic labor in households, leisure and play, and all manner of life-style concerns; the use of autobiography and the personal voice; and postcolonial cultural critique and the analysis of "race."[53]

An important effect of this wave has been the reopening of old debates about the opposition of "high" and "low" culture, with a notable commitment to engaging popular culture in nondismissive, nonpatronizing ways. Taking popular culture seriously, as manifesting real needs and aspirations, as something to be decoded imaginatively in that light, however banal and apparently trivial the contents, has become a central tenet of these discussions, and here it is feminist writing that has been showing the way. Given the understandable and strategically necessary hostility to popular culture in the heyday of the women's liberation movement in the late 1960s and early 1970s, this is a noteworthy turn of affairs, for in that earlier moment, the power of conventional sex-gender signs in everything from makeup to romantic fiction was taken as evidence of backwardness, oppression, and male exploitation in some transparent and self-evidently indictable way. Against this earlier confrontationism, we have seen growing efforts to get inside popular culture to explore more sympathetically how cultural production works on needs in appealing and contradictory ways, from soap opera to MTV. The emergence of a discourse during the 1980s around "pleasure" and "desire" as categories of political understanding, beyond their immediate place in the politics of sexuality in the stricter sense, has been a major symptom of this move and signifies a rethinking of the "popular" in popular culture much larger than the specifically feminist discussion. It implies a more positive engagement with popular culture than either the "mass culture" or the "folk culture" oriented traditions of analysis have tended to allow. It conjoins with the post-Foucauldian develop-

---

53. Among the most useful introductions to cultural studies are the following: Patrick Brantlinger, *Crusoe's Footprints: Cultural Studies in Britain and America* (New York, 1990); Jim McGuigan, *Cultural Populism* (London, 1992); Fred Inglis, *Media Theory: An Introduction* (Oxford, 1990); and Lawrence Grossberg, Cary Nelson, and Paula Treichler, eds., *Cultural Studies* (New York, 1992).

ments in the theory of power. And it requires a major shift in our understanding of the sites at which political action can begin.[54]

In this sense, culture defines a ground of politics beyond the space conventionally recognized by most political traditions as the appropriate context for policy-making in education and the arts. Indeed, reaching back through the twentieth to the later nineteenth century, it is hard to find a democratic politics (whether of the liberal or socialist Left or of the conservative, as opposed to the fascist, Right) that deliberately and openly validated popular culture in its mass commercialized forms. Historically speaking, the very notion of "high culture" has always been counterposed to something else that is less valued, to culture that is "low." In the late nineteenth and twentieth centuries, the construction of this cultural "other" has taken two main forms, although both have been heavily overdetermined by gendered assumptions of value and capacity, as my discussion of gender studies pointed out. One is the colonialist representation of non-Western peoples, which externalizes the distinction between high and low within racialized frameworks of cultural superiority, even (or especially) when the differences concerned have become internal to the Western society. But the second has been produced inside Western cultures themselves and has generally been identified with the "mass," with an idea of popular culture in which "the popular" has been dissociated from romantic notions of authenticity and the folk and has become attached to the commercialized culture of entertainment and leisure in ways that imply corruption rather than preservation, artificiality as opposed to naturalness, vulgarity rather than virtue. This idea of mass culture has been further linked to ideas of the city and a distinctive twentieth-century structure of public communication based on such cheap technologies of film, radio, gramophone, photography, television, motorization, pulp fiction, mass advertising, and magazines.

It is worth remaining briefly with this set of associations. With the idea of the mass has invariably come a sense of decline, of corruption and moral danger—a negative imagery of "un-culture" and disorder, of drunkenness, gambling, unregulated sexuality, violence, criminality, and unstable family life, an imagery organized around social anxieties about youth in explicitly gendered ways. The political valence of this thinking has always been complex. The opposition of "high" and "low" is neither Right nor Left in itself.

---

54. See Judith Williamson, *Consuming Passions: The Dynamics of Popular Culture* (London, 1986); Lorraine Gammon and Margaret Marshment, eds., *The Female Gaze: Women as Viewers of Popular Culture* (London, 1988); Tania Modleski, *Loving with a Vengeance: Mass-Produced Fantasies for Women* (New York, 1982); E. Ann Kaplan, *Rocking around the Clock: Music Television, Postmodernism, and Consumer Culture* (New York, 1987); and Laura Kipnis, *Ecstasy Unlimited: On Sex, Capital, Gender, and Aesthetics* (Minneapolis, 1993). See also Stuart Hall, "Notes on Deconstructing 'the Popular,'" in *People's History and Socialist Theory*, ed. Raphael Samuel (London, 1981), 227–39.

Thus the socialist tradition has drawn just as sharp a line between, on the one hand, the ideal of an educative and uplifting culture of the arts and enlightenment and, on the other hand, an actually existing popular culture of base gratification, roughness, and disorder, which (in the socialist mind) the commercialized apparatus of mass provision has been only too glad to exploit. Socialist cultural policies, no less than liberal ones, have always stressed the virtues of self-improvement and sobriety over the disorderly realities of much working-class existence. For socialists, places of commercial popular entertainment—music halls, circuses, fairs, and all kinds of rough sports in the later nineteenth century; followed by the dance hall and the picture palace in the early twentieth century; and dance clubs, rock concerts, and commercial television since 1945—have been a source of frivolity and backwardness in working-class culture; and against this machinery of escapist dissipation, they counterposed the argument that working people should organize their own free time collectively and in morally uplifting ways. More recently, with the late-twentieth-century crisis of the inner city, this opposition has been transcribed into the racially constructed image of the immigrant urban poor, which is itself historically reminiscent of an earlier subset of the dominant high/low binarism, namely, the xenophobic reaction against Eastern European Jewish immigrants before World War I. To this extent, socialists, liberals, and conservatives have inhabited a common discourse. The precise boundaries between the "high" and the "low," the "cultured" and the "not," have been differently drawn, but the power of the distinction per se seems hegemonic.[55]

However, although "official" politics failed to respond positively or creatively to the mass-culture phenomenon in the early twentieth century, this does not mean that mass culture was not producing powerful meanings in eminently political ways. Indeed, the new apparatus of the "culture industry" (to use one of its familiar pejorative names)—from the razzmatazz of the

---

55. A stimulating framework for thinking about these issues is provided by James Naremore and Patrick Brantlinger, eds., *Modernity and Mass Culture* (Bloomington, 1991); and Andreas Huyssen, *After the Great Divide: Modernism, Mass Culture, Postmodernism* (Bloomington, 1986). A particular framing of the high/low issue at the turn of the century was provided by the complex and variegated repertoire of contemporary theories of degeneration, and while the German historiography of health and race, articulated especially around eugenicist ideas, gives some access to this, there is still much work to be done. See especially Weindling, *Health, Race and German Politics;* Woodruff D. Smith, *Politics and the Sciences of Culture in Germany, 1840–1920* (New York, 1991). For suggestive work in other national fields, see Daniel Pick, *Faces of Degeneration: A European Disorder, c.1848-c.1918* (Cambridge, 1989); Robert A. Nye, *Crime, Madness, and Politics in Modern France: The Medical Concept of National Decline* (Princeton, 1984); Susanna Barrows, *Distorting Mirrors: Visions of the Crowd in Late Nineteenth-Century France* (New Haven, 1981); Ruth Harris, *Murders and Madness: Medicine, Law, and Society in the fin de siècle* (Oxford, 1989); Judith R. Walkowitz, *City of Dreadful Night: Narratives of Sexual Danger in Late-Victorian London* (Chicago, 1992); and Greta Jones, *Social Hygiene in Twentieth Century Britain* (London, 1986).

cinema and the dance hall to the rise of spectator sports, the star system, and the machineries of advertising and fashion—proved remarkably effective in servicing a private economy of desire, beginning in the 1920s and expanding its hold on the popular imagination ever since. This is where the recent validating of popular culture in cultural studies makes its point. The emerging popular culture could no longer be so easily dismissed as an empty and depoliticized commercial corruption of traditional working-class culture (the typical Left critique) but on the contrary claimed a democratic authenticity of its own. Some cultural practitioners of the 1920s could see this. It was precisely the new technologies and media of communication and their mass audiences that excited the German left-modernists, such as Walter Benjamin, Bertolt Brecht, Erwin Piscator, and John Heartfield. No less than the Russian futurists and other avant-gardes in the aftermath of 1917, they used popular forms, such as circus and cabaret; worked through new technical media, such as posters, photographs, and film; and celebrated the mass reproducibility of their work, whereas conventional artists continued to sanctify the value and uniqueness of the individual creation. Benjamin's now classic essay of 1936, "The Work of Art in the Age of Mechanical Reproduction," is a brilliant meditation on the actuality of popular culture, while by the end of the 1920s, the practice of someone like Brecht was suffused with the same recognitions. While cultural conservatives of all stripes (Left as well as Right) could only counterpose the vulgarities of the cinema and other mass entertainments to the "true" values of art, Brecht found them the source of an artistic breakthrough. The raucousness, cigar smoke, and plebeian tones of the boxing hall were the epitome of all that the "bourgeois" theater abhorred, and sport became the model for how such public performance could be reformed, "with the stage as a brightly lit ring devoid of all mystique, demanding a critical, irreverent attitude on the part of the audience."[56]

How should we respond to these discussions as historians working specifically on the *Kaiserreich*? Most obviously, the discourse of the "mass" (mass society, mass culture, mass public, the rise of the masses) can be historicized confidently within the later nineteenth century, with a distinct set of beginnings in the years between the 1880s and 1914. As suggested above, this discourse not only articulated anxieties about social boundaries and the pressure of democracy on existing constitutional arrangements; it was also organized by misogynist constructions of the urban mass public as dangerously feminine. Whereas "mass" had already acquired its positive inflections in the usages of the Left, with its connotations of power in numbers, solidarity, and popular democratic strength, in the language of democracy's critics, it implied "low-

---

56. John Willett, *The New Sobriety, 1917–1933: Art and Politics in the Weimar Period* (London, 1976), 103. For Benjamin's essay, see his *Illuminations* (New York, 1968), 219–53.

ness" and "vulgarity," the threat of the "rabble" and the "mob," whose instincts were only "low, ignorant, unstable," and whose political preferences were "uninstructed," ripe for manipulation by the dominant interests and the defenders of the status quo.[57] Moreover, as I have argued above, such discomforts also permeated the sensibility of the Left, with its cultural languages of sobriety and uplift—reflecting essentially the fear that, left to itself, the new mass public would be seduced by the city's pleasures and excitements, prey to unscrupulous agitators of the political Right, no less than to the hucksters and charlatans of a tawdry commercialism. Finally, the transformation of the public sphere—that reshaping of the political nation initiated so powerfully by the popular mobilizations of the 1890s—is the structural context of this new contentiousness around the appearance and allegiances of the urban mass public. Here the opportunities for cultural analysis are adumbrated by a set of social histories that are themselves still imperfectly researched and understood: the rise of a national reading public, the massive expansion of the popular press, the establishment of comprehensive postal communications and the later introduction of the telephone, the building of railway branch-lines and minor roads, the spread of libraries, the burgeoning of voluntary associations, and the unprecedented availability of cheap reading matter, soon to be extended by the new technologies of printing, radio and film.

But whereas an essay such as Rosenhaft's marks out the possible ground for a cultural history that would engage these opportunities, it is still hard to find a literature for the *Kaiserreich* where they have been realized.[58] There has been some turning to cultural history in an older sense, in particular to the history of the arts, in which some effort is made to giving the latter a stronger social and political context, but this locates itself rather firmly on the "high" cultural side of the distinction.[59] Moreover, to a very great extent, the con-

---

57. Here I am citing from "Masses," in Williams, *Keywords,* 192–97.

58. Rosenhaft, "Women, Gender, and the Limits of Political History."

59. See especially Peter Paret, *The Berlin Secession: Modernism and Its Enemies in Imperial Germany* (Cambridge, Mass., 1980); Peter Jelavich, *Munich and Theatrical Modernism: Politics, Playwriting, and Performance, 1890–1914* (Cambridge, Mass., 1985); Maria Makela, *The Munich Secession: Art and Artists in Turn-of-the-Century Munich* (Princeton, 1990); and Katherine Roper, *German Encounters with Modernity: Novels of Imperial Berlin* (Atlantic Highlands, N.J., 1991). Robert Eben Sackett, *Popular Entertainment, Class, and Politics in Munich, 1900–1923* (Cambridge, Mass., 1982), gets closer to the sphere of popular culture. The enormously influential model for such works has been the essays of Carl E. Schorske, collected as *Fin-de-siècle Vienna: Politics and Culture* (New York, 1981). The main impetus toward a different kind of discussion may be found in journals such as *New German Critique, Critical Inquiry, Cultural Critique, Representations, New Formations,* and *Public Culture.* For more traditional, but sophisticated contributions inside Germany itself, ·see Vittorio Magnago Lampugnani, ed., *Moderne Architektur in Deutschland 1900 bis 1950: Reform und Tradition* (Stuttgart, 1992); and the series Kunst, Kultur und Politik im Deutschen Kaiserreich, under the direction of Stephan Waetzoldt, including Ekkehard Mai and Stephan Waetzoldt, eds., *Kunstverwaltung, Bau- und Denkmal-*

tinuously expanding literature on working-class culture has remained bounded by the older institutional perspectives, in which the associational topography of organized Social Democratic and, to a lesser degree, Catholic activity within the working class sets the agenda; and so here, too, there is little sign of a cultural-studies breakthrough.[60] The greatest potential for the latter is certainly in the area of *Alltagsgeschichte,* and here the essays of Alf Lüdtke, a number of innovative monographs, and a larger body of work in progress have been showing the way.[61] Work within women's history, on the history of popular consumption, and on the practical context of commercialized leisure and enjoyment will be especially important in this respect.[62] The study of youth and

Politik im Kaiserreich (Berlin, 1981); Ekkehard Mai, Hans Pohl, and Stephan Waetzoldt, eds., *Kunstpolitik und Kunstförderung im Kaiserreich* (Berlin, 1982); Ekkehard Mai, Jürgen Paul, and Stephan Waetzoldt, eds., *Das Rathaus im Kaiserreich: Kunstpolitische Aspekte einer Bauaufgabe im 19. Jahrhundert* (Berlin, 1982); and Ekkehard Mai et al., eds., *Ideengeschichte und Kunstwissenschaft: Philosophie und bildende Kunst im Kaiserreich* (Berlin, 1983). For a valuable general conspectus in this older mode, see Wolfgang J. Mommsen, "Kultur und Politik im deutschen Kaiserreich," in Wolfgang J. Mommsen, *Der autoritäre Nationalstaat: Verfassung, Gesellschaft und Kultur im deutschen Kaiserreich* (Frankfurt, 1990), 234–56; and for a suggestive anthology of broadly constructed essays, August Nitschke, et al., eds. *Jahrhundertwende: Der Aufbruch in die Moderne, 1880–1930,* 2 vols. (Reinbek, 1990).

60. For a useful guide to the relevant literature, see Ritter and Tenfelde, *Arbeiter im Deutschen Kaiserreich,* 781–838, which, however, observes the older structural hierarchy of significance, in which social structure, political economy, material standard of living, and state-political context possesses determining priority, as against the more epiphenomenal status of "culture" (symptomatically confined to the final chapter of the book).

61. See Alf Lüdtke, "Cash, Coffee-Breaks, Horseplay: *Eigensinn* and Politics among Factory Workers in Germany circa 1900," in *Confrontation, Class Consciousness and the Labor Process: Studies in Proletarian Class Formation,* ed. Michael Hanagan and Charles Stephenson (New York, 1986), 65–95; Alf Lüdtke, "Organisational Order or *Eigensinn*? Workers' Privacy and Workers' Politics in Imperial Germany," in *Rites of Power: Symbolism, Ritual, and Politics since the Middle Ages,* ed. Sean Wilentz (Philadelphia, 1985), 303–33; Lüdtke, *Alltagsgeschichte;* Franz-Josef Brüggemeier, *Leben vor Ort: Ruhrbergleute und Ruhrbergbau, 1889–1919* (Munich, 1984); Adelheid von Saldern, *Auf dem Wege zum Arbeiter-Reformismus: Parteialltag in sozialdemokratischer Göttingen (1870–1920)* (Frankfurt a.M., 1984); Richard J. Evans, ed., *Kneipengespräche im Kaiserreich: Die Stimmungsberichte der Hamburger Politischen Polizei, 1892–1914* (Reinbek, 1989). For an older work anticipating some of the more recent directions, see Erhard Lucas, *Zwei Formen von Radikalismus in der deutschen Arbeiterbewegung* (Frankfurt, 1976).

62. These references cannot be exhaustive, but see Kathleen Canning, "Gender and the Culture of Work: Ideology and Identity in the World behind the Mill Gate, 1890–1914," in Jones and Retallack, *Elections, Mass Politics, and Social Change,* 175–99; Dorothee Wierling, *Mädchen für alles: Arbeitsalltag und Lebensgeschichte städtischer Dienstmädchen um die Jahrhundertwende* (Berlin, 1987); Ulrich Wywra, *Branntwein und "echtes" Bier: Die Trinkkultur der Hamburger Arbeiter im 19. Jahrhundert* (Hamburg, 1990); Lynn Abrams, "From Control to Commercialization: The Triumph of Mass Entertainment in Germany, 1900–1925?" *German History* 8 (1990): 278–93; Gary Stark, "Cinema, Society, and the State: Policing the Film Industry in Imperial Germany," in *Essays on Culture and Society in Modern Germany,* ed. Gary Stark and

sexuality should also be mentioned.[63] Finally, the deepening of perspectives on the transformation of the countryside—presently conceived mainly via the demographics of the rural-urban transition, the economics of agricultural crisis, and the dynamics of agrarian political mobilization—so that urbanization may be treated as a cultural process, will also provide rich opportunities.[64] In all of these respects, the current growth of interest in theories of civil society and the public sphere may be expected to have an increasingly salient influence.[65]

The concepts and approaches developed within cultural studies have enormous potential when applied to these histories. For this specifically late-nineteenth-century context, the new cultural history might mean a critical return to some of the older questions of the traditional intellectual history, but with a set of methodological intentions fundamentally different from the ones guiding the canonical works of German intellectual history of the 1960s, which were obsessed with finding a linear ancestry for Nazism, and which broadly reproduced the assumptions about the masses' irrational vulnerabilities mentioned above. In effect, those older questions of cultural and intellectual history

---

B. K. Lackner (College Station, 1982), 123–66; David A. Welch, "Cinema and Society in Imperial Germany, 1905–1918," *German History* 8 (1990): 28–45; and Nancy R. Reagin, "'A True Woman Can Take Care of Herself': The Debate over Prostitution in Hanover, 1906," *Central European History* 24 (1991): 347–80. For critical guides to the general possibilities of *Alltagsgeschichte,* see Eley, "Labor History, Social History, *Alltagsgeschichte*"; and David Crew, *"Alltagsgeschichte:* A New Social History 'From Below?'" *Central European History* 22 (1989): 394–407.

63. See Peukert, *Grenzen der Sozialdisziplinierung;* Linton, *"Who Has the Youth, Has the Future";* and for the Weimar years, Elizabeth Harvey, "Serving the Volk, Saving the Nation: Women in the Youth Movement and the Public Sphere in Weimar Germany," in Jones and Retallack, *Elections, Mass Politics, and Social Change,* 201–21.

64. Among existing work, see especially Blackbourn, *Class, Religion and Local Politics;* Applegate, *A Nation of Provincials;* and Werner K. Blessing, *Staat und Kirche in der Gesellschaft: Institutionelle Autorität und mentaler Wandel in Bayern während des 19. Jahrhunderts* (Göttingen, 1982).

65. Much of the impetus for this discussion has been provided by the remarkably delayed translation of Jürgen Habermas's great classic, *Strukturwandel der Öffentlichkeit* (Neuwied, 1962), as *The Structural Transformation of the Public Sphere* (Cambridge, Mass., 1989), for which see Calhoun, *Habermas and the Public Sphere,* which originated as a conference to mark the English-language publication. The other key work, simultaneously companion to, and critique of, Habermas's book, is Oskar Negt and Alexander Kluge, *Öffentlichkeit und Erfahrung: Zur Organisationsanalyse von bürgerlicher und proletarischer Öffentlichkeit* (Frankfurt, 1972), belatedly translated as *The Public Sphere and Experience* (Minneapolis, 1993), for which see Miriam Hansen, "Unstable Mixtures, Dilated Spheres: Negt and Kluge's *The Public Sphere and Experience,* Twenty Years Later," *Public Culture* 5 (Winter 1993): 179–212. See also Craig Calhoun, "Civil Society and the Public Sphere," ibid., 267–80; Bruce Robbins, ed., *The Phantom Public Sphere* (Minneapolis, 1993); John Keane, *Democracy and Civil Society* (London, 1988); John Keane, ed., *Civil Society and the State: New European Perspectives* (London, 1988); Landes, *Women and the Public Sphere;* and Jean Cohen and Andrew Arato, *Civil Society and Political Theory* (Cambridge, Mass., 1992).

may now be reclaimed, but within a densely grounded and richly textured context of social analysis, sharpened by the explicitly theorized frameworks of cultural studies. Unfortunately, whether in relation to the 1920s or to the *Kaiserreich,* such work has barely begun. A number of the essays in this volume move the discussion suggestively forward in this regard, from the essays by Maynes and Spohn on aspects of the culture of the working class, and Blackbourn's on the dynamics of popular religious belief, to Davis's and Domansky's reflections on the gendered cultural context of popular experience in World War I, and the contributions specifically on cultural history by Trommler and Koshar.

Breaking the Frame?

So *is* there a history of the *Kaiserreich?* In an obvious sense, through the availability of general or synthetic accounts, we may answer yes, but not to the degree that we might have expected given the explosion of interest in the period before 1914 during the 1960s and 1970s, and the associated proliferation of research. Wehler's early effort at incorporating the West German revisionism into a single-volume textbook remains the key benchmark, in English as well as in German. Various general textbooks also appeared in Germany during the 1980s, usually within a more general series. But none of them makes a distinctive contribution relative to the body of argument and interpretation outlined in the first part of this introduction or measured by the alternative framings suggested in the second part. Much more imposing, and infinitely suggestive, is Thomas Nipperdey's two-volume history, which assembles an immense array of particular learning within an overall framework that has yet to be assimilated in its potential effects. Otherwise, in English there is a perhaps surprising dearth of synthetic activity, given the opening up of the field discussed above. On the other hand, both Blackbourn and Thomas Childers are preparing general textbook accounts.[66]

More fundamentally, it is less clear that the *Kaiserreich* has a history in place, and this is so in a double sense. On the one hand, many pieces of the picture are still missing, in the sense of the "gaps" that historians have traditionally taken as the principal incitement to new research and thought. The strongest single orientation of the post-sixties social history, the history of labor and the working class in all their dimensions, has made good one such deficit, though without much direct engagement with the explicit legacies of

---

66. See Hans-Ulrich Wehler, *Das Deutsche Kaiserreich, 1871–1918* (Göttingen, 1973), translated by Kim Traynor as *The German Empire, 1871–1918* (Leamington Spa, Warwickshire, and Dover, N.H., 1985); Thomas Nipperdey, *Deutsche Geschichte, 1866–1918,* vol. 1, *Arbeitswelt und Bürgergeist* (Munich, 1990); and vol. 2, Machtstaat vor der Demokratie (Munich, 1992). See also Michael Sturmer, *Das ruhelose Reich: Deutschland, 1866–1918* (Berlin, 1983).

interpretation identified at the beginning of this introduction. Other social groups, such as the peasantry, the *Mittelstand,* the professions, and the various fractions of the new petite bourgeoisie, whose realities demand inclusion if our knowledge and understanding of the *Kaiserreich* are to be well rounded, have also received valuable, though less extensive, attention.[67] The history of women and the situating of such work within analyses of gender have also begun, and this volume is strongly committed toward capturing and further elaborating that particular set of directions within current discussion and research, both through Quataert's general introduction and through individual contributions. In other respects—for instance, the history of the political parties or the study of the regions—the contents of our collection are less generously endowed, although Retallack's does extremely important work in both directions, and a great deal still remains to be done.

But as I have taken some pains to suggest, this question is not simply one of "gaps" or "missing pieces" in the conventional sense, as if the amassing of empirical knowledge alone could "complete" the picture. It is also a matter of perspective. My emphasis above on the potential value of theories and approaches emanating from the reception of Foucault, the discussion of gender, and the growth of cultural studies has attempted to make some of this argument. More pointedly, I would suggest that the familiar boundedness of the *Kaiserreich* within the conventional chronology of the period (1871–1914–18) has now become extremely fluid, so that our questions and knowledge are spilling around at either end of that time. Foundationally, I would argue, it is far less clear than we once assumed exactly what "Germany" meant within the territorialized and legal-constitutional framing established by the Bismarckian Prusso-German settlement of 1866–71. The ordering of profound differences within the populations encompassed by the new national state—regional, religious, and ethnic, as well as the social, cultural, and gender differences explored above—and thus the imagining and fashioning of a coherent and integrated national-German culture were a priority of state intervention, associational initiative, and public discourse that extended throughout the imperial period as a whole and certainly lacked already instituted forms when the empire was originally created. "Making Germans" was a divided and divisive project of national pedagogy whose complicated histories outgrow the conven-

---

67. For work on the peasantry, see Richard J. Evans and W. R. Lee, eds., *The German Peasantry: Conflict and Community in Rural Society from the Eighteenth to the Twentieth Centuries* (New York, 1986); and Robert G. Moeller, ed., *Peasants and Lords in Modern Germany: Recent Studies in Agricultural History* (London, 1986). For the professions, see Cocks and Jarausch, *German Professions.* For the *Mittelstand* and petite bourgeoisie, see David Blackbourn, "Between Resignation and Volatility: The German Petty Bourgeoisie in the Nineteenth-Century," in David Blackbourn, *Populists and Patricians: Essays in Modern German History* (London, 1987), 84–113.

tional periodizing in which the history of the *Kaiserreich* per se is usually inscribed.[68]

But if the history of the *Kaiserreich* thus acquires indeterminacy in its origins and assumed foundations, it also exceeds the conventional boundaries in its later phase, when the contexts of significance become increasingly defined by ideas, problems, and logics of development that spread across the early twentieth century at large, embracing the Weimar as well as the Wilhelmine times. As several of this volume's essays remind us, including those by Hong, Davis, and Domansky, World War I remains a watershed and a very powerful originary context in its own right relative to the histories of Weimar. But at the same time, in a variety of key areas—including the growth of corporative logics in the management of national economic policy, the state's regulative interest in the family as the vital site for the health of the national body, the interest in education and other areas of social policy under the sign of national efficiency, and the turning to science as the primary solvent of social problems—we are dealing with histories that already cohered in the two decades before 1914 and lend a certain unity to the whole period between the turn of the century and the collapse of Weimar. In other areas, such as German colonialism or the main patterning of industrial relations or the principal directions of liberal political renovation, pre-1914 histories were certainly powerfully disrupted by the impact of World War I, but the course of events in the 1920s was nonetheless heavily determined by the character of the prewar developments. Finally, despite the generative importance of the revolutionary conjuncture of 1918–19 and the larger impact of the wartime experience, the political alignments of Weimar, particularly the radicalized politics of the Right, were strongly prefigured in the situation immediately prior to 1914.

We have reached an important moment of historiographical transition. The established framing of the *Sonderweg,* which provided so much of the excitement and controversy in the history of the *Kaiserreich* in the 1970s and 1980s, may have exhausted much of its usefulness. The primary questions of the post-Fischer West German revisionism, concerning such issues as the continuity of elites from Bismarck to Hitler, the alliance of iron and rye, the manipulative techniques of social imperialism, the weakness of liberalism, and the primacy of preindustrial traditions, have also outrun their course. To produce new knowledge and new questions, we need a different kind of comparative framing—more explicit, more specifically organized around manageable bi- or transnational questions, more securely grounded in the current historiographical contexts of the other countries, and more carefully historicized

---

68. See Geoff Eley, "State Formation, Nationalism, and Political Culture: Some Thoughts on the Unification of Germany," in Eley, *From Unification to Nazism,* 61–84; James J. Sheehan, "What Is German History? Reflections on the Role of the *Nation* in German History and Historiography," *Journal of Modern History* 53 (1981): 1–23; and Applegate, *A Nation of Provincials.*

rather than dependent on the ahistorical typologizing of a universalizing social science. We need to rethink the possible meanings of twentieth-century German modernities. We need to draw more self-consciously on the stimulus provided by current theoretical debate. We need to break discussion out of its established periodizations to see how else the questions may now be formed. In the end, therefore, we need both to deepen and to transgress the given ways of thinking, and this volume is conceived as a modest contribution to that task.

Introduction 2: Writing the History of Women and Gender in Imperial Germany

Jean H. Quataert

The history of women and gender in Imperial Germany raises a number of complicated issues at the very heart of current historical reevaluation. Its challenge has helped shape a series of debates, some of which speak specifically to questions in the German past, while others relate equally to larger conceptions about the discipline itself. Indeed, the subbranch of gender displays a Janus face, encouraging simultaneously a national as well as a comparative perspective. And some practitioners in the field are pushing beyond traditional disciplinary borders as well, drawing heavily on new theories and methods in anthropology, literary criticism, and feminist studies.[1]

Without a doubt, since the 1978 publication of Richard Evans's *Society and Politics in Wilhelmine Germany,* which launched challenging new interpretive approaches to the study of Imperial Germany, women's history has established a more significant presence on the German historiographical scene.[2] But this change has been neither easy nor complete. In the first place,

---

1. For an insightful collection of interdisciplinary essays describing a variety of methods useful for analyzing historical questions, see H. Aram Veeser, ed., *The New Historicism* (New York and London, 1989). For the intellectual crossover between anthropologists and social historians, see, among others, Hans Medick and David Warren Sabean, eds., *Interest and Emotion: Essays on the Study of Family and Kinship* (Cambridge, 1984). One of the most persuasive women's historians using poststructuralist theories is Joan Scott, *Gender and the Politics of History* (New York, 1988). Also consult Jane Caplan et al., "Patrolling the Borders: Feminist Historiography and the New Historicism," *Radical History Review* 43 (Winter 1989): 23–43; and in the same volume Judith Newton, "Family Fortunes: 'New History' and 'New Historicism,'" 5–22. A readable introduction to these complicated new theories is Jonathan Culler, *On Deconstruction: Theory and Criticism after Structuralism* (Ithaca, 1982); and Alice A. Jardine, *Gynesis: Configurations of Woman and Modernity* (Ithaca, 1985).

2. Richard J. Evans, ed., *Society and Politics in Wilhelmine Germany* (New York, 1978).

the powerful conservative tradition of historical interpretation in Germany, which privileges themes of statecraft, diplomacy, and decision making "on high," perhaps not surprisingly continues to maintain the old historic record by excluding women. Less justifiably, however, it still ignores the ingrained gendered world of its main subjects.[3] Second, the dominant paradigm shaping the writing of German social history since the early 1970s, the critical school of historical social science, has remained largely intact and closed to the newer interpretive and methodological challenges inherent in the perspective of gender. Indeed, in the vitriolic debates over the very nature of social history that began to invade the historical journals in Germany in the 1980s, practitioners of historical social science clung steadfastly to their original theoretical and epistemological assumptions—and they continue to do so.[4] Theirs is a grand conception of historic transformation, captured most fully by the broad structural changes and processes affecting the state, the law, and the economy as well as culture. Historical reality becomes the sum total of its discrete parts,

---

3. Charles S. Maier, *The Unmasterable Past: History, Holocaust, and German National Identity* (Cambridge, Mass., 1988), deals sensitively with the recent conflict among historians, along the way cataloguing the contemporary historiographical camps in Germany. In addition, consult Wolfgang J. Mommsen, "Gegenwärtige Tendenzen in der Geschichtsschreibung der Bundesrepublik," *Geschichte und Gesellschaft* 7 (1981): 149–188; and Roger Fletcher, "History from Below Comes to Germany: The New History Movement in the Federal Republic of Germany," *Journal of Modern History* 60 (September 1988): 557–68. For examples of history writing in the more conservative tradition, see, among others, Andreas Hillgruber, *Deutsche Grossmacht- und Weltpolitik im 19. und 20. Jahrhundert* (Düsseldorf, 1979); and Josef Becker and Andreas Hillgruber, eds., *Die Deutsche Frage im 19. und 20. Jahrhundert* (Munich, 1983).

4. Jürgen Kocka, "Theorien in der Sozial- und Gesellschaftsgeschichte: Vorschläge zur historischen Schichtungsanalyse," *Geschichte und Gesellschaft* 1 (1975): 9–42; W. Schieder and V. Sellin, eds., *Sozialgeschichte in Deutschland*, 4 vols. (Göttingen, 1986–87); Winfried Schulze, "Gesellschaftsgeschichte in der Kritik: Eine 'Synthese von Ranke und Marx'? Bemerkungen zu Hans-Ulrich Wehlers 'Deutsche Gesellschaftsgeschichte,'" *Geschichte und Gesellschaft* 14 (1988): 392–402; and in the same volume, Thomas Nipperdey, "Wehlers Gesellschaftsgeschichte," 403–15. The theoretical debates over the nature of social history have been between the practitioners of historical social science on the one hand and those favoring a history of daily life (*Alltagsgeschichte*) on the other. I discuss some aspects of these debates below in this overview. Among many other examples of the exchange, consult Jürgen Kocka, "Historisch-anthropologische Fragestellungen—ein Defizit der historischen Sozialwissenschaft?" in *Historische Anthropologie*, ed. Hans Süssmuth (Göttingen, 1984), 73–83; and in the same volume, Hans Medick, "Vom Interesse der Sozialhistoriker an der Ethnologie: Bemerkungen zu einigen Motiven der Begegnung von Geschichtswissenschaft und Sozialanthropologie," 49–56. See as well the chapters in Alf Lüdtke, *Alltagsgeschichte: Zur Rekonstruktion historischer Erfahrungen und Lebensweisen* (Frankfurt and New York, 1989); and the review article by Geoff Eley, "Labor History, Social History, *Alltagsgeschichte:* Experience, Culture, and the Politics of the Everyday—A New Direction for German Social History," *Journal of Modern History* 61 (June 1989): 297–343. See also the "Diskussionsforum" by Klaus Tenfelde, "Schwierigkeiten mit dem Alltag"; and Jürgen Kocka, "Zurück zur Erzählung? Plädoyer für historische Argumentation," *Geschichte und Gesellschaft* 10 (1984): 376–408.

which are labeled "politics," "society," or "culture" and analyzed separately by employing social-science theories, methods, and categories. While admittedly complex and nuanced, the school is self-consciously theoretical and, above all, materialist, seeing human consciousness, attitudes, and behavior as a product of concrete material and structural forces. Thus, the primary influences shaping human agency are socioeconomic, and the determining explanatory category in this framework is class (or, for earlier periods, estates and social orders). Indeed, sex (or gender) is assigned a secondary status, part of a range of variables such as region, religion, or ethnicity that are included to capture society's acknowledged diversity but are given no independent role in the hierarchy of causality. Nonetheless, partly as a result of the greater presence of women's history nationally and internationally, many of the historical social scientists in Germany now seem to pay more explicit attention to gender as a (dependent) variable and include greater discussion of the female component of a social or occupational group under scrutiny. But the potential of gender analysis to challenge fundamental interpretive assumptions as well as broaden the basic components of class analysis, as the chapter by Kathleen Canning in this volume demonstrates clearly, is unacknowledged among these influential historians of German society and politics.[5]

Other factors also worked to retard the impact of women's history in Germany. During the 1980s, the historical profession was all but consumed by an interpretive controversy over Germany's so-called unique path of development (the *Sonderweg* debate).[6] At stake was nothing less than the prevailing societal understanding of the National Socialist experience within the larger context of German history. The debate centered in good measure on Imperial Germany, which, according to one of the lines of analysis, provided the direct structural foundation for the subsequent descent into fascism. Testing and

5. A good example of the attention given to sex differences as part, however, of a series of dependent variables that dissect society is Jürgen Kocka, *Weder Stand noch Klasse: Unterschichten um 1800* (Bonn, 1990). See also Ulrich Engelhardt, "Frauen in der Sozialgeschichte: Eine ungeschriebene Geschichte?" in Schieder and Sellin, *Sozialgeschichte,* 4:156–78. For an analysis of women's history and an assessment of the significance of gender as an analytic category, see Gisela Bock, "Geschichte, Frauengeschichte, Geschlechtergeschichte," *Geschichte und Gesellschaft* 14 (1988): 364–91; as well as her "Frauenforschung—das Ende der Vernunft in der Geschichte?" *Geschichtsdidaktik* 1 (1982): 105–9. Finally, consult the chapter by Kathleen Canning in this volume, "Gender and the Politics of Class Formation: Rethinking German Labor History."

6. The controversy is very well known in German history, and many of the arguments are reflected in this volume. For examples of the alternative positions see Hans-Ulrich Wehler, *The German Empire, 1871–1918,* trans. Kim Traynor (Leamington SA, Warwickshire, and Dover, N.H., 1985); and David Blackbourn and Geoff Eley, *The Peculiarities of German History: Bourgeois Society and Politics in Nineteenth-Century Germany* (Oxford and New York, 1984). Among other reviews, see Jane Caplan, "Myths, Models and Missing Revolutions: Comments on a Debate in German History," *Radical History Review* 34 (1986): 87–99.

critiquing this assumption generated considerable detailed research on a host of important topics on the regime, including the relationship between the state and civil society, the dynamics of the democratization process, as well as the character of official and unofficial clubs and associations. The historiographical conflict, however, was carried on essentially without reference to women or gender themes, and the simultaneous takeoff of women's history in the 1980s occurred basically independently of, and peripherally to, this important debate. Evans early on came the closest to integrating women's issues into the broader arguments over the nature of the Imperial German state and society. In his contribution to the 1978 edited volume on the Wilhelmine state, he confronted head-on two divergent interpretations of politics that foreshadowed the more classic *Sonderweg* divisions and tested the assumptions of each with reference to the feminist movement in Wilhelmine Germany. Did bourgeois feminism represent an authentic emancipatory movement capable of introducing meaningful democratic reforms into the German polity? His conclusions essentially straddled the fence; the complexity of women's organized feminist activity confirmed neither the hypothesis about the tenacity of German illiberalism nor assumptions about the potential for significant political change in the Imperial German polity.[7] Ironically, however, his undertaking set a different and unanticipated research agenda that helped shape the writing of German women's history in the subsequent decade. It stimulated debate about the definition and characteristics of German feminism rather than encouraging an equally essential inquiry of how a study of organized feminism (i.e., women's history more generally) might shed new light on the course of German history.

Finally, there also are institutional barriers that restrict the number of women's historians in the academy and in research collectives. The German professorate is undeniably conservative. A highly restrictive guild, it operates through personal recommendations and cooptation. Sexist prejudices along with the misgivings of a number of schools of thought about gender analysis have meant that women consistently have been overlooked for entry-level appointments. And jobs have been scarce in the last years of recession. Hans-Jürgen Puhle's question, which he raised in 1981, of why there are so few women historians finds an echo more than a decade later.[8]

The field of women's history, therefore, has been the quintessential "outsider" in the academy, a status that it probably shares with a close relative, the

---

7. Richard J. Evans, "Liberalism and Society: The Feminist Movement and Social Change," in Evans, *Society and Politics*, 186–214. See also Ute Gerhard, "A Hidden and Complex Heritage: Reflections on the History of Germany's Women's Movements," *Women's Studies International Forum* 5, no. 6 (1982): 561–67.

8. Hans-Jürgen Puhle, "Warum gibt es so wenige Historikerinnen?" *Geschichte und Gesellschaft* 7 (1981): 364–93. Even the restructuring of German academic life after reunification has not appreciably improved the situation for women.

theoretically challenging alternative approach to social history known in Germany as *Alltagsgeschichte* (the history of daily life). The academic climate in Germany, indeed, has been less hospitable to intellectual experimentation with themes of sex and gender than, for example, in North America, Britain, or France. And several distinct characteristics of German women's history follow from its relative institutional isolation and numerical weakness. On the one hand, practitioners essentially have remained within their own sphere of study, carrying on fruitful dialogues among themselves and with women's historians working in other national contexts. As has been indicated, however, debates in the field of women's and gender history seldom confront directly the more mainstream issues being debated in German history. On the other hand, research in German women's history rarely has set an international agenda. Its relatively thin contribution to theory and method is revealed clearly in the recent article on history, women's history, and gender studies by Gisela Bock, one of the leading practitioners of women's history today in Germany.[9] Focusing on the evolution of women's history generally, Bock refers only minimally to studies drawn from German women's history that have been truly pathfinding. It appears that feminist theory and praxis in history have been shaped more actively by the work of women's historians in other national contexts.

And yet recent events in Central Europe clearly have overtaken their historians and transformed the context for writing history in ways that open new possibilities for greater attention to themes in women's history and gender studies. It seems as if the *Sonderweg* controversy now has run its course; historians need to move beyond its framework, categories, and lines of analysis.[10] And clearly, German unification invites new questions about the German past and new perspectives from which to view it. Whether women's history in this reunification era will become truly an "insider," however, remains open and contested. But two decades of research undoubtedly place the field in a

---

9. Bock, "Geschichte," 364–91.

10. The debate over Germany's so-called unique development has been extraordinarily fruitful but not fully conclusive. Historians who confront the divergent interpretations in their specific case studies usually end up confirming part of the hypotheses of each camp. An excellent example is Michael John, "The Peculiarities of the German State: Bourgeois Law and Society in the Imperial Era," *Past and Present* 119 (1988): 105–13. But even more to the point are the limitations of analysis when framed solely within the categories of the *Sonderweg* debate. For example, corporatist language harking back to an earlier age was decidedly "modern" in the crisis-laden economy and society of Weimar. To label social groups that employed older political vocabulary "preindustrial vestiges" neglects the shift in the content of language over time and also severely limits the nature of the questions that are asked of the material. Thomas Childers begins the process of reevaluation, although he could ask additional questions of the data to move the discussion forcefully outside the framework of the *Sonderweg* debate; see Thomas Childers, "The Social Language of Politics in Germany: The Sociology of Political Discourse in the Weimar Republic," *American Historical Review* 95, no. 2 (April 1990): 331–59.

position to claim a more acknowledged role in the construction of the past and the shaping of shared social memory. This chapter, then, describes the broad contours of women's history and gender studies over the last several decades and assesses their impact on the study of the Imperial German state and society. What major questions have preoccupied German women's historians? What new interpretations of Imperial Germany come from the perspective of women's history? To what extent has the inherited picture been supplemented, complemented, or transformed? And what about the future? How might women's history be more fully integrated into and, in turn, help shape major debates in the history of the Second Empire?

Of course, an immediate paradox confronts any effort to analyze women's history within the context of a particular political regime such as Imperial Germany. Distinct subfields of history develop their own chronological divisions and turning points. Traditional political markers, such as the dates of individual regimes—1871 to 1918 in the case of Imperial Germany—may not be the most appropriate framework for organizing historical material on women's lives and gender themes. One early hallmark of historical social science was the shift away from 1870/71 as the significant date in consolidating the Second Empire. Rather, the new social historians of the 1960s stressed 1879 and the passage of important tariff agreements that, in their interpretive scheme, solidified the political alliance of "grain and iron"—in social terms, joining the feudal aristocracy with the industrial middle class in a political coalition that subsequently dominated high politics in Imperial Germany.[11] Similarly, the newest social historians investigating people's daily lives push beyond the standard political demarcation dates. The history of daily life has its own chronology; memory, it appears, is more fluid than the neat political divisions imposed on the past. And women's history, too, challenges inherited periodization based on standard political events such as revolutions or distinct governing administrations. Turning points turn less sharply when women's experiences are included in the equation; and political transitions often leave larger secular demographic or familial trends virtually unscathed. Several chapters in this volume propose alternative organizing constructs that come from looking at history through the perspective of gender. Young Sun Hong, for example, notes that states' power implicitly rests on an "ideal" configuration of civil society—of so-called proper family and work life, gender roles,

---

11. See particularly Wehler, *The German Empire*, 32–39; and Hans-Ulrich Wehler, *Krisenherde des Kaiserreichs, 1871–1918* (Göttingen, 1979). Consult as well the articles in Helmut Böhme, ed., *Probleme der Reichsgründungszeit, 1848–1879* (Cologne and Berlin, 1968); Helmut Böhme, *Deutschlands Weg zur Grossmacht: Studien zum Verhältnis von Wirtschaft und Staat während der Reichsgründungszeit, 1848–1881* (1966; reprinted, Cologne, 1972); and Hans Rosenberg, *Grosse Depression und Bismarckzeit: Wirtschaftsablauf, Gesellschaft und Politik in Mitteleuropa* (Berlin, 1967).

and leisure activities. Under the strains of World War I in Germany, there was a perceived breakdown of that society, threatening the legitimacy of the state, which led powerful private welfare agencies and actors as well as public officials to reformulate notions of public relief and social responsibility. Politicization of the sphere of social reproduction at once shaped and undermined the Wilhelmine and Weimar states, linking the late imperial, Weimar, and early Nazi eras in ways that speak to a twentieth-century crisis of modernity transcending political regimes. And Elisabeth Domansky, writing from the perspective of an "all-encompassing process of militarization of twentieth-century Europe," sets her analysis in an intriguing chronology. One hallmark of the modern age, as she sees it, is a fundamentally new relationship between production, reproduction, and destruction. In her analysis, this new triad originated in the discursive context of the "culture of scientism" in the 1880s; and World War I becomes a "radical rupture" in German history, no longer the "link" between the Second and Third empires but rather the precondition for National Socialist advances in Germany.[12]

And yet—and this is the other side of the paradox—distinct political worlds, such as that of Imperial Germany, undeniably exercise a formative impact on individual consciousness and action. While social trends and movements may indeed transcend the particular political regime, social experience, in turn, is influenced directly by the dominant political structures and values that comprise a particular polity. The legal political infrastructure of a state limits and channels activities within a given, although admittedly contested, setting. For example, state decisions on the distribution of entitlements placed limited disposable income in the hands of retired men—and slighted older women—in the Wilhelmine era, whereas under Nazi social policy, revenue disbursement promoted nuclear family formation.[13] The crafting of history,

---

12. A good indication of the new chronology that characterizes the history of daily life is found in glancing through the book review section of, for example, the *Internationale wissenschaftliche Korrespondenz zur Geschichte der deutschen Arbeiterbewegung,* 27, nos. 1–4 (1991), or recent reviews in the 1990–91 volumes of the *American Historical Review.* The same is true in women's history. The classic essay questioning not only a dominant interpretation but also the relevance of standard periodization in Western civilization is Joan Kelly's "Did Women Have a Renaissance?" reprinted in her book *Women, History, and Theory: The Essays of Joan Kelly* (Chicago, 1984), 19–50. For a reconceptualization of the standard categories and turning points in the history of the West from the women's perspective, see the ambitious study by Bonnie S. Anderson and Judith P. Zinsser, *A History of Their Own: Women in Europe from Prehistory to the Present,* 2 vols. (New York, 1988). In addition see Hong's chapter in this volume, "The Contradictions of Modernization in the German Welfare State: Gender and the Politics of Welfare Reform in World War I Germany," as well as the one by Elisabeth Domansky, "Militarization and Reproduction in World War I Germany."

13. See particularly Jean H. Quataert, "Social Insurance and the Family Work of Oberlausitz Home Weavers in the Late Nineteenth Century," in *German Women in the Nineteenth Century: A Social History,* ed. John C. Fout (New York, 1984), 270–94; and Tim Mason, "Women

then, is a delicate task that acknowledges the essential "arbitrariness" of the standard periods in history and at the same time recognizes the diverse ways in which distinct political realms interpenetrate social and daily life. How well has women's history met this challenge?

The contributions of women's history to the study of Imperial Germany could be said to fall into four broad, though often overlapping, areas of inquiry. These are (1) the history of organized feminism, (2) the study of the nature and characteristics of women's work, (3) a social history that includes attention to women's daily lives, and (4) an inquiry on women, war, and nationalism. What follows is a brief synopsis of major works and interpretive lines in each category. The examples are by no means exhaustive but are designed rather to capture a range of themes, methods, and approaches that characterize the topics. Taken together, they illustrate the state of current research and suggest additional imperatives, if the field truly is to shake up the inherited picture.

By far, the largest body of research in German women's history is on organized feminism—the history of the women's movements and the multiple, complex, often contradictory efforts by women to shape their political, economic, social, and familial worlds through collective public action. The literature is implicitly comparative, seeking to understand the German experience within a broader Western feminist spectrum that typically includes an Anglo-Saxon and a French model. Authors have tended to incorporate the point made early on by Amy Hackett about feminism molding itself to distinct national contexts and political cultures.[14] The studies extend essentially from the early nineteenth century well into the twentieth and together offer a historical continuum of women's feminist activism with the breakdown of corporate and feudal structures and the transition to a class society and the market economy in Central Europe. Much of this literature privileges the approximate time frame of Imperial Germany, for midway into the decade of unification (1865) the first systematic efforts at coordinated feminist organization took place, while chronologically at the start of the Wilhelmine era (1894), the umbrella organization of bourgeois feminism (the Federation of German Women's Organizations) was founded, which subsequently oversaw autonomous feminist life until its demise by National Socialism in 1933.[15]

---

in Germany, 1925–1940: Family, Welfare and Work," *History Workshop Journal,* 1976, nos. 1–2:74–113. In an important article discussing the struggle over historical memory in the recent German "conflict among historians," Mary Nolan makes the telling point that "private" life is at all times "politicized" and specifically political. See Nolan, "The *Historikerstreit* and Social History," *New German Critique* 15, no. 44 (Spring/Summer 1988): 51–81.

14. Amy Hackett, "The German Women's Movement and Suffrage, 1890–1914: A Study of National Feminism," in *European Social History,* ed. Robert J. Bezucha (Lexington, Mass., 1972).

15. Among the most important works in this first category are Richard J. Evans, *The Feminist Movement in Germany, 1894–1933* (London, 1976); Barbara Greven-Aschoff, *Die bür-*

A number of distinct lines of analysis characterize the literature on the German women's movements. As already indicated, women's historians have been interested primarily in assessing the nature of German feminism as both ideology and praxis. Recognizing that German feminism from the 1860s on took two distinct ideological and social-organizational forms—an autonomous bourgeois feminist movement and a socialist women's movement—historians' efforts have been to place bourgeois feminism within the admittedly complicated history of German liberalism on the one hand, and within the porous subculture carved out by socialists and free trade unionists on the other.[16] What new understandings of German liberalism and social democracy are revealed by a study of the feminist experience? What does this history say about class relations in the Central European context? In addition, the same historians typically scrutinize the tactics, strategies, and goals of the two groups of feminists to understand the social and cultural components of mobilization as well as the outer limits of their struggles for change.

Much of the literature followed the lines of analysis put forth in the late 1970s and early 1980s by influential women's historians of bourgeois feminism, such as Evans and Barbara Greven-Aschoff or, in the case of the socialist women's movement, by Heinz Niggemann, Werner Thönnessen, and Jean Quataert. Only recently has the conception been seriously challenged, and the new reading offers a compellingly different understanding of German femi-

---

gerliche Frauenbewegung in Deutschland, 1894–1933 (Göttingen, 1981); Herrad-Ulrike Bussemer, *Frauenemanzipation und Bildungsbürgertum: Sozialgeschichte der Frauenbewegung in der Reichsgründungszeit* (Weinheim, 1985); Catherine N. Prelinger, *Charity, Challenge and Change: Religious Dimensions of the Mid-Nineteenth-Century Women's Movement in Germany* (Westport, Conn., 1987); Irene Stoehr, "Organisierte Mütterlichkeit: Zur Politik der deutschen Frauenbewegung um 1900," in *Frauen suchen ihre Geschichte: Historische Studien zum 19. und 20. Jahrhundert*, ed. Karin Hausen (Munich, 1983); Bärbel Clemens, *Menschenrechte haben kein Geschlecht! Zum Politikverständnis der bürgerlichen Frauenbewegung* (Pfaffenweiler, 1988); and Margrit Twellmann, *Die deutsche Frauenbewegung: Ihre Anfänge und erste Entwicklung: Quellen, 1843–1889*, 2 vols. (Meisenheim, 1972). For studies that continue the analysis into the German Federal Republic, see the articles by Robert Moeller, "Protecting Mother's Work: From Production to Reproduction in Postwar West Germany," *Journal of Social History* 22, no. 3 (Spring 1989): 413–37; and "Reconstructing the Family in Reconstruction Germany: Women and Social Policy in the Federal Republic, 1945–1955," *Feminist Studies* 15, no. 1 (Spring 1989): 137–69; and his book *Protecting Motherhood: Women and the Family in the Politics of Postwar West Germany* (Berkeley and Los Angeles, 1992).

16. For examples of the literature on the socialist women's movement, see Jean H. Quataert, *Reluctant Feminists in German Social Democracy, 1885–1917* (Princeton, 1979); Werner Thönnessen, *Frauenemanzipation: Politik und Literatur der deutschen Sozialdemokratie zur Frauenbewegung, 1863–1933* (Frankfurt a.M., 1969); Heinz Niggemann, *Emanzipation zwischen Sozialismus und Feminismus: Die sozialdemokratische Frauenbewegung im Kaiserreich* (Wuppertal, 1981); Alfred Meyer, *The Feminism and Socialism of Lily Braun* (Bloomington, 1986); and Sabine Richebacher, *Uns fehlt nur eine Kleinigkeit: Die deutsche proletarische Frauenbewegung, 1890–1914* (Frankfurt a.M., 1982).

nism in both its national and comparative Western perspectives.[17] The older orthodoxy was consistent with the *Sonderweg* argument; and its revision, if adopted, promises to inaugurate a new interpretive climate in German women's organizational history.

Briefly stated, the dominant interpretation rests on a precise definition of feminism as an egalitarian movement for women's individual autonomy, natural rights, and full equality with men in political, economic, and social life. A product of Enlightenment thought and Anglo-Saxon modification, natural-rights feminism, however, never was adopted fully in Germany. Indeed, liberal feminist thought and practice was a victim of the basically authoritarian climate that characterized German political culture and diverted the larger liberal middle-class movement away from democracy and other political reforms as well. For some women's historians, only in the 1860s were bourgeois feminists consistently "liberal," but the increasingly nationalist climate after German unification and the "refeudalization" of the ruling groups essentially forced a retreat from the liberal theory of emancipation.[18] Other historians argue for a radicalization of bourgeois feminism between 1894 and 1908, when activists fought for politically charged goals, such as female suffrage and a new sexual morality, including the right to abortion, which expressed classically liberal individualistic feminist values. But the experiment proved short-lived; it, too, was victimized by the German ambivalence toward liberalism.[19] These historians, starting at different points, nonetheless draw the same conclusions. The wider illiberal climate of Imperial Germany transformed feminism, ideologically and strategically, into a tepid movement (certainly in comparison with England or America) based on notions of distinct male and female values, contributions, and proper roles. Indeed, this belief in separate spheres of activity for the sexes ultimately proved fatal, for it offered no authoritative position from which to challenge the antifeminist stance of National Socialism, which coopted and increasingly dominated the discourse about innate gender differences. Tragically, the argument continues, leaders of the bourgeois feminist movement colluded in their own demise. For their part, the historians of German social democracy highlight a wide spectrum of feminist ideals and goals in the subculture that defy the standard inherited criteria for the label *radical* based on the conceptual tools of class analysis. For example, the feminist commitment to birth control as a way to improve women's life chances was viewed skeptically by radical socialists hostile to what they per-

---

17. A persuasive new interpretation of German feminism, which I deal with shortly below, is Ann Taylor Allen, *Feminism and Motherhood in Germany, 1800–1914* (New Brunswick, N.J., 1991).

18. Bussemer, *Frauenemanzipation und Bildungsbürgertum,* 170–72, 188, 245–48.

19. Evans, *The Feminist Movement,* 35ff.; and Greven-Aschoff, *Die bürgerliche Frauenbewegung,* 149.

ceived as selfish individualism and a failure to recognize poverty as a function of the maldistribution of wealth, not of numbers of children.[20] Radical socialists were not necessarily radical feminists. And these authors uncover extensive antifeminist sentiments in the party and unions that also undercut collective efforts to counter the growing threat by the radical Right.[21]

Ann Taylor Allen's book *Feminism and Motherhood in Germany* offers a dramatically different and highly persuasive reading of this same feminist experience in the middle-class milieu. Essentially she turns the standard interpretation of liberal feminism on its head. Allen demonstrates the centrality of maternalist thinking in German feminism from the early nineteenth century on and, through biographical sketches of key leaders, shows how this belief in distinct female values and spheres was eminently compatible with personal growth and individual autonomy. Belief in gender difference, to be sure, produced accommodating and moderate politics, for example over poor law relief and reform; but it also underpinned radical efforts to dissociate motherhood from the family and broaden public responsibility and financial support for single mothers and their offspring. And, in a complete reversal of the standard canon, Allen shows how the German women's movement in numerous instances proved much more radical than its Anglo-Saxon counterpart. This was certainly true in the wide-ranging debates over marriage and mothers' and children's welfare, as well as reproductive issues.[22] Her work spurs German women's historians to ask new questions about the nature of German feminism no longer caught in the illiberal cycle that predetermined the political outcome; it forces a new look at the feminist uses of motherhood and the family in the socialist subculture (which Allen does not address herself); and it encourages much more careful comparative inquiry, which should dissolve the facile labels of "timid," "weak," and "coopted," which historians have placed on German bourgeois feminism. A logical and necessary question concerns how this revision itself alters the standard assessment of German liberalism.

Several other interpretive strands round out the full picture of the history

---

20. Ulrich Linse, "Arbeiterschaft und Geburtenentwicklung," *Archiv für Sozialgeschichte* 12 (1972): 205–271; Quataert, *Reluctant Feminists,* 96–99.

21. For documentation, see Niggemann, *Emanzipation;* and Thönnessen, *Frauenemanzipation.* On a related topic, see Hubert van den Berg, "'Frauen, besonders Frauenrechtlerinnen, haben keinen Zutritt!' Misogynie und Antifeminismus bei Erich Mühsams," *Internationale wissenschaftliche Korrespondenz* 28, no. 4 (December 1992): 479–510. For a devastating critique of the Left for its failure to develop a gender-balanced political position, see Beatrix Campbell, *Wigan Pier Revisited: Poverty and Politics in the Eighties* (London, 1984).

22. Allen, *Feminism,* 186–87, 204, specifically; but every chapter in the book places German women's historic choices, behavior, and experiences in a carefully analyzed comparative context. Allen consults the best of the literature on North America, England, and France. The end result truly is quite unexpected, as it compellingly challenges the inherited picture of the conservative German bourgeois women's movement.

of Germany's women's movement. A number of historians have raised questions about the causal relationship between the movement for women's emancipation and the ongoing process of social change in Central Europe. What factors were instrumental in mobilizing women of diverse social and ethnic groups? Answers here range from demographic change (a decline in marital fertility) to shifting occupational structures to new family forms and norms as well as to the spread of mass education and effective birth control technologies.[23] An interesting corollary concerns the impact, in turn, of organized feminism on the pattern and pace of social change. To what extent did women's activism itself channel social change in directions favorable to widening access to work, education, or leisure activities? Other historians link their focus on women's organizational life to questions about state formation, an approach that promises to integrate German women's history more directly into wider historical debates. But here the results are mixed, revealing a general shortcoming of the field of German women's history as it is often practiced. For example, on the one hand, a detailed case study of Bremen in the late Wilhelmine through Weimar eras fleshes out the shifting political terrain of a local women's movement. Basing their entry into the public arena on shared notions of female culture and honor (a point that, by the way, reinforces Allen's argument), local bourgeois women carved out a whole new arena of social work in movements for educational reform, temperance, and the abolition of state-sanctioned prostitution; their activism in the public limelight found widespread acceptance and encouraged cross-class identification and collaboration.[24] Bourgeois women were an increasingly important presence in shaping the new interventionist states (on the local level) in Germany. On the other hand, Ute Frevert's broader study of the bourgeois component of German women's experiences also catalogues middle-class involvement in social work, private charity, poor law reform, and public welfare agencies.[25] Not explicitly

---

23. See Barbara Greven-Aschoff, "Sozialer Wandel und Frauenbewegung," *Geschichte und Gesellschaft* 7 (1981): 328–46; Vera Klinger, "Frauenberuf und Frauenrolle: Zur Entstehung geschlechtsspezifischer Ausbildungs- und Arbeitsmarktstrukturen vor dem Ersten Weltkrieg," *Zeitschrift für Pädagogik* 35 (1989): 515–34; Karin Hausen, "Die Polarisierung der 'Geschlechtscharaktere'—Eine Spiegelung der Dissoziation von Erwerbe- und Familienlegen," in *Sozialgeschichte der Familie in der Neuzeit Europas,* ed. Werner Conze (Stuttgart, 1976), 363–93; Karin Hausen, "Grosse Wäsche: Technischer Fortschritt und sozialer Wandel in Deutschland," *Geschichte und Gesellschaft* 13, no. 3 (1987): 273–303; James C. Albisetti, *Schooling German Girls and Women: Secondary and Higher Education in the Nineteenth Century* (Princeton, 1988); James Woycke, *Birth Control in Germany, 1871–1933* (New York, 1988); and John E. Knodel, *The Decline of Fertility in Germany, 1871–1939* (Princeton, 1974).

24. Elisabeth Meyer-Renschhausen, *Weibliche Kultur und soziale Arbeit: Eine Geschichte der Frauenbewegung am Beispiel Bremens, 1810–1927* (Cologne, 1989).

25. Ute Frevert, *Women in German History: From Bourgeois Emancipation to Sexual Liberation,* trans. Stuart McKinnon-Evans (Oxford and New York, 1989).

presented as a study of state formation, the accumulated evidence nonetheless clearly documents women's considerable participation in the reshaping of Germany's traditional poor relief system and the more modern welfare institutions of the Imperial and Weimar states. But ironically the analysis remains too abstract, even though rooted in a valid empirical base. And the problem—which Frevert shares with other practitioners of German women's history—lies in the way the questions are framed. They are not posed in terms of the specific *German* state or emerging civil society. Not enough attention is given to the specifics of the Imperial German authoritarian state—e.g., that professionalization took place under state sponsorship in Germany, not "free" of it—or to those of the Prussian police state or the Saxon state, for that matter, which, reversing all trends toward greater democratization in Europe, actually restricted voting rights for male citizens in 1896.[26] Thus, Frevert's study essentially misses two opportunities. First, it fails to engage the wider literature on the German state and challenge existing interpretations by including women's experiences and a gender perspective. And second, because it has not grappled with the complex nature of the German states in detail, implicit comparisons with, for example, the "limited state" of North America or the centralized administrative world of the French polity are not possible from the data presented.

The second broad category of research in German women's history revolves around the nature and meaning of work for occupationally, socially, and ethnically diverse groups of women. It is here that German-born women's historians—Bock, Barbara Duden, and Gertraude Kittler, to mention the early pioneers—have made their most original theoretical contribution, insights that have the added potential to challenge, from the perspective of work experiences, the periodization of modern German history.[27] These authors offer an excursion into the evolution of the housewife role, a rather "modern" in-

---

26. For interesting studies on state involvement in constituting the German professions, see Geoffrey Cocks and Konrad H. Jarausch, *The German Professions, 1800–1950* (New York, 1990); and David Blackbourn and Richard J. Evans, eds., *The German Bourgeoisie: Essays on the Social History of the German Middle Class from the Late Eighteenth to the Early Twentieth Century* (London and New York, 1991). For a fascinating study of the Prussian state, see Alf Lüdtke, *Police and State in Prussia, 1815–1850* (Cambridge and New York, 1989). Paul St. Clair is examining the Saxon state and grass-roots mobilization in the imperial and Weimar eras; his working paper "The 1896 Revision of the Saxon Electoral Law and Its Effects on the Socialist Party" is in progress.

27. Gertraude Kittler, *Hausarbeit: Zur Geschichte einer "Natur-Ressource"* (Munich, 1980); Gisela Bock and Barbara Duden, "Arbeit aus Liebe—Liebe als Arbeit: Zur Entstehung der Hausarbeit im Kapitalismus," in *Frauen und Wissenschaft: Beiträge zur Berliner Sommeruniversität für Frauen, Juli 1976* (Berlin, 1977), 118–99; Ulla Knapp, *Frauenarbeit in Deutschland: Hausarbeit und geschlechtsspezifischer Arbeitsmarkt im deutschen Industrialisierungsprozess* (Munich, 1984). It is interesting that Frevert, *Women in German History,* utilizes an unimaginative standard chronology instead of rethinking the narrative by employing the theoretical insights and reformulating potential of these studies.

vention, as they see it, among the bourgeoisie of the nineteenth century, solidified only, however, with the widespread adoption of labor-saving household appliances in the rationalized climate of high capitalism in the 1920s. Underlying the work is the effort to conceptualize theoretically—based on the historical specificity of the German case—the importance of women's nonremunerated labor to capitalist development and accumulation, the intersection over time of capitalist and patriarchal interests and values, and the often simultaneous mobilization of women's labor for market and private consumption purposes. In the process, the studies provide a wealth of fascinating information on evolving definitions of "work," structural changes in household composition, and the decline of the domestic service sector as a significant employer of women, with the resultant pressures on middle-class housewives to become their own servants. Indeed, much of the literature in this second category of German women's history—the theme of work—tends to be self-consciously challenging, offering new ways to conceptualize the standard interpretations of labor history and its cherished categories. The hallmark here is less a "herstory"—a supplement to the study of class relations or labor experiences—than a successful endeavor to transform the field's operative assumptions, methods, and tools of analysis. A few examples will illustrate the point.

In her study of women's domestic employment in the imperial period, Barbara Franzoi challenges the predominant picture of German industrialization, arguing from the German case for a rethinking of economic history and the place of the so-called industrial revolution in the process of industrial transformation.[28] Late-nineteenth-century capitalism was not solely about factories, steam engines and power, or proletarians but equally about labor-intensive hand production, small yet competitive sweatshops and home manufacture, and extensive children's and women's labor. Norms about women's

---

28. Barbara Franzoi, *At the Very Least She Pays the Rent: Women and German Industrialization, 1871–1914* (Westport, Conn., 1985). Similar efforts to rethink the lines of European economic development have also been occurring in other national contexts. Among the best known in the English case is Raphael Samuel, "The Workshop of the World: Steam Power and Hand Technology in mid-Victorian Britain," *History Workshop* 3 (1977): 6–72; for French history, see Rondo Cameron, "A New View of European Industrialization," *Economic History Review* 38, no. 1 (1985): 1–23; and, in the case of North America, Delores Greenberg, "Reassessing the Power Patterns of the Industrial Revolution: An Anglo-American Comparison," *American Historical Review* 87 (1982): 1237–61. The parallel German contribution to the "protoindustry" debate raging in the 1980s reinforced this step toward new interpretations and approaches in economic history. See, among others, Peter Kriedte, Hans Medick, and Jürgen Schlumbohm, *Industrialisierung vor der Industrialisierung: Gewerbliche Warenproduktion auf dem Land in der Formationsperiode des Kapitalismus* (Göttingen, 1977); and Jean H. Quataert, "A New View of Industrialization: 'Protoindustry' or the Role of Small-Scale, Labor-Intensive Manufacture in the Capitalist Environment," *International Labor and Working-Class History*, no. 33 (Spring 1988): 3–22.

primary familial responsibilities ensured the presence of a large, unskilled, and poorly paid female labor force that moved in and out of remunerative work in factories, workshops, and the home, reflecting the pressures of the individual life- and family cycle. A whole range of light industries, such as garment- and hat-making could survive in the highly competitive urban environment only by tapping this flexible and vulnerable workforce.

Not only has the interpretive grid surrounding the economy become more nuanced and balanced when the perspective includes women and gender; the operative tools of analysis are often recast. In another thought-provoking study, Carole Adams offers a history of clerks in sales and office work in Wilhelmine Germany.[29] In constructing a social profile of the occupation, Adams pays careful attention to gender distinctions in terms of skills, education, and work careers; analyzed are the areas of differences and similarities among the life and work conditions of male and female clerks. The study, as do many others in this second category of women's history, actually straddles both divisions, for Adams examines the connection between work experience and political mobilization in the bourgeois feminist Clerks' Aid Association and in its competitor, the socialist Central Alliance. But Adams's most novel contribution to the literature concerns what she sees as a dynamic, unresolved tension between class and gender that characterized the politics of the profession. Female clerks from middle-class backgrounds sought to preserve skills and status, colluding with male clerks against working-class women moving into sales. Here the rewards of professionalization favored class solidarity over feminist collaboration. And socialists, joining both men and women in one association, proved insufficiently sensitive to gender issues to promote women's sustained involvement in the organization. Similarly, Quataert's study of rural industrialization and political mobilization in the weaving villages of the Saxon Oberlausitz recasts the traditional understanding of politics by moving away from a focus on political parties, unions, and formal associations. A women's perspective not only encourages interest in the household as a rewarding, though typically neglected, unit of analysis in industrial labor history; it also compels new understanding of collective protest that operated independently of the parties claiming to represent their working-class constituency.[30] And Canning's chapter in this volume, as noted earlier, offers another instructive example in full detail of the ways in which gender analysis challenges and redefines concepts of class and class formation, those key analytic tools "in the vocabulary of social and labor history."

---

29. Carole Elizabeth Adams, *Women Clerks in Wilhelmine Germany: Issues of Class and Gender* (Cambridge, 1988).

30. Jean H. Quataert, "The Politics of Rural Industrialization: Class, Gender, and Collective Protest in the Saxon Oberlausitz of the Late Nineteenth Century," *Central European History* 20, no. 2 (June 1987): 91–124.

The gender perspective has begun to intrude into studies of middle-class life, work, and family forms in Germany as well, although the truly pathfinding and widely consulted research on the theme still is on the English and North American bourgeoisie.[31] German historians have been slower to take up the challenge but now are turning to the task. Blackbourn and Evans's edited collection *The German Bourgeoisie* fails to include a specific chapter on bourgeois *women's* work and life experiences; however, it acknowledges the importance of gender—of gender work roles, notions of sexuality, and the interplay of family and business commitments—in structuring and positioning middle-class existence between the aristocracy and the plebeians. Equally to the point, Frevert's contribution in the collection provides the other side of gender analysis by showing how notions of masculinity—in her case, ideas about honor "as the highest of all human, 'manly' possessions"—were central in shaping attitudes and behavioral patterns among professional men.[32] Marion Kaplan's study of the Jewish middle class rests on an intriguing mix of class, gender, and ethnic variables in the construction of the Jewish bourgeoisie, which comprised 85 percent of the Jewish population in the imperial period.[33] Primarily a study of women's place in the shaping of their class, Kaplan's book depicts the multiple sources of identity (female, Jewish, and bourgeois) that had to be reconciled—or at least at a truce. A rich and sensitive study, it captures the private, day-to-day basis of Jewish identity, which was anchored in the ritual of family life—through which women simultaneously sought to acculturate to the wider *German* meaning of bourgeois existence and safeguard their traditions and specific ethnic values and beliefs. The work is filled with all manner of details on Jewish women's daily existence, including the food they prepared, the furnishings they bought, the marriage markets they confronted, and their need to carve out leisure space. It captures as well the outside world for Jewish women, their efforts to study, work, and organize. But in the main it is a social

---

31. The most innovative and cited studies have been Leonore Davidoff and Catherine Hall, *Family Fortunes: Men and Women of the English Middle Class, 1780–1850* (Chicago, 1987); Mary P. Ryan, *Cradle of the Middle Class: The Family in Oneida County New York, 1790–1865* (Cambridge, 1981); and Carroll Smith-Rosenberg, *Disorderly Conduct: Visions of Gender in Victorian America* (New York, 1985).

32. Blackbourn and Evans, *The German Bourgeoisie.* Frevert's chapter is entitled "Bourgeois Honour: Middle-Class Duelists in Germany from the Late Eighteenth to the Early Twentieth Century," 255–92. Also consult Cocks and Jarausch, *The German Professions;* and Charles E. McClelland, *The German Experience of Professionalization: Modern Learned Professions and Their Organization from the Early Nineteenth Century to the Hitler Era* (Cambridge, 1991).

33. Marion A. Kaplan, *The Making of the Jewish Middle Class: Women, Family, and Identity in Imperial Germany* (New York, 1991). Kaplan's study is a welcome and significant contribution to women's history, which in Germany as elsewhere, while consistently sensitive to class divisions, tends to favor the ethnic majority. German reunification and the integration of the dwindling Sorb population of East Saxony into the larger nation offer new contexts to rethink issues of gender, class, and ethnicity.

history at its best, although it also demonstrates the fluidity that exists between the distinct "categories" of German women's history designated in this essay.

The third broad area of research, then, is a social history that, at least by the titles of published works, claims to shade partially into *Alltagsgeschichte*. A number of clarifications are in order at the outset. Much of women's history in its wider, international context has involved a social history of women's daily existence, originally among the inarticulate, less privileged groups in society but gradually rising up the social ladder. And German history is no exception. The articles and books on topics concerning imperial women's social worlds are too extensive to capture here in any detail. But among other themes, the studies map out changing family forms and demographic patterns as well as distinctly varied timing in the adoption of birth-control technologies and new standards of health among urban and rural women in the different regions of Germany. They look at private space, household furnishings, and apportionment of time in the daily routine of middle-class housewives and their servants. Child-rearing practices, changing recreational patterns and the multiple implications of the growing societal preoccupation with "normal" sexuality are also discussed. Previously spurned topics, such as prostitution and state-sanctioned vice or female homicide and criminality emerge confidently on the stage of legitimate history.[34]

The accumulated research, undeniably, has enriched the historical record. But as elsewhere in the discipline, a justifiable sense of unease has permeated the field of women's social history. Skeptics point to its lack of clear focus and failure to connect back into broader political and economic contexts. The most trenchant critic of standard social-historical practices has been the American women's historian Joan Scott, whose commitment to gender as an analytical

---

34. Among possible examples in this broad category are, on family forms and fertility, John Knodel, *Demographic Behavior in the Past: A Study of Fourteen German Village Populations* (Cambridge, 1988); William H. Hubbard, *Familiengeschichte: Materialien zur deutschen Familie seit dem Ende des 18. Jahrhunderts* (Munich, 1983); Arthur Imhof, "From the Old Mortality Pattern to the New," *Bulletin of the History of Medicine* 59 (Spring 1985): 1–29; Peter Borscheid, "Romantic Love or Marital Interest: Nineteenth Century Marriages in Germany," *Journal of Family History* 11, no. 1 (Spring 1988): 157–92. On health and birth-control practices, see Reinhard Spree, *Health and Social Class in Imperial Germany: A Social History of Mortality, Morbidity and Inequality,* trans. Stuart McKinnon-Evans (Oxford and New York, 1988); and Woycke, *Birth Control.* For a new look at household space, work, and leisure, consult Sibylle Meyer, "The Tiresome Work of Conspicuous Leisure: On the Domestic Duties of the Wives of Civil Servants in the German Empire (1871–1918)," in *Connecting Spheres: Women in the Western World, 1500 to the Present,* ed. Marilyn J. Boxer and Jean H. Quataert (New York, 1987). See also Stefan Bajohr, "Uneheliche Mütter im Arbeitsmilieu Braunschweig, 1900–1930," *Geschichte und Gesellschaft* 7, nos. 3–4 (1981): 474–506; Eric A. Johnson, "Women as Victims and Criminals: Female Homicide and Criminality in Imperial Germany, 1873–1914," *Crime and Justice History* 6 (1985): 151–75; and Richard J. Evans, "Prostitution, State and Society in Imperial Germany," *Past and Present* 70 (February 1976): 106–29.

category is her point of departure for serious historical reconceptualization. Scott decries the "lack of synthesis" in social history and its descent into mere description: it "does not address dominant disciplinary concepts or at least do[es] not address these concepts in terms that can shake their power and perhaps transform them."[35] This failure accounts for the discrepancy between the undeniably high quality of much of women's history and its marginality. Scott's own solution is an insistence on poststructural analysis, uncovering difference through linguistic theories of signification and thus subjecting the basic categories of historical analysis—fundamental ones, such as "women" and "men"—to thorough critique in order to determine how and under what historical contexts their diverse meanings are produced. M. J. Maynes's chapter in this volume, although rooted in social-science assumptions about women's lived experiences, nonetheless meets Scott's challenge, for hers is a social history with the politics left in. Maynes ties in the childhood experiences of Central European working-class men and women at home and in school with the construction and usage of social identity and political values and belief systems. In addition, she offers meaningful comparisons with the French case.[36]

The German variant of social history which shuns emphasis on larger structures and such abstract processes as industrialization and modernization in favor of the subjective dimensions of ordinary people's lives, *Alltagsgeschichte,* also offers women's historians a viable interpretive model to follow. Judging from a number of titles in German women's history, some authors, indeed, are looking at women's daily-life histories.[37] But words can be deceiving. Despite the call for a mutually beneficial theoretical exchange—a sensitivity toward gender in capturing subjective experience in historical miniature—many of the texts in women's history still are deeply materialist, grounded in the material conditions of life and the behavioral patterns and daily routines that are assumed to follow logically. A different set of theoretical postulates is needed to characterize a true merging of the two fields. According

---

35. Scott, *Gender and the Politics of History,* 30; see also Joan Scott, "Women's History" in *New Perspectives on Historical Writing,* ed. Peter Burke (University Park, 1991), 57; and Lynn Hunt, ed., *The New Cultural History* (Berkeley and Los Angeles, 1989), 9, which makes similar points about impact and marginality in a different context.

36. M. J. Maynes, "Childhood Memories, Political Visions, and Working-Class Formation in Imperial Germany: Some Comparative Observations," in this volume.

37. Rosmarie Beier, *Frauenarbeit und Frauenalltag im Deutschen Kaiserreich: Heimarbeiterinnen in der Berliner Bekleidungsindustrie, 1880–1914* (Frankfurt and New York, 1983); Ulla Knapp, "Frauenpolitik und proletarischer Frauenalltag zwischen 1800 und 1933" (Ph.D. diss., University of Wupperthal, 1983); Ulla Knapp, *Alltag und Politik: Vorträge zur Geschichte der Braunschweiger Arbeiterschaft* (Braunschweig, 1990); and Karen Hagemann, *Frauenalltag und Männerpolitik: Alltagsleben und gesellschaftliches Handeln von Arbeiterfrauen in der Weimarer Republic* (Bonn, 1990).

to the agenda proposed by Dorothee Wierling and Alf Lüdtke, two prominent practitioners of *Alltagsgeschichte,* collaboration requires, on the one hand, attention to concrete relations between the sexes and to the multiple meanings of the gender hierarchy in specific contexts. On the other hand, the focus on people's subjective worlds and on different understandings of social behavior captures the contradictory impact of so-called larger processes of historical change on daily life. This approach, for example, does not assume a correlation between industrialization and the adoption of increasingly rational attitudes; it therefore assesses with sensitivity varying modes of behavior. Simultaneously, inclusion of gender means that the larger structures and categories themselves constantly are called into question, dissolving the lines between public and private, demonstrating multiple forms and axes of power, and reformulating notions of work to include paid and unpaid labor.[38] Theirs is a challenging agenda for the 1990s that points to a fruitful area of future research.

The fourth and final category—women, war, and nationalism—is less a full-fledged division replete with illustrative references and citations than a highly promising subject that also might guide future research in German women's history. Imperial Germany, after all, was framed by two distinct periods of warfare, and in the interim era of peace, nationalist agendas moved to the forefront of political struggle. Three separate wars in the 1860s led up to the proclamation of the Second Empire in January 1871 at Versailles, and World War I, the first total war, so seriously strained the legitimacy of the imperial state that it collapsed even before the armistice in 1918. The war decade, however, is poorly integrated into the history of the early imperial period. Demographers of Imperial Germany, for example, explicitly exclude the war years in their models, apparently preferring so-called normal causal factors, such as urbanization, secularization, or migration rates, to explain shifts in fertility and eschewing the short-term, jarring demographic shocks of wartime. Their preference is symptomatic, for the historian of the imperial period typically begins the narrative in the first years of peace. Roger Chickering, for example, who has analyzed women's patriotic activities, casts his gaze forward from 1871, even though his main subject, the Women's Patriotic Association (Vaterländischer Frauenverein), originated five years earlier and, more importantly, set its peacetime agenda in wartime.[39] The lines between war and peace are fluid, indeed. Peacetime was not devoid of war; war lived on in German collective memory through a variety of mediums, a point well made

---

38. Dorothee Wierling, "Alltagsgeschichte und Geschichte der Geschlechterbeziehungen: Über historische und historiographische Verhältnisse," 169–90; and Alf Lüdtke, "Einleitung: Was ist und wer treibt Alltagsgeschichte?" 9–47, both in Lüdtke, *Alltagsgeschichte.*

39. Knodel, *The Decline of Fertility in Germany,* 58; and Roger Chickering, "'Casting Their Gaze More Broadly': Women's Patriotic Activism in Imperial Germany," *Past and Present* 118 (February 1988): 156–85.

by Wolfgang Natter in his study "Literature for the Warrior: Literature at War, 1914–1918." He shows that the wider political crisis of the Weimar Republic was reflected in heated controversy over the meaning of the war found in diverse texts. The earlier wars of unification, too, were relived over and over again, in men's and women's war memoirs published at varying dates in the imperial period, in the histories of the war that retold war's stories, in the artistic monuments and statuary glorifying war that increasingly marked public space, and in commemorative festivities and rituals celebrating specific battles and peaces.[40] Gender symbols were powerful ingredients in these representations of war and peace, and patriotic women played a central role in keeping alive the memory of war and continuously reintegrating the war culture into an evolving nationalist construction of "Germany." As Geoff Eley notes in his introduction to this volume, we actually know very little about the making of German national identity—whether from the top down, involving the world of official nationalism; or from a localist perspective, that of grass-roots receptivity—or of the redefinition of notions of Germanness "from below." Nationalism is a set of concrete (although contested) characteristics defining state and people; it also is a constructed imagining of a sovereign community, a new consciousness that binds people together by excluding others. Gender is a vital component in the play of nationalist politics and identities. The chapter by Lora Wildenthal demonstrates the centrality of gender to the nationalist project.[41] After the disastrous and destabilizing colonial wars of 1904–7, colonialist women and men formulated a new definition of Germanness against native populations on the one hand (i.e., in racial terms) and other colonial powers on the other. Rooted in acclaimed German virtues of hard work, morality, and purity, its very success required the immigration of white German women to the colonies, engaging in what was then acknowledged as significant familial, cultural, and national work.

It was once an uncontested truism that "war was men's business, not

---

40. Wolfgang Nalter, "Literature for the Warrior: Literature at War, 1914–1918," paper presented at the conference "The Kaiserreich in the 1990s: New Research, New Directions, New Agendas," University of Pennsylvania (February 1990). Jean H. Quataert, "Women's Work and the German States in War and Peace-Time, 1861–1890" (Paper presented at the conference "On the Road to Total War: The American Civil War and the German Wars of Unification, 1861–1871," Washington, D.C., 1–4 April 1992).

41. Her chapter is an important contribution to the role of colonialism in the ongoing formulations of German national identity, a little-known subject, as she indicates. See "'She Is the Victor'": Bourgeois Women, Nationalist Identities, and the Ideal of the Independent Woman Farmer in German Southwest Africa," in this volume. Also, Krista O'Donnell, "The Colonial Woman Question: Gender, National Identity, and Empire in the German Colonial Society Female Emigration Program, 1896–1914," Ph.D. diss., Rinehamtor University, in progress.

ladies';"[42] and the topics of war, diplomacy, military strategy and tactics are time-honored subjects in German history. But these traditional historical themes now are facing an intrusion by the gender perspective, as is the whole discussion of nationalist politics and identity. In reading war's texts, experiences, and rituals, many authors, as Natter does, fruitfully employ innovative methods drawn from literary criticism and the new historicism. Hong's chapter in this volume demonstrates how different historical agents read the severe economic and social tensions of World War I in ways that pushed the German welfare state in new and contested directions. Other historians also are testing new interdisciplinary approaches. At the conference on Imperial Germany of 1990, Elisabeth Domansky offered an intriguing analysis of the organization of war, but not, as it is commonly understood, to mean the material institutions, structures, and policies of war. Rather, she analyzed the gender symbolism binding the diverse discourses about the war. Soldiers, for example, spoke of emasculation and, in an ironic role reversal, endowed the home front with male qualities of agency, strength, and control. Working-class women described a similar sexual fear, in their case a loss of femininity under the strains of civilian mobilization and economic dislocation. Such sentiment, however, was directed against the ruling classes and became the foundation for a strategy of resistance and revolt in the name of the threatened working-class family. Domansky's contribution to this collection is a provocative essay exploring the fundamental restructuring of gender relations that resulted from the militarization of German society in the twentieth century. In her reading, male supremacy was recast from its patriarchal basis in the bourgeois family structure—in which men monopolized economic power in the public arena—into a new military system of male domination, reflecting their monopoly over state violence, that is, their role as soldiers. The shift was a necessary corollary to the growing importance of women's reproductive role, a new way to "disempower" women, given their centrality as a valuable national resource. Domansky seems to return us to the *Sonderweg* thesis, for she argues for something distinctive and unique about the German experience. Her essay, nonetheless, is designed precisely to stimulate new thinking about, and experimenting with, historical categories. Similarly, Belinda Davis's contribution here is methodologically and theoretically innovative. Her chapter is as much a commentary on the way historians construct history—i.e., a self-conscious usage of analytic concepts—as an investigation of a specific content at a particular moment in time. Davis overcomes the limitations of Jürgen Habermas's for-

---

42. The phrase comes from the movie *Gone with the Wind* and is the opening line in the introduction to an excellent collection of essays on gender and war. See Margaret Randolph Higonnet et al., eds., *Behind the Lines: Gender and the Two World Wars* (New Haven, 1987), 1.

mulation of the public sphere in ways that make it relevant for women's history and gender analysis in wartime Berlin. Managing "public opinion," as government officials acknowledged, was essential to conducting total war, but it was a complicated task, since public identities were unstable. "No fixed opposition" existed between public and private, bourgeois and worker, or even man and woman; indeed, there were no fixed identities at all but rather wartime roles (such as the "soldiers' wife" and the "woman of little means") constructed out of specific ideological, juridical, and "performative" contexts. Although unstable, they nonetheless were powerful agents shaping events in the name of patriotism, endowed by the public with the legitimacy to speak for the general good, and demonstrating "the power of . . . women over the state gained through their activity in the 'public sphere.'" [43]

Indeed, a promising link in the theme of women and war is the state. Karin Hausen, the eminent German women's historian, describes the ambiguous response of the German welfare state to its war widows of World War I. She captures graphically the underlying gendered biases inherent in the social policy and pension schemes formulated in the so-called general interest. And for the long years of peace, Quataert examines the mechanisms of power whereby official nationalists after 1871 sought to create meaningful identifications with the nation—sought, indeed, to orchestrate dispositions among the citizenry that were designed to transform the *state* into a *nation*. Her focus is on the workings of a "gender war ideology," a set of gendered practices that originated in the war of liberation against Napoleon I. In the last third of the nineteenth century, this ideology functioned by evoking a dual conception of the state as war-making machine but also as caring institution—caring for its soldiers at war, its veterans and disabled, and its needy in general. The cumulative effect of public philanthropic activity under the guise of this ideology in peacetime served to instill identification with a caring state that made war in its name that much more possible.[44] Taken together, this research on women, war, nationalism, and the state raises a host of questions that are central to the historical discipline and have the potential to shape and reshape the debates in German history in creative new ways. For example, how was nationalism internalized in the body politic of the newly constituted nation-states? What

---

43. Elisabeth Domansky, "World War I as Gender Conflict in Germany" (Paper presented at the conference "The *Kaiserreich* in the 1990s: New Research, New Directions, New Agendas," University of Pennsylvania, 23–25 February 1990); Elisabeth Domansky, "Militarization and Reproduction in World War I Germany," in this volume; and Belinda Davis, "Reconsidering Habermas, Gender, and the Public Sphere: The Case of Wilhelmine Germany," in this volume.

44. Karin Hausen, "The German Nation's Obligations to the Heroes' Widows of World War I," in Higonnet, *Behind the Lines,* 126–40; and Jean H. Quataert, "Gender in the Construction of Germany's War Culture: Patriotic Women's Work, 1871–1914" (Paper presented at the conference "Cultural Dimensions of War and Human Conflict," Rutgers Center for Historical Analysis, 4–5 March 1994).

was the role of women in this complex spread of new values? After all, with few exceptions, women throughout Europe were denied full rights of citizenship until after World War I at the earliest. How were women mobilized for the war effort, and for other nationalist purposes, for that matter? What did women and men later on make of those experiences? How powerful are war's emblems and identities to filter experience? Through what symbols and metaphors do nations express their political goals in wartime? Scott has put it boldly: What does a history of women reveal about the politics of war?[45]

This chapter certainly has come full circle. It began with a recognition of the roadblocks to writing women's history in the German national context. Using Imperial Germany as its main example, it nonetheless pointed to the multiple interpretive contributions that the women's and gender perspective has given the study of this important era. Women's history has provided a needed supplement to the inherited picture of the past; it also has reformulated standard interpretations and broadened our understanding and usage of dominant categories and tools of historical analysis. And some women's historians, indeed, have pushed beyond the borders of history, stepping into new linguistic terrain to challenge the fundamental sociological foundations of the modern association of history and the social sciences. There clearly is not one dominant or even typical women's or gender perspective. The field is rich and diverse and promises to play an important role in the ongoing political effort to construct new narratives of the German past.

---

45. Joan Scott, "Rewriting History," in Higonnet, *Behind the Lines,* 30. Scott's point, indeed, is that political history and women's history can be linked closely through analyses of gender in the political discourses around war and peace.

German History and the Contradictions of Modernity: The Bourgeoisie, the State, and the Mastery of Reform

Geoff Eley

Modernization, Modernity

Perhaps surprisingly, in light of the bitterly conducted critiques of the 1960s and 1970s, "modernization theory" seems alive and well. Two decades ago, a generation of radical social scientists—mainly Marxist, and often from a third-world perspective—attacked the patently Eurocentric, unilinear, progressivist, and teleological assumptions on which the developmental modernization theories of the 1950s and 1960s tended to be based, while a related body of historical work questioned the adequacy of the dichotomy of "traditional" and "modern" for analyzing the complexities of historical change, whether within or across particular societies.[1] Of course, it would be wrong to assume that

The evolution of this essay owes much to the ideas and help of Julia Adams, Kathleen Canning, David Crew, Nick Dirks, Young Sun Hong, Rudy Koshar, Amy Nelson, George Steinmetz, Dennis Sweeney, Lora Wildenthal, and John Williams. Of course, they should not be held responsible for the contents.

1. For the most useful critiques, see Dean C. Tipps, "Modernization Theory and the Comparative Study of Societies: A Critical Perspective," *Comparative Studies in Society and History* 15 (1973): 199–266; Anthony D. Smith, *The Concept of Social Change: A Critique of the Functionalist Theory of Social Change* (London, 1973); and John G. Taylor, *From Modernization to Modes of Production: A Critique of Sociologies of Development and Underdevelopment* (London, 1979). For a discussion of modernization theory among historians, see Tony Judt, "A Clown in Regal Purple: Social History and the Historians," *History Workshop Journal* 7 (Spring 1979): 66–94, which unfortunately undermines its case by overstatement and the indiscriminate nature of the attack. In West Germany the response to modernization theory among historians was always much less critical. For the classic affirmation, see Hans-Ulrich Wehler, *Modernisierungstheorie*

modernization theorists and their models just disappeared. The more simplistic versions, it is true, fell into disrepute or entered a crisis of confidence, their assumptions and predictions in disarray. But a large body of policy-oriented work continued as before, while the more sophisticated practitioners retreated, somewhat bloodied, to more moderate and careful ground, often accompanied by reflections on history, to reconsider the originary cases from which the operative developmental models were derived.[2]

Moreover, in the meantime the original ground of the critique has itself become unsure. The superior virtues of the Marxist and related radical counter-positions have become less obvious than in the past. Since the mid-1970s Marxism has also come under attack for its teleological forms of reasoning, not least from a wide range of critics who began their rethinking from within the Marxist tradition's own political and intellectual domain. This Marxist ferment has also been characterized by a pronounced antireductionist turn, so that political and ideological changes can no longer be easily conceived as the logical and dependent consequences of underlying socioeconomic causes in the classic "base-and-superstructure" sense. The main Marxist alternative to modernization-based models of the interrelationship of industrialization and political change—namely, the framework of the transition from feudalism to capitalism—has been little more successful in specifying the causal relationship of particular political histories (such as the English or French revolutions) to structurally determining processes of capitalist developmental change.[3] Recent revisionisms have deconstructed the organizing concept of the industrial revolution itself.[4] Given the uncertainty of the main alternative, therefore, the way has been clear for modernization theory's modest return.

While a less dogmatic, more agnostic understanding of *modernization* has been possible through a loosening of the older polemical fronts, the need to

---

und Geschichte (Göttingen, 1975); and for the beginnings of critique, Hans Medick, "'Missionäre im Ruderboot': Ethnologische Erkenntnisweisen als Herausforderung an die Sozialgeschichte," *Geschichte und Gesellschaft* 10 (1984): 295–314.

2. See especially Charles Tilly, ed., *The Formation of National States in Western Europe* (Princeton, 1975); and Raymond Grew, ed., *Crises of Political Development in Europe and the United States* (Princeton, 1978). See also Wehler, *Modernisierungstheorie,* 58–59.

3. See Rodney Hilton, ed., *The Transition from Feudalism to Capitalism* (London, 1976); and Rodney Hilton, *The Brenner Debate: Agrarian Class Structure and Economic Development in Pre-Industrial Europe* (Cambridge, 1985). I have touched on these issues in Geoff Eley, "In Search of the Bourgeois Revolution: The Particularities of German History," *Political Power and Social Theory* 7 (1988): 105–33. For more recent contributions, see Colin Moers, *The Making of Bourgeois Europe: Absolutism, Revolution, and the Rise of Capitalism in England, France and Germany* (London, 1991); and Heide Gerstenberger, *Die subjektlose Gewalt: Theorie der Entstehung bürgerlicher Staatsgewalt* (Münster, 1990).

4. See David Cannadine, "The Past and the Present in the English Industrial Revolution," *Past and Present* 103 (May 1984): 131–72; Charles Sabel and Jonathan Zeitlin, "Historical Alternatives to Mass Production: Politics, Markets and Technology in Nineteenth-Century Industrialization," *Past and Present* 108 (August 1985): 133–76; and for a critical survey of the

conceptualize *modernity* has been imposed by a different kind of intellectual challenge, namely, the philosophical and cultural discourse of postmodernism. By now the range of theory and commentary encompassed by the latter in the English-speaking world has become vast, and any full discussion goes beyond the bounds of this essay. For our purposes, we may briefly list three dimensions of critique, while noting their fuller elaboration in a more specifically poststructuralist theoretical context: a critique of the universalist values and foundational categories of the Enlightenment philosophical tradition; a critique of the familiar "grand narratives" of modern historical development, of progress and emancipation (such as the industrial revolution, the rise of democracy, the triumph of science over nature, the emancipation of the working class, the victory of socialism, and the equality of women); and a critique of the idea of the coherently centered and rationally acting individual subject.

As such, the postmodernist perspective implies a conception of modernity now in dissolution or supersession that both the modernization theorists and their Marxist critics have held in common—one constructed epistemologically around totalizing notions of transcendent truth and the universalizing metanarrative of the rise of "Western civilization" and "man's" mastery over nature, in a way that allowed the world and its future to be *known* in a scientific, historical, and predictive sense. Such an understanding of modernity implied a strongly centered notion of identity and agency, of directionality in history, of the power of knowledge to shape the environment, and of the progressive impact of the West on the rest of the world (even where such transformations were acknowledged to have proceeded through immediately destructive and exploitative encounters). There is much diversity of perspectives among and within these intellectual traditions, of course—liberal, Marxist, and others. But some version of the above that combines assumptions about the reasoning individual with the overarching logics of universal rationalization, economic progress, and the West's expansion in the world has been constitutive for the main forms of social theory since the end of the last century. As Nelly Richard says,

> With regard to its economic programme and its cultural organization, this concept of modernity represents an effort to synthesize its progressive and emancipatory ideals into a globalizing, integrative vision of the individual's place in history and society. It rests on the assumption that there exists a legitimate center—a unique and superior position from which to establish control and to determine hierarchies.[5]

---

literature on protoindustrialization, Geoff Eley, "The Social History of Industrialization: 'Proto-Industry' and the Origins of Capitalism," *Economy and Society* 13 (1984): 519–39.

5. Nelly Richard, "Postmodernism and Periphery," *Third Text* 2 (1978/79): 6.

This critique of the Enlightenment tradition is a highly charged political project, and it is no accident that in the English-speaking world its impetus has come increasingly from feminists, African Americans, other minorities, and the third-world critics of colonial and postcolonial forms of power—that is, precisely the voices historically most effectively silenced by the progressive Enlightenment-derived cultural and political traditions. Of course, the liberal and conservative upholders of the values of the West are unlikely to be moved by such voices from the margins, as controversies currently raging over the university curriculum in the United States eloquently confirm. Such debates, which focus around the established conception of "Western civilization" and its cultural authority, are the opposite of an abstract or academic affair but rather grow from political demands for a fresh review of discriminatory structures and practices, typically precipitated by some incident or revelation of racist and/or sexist excess. At the same time, calls for nonsexist and antiracist education, "diversity," multiculturalism, and the validation of difference have entailed a radical and wide-ranging philosophical and theoretical debate that elicits increasingly aggressive reassertions of the old truths, as in the current charges in the United States that the advocates of "diversity" are seeking to impose a single standard of politically correct attitudes. The Salman Rushdie affair has been particularly interesting in this respect. While Rushdie himself speaks from within the postcolonial discourse of indeterminacy, his sentence to death by the Ayatollah Khomeini (14 February 1990) has ironically produced an outpouring of Eurocentric moralizing. Aside from the purer civil-libertarian positions and a large amount of more nuanced commentary, Rushdie's defense has called forth some startling restatements of the "Western" tradition, drawn in sharp contradistinction to the irrational and dangerous third-world Other, in this case the demonized forces of fundamentalist Islam.[6]

Once we turn to German intellectual life, we find "Western values" especially strongly centered. The Enlightenment tradition has no shortage of critics—both from a "Green" political and cultural discourse on the Left and from the partisans of German "identity" on the Right. But on the whole, it is still the strong orientation toward the values of the West—from the market-oriented ideology of the Free Democrats (FDP) and the Christian Democrats

---

6. For the Rushdie affair, see Talal Asad, "Multiculturalism and British Identity in the Wake of the Rushdie Affair," *Politics and Society* 18 (1990): 455–80; Carol A. Breckenridge and Arjun Appadurai, "Editors' Comments," and Vinay Dhardwadker, "'Offensive Books' and the Rhetoric of Outrage," *Public Culture* 1, no. 2 (Spring 1989): i–v, 76–79; Gayatri Chakravorty Spivak, Peter van der Veer, Feroza Jussawalla, Charles Taylor, David Hollinger, and Michael M. J. Fischer/Mehdi Abedi, "The Rushdie Debate," *Public Culture* 2, no. 1 (Fall 1989): 79–127; and Timothy Brennan, *Salman Rushdie and the Third World: Myths of the Nation* (New York, 1989). For the current controversy over political correctness, see "Taking Offense: Is This the New Enlightenment on Campus or the New McCarthyism?" *Newsweek,* 24 Dec. 1990, 48–55.

(CDU) center to the welfare statism of the Social Democrats (SPD), and the obdurate rationalism and philosophical modernism of most liberal and social democratic intellectuals—that leaves us most impressed. Here, of course, the unavoidable context of such discussion—until the *annus mirabile* of 1989, at least—has remained the experience and legacy of the Third Reich. For Jürgen Habermas, especially, an explicit, systematic, and continuously reaffirmed allegiance to the "political theory of the Enlightenment" has become the unavoidable antidote to Germany's baleful pre-1945 past. In this case an abstract and normative constitutionalism deriving from the historic break of 1945–49—the necessity of a "constitutional patriotism," or a postconventional identity based on rationalist adherence to an idealized construction of the liberal political community of the West—became for Habermas the only permissible form of a German collective identity, because more traditional appeals to history and nationality ("identity" and "meaning," as privileged in the discourse of the intellectual Right) became morally forfeited due to the years 1933–45. The sense of a new beginning, of strict demarcation against certain older German continuities or traditions—political romanticism, decisionism, and diverse illiberalisms and antimodernisms—has been crucial to Habermas's conception of how postwar German democracy needs to be thought. As he insisted during the *Historikerstreit,*

> The only patriotism that will not alienate us from the West is constitutional patriotism. Unfortunately, a commitment to universal constitutional principles based in conviction has only been possible in German national culture since—and because of—Auschwitz. Anyone who wishes to expunge the shame of this fact with facile talk of "guilt-obsession," anyone who wants to recall the Germans to more conventional forms of national identity, destroys the only reliable basis of our tie to the West.[7]

Thus for Habermas certain ideas are irredeemably contaminated by their associations with the past, and this connotative chain precludes the opening of the contemporary agenda toward the discourse of postmodernism. For him, critiques of the Enlightenment are inseparably linked—logically and historically—to politically destructive and reactionary agendas. His worst fear is that the late-twentieth-century crisis of modernity, rightly defined by the catastrophe of scientific domination over nature, will open the door for irrationalism and a rehabilitated tradition of the antidemocratic Right. And, of course, such voices have certainly been heard. At one intellectual retreat orga-

---

7. Jürgen Habermas, "Eine Art Schadensabwicklung: Die apologetischen Tendenzen in der deutschen Zeitgeschichtsschreibung," *Die Zeit,* 11 July 1986, reprinted in *"Historikerstreit": Die Dokumentation der Kontroverse um die Einzigartigkeit der nationalsozialistischen Judenvernichtung* (Munich, 1987), 75–76.

nized by the CDU soon after returning to government in 1983, "German Identity Today," the conservative philosopher Günther Rohrmoser counter-posed to the Enlightenment what he called a specifically German "answer to . . . modern society and the problems of human alienation connected with it." In the late twentieth century, Rohrmoser argued, the Enlightenment tradition's moral hegemony could no longer persuade. The "project of modernity" was in crisis, and a certain heritage of critique should now come into play: "Is it really the case that the answers of an ideologically exhausted liberalism and a social-ism that has failed in all its variants are better than those we can derive from the memory of the greatest philosophical and cultural achievements of the Ger-mans?" In fact, the post-1945 determination to treat "the difference between the Germans and all the ahistorical-abstract traditions of the West founded on natural law" as "nothing but an error" has produced only "the neuroticization of our national self-understanding."[8] Here the seamless unity of political ro-manticism, appeals to identity, and historical apologetics feared by Habermas—the harmful consequences of departing from the Enlightenment tradition—clearly seems to be at work.

In this respect Habermas speaks for a substantial body of German histor-ical opinion, basically those responsible for the main innovations of the 1960s and 1970s, including Hans Mommsen and other so-called structuralist histo-rians of Nazism, Wolfgang Mommsen and the labor historians, and Hans-Ulrich Wehler, Jürgen Kocka, and other members of the so-called Bielefeld network. But is that really all there is to say? Can we really lump together all the present hesitancies and reservations about the Enlightenment tradition in all its dimensions and mark them negatively as danger, a reemergence of tainted German traditions from before 1945, so that "precisely in [Germany] a 'grand coalition' of critics of Enlightenment has formed, a coalition in which the brown, black, and green fringes meet?" as Habermas has put it?[9] Quite apart from the merits of current philosophical and theoretical critiques them-selves (which, after all, many on the Left have found compelling), enthroning the Enlightenment so intransigently also leads to a highly artificial *historical* account of the nineteenth and twentieth centuries, one in which the complexity of the processes that actually moved progressive or democratic change is flattened. Moreover, as feminist and postcolonial critics have taught us, "the political theory of the Enlightenment" also involved silences and suppressions, so that the founding moments of modern democratic advance became predi-cated on the gendering of political capacities, the social qualification and

---

8. Cited by Jürgen Habermas, "The New Intimacy between Politics and Culture: Theses on Enlightenment in Germany," in *The New Conservatism: Cultural Criticism and the Historians' Debate,* by Jürgen Habermas, ed. and trans. Shierry Weber Nicholsen (Cambridge, Mass., 1989), 199.

9. Ibid.

limitation of citizenship, and the exploitative domination of some peoples by others. Social improvement and cultural goods involved similar privilegings and exclusions, whereby certain constructions of value, agency, and interest were centered at the expense of others. The great movements of modern reform since the French Revolution were constituted from fields of contradiction in this way.

If that is so, then Habermas's connections look less automatic. Once we accept that the story of the Enlightenment tradition is one of contradictory movement and effects, so that the ideals of progress, rationalism, and science may be treated problematically as well as affirmatively, then the issue of negative continuities (which Habermas locates in political romanticism and right-wing anti-Enlightenment oppositions) can be very differently posed. Such dangers can be found not only in the various forms of conservatism and right-wing anti-Enlightenment critique, but also—and more insidiously—at the heart of the Enlightenment ideas themselves. It is this point—which destabilizes the rationalist unity of economic and cultural progress that Habermas wishes to hold together, and which problematizes the postwar "anti-totalitarian consensus" on which he believes West German political culture to have been based—that Habermas's affirmative centering of "Western values" tends to obscure.

How, then, are we to judge the category of "the modern"? A full-scale conceptual review would outgrow the terms of this essay, and instead I want to indicate briefly some of the salient present meanings before moving, eclectically and agnostically, to a consideration of some current historiographical issues of the *Kaiserreich*.

The simplest meaning is the one embodied in the following quotation by Lawrence Stone, inscribed by his pupils at the head of his festschrift:

> How and why did Western Europe change itself during the sixteenth, seventeenth and eighteenth centuries so as to lay the social, economic, scientific, political, ideological and ethical foundations for the rationalist, democratic, individualistic, technological industrialized society in which we now live? England was the first country to travel along this road.[10]

Or, as Anthony Giddens puts it: "'modernity' refers to modes of social life or organization which emerged in Europe from about the seventeenth century onwards and which subsequently became more or less worldwide in their influence."[11] This is also the approach of Thomas Nipperdey and Wehler. After

---

10. A. L. Beier, David Cannadine, and James M. Rosenheim, eds., *The First Modern Society: Essays in English History in Honour of Lawrence Stone* (Cambridge, 1989), vii.

11. Anthony Giddens, *The Consequences of Modernity* (Stanford, 1990), 1.

beginning his account with an exhaustive catalogue of particular changes signified by the progressive transition from the "traditional" to the "modern," Nipperdey locates the latter in an epochal conjuncture of underlying conditions: Max Weber's "disenchantment of the world" (*Entzauberung*), where modernization appears as "systematic, purposeful and sustained rationalization," originating in the universalism permitted by the monotheism of Judeo-Christian religion; the universalistic rationality and antiparticularism of Roman law; and the territorial pluralism of the European state-system, which interacted with the consequences of the Protestant Reformation to promote bureaucratic processes of state formation and key institutional autonomies around towns and universities. Together these processes constituted "modernization" as a "key concept of general history": "It is meant to describe the singular process of immensely rapid economic, social, cultural, and political transformation that has worked itself out over the last two hundred years since the dual revolution of the late eighteenth century, the industrial and the democratic revolution, first in the European-Atlantic sphere and then in the whole world."[12]

Wehler takes a similar approach, authorizing his account more explicitly from Weber and defining modernization by a distinctive set of West European peculiarities ("This overall ensemble of special Western conditions"). Wehler also follows Weber in refusing a Marxist or similar materialist privileging of economic and social determinations. But while he maintains political rule, economics, and culture in a dynamic state of reciprocal interaction—as opposed to ordering them around the primacy of, say, state formation or industrialization—the Weberian "rationalization" tends nonetheless to order the account as a capacious portmanteau concept.[13]

What are we to make of such a usage? At one level it reflects a recent and continuing genre of historical sociology focused on the dialectic of capitalism and state making and based particularly in early modern Europe but also including a range of global histories that are seeking in effect to rebuild social theory via a writing of the history of the world.[14] In effect, this amounts to the

---

12. Thomas Nipperdey, "Probleme der Modernisierung in Deutschland," in *Nachdenken über die deutsche Geschichte*, by Thomas Nipperdey (Munich, 1986), 44–64.

13. Hans-Ulrich Wehler, *Deutsche Gesellschaftsgeschichte*, vol. 1, *Vom Feudalismus des Alten Reiches bis zur Defensiven Modernisierung der Reformära, 1700–1815;* vol. 2, *Von der Reformära bis zur industriellen und politischen "Deutschen Doppelrevolution," 1815–1845–49* (Munich, 1987), esp. 1:332ff., 2:589ff.; quotations are taken from 1:334, 333. On the one hand, Wehler maintains a schematic fourfold separation (he adds a fourth sphere, social inequality, to the Weberian trinity); but on the other hand, it is frequently "rationalization" that speaks through the presentation of them all. See 1:14ff.

14. In the former category, Charles Tilly has been preeminent: see his *Coercion, Capital, and European States, AD 990–1990* (Oxford, 1990), *Big Structures, Large Processes, Huge Comparisons* (New York, 1984), and *The Formation of National States*. Among the wider litera-

more careful disengagement of a more manageably specified question (the relationship of capitalist development to processes of state formation) from the overtotalized framework of modernization theory as it was presented in the 1950s and 1960s, a specification assisted by a more open relationship to Marxist theory and originally given powerful impetus by the reception of Barrington Moore's *Social Origins of Dictatorship and Democracy*.[15] On the other hand, the German discussion seems more continuous with the earlier, more totalizing moment of modernization theory—Nipperdey more pragmatically, Wehler in an explicitly theorized way.[16] Moreover, Wehler retains modernization theory's normative ambition, both theoretically-comparatively and politically-ethically, as in the explication of "erkenntnisleitende Interessen" in terms of "the historical origins of our present" and the "imagery of a desirable future."[17] In Wehler's case, the normativity of the West German present (meaning more specifically the consolidated reform values of the 1970s) and of an allied conception of the Western community is palpable.

In other words, "modernity" here is not just a postulated relationship between social change and institutional forms; it is a set of *philosophical* positions about the contemporary world. Here the relations among contemporary commentary, traditions of thought, and the specific histories through which the latter emerged (the historicity of ideas, as opposed to their universalized abstraction) are much less clear and imply notions of origin, linked to arguments about the rise of bourgeois society or the importance of the French Revolution, that historians have come to suspect.[18] At a certain point, there-

ture, see also Mary Fulbrook, *Piety and Politics: Religion and the Rise of Absolutism in England, Württemberg and Prussia* (Cambridge, 1983); Jack A. Goldstone, *Revolution and Rebellion in the Early Modern World* (Berkeley, 1991); and Perry Anderson, *Lineages of the Absolutist State* (London, 1974). For the new genre of global histories, see Anthony Giddens, *A Contemporary Critique of Historical Materialism*, vol. 1, *Power, Property, and the State* (London, 1981), and vol. 2, *The Nation-State and Violence* (Cambridge, 1985); Michael Mann, *The Sources of Social Power,* vol. 1, *A History of Power from the Beginning to AD 1760* (Cambridge, 1986); John A. Hall, *Powers and Liberties. The Causes and Consequences of the Rise of the West* (Oxford, 1985). There is an excellent critical summary of this genre in Perry Anderson, "A Culture in Contraflow—I," *New Left Review* 180 (March–April 1990): 41–78, where the works of W. G. Runciman, Ernest Gellner, and Jack Goody are also added.

15. Barrington Moore, *The Social Origins of Dictatorship and Democracy: Lord and Peasant in the Making of the Modern World* (Boston, 1966).

16. To a great extent this is also a stylistic difference: Nipperdey eschews footnotes, while Wehler saturates his text with the citations and their authority.

17. Wehler, *Deutsche Gesellschaftsgeschichte,* 1:13.

18. For interesting attempts to ground this view historically, see Ferenc Feher, ed., *The French Revolution and the Birth of Modernity* (Berkeley, 1990); and Charles Taylor, *Sources of the Self* (Cambridge, 1990). One classic study is still Jürgen Habermas, *Strukturwandel der Öffentlichkeit* (Neuwied, 1962). For some reflections on the latter, see Craig Calhoun, ed., *Habermas and the Public Sphere* (Cambridge, Mass., 1992), including my own contribution, "Nations, Publics, and Political Cultures: Placing Habermas in the Nineteenth Century," 289–339.

fore, discussions of modernization in the more controlled sense (capitalism and state making) shade into more encompassing claims about modernity whose license is far less dependent on historical argument and research. This is true both of the specifically German discussion, where Habermas has become such a leading voice in the reaffirming of Enlightenment traditions, and in the English-speaking world among those social theorists who seek to hold the ground of classical sociology. Giddens, for example, has offered the concept of "high modernity" against the claims of postmodernity, grounding his discussion of modernity in the themes of "security versus danger" and "trust versus risk." Yet for Giddens the emergence of modernity is abstracted from multidimensional processes of institutional development—relating to the growth of capitalism ("Capital accumulation in the context of competitive labour and product markets"), industrialism ("Transformation of nature: development of the 'created environment'"), the growth of administrative power and surveillance ("Control of information and social supervision"), and military power ("Control of the means of violence in the context of the industrialization of war")—that have a completely nonspecific relationship to the historical contexts in which such a modernity was allegedly produced.[19]

A second complex of meanings is as pervasive to late-twentieth-century vocabulary as the "modernization/modernity" complex, and indeed is inescapably a part of our contemporary common sense, and that is the "modernism/modernity" range of meanings in cultural theory and the arts. While notoriously hard to pin down, modernism here tends to be associated with a concentrated period of formal innovation in writing and the visual arts in the early twentieth century, which experienced a dramatic process of politicized radicalization during and after World War I, before becoming extended to the new mass media of film, radio, photography, and advertising and their technologies, and thereby to a general sensibility of fashion, style, and design. Other arguments relate this burst of creativity to the artist's changing place in society (that is, structurally speaking in relation to the market, private patronage, and the state) and the self-conscious emergence of a radical literary-artistic intelligentsia claiming a distinctive social and political voice (the avant-garde). The argument can be further extended—in both the understanding of the innovators themselves and the theorizing of the subsequent commentators—to the aesthetic and perceptual consequences of the new urban, industrial, and technological conditions of the late-nineteenth- and early-twentieth-century social world. And the most fruitful specifications of this sociological dimension have focused on the metropolis as the crucible and inspiration of the new sensibility,

---

19. See Giddens, *The Consequences of Modernity,* 1–54, 55–59. See also Jörn Rüsen, Eberhard Lämmert, and Peter Glotz, eds., *Die Zukunft der Aufklärung* (Frankfurt a.M., 1988).

leading to a distinctive human condition of fragmentation and individual isolation, which is both producer and product of the emergent modernist discourse. Georg Simmel and Walter Benjamin become the classical theorizers of this metropolitan moment, while the "modern predicament" becomes canonized into a now familiar line of artistic and literary achievements. How exactly this discourse of modernism should be conceptualized in relation to the new one of postmodernism remains an open question.[20]

In this cultural complex of meanings, it will be noticed, the origins of "modernity" migrate from the late eighteenth to the late nineteenth century. In the German context, it is above all the Weimar Republic that defines our perceptions of modernism in this sense. Detlev Peukert has made perhaps the strongest argument for appropriating this Weimar moment of cultural experimentation, characterized as "classical modernity," as the basis for a general analysis of political and social-historical as well as cultural problems of the early twentieth century. In this view, the transition to industrialism in the 1890s created the conditions for "the socio-cultural penetration of modernity": "Since the turn of the century modernity has classically shaped developments in the fields of science and culture, in town planning, in technology, and in medicine, in spiritual reflection, as well as in the everyday world—has rehearsed our present-day way of life, so to speak."[21] Peukert framed this as a specific proposal for the Weimar Republic, but his own broader work reached back to the *Kaiserreich*, and an exploration of this argument would be very fruitful. So far, in the historiography of the *Kaiserreich* the concept of "modernism" has mainly been engaged as its opposite, namely, resistance to modernity or "antimodernism," either as a social history of the casualties of industrialization or as a very conventional intellectual history (as in the "politics of cultural despair"). The positive modernity of the *Kaiserreich,* as opposed to various kinds of traditionalism, is waiting to be explored.[22]

There is a third current of meaning associated with the category of the "modern" in the English-speaking intellectual world, much less so in the German,

---

20. I am most indebted here to the ideas of Raymond Williams, John Berger, and Roy Pascal. See Raymond Williams, *The Politics of Modernism: Against the New Conformists* (London, 1989); John Berger, *Selected Essays and Articles: The Look of Things* (Harmondsworth, 1972), esp. "The Moment of Cubism," 133–62; and Roy Pascal, *From Naturalism to Expressionism: German Literature and Society, 1880–1918* (London, 1973), esp. 152ff. For an important attempt to specify the social and political context of modernism, see also Perry Anderson, "Modernity and Revolution," *New Left Review* 144 (March–April 1984): 96–113.

21. Detlev J. K. Peukert, "The Weimar Republic—Old and New Perspectives," *German History* 6 (1988): 138.

22. For "antimodernism," see Fritz Stern, *The Politics of Cultural Despair* (Berkeley, 1961); and Shulamit Volkov, *The Rise of Popular Antimodernism in Germany: The Urban Master Artisans, 1873–1896* (Princeton, 1978).

namely, the influence of Michel Foucault.[23] Since the early 1980s work in Britain and North America on sexuality (particularly the late-nineteenth- and twentieth-century constructions of sexual categories), on prisons, hospitals, asylums, and other institutions of confinement, on social policy and public health, and on the history of science and the academic disciplines has been shot through with Foucault's inspiration.[24] Aside from helping to open up new areas of empirical research, moreover, Foucault's ideas can claim major theoretical effects that (as my introduction suggests) have helped change and unsettle the ways we have come to think about politics, power, knowledge, and their relationship to the ordering of the social world. There is no point in repeating that theoretical explication here, and it is enough to point to the ways in which the reception of Foucault has tended to shape a particular understanding of what is distinctive about the modern world.

For Foucault, therefore, "modernity" is to be characterized mainly by the third of Giddens's four institutional dimensions, namely, the growth of administrative power and surveillance, although Foucault's understanding of the latter involves the more distinctive conception of disciplinary power linked to a fundamental argument about epistemological change. At the same time, Foucault is no more specific about the precise historical contexts in which this occurred (indeed, behind his exposition seems to lurk an extremely classical argument about capitalist development and the rise of the bourgeoisie), and his dating of the "modern" with the late eighteenth century creates a major ambi-

---

23. The reception of Foucault in the English-speaking world occurred originally along the margins of official academic life, in journals such as *Telos* and the *Partisan Review* in the United States and by a self-conscious avant-garde of post-New Left journals, such as *Economy and Society, Radical Philosophy, Ideology and Consciousness,* and *m/f* in Britain. It was only in the 1980s that his influence extended to historians more generally. In Germany the reception was pioneered in the same way—outside the mainstream of recognized scholarly discussion, in the so-called alternative scene. But by contrast Foucault's German influence has yet to extend very far into historical discussion. See the fascinating article by Uta Liebmann Schaub, "Foucault, Alternative Presses, and Alternative Ideology in West Germany: A Report," *German Studies Review* 12 (1989): 139–53. Wehler certainly sees no reason to dwell on the potential interest of Foucault's ideas: "We can ignore M. Foucault's monomania without further ado." See Wehler, *Aus der Geschichte lernen? Essays* (Munich, 1988), 314.

24. Two reflections on Foucault's significance in the early 1980s—Michael Ignatieff, "State, Civil Society and Total Institutions: A Critique of Recent Social Histories of Punishment," and David Ingleby, "Mental Health and Social Order," both in *Social Control and the State: Historical and Comparative Essays,* ed. Stanley Cohen and Andrew Scull (Oxford, 1983), 75–105, 141–88—afford a pivotal insight into this inspiration: *before* this time, Foucault's impact was surprisingly absent from the remarkable flourishing of social history in areas such as crime, law, and punishment in the 1970s (including Michael Ignatieff's own *A Just Measure of Pain: The Penitentiary in the Industrial Revolution* [London, 1978]; *after,* it becomes hard to imagine such work without it. For excellent commentaries, see Jeffrey Weeks, "Foucault for Historians," *History Workshop Journal* 14 (Autumn 1982): 106–19; and Patricia O'Brien, "Michel Foucault's History of Culture," in *The New Cultural History,* ed. Lynn Hunt (Berkeley, 1989), 25–46.

guity in the light of the actual rhythms and patterns of state-administrative innovation between then and the end of the nineteenth/start of the twentieth century. On the one hand, there clearly were fundamental transformations in the period between circa 1770 and circa 1850, as Foucault and many historians have claimed. But on the other hand, as I argued in the introduction above, in the later time the repertoire of power-producing knowledges also greatly expands, thereby producing the distinctive twentieth-century configuration of state-society relations. In the words of Scott Lash:

> The rationalization of management and the shopfloor, the bureaucratiza-
> tion of the capitalist state, the rationalization of extra-institution practices
> of social workers *vis-à-vis* the mad, criminal, indigent, "idle," and other-
> wise deviant were phenomena contemporaneous with the birth of the
> Welfare State at the end of the nineteenth century. The beginnings of
> nationalism—hence the priority of the social—as well as the centrality of
> demographic concerns, and the ethos of social citizenship, as well as the
> birth of the human sciences themselves, came by most accounts (and even
> at points by Foucault's) rather at the end than at the outset of the nine-
> teenth century.[25]

As Jacques Donzelot and others have argued, the family becomes a particular object of such interventions and expertise, while sexuality provides an especially rich field in the twentieth century for showing such power relations under construction.[26]

Where do these alternative notions of "the modern" leave us? Most obviously, there is a clear convergence between the second and third complexes of meaning outlined above—between Peukert's particular formulation of the argument concerning *cultural* modernity in the period between the turn of the century and the crisis of the Weimar Republic, and Foucault's ideas about the relationship of knowledge, discipline, and power. Moreover, if we take the direction of the last paragraph concerning appropriate periodization, such a definition gains in historical specificity what the first of the three notions—the surviving version of modernization theory—sacrifices to a more normative philosophical conception of modernity. Given the relative exhaustion of a more conventional

---

25. Scott Lash, *Sociology of Postmodernism* (London, 1990), 133.

26. Jacques Donzelot, *The Policing of Families* (New York, 1979); Jeffrey Weeks, *Sexuality and Its Discontents: Meanings, Myths and Modern Sexualities* (London, 1985); Frank Mort, *Dangerous Sexualities: Medico-Moral Politics in England since 1830* (London, 1987); Antony Copley, *Sexual Moralities in France, 1780–1980: New Ideas on the Family, Divorce, and Homosexuality: An Essay on Moral Change* (London, 1989); Denise Riley, *War in the Nursery: Theories of the Child and the Mother* (London, 1983); and Nikolas Rose, *Governing the Soul: The Shaping of the Private Self* (London, 1990).

modernization-theory perspective for generating new knowledge about modern German history—the most recent defense limits itself to measuring the Weimar polity against an ideal type of stable parliamentary representation, an approach that owes nothing to modernization *theory* per se[27]—there are good grounds for exploring what alternative possibilities there might be. In particular, as I have argued elsewhere, it is important to separate the instabilities of the Weimar Republic and their effects—the obstacles to stable governing consensus and a politics of successful parliamentary integration—from the political dynamics of the imperial period, not because the question of continuity should now be dropped but because it needs to be much better conceptualized in nonlinear and nonteleological ways. In what follows I shall offer some thoughts on the capacity of the political institutions of the *Kaiserreich* for stability and viable development. Implicitly, these will engage the underlying theoretical question alluded to above. Of what does "modern" political rule really consist? And in the process, a Foucauldian understanding of modernity's darker side—the importance of disciplinary power—will certainly be in play.

Backwardness and Modernity in the *Kaiserreich*

Since the 1960s, a set of powerful interpretations have dominated perceptions of the *Kaiserreich* among German historians in a general historiographical revisionism that was enormously important in its time but whose characteristic arguments have now begun to limit rather than extend our understanding. In my introduction to this volume, I tried to indicate some of the directions in which transcendence of older fields of interpretation and debate is beginning to occur, and in what follows I want to return to a more detailed explication of this historiographical terrain. In summary terms, revisionist historians of the 1960s developed a powerful deep-structural perspective on the origins of Nazism, stressing how backward political interests—traditional elites and their preindustrial, premodern mentalities—prevented any democratic modernizing of the political system and instead allowed what Ralf Dahrendorf called "authoritarian and anti-democratic structures in state and society" to endure.[28]

On the one hand, the *Kaiserreich* is categorized as "authoritarian" within the generally agreed typology of nineteenth-century regimes. On the other hand, the victory of authoritarianism in the formation of the Imperial German state is thought to have been an aberrant and abnormal interruption of the "process of democratization" that otherwise and in the long run inevitably "accompanies economic growth." In Germany a "truly realistic" appreciation of what a lasting and consistent modernization would require in this respect

27. Gerald D. Feldman, "The Weimar Republic: A Problem of Modernization?" *Archiv für Sozialgeschichte* 26 (1986): 1–26.

28. Ralf Dahrendorf, *Society and Democracy in Germany* (London, 1968), 15.

was precluded after the 1870s by a profound shift in ideological orientations, resulting from the liberals' changed access to government influence once Bismarck turned strongly to the right, from the discrediting of liberal economics and the general "deliberalizing of public and political life" in the post-1873 depression, from the growing aggression and conservatism of German nationalism as a new integrative ideology for the empire, and from the degeneration of the ideal of *Bildung* into a culture of careerism and advancement. This key ideological watershed amounted to a new structure of political values for the German bourgeoisie—"this fundamental change of constellation," in Wehler's words—that displaced liberalism from its previous integrative role, what Wehler calls the "triangular constellation of 'Bildung,' liberalism, and liberal nationalism" that dominated the 1860s. The new bourgeois consciousness (or perhaps false consciousness) responded to a powerful combination of factors: anxieties produced by the irregularities of economic growth and the fears of social unrest but also the manipulation of those fears by the political managers of the "old elite" (Bismarck, later Bernhard von Bülow and Alfred von Tirpitz).[29]

It is hard not to be impressed by the powerful teleology running through this account. "Modernization" in this discourse is avowedly abstracted from the present-day forms of pluralist democracy in the West. As such, it is thought to be built into the structures of economic growth; and to explain why German history diverges from this model until after 1945, German historians have logically been thrown back onto a vocabulary of "wrong turnings," "failures," "blockages," and "mistaken development." As Wehler has baldly put it, "any modern society attempting to be equal to the demands of constant social change" logically requires a constitutional framework of parliamentary democracy.[30] Conversely, the authoritarianism of the imperial state becomes the institutional expression of the "preindustrial traditions" and their modernization-obstructing dominance in the pre-1914 political culture. Thus a

---

29. The quoted phrases are taken from two essays by Hans-Ulrich Wehler, "Industrielles Wachstum und früher deutscher Imperialismus" and "Wie 'bürgerlich' war das Deutsche Kaiserreich?" in Wehler, *Aus der Geschichte lernen?* 269, 213, 215, and 212, respectively.

30. Hans-Ulrich Wehler, "Industrial Growth and Early German Imperialism," in *Studies in the Theory of Imperialism,* ed. Roger Owen and Bob Sutcliffe (London, 1972), 84. I have left this quotation in the original English, because in the recently published translated version cited in footnote 29 above, "Industrielles Wachstum und früher deutscher Imperialismus," Wehler revealingly substitutes "liberaldemokratische Industriegesellschaft" for "modern industrial society." The full statement reads: "Bismarck und die seine Politik unterstützenden Kräfte hatten es versäumt, Möglichkeiten für eine legitime parlamentarische Opposition zu institutionalisieren, wie sie die Verfassungsstruktur einer liberaldemokratischen Industriegesellschaft verlangt, die den Anforderungen des ständigen sozialen Wandels gerecht zu werden versucht." A clearer illustration of the identity in Wehler's mind between "modernity" and "liberal democracy" could hardly be wishe for. See Wehler, *Aus der Geschichte lernen?* 266.

radical disjunction is postulated between "wealth" and "power," between the "modern" basis of the industrial-capitalist economy and the "traditional" political arrangements, which the bourgeoisie in Germany proved incapable of sweeping away. In the long run, stability could only be assured by the development of more "modern" institutional arrangements for containing social conflicts—that is, by "welfare-statist" and parliamentary-democratic replacements for "the rule of an authoritarian leadership and of privileged social groups centering around the pre-industrial elites of the aristocracy."[31] Otherwise, the inescapable dictates of power legitimation in the developed industrial economy could be satisfied only by artificial forms of "secondary integration" that, Wehler has argued, may be conceptualized as "social imperialism," or the diversion of tensions outward into expansionist drives for imperialist accumulation. Thus between the modern economy and the backward state there arose destabilizing contradictions that could only be artificially bridged by manipulative techniques of rule, so long as the "real" solution of "modernizing" democratic reform was not embraced. In this view, the unreformed imperial state was incapable of reproducing itself other than by an escalating procession of crises, culminating eventually in the miscalculated risk of July 1914.[32]

This approach constructs an extraordinarily powerful structural frame for interpreting the history of the *Kaiserreich* that severely restricts the latitude for analyzing particular problems or events within this fifty-year block of time. Moreover, this "permanent structural crisis" itself provides the framing for a larger story, the specifically German "master narrative" of the origins of Nazism, which are thought to be deeply inscribed in the flaws of the *Kaiserreich:*

> Without a transformation of the social structure and the traditional power relationships, without social emancipation, modernization seems not to be possible, if the domestic and foreign peace is to be maintained. The fatal consequences of the government politics through which the political predominance of the preindustrial elites was to be maintained in the period of high industrialization were revealed quite clearly between 1914 and 1929, when these structures crumbled. By that time, these politics had helped create the dangerous conditions that smoothed the way for National Socialism.[33]

---

31. Wehler, "Industrial Growth," 78 ("Industrielles Wachstum," 261).

32. Wehler links this argument explicitly to Habermas's theory of legitimation. See especially Hans-Ulrich Wehler, *Bismarck und der Imperialismus* (Cologne, 1969), 500; Jürgen Habermas, *Technik und Wissenschaft als "Ideologie"* (Frankfurt a.M. ., 1968), esp. 74–80, 83–84, 92, 99; and Jürgen Habermas, *Legitimationsprobleme im Spätkapitalismus* (Frankfurt a.M., 1973).

33. Wehler, "Industrielles Wachstum," 269.

As many readers know, this is the master narrative of German exceptionalism, of the German *Sonderweg,* which performed such an important function in the intellectual politics of the 1960s and early 1970s, and authorized many of the key historiographical breakthroughs of that time. As readers will also remember, this *Sonderweg* thesis also became the object of wide-ranging critical debate in the early 1980s, a discussion that I played some modest part in helping to begin. Now that those polemics have somewhat settled down, it is worth asking what may have changed, with a particular eye to the issues of backwardness and modernity that this essay is seeking to raise.[34]

Rejudging the Bourgeoisie

As my general introduction to this volume pointed out, the German bourgeoisie became the object of massive attention in the 1980s, through which a considerably more positive evaluation of its nineteenth-century achievements began to emerge. In particular, the so-called *Defizit an Bürgerlichkeit,* or lack of bourgeois virtues—with "bourgeois virtues" implying an elusive and ambiguous blend of sociocultural self-assertion and civil courage—has been subject to revision,[35] and there seems to be a much greater willingness to acknowledge the degree to which bourgeois values permeated German society after the 1860s and set the tone of public life. Thus Wehler distinguishes two areas of bourgeois success or collective self-realization under the *Kaiserreich,* in the sense of values that originated sociologically in a specifically bourgeois milieu in the eighteenth and early nineteenth centuries but expanded in the course of the nineteenth century to become universal social and cultural goods. On the one hand, "definite bourgeois organizational forms"—a particular model of the family and the *Verein,* or voluntary association, as the all-purpose medium of sociability, cultural exchange, and public political activity—showed themselves "as extremely generalizable" and acquired normative validity. On the

---

34. This debate was initiated by David Blackbourn and Geoff Eley, *The Peculiarities of German History: Bourgeois Society and Politics in Nineteenth-Century Germany* (Oxford, 1984), and its earlier, German edition, *Mythen deutscher Geschichtsschreibung: Die gescheiterte bürgerliche Revolution von 1848* (Frankfurt a.M., 1980). For an excellent introduction to the wider literature, see David Blackbourn, "The German Bourgeoisie: An Introduction," in *The German Bourgeoisie: Essays on the Early Twentieth Century,* ed. David Blackbourn and Richard J. Evans (London, 1991), 1–45. Compare also Jürgen Kocka's introductory survey, "Bürgertum und bürgerliche Gesellschaft im 19. Jahrhundert: Europäische Entwicklungen und deutsche Eigenarten," in *Bürgertum im 19. Jahrhundert: Deutschland im europäischen Vergleich,* ed. Jürgen Kocka, vol. 1 (Munich, 1988), 11–76, which pretends that Blackbourn and Eley did not exist.

35. This double meaning of *bürgerlich*—as a "society of citizens" and a society "dominated by a confident bourgeoisie" (Dahrendorf, *Society and Democracy,* 397)—is more central to the German etymology of the term than it is to the anglicized use of "bourgeois." It is a particular problem in the German term *bürgerliche Gesellschaft.* Kocka, "Bürgertum und bürgerliche Gesellschaft," is very good on the definitional complexities of nineteenth-century usage.

other hand, "bourgeois norms and values" became culturally dominant—most decisively in the "system of law" but also in "the revolutionary principle of efficiency, orientation toward work, secularization, rationalization of thought and action, autonomy of the individual, individualism per se, and also the association of individuals for the purpose of clarifying their problems in public discussion."[36] We can further extend this reevaluation to the public culture and institutional arrangements of the new German Empire—to the legal and institutional infrastructure of the *Kaiserreich* and to the growth and elaboration of public opinion via the forms of an institutionally complex and legally guaranteed public sphere—while in the dynamically expanding late-nineteenth-century economy, bourgeois values and achievements found their core domain.[37]

Of course, it is in the *political* domain in the stricter sense that the weakness of the German bourgeoisie was always thought to be most clearly revealed: in the economy and civil society, even in the public sphere broadly understood, bourgeois achievements can be shown; but in the state and the political system (so the argument runs), the power of the traditional elites remained as strong as before. Wehler has gone some way toward acknowledging the "bourgeois" character of the imperial polity: "Despite its compromise character, the constitutionalism of the imperial state also incorporated the triumph of bourgeois liberals"; and, despite the moderation and noncombativity of parliamentarian culture before 1914, "there was nonetheless a strong, perhaps irresistible pressure for the continuous revalorizing of the Reichstag." Furthermore, other "experiences in the political domain," such as the progressive expansion of the rule of law, municipal self-government, and public opinion, "must have genuinely nourished the feeling that the *Kaiserreich* was still capable of modernization and, with patience, could still be further reformed in accordance with bourgeois goals."[38] These are major concessions to the critique.

But at the same time, what these revisions leave intact is the central argument regarding the backwardness of the *Kaiserreich's* core political struc-

---

36. Wehler, "Wie 'bürgerlich' war das Deutsche Kaiserreich?" 204–5.

37. In addition to Kocka, *Bürgertum im 19. Jahrhundert;* and Blackbourn and Evans, *The German Bourgeoisie,* see Jürgen Kocka, ed., *Bürger und Bürgerlichkeit im 19. Jahrhundert* (Göttingen, 1987); Jürgen Kocka, ed., *Arbeiter und Bürger im 19. Jahrhundert* (Munich, 1986); Ute Frevert, ed., *Bürgerinnen und Bürger: Geschlechterverhältnisse im 19. Jahrhundert* (Göttingen, 1988); Hannes Siegrist, ed., *Bürgerliche Berufe: Zur Sozialgeschichte der freien und akademischen Berufe im internationalen Vergleich* (Göttingen, 1988); Geoffrey Cocks and Konrad H. Jarausch, eds., *German Professions, 1800–1950* (New York, 1988); Werner Conze and Jürgen Kocka, eds., *Bildungsbürgertum im 19. Jahrhundert,* part 1, *Bildungssystem und Professionalisierung im internationalen Vergleich* (Stuttgart, 1985); and Jürgen Kocka, ed., *Das Bildungsbürgertum in Gesellschaft und Politik* (Stuttgart, 1989).

38. Wehler, "Wie 'bürgerlich' war das Deutsche Kaiserreich?" 206, 208.

tures (to do with the monarchy, the military, aristocratic privilege, Prussian predominance, more ambivalently the bureaucracy—in general the institutionally secured primacy of preindustrial interests and elites), which have always been counterposed to the ideal of modernity, which *was not* attained. After the recession of "vigorous bourgeois politics" since the 1870s, the bourgeoisie accommodated itself to a subordinate political position (the argument runs), or at most to copartnership with the traditional elites, above all due to the rising pressure of the labor movement from below. Even the most acute "bourgeois observers" made this accommodation, that is, "accepted the constitutional monarchy—and not even the parliamentary system in all cases—together with the public role of the aristocracy, the 'military state,' and in most cases the rule of the bureaucracy." Of the necessary presence of a combative bourgeoisie—recognizable in "bourgeois self-assurance, confidence in victory, deliverance from self-doubt, political know-how, resistance to the new dangers from the Right"—there was not much evidence, whether in the final decades before 1914 or in the new environment of the Weimar Republic. To this extent, the master narrative of the *Sonderweg,* the deep-structuralism of the account of the origins of Nazism, is still intact. The advance of the bourgeoisie stopped at the gates of the political system. This was what distinguished German history in the nineteenth century from the successful modernizations of the West. And the long-term consequences were immense. Nazism was

> the bill for bourgeois conservatism and nationalism, for bourgeois timidity before the risky trial of strength, for the deficit of liberal-bourgeois political culture, of successful bourgeois politics, of the bourgeois stamp on state and society in general.[39]

There is, however, a noteworthy shift in the terms of definition between the beginning and the end of Wehler's discussion: while at the start of his essay his concern is quite properly to distinguish the constituent elements in the *social* category of *Bürgertum* qua bourgeoisie—that is, the traditional burgher estate of the towns, the *Bildungsbürgertum,* or educated middle class, and the economic "bourgeoisie" of businessmen, industrialists, and entrepreneurs, in their various regional manifestations, whose tendential unification during the later nineteenth century allows us to use the category in the first place—by the end he is talking more about the weakness of a particular *political* tradition, namely, liberalism. This change of registers occurs in the course of the opening definitional discussion itself as Wehler moves from the three social constituents mentioned above, through the question of the bourgeoisie's demarcation against the petite bourgeoisie (including "old" and "new" *Mittelstand*), to a reflection on the idea of citizenship and a more open-ended discussion of the

---

39. Ibid., 216–17.

term "bürgerliche Gesellschaft," which incorporates precisely the confusing German dualism affirmed by Dahrendorf in *Society and Democracy in Germany*, namely, a "society of citizens" and a society "dominated by a confident bourgeoisie."[40] Moreover, when Wehler sets out to explain the transition from bourgeois self-confidence to bourgeois abnegation—what he calls "the origin of the fatal pathogenesis of the bourgeoisie"[41]—it is not the economic, social, and cultural strength of the bourgeoisie as a social force, which unfolded much as before, but the difficulties and transformations of *political liberalism* that he addresses. In fact, Wehler himself concedes this, commenting that the new political "constellation" that emerged from the 1870s was perfectly capable "of overarching the heterogeneous social situations of the bourgeois social formations," particularly through the emergent forms of nationalism, and acknowledging in effect that the political ideas capable of harnessing allegiances within the bourgeoisie were changing, rather than the bases of bourgeois power and interest themselves.[42]

I have commented on the consequences of this conceptual slippage from the bourgeoisie as a social category to liberalism as a political tradition extensively elsewhere.[43] For one thing, the understanding of liberalism tends to be abstracted inappropriately from the strong forms of liberal democracy (including the latter's welfare-statism) in the late twentieth century, whose possibility is then projected quite unhistorically onto the collective agency of the bourgeoisie of a hundred years before.[44] In the process, the more appropriate context for judging German liberalism, namely, the "modernity" of the time— the European conjuncture of constitutional revision, nation forming, and state making in the 1860s, together with the culture of progress and the general remaking of the social environment for capitalism—gets confused. The demonstrable affinities between a liberal political outlook and a specific configuration of bourgeois interests and aspirations at this particular time is also allowed to license stronger assumptions about the conceptual unity of bourgeois and liberal identities in general, whereas really these are separate phenomena. The common equation of "liberalism" and "democracy" compounds

---

40. Wehler's definitional discussion in this respect is in ibid., 192–202.

41. Ibid., 214.

42. Ibid.

43. See especially Geoff Eley, "The British Model and the German Road: Rethinking the Course of German History before 1914," in Blackbourn and Eley, *Peculiarities*, 75–90; Geoff Eley, "Liberalism, Europe, and the Bourgeoisie, 1860–1914," in Blackbourn and Evans, *The German Bourgeoisie*, 293–317.

44. The problems here are manifold. On the one hand, it is conceptually and empirically extremely doubtful whether the bourgeoisie may be treated as a collective class agent in this fashion, possessing a corporate political consciousness of a unified kind. On the other hand, specifically democratic demands in the nineteenth century came largely from popular movements that the bourgeoisie sought to suppress.

the conceptual mixing of "liberal" and "bourgeois" still further, making the connotative continuum of "bourgeoisie = liberalism = democracy" into an implied causal chain. But specifically democratic impulses originated elsewhere, namely, in the labor movement and other popular traditions. Indeed, the articulation of bourgeois aspirations in the late nineteenth century, including their liberal forms, usually took an exclusionary *anti*democratic turn (as Wehler also sees), and were no less bourgeois for that.

In other words, we should perhaps be willing to consider the possibility that bourgeois interests and aspirations were becoming dominant in the *political* as well as in the socioeconomic and cultural realms, because at present the main argument against this is the failure of the imperial state to acquire a liberal or even a liberal-democratic form. If we can free ourselves from the assumption that the achievement of bourgeois hegemony (in the sense of the political dominance of bourgeois values) can only be conceptualized via the organization of the bourgeoisie's collective political agency within a specifically *liberal* movement or party, then the way would be clear to consider other, nonliberal forms of political articulation; and the social coding of "authoritarianism" in the pre-1914 state as "aristocratic," "preindustrial," and "traditional" rather than "bourgeois" and "modern" would start to look more questionable.[45] In other words, "bourgeois" interests and values could be at work, and "modern" political forms be in play, even if "liberal" ones were not. Why is Wehler unable to see (or unwilling to admit) this possibility?

The answer lies with the avowedly political and prescriptive aspects of Wehler's work. For quite beyond the specificity of the *Kaiserreich* discussion, Wehler wishes to retain the notion of *bürgerliche Gesellschaft* (the untranslatable cross between "bourgeois society" and "civil society") as an enduring good—as "the end utopia of a society of legally equal, educated and propertied, freely competing, possessively individualist, politically capable citizens, oriented toward the eliciting and implementing of the 'rational' common good."[46] "Much of this utopia of an authentic bourgeois society has been realized in the Western societies of the past two hundred years, step by step, with varying tempo and varying intensity and reach, first in the United States, then after the French Revolution in Europe"; and to the extent that it remains unrealized, it may be regarded "as an uncompleted project of Western societies." It is precisely when measured against this ideal, in Wehler's view, that

---

45. The tendency to speak of the bourgeoisie as a collective acting subject (whether its political orientation be liberal or not) is a large part of the problem. As Blackbourn says, "If we present the bourgeoisie as a class that fights its opponents with boxing gloves, then it's easy enough to show that it failed to win an undisputed victory." See Blackbourn's commentary on the original version of Wehler's "Wie 'bürgerlich' war das Deutsche Kaiserreich?" in Kocka, *Bürger und Bürgerlichkeit,* 283.

46. Wehler, "Wie 'bürgerlich' war das Deutsche Kaiserreich?" 199.

German history proves to be a site of omissions and failures, of "ruinous manifestations and pathological developments," of "devastating defeats," and ultimately of the "betrayal of bourgeois society."[47] The normative relationship to a highly presentist version of modernization theory could hardly be more clearly stated.

In fact, Wehler constructs a highly idealized version of *bürgerliche Gesellschaft*. He is unable to move from elucidating the abstract principles of emancipation within the Enlightenment tradition to specifying the equally important privilegings and exclusions which that tradition always entailed. The crucial elision in Wehler's argument comes with the transition from the universalizing claims of bourgeois values as abstract desiderata (whether to do with voluntary association and the family or with the franchise and the rule of law) to the practical exclusiveness of bourgeois ideals in their actual realization—in the transition, that is, from *bürgerlich* qua citizenship and the universals of progress to *bürgerlich* qua the bourgeoisie as a specific class sociology. Where the one was theoretically open to all, the other was constituted by principles and practices of exclusion. Moreover, this discrepancy between the ideal and its forms of realization was bound to become more acute after the 1860s, because the suppressions and silencings required by the pursuit of bourgeois values mattered far more once those ideals had become institutionalized as a set of cultural and societal norms. At one level Wehler also sees the exclusions. He mentions the peasantry, petite bourgeoisie, and working class in this respect, though interestingly he passes by the exclusions of nationality and gender. Yet he largely dismisses their importance. On the one hand, such excluded social groups had no viable counterutopias to offer, in his view; on the other hand, their futures were also bound up in the specifically bourgeois achievements, and they wanted nothing better than to join the ranks of the bourgeoisie themselves. For Wehler, "embourgeoisement" (*Verbürgerlichung*) was, and remains, an unqualified social good.

In some respects Wehler can be veritably starry-eyed. Thus he celebrates the bourgeois capacity for self-criticism ("Thanks to the respect for critical reason, the possibility of self-correction is firmly anchored"), which he finds inscribed in the structures of the *Bildung* tradition itself, and which could function as a constant resource for ethical consistency and reformist self-correction.[48] Here Wehler's argument, with its stress on the back-and-forth of public exchange and the "critical reasoning" of an "enlightened public opinion," derives faithfully from Habermas's theory of the public sphere. Yet, as I have argued elsewhere, the latter is an extremely idealized abstraction from the

---

47. Wehler, "Geschichte und Zielutopie der deutschen 'bürgerlichen Gesellschaft,'" in *Aus der Geschichte lernen?* 251, 255, 252.

48. Ibid., 201.

political cultures that actually took shape at the end of the eighteenth century. Habermas both idealizes the public sphere's bourgeois character by neglecting the ways in which its elitism blocked and consciously repressed possibilities of broader participation and emancipation, and ignores alternative sources of an emancipatory impulse in popular radical traditions. The rise of a bourgeois public sphere was never defined solely by the struggle against absolutism and traditional authority but always addressed the problem of popular containment as well. The classical model of the public sphere was always already being subverted at the very point of its formation as the actions of subordinate classes threatened to redefine the meaning and extent of the "citizenry," whether in France during the revolution, in Britain between the Wilkite agitations and the Jacobinism of the 1790s, or in Germany between the 1840s and 1870s. Moreover, feminist critiques have shown how modern political thought is highly gendered in its basic structures, and how the public sphere was shaped at its inception by a new exclusionary ideology directed against women, a dimension on which Wehler remains largely silent.[49]

In all of these ways, "civil society" (*bürgerliche Gesellschaft*) was very far from the neutral site of rational political communication and exchange in Habermas's and Wehler's sense. Instead, it was an arena of contested meanings, where different—and opposing—publics maneuvered for space, and from which some "publics" (women, subordinate nationalities, the urban poor, the working class, the peasantry) may have been excluded altogether. Moreover, this element of contest was not simply a matter of coexistence, in which such alternative publics participated in a tolerant pluralism of tendencies and groupings. Such competition also occurred in class-divided societies structured by inequality, and consequently questions of domination and subordination— of power, in its economic, social, cultural, and political dimensions—were also involved. This ambivalence, which cannot be easily dealt with in Wehler's idealizing of *bürgerliche Gesellschaft* as a utopian project, returns us to the critique of the Enlightenment tradition discussed at the start of this essay. The Enlightenment project was partial and narrowly based in the above sense, constituted from a field of conflict, contested meanings, and exclusion. In particular, the claim to *rational* discourse, certainly in the social and gendered

49. See especially Carol Pateman, *The Sexual Contract* (Cambridge, 1988); Jean Bethke Elshtain, *Public Man, Private Woman: Women in Social and Political Thought* (Princeton, 1981); Ellen Kennedy and Susan Mendus, eds., *Women in Western Political Philosophy: Kant to Nietzsche* (New York, 1987); Joan B. Landes, *Women and the Public Sphere in the Age of the French Revolution* (Ithaca, 1988); Dorinda Outram, *The Body and the French Revolution: Sex, Class and Political Culture* (New Haven, 1989); Catherine Hall, "Private Persons versus Public Someones: Class, Gender and Politics in England, 1780–1850," in *Language, Gender and Childhood*, ed. Carolyn Steedman, Cathy Urwin, and Valerie Walkerdine (London, 1985), 10–33. I have discussed the difficulties with Habermas's public-sphere concept in general in Eley, "Nations, Publics, and Political Cultures."

exclusiveness of its historical manifestations between the late eighteenth century and World War I, was simultaneously a claim to *power* in Foucault's sense.

Defining the Imperial State

When we turn to the state as such, we find some ambiguity in the prevailing literature. In particular, if the imperial state was not a "liberal" state on the "Western" model, then what kind of state was it? As we have seen, Wehler goes quite far in the modernizing political changes between 1871 and 1914 that he is prepared to allow, but he still stops his catalogue of bourgeois achievements at what he takes to be the core institutions of the political system—the monarchy, the military, and the apparatus of aristocratic privilege in Prussia. As I will argue briefly in my conclusion, it is far from clear whether these actually are to be deemed the *Kaiserreich*'s core political institutions, or whether by 1900 the main site of state activity begins to lie elsewhere, particularly if we take a Foucauldian understanding of power into account. For the moment, however, I want to explore some of the inconsistencies in Wehler's and others' approach to the definition of the state by questioning the conventional identifications of authoritarian = aristocratic and liberal = bourgeois. I want to argue that a state with authoritarian features should not be assumed automatically to express the political dominance of a landowning aristocracy and other preindustrial elites. On the contrary, it might also articulate the interests of the bourgeoisie and might even provide a framework for the latter's social and political hegemony.

In recent writing the imperial state seems to have been given at least four distinct definitions, which cohabit in the work of the two most influential commentators, Wehler and Kocka. The first definition attributes a dominant role to the Junkers as a "preindustrial" ruling group whose unbroken influence explains the political system's specific "backwardness," as that is usually understood. The twin characteristics of backwardness and aristocratic dominance are thought to have had a number of institutional expressions: the executive power of the king-kaiser; the autonomy of the military; the preferential recruitment of the bureaucracy and the officer corps from the aristocracy; the limited powers of the Reichstag; the transmuted seigneurialism of local government east of the Elbe; the effective immunities of the landowners from certain kinds of taxation in the same region; and, of course, the special qualities of the Prussian, as opposed to the Reich, Constitution. At one level such factors might amply justify an "aristocratic" description of the state. But in most discussions the nature of the state/society relationship (that is, the relationship of the aristocracy as a social class to the state as an ensemble of political institutions) is left undertheorized. Sometimes that relationship is conceptualized as direct political control that subordinated state apparatuses and their direction to Junker interests; at other times the apparatuses appear to be given equivalent autonomy in a manner reminiscent of C. Wright Mills's theory of the "power elite," so that "Junkers, bureaucracy, military" appear collectively as "precapitalist ruling strata."[50] In effect, such writing oscillates between two different conceptions of the state, both equally problematic: an instrumentalist one that sees the state as a passive tool available for manipulation by ruling interests and a "subjectivist" one where the state figures as the primary agency, arbitrating the conflicts of classes and social interests and apparently autonomous of their control. There is much theoretical uncertainty here; and talk of "preindustrial traditions," an "autocratic, semiabsolutist shamconstitutionalism," and the "feudalization of the bourgeoisie" has even suggested notions of a state that was primarily feudal.[51]

A more sophisticated variation along these lines is the concept of Bonapartism, adapted by Wehler from Marx and Engels, whereby the state's autonomy is constituted from the political equilibrium of dominant socioeconomic interests (the alliance of "iron and rye"), originally under the directive genius of Bismarck but then achieving an unstable existence of its own.[52] In the *Critique of the Gotha Program,* Marx called the resultant state "nothing but a military despotism, embellished with parliamentary forms, alloyed with a feudal admixture, already influenced by the bourgeoisie, furnished by the bureaucracy, and protected by the police," and this ultimately unsatisfactory "agglutination of epithets" (as Perry Anderson calls it) seems consonant with Wehler's similarly eclectic version. Anderson's own formula places the accent rather differently, arguing that "the German state was now a capitalist apparatus, over-determined by its feudal ancestry, but fundamentally homologous with a social formation" which by the twentieth century was massively dominated by the capitalist mode of production."[53] In Wehler's case the main effect of this Bonapartist definition is certainly to acknowledge the new salience of industrial capital within the German social formation after unification. But this

---

50. C. Wright Mills, *The Power Elite* (Oxford, 1956).

51. Hans-Ulrich Wehler, *Das Deutsche Kaiserreich, 1871–1918* (Göttingen, 1973), 60–63. On the evidence of "Wie 'bürgerlich' war das Deutsche Kaiserreich?" Wehler has now backed away from the "feudalization" thesis, though without yet putting a coherent alternative in its place.

52. See Wehler, *Bismarck,* 455ff.; Michael Stürmer, "Konservatismus und Revolution in Bismarcks Politik," in *Das kaiserliche Deutschland: Politik und Gesellschaft, 1870–1918,* ed. Michael Stürmer (Düsseldorf, 1970), 143ff. In my view, Wehler's arguments withstand the critiques in Lothar Gall, "Bismarck und Bonapartismus," *Historische Zeitschrift* 223 (1976): 618–37; and Alan Mitchell, "Bonapartism as a Model for Bismarckian Politics," *Journal of Modern History* 49 (1977): 181–209 (with comments by Otto Pflanze, C. Fohlen, and Michael Stürmer). The concept also resembles Antonio Gramsci's concept of "Caesarism," but Gramsci's exposition is ultimately too attenuated and schematic, and his description of Bismarck as an example of a "reactionary Caesarism" does not correspond to the concept advocated here; see Quintin Hoare and Geoffrey Nowell Smith, eds., *Selections from the Prison Notebooks of Antonio Gramsci* (London, 1971), 219.

53. Anderson, *Lineages,* 277–78. The Marx citation is also taken from Anderson.

is expressed in such a way as to leave the first, "aristocratic" or "Junkerist" definition intact. Industrial capital may have arrived, but its interests are accommodated within a "traditional" power structure of a basically unreformed kind.

At some variance with these first two approaches is a third definition of the state, stressing the changing forms of economic intervention. Here Wehler proposes a notion of the modern interventionist state that rests on a particular appropriation of Habermas's concept of legitimation. In terms of the latter, "political power is legitimated above all via well-considered state intervention, which seeks to negotiate dysfunctions of the economy, particularly disruptions of economic growth, in order to secure the stability of the sociopolitical system." The new interventionist ideology (which replaces the "discredited ideology of the liberal-capitalist market economy") is meant both to reestablish conditions favorable for economic growth and to secure the acquiescence of the wage-earning masses by suitable "compensations." Government increasingly has no choice but to pursue these aims as the organizing priority of its activity, for otherwise "the ruling elites" would be unable "to preserve the system and their own interests."[54] Wehler dates the start of these processes in the so-called Great Depression of 1873–96, but others associate them with the stronger appearance of "organized capitalism" after that time.[55]

The fourth definition of the imperial state is advanced especially by Kocka in his analysis of World War I and concerns its "relative autonomy" from direct control by the dominant socioeconomic interests. In this view, the capitalist state's autonomy arises logically from the dictates of legitimation, because government now needs a certain latitude both for the purposes of general economic management and for satisfying certain demands of the subordinate classes. Kocka sees such tendencies toward relative autonomy being strengthened during World War I by the well-known processes of corporative interest negotiation.[56]

Taken together, these four perspectives reflect an oddly bifurcated approach to the pre-1914 German state. They maintain a powerful discrepancy between the state as a system of political domination (its constitutional "backwardness," the Junkers' controlling power and institutional privileges, and the

---

54. Wehler, "Industrielles Wachstum," 260–61; and Wehler, *Bismarck,* 500. The quotations are from Wehler's paraphrase of Habermas. See footnote 32 above.

55. See Jürgen Kocka, "Organisierter Kapitalismus oder Staatsmonopolistischer Kapitalismus? Begriffliche Vorbemerkungen," in *Organisierter Kapitalismus: Voraussetzungen und Anfänge,* ed. Heinrich August Winkler (Göttingen, 1973), 19–35. See also my critical discussion in Geoff Eley, "Capitalism and the Wilhelmine State: Industrial Growth and Political Backwardness, 1890–1918," in *From Unification to Nazism: Reinterpreting the German Past,* by Geoff Eley (London, 1986), 42–58.

56. Jürgen Kocka, *Klassengesellschaft im Krieg: Deutsche Sozialgeschichte, 1914–1918* (Göttingen, 1973).

general primacy of "preindustrial traditions") and its role in the economy (namely, its "modern," interventionist character). For example, Wehler's work contains both a strong view of the needs of capital deriving from the logic of industrial growth (as expressed through the concepts of interventionism, organized capitalism, and legitimation), and yet an equally powerful insistence on the ultimate efficacy of specific political traditions: "It was not the industrial economy as such that by itself established the conditions of societal development, because the latter had to unfold in an institutional framework produced and codetermined by political culture, the system of political domination, and the political interests of pre- and nonindustrial social forces."[57] As should be clear from quotations such as this, the political factors are also conceived mainly as linear continuities from an earlier era—that is, inherited structures rather than ones directly generated, produced, or determined by the Bismarckian or Wilhelmine conjunctures themselves. Moreover, it is more than anything else in the contradiction between these two levels of the "social system"—a noncorrespondence between the political and the economic—that the imperial state's structural instability and ultimate collapse are thought to be inscribed, on the grounds that the inherited syndrome of "traditional" authoritarianism consistently worked against the needs of "modern" legitimation.

This dualism has been a defining feature of recent German historiography. It implies that a genuinely "modern" state would be one in which the progressive social predominance of the bourgeoisie was formally consummated in a constitutional liberalization of the state. That would have brought the imperial state into proper alignment with the modern economy, whereas the disjunction that actually persisted (of "modern" economy/"backward" state) proved to be irrational, dysfunctional, and crisis-producing, historians such as Wehler would argue. But why must the authoritarian features of the imperial state be equated automatically with archaism, backwardness, or political inefficiency? Neither the exclusivist, executive, nor aristocratic features of the German polity before 1914—that is, the checks on popular participation, the relative weakness of parliamentary controls, and the privileges of the titular nobility— were at all unusual by the European standards of the time. Indeed, the *Kaiserreich* was more frequently regarded as an exemplary "modern" state—in the technocratic efficiency of its bureaucratic and military machines, in its more interventionist relationship to the economy and society, in the vaunted excellence of its municipal governments, in its system of social administration, and (from a different point of view) in the existence of universal male suffrage and the extent of popular political mobilization. Paradoxically, as we saw, Wehler has gone far in his recent writings to acknowledging the force of precisely

---

57. Hans-Ulrich Wehler, "Der Aufstieg des organisierten Kapitalismus und Interventionsstaates in Deutschland," in Winkler, *Organisierter Kapitalismus,* 49.

these points, conceding the bourgeois transformation and permeation of the political culture in the broadest sense and retaining the "traditionalist" argument mainly for the visible core of the state-institutional complex (consisting of monarchy/army/Prussia).

If that is so, one might argue, then why not go further and question the meaning currently given to the core institutions themselves? Perhaps the answer is to rethink the basis on which "the state" per se is currently being conceptualized in the German discussion—not just by changing the valence of authoritarianism and accepting its compatibility with bourgeois values (its potential "modernity") in the specific circumstances of the *Kaiserreich* but also by specifying what was most important in what the state actually did between the 1870s and 1914, by reflecting on the changing boundaries between state and civil society, and by exploring the larger field of state/society relations. If we undertake this rethinking, in my view, three recognitions become crucial.

First, after two decades of searching state-theoretical discussion, we need to begin from the state's *autonomy* ("relative" or otherwise), as opposed to its dependence on class or other socioeconomic interests in a directly instrumental or expressive way. State policies cannot be reduced to a reflection of dominant social forces or an effect of ruling interests in an epiphenomenal way. We can be very precise about the sociology of the recruitment and behavior of the state managers (the personnel directly in charge of the state), but this is not the same as defining the social character of the state in the sense of its relationship to society. The autonomy of the state has two dimensions: in its character as a particular institutional complex, it becomes a source of independent bureaucratic, military, and judicial initiative; but at the same time it remains a permeable arena in which contending social and political forces interact. As Göran Therborn puts it, the state is both a relatively unified and independently organized system of apparatuses (whose staff can therefore have independent motivations and effects) and "an institution where social power is concentrated and exercised" (and that therefore becomes subject to external intervention).[58]

Second, in a complex social formation, state power cannot be structured in a straightforwardly pyramidal way or around a protected core of "traditional" institutions that somehow retained their immunity to change and their primacy over the state complex as a whole, least of all in the dynamically expanding capitalist society that Imperial Germany was in the process of becoming. State power was constituted not just in the actions and intentions of a set of visible rulers or in the collectively willed domination of a ruling class

58. Göran Therborn, *What Does the Ruling Class Do When It Rules? State Apparatuses and State Power under Feudalism, Capitalism, and Socialism* (London, 1978), 153, 132. See also Bob Jessop, *The Capitalist State* (London, 1982); John Urry, *The Anatomy of Capitalist Societies: The Economy, Civil Society and the State* (London, 1981); and Ann Showstack Sassoon, ed., *Approaches to Gramsci* (London, 1982).

or an aggregate of ruling elites but also in a much broader field of socioeconomic and politicocultural intervention encompassing a complex repertoire of tasks: economic management and social administration in the stricter technical sense; organizing the cooperation of the dominant classes at the national political level and mediating the economic interests of their various fractions into a workable general policy; regulating the relations of dominant and subordinate classes; maintaining the basis of cohesion in society as a whole through a broadly constructed popular consent; and integrating the relations between state institutions in the narrower sense and a richly textured civil society.

And consequently, even in a fully "bourgeois" society (taking Dahrendorf's double sense of a "society of citizens" and a society "dominated by a confident bourgeoisie," or perhaps the more minimalist definition of a society in which the bourgeoisie as the owners and controllers of means of production are the dominant class), we would not expect to find the bourgeoisie directly controlling the state in any straightforward and instrumentalist sense. Its status as a dominant class derives less from any capacity for backstage string-pulling (though this obviously takes place) than from a capacity to ensure that the sum of state interventions (or "the societal content of the actions of the state," in Therborn's words) works predominantly in its favor. If we define the state with Therborn as an institutional complex "which concentrates the supreme rule-making, rule-applying, rule-adjudicating, rule-enforcing, and rule-defending functions" in a society, then the power of a dominant class resides in the capacity "to bring about a particular mode of intervention" of that "special body" in order to secure the conditions in which "the economic, political, and ideological conditions of its domination" in society may be reproduced.[59] In that case, the bourgeoisie "rules" less by the direct wielding or disposal of state power than by restructuring and maintaining the social, institutional, and ideological arena in which politics and governance have to occur—that is, by exercising "hegemony" in the Gramscian and frequently misunderstood sense.[60]

In light of the above, I would argue that the authoritarian parameters of the Imperial Constitution allowed much latitude for maneuver, negotiation, and compromise before the inner limits of the Bismarckian settlement from

---

59. Therborn, *What Does the Ruling Class Do When It Rules?* 145–61.

60. See especially Stuart Hall, Bob Lumley, and Gregor McLennan, "Politics and Ideology: Gramsci," in *On Ideology,* ed. Centre for Contemporary Cultural Studies (London, 1978), 45–76; Ann Showstack Sassoon, "Hegemony, War of Position and Political Intervention," and Christine Buci-Glucksmann, "Hegemony and Consent," both in Sassoon, *Approaches to Gramsci,* 94–115, 116–26; Raymond Williams, *Marxism and Literature* (Oxford, 1977), 108–14; Geoff Eley and Keith Nield, "Why Does Social History Ignore Politics?" *Social History* 5 (1980): 249–72; Geoff Eley, "Reading Gramsci in English: Observations on the Reception of Antonio Gramsci in the English-Speaking World, 1957–1982," *European History Quarterly* 14 (1984): 441–77.

Wehler's point of view (the prerogatives of the monarchy, the survival of the landowning aristocracy, and so on) began to be breached. Within the same limits, the imperial state showed itself adaptable to the tasks that a "modern" state is called upon to perform—securing the conditions of capitalist reproduction, doing the work of legitimation (in the Wehlerian/Habermasian sense), organizing the unity of the dominant classes, and mobilizing the consent of the people. Indeed, I would suggest that the strictly reactionary elements were more isolated in the political system, that the constitution was more flexible, and that the "modernizing" forces had achieved more penetration—in fact, that the "traditional" elements were less "traditional"—than recent historians have been willing to allow.

Modernity's Dark Side

Thus perhaps we should reconsider what exactly the categories of the "traditional" and the "modern" mean, both in general and in the specific context of the *Kaiserreich*. In particular, I have been trying to suggest, the common equation between authoritarianism, right-wing politics, and imperialist foreign policies on the one side and "backwardness," archaism, and "preindustrial traditions" on the other side is highly misleading. It may be, in fact, that precisely the most vigorous "modernizing" tendencies in the *Kaiserreich,* not the recalcitrantly "antimodern" ones, were the most pugnacious and consistent in their pursuit of imperialist and antidemocratic policies at home and abroad. What I want to argue is that Wehler's recent revisions—which abandon the extreme "feudalization" thesis for a picture of bourgeois values reshaping the cultural and institutional world of the empire—should be pushed still further. The complexity that Wehler now sees in the imperial polity and its relationship to the expanding dominance of bourgeois influences should lead us to give up the conceptual framework of the primacy of "preindustrial traditions" altogether. For if we accept the irreducible contingency of political forms and reject the premise that the dominance of a particular social class has a logical or lawlike requirement for one type of state and political culture over another, then we are free to think through the specificity of the imperial state more critically.

I wish to propose five areas in which these possibilities might be explored, areas in which political life disobeyed the binary distinction between "modernizing" liberalism and "backward" authoritarianism that Wehler and others are trying so hard to maintain. The first two of these I have already presented extensively elsewhere; the last three are proposals for the future.

The first area concerns *radical nationalism,* the distinct politics generated by the *nationale Verbände* (especially the *Flottenverein* and the *Alldeutscher Verband* between the late 1890s and 1914), which crystallized as an extraparliamentary "national opposition" to the moderate governmentalism of the conservative party-political establishment before exploding into an open confrontation with the imperial government itself during 1907–8. There were many complexities to radical nationalism as a political formation. But here I want to present its central paradox from Wehler's point of view. On the one hand, radical nationalists were clearly on the right of the political spectrum—despite the populism of their ideology, they were profoundly antisocialist and antidemocratic in the core of their political being and on the face of it corresponded closely to the type of antimodernizing authoritarianism that preserved the *Kaiserreich* in the backwardness of its illiberalism before World War I. But on the other hand, radical nationalists do not fit with this interpretive framework. Sociologically, they were not the casualties or opponents of modernization but mainly the self-confident beneficiaries of Imperial Germany's new industrial civilization. Politically, they committed themselves to the powerful modernity of the new German national state, which they constructed through the discursive novelty of a "German-national" (*deutsch-national*) rhetoric. Most obviously, this new *deutsch-national* ideology was focused on *Weltpolitik* and the naval arms drive, which were thought to be both the logical correlate of German industrial strength in the world market and the condition of the latter's future growth. But it also embraced a range of additional concerns, including an anticlericalism originating in the *Kulturkampf* and a relentless hostility to all particularism (especially that of Catholic Bavaria), both of which expressed a positive desire for a unitary state. The political drive for a strengthening of the centralized state fabric produced a range of specific reformist commitments, including the demand for an imperial system of taxation that could more effectively harness the nation's material resources and the pressure to "nationalize" the school curriculum, which was also linked to the call for a general ideological program of "civic education" (*staatsbürgerliche Erziehung*). At the height of the tensions with the government in 1907–8, radical nationalists also assumed positions that were potentially antimonarchist. In all of these ways, radical nationalism amounted to a modernizing ideology of "national efficiency" (to adapt a British political phrase of the same time) that was extremely subversive of a traditional conservative standpoint. It opened a crucial ideological fracture in the established discourse of right-wing political legitimacy. How the radical nationalist political formation could be fitted into Wehler's framework is just not clear.[61]

---

61. See Geoff Eley, *Reshaping the German Right: Radical Nationalism and Political Change after Bismarck,* 2d ed. (Ann Arbor, 1991); Geoff Eley, "Reshaping the Right: Radical Nationalism and the German Navy League, 1898–1908," *Historical Journal* 21, no. 3 (1978): 327–54; Geoff Eley, "Some Thoughts on the Nationalist Pressure Groups in Imperial Germany," in *Nationalist and Racialist Movements in Britain and Germany before 1914,* ed. Paul Kennedy and Anthony Nicholls (London, 1981), 40–67.

The second area concerns industrial relations and the political and ideological status of the industrial paternalism that dominated heavy industry in the Ruhr, the Saar, and Silesia, and other sectors of large-scale industry before 1914, including shipbuilding and heavy machinery. Briefly, the issue here is whether the industrial paternalism concerned is to be best seen as a "preindustrial" type of authoritarianism (the *Herr-im-Haus* outlook) that involved the taking over of older, preliberal and aristocratic cultural patterns inappropriate to a modern society; or whether it expressed specific forms of capitalist rationality in the sense that it presupposed and was determined by certain conditions of large-scale and well-organized capitalist production. I have discussed this question at some length elsewhere. The point I wish to make here is that there are other ways of interpreting the repressive industrial relations described by the paternalist model than seeing them as a backward impediment to the evolution of the forms of labor conciliation that Wehler identifies with modernity in this respect. In fact, it makes more sense to see company unions, company housing, blacklists, and company welfare schemes as illiberal *and* modern. It was no accident that such practices were adopted by all the most advanced industrial sectors in Germany before 1914, regardless of the employers' particular political affiliations—including a self-consciously liberal employer such as Siemens in the more dynamic electrotechnical sector as well as a reactionary heavy-industrialist such as Krupp. How this question fits with the recent discussion of *Bürgerlichkeit* would be interesting to work out.[62]

Third, it is worth returning to Wehler's grand-interpretive framework of social imperialism in order to recast it—partly again to deconstruct the relationship to conservative politics and manipulative "system-stabilizing" strategies in which he locates it, and partly to broaden our understanding of the ideological and cultural consequences of the new relationship between the colonial and metropolitan worlds. On the one hand, Wehler argues that Germany's later-nineteenth-century imperialism had a conservative function and effect (in terms both of the "ideological consensus" for overseas expansion in the context of the Great Depression, and of Bismarck's manipulative intentions) and draws an explicit contrast between the authoritarian system that social imperialism successfully guaranteed and the alternative developmental possibility of "welfare-statist mass democracy" (*sozialstaatlichen Massendemokratien*), which remained blocked in German history until after 1945.[63]

---

62. Eley, "The British Model and the German Road," 98–126; David F. Crew, *Town in the Ruhr: A Social History of Bochum, 1860–1914* (New York, 1979), esp. 1ff., 119ff., 145–57, 221–24; Dick Geary, "The Industrial Bourgeoisie and Labour Relations in Germany, 1871–1933," in Blackbourn and Evans, *The German Bourgeoisie,* 140–61. Dennis Sweeney's forthcoming University of Michigan Ph.D. dissertation (defended 1994) will also shed much light on this question: "The Social Question, Social Reform, and the German Bourgeoisie: Industry and Politics in the Saar, 1877–1914."

63. Wehler, *Bismarck,* 19.

Yet, historically speaking, it would be very hard to deny the positive relationship between liberal and social-democratic reform politics and imperialism in most periods since the Enlightenment, whether we consider (just to take the British example) the forms of free-trading imperialism, the new liberalism before 1914, or Fabian views of the empire between and after the two world wars. In fact, the most compelling voices of liberal renewal in Germany before 1914 elaborated their reformist projects (in relation to social legislation and political reform) precisely through an engagement with the possibilities of imperialist expansion. In this respect, as in others, neither liberalism nor Wehler's abstract utopia of *bürgerliche Gesellschaft* can be protected against the contamination of imperialism, because imperialism/colonialism as a set of exploitative power relations with the extra-European world were inscribed in the Enlightenment tradition from the beginning.

On the other hand, therefore, it is important to begin exploring the ways in which forms of social relations, patterns of culture, and increasingly racialized discourses of national superiority that were developed in the colonies were powerfully reinserted within the metropolitan society. "Colonial knowledge" in this sense should be a rich field of inquiry, for it has become clear from recent work on British and French colonialism to what extent metropolitan understandings of nationality have been constructed since the eighteenth century via an elaborate encounter with the colonial Other. Forms of colonial representation through literature, museums and exhibitions, entertainment, and popular culture have been especially fruitful in this regard. The gendering of national identity, whether in militarist activities and warfare per se or in the more general ordering of nationalist representations around conceptions of masculinity and femininity, also had key colonialist roots: for example, intensive discussions of colonial intermarriage generated a complex discourse around gender inequalities, sexual privilege, class priorities, and racial superiority, that then became powerfully rearticulated into nationalist discourse at home. This was the *real* ground of social imperialism, arguably—that is, not so much the conscious manipulations by governing elites focused on by Wehler but the more insidious processes of ideological structuration. At all events, this implies a much richer field of relations between colonial and domestic politics. The consequences of imperialism certainly cannot be bracketed from the "modernization" project by identifying social imperialism so unidimensionally with conservative antimodern strategies.[64]

---

64. See Geoff Eley, "Social Imperialism in Germany: Reformist Synthesis or Reactionary Sleight of Hand?" in Eley, *From Unification to Nazism,* 154–67. Otherwise, the most suggestive work has been done outside the German field: e.g., Ann L. Stoler, "Making Empire Respectable: Race and Sexual Morality in Twentieth-Century Colonial Cultures," *American Ethnologist* 16 (1989): 26–51; Ann L. Stoler, "Carnal Knowledge and Imperial Power: The Politics of Race and Sexual Morality in Colonial Asia," in *Gender at the Crossroads: Feminist Anthropology in the Post-Modern Era,* ed. Micaela di Leonardo (Berkeley, forthcoming); Tony Bennett, "The Exhibi-

Fourth, we need to recognize the importance of gender, not just as the kind of formality that acknowledges the previous neglect of women but as the complex and variable construction of sexual difference that affects both women and men, and whose recognition (as my introduction tries to argue) consequently influences our understanding of the world as a whole. The necessity of this perspective certainly needs to be argued for at the level of general theory, but it is important to note that as a "useful category of historical analysis," gender can also change and enrich our understanding of particular questions. I have already alluded to some general examples—the gendering of citizenship and the public sphere and the gendered discourse of class, together with the relationship between masculinity/femininity and nationalist ideology—that can be explored in a specifically German context. But some established questions of German history can also be illuminated by a gender perspective. One of these could be the "social question."

Thus whereas the late-nineteenth-century apparatus of poor relief, charity, and social insurance may have been formally based on a mixture of arguments (Christian responsibility, capitalist rationality, political calculation, national efficiency), they were also predicated upon gendered assumptions in the manner indicated above, particularly regarding the social importance of the family. This was true of national and local state provision, charitable work, and company-provided welfare, all of which reflected definite assumptions about what constituted orderly domestic living arrangements. Moreover, from the 1890s, with changing bases of women's work (waged/unwaged, domestic/industrial, blue-collar/white-collar), the growth of urban living, the rising industrial and parliamentary strength of labor, and the manifold concerns regarding German national efficiency, the discourse of social reform became charged with new meanings, not least through the involvement of new forms of professional expertise in social policy and the pressure of the emergent women's movement. When we add certain other issues, including child and maternal welfare, public health, policies for the control of youth, and the general regulation of morality and sexuality, we have an especially promising field for gender-sensitive analysis. Of course, World War I, the Weimar discourse of the "new women," and the Nazi counterrevolution produced a series of radicalizations around these issues, and the valuable contribution of women's history to our grasp of these later moments should reemphasize the need for similar

---

tionary Complex," *New Formations* 4 (Spring 1988): 73–102; Anna Davin, "Imperialism and Motherhood," *History Workshop Journal* 5 (Spring 1978): 9–57; John M. MacKenzie, ed., *Imperialism and Popular Culture* (Manchester, 1989); J. A. Mangan, ed., *Making Imperial Mentalities: Socialization and British Imperialism* (Manchester, 1990); Susan Thorne, "Protestant Ethics and the Spirit of Imperialism: Liberal Nonconformity and the Making of an Imperial Political Culture in Nineteenth-Century Britain" (Ph.D. diss., University of Michigan, 1990). Lora Wildenthal's University of Michigan Ph.D. dissertation (in progress) on women and German colonialism will be an important contribution.

analysis of the *Kaiserreich*.[65] My point is that none of these areas unambiguously involved an enlargement of women's rights or political capacities in the liberal sense, but the meaning was nonetheless "modern" for that.

This *ambivalence* of reform and the difficulties of assimilating the actual "modernizing" initiatives of the turn of the century to the progressive or liberal-democratic normativity against which Wehler insists on measuring the German past bring me to the last of my proposals, which concerns the dynamics of disciplinary power in Foucault's sense—that is, the framing and application to the "social body" of new knowledges of science and ambitions of control. Here we connect back to the question of imperial continuities with Nazism, though not in the sense, claimed by Wehler, of deficits of modernity producing pathologies that were the condition of Nazi success. On the contrary, I would argue, it was precisely the most striking manifestations of modern scientific and technocratic ambition in the sphere of social policy that laid the way for Nazi excess. For example, there is a growing literature on the eugenicist consensus that formed the disquieting background to Nazi racism between the late nineteenth century and the 1920s, and in whose light Nazi anti-Semitism has increasingly appeared as the most virulent form of a much more extensive biological politics that systematically naturalized and essentialized social, cultural, and political phenomena under the sign of race. In Robert Proctor's view, "the ideological structure we associate with National Socialism was deeply embedded in the philosophy and institutional structure of German biomedical science." Consequently, if we take a broad view of the biomedical sciences as an ideological field, according to which the Nazis'

---

65. See Renate Bridenthal, Atina Grossmann, and Marion Kaplan, eds., *When Biology Became Destiny: Women in Weimar and Nazi Germany* (New York, 1984); Gisela Bock, *Zwangssterilisation im Nationalsozialismus: Studien zur Rassenpolitik und Frauenpolitik* (Opladen, 1986); Ute Daniel, *Arbeiterfrauen in der Kriegsgesellschaft: Beruf, Familie und Politik im Ersten Weltkrieg* (Göttingen, 1989); Carola Sachse, *Siemens, der Nationalsozialismus und die moderne Familie: Eine Untersuchung zur sozialen Rationalisierung in Deutschland im 20. Jahrhundert* (Hamburg, 1990); Detlev J. K. Peukert, *Grenzen der Sozialdisziplinierung: Aufstieg und Krise der deutschen Jugendfürsorge 1878 bis 1932* (Cologne, 1986); Detlev J. K. Peukert, *Jugend zwischen Krieg und Krise: Lebenswelten von Arbeiterjungen in der Weimarer Republik* (Cologne, 1987); Derek S. Linton, *"Who Has the Youth, Has the Future": The Campaign to Save Young Workers in Imperial Germany* (Cambridge, 1991); Richard Wall and Jay Winter, eds., *The Upheaval of War: Family, Work and Welfare in Europe, 1914–1918* (Cambridge, 1988); David F. Crew, "German Socialism, the State and Family Policy, 1918–33," *Continuity and Change* 1 (1986), 235–63; Young Sun Hong, "The Politics of Welfare Reform and the Dynamics of the Public Sphere: Church, Society, and the State in the Making of the Social-Welfare System in Germany, 1830–1930" (Ph.D. diss., University of Michigan, 1989); Cornelie Usborne, *The Politics of the Body in Weimar Germany* (London, 1992); Atina Grossmann, *Women, Family, and the Rationalization of Sexuality: German Sex Reform, 1925–1935* (New York, 1992); Klaus Theweleit, *Männerphantasien*, 2 vols. (Frankfurt a.M., 1977–78). The phrase at the start of the preceding paragraph is taken from Joan Scott's crucial essay "Gender: A Useful Category of Historical Analysis," in *Gender and the Politics of History*, by Joan Scott (New York, 1988), 28–50.

racial programs (from genocide to the anticipatory treatment of the Gypsies and the 1939 euthanasia program, back through population policies aimed at women and the 1933 sterilization law) were authorized by much longer traditions of racial hygiene from before 1914, then the Judeocide appears as the most vicious part "of a larger attempt . . . to medicalize or biologize various forms of social, sexual, political, or racial deviance."[66] Moreover, we know from the work of Paul Weindling and others on the origins, rise, and mature elaboration of the eugenicist complex between the 1870s and 1945 that this was a restlessly aggrandizing ideological field. It convened biomedical knowledge, public health, and racial thought on the ground of social policy, and it was there that not only the politics of the family and motherhood but also the most progressive achievements of the Weimar welfare state were completely embedded.[67]

Perhaps the key point to emerge from this recent literature concerns the "normality" of racial science in the Kuhnian sense. Far from corrupting "true" science by the intrusion of irrational and anti-intellectual pressures from the outside, Nazism worked within an established eugenicist paradigm by appealing to the existing "imagery, results, and authority of science."[68] Rather than politicizing science in some illegitimate sense, Nazism worked upon traditions of discourse that had connected science to politics since the *Kaiserreich*. Not just entire nationalities (Jews, Gypsies, Poles, and other Slav groups) but also entire social categories (gays, the handicapped, and mentally ill), various groups of the socially incompetent and incurably ill, and then Polish intellectuals, Soviet prisoners of war, "political commissars," and others) became slated for racist and eugenicist attack. This was possible because of the prior diffusion of eugenicist and related ideologies of social engineering, which to a great extent had permeated the thinking of the social-policy and health-care professions long before the Nazis arrived.

In both respects the ground for Nazi racism was discursively laid—not in the limited sense of "linguistic" preparation but by an entire institutional apparatus and system of practice aimed at defining deviant or "worthless" catego-

---

66. Robert Proctor, *Racial Hygiene: Medicine under the Nazis* (Cambridge, Mass., 1988), 6–7.

67. Paul Weindling, *Health, Race and German Politics between National Unification and Nazism, 1870–1945* (Cambridge, 1989); Gerhard Baader and Ulrich Schultz, eds., *Medizin und Nationalsozialismus: Tabuisierte Vergangenheit—Ungebrochene Tradition?* (Berlin, 1980); Benno Müller-Hill, *Tödliche Wissenschaft: Die Aussonderung von Juden, Zigeunern und Geisteskranken, 1933–45* (Reinbek, 1984); Götz Aly and Karl Heinz Roth, *Die restlose Erfassung: Volkszählen, Identifizieren, Aussondern im Nationalsozialismus* (Berlin, 1984); Ernst Klee, *"Euthanasie" im NS-Staat: Die "Vernichtung lebensunwerten Lebens"* (Frankfurt a.M., 1983); and Hans-Walter Schmuhl, *Rassenhygiene, Nationalsozialismus, Euthanasie: Von der Verhütung zur Vernichtung "lebensunwerten Lebens," 1890–1945* (Göttingen, 1987).

68. Proctor, *Racial Hygiene*, 283.

ries of people and at restructuring popular assumptions about what an acceptable social policy could be. This is where my two earlier points concerning colonial knowledges and the importance of gender also converge. Work by Michael Burleigh and Woodruff Smith has shown how the disciplines of anthropology and ethnology also helped to compose the ideological context from which the specifically Nazi project could come.[69] Likewise, Gisela Bock influenced our understanding of the race/gender connection in her study of Nazi sterilization policy; Claudia Koonz saw the Third Reich doubly ordered around the naturalized poles of biological distinction, male/female and Aryan/non-Aryan, in a "social order founded on race and gender"; and the programmatic collection of essays *When Biology Became Destiny* successfully made the case for seeing "biological politics" as a unifying principle of Nazi practice. The logical imbrication of these two categories is perhaps clear enough—centering one's understanding of society around a biologically constructed concept of race had immediate consequences for how one understood the place of women, given the key importance of sexuality, family, and reproduction to both—and the Nazis' racial policies do seem to have been prefigured very strongly in a complex of policies affecting reproduction (such as population, welfare, family, motherhood, euthanasia, and sterilization) that go back to the late *Kaiserreich.*[70] Consequently, we need to recognize once again that Wehler's understanding of modernizing reform as a set of abstract liberal-democratic desiderata and the discourse of modernizing reform as we actually encounter it in the early twentieth century *simply do not fit.* Instead, the Nazis' racialized policies were continuous with what passed as the ruling knowledge of the time and were less an eruption of the irrational than an extreme form of technocratic reason. If we are to understand the origins of Nazism, therefore, it is not to the *Kaiserreich*'s deficient modernization that we must look but to early-twentieth-century modernity's dark side—to "the genesis of the 'Final Solution' in the spirit of science," in Detlev Peukert's compelling phrase.[71]

69. Michael Burleigh, *Germany Turns Eastwards: A Study of Ostforschung in the Third Reich* (Cambridge, 1988); Woodruff D. Smith, *The Ideological Origins of Nazi Imperialism* (New York, 1986); and Woodruff D. Smith, *Politics and the Sciences of Culture in Germany* (New York, 1991).

70. Bock, *Zwangssterilisation;* Claudia Koonz, *Mothers in the Fatherland: Women, the Family, and Nazi Politics* (New York, 1987); Bridenthal, Grossmann, and Kaplan, *When Biology Became Destiny.*

71. Detlev J. K. Peukert, "The Genesis of the 'Final Solution' from the Spirit of Science," in *Reevaluating the Third Reich,* ed. Thomas Childers and Jane Caplan (New York, 1993), 234–52.

Gender and the Politics of Class Formation: Rethinking German Labor History

Kathleen Canning

Class formation is one of the most important markers of the economic and social transformation of nineteenth-century Europe, of the dissolution of feudal estate society and the rise of a modern, industrial urban society. "Class" is also a keyword in the vocabulary of social and labor history, one that occupies a central place in the process of rethinking and recasting the conceptual framework of social history that is currently under way in the United States, Britain, and France.[1] The emergence of gender as a category of historical analysis and the growing importance of language in the theory and practice of social history have undermined the stability of the historical and analytical vocabulary of social and labor history, especially of the concepts of experience, agency, and class. The "linguistic turn," combined with the theoretical innovations of feminist history, has resulted in a "disorienting" epistemological crisis in social

This essay was previously published in *American Historical Review* 97, no. 3 (June 1992): 736–68. Earlier versions of this essay were presented to the Program on the Comparative Study of Social Transformation at the University of Michigan, at the 1989 meeting of the Social Science History Association, and at the conference "The *Kaiserreich* in the 1990s: New Research, New Directions, New Agendas," held at the University of Pennsylvania in 1990. I would like to thank Jane Caplan, David Crew, Laura Downs, Geoff Eley, Karin Hausen, Carol Karlsen, Vernon Lidtke, Hubert Rast, Sonya Rose, Adelheid von Saldern, David Scobey, Bill Sewell, Wilfried Spohn, Margaret Somers, and finally, the anonymous American Historical Review reviewers for critical questions, helpful suggestions, and fruitful discussions concerning this essay.

1. Patrick Joyce, "In Pursuit of Class: Recent Studies in the History of Work and Class," *History Workshop* 25 (Spring 1988): 175; and Lenard Berlanstein, "Working with Language: The Linguistic Turn in French Labor History: A Review Article," *Comparative Studies of Society and History* 33 (April 1991): 439. See also Raymond Williams, *Keywords: A Vocabulary of Culture and Society* (New York, 1983).

history, during which the concepts of class and class formation have been challenged and redefined.[2]

"Class" in its Marxist or Weberian versions has usually designated a relationship to the process of production and a corresponding social identity. Since the 1963 publication of E. P. Thompson's classic work, *The Making of the English Working Class,* many historians have also embraced the view of class as a cultural relation. During the 1980s, the works of William H. Sewell, Jr., Gareth Stedman Jones, William Reddy, and Patrick Joyce brought the cultural dimensions of class into sharper focus. Sewell and Stedman Jones, for example, shifted the emphasis of labor history away from socioeconomic causality toward political language, ideology, rhetoric, and representation, away from a notion of class as a "social fact" to one of class as a postulated "social identity."[3] Reddy's *Money and Liberty in Europe* emphatically rejected the "simple pairings of social classes with political factions" and dispensed with a view of the "means of production as an unambiguous marker of class identity."[4] In *Visions of the People,* Joyce distinguished carefully between the

2. See, for example, Joan W. Scott, "Gender: A Useful Category of Historical Analysis," *American Historical Review* 91 (December 1986): 1053–75; John Toews, "Intellectual History after the Linguistic Turn: The Autonomy of Meaning and the Irreducibility of Experience," *American Historical Review* 92 (October 1987): 879–907. On the linguistic turn in German history, see Peter Schöttler, "Historians and Discourse Analysis," *History Workshop* 27 (Spring 1989): 37–65; and the following essays in *Central European History* 22 (September–December 1989): Michael Geyer and Konrad Jarausch, "The Future of the German Past: Transatlantic Reflections for the 1990s," 229–59; Jane Caplan, "Postmodernism, Poststructuralism, and Deconstruction: Notes for Historians," 260–78; and Isabel V. Hull, "Feminist and Gender History through the Literary Looking Glass: German Historiography in Postmodern Times," 279–300. On the epistemological crisis, see Bryan Palmer, *Descent into Discourse: The Reification of Language and the Writing of Social History* (Philadelphia, 1990), 78–86, in which Palmer describes being "quite shaken" by Scott's deconstructive challenge. Berlanstein's view of the linguistic turn is more sympathetic but also points to the disorienting effects of Scott's work on the field of social history in his "Working with Language," 439.

3. Geoff Eley, "Is All the World a Text? From Social History to the History of Society Two Decades Later," in *The Historic Turn in the Human Sciences,* ed. Terence J. McDonald (Ann Arbor, forthcoming), 18–19. On the shift away from socioeconomic causality, see Berlanstein, "Working with Language," 428–29. The works referred to here are William H. Sewell, Jr., *Work and Revolution in France: The Language of Labor from the Old Regime to 1848* (Cambridge, 1980); and Gareth Stedman Jones, *Languages of Class: Studies in English Working Class History, 1832–1982* (Cambridge, 1983). A valuable discussion of class in German labor history can be found in David Crew, "Class and Community: Local Research on Working-Class History in Four Countries," in *Arbeiter und Arbeiterbewegung im Vergleich: Berichte zur internationalen historischen Forschung,* ed. Klaus Tenfelde (Munich, 1986), 279–80. For a discussion of experience, see William H. Sewell, Jr., "How Classes Are Made: Critical Reflections on E. P. Thompson's Theory of Working-Class Formation;" in *E. P. Thompson: Critical Perspectives,* ed. Harvey J. Kaye and Keith McClelland (Philadelphia, 1990), 50–77; Joan Wallach Scott, "The Evidence of Experience," *Critical Inquiry* 17 (Summer 1991): 773–97.

4. William Reddy, *Money and Liberty in Modern Europe: A Critique of Historical Understanding* (Cambridge, 1987), 30–31.

"consciousness of class" and the consciousness of *a* class, emphasizing, for example, that the working class in Lancashire was more likely to embrace populism than to manifest "class consciousness." Although Joyce concluded that class was "only one of the ways in which people patterned and gave meaning to the social order," he explicitly "pull[ed] back from the verge of denying class."[5] Instead, the culturalist approach to labor history seeks to redefine class by historicizing it, by attending to the "actual terms in which contemporaries talked about the social order."[6] Thus, while class is retained as an analytical category, the culturalist labor histories of the 1980s recast it as a remarkably elastic concept.

At the same time, recent attempts to establish the relationships among and between the distinct social identities of gender, race, ethnicity, and class have created a different kind of "crisis of the concept of class,"[7] one that reveals the ways in which class subsumes these identities and differences. Women and gender have presented a perplexing problem for histories of class since the late 1960s, when feminist scholarship began to challenge prevalent historical and sociological paradigms. Labor historians and political theorists often attempted to fit women into prevalent notions of class, some by arguing that women formed a separate class of their own, others by examining the ways in which (female) gender presented an obstacle to the formation of a cohesive class unit. Still others circumvented the dilemma of "sex and class" by ascribing to women the same class position, identity, and interests as those of their fathers or husbands. Feminist historians sought to transcend this theoretical impasse by formulating a "doubled vision" of society, one that emphasized the simultaneity of sex and class in the lives of both men and women.[8] In dissolving the myth of a "natural" division between public and private, between women and men, and in analyzing the ways in which these divisions were "socially constructed and socially imposed," this doubled vision prepared the way for the shift toward "the self-conscious study of gender," even if it left the concept of class intact.[9]

---

5. Patrick Joyce, *Visions of the People: Industrial England and the Question of Class, 1848–1914* (Cambridge, 1991), 5, 13–23, 329–31. See also Patrick Joyce, *The Historical Meanings of Work* (Cambridge, 1987).

6. Joyce, *Visions of the People,* 1. See also Reddy's exploration of the many possible ways in which the concept might be redefined, all of which, in his view, "are equally successful, none of which is evidently superior to any of the others"; Reddy, *Money and Liberty,* 30.

7. Reddy, *Money and Liberty,* 30.

8. The term "doubled vision" is from Joan Kelly's important essay "The Doubled Vision of Feminist Theory," in *Women, History, and Theory: The Essays of Joan Kelly,* by Joan Kelly (Chicago, 1984), 51–64, first published in *Feminist Studies* 5 (Spring 1979): 216–27. See also Judith L. Newton, Mary P. Ryan, and Judith R. Walkowitz, eds., *Sex and Class in Women's History* (London, 1983), esp. the introduction, 1–15.

9. Joan Kelly, "The Social Relations of the Sexes," in Kelly, *Women, History, and Theory,* 6, refers to the social construction of these divisions. Newton et al. refers to the "self-conscious study of gender" in *Sex and Class,* 4.

Parallel to the culturalist labor historians' critical engagement with class during the last decade, feminist labor historians explored the role of sexual difference in shaping the process of working-class formation. British historian Sally Alexander's study of women's work in nineteenth-century London led her to issue a radical call in 1984 for "feminist history . . . to emancipate itself from class as the organizing principle of history, the privileged signifier of social relations and their political representations."[10] Yet this call may have been somewhat premature, at least in the United States, for an "emancipation from class" necessitated the development of alternative conceptual tools. Joan Scott's influential article "Gender: A Useful Category of Analysis," published in 1986, established a theoretical framework for the shift from women's history to gender history. In refining the analytical concept of gender, Scott made a convincing case for its usefulness to historians in general and also for its potential to destabilize and displace established categories like class.[11] Her subsequent critique of Stedman Jones's *Languages of Class* made explicit the ways in which "concepts such as class are created through differentiation" and argued that "gender becomes so implicated in concepts of class that there is no way to analyze one without the other."[12] The appearance in the next year of *Family Fortunes,* by Catherine Hall and Leonore Davidoff, offered a powerful historical example of the ways in which gender and class worked together in shaping middle-class identity in nineteenth-century England.[13]

This process of rethinking class, of exploring its cultural dimensions, of analyzing it in relation to gender, race, and ethnicity, which characterizes recent British, French, and American labor historiography, has had little or no impact thus far on German labor history. Far from engagement with an epistemological crisis or a new interrogation of established concepts and categories, Germany's preeminent labor historians have recently begun a massive project

---

10. Sally Alexander, "Women, Class, and Sexual Differences in the 1830s and 1840s: Some Reflections on the Writing of a Feminist History," *History Workshop* 17 (Spring 1984): 133–49. See also Sally Alexander, *Women's Work in Nineteenth-Century London* (London, 1983); Barbara Taylor, *Eve and the New Jerusalem: Socialism and Feminism in the Nineteenth Century* (New York, 1983); and Patricia Hilden, *Working Women and Socialist Politics in France, 1880–1914: A Regional Study* (New York, 1986). Jean H. Quataert, *Reluctant Feminists in German Social Democracy, 1885–1917* (Princeton, 1979); and Laura Strumingher, *Women and the Making of the Working Class, Lyon, 1830–1870* (St. Albans, Vt., 1979) addressed some of the same issues during the late 1970s.

11. Scott, "Gender: A Useful Category."

12. Joan Scott, "On Language, Gender and Working-Class History," in *Gender and the Politics of History,* by Joan Scott (New York, 1988), 60. This essay was first published in *International Labor and Working Class History* 31 (1987): 1–13.

13. Leonore Davidoff and Catherine Hall, *Family Fortunes: Men and Women of the English Middle Class, 1780–1850* (Chicago, 1987). An interesting discussion of the book can be found in Judith Newton, "*Family Fortunes:* 'New History' and 'New Historicism,'" *Radical History Review* 43 (1989): 6–11.

of synthesizing and summarizing the findings and accomplishments of this expansive field in a new and definitive series titled History of Workers and the Workers' Movement in Germany since the End of the Eighteenth Century.[14] Indeed, German labor history, as an elemental part of the "historical social science" that was founded in Germany during the 1960s and 1970s, remains confined within a Weberian paradigm of modernization. Central to this paradigm is an *Entwicklungs- und Verlaufsmodell* of class formation, a model that outlines the progressive advancement of the various stages of class formation, which is shaped less by human actors than by structures and processes (for example, by changing market relations and the expansion of wage labor).[15] Thus the story of German working-class formation is most often analyzed as *Strukturgeschichte* (structural history) and has only recently begun to incorporate *Erfahrungsgeschichte* (the history of the experiences of the participants in this process). Aside from this recent concession to the history of experience, German labor history has remained remarkably impermeable not only to the linguistic turn but also to the important insights and challenges of the anthropologically oriented *Alltagsgeschichte,* a history of everyday life that dissolves the boundaries between workplace, household, and community in its exploration of experience and identity formation, as well as to the achievements of women's history and gender history.[16]

In the United States and England, feminist history has played a pivotal

---

14. Gerhard A. Ritter, ed., Geschichte der Arbeiter und der Arbeiterbewegung in Deutschland seit dem Ende des 18. Jahrhunderts. The volumes that have appeared thus far include vols. 1 and 2, by Jürgen Kocka, *Weder Stand noch Klasse: Unterschichten um 1800* (Bonn, 1990), and *Arbeitsverhältnisse und Arbeiterexistenzen: Grundlagen der Klassenbildung im 19. Jahrhundert* (Bonn, 1990); and vols. 9, 10, and 11, by Heinrich August Winkler, *Von der Revolution zur Stabilisierung: Arbeiter und Arbeiterbewegung in der Weimarer Republik 1918 bis 1924* (Bonn, 1984), *Der Schein der Normalität: Arbeiter und Arbeiterbewegung in der Weimarer Republik 1924 bis 1930* (Bonn, 1988), and *Der Weg in die Katastrophe: Arbeiter und Arbeiterbewegung in der Weimarer Republik 1930 bis 1933* (Bonn, 1987). Additional volumes by Ritter, Kocka, and Klaus Tenfelde are due to appear in the next several years.

15. Kocka, *Weder Stand noch Klasse,* 33. See also Konrad Jarausch's assessment of German social history in his essay "Towards a Social History of Experience: Postmodern Predicaments in Theory and Interdisciplinarity," *Central European History* 22 (September–December 1989): 427–43.

16. For a provocative example of *Alltagsgeschichte,* see Alf Lüdtke, "Organizational Order or *Eigensinn*? Workers' Privacy and Workers' Politics in Imperial Germany," in *Rites of Power: Symbolism, Ritual, and Politics since the Middle Ages,* ed. Sean Wilentz (Philadelphia, 1985), 303–33. Important discussions of this approach can be found in David Crew, *"Alltagsgeschichte:* A New Social History from Below?" *Central European History* 22 (September–December 1989): 394–407; Geoff Eley, "Labor History, Social History, *Alltagsgeschichte:* Experience, Culture, and the Politics of the Everyday—A New Direction for German Social History?" *Journal of Modern History* 61 (June 1989): 297–343; and Dorothee Wierling, "Alltagsgeschichte und Geschichte der Geschlechterbeziehungen," in *Alltagsgeschichte: Zur Rekonstruktion historischer Erfahrungen und Lebensweisen,* ed. Alf Lüdtke (Frankfurt and New York, 1989), 169–90.

role in dissolving the "grand narrative histories" of state institutions, national events, and socioeconomic structures, of class and class formation.[17] In Germany, by contrast, the relationship between feminist history and historical social science is marked by "mutual distancing."[18] As a result, many of the historical monographs on women's work, everyday lives, and political movements have been produced in relative isolation from the mainstream of historical social science. Many social and labor historians, in return, regard women's history as too specialized to be relevant to the discipline in general or to their synthetic histories of work, working-class formation, or *Gesellschaftsgeschichte* (history of society).[19] The recent shift to *Geschlechtergeschichte* (gender history), which professes more explicit theoretical aims than women's history and which obviously seeks to engage "mainstream" history, has changed little in this regard. Many German social historians continue to resist the notion that the "magic weapon of gender history," as one of their eminent representatives scornfully termed it, might be relevant to their own enterprise.[20] Binary oppositions such as private/public or family/factory continue to pervade recent accounts of class formation, and the conceptual framework of German social history remains closed to the potentially disruptive effects of gender.

This "mutual distancing" between German labor history and the history of women and gender has had several important consequences. The most obvious is that the experiences of male industrial workers continue to shape the theory and practice of German labor history. Also, gender is either wholly absent or figures in only a minor way in theoretical models and historical accounts of working-class formation. Yet the shortcomings of German labor history cannot be remedied merely through an *ergänzende Geschichtsschreibung,* by retrieving the rest or the other (the women's) side of the story. In fact, feminist historians of Germany have recently pointed out that this kind of historical

---

17. Hull, "Feminist and Gender History," 279.

18. Ute Frevert, "Klasse und Geschlecht—Ein deutscher Sonderweg?" in *Nichts als Unterdrückung? Geschlecht und Klasse in der englischen Sozialgeschichte,* ed. Logie Barrow, Dorothea Schmidt, and Jutta Schwarzkopf (Münster, 1991), 262.

19. Frevert, "Klasse und Geschlecht," 261–62; Eve Rosenhaft, "Geschichten und ihre Geschichte: Ein Nachwort," in Barrow et al., *Nichts als Unterdrückung?* 248. Women and gender appear only in disparate footnotes in Hans-Ulrich Wehler's otherwise comprehensive *Deutsche Gesellschaftsgeschichte,* of which volumes 1 and 2 have appeared thus far (Munich, 1987). Kocka's *Weder Stand noch Klasse* and *Arbeitsverhältnisse* investigate the living and working conditions of female servants, agricultural workers, and employees in domestic and factory textile production only to conclude that the nature of their employment excluded them from the process of class formation.

20. Hans-Ulrich Wehler, "Der deutsche Weg: Geoff Eleys Revisionsversuche," *Frankfurter Allgemeine Zeitung* 71 (25 February 1991). Wehler uses the polemical term "die Wunderwaffe der Geschlechtergeschichte."

enterprise merely serves to reinforce their "outsider status."[21] Instead, they emphasize the important task of integrating gender history into *Gesellschaftsgeschichte*. Dorothee Wierling, for example, argues that the success of gender as a category of historical analysis hinges on this very process of integration, by which social historians incorporate gender into their conceptual framework and gender history constitutes itself as an essential part of *Gesellschaftsgeschichte*.[22]

This study seeks to analyze prevalent paradigms of class formation, to critique their neglect of gender, and to explore the implications of bringing gender into the existing models. I will suggest that the two forms of absence— theoretical and historical-empirical—are related, and I propose to evaluate the theoretical concepts of class and class formation in terms of a historical case study of male and female textile workers in Germany between 1880 and 1930. This attempt to insert gender as a category of historical analysis and women as historical subjects into prevalent models of class formation results not in the seamless integration that Wierling imagines but in the transformation of the model itself.

Despite the growing interest of historians in the intersections of class with identities of gender, race, ethnicity, and religion, these concepts have had a negligible role in recent theoretical debates among historians and sociologists on working-class formation. Even recent bids to revise both old Marxist and newer Thompsonian orthodoxies—such as the 1986 collection of essays *Working-Class Formation: Nineteenth-Century Patterns in Western Europe and the United States,* edited by Ira Katznelson and Aristide Zolberg— overlook or subsume these categories.[23] The absence of women and gender in prevalent models of class formation is rendered even more provocative by

---

21. Frevert, "Klasse und Geschlecht," 262; Rosenhaft, "Geschichten und ihre Geschichte," 248.

22. Wierling, "Alltagsgeschichte," 173.

23. Ira Katznelson and Aristide R. Zolberg, eds., *Working-Class Formation: Nineteenth-Century Patterns in Western Europe and the United States* (Princeton, 1986). The essays in this volume seek to revise both Marxist orthodoxies and Thompson's "culturalist-experientialist" approach. It has remained an influential and valuable collection since its publication, not least because of its theoretical and comparative approach to the historical problem of class formation in France, Germany, and the United States. Notable exceptions to the charge of neglecting gender, ethnicity, religion, and race in theoretical and historical investigations of working-class formation include Vernon L. Lidtke, "Burghers, Workers and Problems of Class Relationships, 1870 to 1914: Germany in Comparative Perspective," in *Arbeiter und Bürger im 19. Jahrhundert,* ed. Jürgen Kocka (Oldenbourg, 1986), 29–46; Jean H. Quataert, "The Politics of Rural Industrialization: Class, Gender, and Collective Protest in the Saxon Oberlausitz of the Late Nineteenth Century," *Central European History* 20, no. 3 (June 1987): 91–124; and Wilfried Spohn, "Religion and Working-Class Formation in Imperial Germany, 1871–1914," *Politics and Society* 19 (1991): 109–32.

the prominence of both women and ideologies of gender in the recent literature on middle-class formation. As the studies by Mary Ryan on the United
States, Bonnie Smith on France, Davidoff and Hall on England, and Ute
Frevert on Germany have shown, home and hearth are central locations of
middle-class formation.[24] The ideology of domesticity, which ascribed sharply
differentiated roles to men and women in the public and private spheres, was
a key aspect of the social identity of the German *Bürgertum* and the Victorian middle classes. The site of working-class formation, by contrast, was the
predominantly male sphere of industrial production, and the universalizing
claims of "class" effaced women's paid and unpaid labor. While sexual
difference is viewed as a constitutive factor in middle-class formation, it
is disguised and obscured in most historical accounts of working-class formation.

I intend to reevaluate prevalent theories of class formation from the perspective of gender, to analyze in theory and in one specific historical context
the complex relationships between gender and class. My focus is the "levels
approach" to class formation, as outlined in its theoretical dimensions by
Katznelson and in its historical dimensions by German historian Jürgen
Kocka.[25] German labor historians first became familiar with the levels approach to class formation with the East German publication of Hartmut
Zwahr's study of Leipzig metal workers in 1978.[26] Kocka formulated a similar
four-tiered model of class formation in his *Lohnarbeit und Klassenbildung,*
one that resonates in his essay in *Working-Class Formation* and that appears to
coincide with Katznelson's conceptualization in most points.[27] In dividing the
process of class formation into a series of levels and inserting levels of social
and cultural formation between economic and political class-formation, advo-

---

24. Mary P. Ryan, *Cradle of the Middle Class: The Family in Oneida County, New York,
1790–1865* (Cambridge, 1981); Bonnie G. Smith, *Ladies of the Leisure Class: The Bourgeoises of
Northern France in the Nineteenth Century* (Princeton, 1981); Davidoff and Hall, *Family Fortunes;* and Ute Frevert, *Bürgerinnen und Bürger: Geschlechterverhältnisse im 19. Jahrhundert*
(Göttingen, 1988). See also Mary Poovey, *Uneven Developments: The Ideological Work of Gender
in Mid-Victorian England* (Chicago, 1988).

25. Ira Katznelson, "Working-Class Formation: Constructing Cases and Comparisons," and
Jürgen Kocka, "Problems of Working-Class Formation: The Early Years, 1800–1875," both in
Katznelson and Zolberg, *Working-Class Formation,* 3–41, 279–351.

26. Hartmut Zwahr, *Zur Konstituierung des Proletariats als Klasse: Strukturuntersuchung
über das Leipziger Proletariat während der Industriellen Revolution* (Berlin, 1978).

27. Jürgen Kocka, *Lohnarbeit und Klassenbildung: Arbeiter und Arbeiterbewegung in
Deutschland, 1800–1875* (Bonn, 1983). See especially chap. 2, "Die Weberianische Verwendung
eines Marxschen Klassenbegriffs," 23–30. Kocka's model of class formation is explicated in
greater detail in his *Weder Stand noch Klasse* and *Arbeitsverhältnisse.* Kocka's additional forthcoming volumes include vol. 3, *Arbeiterleben und Protest: Entstehung einer sozialen Klasse;* and
vol. 4, *Zwischen Volksbewegung und Klassenbewegung: Arbeiterorganisationen vom Vormärz bis
1875* of the project *Geschichte der Arbeiter und der Arbeiterbewegung.* See note 14.

cates of the levels approach challenge the old orthodox Marxist "class-in-itself-and-class-for-itself" teleology. At the same time, they offer something clearer than E. P. Thompson's notion of experience as a mediating factor between production or capitalist structure and the process of class formation.

Despite the common framework of levels or stages in the process of class formation, it is important to point to several significant differences between Zwahr on the one hand and Kocka and Katznelson on the other. According to Zwahr's model, the various levels represent a linear, chronological development. Level one, or economic formation, during which the capitalist economy developed and wage labor became the principal form of manual labor, brings about the second level of social formation, at which developing webs of familial, marital, social, and communal ties bound workers together within occupational groups and across traditional barriers of trade and skill. The progressive development of levels one and two created the conditions for level three, the emergence of a class-conscious proletariat imbued with the ideology of Marxism. While Katznelson and Kocka propose similar versions of levels one and two, their models offer a much more nuanced approach to "political" class formation, which in Zwahr's version is marked by the founding of a class-conscious labor union or workers' party. Both Katznelson and Kocka introduce an additional level between social and political class formation, one that encompasses a common social or cultural identity or the disposition to behave as a class. Kocka, for example, offers an interesting analysis of the "language of class," in particular of the emergence of the concepts of *Arbeiter* (worker) and *Arbeiterklasse* (working class) as positive terms of self-identification by the 1860s in Germany.[28] The fourth level encompasses class-conscious collective action that involves confrontation with other classes or the state and that, unlike Zwahr's third level, has no prescribed ideological content.

An additional important innovation in Kocka's model, as well as in Mary Nolan's contribution to the Katznelson and Zolberg volume, is the analysis of the role of the state in the process of working-class formation. Kocka points to the ways in which between 1800 and 1870 "governments of the larger [German] states facilitated the gradual intrusion of capitalist principles into the feudal structure of large-scale agriculture." At the same time, government policies toward trade and guilds "weaken[ed] traditional corporate identities" and helped journeymen "to identify [themselves] as workers instead of as members of particular crafts or special skill groups."[29] Nolan argues in a similar vein that the newly unified German state "made workers a prime object of policy" in the wake of the depression of 1873. In placing workers "at the center of political debate" about the social question, state policy, "in both its

---

28. Kocka, "Problems of Working-Class Formation," 327.
29. Ibid. 289–91, 311.

repressive and paternalistic forms . . . promoted not only working-class political opposition, but the very process of working-class formation."[30]

Finally, in postulating an open-ended relationship among the four levels of working-class formation, in particular the absence of necessary stages or a natural progression from one level to the next, both Katznelson and Kocka disavow the teleology of Zwahr's model.[31] However, critics of the Katznelson and Zolberg volume have noted a lingering teleology in the revised levels approach. First, capitalist industrial development follows a unilinear path in this schema, and the notion of proletarianization appears as a starting point instead of a historical process to be analyzed. The structure of production is equated with economics, while the state, culture, ideology, gender, law, and religion are viewed as intervening variables rather than constitutive elements of production.[32] Moreover, economic structures figure as the motor of this model in that human agency and collective action are viewed as mere responses to material and social circumstances. Kocka, for example, points to the ways in which "the opportunities or risks for . . . [wage] workers are determined by markets and market changes. . . . Their work is determined by those who possess all this in the form of capital and who, on this basis, employ and direct them."[33] Politics and the activities of human actors are displaced to levels three and four, and their importance in shaping economic or social structures is neglected.[34] Despite its firm rejection of teleology, Kocka's narrative conveys a strong sense of a progressive development toward class, one that is marked by the emergence of labor unions in the 1860s and the founding of the Social Democratic Party (SPD) in 1875.[35]

Also problematic is Kocka's view that class formation advances when "non-class" lines of differentiation—ethnicity, nationality, religion, and gender—which run "next to, over, under or across class divisions," are relatively weak, while the relative strengthening of these "non-class" differentia-

---

30. Mary Nolan, "Economic Crisis, State Policy, and Working-Class Formation in Germany, 1870–1900," in Katznelson and Zolberg, *Working-Class Formation,* 360–61.

31. Kocka, *Lohnarbeit und Klassenbildung,* 27–29; Kocka, "Problems of Working-Class Formation," 283; and Katznelson, "Working-Class Formation," 17.

32. Margaret R. Somers, "Workers of the World, Compare!" *Contemporary Sociology* 18 (May 1989): 328–29; Joyce, "In Pursuit of Class," 172; and Michael Sonenscher's review of *Working-Class Formation* in *Social History* 13 (October 1988): 386. See also John Breuilly, "The Making of the German Working Class," *Archiv für Sozialgeschichte* 27 (1987): 546, 550, in which he reviews Kocka's *Lohnarbeit und Klassenbildung.*

33. Kocka, "Problems of Working-Class Formation," 281–82; see also Somers's astute observations on this point in "Workers of the World," 328.

34. Somers, "Workers of the World," 328–29. Sonenscher refers to the analysis of politics in the essay collection as a study of "politics with much of the politics left out." See his review in *Social History* 13 (October 1988): 387.

35. Kocka, "Problems of Working-Class Formation," 349. In his *Weder Stand noch Klasse,* Kocka refers to the "Voranschreiten der Klassenbildung," 162.

tions points to a process of class devolution.[36] In establishing dichotomies and oppositions between these various lines of social differentiation, he misses the contiguity of these differences in the formation of complex social identities. The implication of his argument is that working-class formation necessitates the relative weakening of other forms of identification. Again, this analysis of working-class formation presents a striking contrast to the literature on gender and middle-class formation, including Kocka's own observations on the German *Bürgertum*, which suggest that sexual difference and its explicit articulation were constitutive factors thereof.[37] Thus, however salutary the "shift from teleological to analytical" in these revised models of class formation, the relationships among the various levels of class, and between "non-class" and "class" distinctions, remain indefinite in Katznelson's and Kocka's models, a situation that both authors hope to remedy by emphasizing the need for "empirical research." My historical case study of the relationships between gender and class among textile workers in Wilhelmine and Weimar Germany suggests, however, that the attempt to find a place for gender and women in this model of class formation disarranges teleologies, blurs boundaries between levels, or breaks apart the model altogether.

The history of the factory workplace, unions, and strikes in the textile industry of the Rhineland and Westphalia is rife with conflicts of gender and class. Gender was at the heart of the transition from home weaving and spinning to mechanized mills, as revealed in the dramatic campaigns of weavers across the Rhineland against "feminization" (*Verweiblichung*) and "displacement" (*Verdrängung*) during the 1880s and 1890s. The first Social Democratic and Catholic textile unions were founded under the shadow of this perceived social dislocation. Despite their divergent ideological traditions, the two organizations shared perceptions of the changing world of industrial relations, of feminization and male displacement. Even if these perceptions and experiences were mediated differently—one in the language of class, and the other in the language of estate and religion—both were influenced primarily by gender, specifically by the male experience of industrialization. Gender remained a point of contention and conflict as the textile industry became the largest factory employer of women and as the two textile unions organized the largest female contingents within the Socialist and Christian union confederations.

---

36. Kocka, *Lohnarbeit und Klassenbildung,* 29. I am using the term "non-class" for Kocka's term "nicht klassenmässige Trennungslinien." Kocka makes the same argument more forcefully in his *Weder Stand noch Klasse,* 38–39.

37. Jürgen Kocka, foreword to Frevert, *Bürgerinnen und Bürger,* 9. In his estimation, "There are many indications that, in addition to the class differences between the owners of the means of production and wage workers, sexual difference is one of the constitutive elements of the structural inequality of bourgeois society."

The starting point of my study is the emergence after 1890 of Social Democratic workers' organizations that defined themselves in terms of "class" against employers and the state. The Deutscher Textilarbeiterverband (German Textile Workers' Union, or DTAV) formed a part of that collective self-definition through its membership in the confederation of "free" trade unions and its close ties to the Social Democratic Party. I would argue that class, as the primary political identity postulated among German workers, had a singular kind of discursive power in Germany between 1890 and 1930, not least because of the predominance of the SPD and its unions among German workers. Class as political rhetoric permeated the discourses of Social Democracy, Catholicism, and liberal Protestant social-reform efforts and echoed from the outposts of rural union locals to provincial and national parliaments. Even those who opposed the self-conscious "working class" embraced its vocabulary in articulating that opposition.

The definition of class in terms of gender, indeed, the fragmentation of class by gender, is evident throughout the history of the DTAV, from its formation during the 1890s to turning points in the early twentieth century when "class" had to be reconstituted: during World War I, the revolution of 1918, and the demobilization of 1918–19; during the crisis of inflation and unemployment of 1923–24, and again during the final years of the Weimar Republic. One side of this story is the articulation of male class identities, particularly in times of crisis, when men, threatened with unemployment or wage cuts, explained social dislocation in terms of female competition. Waves of "proletarian anti-feminism" prompted weavers' strikes against the hiring of female "wage cutters" during the 1880s and 1890s and accompanied government campaigns against female "double earners" to secure jobs for men during the acute crises of demobilization, inflation, and depression of the Weimar Republic.[38] The other side of the story—the ways in which women confronted and eventually (after World War I) appropriated the rhetoric of class—shows that the boundaries of class were seldom fixed, that class formations and the exclusions on which they were based were continually contested and transformed. Although this particular story uncovers women who engaged and challenged the union bureaucracy, it is important to emphasize two points: class had meaning for women who remained aloof from the organized labor movement, and gender is central to the history of class, even where women do not enter traditional "male" political arenas. The active presence of women in

38. "Proletarian anti-feminism" is a term from Werner Thönnessen, *Frauenemanzipation: Politik und Literatur der deutschen Sozialdemokratie zur Frauenbewegung, 1863–1933* (Frankfurt, 1969), 5–7, 84, 147. See also Mary Nolan's case study "Proletarischer Anti-Feminismus, dargestellt am Beispiel der SPD-Ortsgruppe Düsseldorf, 1890–1914," in *Frauen und Wissenschaft: Beiträge zur Berliner Sommeruniversität* (Berlin, 1976), 356–77.

the German Textile Workers' Union only makes this story of contested boundaries and meanings more compelling.

The first task in analyzing the role of gender in the economic formation of the German working class (level one) is to determine the quantitative and qualitative participation of women in the process of production, to explore the changing contours of the female work force between 1880 and 1930, and to ask how the steady expansion of the female labor market might have influenced the relationships between men and women in the process of class formation.[39] Second, it is necessary to confront the texts and subtexts of labor historiography regarding women's work. The fact that women occupied a central place in the ranks of the first industrial workers across Europe raises questions about why women workers who appear in the history of factories and workshops (at level one) are invisible in histories of the labor movement and collective action (levels three and four).[40]

Overcoming this invisibility in German labor history requires close attention to the gendered narratives of labor movement sources and to their uncritical assimilation by historians. German labor history has accepted and reproduced a working-class ideal type, one that filled the pages of the union press and shaped the union's public representation and appeal. This ideal type was male and Protestant; his identification with job or craft—a prerequisite for the development of class consciousness—was based on skill acquired through formal apprenticeship training, relatively well-paid employment in an economically vital and highly productive industry, and long-term job stability. Implicit in the construction of this male ideal type was its opposite, the typical female factory worker: unskilled, "willig und billig" (submissive and cheap), and employed on a temporary or irregular basis. The canon of German labor history implies that women workers failed to appear at levels three or four because of the ways in which they participated in production: their youth, lack of formal

39. It is important to analyze the entry of women into new industries as well as the "feminization" of already established industrial sectors. Important studies of sexual segregation in the German industrial labor market include Stefan Bajohr, *Die Hälfte der Fabrik: Geschichte der Frauenarbeit in Deutschland, 1914 bis 1945* (Marburg, 1979); Walter Müller, Angelika Willms, and Johann Handl, eds., *Strukturwandel der Frauenarbeit, 1880–1980* (Frankfurt, 1983); and R. Stockmann, "Gewerbliche Frauenarbeit in Deutschland, 1875–1980," *Geschichte und Gesellschaft* 11 (1985): 447–75.

40. The highly politicized silk weavers of Lyon, for example, were some 70-percent female. See Robert J. Bezucha, *The Lyon Uprising of 1834: Social and Political Conflict in the Early July Monarchy* (Cambridge, Mass., 1974); Strumingher, *Women and the Making of the Working Class;* and Ivy Pinchbeck, *Women Workers and the Industrial Revolution, 1750–1850,* 3d ed. (London, 1981). On the invisibility of women at levels three and four, see Alexander, "Women, Class, and Sexual Differences"; Dorothy Thompson, "Women and Nineteenth Century Radical Politics: A Lost Dimension," in *The Rights and Wrongs of Women,* ed. Juliet Mitchell and Ann Oakley (Harmondsworth, Eng., 1976), 112–38; Taylor, *Eve and the New Jerusalem;* Joan Scott, "Women in *The Making of the English Working Class*," in Scott, *Gender and the Politics of History,* 68–90.

skill training, and highly fluctuating work patterns precluded the formation of work identities.[41] German labor historiography is characterized by two underlying and contradictory assumptions regarding the relationship between production and class formation. First, the structure of production has a pivotal role in shaping the ways in which male workers viewed or related to their work and formed work identities.[42] At the heart of this relationship between worker and work was the possession of skill—real or mythologized—and the claim to comprehend the labor process as a whole or to assert some measure of control over that process. Political or class consciousness originated in the identities that workers formed in the workplace, in particular in their struggles at the point of production. The second contradictory assumption is that women's work identities, unlike men's, were not shaped primarily by their experience in, and relationship to, production. Marriage and motherhood, not the ten to twelve hours spent on the shop floor, are viewed as constitutive of women's work identities and political behavior.[43]

This view has been reinforced by a "new orthodoxy" in feminist history that has also sought to explain working women's identities and political activities primarily in terms of family values, thus effectively denying the authenticity of women's work experience. While feminist historians have dissolved the boundaries between the private and the public (or political) by uncovering the political fabric of the "private sphere," of consumption, reproduction, and neighborhood networks, some appear to have concluded that "the private" is

---

41. Leading German social historians, such as Ritter and Tenfelde, claim that these attributes of female employment made the presence of large numbers of women in an industry "organisationserschwerend" (detrimental to unionization). See their essay "Der Durchbruch der Freien Gewerkschaften Deutschlands zur Massenbewegung im letzten Viertel des 19. Jahrhunderts," in *Vom Sozialistengesetz zur Mitbestimmung: Zum 100. Geburtstag von Hans Böckler* , ed. Heinz O. Vetter (Cologne, 1975), 101–2. See also Karl Ditt, *Industrialisierung, Arbeiterschaft und Arbeiterbewegung in Bielefeld, 1850–1914* (Dortmund, 1982), 236, who makes a similar argument. Brian Peterson elaborates the reasons why working-class women were unlikely to become politically active, even during the politically charged Weimar period. In his view, young working-class women were apolitical "because of the primacy of the personal," and older women because of the "sheer weight of the double burden of maintaining a household and working." See Brian Peterson, "The Politics of Working-Class Women in the Weimar Republic," *Central European History* 9 (1977): 99. Interestingly, these claims have scarcely been challenged since they were made.

42. "Work identity" is not a term that the nineteenth- or twentieth-century labor movement actually used. I employ it to denote *Berufsinteresse* or *Berufsidentität,* which figures in union sources as a prerequisite to union membership. See, for example, Zentralverband Christlicher Textilarbeiter Deutschlands (hereafter ZCTD), "Warum braucht die Frau die Erziehung zur Gewerbetätigkeit?" *Textilarbeiterzeitung* 12 (22 January 1910): 10. The term is also implicit in more recent German labor historiography.

43. See, for example, Nolan, "Economic Crisis," 377.

the main or the only female political arena.[44] This tendency to confine women workers behind the lines of home and family, to read their activities in the arenas of factory, unions, and strikes as originating in, and oriented primarily toward, the family, underscores the tacit assumptions of German labor historiography that production was mainly a male arena and that neither gender nor women had a significant role in the vibrant political world of the German working classes.[45]

A close examination of textile personnel records challenges the image of the female mill employees as temporary, uncommitted workers. An analysis of male and female career patterns demonstrates that job stability in the textile industry was not a preserve of male workers, nor was instability inherently female. In fact, the yearly turnover rates for male textile workers were higher or nearly identical to those for women and men, and women had similar rates of stability and turnover when they worked in the same shops (weaving, spinning) at a similar level of skill.[46] Women's work patterns did differ from those of men in one important respect: the intersections of "family time"

---

44. Eleanor Gordon refers to this "new orthodoxy" in her article "Women, Work and Collective Action: Dundee Jute Workers, 1870–1906," *Journal of Social History* 20 (1987): 27–28, 44. On the broader theme of the family or the private sphere as a locus of politics, see "Politics and Culture in Women's History: A Symposium," *Feminist Studies* 6 (Spring 1980): 26–63. For a more specific examination of this theme for the working-class family, see Ellen Ross, "Fierce Questions and Taunts: Married Life in Working Class London, 1870–1914," *Feminist Studies* 8 (Fall 1982): 575–602; Temma Kaplan, "Female Consciousness and Collective Action: The Case of Barcelona, 1910–1918," in *Feminist Theory: A Critique of Ideology* , ed. Nannerl O. Keohane, Michelle Z. Rosaldo, and Barbara C. Gelpi (Chicago, 1982), 55–76.

45. Some of the classic works in women's history, such as Joan W. Scott and Louise A. Tilly, *Women, Work, and Family* (New York, 1978); Louise Tilly, "The Family Wage Economy of a French Textile City: Roubaix, 1872–1906," *Journal of Family History* 4 (1979): 381–93; and Alice Kessler-Harris, *Out to Work: A History of Wage-Earning Women in the United States* (New York, 1982), analyze women's participation in the waged labor force as part of "family strategies" or point to the importance of the family in shaping women's union behavior. Additional studies that propose interesting ways of thinking about this problem include Robyn Dasey, "Women's Work and the Family: Women Garment Workers in Berlin and Hamburg before the First World War," in *The German Family: Essays on the Social History of the Family in Nineteenth- and Twentieth-Century Germany,* ed. Richard J. Evans and W. R. Lee (London, 1981), 221–55; and Jean H. Quataert, "Teamwork in Saxon Homeweaving Families in the Nineteenth Century: A Preliminary Investigation into the Issue of Gender Work Roles," in *German Women in the Eighteenth and Nineteenth Centuries: A Social and Literary History,* ed. Ruth-Ellen B. Joeres and Mary Jo Maynes (Bloomington, 1986), 3–23.

46. The personnel records include payroll or wage books and *Arbeiterstammrollen,* in which employers registered vital information on each worker, from eight textile mills in the Rhineland and Westphalia. My total valid sample at present includes approximately 3,600 workers. See Kathleen Canning, "Class, Gender, and Working-Class Politics: The Case of the German Textile Industry, 1890–1933" (Ph.D. diss., Johns Hopkins University, 1988), chap. 3, "The Textile Workforce: Career Patterns and Work Identities."

(particularly childbirth) and "industrial time" necessitated more frequent interruptions of their employment.[47] Contrary to common assumption, female textile workers were more likely to take a temporary leave from work upon marriage or the birth of a first or second child than to give up their jobs entirely. As the numbers of married women workers employed in textile factories increased steadily between 1882 and 1914, married women and single mothers established their own rhythms of work, interrupting employment to give birth, returning to work for a few months, leaving work again to care for a sick child or relative, and returning once again when the family situation permitted. As early as 1874, the factory inspector in one textile town noted that "women who are responsible for a household come to work later and leave work earlier [than the others]. When someone in the family is ill, they do not come to work at all. There is a general unspoken agreement by which married women are treated with lenience. Their situation is therefore a relatively favorable one."[48]

Records from the Mechanische Weberei in Bielefeld confirm that women commonly returned to the mill after childbirth: more than one-third of the women who left their jobs because of pregnancy returned to work within a few months after giving birth.[49] The profile of one woman who undoubtedly belonged to the *Stammarbeiterschaft*, or "core" of the textile work force, illustrates how women workers negotiated the demands of marriage, motherhood, and factory employment. Sofia Budde, weaver, worked at the Weberei for a total of twenty-nine years between 1890 and 1925. Hired as a weaver in 1890 at the age of fourteen, she left her job for the first time in August 1894 because of pregnancy. She returned to the mill two months later, presumably after the birth of her first child, and listed her new (married) name as Sofia Schneider. Two years later, she took a seven-month leave, again because of pregnancy. When Sofia returned to her loom in July 1897, she was twenty-one and the mother of two small children. She stayed on the job until September 1905, when she interrupted her employment for nine months. This time, the reason for her departure was listed as "auf Wunsch" (at her own request), but in view of her lengthy absence, it is likely that she gave birth to another child during these months. Schneider returned to the Weberei in May 1906 and worked the next eleven years without interruption. Her last absence, between 1917 and 1921, was probably necessitated by the disruptions of textile production or changes in her family situation during and after the war. She returned to work again in

47. Tamara Hareven, *Family Time and Industrial Time: The Relationship between the Family and Work in a New England Industrial Community* (Cambridge, 1982).

48. Hauptstaatsarchiv Düsseldorf (hereafter HStAD), Landratsamt Mönchen-Gladbach 710, Bericht des Gewerbeaufsichtsbeamten Mönchen-Gladbachs (14 December 1874), 104–5.

49. Stadtarchiv Bielefeld, Personalbücher der Mechanischen Weberei, 28/1, 29/1. This calculation was made for the entire period covered by the *Arbeiterstammrollen*. 1865–1924.

1921 and departed from the Mechanische Weberei for the last time in 1925 at the age of forty-nine.[50]

The pattern of Sofia Schneider's factory career, as well as the general patterns outlined above, points to the ways in which women continually mediated the demands of family time and industrial time, shaping their own working lives as they interacted with structures (labor markets) and processes (industrial growth, feminization). At the same time, mill owners sanctioned and facilitated these flexible rhythms of work. On the one hand, employers were dependent on married women workers, especially during periods of rapid industrial growth and acute labor shortages, which occurred frequently between 1890 and 1914. On the other hand, these gender-specific work patterns served as one explanation for women's lower wages and subordinate status as a "secondary" work force. These career patterns underscore the importance of expanding definitions of job stability to include those who remained "core workers" despite interruptions in their employment. My conclusion that many women workers were long-term and loyal employees offers no substantive evidence of the kinds of work identities they might have formed, but it does argue against the claim that the brevity of the average female factory career prevented women from developing work identities at all.

Finally, an analysis of level one, or economic formation, should emphasize the role of noneconomic factors, ideological conceptions of gender roles and proper work for men and women, in shaping the structure of textile production—the deployment of textile machinery, the division of labor, and definitions of skill, work time, and wages—especially as its female work force expanded between 1890 and 1914. The social reformers, factory inspectors, entrepreneurs, and labor movement activists who participated in the intensive debates about female factory labor during this period redefined the sexual division of labor as they sought to resolve the growing discrepancy between the continued expansion of the female work force and traditional notions about the character of the sexes. Legislators and factory inspectors, for example, legitimated women's factory employment while attempting to contain it within strict boundaries. They sought to preserve a delicate balance between women's work and family duties, to regulate the work world in order to preserve the family, as the restrictions on women's work time enacted in 1891 and again in 1908 make clear.[51] Textile employers, for their part, adhered to the prevalent norms of

---

50. Stadtarchiv Bielefeld, Personalbücher der Mechanischen Weberei, 28/1, 29/1.

51. The labor code of 1891 excluded women from night work, limited women's regular workday to eleven hours, and extended pregnancy leave to four weeks. It also curtailed their hours on Saturdays and allowed women with families to leave work one half hour early at lunchtime in order to give them adequate time to shop, cook, and clean; HStAD, *Jahresberichte der Königlich Preussischen Gewerberäte* (1892), 328–30 (hereafter HStAD, *Jahresberichte*); and Reichsamt des Innern, *Die Arbeitszeit der Fabrikarbeiterinnen, nach Berichten der Gewerbeaufsichtsbeamten*

women's work in creating a female work force on which their industry was dependent but which was "secondary" in terms of wages and skill. At the same time, however, they challenged prevailing notions of sexual difference by actively recruiting married women workers and by rewarding them for long-term employment. Mill owners responded to the moral outcry against female factory labor with an array of paternalist "welfare" measures, such as cooking, sewing, and housekeeping classes, factory kindergartens, and company dormitories, measures that aimed to import the home into the factory, to make factory work compatible with the ideology of domesticity.

Male labor leaders and union members inserted their own fears of social and sexual disorder, of the dissolution of family, femininity, and masculinity, into their campaigns for work-time reductions and wage increases. Their visions of domesticity were expressed in the image and rhetoric of the male breadwinner that marked these campaigns.[52] Even if most women workers took jobs out of economic necessity, many of them spurned the ideology of women's work that sought to restrict wage labor in favor of motherhood and housework. They came face-to-face with this ideology each time they transgressed gender boundaries: when they accepted jobs in "men's shops" or launched wildcat strikes without the support of male colleagues or union leaders. Women workers upheld their own visions of domesticity as they fought to imprint the factory regime with their needs as mothers and wives, raising frequent demands for longer lunch breaks, shorter work days, and better health and safety protection. Their visions often collided with those of male workers and employers: women resisted the representation of woman worker as mother, for example, when it was invoked to justify the discrepancy between male and female wages.

This brief explication of the ideological underpinnings of the structure of production illustrates the difficulty in extricating "economic formation" from politics, from conflicts between state and industry, mill owners and workers, women and men. Ultimately, it casts doubt on the efficacy of the levels approach and points to the fragility or artificiality of the divisions among the various levels.

Level two, or the social formation of class, refers to webs of social relations that formed around common interests and experiences at work and in the realms of family and residential community. In each case, social class forma-

---

(Berlin, 1905). In 1908, the state again amended the industrial labor code, restricting women's work day to ten hours maximum during the first five days of the week and to eight hours on Saturday; HStAD, *Jahresberichte* (1910), 420.

52. One example is in DTAV, "Wann werden wir den freien Sonnabendnachmittag haben?" *Der Textilarbeiter* 25, no. 34 (15 August 1913): 266–67. The Social Democratic Textile Workers' Union formulated its arguments in favor of Saturday restrictions in terms of women's domestic responsibilities.

tion acts as a site of social interaction, of communication about the ways in which class is experienced in its economic and social dimensions; it is a site where common interests are identified, if not yet acted on. Zwahr defines social class formation in terms of the increasingly complex networks of familial, marital, social, and communal ties that bound workers together within occupational groups as well as across traditional barriers of skill.[53] Kocka and Katznelson both seem to suggest that common interests arising from shared experiences in the workplace are essential elements of social class formation. Kocka, for example, emphasizes the importance of "a joint socio-economic position" on which "structural presuppositions of common interests" were formed, while Katznelson argues that social class formation was "determined in part by the structure of capitalist development," by workplace social relations and labor markets.[54] Zwahr proposes a different view, one that postulates a more flexible relationship between economic and social formation. His analysis of level one, the sphere of production, considers the diversity of experience and the barriers of skill, wage, and status that had to be overcome in order for class formation to advance. Social formation takes place as those barriers are crossed and different experiences transcended, as workers marry or choose godparents for their children across skill levels, as they congregate in urban neighborhoods, forging a common class identity that is not exclusively determined by production.[55]

The family is central in each of these versions of social class formation, although it figures in several different, often contradictory ways. The family served as an agent of transmission by which one generation passed wage labor status and class consciousness on to the next. Zwahr's notion of a "born proletariat" is illustrative of this point, for it distinguishes between the first generation of workers, who were born into the proletariat, and their fathers, who had been born into artisanal families and had suffered the dislocation and distress of proletarianization. In Leipzig, the "born proletariat" formed the vanguard of the emergent working class; it was the first to embrace Marxism and to establish class-conscious organizations. Thus, in Zwahr's schema, the family is viewed as a locus of transmission of class identity, a site of socialization and politicization.

While Kocka and Katznelson might agree that the family serves to transmit class culture and consciousness, their emphasis on the legendary "separation of home and work" as an essential aspect of class formation raises provocative questions about the enduring importance of family and household in the process. In the historical narratives of modernization, urbanization, and capitalist formation, the "separation of home and work" had political conse-

---

53. See Zwahr, *Zur Konstituierung,* 115–89, esp. 163–89.

54. Katznelson, "Working-Class Formation," 16; Kocka, "Problems of Working-Class Formation," 282.

55. Zwahr, *Zur Konstituierung,* 163–89.

quences in the division it effected between private and public. These narratives displaced politics onto the public realm, stripping family and household of their economic and political significance, of their "socializing and educative functions."[56] They also effaced the relations of power and dominance in families and households and rendered invisible the struggles within them over production, consumption, reproduction, and sexuality. The emphasis on this separation erases the importance of wage labor within many "modern" working-class households, in which women took in sewing, washing and ironing, or provided boarding, lodging, or child care. Furthermore, in making the home/workplace dichotomy an essential and universal marker of class formation, Kocka and Katznelson obscure the specifically gendered meaning of this purported separation "between work and non-work."[57]

Considering the prominence of family, household, and community in these innovative approaches to class formation, it is indeed remarkable that gender and women remain invisible. While Zwahr's focus is the Leipzig metalworking industry, in which only negligible numbers of women worked during the nineteenth century, he also overlooks women in his analysis of families and communities.[58] Women are perplexingly absent in his discussion of the born proletariat, even though they performed the reproductive labor of class formation: marrying working-class men, giving birth to "born proletarians," and nurturing the development of class consciousness in their children as they shaped and passed on class traditions, cultures, and self-definitions. Moreover, many women who were not themselves employed outside the home took an active role not only in the proverbial food riots but also in strikes and other forms of protest that involved members of their families or communities.

The authors of the levels approach to class formation assume that the shared interests of family and community superseded the divisions within them and, similarly, that shared class identities transcended the fissures of gender

---

56. Richard J. Evans, "Politics and the Family: Social Democracy and the Working-Class Family in Theory and Practice," in Evans and Lee, *The German Family*, 256. For examples of this narrative, see Kocka, "Problems of Working-Class Formation," 317–19; *Kocka, Weder Stand noch Klasse*, 16; Kocka, *Arbeitsverhältnisse*, 143, 478, 517; and Katznelson, "Working-Class Formation," 16.

57. Kocka, "Problems of Working-Class Formation," 319. Certainly this difference "became more systematic and pronounced" for male workers, while few working-class women were able to enjoy a sphere of "nonwork." Kocka points out that most wives of workers contributed something to the family income (as servants, washing women, part-time domestic workers, petty traders) yet continues to emphasize the importance of the "separation of home and work" (317–19). Jean Quataert's work, by contrast, underscores the political and economic significance of the household. See in particular Quataert, "Teamwork."

58. The same can be said for Kocka's examination of marriage patterns, in which gender plays an obviously important role. See Jürgen Kocka, "Family and Class Formation: Intergenerational Mobility and Marriage Patterns in Nineteenth-Century Westphalian Towns," *Journal of Social History* 17 (Spring 1984): 411–33.

within family and household and those of ethnicity, religion, and gender within residential communities. The persistence and prevalence of "non-class" distinctions within families and communities raise fundamental questions about social cohesion as the outcome of social class formation: how did the experience of "class" differ between husbands and wives, sons and daughters, between generations within families; between Catholics and Protestants, Poles and Germans, between residents of industrial cities and of rural mill villages? These questions call for a more complex view of family, household, and community that considers the ways in which economic and social class formation are intertwined in these realms, explores the gendered fabric of household and community, and imparts to gender a decisive role in class formation, even where women did not participate in production to the same extent or in the same ways that men did. This is an endeavor that promises to dissolve the divisions between the four levels of class formation.

The third level of class formation as defined by Kocka and Katznelson is also the most elusive. Kocka envisions the development of a common social identity grounded in the awareness or consciousness of a shared socioeconomic position. This social identity encompasses "some degree of internal cohesion and mutual communication, common experiences and dispositions, common fears and aspirations, manifest interests and loyalties, something like a common consciousness as a class—distinguished from the members of other classes."[59] Katznelson's definition of this level in terms of "shared dispositions" is similar. In his schema, shared dispositions are not necessarily "class dispositions"; they can also denote shared understandings of the social system or shared values of justice and goodness. Thus this level has an obvious cultural dimension in that it represents the ways in which "people construct meaning to make their way through the experienced world" or "the cultural configurations within which people act."[60]

The unbound configuration of level three can perhaps be made concrete by analyzing one kind of shared disposition: work identities, or the ways in which men and women related to and located themselves within the sphere of their waged work, a domain that encompassed their machines, the products of their labor, social networks on the shop floor, and even the physical space of the mill. Although work identities are admittedly difficult to measure or document empirically, it is possible to read a variety of sources "against the grain"—factory inspectors' reports, police and newspaper accounts of unrest, personnel records, and female social reformers' observations of mill life—in order to explore the ways in which workers viewed and utilized their jobs, as expressed

---

59. Kocka, "Problems of Working-Class Formation," 282.
60. Katznelson, "Working-Class Formation," 18–19.

both in the rhythms of their mill careers and in their work ethics. Other dimensions of work identities include individual and collective self-definitions, through which workers both resisted and sought accommodation with the factory regime and the dominant ideology of gender roles that underlay it. Central to this inquiry is the assumption that work identities were embedded in, but not determined by, the structure of production. For integral to the concept of work identity is the possibility of agency, which is revealed in the ways in which workers sought to position themselves within, and sometimes to distance themselves from, the constraints of the structure of production.[61] The significance of the workplace in this process of identification does not imply the existence of a firm boundary between shop-floor experience and family or community. Instead, the concept of work identities includes an exploration of the way in which identities were shaped by the continual intersections of family time and industrial time.

Of pivotal importance in imagining how women formed work identities and developed a sense of *Berufsethos* are questions about how they viewed and utilized their jobs and about why women went to work and remained at work in the textile mills. In most cases, it was not an abstract work ethic or loyalty to the loom that drove women (single, married, or widowed) into the factory. Regardless of the pride that textile workers may have found in the products of their labor, most women worked out of dire economic necessity, as did most men.[62] However, the mill job also represented for women with families a complex network of support that extended beyond the monetary value of the wages they earned. The camaraderie and sociability of the shop floor and the solidarity of sharing the experiences of pregnancy, birth, illness, or widowhood were an important part of women's work experience. Observers noted that the gossip and chatter of the shop floor often drew women back to work after marriage or the birth of a child. Strike reports also offer insight into the significance of workplace friendships and loyalties in shaping work cultures.[63]

---

61. Agency, like class and experience, remains a point of contest between social historians who salute the linguistic turn and thus emphasize the ways in which agency was always "discursively constructed," and those who continue to uphold a notion of agency that denotes the actions and interventions of human beings in the making of their own history. On this point, see Scott, "The Evidence of Experience," 777–78, 792–93; Parveen Adams and Jeff Minson, "The 'Subject' of Feminism," in *The Woman in Question: M/f,* ed. Parveen Adams and Elizabeth Cowie (Boston, 1990), 91–93.

62. Factory inspectors undertook an extensive study of married women's factory employment in 1899 that refuted the popular notion that most women worked not for the bare necessities but in order to attain the "extras," such as clothes, tobacco, and alcohol; HStAD, *Jahresberichte* (1899), 509, 513, 604.

63. One social reformer who conducted an academic study of textile workers in a Rhenish textile town pointed out that the female worker went back to the mills after marriage not out of

While most women worked out of economic necessity, those who worked for several years at one job undoubtedly took pride in their work. Minna Wettstein-Adelt, a social reformer who disguised her identity and went to work in a textile mill, offered insights into the work ethic among women weavers: "Many of these girls work enthusiastically, especially those who follow the completion of a whole piece, like those who weave smaller rugs or single fitted curtains. They love their machines, like one loves a loyal dog. They clean them until they shine and decorate them with colorful ribbons, holy cards, and other trinkets that their suitors won for them at last summer's fair."[64] The records of one charitable foundation, the Diergardt Stiftung of Viersen, also reveal that female textile workers expressed their pride in work through factory rituals, especially festive celebrations of employment anniversaries and awards for diligence. The female colleagues of Frau Schmitz, a reeler who received the Diergardt award on her twenty-fifth anniversary on the job, decorated her machine with flowers and ribbons, presented her with the gift of an armchair, and composed songs in her honor.[65] The centrality of the machine in these festive ceremonies offers testimony of the identification of women with their work and pride in the products of their labor.

Work identities can also be viewed as the location of individual and collective self-definition vis-à-vis employers, the state, and male workers. One manifestation of collective identities was the manner and style of workers' dress. Shop-floor "fashions" signified women workers' awareness of their place in the process of production and in the moral regime of the mills. Female weavers reportedly dressed in a prim manner, which may have reflected their sense of belonging to the elite of female workers. Their distinct dress code may also be explained by the presence of large numbers of older, married women in the ranks, who were often portrayed by employers as the custodians of the younger, more unruly women workers. Female spinners, by contrast, usually young and single and considered to be the insolent and unruly force among female textile workers, often dressed in disorderly clothing yet manifested

---

necessity but because she "misse[d] the 'events' in the factory workroom, the company of others, to which she has been accustomed since she was thirteen or fourteen years old"; Marie Bernays, *Auslese und Anpassung der Arbeiterschaft der geschlossenen Grossindustrie: Dargestellt an den Verhältnissen der "Gladbacher Spinnerei und Weberei A. G." zu München-Gladbach im Rheinland* (Leipzig, 1910), 200. Police reports also indicate that women workers launched strikes to express their solidarity with female colleagues who had been fired or penalized; HStAD, Regierung Düsseldorf, no. 24706, no. 24693: "Bericht der Polizeiverwaltung von 26.11.1900"; no. 24704: "Bericht der Polizeiverwaltung von 25.2.1910."

64. Minna Wettstein-Adelt, *3½ Monate Fabrikarbeiterin* (Berlin, 1893), 20.

65. Stadtarchiv Viersen, Diergardt Stiftung III/056, 1904–1912: "Ehrungen und Belohnungen für Fabrikarbeiter aus der zu Mönchengladbach bestehenden Diergardt Stiftung, 1904–1912": Brief von C. H. Goeters an den Bürgermeister Stern von Viersen (4 April 1905).

their own chic style.[66] It is likely that the high temperatures and dampness of the spinning shops had something to do with female spinners' "disorderly" dress. But the stylish character of that disorder may also have expressed a rebellion against the moral claims of the factory regime. The clothing that female spinners and weavers wore expressed their sense of belonging to a class of factory workers and distinguished them from other social classes.

A story from 1905 of one young woman who inadvertently violated the dress code illustrates this point: the young woman was Danish, and according to her country's custom, she wore a hat on the way to and from work and blouses with long sleeves while at work, both emblems of "respectability" among German middle-class girls. Her appearance caused a sensation on the streets and in the mill, distracted several female workers from their jobs, and provoked demands from several of them that she remove the hat or leave the workplace. The *Obermeister* averted a spontaneous walkout by promptly firing the young woman.[67] While enforcing their own rigid, class-based code of dress in the mills, female textile workers on Sundays frequently donned their prettiest dresses and did not disdain to wear hats, gloves, and jewelry or to carry parasols. The discrepant dress codes of workdays and holidays underscore the significance of shop-floor "fashion" in female work culture and in the formation of social class identity.

Women workers also developed their own moral code in response to employers' attempts to regulate morality and virtue through institutions of tutelage. A central component of workplace culture, this moral code allowed for both accommodation and resistance to the factory regime. Female mill workers expressed and enforced their own sexual mores at work, especially when they worked in predominantly female shops. Beyond the frankness about sexual experiences and the acceptance of out-of-wedlock pregnancies, recounted by middle-class observers, women workers also delimited their space in the mill by sexual horseplay, including the initiation of newcomers in sexual games and gestures. Wettstein-Adelt, for example, described her shock at the obscene behavior of her female coworkers, one of whom frequently expressed anger or displeasure by lifting her skirts and pulling down her underwear.[68]

Women workers also asserted and defended their own definitions of sexuality in their individual and collective protest against rape or molestation by managers and supervisors, apparently a common enough feature of shop-floor

---

66. Marie Bernays, "Berufsschicksale moderner Industriearbeiter," part 2, *Die Frau* 18 (December 1910): 212–15.

67. DTAV, *Der Textilarbeiter* 17, no. 41 (13 October 1905), local report from Mönchen-Gladbach.

68. Wettstein-Adelt, *3½ Monate,* 31. Alf Lüdtke's work on *Eigensinn* has influenced my reading of my sources on dress code and sexuality. See in particular his essay "Organizational Order."

life. This resistance took various forms, ranging from reporting the rape to the factory inspector or the union to collecting stories and passing the word through the mill in an attempt to protect female colleagues from subsequent assaults. Women frequently engaged in collective action to enforce and defend their own code of morality. In 1905, male and female workers in a Bocholt mill went on strike to demand the firing of an overseer who had raped several female employees.[69] The issue of rape led to a turbulent confrontation in the government district of Düsseldorf in 1902 when an angry crowd of both male and female workers assembled in front of the home of a master weaver who had assaulted a female subordinate. One worker was killed in the resulting melee, and four others received jail sentences.[70]

My analysis of work identities focuses on the multiple meanings that women and men derived from their experiences of work. It coincides in many respects with Katznelson's analysis of cultural formation as "shared dispositions" or Kocka's notion of common fears, aspirations, interests, and loyalties. But I place gender at the center of my analysis of cultural class formation in order to illustrate that these meanings and identities were far more complex than a "consciousness of a shared socio-economic position."[71] The world behind the mill gate was just as likely to be rent apart by gender divisions as it was to be welded together by class identification. My critique posits a flexible and historically specific notion of class, one that locates "cultural" identities of class not only in conflicts about wages or work time but also in confrontations about pride and honor, gossip and respectability, bodies and sexuality. It inserts into level three of the model of class formation experiences and meanings that had no necessary consequences for level four, the formation of workers into a political class. Indeed, labor leaders sought to expunge many of the experiences analyzed here from the realm of organized labor politics.

The culmination of the process of class formation in each of the models discussed here is the political expression of a collective class identity (level four). Zwahr views political class formation as the development of a class-conscious proletariat that has embraced a specific ideology, that of scientific Marxism, while Katznelson and Kocka focus on the organizational form rather than on its ideological content. A political class is one that is "organized and that act[s] through movements and organizations to affect society and the position of the class within it" or one that "may act collectively and perhaps

---

69. ZCTD, *Der christliche Textilarbeiter* 17, no. 27 (8 July 1905), local report from Bocholt. The workers also raised the demand for higher wages in this strike. See also Wettstein-Adelt's accounts of sexual harassment in textile mills in *3½ Monate,* 28–29.

70. For additional reports of sexual abuse and workers' demands to fire perpetrators, see HStAD, *Jahresberichte* (1902), 327; (1905), 265; (1912), 367–68.

71. Kocka, "Problems of Working-Class Formation," 282.

organize in conflict with other classes and perhaps the state."[72] Introducing gender into the level of political class formation requires, first, a critical engagement with the assumptions of German labor history regarding women workers' proclivity (or lack thereof) toward political activism. This inquiry is best located in a largely (but by no means exclusively) "female sphere" of industry, such as textiles, where significant numbers of women worked, joined unions, and went on strike. In examining the encounters between women and the organized labor movement, I intend not only to document but also to explain the varying patterns of union membership and the divergent goals of male and female activists. I prefer to resist easy references to women's "nature" and seek instead to uncover the ways in which the politics of class might have inhibited the participation of women in the organized labor movement.

Female activists in the textile unions, reporting on their recruiting efforts among women workers, often recounted the difficulties in winning women's loyalties to the union. Many women, torn between the double burdens of work and care of family and household, were unable to find the time to devote to union meetings or organizing campaigns, as is poignantly illustrated by women workers' accounts in *Mein Arbeitstag—mein Wochenende* (My working day— my weekend), published by the DTAV in 1930.[73] Others could not afford the expense of dues, even if they were less expensive for women. Still others were constrained by familial authority structures, by the sanctions of fathers or husbands against political engagement on the part of their daughters or wives. A close reading of union newspapers and conference minutes reveals another barrier to women's participation in, or long-term commitment to, union politics: the "anti-feminist" sentiment of many male unionists, expressed occasionally in strikes against the hiring of female weavers, in recurrent resistance to the demand for equal pay for equal work, and in the persistent reluctance of union functionaries to grant women a permanent place in the union bureaucracy.[74] This "anti-feminism," juxtaposed with the DTAV's claim to represent

---

72. Katznelson, "Working-Class Formation," 20; and Kocka, "Problems of Working-Class Formation," 283.

73. DTAV, *Mein Arbeitstag—mein Wochenende* (Berlin, 1930). A new edition has recently been published with an excellent introduction by Alf Lüdtke: *Mein Arbeitstag—mein Wochenende: Arbeiterinnen berichten von ihrem Alltag, 1928* (Hamburg, 1991).

74. Thönnessen, *Frauenemanzipation;* Nolan, "Proletarischer Anti-Feminismus." Martha Hoppe became the first paid female union secretary in 1908, but she was consistently denied the right to vote in the union's executive committee; DTAV, *Protokoll der 9. ordentlichen Generalversammlung, abgehalten 1908 in Leipzig,* 9. Union leaders continued to oppose integration of women into all levels of union administration until 1927, when Elsa Niwiera became director of the Women's Bureau and a full-fledged member of the executive with the right to vote on all union affairs. See DTAV, *Protokoll des 14. Verbandstages, abgehalten 1921 in Breslau,* 90–91, 146, 215–18, 259–60; DTAV, *Protokoll des 16. Verbandstages, abgehalten 1927 in Hamburg,* 53, 108, 219; DTAV, *Jahrbuch 1927* (Berlin, 1928), 194–95.

all textile workers, made the union an intensely contradictory arena for the unorganized women workers, whom the union sought to recruit, and for the committed female union activists, who confronted this sentiment at every level of the union bureaucracy. On the one hand, the DTAV adhered to the SPD's view of waged work as an essential prerequisite of women's emancipation and frequently defended the right of women to paid employment on these grounds.[75] On the other hand, in both its internal discourse and its appeal to the public, the union created and upheld an image of the working woman as a wage cutter or strikebreaker, a ruthless competitor, a volatile, unreliable ally, or a passive, apathetic victim of capitalist exploitation. Female activists pointed to the powerful effects of this negative imagery on the political behavior of women workers, many of whom responded to these representations by remaining aloof from the organized labor movement or by articulating their demands in other forms, such as spontaneous strikes.[76]

Despite the many possible reasons why women workers may not have been inclined to embrace a vocabulary of class or to express their concerns by participating in "class-conscious" organizations or actions, membership statistics reveal that significant numbers of women workers surmounted familial and social barriers and joined the DTAV. In 1897, a few years after the DTAV's first congress, approximately 2,400 women comprised a mere 11 percent of its membership. During the next decade, the union experienced a process of feminization that paralleled the transformation of the textile work force, and by 1907, women represented 37 percent of DTAV rank and file. As the union continued to grow before World War I, this figure remained relatively constant (see graph). Between 1913 and 1919, female membership more than tripled as women came to dominate the union during the war. It increased again dramatically between 1919 and 1923, when nearly one-half million women belonged to the DTAV.[77] As the table illustrates, by 1925 the unionization rate for female textile workers had surpassed that of men: 30 percent of female textile workers, compared to 24.5 percent of their male colleagues, belonged to the DTAV. Furthermore, women went out on strike in numbers that equaled, and during the years 1919 to 1924 even exceeded, those of male textile workers.[78] What implications do these numbers have for analyzing the role of gender in

75. Thönnessen, *Frauenemanzipation*, 41–48; on the diverging views of women's emancipation between the "Lassalleans" and "Eisenachers" within the early SPD, see 13–16, 32–34.

76. DTAV, *Protokoll der 10. Generalversammlung, abgehalten 1910 in Berlin*, 237, 241; DTAV, *Protokoll der 12. Generalversammlung, abgehalten 1914 in Dresden*, 113. Also see DTAV, "Warum sind die Frauen so schwer für die Gewerkschaft zu gewinnen?" *Der Textilarbeiter* 20, no. 42 (16 October 1908); and "Die Meinung einer Kollegin zur Arbeiterinnenfrage," *Der Textilarbeiter* 22, no. 36 (9 September 1910): 283.

77. DTAV, *Jahrbuch 1927*, 147.

78. Canning, "Class, Gender, and Working-Class Politics," chap. 6, 357–65.

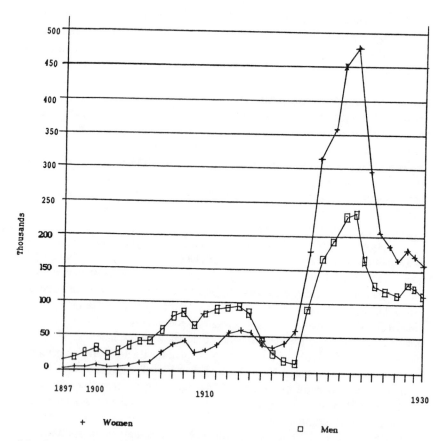

Membership: Socialist Textile Union. Male and female workers, 1897–1930. Data from DTAV, *Jahrbuch 1927,* 147; *Jahrbuch 1932,* 65.

the process of political class formation? Do they signify or attest to the acquisition of "class identities" on the part of female union members and strikers? If so, how did the experiences, identities, and languages of class differ between men and women, and in what ways did the divergence between them fracture the unity of the "organized working class"? In what sense can the moments of solidarity be related to the moments of conflicting interests between men and women? How did women position themselves within this class? Did they make their own meanings, formulate their own agendas, stake a claim to their own space within the labor movement?

Women emerged in the DTAV with their own political vision only after 1908, when the union appointed Martha Hoppe as its first female secretary and

TABLE 1. Percentage of Unionized Textile Workers (German Empire)

	1895	1907	1925
Male Employees in Textile Industry	517,230	529,008	514,858
Male Members in Textile Unions/Percentage of Those Employed			
DTV (Social Democratic)	n.a.	74,883	126,172
		(14.2%)	(24.5%)
ZCTD (Christian)	n.a.	29,288	32,986
		(5.5%)	(6.4%)
Total (both unions)	n.a.	104,171	159,158
		(19.7%)	(30.9%)
Female Employees in Textile Industry	427,961	528,235	681,262
Female Members in Textile Unions/Percentage of Those Employed			
DTV (Social Democratic)	n.a.	43,250	204,504
		(8.2%)	(30.0%)
ZCTD (Christian)	n.a.	12,628	45,585
		(2.4%)	(6.7%)
Total (both unions)	n.a.	55,878	250,089
		(10.6%)	(36.7%)

Sources: DTAV, *Jahrbuch 1927* (Berlin, 1928): 147; ZCTD, *Jahrbuch 1932* (Düsseldorf, 1932): 65; Wilhelm Böhmert, "Wandlungen der deutschen Volkswirtschaft 1882–1907: Ergebnisse der Berufs- und Betriebszählungen," *Arbeiterfreund* 48 (1910): 24–25, 136, and George Neuhaus, "Die berufliche und soziale Gliederung im Zeitalter des Kapitalismus," *Grundriß der Sozialökonomik* 9: 399, 424–25.

officially addressed the "woman question" at its congress that year.[79] Early on, female activists in the union sought to expose the disparity between the DTAV's official program and the practice of the male rank and file in the everyday life of the union. The activities of female unionists—who worked under Hoppe's leadership to fulfill the demands of women workers for a more equitable wage, a shorter workday, expanded health and safety protection, and equal representation in the union bureaucracy and press—fueled the anti-feminist sentiments of male members and union leaders. Indeed, the most significant encounters between male and female union activists took place on the terrain of imagery and rhetoric as each group upheld its own vision of sexual difference and inscribed it with distinct political meanings.

At the center of these conflicts about equality and sexual difference in the DTAV was the contested notion of *weibliche Eigenart,* or the "particularity" of the female sex. In one sense, this term embodies the profound ambivalence of

---

79. DTAV, *Protokoll der 9. Generalversammlung 1908,* 9, 209; Canning, "Class, Gender, and Working-Class Politics," 329–32. The year 1908 also represents a turning point in the relationship between women and men in the DTAV because of the repeal of the Prussian Law of Association, which had impeded women's participation in associations that could be viewed as "political."

party and union regarding the relevance of sexual difference for the politics of class. For example, female SPD leaders and functionaries could assert at one moment that "proletarian men" and "proletarian women" had fundamentally "the same interests" and that the Social Democratic struggle sought to join "all of the exploited, regardless of sex."[80] In the next moment, however, they recognized women's distinct experiences at work, the particularity of the double burden of waged work and housework or child rearing, and women's political inexperience and precarious legal status and issued an urgent call for separate institutions for women within the union. Interestingly, the socialist-feminist movement and the middle-class feminist movement ascribed similar meanings to the term *Eigenart*, despite the open animosity between the two. Both proposed a politics of *Eigenart* based on women's particular existence, activities, sentiments, and consciousness, which were not less than, merely different from, men's. As a political slogan in both movements, *Eigenart* refused the vision of a "seamless integration of women into male spheres of employment or politics" that would necessitate the loss of female identity.[81] Instead, the politics of *Eigenart* demanded a place for a specifically female identity in the spheres of formal and informal politics.

Male labor leaders also embraced a notion of female *Eigenart*, one that disparaged female particularity as an impediment to their organizing efforts. Male leaders of the DTAV, for example, employed two distinct, often contradictory arguments against incorporating female *Eigenart* into the politics of class. When faced with a challenge from within or with the prospect of restructuring the union on behalf of women, they vigorously denied women's special needs, asserting that equality between the sexes already existed in the union and offering as evidence only their own practice of refusing preferential treat-

---

80. Ottilie Baader, "Bericht der Sozialdemokratischer Frauen Deutschlands an die Internationale Konferenz Sozialistischer Frauen," in *Frauenemanzipation und Sozialdemokratie,* ed. Heinz Niggemann (Frankfurt, 1981), 128–30. See also discussions within the SPD of protective legislation for women workers in Karin Bauer, *Clara Zetkin und die proletarische Frauenbewegung* (Berlin, 1978), 125; and Quataert, *Reluctant Feminists,* 39–45. Richard J. Evans, *Sozialdemokratie und Frauenemanzipation im deutschen Kaiserreich* (Berlin, 1979), 44–50, discusses this ambivalence in August Bebel's *Die Frau und der Sozialismus* (1910).

81. Irene Stoehr, "'Organisierte Mütterlichkeit': Zur Politik der deutschen Frauenbewegung um 1900," in *Frauen suchen ihre Geschichte: Historische Studien zum 19. und 20. Jahrhundert,* ed. Karin Hausen (Munich, 1983), 222–23, 228–29. For additional discussion of *Eigenart* in the middle-class women's movement, see Helene Lange, "Steht die Frauenbewegung am Ziel oder am Anfang?" *Die Frau* 29 (November 1921): 33–46; and Barbara Greven-Aschoff, *Die bürgerliche Frauenbewegung in Deutschland, 1894–1933* (Göttingen, 1981), 37–43. Various Social Democratic versions of *Eigenart* can be found in Käthe Duncker's contribution to the debate on the SPD's conference on women: "Autonomie oder Integration in die Partei? Debatte auf der Frauenkonferenz 1908," in Niggemann, *Frauenemanzipation und Sozialdemokratie,* 139; Lily Braun, *Die Frauenfrage: Ihre geschichtliche Entwicklung und wirtschaftliche Seite* (1901; reprint, Berlin, 1979), 199–200, 207; and Bauer, *Clara Zetkin,* 130.

ment to one sex. But when pressed to explain the varying patterns of men's and women's union or strike participation, male unionists admitted that women had particular duties—housework and child rearing, for instance—that bound them to the home and a state of perpetual backwardness, which they did not propose to change. Thus, in the official union rhetoric, *Eigenart* signified passive, apolitical women workers who were, at best, a costly burden on the labor movement and who, in the worst instances, betrayed the union's struggle by acting as wage cutters and strikebreakers.[82] Male union leaders implemented the rhetoric of *Eigenart* in order to deny women entry into, to define women out of, the realm of class. In their view, accommodating female *Eigenart* in the sense defined by female activists would divide the labor movement and divert its leaders' attention from the union's principal goals. In the view of male leaders, the unions could afford neither. Instead, women were to shed their *Eigenart,* their gender, in order to join the working class.

Female union activists, by contrast, articulated a concept of *Eigenart* that acknowledged the simultaneity of work and family in shaping women's work identities. They perceived a political potential in these overlapping identities that was overlooked, often scorned, by men. Conceding that women workers lagged far behind men in terms of associational traditions, practical experience, political understanding, and self-confidence, women activists sought to create a space within the DTAV in which female *Eigenart* would be respected, in which it could become the basis not of female backwardness, as male leaders argued, but of political mobilization. The politics of *Eigenart* did not represent a rejection of the politics of class so much as a contest of the boundaries established by male leaders. Women insisted, for example, not on separate organizations but rather on their own space within the union, a space in which the renunciation of gender was not a prerequisite of class. They urged the union to formulate its women's program in terms of *Eigenart* "until the transformation is complete, until our female colleagues feel that they have equal rights and equal duties."[83] Intrinsic to their political concept of *Eigenart* was a critique of the universalist claims of class and its focus on production, a refusal of the dichotomy between women's work for wages and their work as mothers and wives. In claiming special consideration of women workers as mothers and wives, female union activists challenged the dominant identity and ideology of class in the German Social Democratic labor movement.

Prior to World War I, especially between 1908 and 1914, female activists in the DTAV sought recognition of female *Eigenart* in their everyday struggles in the mills for higher wages and a shorter workday and for greater protection

---

82. DTAV, *Protokoll der 10. Generalversammlung 1910,* 87, 120, 135–36; and DTAV, *Protokoll der 12. Generalversammlung 1914,* 118. See also DTAV, "Für die Frauen, von den Frauen," *Der Textilarbeiter* 21, no. 1 (1909): 5.

83. DTAV, *Protokoll der 10. Generalversammlung 1910,* 234–35.

of pregnant workers and, through their campaigns within the union, to hold separate women's meetings, to establish a women's supplement to the union paper, and to increase the number of women in the higher echelons of union administration. Although they made modest gains in these areas, women remained a minority in the union, and negative images of women workers continued to pervade union rhetoric. The discordance between these images and women's own identities may explain why many more women workers sought to redress their grievances in strikes rather than through union activity.[84] Despite the predominance of women in the textile mills and the growing number of women in the DTAV before the war, female activists' efforts to redefine the politics of "class," embedded in male notions of work ethos, skill, and wage, remained largely unsuccessful. Yet they seeded the ground for a postwar transformation of union politics. On the eve of the war, one female organizer predicted that the growing presence of women would fundamentally change the face of the unions: "The future in our organization belongs to women. . . . It is even possible that men will one day have to fight themselves for equality in our organization."[85]

The upheaval of war, revolution, and demobilization transformed the experiences of female factory workers and the discourses about women's work. These moments of rupture are crucial in understanding the feminization of union politics that occurred during the mid-1920s in the DTAV. First, the boundaries between *Frauen- und Männerindustrien* (female and male industries) dissolved as thousands of male workers left for the front and women were transferred to previously male sectors of production. Many of those who remained in the textile mills, as well as those who sought work in the armaments plants, were trained to use and repair complex machinery, to perform "skilled" or supervisory jobs.[86] Then, as the wartime economy became increasingly dependent on women, the state, employers, factory inspectors, and local offi-

---

84. Strikes, rooted in the workplace community, may have represented a less contradictory political arena than unions, one in which women could more easily reconcile their identities as mothers, workers, and wives with their demands for higher wages, shorter working hours, and safer conditions of work. For example, during the years 1902 to 1904, women made up between 17 and 23 percent of DTAV rank and file but 53 percent of participants in so-called offensive strikes. Of male strikers, 78 percent were unionized, while 63 percent of striking women belonged to the DTAV; DTAV, *Protokoll der 7. ordentlichen Generalversammlung, abgehalten 1904 in Linden-Hannover,* 42–45. During 1906–7, women again represented 53 percent of participants in offensive strikes but only 36 percent of DTAV members; DTAV, *Protokoll der 9. Generalversammlung 1908,* 40–43.

85. DTAV, *Protokoll der 12. Generalversammlung 1914,* 113.

86. HStAD, Regierung Düsseldorf, no. 33581: "Bericht der Gewerbeinspektor für Crefeld Stadt und Land und Kreis Kempen von 30.3.1917." According to this report, many women received specialized job training during the war, including some who were trained to maintain and repair textile machines. See also Ute Daniel, *Arbeiterfrauen in der Kriegsgesellschaft: Beruf, Familie und Politik im Ersten Weltkrieg* (Göttingen, 1989).

cials joined efforts to "enlighten women about how urgently their work is needed."[87] Women's work for the fatherland was no longer "secondary" or detrimental to the family, to men's wages, or to masculine work identities. It was imbued, if only for a few years, with the honor and esteem that had otherwise been reserved for skilled male labor.

A parallel process took place within the textile unions as thousands of women assumed leadership of local union posts in the absence of male functionaries. Within a few years, the DTAV became a predominantly female union: by 1916, women had come to comprise approximately 60 percent of members, and this figure increased to nearly 75 percent by 1918. The political rhetoric of the union changed markedly as punitive reprimands of female backwardness gave way to respectful acknowledgment of the fact that women had indeed become "the core of the organization."[88] Moreover, outside the unions, an increasing number of female workers defied the *Burgfriede* (the agreement between the unions and government for domestic peace during wartime). Women comprised 62 percent of industrial strike participants in 1916 and 75 percent in 1917.[89] In sum, the departure of so many men from their families, their jobs, and their union posts may have encouraged the development of a female subculture, a wartime anomaly that allowed the politics of *Eigenart* to flourish, while at the same time women were proving that they could take on "men's jobs" and "men's responsibilities." The extent to which the war had drawn women workers into the arena of labor politics became evident during 1918, when female membership began to expand at unprecedented rates, reversing the ratio between men and women in some locals within a few months.

As women came to predominate in the DTAV, the politics of *Eigenart* acquired a new meaning, and female activists emerged in the union with a renewed energy. However, they faced new challenges and new forms of "anti-feminism" when the war came to a close and the government of Wilhelm II collapsed. In view of the tumultuous political and economic conditions at the close of the war, the new Social Democratic government sought not only to reorder the relations between labor and capital in a fundamental sense but also to alleviate the urgent problems of unemployment and unrest by recasting the

---

87. HStAD, Regierung Düsseldorf, no. 33485, correspondence marked 174/8 1917. This correspondence is damaged, but it seems likely that it was compiled by a local *Kriegsamtstelle* in the Rhineland for the *Regierungspräsident* in Düsseldorf.

88. DTAV, *Protokoll der 13. Generalversammlung, abgehalten 1917 in Augsburg,* 127–29; DTAV, *Jahrbuch 1914–1915* (Berlin, 1916), 282, 307; and DTAV, *Jahrbuch 1917* (Berlin, 1918), 72–74. The number of women who held union posts grew from approximately 1,800 in 1913 to 3,000 in 1917.

89. DTAV, *Jahrbuch 1916* (Berlin, 1917), 95–97; *Jahrbuch 1917,* 63–71. Only 26 percent of those involved (male and female) in 1916 and only 36 percent in 1917 were union members.

sexual division of labor. The demobilization decrees aimed to return veterans to their jobs as quickly as possible and called for the immediate dismissal of women whose male family members could now earn a living. Demobilization marked a sudden and powerful transformation of the social climate surrounding women's work. Government and unions unleashed vigorous campaigns against the so-called *Doppelverdiener* (double earners).[90] The juxtaposition of the rapid erosion of economic rights with the newly acquired right to vote, both of which were cloaked in the rhetoric of civic equality for the sexes, profoundly affected female textile workers' views of work and politics. Between December 1918 and the end of 1920, female membership in the DTAV increased by more than 450 percent; approximately 260,000 women joined the union. Tens of thousands of women joined male colleagues and workers from other industries in militant political strikes that shut down the entire Rhineland and the Ruhr between 1918 and 1920.

These experiences, in both their social and discursive dimensions, form the backdrop for the feminization of politics and the articulation of new political identities during the Weimar Republic. While the numbers of new female members skyrocketed, the union found itself embroiled in internal conflicts when union leadership and rank and file split between the radical Independent Social Democratic Party (USPD) and the majority Social Democratic Party. Enmeshed in conflict and imbued with the new rhetoric of civic gender equality, the DTAV executive voted in 1919 to dismantle the Women's Bureau: its members concluded "that a special type of training for women was not necessary."[91] Male union leaders, who had long ago mastered the rhetoric of equality, which rendered female *Eigenart* superfluous, even reactionary, now pointed to women's experiences of war, revolution, and democracy as proof of their "equal" abilities and status.

When the postwar political crisis had subsided, DTAV leaders faced new challenges from the union's female members, now backed by the presence of many more active women. They reasserted their earlier demands for a female representative to the union's executive, disrupting union conferences during the early 1920s with their expressions of outrage about the union's refusal to allow secretary Martha Hoppe the right to vote. Moreover, the postwar politics

---

90. ˙Richard Bessel, "'Eine nicht allzu grosse Beunruhigung des Arbeitsmarktes,' Frauenarbeit und Demobilmachung in Deutschland nach dem Ersten Weltkrieg," *Geschichte und Gesellschaft* 9 (1983): 211–29; Susanne Rouette, "'Gleichberechtigung' ohne 'Recht auf Arbeit': Demobilmachung der Frauenarbeit nach dem Ersten Weltkrieg," in Christiane Eifert and Susanne Rouette (eds.), *Unter allen Umständen: Frauengeschichte(n) in Berlin* (Berlin, 1986), 159–82; and Susanne Rouette, "Die sozialpolitische Regulierung der Frauenarbeit: Arbeitsmarkt- und Fürsorgepolitik in den Anfangsjahren der Weimarer Republik; Das Beispiel Berlin" (Phil. dissertation, Technische Universität Berlin, 1991).

91. DTAV, *Protokoll des 14. Verbandstages, abgehalten 1921 in Breslau*, 146.

of *Eigenart* insisted that the union address women's reproductive burdens—pregnancy, birth control, abortion, and housework. Between 1925 and 1928, the female body emerged in the arena of class politics when the DTAV investigated the conditions of pregnant workers and presented its shocking findings to the Reichstag in 1925; when it organized demonstrations against Paragraph 218, the restrictive abortion law; and, finally, when it placed housework at the center of its women's program, sponsoring an essay contest for female textile workers on the relationship between waged work and housework in 1928 and publishing the collected essays in 1930.[92] The appearance of a politicized female body in the sphere of union politics stands in stark contrast to the prewar politics of class. In forging a political link between the home and the workplace, the private body and the social and political body, female activists in the DTAV fostered the formation of a female political identity within the organized labor movement. In uncovering the political meanings of sexual difference, which divided the labor movement, they resisted and transformed the ideology of class.

This brief overview of the relationship between gender and class in the DTAV portrays a union movement that had, at certain points in its history, taken on the form of political class spelled out in Katznelson and Kocka's fourth level. Central to the appropriation of the ideology and identity of class were the boundaries that it drew around itself of religion, ethnicity, and gender. While exclusion and subordination were intrinsic to the process of class formation, the DTAV's gendered boundaries were seldom fixed. This is particularly clear in the case of the textile union, where the steady growth of female membership, the emergence of a core of female activists, and their articulation of female *Eigenart* periodically challenged and destabilized the content of union policies, the structure of union hierarchies, and ultimately the politics of class.

In this discussion of the levels approach, I have sought to uncover the presence of women and to argue for the relevance of gender at each level of class formation. Serious questions about the usefulness of this approach arise when it is viewed from the perspective of gender and subjected to empirical and historically specific examination. The lens of gender permits specific insights into the arbitrary nature of the divisions among the four levels, as the discussions of economic and social class formation show. More specifically, the use

92. DTAV, *Umfang der Frauenarbeit in der deutschen Textilindustrie: Erwerbsarbeit, Schwangerschaft, Frauenleid* (Berlin, 1925); Max Hirsch, *Die Gefahren der Frauenerwerbsarbeit für Schwangerschaft, Geburt, Wochenbett und Kindesaufzucht mit besonderer Berücksichtigung der Textilindustrie* (Berlin, 1925); DTAV, *Protokoll vom 1. Kongress der Textilarbeiterinnen Deutschlands, abgehalten am 11. und 12. Oktober 1926 in Gera*, 4–12; DTAV, *Mein Arbeitstag—mein Wochenende*.

of gender as a category of historical analysis dissolves the sense of progress that is implicit in the notion of levels by revealing, for example, that the "dispositions or identities" purportedly formed at level three often contradict or challenge the goals and visions of the organized labor movement that represent level four. A consideration of the role of politics and ideology in shaping the process of economic class formation further diffuses this sense of progress among the various levels. Finally, the concept of gender resists the inherent tendency of this approach to reduce class politics to the singular dimension of waged work and uncovers the ways in which reproductive issues, as one example, transformed the ideology of class in the DTAV during the 1920s.

This critique appears to open an endless series of questions regarding the continued usefulness of our conceptual vocabulary, in particular the terms "class formation" and "class." One is whether a new and gendered view of class will bring about a Thompsonian revival of historical narratives that are "so complex, so permeated with social particularities and the subjective sentiments of the people in [the] story" that they cannot be reduced to abstract models.[93] In refraining from formulating alternative models that propose to integrate differences of gender, race, religion, or ethnicity, I conclude with a view of class that is "destabilized" yet historically specific. It calls for careful delineation between class as an analytical concept and class as a postulated identity or ideology, which is always embedded in specific historical settings. Thus "theorizing" class and class formation at this juncture might mean transcending the "social particularities" of class formations not through the establishment of new models but by linking or comparing, for example, different historical encounters between gender and class, or distinct ways in which populist or nationalist identities overlapped with those of class.

Attention to the historically specific ideologies and identities of class, approaching class "from the perspective not of teleology, but of . . . genealogy," requires neither the construction of a new model nor the revival of a historical narrative.[94] Rather, it demands a weaving of theory into historical research, a continual rethinking of our analytical categories grounded in a close reading of historical social vocabulary. In granting history an important place in the work of theoretical renovation, I have tried to move beyond the epistemological crisis engendered by the linguistic turn in history toward new visions of class and a historical language that embraces rather than obscures the conflictual meanings of class.

In emphasizing conflictual meanings, my study conceives of class as more than a "discursive construction." It also explores class as an identity and an ideology that was shaped as women and men assigned and contested the

---

93. Lidtke, "Burghers, Workers," 29.
94. Scott, "Women in *The Making of the English Working Class*," 85, 88.

meanings of class. Furthermore, attending to this process of assigning and contesting meanings makes gender visible where it otherwise might remain concealed.[95] In the case of the German Textile Workers' Union, gender, embodied in the politics of *Eigenart,* did not represent an obstacle or a barrier to class formation as much as a contest of the boundaries established by male leaders. If class formation is viewed as a series of makings and remakings, as a process that was constantly contested, either explicitly by those who opposed it or implicitly by those who stood outside it and who appeared as the "other" or the "backward," then gender appears to constitute a continual point of contest, a renewed disordering of the process of class formation.[96] The dichotomies of class and gender, of class and "non-class" distinctions, which are integral to most historical accounts of class formation, obscure the ways in which women appropriated and transformed the vocabulary and ideology of class by inflecting its universal claims, exposing its masculine character, and inscribing class with their own meanings. The alternative to this dichotomous view is one of class formation as a series of short-lived resolutions, new destabilizations, and redefinitions in which gender both shapes and contests class.

---

95. Scott's deconstructive reading of E. P. Thompson's *Making of the English Working Class* offers one excellent example of how this might be done.

96. Mary Nolan's suggestion that the working class must re-create itself at each stage of industrial capitalism, as the economy and labor force are restructured, as political institutions and forms of hegemony change, prompted me to consider the place of gender in this process. Mary Nolan, *Social Democracy and Society: Working-Class Radicalism in Düsseldorf, 1890–1920* (Cambridge, 1981), 2. On this point, see Sewell's critique of Thompson, "How Classes Are Made," 68.

Childhood Memories, Political Visions, and Working-Class Formation in Imperial Germany: Some Comparative Observations

M. J. Maynes

Wir haben früh erfahren
Der Arbeit Frongewalt
In düstern Kinderjahren
Und wurden früh schon alt
Sie hat an unserm Fuss geklirt
Die Kette, die nur schwerer wird . . .
—"Dem Morgenrot entgegen," quoted by Karl Grünberg

The relationship between the history of national political development and that of everyday life is everywhere a troubled one. While some social-historical research can still be castigated for leaving the politics out, it is also true that for important strains within social history, particularly those influenced by neo-Marxist or feminist theory, making connections between everyday life and the realm of politics has long been important. But it has not been easy. Making these connections has involved considerable conceptual and practical difficulty, particularly in the case of Central European historiography, where the innovations associated with social history and women's history came relatively late and often faced considerable institutional resistance.

Nevertheless, perhaps because of the continued preponderance of state-centeredness in German historiography, the separatism that characterized the development of social-historical approaches in other fields is less noticeable in the German case. It is not surprising, then, that some of the best examples of historical research that makes connections between the social and the political realms have come out of the recent ferment in German historiography, although it is equally clear that the project of integrating important dimensions of social life into the master narratives of German history is in its early stages. Even the latest reconceptualizations of the nature of political and societal development in Imperial and Weimar Germany are only beginning to incorporate family history, gender relations, popular cultural phenomena, and perspectives "from below" into historical interpretations.

In this essay, I would like to concentrate on one area of intersection between social and political history—namely, the investigation of class formation as a social-historical and political process. Historians of class relations, no longer restricting themselves to studies of the industrial workplace and the workers' parties, are more likely to conceptualize class position and class identity as multifaceted, constructed through historically specific experiences, and evident at different sites. I shall explore two such sites of class formation: the working-class family and the elementary school. I shall address the question of how childhood experiences reverberated in formulations of social identity and political orientation. The evidence I shall use is drawn from the autobiographies of workers whose childhoods were lived before World War I. This evidence suggests, I believe, not only that workers often built upon, used, and reinterpreted childhood experiences in political contexts but also that the specific flavor of working-class politics in Imperial Germany was shaped by aspects of the history of childhood peculiar to Central Europe in the late nineteenth century. This latter argument is, implicitly at least, a comparative one. Although I shall not develop the comparison fully, I will refer to analogous evidence about France to illuminate German particularities.

Metaphors of Childhood Suffering as Class Injury

One distinguishing feature of the German-language memoir literature that recounts working-class childhood in the late nineteenth century is its grimness. In most of these accounts,[1] variants on a single theme recur: what was missing from the author's childhood, how it was different from, and worse than, that of more privileged children, and how it failed to live up to the standards of a proper childhood.

Many authors employed the metaphors of paradise and light that suffused

---

1. The memoirs on which this essay are based are drawn from a set of working-class autobiographies that I have been collecting for several years. At the time this essay was written, the set included sixty memoirs of varying lengths published between 1854 and 1976. Among the thirty-four German-language texts, only five describe childhoods in largely positive terms. The rest either dwell on the hardships suffered by the author as a child or describe only minor aspects of, or periods during, childhood in positive terms. I have subsequently published a book based on ninety memoirs—*Taking the Hard Road: Lifecourse in French and German Workers' Autobiographies in the Era of Industrialization* (Chapel Hill, N.C., 1995).

the dominant imagery of childhood by this era only to negate them. For example, Franz Lüth, an agricultural day laborer born in Mecklenburg in 1870, put it this way:

> The happiest days of a person's life, the golden years of childhood, passed slowly, joylessly, and full of despair for small and needy Franz. At home, he was so overloaded with work that not an hour of free time was left. (Lüth, 11)

Anna Altmann, who was active in the Austrian socialist women's movement, made an explicit comparison between her remembered childhood of the 1850s and the imagined childhood of the "class enemy":

> The garlands woven by the proletariat on the path through life aren't like those of the rich and fortunate, because by the cradle of the proletarian child there stand behind the actual parents a second couple—Father Sorrow and Mother Need—who also claim their rights. Today when I recall in my mind's eye from well beyond the midday of my life pictures of the past, the first to emerge are the dark shadows of my ruined youth. The golden days that the children of the rich enjoyed under the protection of their guardians were never granted to me nor to many hundreds of others. (Altmann, 23)

Heinrich Dikreiter, born in Strasbourg in 1865 and raised in orphanages after his mother's death, eventually also learned that he had missed out on something during his earliest childhood years:

> All that brightens a child's life—fairy tales and storybooks, toys and things like that—were foreign to us. (Dikreiter, 15)

Only a brief stay in the particularly well administered orphanage in Constance stood out as "the one bright star in the darkness of his sad childhood years" (Dikreiter, 21). Adelheid Popp, who was born in 1869 into a family of village weavers in Austria, employed the same commonplace:

> No bright moment, no sunbeam, no hint of a comfortable home where motherly love and care could shape my childhood, were ever known to me. (Popp, 1)

With few exceptions, German workers' accounts of childhood suggest the brutal contrast between the experiences of Central European working-class children in the late nineteenth century and the dominant ideals defining childhood in other milieus.[2]

While the rhetorical claim of having missed out on childhood often relies on implicit standards, some autobiographers are quite explicit about where they discovered the standards against which their own childhoods were found wanting. Alwin Ger, for example, born in 1857 into a Saxon mining family, encountered the world of middle-class childhood in the bedroom of his employer's children when he went off as a machine factory apprentice. The oldest son was in a *höhere Bürgerschule,* and his room was filled with atlases, science books, and equipment.

"I experienced," Ger recalled, "unbounded joy at the intellectual discovery I'd made, and at the same time it dawned on me for the first time, as I glimpsed the teaching materials here at the disposal of the children of the propertied, how boundlessly pitiful was the schooling that we kids had had. (Ger, 134)

Anna Meier only had to look out of her window, she recalled:

whenever the other kids were running around in the streets in their childish high spirits, and I would direct my gaze longingly out the window, I would be reminded by a slap from my mother that I had work to do. (Maier, 107)

Other workers recalled glimpses of other kinds of childhood seen through toyshop windows at Christmastime or in the *Kinderzimmer* of the bourgeois homes in which they were employed as domestic servants.

I have argued elsewhere[3] that part of the explanation for why the German working-class autobiographies of the pre-World War I era recall childhood in such brutal terms is the contemporaneous juxtaposition of very different childhood experiences and norms that characterized the late nineteenth century in

---

2. For historical accounts of the evolution of childhood in Germany, see Michael Mitterauer and Reihard Sieder, *The European Family: Patriarchy and Partnership from the Middle Ages to the Present* (Chicago, 1982); Ingeborg Weber-Kellermann, *Die Kindheit: Kleidung und Wohnung, Arbeit und Spiel* (Frankfurt, 1979); Donata Elschenbroich, *Kinder werden nicht geboren* (Frankfurt, 1977); and Jürgen Schlumbohm, *Kinderstuben: Wie Kinder zu Bauern, Bürgern, Aristokraten wurden* (Munich, 1982). For a review of the historical research on the history of childhood in Germany, see Mary Jo Maynes and Tom Taylor, "The History of Childhood in Germany," in *Children in Comparative and Historical Perspective: An International Handbook,* ed. N. R. Hiner and J. Hawes (Westport, Conn., 1991).

3. I have developed the comparative argument about the effects of different demographic and family-economic regimes in France and Central Europe in "The Contours of Childhood: Demography, Strategy and Mythology of Childhood in French and German Lower-Class Autobiographies," in *The European Experience of Declining Fertility, 1850–1970: The Quiet Revolution,* ed. Louise Tilly, John Gillis, and David Levine (New York and London, 1992).

Central Europe. In particular, large working-class families, with their continued reliance on child labor, coexisted with middle-class families, which were becoming smaller and more child-centered. Furthermore, the enforcement of obligatory schooling laws in Central Europe increased pressure on working-class children, even as in bourgeois circles the emergence of the child-centered family placed new emphasis on childhood as a privileged moment in life.

The autobiographies I have studied suggest that this contrast between what childhood was supposed to be like and what it actually was, was interpreted, in the era of the rise of socialism in the German-speaking world, as a political grievance. Even late in the nineteenth century, "normal" childhood was still denied many working-class children, and its persistent elusiveness fed into an emergent social critique and provided an incentive for political activism aimed at least in part at making childhood a possibility for future generations of workers. Recounting a harsh childhood in such a context constituted a political statement, a contribution to the discourse on class confrontation. Some authors made the claim explicit. Thus, according to Altmann,

Our whole struggle is aimed only toward this—to create a better future for our children. It's a mistaken opinion when people say: I had to suffer, so my kids should face the same.

The only legacy that the proletariat can leave behind for its children is to work for their better living conditions. (Altmann, 60–61)

Maier mentioned her dedication to winning mothers over to socialism "so that the children of the proletariat will in the future experience more joy in childhood than [she] had had" (Maier, 109). Although many of the contours of childhood still eluded late-nineteenth-century workers and their children, they were nevertheless familiar enough to serve as a model to pursue and even a motive for political action.

But there is another politically pertinent dimension to these stories as well. Their actual villains tend to be not the abstract social inequalities that provide the explicit theoretical frame for many of them but rather actual individuals, often parents, who acted as the immediate embodiment of class injury. The texts thus reveal an ambivalence vis-à-vis working-class identity, which other analysts of German working-class political culture of this era have noted. Indeed, the socialist effort to create a "respectable" proletarian culture and a new kind of family life reflected this ambivalence toward the working-class family.[4] On the one hand, socialist theory elevated the working classes to

---

4. There are many works on the German socialist movement that address the problematic character of its "revolutionary" identity and of the relations between the socialist leadership and the workers. These analyses date back as far as the turn-of-the-century revisionist debate and

a position of moral authority and historical ascendancy. On the other hand, as historians of the workers' movement have noted, many socialist programs aimed at making possible for workers the cultural and familial attainments characteristic of bourgeois life. Even more problematic is the inference one might draw from the childhood tales that many workers emerged from the deprivations of childhood with psychological damage. The stories of child-hood, in other words, could serve simultaneously to condemn the social system that led to the deprivations that working-class children experienced and to confirm the superiority and desirability of bourgeois cultural and family practices.[5]

Schooling and Political Authority

Accounts of schooling suggest that childhood encounters outside the family. also left political imprints. Karl Grünberg's memoirs are emblematic. As an eight-year-old schoolboy, Grünberg had gotten caught in a clash of wills be-tween his mother and his teacher, Kittner. This classroom "battle of the lunchbox" appears in Grünberg's autobiography as the opening foray in a life of struggle that would repeatedly pit him against authorities. One day Kittner tripped over the large metal lunchbox that Grünberg had brought to school and in his fury banned the box from his classroom. Grünberg's mother insisted on his carrying it the next day since she knew it was his right. It was without a doubt true, Grünberg recalled, that,

right was also on our side in this case. But [my mother] forgot in the process that the one she challenged pulled more weight and that the

---

Robert Michels's early-twentieth-century study *Political Parties: A Sociological Study of the Oligarchical Tendencies of Modern Democracy* (New York, 1915) and include, among others, Gunther Roth, *The Social Democrats in Imperial Germany* (Totowa, N.J., 1963); Dieter Groh, *Negative Integration und revolutionärer Attentismus: Die deutsche Sozialdemokratie am Vor-abend des ersten Weltkriegs* (Frankfurt, 1973); and Vernon Lidtke, *The Outlawed Party: Social Democracy in Germany, 1878–1890* (Princeton, 1966). Examples of a variety of approaches to the history of the working classes outside of the organized socialist and trade-union movements can be found in Werner Conze and Ulrich Engelhardt, eds., *Arbeiterexistenz im 19. Jahrhundert* (Stutt-gart, 1981); Jürgen Reulecke and Wolfhard Weber, eds., *Fabrik, Familie, Feierabend: Beiträge zur Sozialgeschichte des Alltags im Industriezeitalter* (Wuppertal, 1978); and Richard J. Evans, ed., *The German Working Class, 1888–1933: The Politics of Everyday Life* (London, 1982).

5. Contemporaries were well aware of the double edge of memoir literature that empha-sized the victimization of workers. Some socialists were critical of the emergent social-psychological analysis implicit in the works of reformers such as Adolph Levenstein and Eugen Rosenstock. For a discussion of this early social-psychological analysis of workers' lives, see Alfred Kelly's introduction to *The German Worker: Working-Class Autobiographies from the Age of Industrialization* (Berkeley, 1987), 6ff.; and Joan Campbell, *Joy in Work, German Work: The National Debate, 1800–1945* (Princeton, 1989), especially chaps. 4 and 5.

conflict that was about to start would literally be fought out on the back of a small eight-year-old boy who was fully in the power of this teacher. (Grünberg, 23)

Grünberg would long bear the scars of this encounter. He began to stutter, and his life at school was a torment. The image of Kittner's "boot camp" (*Dressuranstalt*) takes a prominent role in the memoirs as a symbol of the abuse of authority.

Grünberg's account is more vivid than most, but its elements are repeated in a great number of school narratives of this epoch. Lüth recalled that he had no one in his Mecklenburg village to stick up for him, "including his teacher, whose anger hailed down on him; the orphaned child stood defenseless against him" (Lüth, 9). For Ger the memory of schooling was "the most miserable" of all his childhood recollections. He was taught by "an old embittered bachelor who mistrusted everyone and everything in the world, including the female sex" (Ger, 59). To one extent or another, the story of the authoritarian, conservative, and vindictive schoolteacher who kept order in the classroom through liberal use of the cane is the account of the majority of the male working-class autobiographers who passed through the German elementary schools before World War I.

A few men told different stories. For example, Wilhelm Kaisen, who was born in 1887 in a suburb of Hamburg, contrasted his "teacher" with the harsh and hated "schoolmaster" of the pervasive stereotype. And Dikreiter recalled that his transfer in the 1870s to the Constance city orphanage was like entering a new world:

the beginning of an education as a future German citizen of liberal hue. The head of the institution in which boys and girls were raised together without damage to body or soul offered me his friendly hand as I entered his realm and treated me immediately in a very familiar manner. (Dikreiter, 19)

If the accounts of Kaisen and Dikreiter reveal glimpses of a more benign pedagogy (at least in the German states on the periphery of Prussia), among the mass of accounts of German working-class boyhoods of the nineteenth century, such positive recollections of schooling are rare.[6]

---

6. Margarete Flecken comes to similar conclusions about the character of teachers portrayed in the German worker autobiographies she surveys, but she argues that there is a consistent tendency for the urban schools to be portrayed more positively than the rural schools. I would add that regional differences need to be taken into account. Conversely, Grünberg's Berlin experience suggests that not all cities provided such positive school environments. See Margarete Flecken, *Arbeiterkinder im 19. Jahrhundert* (Weinheim and Basel, 1981), esp. 138–56; and R. Bölling, *Sozialgeschichte der deutschen Lehrer* (Göttingen, 1983), 88–91.

The stereotypical drillmaster was, moreover, a figure far more prominent in boys' life stories than in girls'. German accounts of working-class girlhood (most of which are not drawn from Prussia) tend to present teachers in a softer light. In some, to be sure, the classroom tyrant does make his appearance. Annaliese Rüegg's elementary schoolteacher pulled her hair and treated her badly:

> Whether I was clever or not, I never knew. I only knew that the richer and better-dressed children sat in the front rows and were the focus of most of the teacher's attention. . . . Because I knew that I was going to work in the factory later in life I thought—Why bother? You can clean machines and tie loose threads without knowing spelling and geography. And the factory owner will calculate my wages without my help. (Rüegg, 17)

Rüegg's account, despite its critical portrait of the schoolmaster, is marked by a humor that distinguishes it from the unmitigated bitterness that characterized most of the men's recollections. Yet Rüegg's account is far more negative than those of other women. Aurelia Roth, for example, echoed a recurrent theme when she recalled her school in the Jizera Mountains of Austria as preferable to home:

> I often had to miss school to work. That was for me the biggest sacrifice I ever had to make. I had very little time for studying, even less for play, but what sickened me the most was when I had to miss school. . . . I didn't want to stay at home; I liked it better at school. The teacher always liked me because I was so attentive. (Roth, 52–53)

Even more poignant is Lena Christ's account of her teacher as her defender, however ineffective, against the abuse she suffered at her mother's hands. Christ, who was the illegitimate child of a servant, had moved to her mother's home in Munich in the late 1880s after spending her early childhood with her grandparents in rural Bavaria. She found cruel treatment awaiting her there. School provided defenders, however ineffective:

> My teachers took my part, and once when I came to school in the morning barefoot, my mistress sent me home with a note in which she reproached my mother. But this only had the consequences of a new punishment. . . . Because I wore a dress with short sleeves, when I returned to school my teacher noticed the black-and-blue marks on my arms as well as on my neck and face, and despite my fear of further punishment, I had to report the whole truth to the principal, who was called in. A letter to my mother brought the result that I received nothing to eat for the whole day and had

to spend the night in the corridor of our building, kneeling on a log. (Christ, 52–53)

Many girls (and a few boys) contrasted the relative leisure of school with the continual labor expected at home. They were required both to contribute to the family income and to help with domestic chores such as cooking, cleaning, and care of siblings. Anna Perthen, for example, recalled:

As the oldest, instead of playing or studying after school, I had to take care of children, sew buttons, or gather wood in the forest. . . . When I was twelve years old, I had to go into a textile factory, where the workday lasted from five in the morning until seven in the evening. In the afternoon from four to six we went to the factory school. . . . There wasn't much learning going on, of course, we thought of these two hours more as rest. (Perthen, 113)

In girls' recollections, there is virtually no allusion to the realm of freedom in home or street life that provided an opposition to the confinement, discipline, and restrictions of the schoolroom. For girls, home was portrayed as the site of most intense discipline, a depiction that is most extreme in the case of Christ, whose mother grew obsessively concerned with a propriety that demanded submissiveness, self-discipline, and modesty on the part of her daughter.[7]

School's relatively greater appeal to girls was increased due to the more gentle treatment they apparently commanded there—from male teachers, but especially from the growing number of female teachers, who toward the end of the nineteenth century were deemed particularly suitable for instructing girl pupils. Women teachers in religious orders had long been common in Catholic areas of Europe, but lay women teachers, often recruited from among the daughters of the middle classes (in contrast with the more modest social origins of their male colleagues), appeared throughout Germany by the closing decades of the nineteenth century as a cheaper solution to the mushrooming demand for elementary teachers that accompanied population growth and increasing schooling.[8] Different experiences at home, based in part on gender-

---

7. Certainly girls' freedom of movement relative to boys' was more restricted with sexual maturity. For a parallel discussion of the connections between staying at home and working-class respectability based on oral histories gathered from Viennese workers, see Robert Wegs, "Adolescence and Working-Class Youth in Vienna, 1890–1938" (Paper given at the Social Science History Association Meeting, New Orleans, 1 November 1987). A slightly different version of this paper was published as "Working-Class Adolescence in Austria, 1890–1930," *Journal of Family History* 17 (1992): 439–50.

8. See James Albisetti, "Women and the Professions in Imperial Germany," in *German Women in the Eighteenth and Nineteenth Centuries: A Social and Literary History*, ed. Ruth-Ellen

specific expectations about comportment and work roles, and different pupil-teacher relations in the classroom, based on gender-specific relations between pupils and teachers, both contributed to the contrasting school experiences of girls and boys.

Schooling and Political Development in Germany

How do these school stories correspond to larger themes of political development in Germany? By the late nineteenth century throughout much of Europe, the schoolroom had become not only a defining institution of childhood but also an important site of political socialization for lower-class children. In Central Europe, the reform of the schools that began in the late eighteenth century had dramatic consequences for childhood. School enrollment was pushed toward universality at a very early date: by the early nineteenth century in the southwest and throughout Prussia by midcentury, children routinely attended school for at least part of the legally mandated period (generally from age six to thirteen or fourteen). Schooling had become virtually inescapable for all school-aged children by roughly the 1880s—earlier in Germany than virtually anywhere else in Europe.

The political character of the schools varied among the different German states over the course of the nineteenth century. Throughout Central Europe, state authorities had developed an early interest in, and control over, the schools, generally through the state-church bureaucracies established by the end of the eighteenth century. The influence of this state control varied, however, with the political climate and particular state policy. In Prussia, the largest of the German states, there were several moments of political contest over the school system, most notably during the revolutionary and Napoleonic reform era, around the epoch of the 1848 revolts and in the *Kulturkampf* era of the 1870s. During these periods, traditional pedagogy and classroom relations, deemed so crucial for building the character of future citizens, came under scrutiny. But the liberal critique of the disciplinarian classroom met with little success in Prussia before the twentieth century. The neohumanism of the early nineteenth century was forgotten in the emphasis on rote learning and strict discipline taught in the normal schools of the *Vormärz*. The defeat of the 1848 revolt also had pedagogic repercussions, as the emphasis of educational policy

---

B. Joeres and M. J. Maynes (Bloomington, 1986), 94–109, as well as his *Schooling German Girls and Women* (Princeton, 1988). In Prussia, according to Albisetti, the number of female elementary teachers increased nearly tenfold between 1878 and 1901, from around 1,500 to nearly 14,000. As R. Bölling points out, roughly a fifth of the teachers of the German Empire were women by the turn of the century, with women being most common in the teaching corps of urban areas of the west and Catholic areas of the south; Bölling, *Sozialgeschichte,* 99.

throughout the second half of the nineteenth century was upon the teaching of discipline, piety, and civic loyalty above all else.[9]

Teachers trained during these repressive periods would dominate in the classrooms of Prussia until the century's end. In contrast with pedagogic theory developed in some other European countries by the early nineteenth century, law and practice in Prussia continued to rest on the maintenance of the teacher's authority through the use of corporal punishment. Historians of education have pointed to the persistent place of corporal discipline in Prussian school regulations well into the era of organized capitalism. Jürgen Reulecke, for example, noted that

> in 1898 a royal district court confirmed in finest official German that "moderate welts on the seat" and "mild headaches" were manifestations "that could result from corporal punishments that to some extent accomplished their goal of physical displeasure and pain without the level of permissible punishment being overstepped."

There were even exact guidelines for the instrument of discipline: it should be "a pliant, smooth stick that was not more than one centimeter thick.[10]

Prussia, of course, was not all of Germany. But several other German states followed suit. In Bavaria, the second largest German state, the political reaction of the 1820s followed a similar logic to that of Prussia. Bavarian teachers should themselves be agents of the state's insistence on the teaching of piety, loyalty, and obedience. The reaction of the 1850s also paralleled the Prussian reactionary reforms, which it followed by three years. In Bavaria "a solid moral development, which alone would preserve the ignorant masses from the dangers of a scientific education," was more important for elementary

---

9. For discussions of the political character of educational institutions in Germany, see Anthony LaVopa, *Prussian Schoolteachers: Profession and Office, 1763–1848* (Chapel Hill, 1980); James Albisetti, *Secondary School Reform in Imperial Germany* (Princeton, 1983); Marjorie Lamberti, *State, Society and the Elementary School in Imperial Germany* (Oxford, 1989); as well as Bölling, *Sozialgeschichte;* and Albisetti, *Schooling*. Both Albisetti and Lamberti discuss the successes and failures of various efforts to reform pedagogy during the imperial era. Albisetti finds evidence of limited success of reform at the secondary level, whereas Lamberti's study of elementary schooling emphasizes institutional persistence. In her view, school reform efforts failed because of the association of reformers with unpopular stances on the role of religion in the schools. While this analysis corrects earlier overemphasis of the power of state bureaucracies, her evidence nevertheless supports the view that Prussian elementary school bureaucracies were particularly conservative institutions during the Second Empire.

10. Jürgen Reulecke, "Von der Dorfschule zum Schulsystem," in Reulecke and Weber, *Fabrik,* 260. For an analysis of the political order of the Prussian classroom, see F. Meyer, *Schule der Untertanen: Lehrer und Politik in Preussen, 1848–1900* (Hamburg, 1976).

schoolteachers than a solid general education. Behind this caution lay a fear of mass mobilization through education.[11]

More liberal traditions took root in some localities in Prussia and in other German states, and in these areas educational policy reflected a different perception of the proper character of classroom relations. In Baden, for example, where an activist teaching corps was part of the relatively liberal and anticlerical coalition behind reform, school policy bore a far less conservative stamp than elsewhere. Even more dramatically, in Bremen and Hamburg, which as large city-states evolved according to a different political dynamic and where there were active workers' movements, classroom politics could be very different indeed. Schoolteachers were even among the earliest recruits of socialist movements in these localities.[12] Moreover, the influx of middle-class women into the teaching profession throughout Germany in the second half of the nineteenth century certainly undermined aspects of the drillmaster image. Still, these alternative developments seem to have done little to undermine the stereotype. The teacher as tyrant, the pedagogy of suppression, seem to have held as the dominant image of German boys' schools long after the emergence of the industrial capitalist order.

It is more to the point, perhaps, to underscore the aim of circulating such images and the role they played in the discourse about worker-state relations. Working-class children and adults living in late-nineteenth-century Germany did not have to look far to find political frameworks in which to interpret their educational experiences. Pronouncements on the subject of popular education made by the socialist leader Wilhelm Liebknecht in 1872 opened the critique of the state and its educational institutions that would shape socialist thought on the subject throughout the Second Empire. Liebknecht proclaimed that the schools of the German state existed to inculcate in their pupils the blind acceptance of authority and blind obedience that they would later have to display in the barracks.[13] The emergent socialist analysis of the schools in turn shaped the perceptions and recollections of pupils who were familiar with the

---

11. Bölling, *Sozialgeschichte,* 59. For Bavaria, see also Werner K. Blessing, "Allgemeine Volksschulbildung und politische Doktrination im bayerischen Vormärz," *Zeitschrift für Bayerischen Landesgeschichte* 37 (1974): 479–568.

12. See Bölling, *Sozialgeschichte,* for a good discussion of regional and state variations in the political character of the teaching corps.

13. For a brief overview of educational policy in the German Social Democratic Party, see my *Schooling in Western Europe: A Social History* (Albany, 1985), chap. 6. Particular aspects of the problem are addressed in J. M. Olson, "Radical Social Democracy and School Reform in Wilhelmine Germany," *History of Education Quarterly* 17 (1977): 3–16; N. Schwarte, *Schulpolitik und Pädagogik der deutschen Sozialdemokratie* (Cologne, 1980); K. Birker, *Die deutsche Arbeiterbildungsvereine, 1840–1870* (Berlin, 1973); W. Wendorff, *Schule und Bildung in der Politik von Wilhelm Liebknecht* (Berlin, 1978); and V. Lidtke, *The Alternative Culture: Socialist Labor in Imperial Germany* (New York, 1985).

socialist commonplaces. Several of the autobiographies use the motif of the authoritarian school to subvert the disciplinary intent of the pedagogic practice. In Grünberg's case, for example, the autobiographical interpretation of his torment at school is placed in the context of an evolving narrative of critique of the authoritarian state. Moreover, the memory of his own personal battle in the classroom is explicitly linked with political satires that he would encounter in the broader culture as an adult:

> From what I have said it is clear that this teacher was a typical "ele-
> mentary school bully" of the sort that I'd get to know in the excellent
> school comedy *Flachsmann als Erzieher*. (Grünberg, 22)

The memory of persecution and of his response to it would be an important element of Grünberg's definition of himself as rebel. Similarly, Ger, Lüth, Georg Werner, and other German men would tell the stories of their pedagogic drillmasters in terms that both fed into and reflected their later interpretations of the politically repressive function of schooling. Ger, for example, included in his memoirs a diatribe against the school and church which "designed everything in the education of these poor people to suppress the training of reason" (Ger, 17), an account that echoes Liebknecht's charge against the German schools. Werner claimed that bad treatment at the hands of one of his teachers resulted in "his awakened will to resistance" (Werner, 14). Certainly not all of the German boyhood accounts marked by oppressive teaching culminated in socialist careers, nor were all socialists badly taught. But a strong connection between the depiction of boyhood first encounters with state authority in the schools and the socialist critique of the repressive character of the state is certainly suggested.

In this context, the differing emphases of the accounts of schooling found in German women's autobiographies also takes on an additional dimension and suggests some of the ways in which the gender differences fed into class identity in very essential ways. As "good" pupils who appreciated and were appreciated by their teachers, the girls may well have been less subject to discipline than boys were (although it is important to note that many male autobiographers were self-reported star pupils as well). Even more to the point, the narrative of rebellion that informed many of the working-class male texts, in which the school story plays so important a part, had little pertinence for women—even female militants. The school's emphasis on submissiveness, considered as the emblem of political and economic oppression when forced upon boys in the classroom and adult men in the barracks and the factory, may have appeared more "natural" when applied to women and girls. In other words, parallel to the more obvious sex discrimination that marked socialist practice and affected the participation of women in the socialist movement, there ran at a deeper level a construction of the process of "coming to class awareness" that rested on contradictions between masculinity and submission to authority that simply did not pertain to women.[14] Women did certainly offer examples of rebellion, but their rebellions typically occurred as adults and centered around unjust practices in the workplace or assaults of their sexual inviolability or contradictory practices around working-class motherhood. Harassment in the classroom was rarely part of German women's narrative of growing up rebellious. Most women, even socialist women, did not allude to the socialist critique of the state in interpreting their experiences at school. They had to look elsewhere for the origins of their insubordination.

The French Comparison

A quick exploration of lower-class autobiographical representations in France in this same epoch suggests that the grimness of proletarian childhood was especially pronounced in (if not peculiar to) German-language texts. There are a few French accounts of childhoods marked by cruelty, neglect, and exploitation,[15] but these tales are notably rare and date from early in the nineteenth

---

14. For a full discussion of the place of women in the German socialist movement, see Heinz Niggemann, *Emanzipation zwischen Sozialismus und Feminismus: Die sozialdemokratische Frauenbewegung im Kaiserreich* (Wuppertal, 1981); and Jean H. Quataert, *Reluctant Feminists in German Social Democracy, 1885–1917* (Princeton, 1979), both of whom underscore the many barriers to female participation in the socialist movement. The question of a specifically female version of working-class identity in Germany is also fully explored by Kathleen Canning in "Gender and the Politics of Class Formation: Rethinking German Labor History," *American Historical Review* 97 (1992): 736–68.

15. Again, the tendency of the autobiographies can be specified more precisely. Only three of the twenty-six French autobiographers report childhoods dominated by excessive work and neglect. The others alternate between discussions of work and other pastimes, discipline, and shows of affection. Of course, we need to take into account who ended up writing autobiographies and what sorts of childhood experiences may have been especially likely to have connections with the autobiographical urge. These autobiographers emerged from across a broadly conceived spectrum of manual occupations. Parents of the autobiographers in my study not only were in "core" working-class occupations of the industrial era (miners, factory workers, railroad workers) but also included the upwardly and downwardly mobile, the service workers who proliferated in the growing cities, and the agricultural workers in various situations whose children fed into urban migrant streams. The sample included a greater proportion of factory workers among the parents of the autobiographers in the German sample and a greater proportion of agricultural families in the French. While these differences certainly help to account for some of the contrasting childhood experiences recorded, it is important to note that this difference reflects (though it exaggerates slightly) the respective character of the labor force of French- and German-speaking regions in the nineteenth century, stemming from the somewhat different character and pace of industrialization in France and Central Europe. For example, mid-nineteenth-century occupational censuses of France and Prussia indicate that 52 percent and 55 percent of the respective workforces were still employed in the primary sector. In France, this proportion fell only gradually to 42 percent by the

century. Much more common are stories of surprisingly sentimental home lives and warm relationships with mothers (and often fathers), even in the face of material deprivation. Louis Lecoin's story illustrates the point well. Lecoin was the third of seven children of a day laborer and was born in 1888. The family lived from hand to mouth, and all of its members had to contribute in various ways to its survival. Still, Lecoin explicitly rejected the conclusion that his childhood was exclusively a time of suffering:

> Am I, despite myself, going to claim to be a child martyr and have you believe that my early years passed in gloom, without horizon, without brightness, with no joy? That would be false!
> In the first place, my parents never treated me badly. (Lecoin, 17)

Lecoin remembered that he never blamed his parents for their poverty, nor did their struggle for survival make him sad. Instead, he suggests, the joint struggle created enormous solidarity among family members and, he felt, a special appreciation of children for their parents not felt by upper-class children:

> I have kept from my early childhood, which was very fine despite every-thing and even though it took place in the blackest poverty, the impression that the poor possess one advantage over the rich, in any case a noticeable compensation—I think that the kids of poor folks feel a closer and better affection for their parents—but have I observed well? (Lecoin, 13)

To take some other examples, Jean-Baptiste Dumay, half-orphaned before birth in 1841 by his father's death in a mining accident, recounted a relatively carefree childhood. In Jean Guehenno's memoir of growing up at the turn of the century in a Breton shoemaking family, the author's criticism of the intel-lectual narrowness of proletarian existence is tempered by nostalgia for what he had lost in his move from the shoe factory to the Academie française:

> I can still hardly believe that I never lack for bread or liberty. I've even come to believe that my security represents a sort of impoverishment . . . all that is forceful and clear in my life originated in my earlier exis-tence. . . . I've even taken to talking like my father . . . to saying "we" as he did, generously and as if this "we" embraced the universe, all of humanity. (Guehenno, 15)

---

century's end, whereas in Prussia, the proportion dropped more steeply to 34 percent. A fuller analysis of these occupational-structural differences can be found in Hartmut Kaelble, "Ab-weichung oder Konvergenz? Soziale Mobilität in Frankreich und Deutschland während des 19. und 20. Jahrhunderts," in *Aspekte der historischen Forschung in Frankreich und Deutschland*, ed. Gerhard A. Ritter and Rudolf Vierhaus (Göttingen, 1981).

As I mentioned earlier, there were elements of the family economy that by the late nineteenth century differentiated the French from the Central European working-class experience of growing up. Lecoin came from a large family, but both Dumay and Guehenno were from one-child families, which were becoming increasingly common in France. A changing family strategy made possible the generalization of child-centered family life that in Central Europe seemed to have been more restricted to middle-class milieus. Both the material and the psychological impact of this difference are recognizable in the proletarian autobiographies. Not only were French childhood accounts less centered on deprivation and relentless work than their German counterparts; they also were less likely to complain of the emotional bleakness and even abuse so common in the German stories.

Similarly, the encounter with repressive authority in the classroom so significant in German male autobiography is apparently distinctive of the German genre. At least as striking as the different schooling stories told in German autobiographies by men and women is the contrast between the German accounts overall and the French, a contrast that mirrors and amplifies the culturally specific autobiographical portrayals of childhood in the family context that I pointed out above.

The French public school *instituteurs* played an increasingly important role in memoirs dating from the mid-nineteenth century and later were typically recalled with respect and affection. For example, René Bonnet lived on the eve of World War I with his grandparents in a small village in the Limousin while his parents worked in Paris. He did not start school until he was almost eight years old because his grandparents knew he felt some anxiety about it. His fear was countered by the sympathy and sensitivity of his teacher:

> from the first lessons, Mr. Chalard realized that I was timid, and he contrived to build my self-confidence. He avoided asking me troublesome questions to which I might not know how to reply. (Bonnet, 17)

Georges Dumoulin, the son of day laborers in a small town in northern France, recalled his schooling in the 1880s in the most glowing terms:

> What beautiful years of my life! How sweet it is to recall them even now, these years of conquest, of reward, in the course of which all the satisfactions of self-esteem were bestowed upon my sensitive nature! I consecrated a veritable cult to my teacher, Charles Latour. He ran the school like a father, and he loved me like one of his children. It was he who gave me the books, the school supplies that my parents couldn't afford to buy, and above all the good advice that was aimed at helping me to avoid suffering because of my situation. (Dumoulin, 18)

For French working-class girls, *institutrices* could be equally significant figures. As in Germany, lay women teachers were recruited in increasing numbers in the closing decades of the nineteenth century to teach the growing number of female elementary pupils. In France, too, they were often recruited from among the ranks of the middle class, and their elevated social status seems often to have been an element in the girls' admiration. Madeleine Henrey recalled her schoolmistress as a particularly powerful influence during her girlhood in a working-class district of Paris on the eve of and during World War I:

> . . . my mother decided to send me to the state schools. I was twelve and terribly backward, and the drastic change was at first very upsetting, but I was so very conscious of my apparent ignorance, so determined to do better than the other girls, that I began to climb higher in the class by sheer hard work. . . . Mlle Foucher encouraged me. Of Alsatian descent, she was ardently patriotic, of rare intelligence and humanity. Her lessons acquired polish and extreme simplicity. Young, pretty, elegant, always beautifully shod, she seemed to dress for us. This combination of beauty and intelligence has ever seemed to me the most desirable thing on earth. . . . She was ours. We loved her. (Henrey, 206–8)

Even the more humble village *institutrice* could get results. The foundling Angelina Bardin, who was raised in a foster home in the Sarthe on the eve of World War I, recalled the combination of emotional involvement and intellectual seriousness that characterized her teachers in the village schools. When she first entered school, she was extremely frightened:

> I clung next to a wall, so as not to see anyone. My young teacher leaned over to me and stroked my hair. . . . Hidden by her white shawl, I didn't move. . . . The fringes of the wool shawl rubbed against my face; I counted them. I knew how to count to ten. . . . It was a great effort, one that left you a bit short of breath. Mademoiselle said to me then: Why are you afraid if you know how to count to ten? The justice of this remark made me raise my head. She repeated to me that when you knew how to count to ten, you didn't have to be afraid of anyone. (Bardin, 27–28)

The political history of schooling in France apparently bequeathed autobiographers from the lower classes a very different national mythology. In the France of the Third Republic, the schools were among the most important institutions forming the basis of a new political consensus around a liberal program. The battle over the schools was portrayed as the struggle between reactionary, clerical darkness and enlightenment for the masses. A belief in liberating knowledge and the opportunity for improvement through education to all was one of the founding and supporting myths of the republic.

This mythology had roots that went back to the epoch of the revolution; throughout the various moments of contention over the French state that punctuated the period from 1789 to 1871, debates over schooling held a prominent place in political discussion. Historical analyses of these debates and of subsequent educational policy have suggested discrepancies between hopes centered on schooling and social and political practice. But whatever retrospective analysis has to say about the realities that contradicted the Third Republic's dominant school mythology, it nevertheless appears from the autobiographies to have been quite solid and extensively held.[16]

Schools were made free, obligatory, and lay shortly after the triumph of the republic. The school administrators of the republican era aimed to integrate working-class children into the vision of interclass solidarity and cooperation that underlay Third Republican *solidarist* strategy. The people who recorded their memories of these schools suggest that to a great extent the solidarist view was indeed embodied in the image of the teacher. Autobiographical portraits of the *instituteurs* and *institutrices* of the Third Republic indicate that they were often seen as class mediaries in precisely the fashion that the ideology of *solaridisme* required.

The reading of these childhood memoirs against the background of the political culture in which they were written highlights their political significance. It is telling, for example, that Lecoin, who described the most impoverished of the French childhoods, nevertheless explicitly rejected the title of "child martyr." The French accounts in general, while recognizing material deprivation, locate the impact of economic brutality later in life and for the most part outside of the family and the school. For many of the German autobiographers in similar circumstances, in contrast, it seems to have been precisely to *claim* the title of child martyr that childhoods were recounted in the first place. German autobiographers, especially those who wrote as part of the great outpouring of life stories that flowed from the years of socialist growth in the early decades of the twentieth century, had a distinct political motivation for emphasizing the misery of childhood for working-class children. The continued elusiveness of proper childhood that is suggested in the German accounts contributed to the formulation of a social critique; it became the basis of a political claim. Missing out on the "golden years" of childhood became for

16. There is a broad overview of the historical analysis of French political life in the nineteenth century in Roger Magraw, *France, 1815–1914: The Bourgeois Century* (London, 1983). For specific discussion of the Third Republic and the role of educational reform in republican ideology and political strategy, see Sanford Elwitt, *The Making of the Third Republic: Class and Politics in France, 1869–1884* (Baton Rouge, 1975); as well as Katherine Auspitz, *The Radical Bourgeoisie* (Cambridge, 1982).

many Germans a first step on the life course to rebelliousness. To develop an insight suggested by George Steinmetz, the politicization in class-analytic terms of even the earliest childhood memories suggests the relative thoroughness of the process of class formation for German proletarians of this epoch.[17] However, the autobiographies also provide evidence of their authors' ambivalence vis-à-vis working-class identity. In the German accounts, authors often approached and crossed the fine line between documenting the effects of childhood deprivation and condemning the culture that that deprivation nurtured.

Writers of autobiographies recounted their childhoods in or after the lingering heat of political discussion about the character of dominant norms, about family and working-class patterns, and about the nature and aims of schooling. These memories thus reflect both contrasts in family and schooling patterns apparent by the late nineteenth century in France and Central Europe and also differences in the degree to which such experiences were incorporated into a political discussion in which class was a central dimension in the analysis of even very private experiences. There is at least a suggestion here that many French workers had carved out for themselves a realm of private satisfaction and personal ambition and had tempered certain of the most extreme consequences of the dislocation of industrial capitalism through family strategy. Contemporaneous German proletarian life stories, in contrast, politicize earlier stages of the life course and recount lives where every experience is marked by class difference. The autobiographical narratives signal some important aspects of class formation, rooted in the dynamics of family, gender, and child socialization, that need to be more fully addressed in historical class analysis. They also demonstrate the extent to which political consciousness is formed not only through the self-conscious activities of workers' organizations but also through family and socialization processes often relegated to a prepolitical stage of class formation.

Autobiographical Texts Cited

Altmann, Anna. 1912. "Blätter und Blüten." In *Gedenkbuch. 20 Jahre österreichische Arbeiterinnenbewegung,* ed. A. Popp. Vienna. 23–34.
Bardin, Angelina. 1956. *Angelina. Une fille des champs.* Paris.
Bonnet, Marcelin René. 1954. *Enfance Limousin.* Paris.
Christ, Lena. 1921. *Erinnerungen.* Munich.

---

17. George Steinmetz, "Reflections on the Role of Social Narratives in Working-Class Formation: Narrative Theory in the Social Sciences," *Social Science History* 16 (Fall 1992): 489–517.

Dumay, Jean-Baptiste. 1976. *Mémoires d'un militant ouvrier du Creusot, 1841–1905.* Grenoble.

Dumoulin, Georges. 1938. *Carnets de Route. (Quarante anneés de vie militante).* Lille.

Ger(isch), Alwin. 1918. *Erzgebirgisches Volk. Erinnerung von A. Ger.* Berlin.

Grünberg, Karl. 1969. Episoden. *Sechs Jahrzehnte Kampf um den Sozialismus.* Berlin.

Guehenno, Jean. 1961. *Changer la vie. Mon enfance et ma jeunesse.* Paris.

Henrey, Mrs. Robert. 1950. *The Little Madeleine. The Autobiography of a Young Girl in Montmartre.* New York.

Lecoin, Louis. 1965. *Le cours d'une vie.* Paris.

Lüth, Franz. nd (1908) *Aus der Jugendzeit eines Tagelöhners,* ed. W. H. Michaelis. Berlin.

Maier, Anna. 1912. "Wie Ich Reif Wurde." In *Gedenkbuch. 20 Jahren österreichische Arbeiterinnenbewegung,* ed. A. Popp. Vienna. 107–9.

Perthen, Anna. 1912. "Der Anfang in Bodenbach." In *Gedenkbuch. 20 Jahren österreichische Arbeiterinnenbewegung,* ed. A. Popp. Vienna. 113–16.

(Popp, Adelheid). 1909. *Die Jugendgeschichte einer Arbeiterin.* Munich.

Roth, Aurelia. 1912. "Eine Glasschleiferin." In *Gedenkbuch. 20 Jahre österreichische Arbeiterinnenbewegung,* ed. A. Popp. Vienna. 52–61.

Rüegg, Anneliese. 1914. *Erlebnisse einer Serviertochter. Bilder aus der Hotelindustrie.* Zurich.

Werner, Georg. 1958. *Meine rechnung Geht in Ordnung, 1877–1957.* Berlin.

Religion and Working-Class Formation in Imperial Germany, 1871–1914

Willfried Spohn

Introduction

Until recently, religion and secularization have not been major topics either within studies of the labor history of specific nations or within comparative historical-sociological approaches to working-class formation.[1] This is due to deep-rooted sociological and Marxist notions that equate class consciousness with secularism and conceive of religion as an opponent of, and limitation on, working-class formation.[2]

Because most national labor histories have been written by labor-movement intellectuals and their academic followers and most labor movements have been shaped by anticlerical and secular ideologies,[3] the relationship of religious institutions and mentalities to working-class formation has

This essay has been published in *Politics and Society* 119, no. 1 (1991): 109–32. The version here contains only minor changes. For critical and helpful discussion, I want to thank particularly Margaret Levi and Mary Nolan.

1. See especially Eric J. Hobsbawm, *Worlds of Labour: Further Studies in the History of Labour* (London: Weidenfeld and Nicolson, 1984); Eric J. Hobsbawm, *The Age of Empire* (New York: Pantheon Books, 1988); Ira Katznelson and Aristide R. Zolberg, eds., *Working-Class Formation: Nineteenth-Century Patterns in Western Europe and the United States* (Princeton: Princeton University Press, 1986); and Jürgen Kocka, ed., *Europäische Arbeiterbewegungen im 19. Jahrhundert: Deutschland, Österreich, England und Frankreich im Vergleich* (Göttingen: Vandenhoeck und Ruprecht, 1983).

2. See the introduction to Richard Evans, ed., *The German Working Class, 1888–1933: The Politics of Everyday Life* (London: Hutchinson, 1982).

3. Eric J. Hobsbawm, "Labour History and Ideology," in Hobsbawm, *Worlds of Labour,* 1–14.

been neglected. One major exception is the British case, where religious traditions have played a significant role in the labor movement and consequently have been a prominent theme of British labor history.[4] But especially in the German case, which was shaped by atheistic ideology and provided the historical paradigm for Marxist class notions, the reference to religion has seemed to be a contradiction in terms. As studies on working-class culture, popular religion, and the social history of religion show, however, this state of affairs is changing.[5]

Not surprisingly, recent comparative historical and sociological approaches have followed the same pattern. A major exception is the British historian Eric Hobsbawm, who raises the question of the relationship between religion and working-class formation in a comparative perspective.[6] A more typical example is Barrington Moore, who does not include the analysis of religion in his historical sociology of the German working class, although he aims to describe working-class mentalities as cultural clues to obedience and revolt.[7]

The most systematic recent historical-sociological approach to working-class formation, by Ira Katznelson, Aristide Zolberg, and associates, lacks any systematic treatment of religion and secularization.[8] In that collection of essays, working-class formation is seen to occur historically and theoretically on four levels: the economic structure of wage labor, social life, cultural dispositions, and collective action. The variations in working-class formation are viewed as the result of three clusters of economy-, society-, and policy-centered factors. Religion is included—albeit not systematically—as a society-centered institutional and mental context. But religion should also be conceived of as a component of working-class formation with regard to the religious aspects of working-class life, cultural dispositions, and political ori-

---

4. Hugh McLeod, *Religion and the Working Class in Nineteenth Century Britain* (London: Macmillan, 1984); see also the classic study by Edward P. Thompson, *The Making of the English Working Class* (Harmondsworth: Penguin, 1968).

5. See Richard Evans, ed., *Religion and Society in Germany: European Studies Review* 12, no. 3; Hugh McLeod, *Religion and the People of Western Europe, 1789–1970* (Oxford: Oxford University Press, 1981); Gerhard A. Ritter, *Arbeiterkultur* (Königstein/Ts.: Athenäum, 1979); and Wolfgang Schieder, "Religion in der Sozialgeschichte," in *Sozialgeschichte in Deutschland: Entwicklungen und Perspektiven im internationalen Zusammenhang,* vol. 3, *Soziales Verhalten und soziale Alktionsformem in der Geschichte,* ed., Wolfgang Schieder and V. Sellin (Göttingen: Vandenhoeck und Ruprecht, 1987).

6. Eric J. Hobsbawm, "Religion and the Rise of Socialism," in Hobsbawm, *Worlds of Labour,* 33–48.

7. Barrington Moore, Jr., *Injustice: Social Origins of Obedience and Revolt* (Cambridge: Cambridge University Press, 1978).

8. Katznelson and Zolberg, *Working-Class Formation.*

entations;[9] and religion should be analyzed not only in its restraining but also in its enabling role.[10]

The studies of nineteenth-century German working-class formation by Jürgen Kocka and Mary Nolan explain the dominance of the socialist-Marxist labor movement chiefly by reference to the belated but rapid and crisis-prone capitalist industrialization in the second half of the nineteenth century, the authoritarian imperial state's simultaneous use of repression and social integration, and the political weakness of German liberalism when simultaneously confronted with nation building, democratization, and the social question.[11] The religious conditions and components of working-class formation are described to a certain degree, but mainly with reference to the Catholic church's ability to limit social democracy's organizational efforts.[12]

These explanations for the pattern of working-class formation in Imperial Germany are insufficient, because various characteristics of that pattern can be fully understood only when religion and secularization are taken into account as contexts and components of working-class formation. First, the overall pattern of working-class formation in Imperial Germany, with its dominant Social Democratic (mostly Protestant) pole and its smaller Christian (mostly Catholic) counterpole, is also structured along confessional lines. The differing relationships of the Protestant and Catholic churches to the working class, the differing effects of both state churches on the secularization of the working class, and the connections between secularization and secular religion were decisive.

---

9. Certainly the analytical model of Katznelson and Zolberg is highly useful for comparative purposes, but it can easily have a structuralist bias; see the stimulating criticism by Margaret R. Somers in "Workers of the World, Compare!" *Contemporary Sociology* 18, no. 3 (1989): 325–29. See also my own discussion of Jürgen Kocka's Marxian-Weberian class model from a Thompsonian perspective: Willfried Spohn, "Klassentheorie und Sozialgeschichte: Ein kritischer Vergleich der klassengeschichtlichen Interpretationen der Arbeiterbewegung durch Edward P. Thompson und Jürgen Kocka," *Prokla: Zeitschrift für politische okonomie und sozialistische Politik* 61 (1985): 126–38. See also Jürgen Kocka, *Weder Stand noch Klasse. Unterschichten um 1800* (Berlin: Dietz, 1991) and Jürgen Kocka, *Arbeitsverhöltnisse und Arbeiterexistenzen. Grundlagen der Klassenbildung 1800–1870* (Berlin, 1991).

10. For this distinction, see Raymond Williams, *Marxism and Literature* (Oxford: Oxford University Press, 1977).

11. Jürgen Kocka, "Problems of Working-Class Formation in Germany: The Early Years, 1800–1875," in Katznelson and Zolberg, *Working-Class Formation* and Kocka, *Europäische Arbeiterbewegungen.*

12. Mary Nolan, "Economic Crisis, State Policy, and Working-Class Formation in Germany, 1870–1900," in Katznelson and Zolberg, *Working-Class Formation;* Mary Nolan, *Social Democracy and Society: Working Class Radicalism in Düsseldorf, 1890–1920* (Cambridge: Cambridge University Press, 1981).

Second, the limits on Social Democracy's organizational efforts were set primarily by the formation of a Catholic working-class milieu, with its own religious working-class identity, rather than by the institutional strength of the Catholic church. In this respect, religious mentalities and attitudes are essential cultural and political components of working-class formation. And the same holds true for socialist labor. At the center of its cultural dispositions and political orientations, as expressed by its Marxist-atheistic worldview were secularized Protestant-Lutheran working-class mentalities, which displayed strong elements of a secular religion.

As a result, the religious components of working-class formation in Imperial Germany contributed to the fundamental political divisions between the various working-class currents. This had a crucial long-term impact on the history of working-class formation in twentieth-century Germany.

The article is based on sources such as worker autobiographies, local newspapers, poems, songs, the writings of political and religious intellectuals, and local and regional studies. In the following I present an outline of arguments and considerations for interpreting these complex historical sources.

Religious Determinants of Working-Class Formation

Imperial German society was structured by five so-called social-moral milieus, which were characterized by a certain (albeit generically and regionally different) "pillarized" linking of social and cultural life-worlds with relatively stable political orientations.[13] These were the mainly Prussian agrarian milieu represented by the Conservative Party, the primarily urban middle-class milieu with its National Liberal Party and its Left-Liberal Party, the predominantly urban working-class milieu and social democracy, the socially mixed Catholic milieu and the Center Party, and the minority cultures with their respective ethical-political representations.

The pattern of working-class formation roughly followed these five social-moral milieus and correspondingly consisted of Evangelical, liberal, socialist, Catholic, and ethnic working-class milieus.[14] Although these

---

13. This notion has been introduced to describe the relatively stable social units in Imperial Germany, which were characterized by the coincidence of economic situation, regional tradition, religion, cultural orientation, and political representation. See Parteiensystem und Sozialstruktur: Zum Problem der Demokratisierung der deutschen Gesellschaft," in *Wirtschaft, Geschichte und Wirtschaftsgeschichte,* ed. Wilhelm Abel (Stuttgart: Klett und Cotta, 1966), 371–93. Gerhard A. Ritter, *Die deutschen Parteien, 1830–1914* (Göttingen: Vandenhoeck und Ruprecht, 1985); and James J. Sheehan, "Klasse und Partei im Kaiserreich: Einige Gedanken zur Sozialgeschichte der deutschen Politik," in *Innenpolitische Probleme des Bismarck-Reiches,* ed. O. Pflantze (Munich: Oldenbourg, 1983), 1–24.

14. Josef Mooser, *Arbeiterleben in Deutschland, 1900–1970* (Frankfurt: Suhrkamp, 1984).

working-class milieus were integrated into the more comprehensive ones, each had its own culture with its own party, trade union, press, and associations. This internal integration also formed boundaries, that were drawn not only by opposing orientations, social barriers, regional peculiarities, and ethnic identities but also by confessional differences.

The dominant element of the working class was socialist. Because it was socially and politically discriminated against by state and church, the socialist labor movement reacted by developing a radically oppositional, Marxist, and atheistic ideology.[15] It tended to represent dependent artisans and journeymen, skilled more than unskilled industrial workers, mainly in the northern German urban-industrial centers. It recruited predominantly from Protestant working-class areas. The smaller counterpole was formed by the Catholic working-class milieu, which represented artisans, journeymen, and skilled and unskilled workers mainly in Rhineland-Westphalia, the Saarland, and Silesia.[16]

In comparison to the socialist and Catholic labor movements, the liberal working-class milieu could develop only to a very limited extent. It consisted mainly of artisans and skilled workers in old industrial and urban centers, was organized in the Hirsch-Duncker trade unions, and was overwhelmingly Protestant.[17] The Evangelical working-class milieu also remained insignificant.[18] It was comprised of artisans and workers in small towns and in confessionally mixed industrial communities. Among the ethnic minorities, the Polish miners were the most successful in developing their own separate working-class culture,[19] whereas the relatively few Jewish workers were generally oriented toward social democracy.[20]

Thus working-class formation in Imperial Germany was patterned in

---

15. See W. L. Guttsman, *The German Social Democratic Party, 1875–1933* (London: Allen and Unwin, 1981); and Vernon Lidtke, *The Outlawed Party: Social Democracy in Germany, 1878–1890* (Princeton: Princeton University Press, 1966).

16. See Eric Born Brose, "Christian Labor and the Politics of Frustration in Imperial Germany" (Ph.D. diss., Columbia University, 1978); Klaus-Michael Mallmann, *Die Anfänge der Bergarbeiterbewegung an der Saar, 1848–1904* (Saarbrücken: Minerva, 1981); Lawrence Schofer, *The Formation of a Modern Labor Force, Upper Silesia, 1865–1914* (Berkeley: University of California Press, 1975); and Klaus Tenfelde, *Sozialgeschichte der Bergarbeiterschaft an der Ruhr im 19. Jahrhundert* (Bonn: Verlag Neue Gesellschaft, 1977).

17. See Werner Conze, *Die Möglichkeiten und Grenzen der liberalen Arbeiterbewegung in Deutschland* (Heidelberg: Winter, 1965).

18. See Bruno Feyerabend, "Die evangelischen Arbeitervereine" (Ph.D. diss., University of Frankfurt, 1955).

19. See Elke Hausschildt, "Polish Migrant Culture in Imperial Germany," *New German Critique* 46 (Winter 1989): 155–71; Christoph Klessmann, *Polnische Bergarbeiter im Ruhrgebiet, 1870–1945* (Göttingen: Vandenhoeck und Ruprecht, 1978); and Richard C. Murphy, *Gastarbeiter im Deutschen Reich: Polen in Bottrop, 1891–1933* (Wuppertal: Hammer, 1982).

20. See Robert Wistrich, *Socialism and the Jews: The Dilemma of Assimilation in Germany and Austria-Hungary* (East Brunswick, N.J.: Associated University Presses, 1982).

asymmetric ways between socialist and Catholic labor. With respect to the religious structures involved, secular-irreligious worldviews displayed a relatively strong influence compared with confessional religiosity. At the same time, confessional dualism had its impact not only directly on the relationship between Catholic and Evangelical labor but also indirectly on the relationship between Christian (mostly Catholic) labor and socialist (mostly secularized Protestant) labor. Thus working-class formation was constructed along confessional lines, as some figures show.

Given a rough overall ratio of 2 : 1 between Protestants and Catholics, the ratio between Protestant and Catholic workers was an estimated 2.5 : 1.[21] This indicates that capitalist industrialization together with proletarianization was developing more rapidly in Protestant, Prussian north German regions than in the Catholic south and west. Moreover, Catholic workers were employed more in such industries as woodworking, textile production, and mining, which still had a certain affinity to agricultural and protoindustrial modes of production and ways of life.

Within this economic structure, the socialist workers decisively outnumbered the Catholic ones. In terms of trade union membership, the ratio was about 7 : 1 in 1913,[22] but in terms of overall participation in working-class organizations, it was an estimated 4 : 1.[23] This reflects the fact that the Catholic working-class milieu lost about one-third of Catholic workers to the socialist milieu[24] but was able to integrate two-thirds of them into the Catholic working-class culture, not so much into the trade unions as into broader associational networks.

This transfer of Catholic workers affected the predominant confessional construction of both working-class cultures only marginally. With respect to voting behavior, support for the Center Party was drawn almost exclusively (90 percent) from Catholic precincts,[25] whereas the Social Democratic Party

21. There is no comprehensive study of the relationship between social structure and religious orientations for nineteenth-century Germany. Therefore I have to confine myself to some rough estimates, here with reference to the introduction by Richard Evans to *Religion and Society in Germany* and Gerd Hohorst, Jürgen Kocka, and Gerhard Ritter, *Sozialgeschichtliches Arbeitsbuch: Materialien zur Statistik des Kaiserreichs, 1870–1914* (Munich: Beck, 1975), 55, 73.

22. The free trade unions had 2.55 million and the Christian unions had 0.34 million members. See Mooser, *Arbeiterleben*, 192–93.

23. See Thomas Nipperdey, *Religion im Umbruch: Deutschland, 1870–1918* (Munich: Beck, 1988), 58.

24. See ibid., 61–62; and Gerhard Ritter, "Zur Strategie der sozialdemokratischen Wahlrekrutierung im Kaiserreich," in *Wählerbewegung in der deutschen Geschichte: Analysen und Berichte zu den Reichstagswahlen, 1871–1933*, ed. Otto Büsch, Monika Wölk, and Wolfgang Wölk (Berlin: Colloquium Verlag, 1978), 313–24.

25. Gerhard A. Ritter and Merith Niehuss, *Wahlgeschichtliches Arbeitsbuch: Materialien zur Statistik des Kaiserreichs, 1871–1918* (Munich: Beck, 1980), 99–101; and Johannes Schauff,

gained approximately 80 percent of its votes from Protestant areas, and its Catholic votes came from more secularized urban centers.[26] Even more revealing, approximately 80 percent of Social Democratic and free trade union members came from Protestant backgrounds, whereas about 90 percent of the formally interconfessional Christian trade union members came from Catholic ones.[27]

The confessional structuring of working-class formation can be explained only to a certain extent by the differing industrialization patterns and their consequences for working-class life-worlds in Protestant and Catholic regions.[28] It can be generally assumed that industrialization together with proletarianization, migration, and urbanization tendentially disintegrated traditional, religious life-worlds and that these processes were an essential precondition for secularized working-class mentalities. Therefore, the stronger industrialization of Protestant regions in Imperial Germany should have led to a more secularized Protestant working class; and, conversely, the weaker industrialization of Catholic regions should have resulted in stronger traditional, religious bonds. Industrialization did not differ to such an extent in Protestant and Catholic regions, however, that this alone could explain why Protestant workers were overwhelmingly organized in a secularized labor movement, whereas the majority of Catholic workers were organized in a religious labor movement.

In order to explain that difference, one must ask how traditional religiosity among the lower classes was transformed during the process of industrialization. Two interrelated aspects are involved here. On the one hand, this cultural-mental change is determined by more comprehensive societal, institutional, and cultural developments; on the other hand, it is also a component of working-class formation, a result of how workers used or rejected religious systems of meaning in the construction of their identities.

I will turn first to the religious context of the transformation of working-class religiosity. Three characteristics of nineteenth-century German religious history were decisive: the impact of the state churches on the process of working-class secularization, the influence of confessional dualism on the

---

Die deutschen Katholiken und die Zentrumspartei: Eine politisch-statistische Untersuchung der Reichstagswahlen seit 1871 (Cologne: Bachem, 1928).

26. Alois Klöcker, "Konfession und sozialdemokratische Wählerschaft," in Büsch et al., *Wählerbewegung in der deutschen Geschichte,* 197–207.

27. Michael Schneider, *Die christlichen Gewerkschaften, 1894–1933* (Bonn: Verlag Neue Gesellschaft, 1982).

28. On the pattern of nineteenth-century German industrialization, see Willfried Spohn, *Weltmarktkonkurrenz und Industrialisierung Deutschlands, 1870–1914* (Berlin: Olle und Wolter, 1977); and Hubert Kiesewetter, *Industrielle Revolution in Deutschland, 1815–1914* (Frankfurt: Suhrkamp, 1989).

unevenness of this process, and the importance of secular religions for working-class secularization.

With respect to working-class secularization, it was crucial that the Protestant and Catholic churches had been established as *Amtskirchen* (state churches) at the beginning of the nineteenth century, completing the already close link between churches and territorial absolutist states that emerged from the Reformation and the Counter-Reformation.[29] As a result, religious affairs on all levels were subject to close state control, newly emerging religious currents were either integrated or suppressed, and independent religious sects remained relatively weak. Formal church membership remained extensive until the end of the imperial era, although the middle class became estranged from the churches after the Revolution of 1848, and the working class did so after the foundation of the Bismarckian empire.[30]

Some general ecclesiastical data indicate that after the turn of the century, denominational identity continued to be a self-evident, common part of life.[31] In 1905, for example, formal church membership among the country's 66 million inhabitants was 62 percent Protestant, 36.7 percent Catholic, 0.8 percent other Christian, 1 percent Jewish, and only 0.03 percent without confession. While these figures inform us primarily about confessional distribution and compulsory church membership, others show that participation in ecclesiastical life-cycle ceremonies, such as baptism, confirmation, marriage, and funeral rites, was a high 90 to 97 percent (with the single exception of 60 percent in Berlin, the most secularized German city). These figures point to the obligatory character of church rituals and to the cultural barriers against abandoning them.

Other general indicators, however, reveal a markedly low level of working-class religiosity in urban and industrial centers. Holy communion statistics for 1906–8 show that, although participation in villages and small towns remained quite high, only 7 to 15 percent of church members in the larger German cities took communion. Similarly, only 10 to 20 percent of

---

29. See Werner Conze, "Religion und Kirche," in *Handbuch der deutschen Wirtschafts- und Sozialgeschichte*, vol. 2, ed. H. Aubin and W. Zorn, 478–520 (Stuttgart: Klett and Cotta, 1976); Evans, Introduction to *Religion and Society in Germany;* Thomas Nipperdey, *Deutsche Geschichte, 1800–1860: Bürgerwelt und starker Staat* (Munich: Beck, 1984); Franz Schnabel, *Deutsche Geschichte im 19. Jahrhundert*, vol. 4 (Freiburg: Herder, 1937); and Hans-Ulrich Wehler, *Deutsche Gesellschaftsgeschichte, 1700–1815, 1815–1848/49* (Munich: Beck, 1987).

30. See Owen Chadwick, *The Secularization of the European Mind* (Cambridge: Cambridge University Press, 1975).

31. For the following figures, see Vernon Lidtke, "Social Class and Secularization in Imperial Germany: The Working Classes," *Yearbook of the Leo Baeck Institute* 25 (1982): 21–40, especially 23–25; and Hugh McLeod, "Protestantism and the Working Classes in Imperial Germany," *European Studies Review* 12, no. 3 (1982): 323–44.

church members in the larger cities attended services.[32] Some regional and local studies suggest that church membership and participation by workers followed the general uneven pattern between countryside and cities on a slightly lower level.[33] The workers' widespread estrangement from church and religion in urban and industrial areas is also suggested by their rapidly growing support for the Social Democratic Party, which was known for its atheistic anticlericalism and which gained 34 percent of the votes in the Reichstag election of 1912.[34] Contemporary empirical surveys of workers' religious consciousness further support this. According to Adolf Levenstein's 1912 study, 6.2 percent of workers questioned were irreligious, 50.1 percent indifferent, and only 12.1 percent religious (the remaining 31.6 percent did not answer).[35]

With regard to the confessional patterning of working-class formation, it was crucial that secularization was far more a Protestant than a Catholic phenomenon. Participation in church life, from church attendance and holy communion to life-cycle ceremonies, was considerably higher in Catholic regions than in Protestant ones.[36] The reason for this was not only that industrialization, urbanization, and proletarianization developed more in Protestant (mostly northern German) areas than it did in Catholic (mostly southern German) ones. This phenomenon was also connected to the substantially different

---

32. Lidtke, "Social Class and Secularization in Imperial Germany," 24–25.

33. See David Blackbourn, *Class, Religion, and Local Politics in Wilhelmine Germany: The Center Party in Württemberg before 1914* (New Haven: Yale University Press, 1980); David Crew, *Town in the Ruhr: A Social History of Bochum, 1860–1914* (New York: Columbia University Press, 1979); Stephen Hickey, "The Shaping of the German Labor Movement: The Miners in the Ruhr," in *Society and Politics in Wilhelmine Germany,* ed. R. Evans, 210–39 (London: Hutchinson, 1978); and Hsi-Huey Liang, "The Social Background of the Berlin Working-Class Movement" (Ph.D. diss., University of Michigan, Ann Arbor, 1980); Werner K. Blessing, *Staat und Kirche in der Gesellschaft: Institutionelle Autorität und mentaler Wandel in Bayern während des 19. Jahrhunderts* (Göttingen: Vandenhoeck und Ruprecht, 1982); Paul Göhre, *Drei Monate Fabrikarbeiter und Handwerkbursche* (Leipzig: Grünow, 1891); Rainer Marbach, *Säkularisierung und sozialer Wandel im 19. Jahrhundert* (Göttingen: Vandenhoeck und Ruprecht, 1978); Otto Neuloh, *Vom Kirchdorf zur Industriegemeinde: Untersuchungen über den Einfluss der Industrialisierung auf die Welstordnung der Arbeitnehmer* (Cologne: Grote, 1967).

34. Hohorst et al., *Sozialgeschichtliches Arbeitsbuch,* 175.

35. Adolf Levenstein, *Die Arbeiterfrage* (Munich: Reinhardt, 1912); see also the contemporary studies of Günther Dehn, *Die religiöse Gedankenwelt der Proletarierjugend in Selbstzeugnissen dargestellt* (Berlin: Furche, 1924); Wilhelm Ilgenstein, *Die religiöse Gedankenwelt der Sozialdemokratie* (Berlin: Vaterländische Verlags- und Kunstanstalt, 1914); Paul Piechowski, *Proletarischer Glaube: Die religiöse Gedankenwelt der organisierten deutschen Arbeiterschaft nach sozialistischen und kommunistischen Selbstzeugnissen* (Berlin: Dietz, 1927); and Martin Rade, "Die sittlich-religiöse Gedankenwelt unserer Industriearbeiter," in *Die Verhandlungen des neunten Evangelisch-sozialen Kongresses Berlin 1898* (Göttingen: Vandenhoeck und Ruprecht, 1898).

36. Lidtke, "Social Class and Secularization in Imperial Germany," 23–28.

relationship of church, state, and working class in each confession. It was in their reaction to the social question that the most important contrast between Protestantism and Catholicism emerged during the nineteenth century. Although both churches were state churches, the Protestant church was especially connected with the Prussian state and then with the imperial state.[37] This so-called marriage of throne and altar was one of the main reasons for the sharp anticlerical and antireligious tendencies among the Protestant population in particular. The close institutional connection with the state was bound up with a Lutheran theological tradition that strongly separated world and God, public and private, and state and church. Accordingly, Lutheranism assigned the social question to the state and left care for the inner spirit to the church.[38] This theology set strong limitations on any social activism. Protestantism, which centered on the more middle-class vicarage, was hostile to any collective association of working-class interests, and in turn workers strongly rejected the church as well.

The Catholic church reacted quite differently to the social question.[39] This was not merely a consequence of its minority status in Prussian Germany and the attacks on it during the *Kulturkampf.* It was also a consequence both of a more plebeian clergy and of a different type of religiosity and theology that did not separate world and God but instead advocated a religiously motivated commitment to the world.[40] Within this theological framework, a form of "social Catholicism" was able to develop. Social Catholicism led not only to the formulation of Catholic social doctrine but also to an active articulation of workers' needs and wants.

Given the widespread secularization of Protestant workers, it is essential to interpret the cultural meaning of working-class secularization. If we conceive of religion as a belief system constituted by experiences of the sacred and of secularization as a process by which religious institutions, practices, and consciousness lose their religious significance and are replaced by alternative institutions and belief systems,[41] we must emphasize two aspects of working-class secularization in Imperial Germany.

37. See R. M. Bigler, *The Politics of German Protestantism* (Berkeley: University of California Press, 1972); and William O. Shanahan, *Der deutsche Protestantismus vor der sozialen Frage, 1815–1871* (Munich: Piper, 1962).

38. See Ernst Troeltsch, *Die Soziallehren der christlichen Kirchen und Gruppen* (Tübingen: Siebeck und Mohr, 1922); and W. Reginald Ward, *Theology, Sociology and Politics: The German Protestant Social Conscience, 1890–1933* (Bern: Peter Lang, 1979).

39. See Martin Greschat, *Christentum und Gesellschaft: Das Zeitalter der Industriellen Revolution* (Stuttgart: Kohlhammer, 1980).

40. See Troeltsch, *Die Soziallehren der christlichen Kirchen und Gruppen.*

41. See Alasdair MacIntyre, *Secularization and Moral Change* (Oxford: Oxford University Press, 1967); Lidtke, "Social Class and Secularization in Imperial Germany," 21–22; Guenther Roth and Wolfgang Schluchter, *Max Weber's Vision of History, Ethics and Methods* (Berkeley:

First, all the empirical indicators tell us more about declining church-associated religiosity than about dechristianization as such. The markedly low level of church service and holy communion attendance does not imply a corresponding working-class irreligiosity. Workers in the new urban and industrial centers who had recently emigrated from still-pious villages and small towns often retained their traditional religious needs and beliefs but were unable to satisfy them within new surroundings.[42] Support for Social Democracy, either by voting or joining socialist organizations, did not necessarily imply an endorsement of atheism. Indeed, formal disaffiliation from the church—vehemently urged by Social Democracy after the turn of the century—was only minimally successful.[43] Moreover, within the working-class family, it was mainly men who were irreligious, while women tried to pass along traditional attitudes to their children.[44] Thus there is a danger in believing contemporary opinion, which overrated working-class dechristianization because it seemed to threaten the moral order of state and society.

Second, working-class secularization was characterized not only by secular irreligiosity but also by alternative secular-religious belief systems. By "secular religion," I mean religious resurgences of the sacred in the secularized world, especially in the realm of politics.[45] By the mid-nineteenth century, the German *Bildungsbürgertum,* the educated middle class, had already turned to a belief system with strong secular-religious components. Precisely because of the close link between state and church and their mutual control of religious life, political and religious issues were closely related within the liberal-democratic opposition movement during and after the Revolution of 1848. Radical liberalism went hand in hand with radical freethinking, which had originated in demands for religious autonomy for individuals and dissenting sects, promoted rational theology against revealed religion, and turned into a

University of California Press, 1979); Max Weber, *Wirtschaft und Gesellschaft* (Tübingen: Siebeck und Mohr, 1964); Max Weber, *Gesammelte Aufsätze zur Religionssoziologie* (Tübingen: Siebeck und Mohr, 1988); and Bryan Wilson, *Religion in Sociological Perspective* (Princeton: Princeton University Press, 1982).

42. For Berlin, see Jörg Kniffka, Das kirchliche Leben in der Mitte der zwanziger Jahre: Eine Untersuchung der kirchlichen Teilnahme und ihrer Motivation in evangelischen Arbeitergemeinden von 1924 bis 1927" (Ph.D. diss., University of Münster, 1971); see also Hugh McLeod, "Religion in the British and German Labour Movements, 1890–1914: A Comparison," *Bulletin of the Society for the Study of Labour History* 51, no. 1 (1986): 25–28.

43. Lidtke, "Social Class and Secularization in Imperial Germany," 25.

44. See Ruth-Ellen B. Joeres and Mary Jo Maynes, eds., *German Women in the Eighteenth and Nineteenth Centuries: A Social and Literary History* (Bloomington: Indiana University Press, 1986); and John C. Fout, ed., *German Women in the Nineteenth Century: A Social History* (New York: Holmes and Meier, 1984).

45. See Jean-Pierre Sironneau, *Sécularisation et religions politiques* (The Hague: Mouton, 1982).

belief in pantheistic or Christian humanism.[46] During the imperial era, this humanism fused with beliefs in science, social Darwinism, and cultural nationalism.[47]

Following the middle class, working-class secularization was strongly connected with the creation of alternative belief-systems. The secular segments of the working class, who were influenced by liberal, free-religious, and then social-Darwinistic humanism, combined the bourgeois secular-religious traditions with socialism and later Marxism. Thus if we look more closely at Levenstein's study cited above,[48] we see that the types of working-class consciousness categorized as irreligious and indifferent often express a close affinity to the popular philosophy of nature, social Darwinism, and socialism.[49]

Having outlined the ways in which religious institutions and mentalities influenced the peculiar pattern of working-class formation in Imperial Germany, I will now turn to the question of how religious and secularized mentalities became components of working-class identities.

Christian Labor and Religion

Popular mentalities in preindustrial Germany were predominantly religious.[50] Before the Revolution of 1848, when religious and ecclesiastical bonds were largely intact, the increasing pauperization of the lower class was often accompanied by deepening piety, and the political and social criticism of human misery was frequently articulated in Christian popular language. This religious socialism had many colors—ecclesiastical, conservative, sectarian, radical, and, above all, antiliberal. Based on the idea of an integrated Christian social order, Christian socialism was a reaction by church officials against the widespread deterioration of social conditions and the alarming anticlerical and democratic tendency of artisans and workers. Although it mixed social com-

---

46. See Jörn Brederlow, *"Lichtfreunde" und "Freie Gemeinden": Religiöser Protest und Freiheitsbewegung im Vormärz und in der Revolution von 1848/49* (Munich: Oldenbourg, 1976); and Friedrich W. Graf, *Die Politisierung des religiösen Bewusstseins: Die bürgerlichen Religionsparteien im Deutschen Vormärz: Das Beispiel des Deutsch-Katholizismus* (Stuttgart: Frommann-Holzboog, 1978). See generally Jürgen Kocka, ed., *Bürgertum im 19. Jahrhundert*, 3 vols. (Munich: Deutscher Taschenbuch Verlag, 1988).

47. See George L. Mosse, *The Crisis of German Ideology: Intellectual Origins of the Third Reich* (1964; reprint, New York: Schocken Books, 1981); Gabriel Motzkin, "Säkularisierung, Bürgertum und Intellektuelle in Frankreich und Deutschland während des 19. Jahrhunderts," in Kocka, *Bürgertum im 19. Jahrhundert:* 141–71; and Helmuth Plessner, *Die verspätete Nation* (Stuttgart: Kohlhammer, 1959).

48. Levenstein, *Die Arbeiterfrage.*

49. Alfred Kelly, "Darwinism and the Working Class in Wilhelmine Germany," in *Political Symbolism in Modern Europe*, ed. S. Drescher, D. Sabean, and A. Sharli (New Brunswick, N.J.: Transaction Books, 1982).

50. See Hobsbawm, "Religion and the Rise of Socialism."

mitment, paternalistic welfare, and authoritarian patronage from above, it was also based on deepening popular piety.[51]

From the beginning, however, the difference between the Protestant and Catholic varieties of Christian socialism was striking. Among Protestants, for example, Heinrich Wichern, the founder of modern organized charity within the Lutheran church, was one of the few who realized that practical commitment was necessary to solve the social question. But characteristically he called his enterprise the Innere Mission (Inner Mission), thus emphasizing inward moral evangelization instead of institutional change by social reform, which Lutheranism defined exclusively as the task of the state.[52] Among Catholics, fundamental criticism of liberal capitalism was much more marked, and some notions of the collective rights of the "working estate" were recognized, however vaguely. For this reason, a range of Catholic associations for journeymen, artisans, and workers was established; these were connected most prominently with Adolf Kolping, a worker-priest, and Emmanuel Ketteler, a socially committed bishop. Social reform was not seen exclusively as a responsibility of the state, and the Christian ethos was directed less toward inward spirituality than toward collective practical morality.[53]

In contrast to Lutheranism, Catholicism fostered the collective organization of workers although there was much conflict between the religious-patriarchal limitations set by the church and the demands put forward by Catholic workers. The development of Catholic labor was strongly influenced by the precarious situation of the Catholic population as a whole after the foundation of the Bismarckian empire. The *Kulturkampf* in particular forced Catholics into a social ghetto, which strengthened the internal cohesion of the Catholic milieu and facilitated the social integration of Catholic workers.[54] But these conditions alone do not explain the strength of Catholic workers' organizations. Catholic social thought and activist priests were equally important.

51. See Greschat, *Christentum und Gesellschaft;* Schnabel, *Deutsche Geschichte im 19. Jahrhundert;* and Jonathan Sperber, *Popular Catholicism in Nineteenth Century Germany* (Princeton: Princeton University Press, 1984).

52. See Günther Brakelmann, *Kirche, soziale Frage und Sozialismus* (Gütersloh: Bertelsmann, 1977); and Shanahan, *Der deutsche Protestantismus vor der sozialen Frage.*

53. See Alfred Langner, ed., *Katholizismus, Konservative Kapitalismuskritik und Frühsozialismus bis 1850* (Munich: Schöingh, 1975); Helga Grebing, ed., *Handbuch der politischen Ideen in Deutschland* (Frankfurt: Fischer, 1969); Emmanuel W. Ketteler, *Die Arbeiterfrage und das Christentum* (Mainz: Kirchheim, 1864); and Adolf Kolping, *Der Gesellenverein und seine Aufgabe* (Cologne: Kolping, 1921).

54. See Brose, "Christian Labor"; Hugh McLeod, "Building the 'Catholic Ghetto': Catholic Organizations, 1870–1914," in *Voluntary Religion,* ed. W. J. Shields and D. Wood (Oxford: Oxford University Press, 1986); and Wilfried Loth, *Katholiken im Kaiserreich: Der politische Katholizismus in der Krise des Wilhelminischen Deutschlands* (Düsseldorf: Droste, 1984).

In this context a network of institutions emerged that promoted working-class interests, at least to a certain extent. The Center Party, the political voice of the Catholic population, gradually promoted a number of social-reform measures.[55] The Christian-Social Movement, led by Bishop Ketteler, fostered a wide network of Catholic associations, including savings and credit associations; consumer cooperatives; and workers', journeymen's, and artisans' clubs.[56] But this socialism from above was challenged in the 1870s by a more radical Catholic socialism from below, associated with such figures as the worker chaplains Franz E. Cronenburg in Aachen and Anton Laaf in Essen. Both men, however, were soon discouraged by the *concerted action* of the Center Party and the Catholic church, and shortly afterwards a federation closely connected to Catholic entrepreneurs, Arbeiterwohl (Society for the Workers' Benefit), was established.[57] For Catholic working-class formation, however, the establishment of a Catholic labor movement was more important than any restrictions placed upon it.

During the Wilhelmine period, Catholicism overcame its social and political isolation, the Center Party became one of the pillars of the imperial political system, the papal encyclical *Rerum Novarum* in 1891 endorsed adaptation to a modern industrial society, and the intermediary institutions of the Catholic social-cultural milieu were steadily expanded and consolidated. Within this pillarization of Catholicism, Catholic working-class culture and organizations acquired their definite shape. First, the Katholische Arbeiterbewegung (Catholic Labor Movement) enjoyed a steady growth because the lower clergy in particular was strongly committed to relieving the daily problems of workers. Then the Volksverein für das katholische Deutschland (Popular Society for Catholic Germany) promoted a network of popular associations intended to foster the Catholic faith through religious education and practical courses.[58] Finally, the interconfessional, albeit predominantly Catholic, Christian trade unions were founded in 1894, and after the turn of the century, they emerged as the mass organization of Catholic workers.

To be sure, the independent organization of workers was highly controversial within Catholicism. Conservative, so-called integral Catholic opinion, which was centered in Berlin, wanted to control the trade unions by

---

55. See Ritter, *Die deutschen Parteien.*

56. See Greschat, *Christentum und Gesellschaft;* and McLeod, "Building the 'Catholic Ghetto.'"

57. See Brose, "Christian Labor"; Greschat, *Christentum und Gesellschaft;* August Erdmann, *Die Christliche Arbeiterbewegung in Deutschland* (Stuttgart: Dietz, 1909); and Eberhard Naujoks, *Die katholische Arbeiterbewegung und der Sozialismus in den ersten Jahren des Bismarckschen Reiches* (Berlin: Junker und Dünnhaupt, 1939).

58. Josef Mooser, "Arbeiter, Bürger und Priester in den konfessionellen Arbeiter-vereinen im deutschen Kaiserreich, 1880–1914," in *Arbeiter und Bürger im 19. Jahrhundert,* ed. Jürgen Kocka (Munich: Oldenbourg, 1986).

subordinating them to the Catholic workers' associations. More progressive opinion, based in Mönchengladbach, defeated this attempt, and the Volksverein für das katholische Deutschland became the intellectual center of unionism. Although this trade union dispute caused a major setback in the development of the Christian trade unions, they were one of the main pillars of the Catholic labor movement on the eve of World War I.[59]

Because Catholic workers could develop their class identity within a religious-ecclesiastical framework, their religiosity and piety became an integral part of their political-cultural formation. Of course, when the church—usually personified by the local priest—was hostile to workers' demands, workers often moved toward social democracy.[60] For example, after experiencing a deep religious crisis, the clay miner Nikolaus Osterroth changed "from a praying man to a fighter"—without, however, giving up his ultimate faith in God.[61] But the majority of Catholic workers were able to shape their class consciousness on the basis of religious attitudes that were intellectually articulated within the Catholic social doctrine.

Workers were recognized as a legitimate social estate, and thus the vision of a corporative order of estates was reactivated. Simultaneously the norms of love, justice, and morality were asserted in the face of the industrial-capitalist conditions of work and daily life. Goals included the restoration of the Christian family, the social acknowledgment of the necessity for dignity, just wages, and a Christian industrial order based on responsibility for, and codetermination by, workers.[62] Although Catholic workers by and large shared an attitude of compromise and negotiation, when they regarded the behavior of employers and state agents as unjust, they might riot or strike. Their intense rejection of social democracy as godless, materialist, and motivated by class hatred was based not only on ecclesiastical mobilization from above but also on a social Catholicism from below, which shaped their collective identity.

Within Lutheran Protestantism, the Evangelical working-class movement was extremely limited. This was true for the entire period from 1871 to 1914 and was not merely a result of the marriage of throne and altar. As was mentioned above, it followed from the church's emphasis on charity, moral edification, and inward evangelization and from its definition of social policy as the exclusive task of the state. Moreover, both church and state held strongly

---

59. See Brose, "Christian Labor"; and Schneider, *Die christlichen Gewerkschaften.*

60. See Arpad Horvath, *Sozialismus und Religion* (Bern: Peter Lang, 1987); and Nolan, "Economic Crisis."

61. See Nikolaus Osterroth, *Vom Beter zum Kämpfer* (Berlin: Dietz, 1921); and Alfred Kelly, ed., *The German Worker: Working-Class Autobiographies from the Age of Industrialization* (Berkeley: University of California Press, 1987).

62. See Bundesverband der Katholischen Arbeitnehmer-Bewegung Deutschlands, ed., *Texte zur katholischen Soziallehre,* 2 vols. (Kevelaer, Ger.: Bercker, 1976).

patriarchal attitudes and fostered evangelical moralization as a weapon against the evil of social democracy.

To be sure, there was also Protestant social commitment. Friedrich Bodelschwingh, for example, established the Bethel asylums for disabled persons; Friedrich Siegmund-Schultze organized a settlement movement in Berlin; and Protestant pastors and intellectuals, organized in the Verein für Sozialpolitik and the Evangelisch-sozialer Kongress, influenced Bismarckian and Wilhelmine social policy.[63] Between church charity and state welfare policy, however, there was little room for the collective mobilization of working-class interests.[64]

As a result, the Evangelical workers' associations were not founded until the 1880s and failed to develop significantly thereafter.[65] Moreover, the attempts by Adolf Stoecker, the influential anti-Semitic Prussian court chaplain during the Bismarckian period, to found a Christian-social workers' party and by Friedrich Naumann to organize a national-social party both failed. This was not only because support by the workers was lacking but also because the Protestant church and the imperial state discouraged them.[66] Promotion of a common Christian labor movement on the basis of interconfessional Christian unions was only partially successful, because the Evangelical workers' associations were often confessionally opposed to the Catholic labor movement.[67] Finally, the more radical workers within the Evangelical workers' associations, as well as some Protestant socialist pastors, such as Paul Göhre and Christoph Blumhardt, eventually defected to social democracy.[68]

Secular Labor and Religion

The radicalization of preindustrial religious socialism was not attractive for the first autonomous German labor movement, which emerged during the revolutionary years of 1848 and 1849. The "Gospel of the Poor Sinner" by Wilhelm Weitlung, for example—which Marx first praised as an authentic form of socialism and then dismissed as unscientific—outlined a radical religious com-

63. See Harry Liebersohn, *Religion and Industrial Society: The Protestant Social Congress in Wilhelmine Germany,* Transactions of the American Philosophical Society vol. 76, part 6 (Philadelphia: American Philosophical Society, 1986); and Ward, *Theology, Sociology, and Politics.*

64. See Brakelmann, *Kirche, soziale Frage und Sozialismus;* Hans-Dieter Denk, *Die christliche Arbeiterbewegung in Bayern bis zum Ersten Weltkrieg* (Mainz: Matthias-Grünewald, 1980); and Feyerabend, "Die evangelischen Arbeitervereine."

65. See Walter Frank, *Hofprediger Adolf Stoecker und die christlich-soziale Bewegung* (Hamburg: Hanseatische Verlagsanstalt, 1939).

66. See Ward, *Theology, Sociology, and Politics.*

67. See Schneider, *Die christlichen Gewerkschaften.*

68. See Ernst Adam, "Die Stellung der deutschen Sozialdemokratie zu Religion und Kirche bis 1914," (Ph.D. diss., University of Frankfurt, 1930); Paul Göhre, *Wie ein Pfarrer Sozialdemokrat wurde* (Berlin: Vorwärts, 1900); and Horvath, *Sozialismus und Religion.*

munism that was based on popular religiosity.[69] Weitlung, however, was unable to shape the emerging labor movement; instead, he was rejected because of his authoritarian messianism.[70] In Germany religious utopian socialism lost its influence at a relatively early date.[71]

Instead, the Allgemeine deutsche Arbeiterverbrüderung (General German Workers' Brotherhood), the first unified working-class movement, which existed for a short time during the Revolution of 1848, was shaped by "bourgeois" humanist anticlericalism. It adhered to a free-religious or freethinking, liberal-democratic, and social-reform oriented socialism that emerged under the influence of socially committed burghers who were leading members of the German Catholic and free Protestant communities. Stefan Born, the chief figure of the Allgemeine deutsche Arbeiterverbrüderung, was typical in combining a Christian spirit of brotherhood with moderate anticlericalism. In contrast, the radical atheism of the left-wing Hegelians and of Marx and Engels played only a marginal role; it seemed to disrupt worker solidarity and divert energies from practical tasks.[72]

Although the Allgemeine deutsche Arbeiterverbrüderung was soon repressed, many of its local cells survived in the larger German towns and preserved their traditions until the 1860s, when a decisive, although limited, liberalization of political life evolved. All signs point to the continuing and even broadening influence of liberal-democratic, free-religious, and humanist thinking within the workers' and artisans' associations.[73] Free religiosity meant rational theology, the philosophy of nature, rationalist criticism of the Bible, and free, individual religious practice that tended more to humanist deism than to militant atheism. Free-religious thinkers commonly acted as wandering preachers in the artisans' and workers' associations.[74] The prevailing idea of emancipation within these associations was shaped by a bourgeois

---

69. Wilhelm Weitling, *Das Evangelium des armen Sünders: Die Menschheit, wie sie ist und wie sie sein sollte* (Reinbek: Rowohlt, 1971).

70. See Wolfram von Moritz, *Wilhelm Weitling: Religiöse Problematik und literarische Form* (Frankfurt: Lang, 1981); Wolfgang Schieder, *Die Anfänge der deutschen Arbeiterbewegung* (Stuttgart: Klett, 1963); and Carl Wittke, *The Utopian Communist* (Baton Rouge: Louisiana State University Press, 1953).

71. See Gian Mario Bravo, "Die internationale Frühsozialismus Forschung," in *Arbeiter und Arbeiterbewegung im Vergleich: Berichte zur internationalen historischen Forschorg*, ed. Klaus Tenfelde, *Historische Zeitschrift*, Sonderheft 15 (Munich: Oldenbourg, 1986).

72. See Frolinde Balser, *Social-Demokratie, 1848/49–1863: Die erste deutsche Arbeiterorganisation "Allgemeine deutsche Arbeiterverbrüderung" nach der Revolution* (Stuttgart: Klett, 1962); and Stefan Born, *Erinnerungen eines Achtundvierzigers* (Berlin: Dietz, 1978).

73. See Toni Offermann, *Arbeiterbewegung und liberales Bürgertum in Deutschland, 1850 bis 1863* (Bonn: Verlag Neue Gesellschaft, 1979).

74. See Heiner Grote, *Sozialdemokratie und Religion* (Tübingen: Siebeck und Mohr, 1968); and Günter Kolbe, "Demokratische Opposition im religiösen Gewande und antikirchliche Bewegung im Königreich Sachsen"FS (Ph.D. diss., University of Leipzig, 1964).

humanism, which stressed political liberation and the social improvement of workers by education, ennoblement, and moral edification.[75] In this sense, the free-religious attitudes of August Bebel and Wilhelm Liebknecht, the leaders of the VDAV (United German Workers' Association), and the religious tolerance of Ferdinand Lassalle,[76] the founding father of the ADAV (General German Workers' Association), may be regarded as representative of the religious sentiments within the workers' and artisans' associations of the 1860s. How did the socialist movement become militantly atheistic at the beginning of the Bismarckian empire?

The humanist and freethinking traditions of social liberalism within the artisans' and workers' associations were transformed into an atheistic socialism when the liberalism of the National Liberals abandoned its principled opposition to the Prussian authoritarian state and became a pillar of German unification and the Bismarckian empire.[77] In Imperial Germany, both the liberal artisans' and workers' associations and the Hirsch-Duncker trade unions remained attractive only for more skilled and prosperous Protestant artisans and workers. Their continued adherence to free religiosity was indicated by their political orientation toward the Left-Liberal "Freethinkers" Party.[78]

The overwhelming majority of the artisans' and workers' associations, however, turned to the socialist labor movement, which was centralized when the ADAV and VDAV merged to form the SAP (the Socialist Workers' Party) at Gotha in 1875, which was connected with the *freie Gewerkschaften* (free trade unions).[79] Ironically, it was social democracy's attachment to liberal-democratic and freethinking humanism as well as to the Christian values of brotherhood and social justice that inspired this separation from liberalism, the Protestant church, and the Christian state. It was moral disappointment with these political and religious authorities, which simultaneously legitimized themselves through universal humanist and Christian values and rejected these values as illegitimate for the workers, that fueled the chiliastic mood of the

---

75. See Brigitte Emig, *Die Veredelung des Arbeiters: Sozialdemokratie als Kulturbewegung* (Frankfurt: Campus, 1980); Gustav Mayer, *Radikalismus, Sozialismus und bürgerliche Demokratie* (Frankfurt: Suhrkamp, 1969).

76. Religions tolerance was a consequence of Lassalle's enlightened Judaism; see Robert Wistrich, *Revolutionary Jews from Marx to Trotsky* (London: George Harrap and Co., 1976).

77. See John Breuilly, "Liberalismus oder Sozialdemokratie? Ein Vergleich der britischen und deutschen politischen Arbeiterbewegungen zwischen 1850 und 1875," in Kocka, *Europäische Arbeiterbewegungen*, 129–66; Conze, *Die Möglichkeiten und Grenzen der liberalen Arbeiterbewegung;* and James J. Sheehan, *German Liberalism in the Nineteenth Century* (Chicago: University of Chicago Press, 1978).

78. See K. Goldschmidt, *Die deutschen Gewerkvereine (Hirsch-Duncker)* (Berlin: Dietz, 1907).

79. See Werner Conze and Dieter Groh, *Die Arbeiterbewegung in der nationalen Bewegung* (Stuttgart: Klett, 1968); and Mayer, *Radikalismus, Sozialismus und bürgerliche Demokratie.*

emerging socialist movement. The consequence was the radicalization of social liberalism into socialism and of free religiosity into militant atheism. This radicalization did not mean a simple negation of the humanist and free-religious tradition but rather its chiliastic intensification and transformation, based on a Lutheran-pietist, working-class ethic. Atheistic socialism represented a secular religion of redemption, which was most popular in Protestant working-class milieus.

Bebel, the uncontested Social Democratic leader from 1875 until his death in 1913, most forcefully articulated this radicalization.[80] In his early writings in the 1870s, he stressed that Christianity is made by men, compensates earthly misery with a heavenly world, rests on stupidity and superstition, and legitimizes the existing social order. He argued that such morally good values as brotherly love, general humanism, social equality, and mutual tolerance are not in fact strictly Christian values and that the abolition of Christianity is a decisive prerequisite for the advancement of men, of the working class, and of women.[81] Bebel's ethical atheism was a radicalized free-religious humanism that simultaneously departed from it and transformed it into an atheistic socialism fueled by a working-class ethic that stressed brotherly love, social justice, and social equality.

Although Bebel claimed that these values were in fact anti-Christian, the Social Democratic rank and file continued to express them in the language of either a traditional popular Christian socialism or a popular free-religious socialism.[82] On the one hand, Jesus as an artisan and a worker was regarded as the first socialist who fought for the poor and oppressed, promising them equality, liberation, and redemption, only to be betrayed by his followers, the church, and its priests. On the other hand, church festivals, especially Christmas, Easter, and Pentecost, were reinterpreted in a free-religious way by incorporating them into a humanistic religion of nature. But their Christian meaning was simultaneously intensified by stressing their usurpation by the rich and the hope of salvation connected with them. Christian chiliastic motifs were frequently present when the Last Judgment (that is, revolution) seemed near and the rich would be condemned and the poor redeemed. The same mood reigned within the free-religious communities, whose working-class members were often Social Democrats as well. Messianic hopes emerged even within the Lassallean cult, which was especially popular in Protestant sectarian mi-

---

80. See Vernon Lidtke, "August Bebel and German Social Democracy's Relation to the Christian Churches," *Journal for the History of Ideas* 27, no. 2 (Summer 1966): 245–64.

81. August Bebel, *Christentum und Sozialismus* (Hottingen-Zürich: Volksbuchhandlung, 1887); August Bebel, *Die Frau und der Sozialismus* (Hottingen-Zürich: Volksbuchhandlung, 1879); see also Horvath, *Sozialismus und Religion.*

82. See Grote, *Sozialdemokratie und Religion.*

lieus.[83] And in many workers' autobiographies, joining the Social Democratic organizations was described as a conversion to socialism.[84]

These various free-religious, chiliastic hopes were most clearly articulated by the so-called worker-philosopher Jose Dietzgen, who declared socialism itself to be a religion of salvation.[85] Others spoke of a substitute religion, referred to Social Democracy as a sect, or called it an alternative church.[86] All these parallels to religion, however—which quite adequately expressed the secular-religious aspects of emerging Social Democratic socialism—became increasingly suspect and "illogical" within the context of the prevailing atheistic discourse of the party leadership. It was because of these contradictions, and not as a statement of religious tolerance, that the Socialist Workers' Party developed the compromise formula "religion is a private matter" in the Gotha party program.[87]

From 1878 to 1890, when all Social Democratic organizations were banned under the Antisocialist Law,[88] the popular Christian and free-religious notions that inspired socialist atheism were still widespread. Comparisons of the socialists with the early Christians and of their respective oppressors became popular, and socialist writers exhibited a growing interest in the history of early Christianity.[89] Not surprisingly, socialist writers toned down their hostility to church and religion, partly to avoid further cause for persecution, partly because any immediate transition to socialism seemed unrealistic in view of the weakness of the socialist movement.

Within this context, Marxism came to be adopted and institutionalized in the Erfurt program of 1891.[90] It fulfilled the need for a scientifically proven socialist worldview, expressed the tamed and more pragmatic chiliastic hopes, and addressed the economic and social problems of the workers. In addition, it justified scientifically rather than morally socialist atheism. It was now viewed as a natural law that Christianity and religion would vanish as modes of production evolved. Primitive societies practiced magical religion; feudalism, Catholicism; and capitalism, Protestantism; but socialism would generate athe-

83. See ibid.; and Horvath, *Sozialismus und Religion.*

84. See W. Emmerich, ed., *Proletarische Lebensläufe,* 2 vols. (Reinbek: Rohwolt, 1974, 1975); Jochen Loreck, *Wie man früher Sozialdemokrat wurde* (Bonn: Verlag Neue Gesellschaft, 1977); and Kelly, *The German Worker.*

85. Josef Dietzgen, *Die Religion und die Sozialdemokratie* (Berlin: Vorwärts, 1875).

86. See Grote, *Sozialdemokratie und Religion.*

87. See ibid.; and Lidtke, "Social Class and Secularization in Imperial Germany."

88. See Lidtke, *The Outlawed Party.*

89. See Horvath, *Sozialismus und Religion.*

90. Karl Kautsky, *Das Erfurter Programm* (Stuttgart: Dietz, 1892); Erich Matthias, *Kautsky und der Kautskyanismus* (Tübingen: Siebeck und Mohr, 1957).

ism.[91] Within this framework, any parallels between socialism and religion were rejected, and even the ethical presuppositions of socialism were suppressed. They found an echo only in some marginal positions that either viewed the materialist worldview as a substitute religion or that supported an ethical socialism.[92]

Religion was again confirmed as a private affair. This formula of religious tolerance, however, was at odds with the predominantly atheistic attitude within the Social Democratic Party—a discrepancy that led to frequent and fierce disputes between Protestant pastors and party officials.[93] But this compromise served to accommodate divergent attitudes toward religion within the party, its affiliated organizations, and its working-class constituency.[94] Within the party, the freethinkers' atheistic fundamentalism no longer satisfied the political requirements of a mass party.[95] In addition, a religious socialism emerged, mainly supported by Protestant pastors who entered the party to fight for real tolerance in religious matters.[96] And finally the free trade unions, which represented a large and increasing working-class constituency, demanded strict religious neutrality because antireligious attitudes could damage working-class unity by alienating workers who were practicing Christians.[97]

Thus in the Wilhelmine period the religious dimensions of socialist working-class culture exhibited the same cultural complexity and diversity that was characteristic of the entire alternative culture of socialist labor.[98] On the one hand, the secular-religious identity of socialist labor was embodied in the movement's distinctive rites and symbols as well as in the free-religious transformations of the traditional life-cycle ceremonies and church festivals. On the other hand, these cultural transformations had obvious limits. Socialist rites often overlapped with traditional ones (for example, demonstrations on May Day incorporated religious processions),[99] and free-religious adaptations of

---

91. See Anton Pannekoek, *Religion und Sozialismus* (Bremen: Buchhandlung der Bremer Bürger-Zeitung, 1905).

92. See Bo Gustafsson, *Marxismus und Revisionismus* (Frankfurt: Europäische Verlagsanstalt, 1972).

93. See Horvath, *Sozialismus und Religion.*

94. See Lidtke, "August Bebel and German Social Democracy's Relation to the Christian Churches."

95. See Jochen-Christoph Kaiser, *Arbeiterbewegung und organisierte Religionskritik* (Stuttgart: Klett, 1981); and Hartmut Wunderer, "Freidenkertum und Arbeiterbewegung: Ein Überblick," *Internationale Wissenschaftliche Korrespondenz* 14, no. 3 (Autumn 1978): 1–33.

96. See Rüdiger Reitz, *Christen und Sozialdemokratie* (Stuttgart: Radius, 1983).

97. See Otto Hue, *Neutrale oder politische Gewerkschaften?* (Bochum, 1900).

98. Vernon Lidtke, *The Alternative Culture: Socialist Labor in Imperial Germany* (New York: Oxford University Press, 1985).

99. See Gottfried Korff, "Volkskultur und Arbeiterkultur: Überlegungen am Beispiel der sozialistischen Maifesttradition," *Geschichte und Gesellschaft* 5, no. 1 (1979): 83–102.

church festivals were only partially anchored in workers' sentiments (proletarian Christmas often meant a collective celebration of traditional Christmas). And as the socialist movement and culture gained a mass character, the limits of these secular-religious transformations became even more marked.

Despite the variety and complexity of religious sentiments and attitudes within socialist labor, however, the socialist-Marxist worldview was the dominant element of the socialist political-cultural identity.[100] Marxism was an integral component of socialist chiliasm. Because secularized socialism was mainly a culturally transformed Protestant Christian socialism that began with free-religious humanism and ended with Marxist atheism, it was shaped by Lutheran and pietist attitudes.[101] Scientific socialism separated theory and practice in much the same way that God and world were separated within the Lutheran tradition. Chiliastic hopes were incorporated in the socialist future state, which would accomplish a radical break with contemporary capitalist society and the bourgeois state. At the same time, the future state was a scientifically proven and necessary outcome of history and could not be influenced by people. Thus scientific socialism stressed inward belief in correct doctrine and recognition that the world would follow its historical destiny.

In this way, a Lutheran-pietist quietism accompanied an underlying chiliastic radicalism and a specific ethos of duty and obedience toward the party. Certainly, there was an increasing practical struggle for social reform and political participation by the free trade unions and Social Democratic organizations, and this political pragmatism was especially pronounced in the case of Catholic Social Democrats.[102] Also on the political-intellectual level, differing traditions of Marxism emerged; Jewish Marxists in particular developed a more unorthodox, utopian Marxism.[103] Nonetheless, the Lutheran features of socialist secularism structured the political culture of socialist labor and presaged the coming schism between the legalist reformation of the Social Democrats and the chiliastic revolutionary sentiment of the communists in the Weimar Republic.[104]

---

100. See Guenther Roth, *The Social Democrats in Imperial Germany* (Totowa N.J.: Bedminster Press, 1963).

101. See Lucian Hölscher, *Weltgericht oder Revolution: Protestantische und sozialistische Zukunftsvorstellungen im deutschen Kaiserreich* (Stuttgart: Klett und Cotta, 1989).

102. See Hans-Josef Steinberg, *Sozialismus und deutsche Sozialdemokratie: Zur Ideologie der Partei vor dem 1. Weltkrieg* (Bonn: Verlag Neue Gesellschaft, 1976).

103. See George L. Mosse, *German Jews beyond Judaism* (Cincinnati: Hebrew Union College Press, 1985); and Wistrich, *Revolutionary Jews from Marx to Trotsky.*

104. See Carl Schorske, *German Social Democracy, 1905–1917* (Cambridge: Cambridge University Press, 1955).

The Pattern of Working-Class Formation—A Summary

I have tried to show in rough outline that religious institutions and mentalities had a decisive impact on the peculiar pattern of working-class formation in Imperial Germany. Religious institutions and mentalities represented an essential precondition and context of working-class formation. First, the state-controlled churches and the corresponding lack of democratization of religious life contributed to the widespread working-class secularization. Second, the different relationships of Protestantism and Catholicism to the state and to the working class fostered the process of secularization more in the Protestant than in the Catholic working classes. Third, working-class secularization was often identical with the cultural transition to alternative, secular-religious belief systems.

To be sure, specific economic, social, and political processes in nineteenth-century German society were also essential for shaping the asymmetric pattern between the dominant socialist labor and the smaller, Catholic movements. Economically, relatively late but rapid capitalist industrialization created in a few generations a large, new, and uprooted industrial working class. Socially, the experience of dependent wage labor and of miserable working and living conditions, which was perceived from a corporate artisan tradition, allowed for an early and broad group identity.[105] And politically, the discrimination against, and repression of, the workers by the authoritarian imperial state—which the mainstream liberal movement supported—provoked the comprehensive and autonomous counterorganization of socialist labor.[106] Only by interweaving religious structures with the economic, social, and political ones, however, can one explain why socialist labor was by and large confined to Protestant workers.

Religious mentalities also played a decisive role in shaping specific working-class identities, and in doing so, they were relevant components of workers' political dispositions and cultures. Thus religious mentalities decisively shaped both segments of the Christian labor movement. The few followers of evangelical labor identified with cultural Protestantism, the Christian monarchy, welfare policy, nationalism, and imperialism. In contrast, Catholic labor, which was often in conflict with clerical restrictions, was shaped by the workers' social Catholicism, which stressed social rights, the

---

105. See Jürgen Kocka, *Lohnarbeit und Klassenbildung: Arbeiter und Arbeiterbewegung in Deutschland, 1800–1875* (Berlin: Dietz, 1983); and Kocka, "Problems of Working-Class Formation in Germany."

106. Kocka, *Europäische Arbeiterbewegungen.*

dignity of labor, just wages, and codetermination within the framework of a Christian social order.

But religious mentalities also indirectly structured the secular currents of the working class. Liberal labor adhered to a secularized Protestant, free-religious, and humanistic social liberalism. In separating from this tradition, socialist labor transformed its heritage into an atheistic, socialist, and Marxist belief-system, but its main cultural features—scientism, moralism, quietism, authoritarianism, and chiliastic radicalism—expressed a Protestant working-class ethic in secular-religious ways.

Working-class identities as constitutive elements of the working-class formation pattern were also shaped by differing economic, social, and cultural experiences, regional peculiarities, and ethnic backgrounds. It is only the open and hidden religious structuring, however, that can explain the cultural components of the respective working-class identities and their mutual relationships. All working-class cultures constructed their identities on a political and ideological, religious, or secular-religious basis, and consequently they were strongly closed off and separated from each other.

Confessional dualism directly structured the conflict between Evangelical and Catholic labor. Although the common defense against atheistic socialist labor should have promoted the unification of both religious camps, cooperation was severely limited. The formally interconfessional Christian unions remained almost exclusively Catholic.

Because of the uneven process of working-class secularization, confessional dualism also indirectly structured the fundamental split between religious (predominantly Catholic) and secular (predominantly Protestant) labor. An overarching national trade union organization was not realized. The Social Democratic workers' perception of the Catholic workers as essentially superstitious, submissive, and cowardly in their conciliatory attitude toward capital and the state was also structured by the Lutheran socialist *Gesinnungsethik* (belief of conviction). The Catholic workers' view of the Social Democratic workers as godless, materialist, and fueled by class hatred was also shaped by Catholic-corporatist *Werkfrömmigkeit* (work piety). So the mutual experience and perception of the other as immoral sharpened the political divisions.

This particular German pattern of working-class formation was an important component of the democratic ambiguities of German modernization. On the whole, all working-class movements (such as unions, associations, and parties or currents within parties) belonged to the social groups that demanded and supported social reform and political democratization. At the same time, however, these democratic orientations were bound to religious and secular-religious identities that reduced democratic procedures to means for their own higher ideological ends. This lack of a democratic *Vergemeinschaftung*—in the sense of an overarching democratic and pluralistic political culture—within the working classes was an essential feature of the pattern of working-class formation in the Kaiserreich. As a part of the authoritarian route of German modernization, this pattern had also an impact on the further development of the working class in twentieth-century Germany.

Apparitions of the Virgin Mary in Bismarckian Germany

David Blackbourn

The history of nineteenth-century Europe was punctuated by episodes in which scores of thousands, sometimes hundreds of thousands, of people flocked to obscure spots where the Virgin Mary had supposedly appeared. These popular movements were likened by contemporaries to the Crusades. They were one of the most obvious signs of the great religious revival of the nineteenth century and served as a counterpoint to the more familiar political upheavals of the time. The best-known example is undoubtedly Lourdes (1858), and most people who think about these events at all probably associate them with predominantly Catholic countries, such as France, Italy, and Ireland, where a number of nineteenth-century apparitions were given official church approval. But Marian apparitions also occurred in Germany, and the essay that follows is mainly concerned with one of them.[1]

Modern apparitions have come in waves. One such wave occurred in the aftermath of the French Revolution, in France itself and in Italy and Germany under French occupation. There was a further set of apparitions in the 1830s and 1840s, this time particularly in France, most notably the visions of the novice nun Cathérine Labouré in Paris (1830) and of two young shepherds in the Alpine village of La Salette (1846). Then, following the celebrated visions of Bernadette Soubirous at Lourdes in 1858, came the most extensive wave of European apparitions in the nineteenth century. In the following twenty years, visions of the Virgin were reported in France, Italy, Ireland, and Bohemia, as well as in Germany. By the twentieth century, the idiom of the Marian apparition had established itself so firmly that it had eclipsed other kinds of religious vision still widely claimed a century earlier: burning crucifixes, bearded and ragged old men, plagues of caterpillars, and celestial omens (although the

---

1. I have completed a book-length study on this: *Marpingen: Apparitions of the Virgin Mary in Bismarckian Germany* (Oxford, 1993 and New York, 1994). In some of the notes below, readers are referred to chapters of this book for evidence and further details.

"Virgin in the sky" at Pontmain in 1871 showed that the new form could accommodate elements of the old.)[2] It was the Virgin Mary who was at the center of the interwar apparitions that followed Fatima in 1917 and of the apparitions that were claimed right across Europe in the second half of the 1940s in Germany, France, Italy, Hungary, Poland, and Romania. The same was true of the new wave of apparitions during the 1980s in Yugoslavia, the Ukraine, Germany, and Ireland, and outside Europe in Egypt and Uganda, Chicago and Nicaragua. Beyond the primacy of the Virgin Mary, modern apparitions became more uniform in other respects: in the nineteenth century, for the first time, the visionaries were predominantly children or women, and it became customary for a "message" to be disclosed by the apparition.[3] Growing uniformity can be linked generally to improved communications but more particularly to the growing standardization of devotional forms. Lourdes especially became a kind of template from which subsequent apparitions took their pattern.[4]

Modern apparitions are not explicable as the result of mere imitation, however, even though this demonstrably played a part. Nor are they susceptible simply of individual-psychological explanation. It is true that there are a number of recurrent motifs that run through the lives of those who claimed apparitions. In the case of the young children and adolescent girls who made up the largest number of seers, we can point to a common pattern of recent emotional upheaval—typically the loss of, or neglect by, a parent—often in conjunction with some other change in life, the crossing of a particular threshold. Sometimes this was a matter of being fostered out or sent to work away from home; sometimes it was associated with beginning school or being on the eve of confirmation. The children concerned were often coming into contact with stories of the Blessed Virgin and her visitations at a time when they were highly susceptible to the comforts and emotional consolations of a "true mother," who would not desert or neglect them. Nor should we forget the fact that these children were frequently poor, or "outsiders" of one kind or another. Many young seers were in farm or domestic service, others belonged to the "dishonorable" profession of shepherd, still others had been forced to come to terms with a recent loss of family respectability, like the young Soubirous, who

---

2. R. Laurentin and A. Durand, *Pontmain: Histoire authentique,* vol. 1, *Un signe dans le ciel* (Paris, 1970).

3. M. L. Nolan and S. Nolan, *Christian Pilgrimage in Modern Western Europe* (Chapel Hill, 1989), 266–89; V. Turner and E. Turner, *Image and Pilgrimage in Christian Culture* (Oxford, 1978); V. Turner and E. Turner, "Postindustrial Marian Pilgrimage," in *Mother Worship,* ed. J. Preston (Chapel Hill, 1982), 145–73.

4. See Blackbourn, *Marpingen,* chap. 1; also H. Thurston, *Beauraing and Other Apparitions* (London, 1934); B. Billet et al., eds., *Vraies et fausses apparitions dans l'Eglise* (Paris, 1973); and M. P. Carroll, *The Cult of the Virgin Mary* (Princeton, 1986), 115–40.

picked rags and collected dirty hospital linen with her father, a bankrupt miller.[5]

The visions bestowed status and authority on the visionaries. In relaying the purported words of the Virgin, they determined who should approach the apparition site, how they should behave, and the procedures that would lead to a miraculous cure. They instructed that chapels be built, told of secrets they could not divulge, and prophesied woe for the sinful (and the skeptical). The new status of the children also offered subversive possibilities. Eugène Barbedette, one of the Pontmain seers, was asked by a group of prominent Catholic laywomen and female religious in Fougères if the Virgin bore any resemblance to one of them. "No," he replied, "compared with the Blessed Virgin you are all ugly."[6] So many of the younger seers had lived Cinderella lives before their apparitions, and they now experienced that happy reversal of fortunes so characteristic of Cinderella and other folktales, with the Mother of God cast in the role of fairy godmother.

Similar considerations apply to adult visionaries: the Romantic writer Clemens Brentano observed that the visionary Anna Katharina Emmerich had been "abandoned by all and ill-treated like Cinderella."[7] The women in question—they were almost always women—had commonly experienced recent illness and bereavement and often occupied a marginal position within the family or community. Adult female seers, like their youthful counterparts, acquired a rare authority as the conduits through which divine dissatisfaction was expressed, and there are plenty of instances where it seems that they were avenging themselves, consciously or unconsciously, on a harsh world. Sometimes they were angry, lashing the mighty for their sins. An eighteen-year-old from Normandy, imprisoned for arson, returned to her village and recounted the dire predictions of the Blessed Virgin about what would happen if a chapel were not constructed in honor of Our Lady of La Salette. The strictures and warnings reported by the servant-visionary Estelle Faguette of Pellevoisin in the 1870s were matched by those of other young Frenchwomen of the period.[8] These messages delivered by the weak to the strong were usually less apocalyptic and extravagant; yet they were always there by implication. The respect conferred by the apparitions gave women a chance normally denied them to

5. On Lourdes, see R. Laurentin and B. Billet, *Lourdes: Dossiers des documents authentiques* (Paris, 1958–66), 1:75 ff, 131–35; Carroll, *The Cult of the Virgin*, 158–59. Generally, see Blackbourn, *Marpingen*, chap. 1.

6. Laurentin and Durand, *Un signe dans le ciel*, 65.

7. J. Hellé, *Miracles* (London, 1953), 191. On Brentano and Emmerich, see H. Graef, *Mary: A History of Doctrine and Devotion* (London, 1963), 2:386.

8. J. Devlin, *The Superstitious Mind: French Peasants and the Supernatural in the Nineteenth Century* (New Haven, 1987), 152–53; R. Ernst, *Maria redet zu uns: Marienerscheinungen seit 1830* (Eupen, 1949), 39–41; and T. de Cauzons, *La magie et la sorcellerie en France* (Paris, 1911), 4:597–617.

slough off harsh responsibilities. Like illness, the status of visionary was a resource of the weak, a means of escape; it also offered a veiled means of protest against real or imagined ill-treatment.

Many of these elements were present in the apparitions that took place in the Bohemian village of Philippsdorf in 1866. Magdalena Kade was a thirty-year-old unmarried weaver's daughter with a long history of illness, including convulsions. Her father died when she was thirteen, and her brother inherited the family home; her mother died in 1861, and in 1864 Kade moved out to live with another family, probably as a servant; in 1865 she was the victim of a series of cruel lampoons written by a fellow villager. Admitted back by her brother because of illness, she lay in bed beneath a picture of the "suffering Mother," surrounded by her brother's lodgers. The apparitions began four weeks after she had returned home. "Cured," as the Virgin Mary had promised, Magdalena Kade became the center of medical attention and prompted a local cult of "Mary the salvation of the sick." Thousands of pilgrims went to the village, and the visionary was feted by visiting priests and persons of influence.[9]

There is value in this approach; it is surely better than presenting the visionaries as a bundle of clinical symptoms. But even if we interpret the individual experiences in this way rather than reduce them to a category such as "hysteria" in the manner of contemporaries, Jean-Marie Charcot and Richard Krafft-Ebing, our explanations remain limited.[10] These were collective as well as individual phenomena. External pressure as well as emotional upheaval usually provides some indication of why the apparitions took place when they did, and external stress of one sort or another certainly suggests why these events enjoyed the resonance they did. If we look at the waves of apparitions, some common elements stand out. One is the background of war and postwar anxiety, from Napoleonic Europe through the visions that stalked the battlefields of Italian unification and the Franco-Prussian War to the wave of apparitions that followed World War II. In content as well as timing, these were intercessions by the "Queen of Peace." It is also apparent that clusters of apparitions occurred at times of political turmoil or when Catholics felt themselves under threat from civil power. This motif recurs from Labouré's appari-

9. F. Storch, *Maria, das Heil der Kranken: Darstellung der ausserordentlichen Vorfälle und wunderbaren Heilungen, welche im Jahre 1866 zu Philippsdorf in Böhmen sich ereignet haben* (Georgswalde, n.d.); P. Sausseret, *Erscheinungen und Offenbarungen der allerseligsten Jungfrau Maria* (Regensburg, 1878), 2:244–49; W. J. Walsh, *The Apparitions and Shrines of Heaven's Bright Queen* (New York, 1904), 4:59–70.

10. Examples in R. Krafft-Ebing, *Lehrbuch der gerichtlichen Psychopathologie* (Stuttgart, 1875), 200–202; and R. Krafft-Ebing, *Lehrbuch der Psychiatrie auf klinischer Grundlage* (Stuttgart, 1879–80), 2:90–93, 116–17; 3:87–90. Compare Carroll, *The Cult of the Virgin;* and M. Oraison, "Le point de vue du médecin psychiatre clinicien sur les apparitions," in Billet et al., *Vraies et fausses apparitions,* 123–47.

tions in the revolutionary France of 1830, through the wave of Marian visions during the secular state-building and anticlerical decades of the 1860s and 1870s, to the explicitly anticommunist message of Fatima in 1917 and the "cold war apparitions" of the 1940s and 1950s.[11]

In the essay that follows, I want to place the German apparitions of the 1870s in several contexts. Is there anything in the lives of the visionaries and their families that might suggest how these events came about? To what extent does economic and social crisis help to explain the popular resonance of the German apparitions, as it clearly does in La Salette, Lourdes, Knock, and many other cases? What is the connection between the apparitions and larger changes in Catholic popular piety in this period, and what can we learn from such episodes about relations between clergy and laity? I attempt, finally, to examine some of the connections between the apparitions and the *Kulturkampf* in Prussia. By looking at a dramatic example of the interplay between piety and politics, one that eventually engaged the attention of army, bureaucracy, judiciary, press, and parliament, I hope to cast some light on Bismarckian Germany from an unfamiliar angle.

Apparitions of the Virgin Mary were widely reported in Germany during the 1870s, especially from the western and eastern margins of the new empire, including Alsace, the Palatinate, the Rhineland, Silesia, and Posen. The three most publicized cases were in Mettenbuch (Lower Bavaria), Dittrichswalde (the Ermland), and Marpingen (the Saarland).[12] I shall concentrate on the last of these, not only because it has the richest and most varied archival evidence but because it also acquired the largest public and political resonance.

Marpingen was a large village with about 1,600 inhabitants situated in the hill country of the northern Saarland, solidly Catholic and largely unremark-

---

11. Detailed argument and references in Blackbourn, *Marpingen,* chap. 1. T. Kselman, *Miracles and Prophecies in Nineteenth-Century France* (New Brunswick, N.J. 1983); and N. Perry and L. Echeverría, *Under the Heel of Mary* (London, 1988) deal extensively with the political context.

12. The extensive printed sources on these cases include, on Marpingen: A. F. von Berg [Adam Fauth], *Marpingen und das Evangelium* (Saarbrücken, 1877); W. Cramer, *Die Erscheinungen und Heilungen in Marpingen* (Würzburg, 1876); F. von Lama, *Die Muttergottes-Erscheinungen in Marpingen (Saar)* (Altötting, n.d.); *Marpingen—Wahrheit oder Lüge?* (Münster, 1877); *Die Marpinger Mutter Gottes-Erscheinungen und wunderbaren Heilungen* (Paderborn, 1877); *Marpingen und seine Gnadenmonate* (Münster, 1877); J. Rebbert, *Marpingen und seine Gegner* (Paderborn, 1877); N. Thoemes, *Die Erscheinungen in Marpingen* (Stuttgart, 1877); on Mettenbuch: B. Braunmüller, *Kurzer Bericht über die Erscheinungen U. L. Frau bei Mettenbuch* (Deggendorf, 1878); on Dittrichswalde: "Die Erscheinungen der unbefleckt Empfangengen in Dittrichswalde," *Der Sendbote des göttlichen Herzens Jesu* 14 (1878): 56–62; "Die Erscheinungen zu Dittrichswalde," *St-Bonifatius-Kalender für das Jahr 1879,* 147–59; on Alsace: "Wunder in Elsass," *St-Bonifatius-Kalender für das Jahr 1893,* 89–104; Berg, *Marpingen und das Evangelium,* 26–27; on Silesia: *Deutsche Allgemeine Zeitung,* 29 August 1876; and on Posen: *Kölnische Zeitung,* 6 September 1876.

able.[13] It was in the diocese and the Prussian administrative district of Trier, part of the Rhine Province, to which that area of the Saarland had belonged since 1834. Marpingen was some miles from the nearest railhead, in St. Wendel, and it was, as one contemporary put it, "not marked on normal maps."[14] True, the village was not quite the isolated community some later depicted. A growing proportion of village men earned their living in the Saar coalfield to the south, peasants conducted business in nearby market towns, and figures as various as the rural postman, notaries, moneylenders, knife grinders, and traveling musicians passed through with news. At the beginning of July 1876, however, attention in Marpingen was centered on haymaking, which had an important place in the annual agricultural cycle. Work began at dawn, and all available hands were pressed into service. Children were no exception, and the village school had a "haymaking-holiday."[15] Those too young to take part or to help with the care of farm animals were given the task of gathering berries or other fruits of the forest.

It was in order to gather bilberries—*Wälen* in the local dialect—that, on the hot Monday of 3 July, a number of young girls found themselves in the Härtelwald, a hilly wooded area with many rocky gullies a few minutes away from Marpingen. There were five girls in all. Three were eight-year-olds and fast friends: Katharina Hubertus, Susanna Leist, and Margaretha Kunz. With them in the woods were Katharina's six-year-old sister, Lischen, and another six-year-old, Anna Meisberger. The girls had separated to look for berries and were not together when the Angelus sounded and they started to make their way home. Between the wood and the village was an area of wild meadow with thick bushes around it. It was here that Susanna Leist suddenly called out, bringing Katharina and Margaretha hurrying to her, and drew her friends' attention to a "figure in white." When the girls reached home, agitated and frightened, all three described seeing a woman in white with a child in her arms. The reactions of parents and neighbors are disputed, but it is clear that the girls remained in a state of excitement. Margaretha slept badly and prayed a lot, Katharina dreamed of the woman in white, and Susanna was reluctant to go to bed at all. The following day they returned to the spot and knelt down to pray. According to their account, after they had recited the Lord's Prayer three times, the apparition appeared again to Margaretha and Katharina—although not to

13. On topography, see W. Bungert, *Heimatbuch Marpingen* (Marpingen, 1980); and K. Höppstädter and H.-W. Herrmann, *Geschichtliche Landeskunde des Saarlandes* (Saarbrücken, 1960), 1:15–16.

14. Cramer, *Die Erscheinungen*, 6.

15. Landesarchiv Saarbrücken, Einzelstücke 107: Zusammenstellung des wesentlichen Inhalts der Untersuchungsacten betreffend die Mutter-Gottes-Erscheinungen in Marpingen, Saarbrücken den 9. August 1878, Kleber Untersuchungsrichter (LASB, E 107), 293.

Susanna, the original seer. "Who are you?" they asked the figure in the local dialect and received the reply: "I am the Immaculately Conceived."[16]

The apparitions continued. The figure, now confidently identified by adults as the Blessed Virgin, instructed that a chapel be built, encouraged the sick to come to her, and asked that water be taken from a nearby spring. Soon there were reports of miraculous healings, and within less than a week thousands of pilgrims were streaming to Marpingen. Reports spoke of twenty thousand in the village, with up to four thousand at the apparition site, singing, praying, and taking away foliage or handfuls of earth. In the words of the parish priest, Lourdes was "feeble compared with the mighty current that here is breaking through all barriers."[17] The three seers subsequently claimed visions in other parts of the village—in their homes, in barns and stables, in the school, in the graveyard and the church—and what they described became more luxuriant. The Virgin appeared with and without the Christ child, sometimes accompanied by angels. She was dressed now in white, now in gold or azure. The apparitions also took on darker tones. On one occasion the girls reported seeing the Virgin clad in black, on another they described a celestial procession passing over the graveyard. The devil also made several appearances. The apparitions were to continue for fourteen months.

Marpingen became a *cause célèbre*. Journalists, priests, and the sellers of pious memorabilia descended on the village, along with pilgrims from Germany and abroad.[18] Supporters and opponents dubbed Marpingen "the German Lourdes," even "the Bethlehem of Germany."[19] "It is an undeniable fact that the whole world is talking about Marpingen," wrote one sympathetic commentator.[20] "Marpingen has become the center of events that have shaken the world," suggested another.[21] The hyperbole was forgivable. A bar brawl in a different part of Germany began when one man insulted another by calling him a "Marpinger." (A local court found him guilty of slander and sentenced him to a fine of fifteen Marks or three days in jail.)[22] One newspaper, linking the themes of the apparitions and the Eastern crisis that was dominating the press, ran an editorial under the headline "Marpingen and Stambul."[23] Bismarck himself made slighting remarks about Marpingen, and his interest

---

16. Accounts of the apparitions can be found in LASB, E 107, 1–14; Bistumsarchiv Trier (BAT), B III, 11, 14/3, 1–49; see also the published sources in note 11 above.

17. LASB, E 107, 424: Jacob Neureuter, notebook entry of 11 July 1876.

18. See Blackbourn, *Marpingen,* chap. 4.

19. LASB, E 107, 484; "An der Gnadenstätte von Marpingen," *Die Gartenlaube* (1877), 669; *Marpingen und seine Gnadenmonate,* 16.

20. *Marpingen—Wahrheit oder Lüge?* 4.

21. *Die Marpinger Mutter Gottes-Erscheinungen und wunderbaren Heilungen,* 13.

22. A report from the town of Deutz in the *Saar- und Mosel-Zeitung,* 17 October 1876.

23. *Breslauer Zeitung,* cited in *Germania,* 13 January 1877.

reflected another element of the village's new celebrity (or notoriety).[24] The apparition movement collided with the machinery of state. The result was a lengthy struggle that was to extend from Marpingen and the surrounding areas of the Saarland to the courtrooms of the Rhine Province and the Prussian parliament in Berlin.

In trying to unpick the beginning of these events, let us start with the visionaries. By common consent, Margaretha (Gretchen) Kunz was the most developed of the three seers and the dominant figure among them. The word that seemed to occur to everyone who met her was *geweckt*—bright or sharp.[25] Her father had died in a mill accident five months before her birth, and it would be surprising if she did not experience some resentment from her brothers and sisters, as the last-born of a large family, another mouth to feed in suddenly straitened circumstances. We know that the life of the family changed after the death of Jacob Kunz. He had owned a share in the Alsweiler mill, and the family belonged to the solid middle peasantry ("cattle-peasants") of Marpingen; one of Margaretha's uncles was a village notable.[26] But the mill was subject to forced sale, his widow was unsuccessful when she challenged this in the courts, and Jacob Kunz left debts. Margaretha's elder brothers went down the pit, and her sister Magdalena became a servant girl in the village.[27] It is worth noting the parallels here with the fourteen-year-old Mathilde Sack, a tailor's daughter who was the central figure in the Mettenbuch apparitions.[28] She also had had to come to terms with a fractured family and a loss of family respectability: her mother had died when Mathilde was eleven, her father had been jailed, and she disliked her stepmother. After leaving to work variously for a goldbeater and a confectioner and in domestic service (she was dismissed by one dissatisfied mistress), Mathilde finally left the unhappy family home when her brother went into the army, going as a farm servant to her aunt in Mettenbuch, where apparitions were reported soon afterward.[29] There are

---

24. Rebbert, *Marpingen und seine Gegner,* 9.

25. LASB, E 107, 87, 99; E. Radziwill, *Ein Besuch in Marpingen* (Berlin, 1877), 3–4. Margaretha also had her mother's heavy physical build (see LASB, E 107, 325), and a photograph of the three shows her dominating the group; see Lama, *Die Muttergottes-Erscheinungen,* 36; Bungert, *Heimatbuch,* 229.

26. The uncle was Stephan Kunz IV, a substantial peasant and auxiliary field guard (*Gehilfs-Feldhüter*): LASB, E 107, 79, 431–32; BAT, B III, 11, 14/4, 117.

27. LASB, E 107, 75, 307; the notary Heß to Edmund Radziwill, 28 November 1876, cited in *Marpingen—Wahrheit oder Lüge?* 13–15.

28. The other (younger) children were "under her influence," said the teacher Mayr: Staatsarchiv Landshut (SAL), 164/2, 1162: Besprechung mit Lehrer Mayr von Berg vom 7. Mai 1877. This general view is borne out by the evidence.

29. Details drawn from Bischöfliches Zentralarchiv Regensburg, Generalia F 115 (BZAR, F 115), Fasc. 4: Untersuchung der Angaben der Mettenbucher Mädchen in Waldsassen—1878 u. 1879, esp. Protokoll aufgenommen im Kloster der Cisterzianerinnen zu Waldsassen am 7. Novem-

echoes in both cases of Soubirous, bankrupted miller's daughter and unhappy farm servant.[30] There is no doubt that the German visionaries felt guilt, fear, and uncertainty in their new roles; but there was also awareness of the new attention they commanded. They jealously guarded the apparition sites, issuing warnings to the parish priests and indicating with a shake of the head that certain individuals should not approach. They spoke of secrets, told pilgrims that a celestial omen would be explained and—in Marpingen—"prophesied" the death of a sick child. Katharina said that she had been told to become a nun.[31] The Mettenbuch seers fashioned for themselves, from devotional scraps and fragments, the image of a better world. They described Mary wearing "gold shoes and white stockings" and "angels, as they ate grilled fish from a golden table"; the Virgin reportedly gave instructions that they make up and drink daily from a concoction that sounds like a rustic ambrosia.[32] The Madonna of Marpingen was more domesticated, as the seers described her appearances in particular houses and other village landmarks. There was doubtless a reassuring element to this: a Blessed Virgin who could be associated with Schäfer's meadow, or with the round stone that stood at the end of the upper village, was rendered benign, placed firmly within a bounded world. Their message that Mary had graced these everyday spots also cast the places themselves in a new light and enhanced the status of the messengers, for through their privileged position the children placed their own stamp vicariously on places and properties that were normally an adult preserve. More directly, the behavior of the Marpingen seers was often puckish and pert to the point of childish malice, especially in the case of Margaretha.[33]

At the same time, the story told by the girls was shaped by adults. Pious accounts later emphasized that the parents had used carrot and stick to try to force the children to back down. Frau Kunz supposedly told Margaretha that if she continued to tell lies, her brother Peter would "beat her half to death" when he came back from work.[34] But the later testimony of the seers makes it clear

ber 1878; and the unnumbered folder labeled Mettenbuch: Mathilde Sack in Waldsassen; additional material in Fasc. 1: Bericht des Pfarramtes Metten (23 July 1877); and Fasc. 1, Beilage 1: Protokoll der Vernehmung der Mathilde Sack, Schneiderstochter, 14 J. alt (25 December 1876).

30. On female farm servants, see R. Schulte, "Dienstmädchen im herrschaftlichen Haushalt: Zur Genese ihrer Sozialpsychologie," *Zeitschrift für bayerische Landesgeschichte* 41 (1978): 879–920.

31. LASB, E 107, 6, 64–65, 184, 129–30, 446; BAT, B III, 11, 14/3, 9–42; Thoemes, *Die Erscheinungen in Marpingen,* 54, 81.

32. SAL, 164/2, 1162: Besprechung mit Lehrer Mayr von Berg vom 7. May 1877; BZAR, F 115, Fasc. 5: Vernehmung des Fr. Xav. Kraus in Regensburg, Nov. 1878. Weitere Vernehmungen in Mettn. Dezbr. 1878.

33. See examples and analysis of all these points in Blackbourn, *Marpingen,* chap. 4.

34. BAT, B III, 11, 14/3, 5; LASB, E 107, 301–4, 322; Cramer, *Die Erscheinungen,* 9; Thoemes, *Die Erscheinungen in Marpingen,* 23.

that they were prompted and encouraged almost from the beginning, as adults reworked the story of a "woman in white" into a recognizable apparition narrative.[35] It is possible to reconstruct how support for the apparitions spread from the upper village, where the visionaries lived, into the rest of Marpingen via family clans and friendship networks—predominantly female clans and networks. Village women played a prominent role in nurturing the apparition movement, although the evidence also suggests that attitudes toward the apparitions were decisively influenced when village notables and other "men of good character" gave their support.[36]

A microlevel analysis of how the apparitions were taken up in Marpingen tells us much about the lines of authority in the village, about the relations of adults and children, men and women, notables and village poor. I have been able to give only the briefest sketch here. The positive local reception of the apparitions is also revealing in other ways. The ease with which a "woman in white" could be transformed into Mary Immaculate casts light on religious change in Marpingen during the third quarter of the nineteenth century. The zeal with which Mary's intercession was greeted tells us something about Catholic anxiety, even desperation, in the 1870s. And the eagerness with which villagers exploited pilgrims commercially indicates the economic plight of Marpingen in the same decade. In following up these points, we need to turn to Marpingen's relations with a larger world, particularly to the ways in which external pressures affected the village and made it more receptive to the apparition story.

One of these pressures affected the villagers as Catholics. In 1834 the latest of its many recent temporal rulers, the duke of Saxe-Coburg-Gotha, sold the small principality of Lichtenberg, to which Marpingen belonged, to the king of Prussia.[37] Thereafter the area belonged to the Rhine Province, subject to Prussian state-building and under the aegis of a Protestant dynasty, a Protestant state church, a Protestant field administration, and a Protestant officer

---

35. BAT, B III, 11, 14/3, 59–65: Margaretha's "confession," 26 January 1889. Frau Leist told the girls on the first evening: "Go back into the woods tomorrow, pray, and if you see her again, ask who she is; if she says she is the Immaculately Conceived, then she is the Blessed Virgin." Susanna, when asked who had suggested they return to the woods, was silent for fifteen minutes, then replied: "It was *not* my mother"; LASB, E 107, 60–61: Leist interrogation on 31 October 1876. On apparitions as "fictions," see J. Kent, "A Renovation of Images: Nineteenth-Century Protestant 'Lives of Jesus' and Roman Catholic Alleged Apparitions of the Blessed Virgin Mary," in *The Critical Spirit and the Will to Believe*, ed. D. Jasper and T. R. Wright (Basingstoke, 1989), 37–52.

36. See details and references in Blackbourn, *Marpingen*, chap. 4.

37. On this background—six changes of sovereignty between the 1760s and 1834—see Bungert, *Heimatbuch*, 94–113, 195–205; M. Müller, *Die Geschichte der Stadt St Wendel* (St. Wendel, 1927), 189–91, 229; and O. Beck, *Beschreibung des Regierungsbezirks Trier* (Trier, 1868–71), 2:66–73.

corps.[38] Some in Berlin clearly believed that Prussia also had a Protestant mission, although few went as far as Foreign Minister Johann Peter Friedrich Ancillon, who called in 1832 for a "Protestantization of the Catholic Rhineland."[39] Anti-Catholic discrimination was endemic, and one Catholic priest declared that he would sooner live under the Turks.[40] Where, as in the case of state forestry or mine officials, the lines of denominational and social conflict coincided, the potential for Catholic alienation and discontent was multiplied. There were numerous signs of this in the decades preceding German unification on Protestant-Prussian terms. The third quarter of the nineteenth century also saw mounting communal tension. The historical patchwork quilt of Protestant and Catholic communities on the western border of Germany and the further intermingling of the denominations through new demographic patterns made this tension especially severe in the Saarland. Marpingen's miners experienced it in the coalfield.[41] All villagers witnessed the fierce denominational struggles (over shared churches, the construction of new buildings, the ringing of church bells) that erupted in villages throughout the area—in Offenbach, Kappeln, Weierbach, Oberreidenbach, and Sien.[42] One of these disputes, beginning in 1863–64 and resurfacing in the 1870s, occurred in Berschweiler, an immediately neighboring village and the birthplace of Margaretha's mother.[43]

What sharpened Catholic feelings in the 1870s was the harshness of the Prussian *Kulturkampf,* a conflict in which eighteen hundred priests were jailed or exiled, wanted notices were issued for bishops, homes were searched, and sixteen million marks' worth of church property was seized.[44] The diocese of Trier was seriously affected. In December 1873 the diocesan seminary was closed down, and in March 1874 Matthias Eberhard became the second Prus-

38. Müller, *Die Geschichte der Stadt St Wendel,* 239–44; R. Vierhaus, "Preussen und die Rheinlande, 1815–1915," *Rheinische Vierteljahrsblätter* 30 (1965): 152–75.

39. F. E. Heitjan, *Die Saar-Zeitung und die Entwicklung des politischen Katholizismus an der Saar von 1872–1888* (Saarlouis, 1931), 17.

40. H. Klein, "Die Saarlande im Zeitalter der Industrialisierung," *Zeitschrift für die Geschichte der Saargegend* 29 (1981): 99.

41. W. Laufer, "Bevölkerungs- und siedlungsgeschichtliche Aspekte der Industrialisierung an der Saar," *Zeitschrift für die Geschichte der Saargegend* 29 (1981): 154–55; K. J. Rivinius, "Die sozialpolitische und volkswirthschaftliche Tätigkeit von Georg Friedrich Dasbach," in *Sozial Frage und Kirche im Saarrevier* (Saarbrücken, 1984), 121–22; K.-M. Mallmann, "'Aus des Tages Last machen sie ein Kreuz des Herrn'? Bergarbeiter, Religion und sozialer Protest im Saarrevier des 19. Jahrhunderts," in *Volksreligiosität in der modernen Sozialgeschichte,* ed. W. Schieder (Göttingen, 1986), 155–56.

42. Landeshauptarchiv Koblenz (LHAK), 403/10611, 251–358, 429–58, 573–715; LHAK, 403/10612, 11–26.

43. LHAK, 403/10611, 517–52.

44. On the repressive aspects of the *Kulturkampf,* see M. Scholle, *Die Preussische Strafjustiz im Kulturkampf, 1873–1880* (Marburg, 1974).

sian bishop to be arrested, receiving a fine of 130,000 marks and a nine-month prison sentence.[45] He died six months after his release from jail, exactly one month before the Marpingen events began. The diocese was, in the emotive phrase of the time, "orphaned." Marpingen was directly affected by the so-called bread-basket law, which removed state subsidies from priests who refused (as virtually all did) to declare support for the government's measures. There is evidence of the strains that this produced in the village.[46] Indirectly, Marpingen watched priests in other Saarland parishes being arrested, particularly in neighboring Namborn, where the hunting down and arrest of Jakob Isbert in July 1874 resulted in one of the most violent episodes of the *Kulturkampf.* Namborn was in the same deanery as Marpingen, and the crowds that stormed the railway station at St. Wendel in an attempt to free Father Isbert included many from surrounding rural areas. The rural mayor who arrested the priest, the anticlerical Wilhelm Woytt, also had responsibility for Marpingen, where he was deeply unpopular. It is a measure of local sentiment that he was known as the Devil of St. Wendel.[47] In the wake of official repression, there was heightened Catholic feeling, partly militant, partly mystical. With each new onslaught, the sense of panic and desperation brought reports of stigmatists and prophets, signs of a collective longing for some kind of supernatural intercession and deliverance.[48]

The *Kulturkampf* was not the only source of pressure and anxiety in Marpingen. Historians disagree about many aspects of the "Great Depression," but no one disputes that 1873 saw the advent of agricultural crisis and industrial recession.[49] Marpingen was hit by both. Land prices had collapsed after earlier speculation, leaving high levels of debt; prices were low, credit was

---

45. F. R. Reichert, "Das Trierer Priesterseminar im Kulturkampf (1873–1886)," *Archiv für mittelrheinische Kirchengeschichte* 25 (1973): 65–105; *Bericht über die Gefangennehmung des Herrn Bischofs Dr. Matthias Eberhard sowie über die Austreibung der Professoren aus dem bischöflichen Priesterseminar zu Trier* (Trier, 1874).

46. The law generally hit poorer, left-bank Rhenish parishes harder. On the Marpingen clerical income, see BAT, 70/3676, 43–46, 81–84; on the tensions that resulted, see BAT, 70/3676a, 158–59: Father Jacob Neureuter to the vicar-general of Trier, 30 October 1893.

47. On Namborn, see LHAK, 403/15716, 12–13; BAT, B III, 11, 14/6[1]: 96–99; K. Kammer, *Trierer Kulturkampfpriester* (Trier, 1926), 156; Müller, *Die Geschichte der Stadt St Wendel,* 270–73; J. Bellot, *Hundert Jahre politisches Leben an der Saar unter preussischer Herrschaft (1815–1918)* (Bonn, 1954); K.-M. Mallmann, "Volksfrömmigkeit, Proletarisierung und preussischer Obrigkeitsstaat: Sozialgeschichtliche Aspekte des Kulturkampfes an der Saar," in *Sozialfrage und Kirche im Saar-Revier,* 211–12.

48. On Elisabeth Flesch, the "blood sweater" of nearby Eppelborn, and other cases, see Blackbourn, *Marpingen,* chap. 3.

49. H. Rosenberg, *Grosse Depression und Bismarckzeit* (Berlin, 1967); G. Eley, "Hans Rosenberg and the Great Depression of 1873–96," in *From Unification to Nazism,* by G. Eley (London, 1986), 23–41.

short, and—in the words of one writer—the moneylenders were active "from three o'clock in the morning until ten o'clock at night."[50] (Villagers would later show a certain insolent pride in parading the visionaries before these same moneylenders and cattle dealers in Tholey.) Bailiffs serving distraint orders and the itinerant poor crowding the highroads testified to the crisis.[51] Marpingen was also severely affected by the industrial recession in the Saarland. By the middle of the 1870s, half of the employed population worked away from the village in the southern Saar coalfield, which developed so fast in the 1850s and 1860s that it was dubbed "black California."[52] The loss or reduction of their income had a demonstrably adverse effect on Marpingen.[53] Indeed, the new way of life of this first generation of miner-peasants marked a significant break in the life of the whole village. The miner-peasants walked to work early on Monday morning and returned late on Saturday night, living effectively as *Gastarbeiter* for six days a week in poor accommodations, subjected to quasi-military discipline by mine officials and distrusted by many indigenous miners as rate-busting rustics (and "backward" Catholics). They lived in two worlds, at home in neither. For those they left behind, central aspects of life were also transformed, including farm work and the organization of it, relationships between husband, wife, and children, and family marriage strategies.[54] The Marpingen seers had brothers and other extended family members who earned a living in this way; many of the "rival children" who later claimed apparitions also had absent fathers and brothers; miners' wives and children were to be prominent in reporting "miraculous" cures.[55] These circumstances are surely

---

50. J. J. Kartels, "Die wirthschaftliche Lage des Bauernstandes in den Gebirgsdistricten des Kreises Merzig," *Schriften des Vereins für Sozialpolitik* 22 (1883): 208; see also H. Horch, *Der Wandel der Gesellschafts- und Herrschaftsstrukturen in der Saarregion während der Industrialisierung (1740–1914)* (St. Ingbert, 1985), 234–38; and Müller, *Die Geschichte der Stadt St Wendel*, 212, on moneylenders and cattle dealers in the area. On earlier speculation by peasant-miners, see O. Beck, *Die ländliche Kreditnoth und die Darlehenskassen im Regierungsbezirk Trier* (Trier, 1875), 112; and J. Müller, *Die Landwirtschaft im Saarland* (Saarbrücken, 1976), 24–27.

51. Testimony of the gendarme Hentschel in *Der Marpinger Prozess vor dem Zuchtpolizeigericht in Saarbrücken*, ed. G. Dasbach (Trier, 1879), 163; Müller, *Die Geschichte der Stadt St Wendel*, 276.

52. Bungert, *Heimatbuch*, 301; and Laufer, "Bevölkerungs-und siedlungsgeschichtliche Aspekte," 154.

53. LASB, E 107, 434.

54. K. Fehn, "Das saarländische Arbeiterbauerntum im 19. und 20. Jahrhundert," in *Agrarisches Nebengewerbe und Formen der Reagrarisierung*, ed. H. Kellenbenz (Stuttgart, 1975), 195–214; M. Zenner, "Probleme des Übergangs von der Agrar- zur Industrie- und Arbeiterkultur im Saarland," in *Sozialefrage und Kirche im Saar-Revier*, 70–71; Bungert, *Heimatbuch*, 303; Horst Steffens, "Einer für alle, alle für einen? Bergarbeiterfamilien in der 2. Hälfte des 19. Jahrhunderts," in *Haushalt und Verbrauch in historischer Perspektive*, ed. T. Pierenkemper (St. Katharinen, 1987), 187–226; K. Hoppstädter, "'Eine Stunde nach der Schicht muss jeder gewaschen sein': Die alten Schlafhäuser und die Ranzenmänner," *Saarbrücker Bergmannskalender*, 1963:77–79.

55. See details in Blackbourn, *Marpingen*, chaps. 4–5.

significant, especially when we put them together with other pieces of evidence. Broken families were, as we have seen, a motif in many apparitions, in Germany and elsewhere. We also know something about the strains that arose in similar commuting villages in Württemberg and in other communities where the adult males were regularly away seeking employment, such as the *Weiberdorf* (village without men) in the Eifel depicted in Clara Viebig's novel of that name.[56] We have the evidence, finally, of a curious parallel to the Marpingen events two years later in the Friuli, when an outbreak of "collective hysteria" arose among the women of Verzegnis at a time when most of the village men were absent as migrant seasonal laborers.[57] These examples suggest that we take seriously the social-psychological dimension involved at Marpingen, where the strain of economic and social dislocation was borne by families.

This angle of approach also requires that we look at the place occupied by women and children in the changing devotional forms and popular piety of the decades before the 1870s. The word "changing" needs to be emphasized, for it would be wrong to regard what happened to Marpingen simply as the "traditional" response of a pious community to the threats posed by a "modern" state and economy. The history of Marpingen earlier in the century shows how misleading that would be. In the 1840s the village was still being described in the most unflattering terms by its parish priest. Lack of interest in church services, card playing, enthusiasm for the tavern, dancing through the night on feast days, unruly young people, the negligent upbringing of children, crude sensuality—these were "quite general" in the parish.[58] Even by the standards of contemporary clerical disapproval, the village seems to have stood out, and events in the first half of the nineteenth century suggest an unusual degree of spite and hostility toward successive parish priests. Father Heinrich Licht had his windows broken; Father Matthias Hoff had serious differences with his flock over dancing and standards in the local school; Father Joseph Bicking, in

---

56. J. Kuczynski, *Geschichte des Alltags des Deutschen Volkes,* vol. 4, *1871–1918* (Berlin, 1982), 414–15; and C. Viebig, *Das Weiberdorf: Roman aus der Eifel,* 7th ed. (Berlin, 1901). On *Weiberdörfer* in the Saarland, see N. Fox, *Saarländische Volkskunde* (Bonn, 1927), 389; Kartels, "Die wirthschaftliche Lage," 197; Steffens, "Einer für alle," 214–16; and for an Austrian example, see E. Viethen, "Tradition und Realitätseignung—Bergarbeiterfrauen im industriellen Wandel," in *Die andere Kultur: Volkskunde, Sozialwissenschaften und Arbeiterkultur,* ed. H. Fielhauer and O. Bockhorn (Vienna, 1982), 241–59.

57. L. Petit, "Une epidémie d'hystéro-demonopathie, en 1878, à Verzegnis, province de Frioul, Italie," *Revue scientifique,* 10 April 1880, 974A–5A. On the dislocation of worker peasantries in the Friuli, see D. R. Holmes, *Cultural Disenchantments: Worker Peasantries in Northern Italy* (Princeton, 1989).

58. Parish priest Father Joseph Bicking, cited in H. Derr, "Geschichte der Pfarrei Marpingen" (Priesterseminar diss., Trier, 1935), 27–29.

the 1840s, had problems over almost everything, meeting with verbal and physical abuse, which may have led him eventually to leave Marpingen.[59] The transformation that occurred in the following generation is essential to an understanding of what happened later. The changes were similar to those described by Jonathan Sperber in his study of popular Catholicism in the Rhineland and Westphalia.[60] In Marpingen, as elsewhere, there was a purposive renewal of piety and a reassertion of clerical control. Religious brotherhoods and sodalities were founded; a well and a shrine linked to the legend of a miraculous image of the Virgin were restored; church attendance improved, and illegitimacy rates fell.[61] The parish priest in 1876 (he had been there since 1864) was Father Jacob Neureuter, one of the new breed of intensely Mariolatrous clergy produced by the more independent seminaries of the 1850s and 1860s, and the cult of the Virgin Mary was central to the religious revival in Marpingen, as it was across Europe. It touched everything—sodalities, hymnals, statuary, even the liturgy—and formed the centerpiece of a recharged, emotionally laden piety.[62] This change was paralleled by two others. One was the "feminization" of Catholicism (much less studied in the German case than in some others).[63] The second was the growing emphasis on the child as a symbol of purity and simple faith. Children, for their part, grew up in a world increasingly suffused with the songs, the flowers, the perfumes, and the images of a cloying piety centered on the Virgin Mary. They were also being prepared

59. Derr, "Geschichte der Pfarrei Marpingen," 11–12, 20–29, 35. Bicking had a further problem with irregular church bookkeeping, a "hateful business"; see BAT, 70/3676, 20: Bicking to the vicar-general, Trier, 25 October 1847. See also Derr, 22–25, 30, 34–37.

60. J. Sperber, *Popular Catholicism in Nineteenth Century Germany* (Princeton, 1984).

61. Derr, "Geschichte der Pfarrei Marpingen," 30–34, 54–63, and table on illegitimacy rates; Thoemes, *Die Erscheinungen in Marpingen,* 9–12; *Die Marpinger Mutter Gottes-Erscheinungen,* 12–13.

62. Marpingen was "teeming with images of the Virgin," said a hostile observer in 1876; Police commissar Leopold von Merescheidt-Hüllessem, cited in *Saar- und Mosel-Zeitung,* 20 December 1876. On "Marianization" in the Trier diocese, see A. Heinz, "Im Banne der römischen Einheitsliturgie: Die Romanisierung der Trierer Bistumsliturgie in der zweiten Hälfte des 19. Jahrhunderts," *Römische Quartalschrift* 79 (1984): 37–92; A. Heinz, "Marienlieder des 19. Jahrhunderts und ihre Liturgiefähigkeit," *Trierer Theologische Zeitschrift* 97 (1988): 106–34; B. Schneider, "Die Trauben- und Johannesweinsegnung in der Trierer Bistumsliturgie vom Spätmittelalter bis zum ausgehenden 19. Jahrhundert," *Archiv für mittelrheinische Kirchengeschichte* 37 (1985): 57–74; K. Küppers, "Die Maiandacht als Beispiel volksnaher Frömmigkeit," *Römische Quartalschrift* 81 (1986): 102–12.

63. H. McLeod, *Religion and the People of Western Europe, 1789–1970* (Oxford, 1981), 28–35; R. Gibson, *A Social History of French Catholicism, 1789–1914* (London, 1989), 104–7, 180–90; F. Lannon, *Privilege, Persecution and Prophecy: The Catholic Church in Spain, 1875–1975* (Oxford, 1987); B. Pope, "Immaculate and Powerful: The Marian Revival in the Nineteenth Century," in *Immaculate and Powerful: The Female in Sacred Image and Social Reality,* ed. C. W. Atkinson, C. H. Buchanan, and M. R. Miles (Cambridge, Mass., 1985), 193–94.

for communion at a younger age, something that may have influenced several German visionaries of the 1870s.[64] These changes were reinforced by the great popular missions held in Germany in the 1850s and 1860s, and they received the warmest encouragement from Pope Pius IX, for whom the cult of the Virgin Mary in general and the doctrine of the Immaculate Conception in particular were major preoccupations.[65]

All of this might suggest a substratum of truth to the charge leveled by officials and liberals, in highly characteristic terms, that clerical inspiration was at work on susceptible women ("madwomen," "hysterical women") and children ("the maids favored by the Deity").[66] In Marpingen we have young girls who had just begun study of the catechism at school, instructed by a parish priest who had placed his own oil painting of the Virgin and child in the local church and sermonized about Lourdes and by a teacher who had also related the story of Bernadette.[67] Moreover, the apparitions began on the very day—3 July 1876—that thirty-five bishops, five thousand priests, and one hundred thousand lay Catholics were gathered for a major "coronation" ceremony at Lourdes.[68] It was a time when details about the Pyrenean apparitions were widely reported in the Catholic press, when Catholics in Marpingen (as elsewhere in Germany) would certainly have been voicing the common lament that the Virgin had not yet graced German soil. Lourdes had an obvious impact on German Catholics. Where such apparitions had been approved as exemplary, the church threw its formidable institutional weight behind them. It showed great organizational flair in promoting the apparitions as official cults, sending in religious orders to run sites such as the Lourdes Domain as specialists and learning from the great exhibitions of the period when it came to the transportation of pilgrims by railway or the use of lighting for dramatic effect. Through sermons, popular pamphlets and the word-of-mouth accounts of those who had been on major "national pilgrimages" (which began in the 1870s), expectations were aroused and the faithful everywhere learnt what the Blessed Virgin "ought" to look like.[69] The effects of this can be seen at Marpingen, where a routinely familiar story about a woman in white was reshaped by local crisis

---

64. On this unexplored subject, see H. Jedin, *Handbuch der Kirchengeschichte*, vol. 6, part 2, *Die Kirche zwischen Revolution und Restauration* (Freiburg i. Br., 1971), 664–65.

65. On missions in the Saarland, see LHAK, 442/6438, 171, 179–83, 241–43, 247–48, 277–80, 307–11, 331–34, 349–50, 399–407, 427–30, 449–64. On Pius IX, see R. Aubert, *Le pontificat de Pie IX (1846–1878)* (Paris, 1950), 466–69.

66. *Saar- und Mosel-Zeitung*, 18 July 1876; and *Nahe-Blies-Zeitung*, 21 October 1876.

67. Radziwill, *Ein Besuch*, 7; Derr, "Pfarrei Marpingen," 43; BAT, B III, 11, 14/3, 55; LASB, E 107, 75–76, 84, 102–4.

68. Cramer, *Die Erscheinungen*, 8.

69. Kselman, *Miracles and Prophecies;* Pope, "Immaculate and Powerful," 185–86; Hellé, *Miracles*, 83–84; and G. Korff, "Formierung der Frömmigkeit," *Geschichte und Gesellschaft* 3 (1977): 356–57.

and the longing for deliverance, by the contingencies of time and place, and not least by the agency of particular adults into a rather different story about Mary the Immaculately Conceived.

At the beginning the responsibility of the clergy was indirect: they followed popular sentiment much more than they led it. This remained true as the apparitions continued, although the degree of clerical enthusiasm should not be underestimated. Very large numbers of priests visited Marpingen. Of the five hundred or so pilgrims in the village on 28 August 1877, around forty were members of the clergy. The exceptionally large crowd six days later included "hundreds" of priests from Germany and abroad.[70] Some idea of the geographical spread can be gleaned from the unlucky twenty who were caught and prosecuted for the illegal celebration of mass in Marpingen. They came not only from the Rhine Province and the nearby Palatinate but from Baden, Westphalia, and East Prussia.[71] Widespread clerical belief in the apparitions is plain: priests wept when the three girls told their story, accompanied triumphant processions of the "miraculously" cured to the visionaries' homes, and took Marpingen water away with them.[72] This is not surprising, given their training and the circumstances of the 1870s. The apparitions must have represented a solace for many, a sign of grace in a cold, hard world "sunk in materialism," and an intercession of such potency that it would jolt the progressives out of their materialist complacency.[73] In the words of one: "I firmly hope and believe that things are still to happen here at which the *Kulturkämpfer* will marvel, as once did Columbus and his fellows when they discovered America."[74] Priests with notebooks became a familiar sight in Marpingen; and by prompting the visionaries (however innocently), as they certainly did, by recording the events, and by publicizing them in the press and in cheap pamphlets, many priests helped to legitimate events that they saw as a great cause.[75]

Yet there were clerical skeptics, too, and with good reason. Among visiting priests and those who corresponded with Neureuter, there was concern at aspects of the visionaries' accounts, particularly the descriptions of the devil: "dark points," in the words of one; "curious matters that make an extremely

---

70. LASB, E 107, 165; *Marpingen und seine Gnadenmonate*, 41.

71. LHAK, 403/15716, 130–31, 134–39, 144–47, 154–55, 158–61. On the difficulty of apprehending them, see LASB, E 107, 168–69.

72. LASB, E 107, 372–73; P. Sausseret, *Erscheinungen und Offenbarungen* (Regensburg, 1878), 2:230; *Saar- und Mosel-Zeitung*, 30 March 1877.

73. Quotation from LASB, E 107, 359–61: Father Klotz to Father Konrad Schneider, 19 August 1876. Schneider was parish priest in Alsweiler, near Marpingen, and spent long periods in the village after the apparitions.

74. Ibid., 364: Father Schneider to Father Bollig, of Mertesdorf, 10 October 1876.

75. BAT, B III, 11, 14/3, 59–65.

unfavorable impression," in the opinion of another.[76] There were further disquieting elements. Pilgrims streamed there without their parish priests in a
manner that seemed dangerously spontaneous. These large unofficial movements of the faithful ran directly counter to the clerical tendency to encourage
more organized and controlled pilgrimages. The pilgrims attracted to the "miraculous" children also showed some inclination to neglect the official site of
Marian devotion in the village (the well and shrine near the church) and flock
instead to the new site in the wood, which lay on the opposite side of the
village. In Marpingen, as elsewhere, there is a local topography of apparitions,
which we should not neglect. Popular faith in the curative powers of water and
of the place itself was strongly tinged with animistic beliefs. At the same time,
the commercial opportunities presented by the pilgrimage trade raised the
specter of that intermingling of the sacred and profane so often criticized by the
clergy—although, it should be said, this problem was touched on by clerical
critics of Marpingen less than one might expect.[77]

The two central issues were undoubtedly "superstition" and clerical control. The emotional drama surrounding the apparitions released popular sentiments that could hardly fail to alarm the clergy. Pilgrims saw processions
"floating through the air"; others believed they had been guided to their goal by
the "miraculous star of Marpingen"; there were reports of imminent plague
from which only those who partook of the water would be spared, of heaven
and hell opening up and of demons roaming abroad.[78] The Marpingen apparitions also triggered numerous imitations. Within the village itself, a score of
"rival children" claimed increasingly extravagant visions.[79] Further local apparitions were reported from Gronig, Wemmetsweiler, Münchwies, and
Berschweiler. In Münchwies a group of children worked themselves into a
religious ecstasy; at one point a group burst in on Neureuter at Marpingen
"bathed in sweat" and asking to take communion. Children and adults saw the
devil standing next to the Virgin and dancing around her in the shape of a dog, a
donkey, and a cow.[80] In Berschweiler a group of a dozen children, mainly girls,
fought violent struggles with the devil in front of large crowds. We are told how

76. *Die Marpinger Mutter Gottes-Erscheinungen,* 24; LASB, E 107, 118–19.

77. On the pilgrims and their conduct, and on the commercialization, see Blackbourn,
Marpingen, chap. 5.

78. *Kölnische Zeitung,* 23 August 1876; Thoemes, *Die Erscheinungen in Marpingen,* 78–
81; Berg, *Marpingen und das Evangelium,* 44; *Saar- und Mosel-Zeitung,* 6 February 1877; Müller,
Die Geschichte der Stadt St Wendel, 274.

79. LASB, E 107, 126–28, 163, 189, 444, 494; *Der Marpinger Prozess vor dem
Zuchtpolizeigericht,* 171–72, 193–96; *Die Marpinger Mutter Gottes-Erscheinungen,* 17;
Marpingen—Wahrheit oder Lüge? 84–85; *Marpingen und seine Gnadenmonate,* 32, 42–43.

80. *Prozess vor dem Zuchtpolizeigericht,* 157 (Neureuter's testimony); LHAK, 442/6442,
73–80: Father Göller to the Landrat of Ottweiler, 22 July 1877; teacher Kill to the Landrat of
Ottweiler, 22 July 1877; the Landrat of Ottweiler to the district governor of Trier, 25 July 1877.

"eleven girls rolled on a bed with convulsive twitches and improper movements, while screaming and shouting about the apparitions they were witness-
ing," performances that commonly went on beyond midnight.[81] A little further
afield, the "Virgin in a bottle" at the Gappenach mill, over which the miller, his
wife, an impoverished tailor, and a woman known as "the nun of Naunheim"
were prosecuted, attracted five thousand pilgrims a day. There was another
Virgin in a bottle at Mühlheim.[82]

Many of these cases, especially the ones involving nocturnal activities,
were an explicit challenge to clerical authority, often accompanied by threats
(especially in Berschweiler and Gappenach). In Münchwies the local priest
criticized the "night-time mischief" of local youth in terms remarkably similar
to those applied in earlier decades to "unruly" Marpingen.[83] Even the original
Marpingen apparitions alarmed some local priests sufficiently that they sermonized against them and warned their parishioners off, without conspicuous
success.[84] While many liberal and Protestant observers argued that the
Catholic clergy should somehow have nipped matters in the bud, a sardonic
reporter in the *Gartenlaube* was more realistic: the clergy was "simply not
master of a movement over which it has long lost any control."[85] This verdict
applies, in more complicated ways, to the parish priests of Marpingen and
Mettenbuch. Both were overwhelmed, in the first place, by the new demands
on them: correspondents who wanted information and "miraculous" water,
pilgrims requiring masses to be said and confessions to be heard, clerical
visitors who "tortured" the parish priests with their questions—not to mention
abusive mail and inquisitive officials.[86] Neureuter in Marpingen and Father
Johannes Anglhuber in Mettenbuch were racked by personal doubts about the
authenticity of the apparitions and troubled by the possibility of childish mischief or diabolical inspiration, although it is clear that both came privately to
believe in them. However, given the formal obligation on any parish priest in
this position to maintain a prudent reserve, both came under enormous pressure
from their parishioners and others to embrace the apparitions wholeheartedly.
The phrases "keep under control" and "do not encourage" echo poignantly

---

81. *Der Marpinger Prozess vor dem Richterstuhle der Vernunft von einem Unparteiischen*
(Vienna, 1881), 29; see also LASB, E 107, 127, 160; *Saar- und Mosel-Zeitung,* 12 January 1878;
St-Paulinus-Blatt, 20 January 1878; *Vossische Zeitung,* 16 January 1878.

82. Berg, *Marpingen und das Evangelium,* 29–30; *Saar- und Mosel-Zeitung,* 27 March, 30
March, 1 April, 5 April, 7 April 1877; *Kölnische Zeitung,* 1 July 1877.

83. LHAK, 442/6442, 76–80: Father Göller to the Landrat of Ottweiler, 22 July 1877.

84. Examples include priests in Tholey, Bliesen, St. Wendel, Illingen, and Hasborn: LASB,
E 107, 75, 201; BAT, B III, 11, 14/5, 126; *Kölnische Zeitung,* 26 July and 3 August 1876.

85. "An der Gnadenstätte von Marpingen," 667.

86. It was the visiting Father Wolf who "tortured me with his questions": *Prozess vor dem
Zuchtpolizeigericht,* 153. On the abusive mail, see *Die Marpinger Mutter Gottes-Erscheinungen,*
21.

through their correspondence, along with "what should I do?" and "I do not know where to turn." There is evidence that Neureuter came close to cracking under the strain.[87]

Whenever claims of apparitions and miraculous cures arose, canon law stipulated that a formal ecclesiastical inquiry be held. Marpingen, Mettenbuch, and Dittrichswalde were subject to such inquiries, and in each case a negative judgment was the result. The church had problems, however, both in conducting its investigations and in getting its judgments to stick. In the case of Marpingen, the *Kulturkampf* had deprived Trier of a bishop, and the diocese was being run by members of the cathedral chapter acting as papal legates and using Latin code names.[88] The chain of command in the diocese was fragile (this was one of Neureuter's problems), and a canonical inquiry was hard to organize. Eventually the task was entrusted to an octogenarian Luxemburg cleric with strong German connections, Titular Bishop Johannes Theodor Laurent of Chersones: in 1878 he deemed the account of the Marpingen seers "unseemly," "unworthy and sacrilegious" and the apparitions themselves inauthentic.[89] However, the interplay of piety and politics made it difficult for the improvised hierarchy in Trier to come out openly against the apparitions, for this would have given a weapon to anticlericals and bitterly disappointed the faithful. As a result, the church sat on the Marpingen findings, storing up future trouble for itself from frustrated advocates of the "German Lourdes."[90] In the short term, though, the decision in Trier may have represented prudent calculation, for in the Mettenbuch case, where Bishop Ignaz Senestrey of Regensburg was free to conduct a textbook inquiry, the pastoral letter rejecting the apparitions failed to quell widespread belief in their authenticity. Regensburg continued to be troubled by the issue through the 1880s.[91] The silent *Kulturkampf* in Bavaria, like the open *Kulturkampf* in Prussia, heightened the popular Catholic propensity to believe in the intercession of the Blessed Virgin, whatever its clergy said.

---

87. Details and references in Blackbourn, *Marpingen,* chap. 6.

88. C. Weber, *Kirchliche Politik zwischen Rom, Berlin und Trier, 1876–1888* (Mainz, 1970), 20–27.

89. BAT, B III, 11, 14/3, 43–49. On Laurent, see K. Möller, *Leben und Briefe von Johannes Theodor Laurent,* 3 vols. (Trier, 1887–89); O. Foesser, "Johann Theodor Laurent und seine Verdienste um die katholische Kirche," *Frankfurter zeitgemässe Broschüren,* n.s., 11 (1890): 153–84; J. Goedert, *Jean-Théodore Laurent: Vicaire apostolique de Luxembourg, 1804–1884* (Luxemburg, 1957).

90. See Blackbourn, *Marpingen,* chap. 11.

91. Details of the inquiry in BZAR, F 115, Fasc. 1: Akten der bischöfl. Commission, vom 21. Sept. bis 14. Nov. 1877, with further materials in supplements and in Fasc. 2; the judgment is in Fasc. 6: Gutacten über die Sache. Entscheidung durch den Hirtenbrief v. 23. Jan. 1879. On the problems that arose, see Fasc. 7: Vollzug der Entscheidung 1879–81; and the unnumbered files Mettenbuch 1881–84, Mettenbuch 1885, Mettenbuch 1887–88, and Mettenbuch 1886–90.

Reactions to the apparitions not only revealed divisions among the lower clergy and between clergy and laity; they also revealed divisions within the laity itself. These had a clear sociological dimension. The miraculous sites attracted large numbers of visitors from the Catholic aristocracy, German and non-German. Spees, Stolbergs, Löwensteins—all the great families were represented in Marpingen.[92] The Princess Helene of Thurn und Taxis patronized both Mettenbuch and Marpingen, traveling to the latter with a retinue of seventeen servants.[93] At the bottom of the social scale, the apparition sites attracted peasants, agricultural laborers, farm and domestic servants, significant numbers of small tradespeople, and—above all in Marpingen—workers. Marpingen became something of a miners' pilgrimage.[94] Conspicuously absent among pilgrims and other supporters of the apparitions were members of the Catholic bourgeoisie, certainly bourgeois men. There were naturally theologians and publicists who were enthusiastic, and a handful of businessmen appear in the record as having visited Marpingen (although not always with any great faith).[95] But in the extensive sources, official and unofficial, hostile and friendly, there is not a single reference to pilgrims who were industrialists or managers, no mention at all of any pilgrim from the middle or higher ranks of the bureaucracy, no pilgrim engaged in the exercise of law, medicine, engineering, or architecture. The social composition of those who went to Marpingen reflects the skewed distribution of Catholics in the overall population. But the striking underrepresentation of the propertied and educated middle classes also says something about Catholics who belonged to those classes. There were, of course, Catholic doctors, lawyers, officials, and businessmen, but they were precisely the Catholics of whom it was complained that they were "too close to the Protestants and lukewarm," that they led worldly lives and read novels.[96] These were the Catholics who distrusted "excessive" Mariolatry and found episodes like Marpingen more embarrassing than inspirational. From the austere academic Franz-Xaver Kraus, who regarded Marpingen, like Lourdes, as an ultramontane nonsense to the factory owner who

92. Müller, *Die Geschichte der Stadt St Wendel,* 275; LASB, E 107, 162, 166, 361–62; *Prozess vor dem Zuchtpolizeigericht,* 84; *Marpingen und seine Gnadenmonate,* 46; *Marpingen—Wahrheit oder Lüge?* 44–45.

93. Fürst Thurn und Taxis Zentralarchiv, HMA 2699, Nr. 2974–78, 3211–17, 2803, 2809–10; HMA 2700, Nr. 3031: bills for trips to Marpingen and Mettenbuch in 1877–78.

94. Blackbourn, *Marpingen,* chap. 4, has a detailed sociological breakdown of the pilgrims to both Marpingen and Mettenbuch. See also Mallmann, "Aus des Tages Last."

95. LASB, E 107, 86–92, 236.

96. E. Gatz, *Rheinische Volksmission im 19. Jahrhundert* (Düsseldorf, 1963), 97–98. Conversely, the skepticism about Marpingen among "thinking" Catholics was exploited by Protestant writers; see Berg, *Marpingen und das Evangelium,* 40.

expressed himself scandalized by the affair, these attitudes were widespread.[97] They were especially prevalent in the educated middle class, and they extended to figures prominent in Catholic public life. Thus Julius Bachem, lawyer, publicist, and leading Center Party politician, did everything possible to distance himself from the supernatural claims on which Marpingen rested.[98]

Yet Bachem defended the inhabitants of Marpingen, in the parliament and in the courts, against charges that arose from events there. This combination of personal skepticism and public defense was not hypocritical but rather another telling sign of the times. It was the great—involuntary—achievement of the Prussian state and their liberal allies that they did so much to paper over the real divisions among German Catholics. The very reasons that made it difficult for the church to win popular support for its rejection of the apparitions were the same ones that tended to bring German Catholics together—for all were tarred with the same brush.[99] To understand this, we have to appreciate the scale of the political and bureaucratic offensive faced by Catholics in the 1870s. Liberals were in many ways the pacemakers here. It was, after all, a left- liberal— the doctor, pathologist, and scientific popularizer Rudolf Virchow—who coined the phrase *Kulturkampf.* And the fierceness with which liberals supported this "struggle of civilizations" demonstrates their heady belief in progress, defined above all against the "dead hand" of the church and Catholic "backwardness."[100] The reactions of liberal politicians and press to Marpingen reveal a boundless contempt and hostility. The apparitions were painted as an example of deception and credulity—the "Marpingen miracle swindle," the "crassest stupidity," "mindless superstition," "a colossal swindle based on stupidity," a product of the "credulous bigoted masses."[101] A darker, pseudo-scientific language also colored these denunciations. Apparition sites were habitually described as a *Sumpf,* or swamp; believers (especially women) were the victims of "mania" or "hysteria"; the episodes were a form of collective

---

97. F.-X. Kraus, *Tagebücher,* ed. H. Schiel (Cologne, 1957), 381: entry of 23 September 1877; *Germania,* 9 February 1877.

98. J. Bachem, *Lose Blätter aus meinem Leben* (Freiburg i. Br., 1910), 65–75; and J. Bachem, *Erinnerungen eines alten Publizisten und Politikers* (Cologne, 1913), 133–42. The same attitude colored Bachem's discussions of Marpingen in court (see *Prozess vor dem Zuchtpolizeigericht*) and in the Landtag; see *Sten. Berichte über die Verhandlungen der durch die Allerhöchste Verordnung vom 3. Oktober 1877 einberufenen beiden Häuser des Landtages. Haus der Abgeordneten* (Berlin, 1878), vol. 2, 46th sitting, 16 January 1878, 1151–59.

99. See D. Blackbourn, "Progress and Piety: Liberals, Catholics and the State in Bismarck's Germany," in *Populists and Patricians,* by D. Blackbourn (London, 1987), 155.

100. Blackbourn, "Progress and Piety."

101. Ludwig Seyffardt, *Sten. Berichte,* 30 November 1877, reprinted in Ludwig Seyffardt, *Erinnerungen* (Leipzig, 1900), 195–96; *Saar- und Mosel-Zeitung,* 16 July 1876; *Nahe-Blies-Zeitung,* 24 August, 5 September, and 28 October 1876; *Kölnische Zeitung,* 20 October 1876.

pathology, an "epidemic popular disease."[102] The apparitions were also, in the view of many liberals, an attempt to foster "hatred" against the Reich and to inflame the "fanatical mob" into "revolutionary upheaval."[103]

Contempt, dehumanizing language, fears for public order—all made it easier for liberals to support repressive measures, urging the government to "proceed with maximum energy against this antistate and treasonable agitation."[104] Among National Liberals, who identified themselves strongly with Bismarck, "energetic measures" were constantly invoked. Energy, strength, endurance, lack of sentimentality were "manly" virtues, the self-image with which National Liberals warmed themselves as they "struggled" (or backed the struggle of the state) against the clerical enemy.[105] Left-liberals such as Virchow and newspapers like the *Frankfurter Zeitung* had greater misgivings about the methods employed in the *Kulturkampf.* The latter argued that Marpingen was a swindle that would have been better dealt with by "manly and honorable words and open discussion" than by repression.[106] Yet they were also committed by the logic of their position to a firm prosecution of the anticlerical struggle in which they so passionately believed. Marpingen provides a perfect instance of the way that progressive liberals allowed Bismarck to wage "proxy wars" (*Stellvertreterkriege*) on their behalf.[107] As a result, the state, which had censored liberal newspapers and dismissed liberal officials in the 1850s and 1860s, was now cast in the role of a progressive cultural steamroller. The price paid by liberals was acquiescence in the repressive measures taken in places like Marpingen.

How, then, did the Prussian state act in Marpingen? The authorities remained ignorant of what was happening for a week. The local gendarme was in jail on an immorality charge, and the only state-appointed official in the village, the *Ortsvorsteher,* provided no information to his superiors.[108] The local *Landrat,* the decisive figure in the Prussian field administration, was on holiday. When his deputy, District Secretary Hugo Besser, and Woytt, the local rural mayor, first heard about Marpingen and the size of the crowds gathering there, they overreacted. Besser panicked, and Woytt seems to have used the

102. For a detailed examination of this language, see Blackbourn, *Marpingen,* chap. 9.

103. *Nahe-Blies-Zeitung,* 7 September 1876. Cf. *Saar- und Mosel-Zeitung,* 24 August 1876; *Kölnische Zeitung,* 26 August and 3 November 1876; *National-Zeitung,* 17 January 1878; *Deutsche Allgemeine Zeitung,* 17 August 1876.

104. *Nahe-Blies-Zeitung,* 7 September 1876. This was entirely typical of National Liberal newspapers.

105. The trope of "manliness" is explored in Blackbourn, *Marpingen,* chap. 9.

106. *Frankfurter Zeitung,* 16 January 1878.

107. R. Aldenhoff, *Schulze-Delitzsch: Ein Beitrag zur Geschichte des Liberalismus zwischen Revolution und Reichsgründung* (Baden-Baden, 1984), 233. Cf. O. Klein-Hattingen, *Die Geschichte des deutschen Liberalismus* (Berlin, 1912), 2:49–55.

108. LASB, E 107, 428.

opportunity to revenge himself on a community that resented his vigorous support of the *Kulturkampf* and was also in dispute over his salary. The result was a halfhearted effort by the two men and a group of gendarmes to read the riot act to four thousand singing and praying pilgrims, followed by a telegram to the nearest garrison, in Saarlouis, requesting assistance.[109] Shortly after noon on 13 July, ten days after the apparitions began, the eighty-strong 8th Company of the 4th Rhenish Infantry Regiment, under Captain von Fragstein-Riemsdorff, arrived in St. Wendel to be briefed by the district secretary. They set off for Marpingen soon after 6 P.M., going cross-country and using forestry tracks. They approached the woods at about 8 P.M., sounded a drumroll, which caused confusion even among the soldiers (some mistook it for the order to load rifles), and proceeded to disperse the crowd with fixed bayonets. The company was then billeted in Marpingen at the village's expense, starting by requisitioning beds, food, hay, and other provisions (including wine) in the early hours of the morning.[110] The commanding officer later observed laconically that "the inhabitants of Marpingen showed themselves to be slack and grudging in the lodging of men and the procuring of necessary provisions, etc., so that energetic action and blunt measures were necessary on my part to regularize the circumstances of the case."[111] Writing in the *Kölnische Volkszeitung*, Matthias Scheeben suggested that the behavior of the military "was worse than that to be expected of troops in an occupied country."[112] Writer and newspaper were later prosecuted for this slur.

The civilian authorities now pursued a dual-track policy, the first part of which aimed to discover the "instigators" of the whole affair. The local *Landrat*, the district governor from Trier, examining magistrates, and public prosecutors descended on the village and began a lengthy round of inquiries and disciplinary measures. Neureuter and two neighboring parish priests had their homes searched and their correspondence seized; all three priests were then arrested and removed from their posts as school inspectors. Two village schoolteachers were transferred away from the village, and further arrests were made. All the women in the village aged between twenty-five and fifty were subject to a mass identification parade to discover who had placed a cross at the apparition site. There were numerous interrogations, especially of the three girls and their parents (Margaretha was questioned twenty-eight times), and the children were removed from their homes and placed under surveillance in an

109. LHAK, 442/6442, 17–20, 133–34; *Prozess vor dem Zuchtpolizeigericht,* 14–15, 149–50; BAT, B III, 11, 14/4, 10.

110. LASB, E 107, 15–19, 31–45; BAT, B III, 11, 14/4, 27; LHAK, 442/6442, 135–41. See also Cramer, *Die Erscheinungen,* 19–21; Bachem, *Erinnerungen eines alten Publizisten,* 135–37; *Marpingen—Wahrheit oder Lüge?* 40–41.

111. LASB, E 107, 437.

112. *Kölnische Volkszeitung,* 26 September 1876.

orphanage in Saarbrücken designed for Protestants.[113] One of the key figures in all of this activity was Leopold Friedrich Wilhelm Freiherr von Meerscheidt-Hüllessem, a senior Berlin detective dispatched to Marpingen by the ministry of the interior at the beginning of October.[114] Meerscheidt was later to play a major part in the surveillance of socialist activities in the 1880s and in compiling the list of suspected homosexuals maintained by the criminal police in Wilhelmine Germany.[115] He operated in the village under a false name, passing himself off (not altogether successfully) as a sympathetic Irish-American journalist with the *New York Herald,* for which role he had been provided with appropriate papers. By happy chance, the cover name chosen for this detective was "Marlow." His activities in Marpingen included those of the *agent provocateur* and recalled the dirty tricks practiced by the Prussian criminal police in the era of Karl Hinckeldey and Wilhelm Stieber during the 1850s.[116] Eventually the efforts of "Marlow" and others led to charges being brought against twenty adults for fraud, aiding and abetting fraud, and public order offences.[117]

The second part of the authorities' actions was aimed at preventing the inhabitants of Marpingen or visitors from turning the Härtelwald into a pilgrimage site. This was to be achieved by heavy policing. Access to the woods was periodically restricted or denied altogether, and they were regularly patrolled, first by the infantry company (withdrawn two weeks later), then by gendarmes and a company of the 8th Rifle Battalion posted to the village in February 1877.[118] More than a hundred villagers were fined for entering the woods, even when they went to cut straw, reach their meadows, or take a shortcut to the railway station in St. Wendel. On one occasion gendarmes seized the heavily pregnant Katharina Meisberger, the only one of a group of fourteen or fifteen women who had failed to flee, and she was "harassed" (*drangsaliert*) to reveal the names of her companions; on other occasions gendarmes surprised people by jumping out from behind bushes. Numerous villagers were also interrogated, and subsequently fined, over the illegal provision of bed and board to pilgrims, an activity that could lead to a late-night

---

113. See details and references in Blackbourn, *Marpingen,* chap. 7.

114. LHAK, 442/6442, 27: minister of interior in Berlin to District Governor Arthur von Wolff in Trier, 30 September 1876.

115. D. Fricke, *Bismarcks Prätorianer: Die Berliner Politische Polizei im Kampf gegen die deutsche Arbeiterbewegung (1871–1878)* (Berlin, 1962), 68–71; J. Haller, *Geschichte der Frankfurter Zeitung* (Frankfurt, 1911), 800.

116. On Stieber and Hinckeldey, see A. Funk, *Polizei und Rechtsstaat: Die Entwicklung des staatlichen Gewaltmonopols in Preussen, 1848–1918* (Frankfurt, 1986), 60–70.

117. See full details in Blackbourn, *Marpingen,* chap. 7.

118. Stadtarchiv St Wendel, Abt. C, 2/56, 134–44, 165–73; LASB, Best. Landratsamt Saarbrücken, 1, 739; LASB, E 107, 156, 350. On the costs, see LHAK, 442/6442, 61–65.

knock on the door, even for those whose barn accommodated, say, a knife grinder who visited the village every year.[119]

There were many examples of arrogance and petty harassment in the treatment meted out to villagers and pilgrims alike, although upper-class pilgrims largely escaped this. Some of the heavy-handedness in Marpingen was the responsibility of particular gendarmes and local officials—the bigoted Mayor Woytt, the hard-line *Landrat* Rumschöttel, the vigorously anti-Catholic District Governor Arthur von Wolff.[120] Yet their individual actions cannot be divorced from a larger system—one that expected the mounted, quasi-military gendarmerie to look down (physically and metaphorically) on the populations they policed, that had placed Rumschöttel in St. Wendel after 1848 as a troubleshooter, and that had weeded out officials less committed to official *Kulturkampf* policy than Wolff.[121] Moreover, other aspects of the state response to Marpingen clearly came from the top, notably the nefarious activities of "Marlow." That the Prussian state should have acted more repressively than its Bavarian counterpart did in Mettenbuch comes as no great surprise, certainly given the circumstances of the 1870s.[122] What might seem more surprising is the severity of the actions in Marpingen compared with Dittrichswalde, where the visionary children were actually Poles. The differences serve as a salutary reminder that the western border was also regarded as extremely sensitive—in some ways more sensitive than the eastern border, because more recently digested into Prussian administration, and because the Franco-Prussian War was so fresh in the memory. Coercion in Marpingen was partly fueled by overheated fears of French plots, in which villagers were cast as the enemy within.[123] There was, then, a larger structural pattern that governed the response to Marpingen; but the contrast between events there and in Dittrichswalde must be explained ultimately as a matter of dynamics or momentum. Initial overreaction in Marpingen was a by-product of poor intelligence and local inflexibility. This led to the early calling in of the army, a fairly widespread feature of Prussian "policing."[124] And once the mailed fist had

---

119. These examples (out of many) in BAT, B III, 11, 14/4, 71, 174–75, 178.

120. The senior Prussian legal official, Karl Schorn, singles out the mishandling of Marpingen by particular individuals in his highly critical account, *Lebenserinnerungen* (Bonn, 1898), 2:259–62.

121. Detailed arguments on this point in Blackbourn, *Marpingen*, chap. 9.

122. The handling of Mettenbuch by district officials in Deggendorf, Regen, and Viechtach, and the responses from the provincial authority in Landshut, can be followed in SAL, 164/2, 1161/4; 164/15, 814; and 164/18, 697.

123. The soldiers who intervened were initially briefed that insurrection was afoot: LASB, E 107, 425. Belief in, and rumors about, a French "plot" colored many subsequent actions: ibid., 29, 150–52, 155, 198.

124. A. Lüdtke, *"Gemeinwohl," Polizei und "Festungspraxis": Staatliche Gewaltsamkeit und innere Verwaltung in Preussen, 1815–1850* (Göttingen, 1982); R. Koselleck, "Die Auflösung

been used, the agencies of the state—army, police, ministry of the interior, field administration, legal bureaucracy—found themselves committed to a position from which it was difficult to withdraw without loss of face. Distinctions should nevertheless be made. The gendarmes and the field administration, with the ministry of the interior ultimately behind it, generally took a harder line than the legal bureaucracy. This had something to do with professional pique among judicial officials in the Saarland that bureaucrats in Trier, Koblenz, and Berlin were interfering in their sphere of competence (the arrival of "Marlow" is a case in point). It may also be related to the larger proportion of Catholics in the judicial branch than in the field administration. In the end, however, there was another distinction: between a ministry of the interior and field administration that pressed for cases to be made, even where (as in Marpingen) it was an uphill struggle, and judicial officials who recognized that it was an uphill struggle and resented the misuse of their time.[125] Marpingen reveals some of these tensions. It also shows how arbitrary bureaucratic actions could be checked by the rule of law. It is significant that the major trials arising out of Marpingen ended in acquittals when courts declined to accept the version of events offered by army officers and by "Marlow."[126] Moreover, like the notorious Zabern case in 1913, when the Prussian army ran amok in an Alsatian garrison town—a case that offers some parallels— Marpingen became a *cause célèbre* not least because public opinion and political exposure made it one.[127] Leading Catholic publicists, such as Georg Dasbach and Edmund Prince Radziwill, wrote about the affair, papers like the *Kölnische Volkszeitung* highlighted the abuses that had taken place, and the conduct of the authorities was the subject of a full-scale debate in the Prussian parliament on a motion tabled by the Center Party.[128] Overreaction and high-handedness there certainly were; but we should recognize that in the Prussian

---

des Hauses als ständischer Herrschaftseinheit," in *Familie zwischen Tradition und Moderne,* ed. N. Bulst, J. Goy, and J. Hoock (Göttingen, 1981), 120–21; and R. Tilly, "Popular Disorders in Nineteenth-Century Germany," *Journal of Social History* 4 (1971): 14, 21.

125. See, for example, LHAK, 442/6442, 113–14: report by Examining Magistrate Emil Kleber on the state of the Marpingen inquiry, 17 September 1877. Kleber's summary of evidence in LASB, E 107, is larded with skeptical notes, especially where the role of Meerscheidt was concerned.

126. On the trial of Scheeben and the *Kölnische Volkszeitung,* whose acquittal was upheld on appeal, see LASB, E 107, 17; BAT, B III, 1, 14/4, 27; LHAK, 442/6442, 135–41; Bachem, *Erinnerungen eines alten Publizisten,* 136; and *Frankfurter Zeitung,* 30 May 1877. On the major trial, at Saarbrücken, see *Prozess vor dem Zuchtpolizeigericht,* esp. 43–50 (the testimony and cross-examination of Meerscheidt), and 275 (Defense Counsel Bachem's savage attack on the policeman, unreproved by the presiding judge). See details of other legal cases in Blackbourn, *Marpingen,* chap. 10.

127. D. Schoenbaum, *Zabern 1913: Consensus Politics in Imperial Germany* (London, 1982).

128. Parliamentary debate in *Sten. Berichte,* sitting of 16 January 1878.

state of the 1870s, there were also limits imposed by the rule of law and political embarrassment.[129]

There is a further point here. One of the most striking features of events in Marpingen was the difficulty faced by the state in successfully exercising its authority. It is clear that a whole range of nominal state officials—the parish priest, schoolteachers, successive local *Ortsvorsteher*, the village watchman, the communal forester—failed, sometimes spectacularly, to cooperate with the gendarmes and investigating authorities.[130] In some cases prudence may have played a part in this. In other communities the lives of those branded as Judases were made very uncomfortable.[131] In Marpingen, the evasive and contradictory statements made by the schoolteacher Magdalene André probably owed something to nervousness of this sort.[132] For the most part, however, non-cooperation resulted from sympathy with local opinion against outside authority. This sympathy only grew as arbitrary measures increased. Conversely, one reason for the brusque interrogations and petty harassment of local people by some officials and gendarmes was undoubtedly frustration caused by the wall of silence they encountered, as the tight-lipped solidarity of villagers compounded the lack of cooperation from minor local officials.[133] Much the same happened in other areas during the *Kulturkampf*, and it raises a final set of questions about the nature of Catholic resistance to the *Kulturkampf*.

The most obvious sign of Catholic resistance was organizational. At the head of the organizations that defended Catholics during the 1870s stood the Center Party, which secured four-fifths of all Catholic votes at the high point of the *Kulturkampf*.[134] The Center Party rested, in turn, on a substructure of associations through which Catholic identity was articulated. These included the clubs, or *Casinos*, of middle-class Catholics, Catholic peasant and journeymen associations, and a host of religious and charitable organizations—Pius associations, Boniface associations, and so on. Bourgeois Catholics played an important leadership role in many of these. Organizations of this kind also gave priests and aristocrats a series of "modern" public roles to bolster the ties of deference that still bound many lower-class Catholics to them. The clergy played an equally crucial role in the development of the Catholic press. The

---

129. On the rule of law, see D. Merten, *Rechtsstaat und Gewaltmonopol* (Tübingen, 1975); Funk, *Polizei und Rechtsstaat;* and H.-J. Strauch, "Rechtsstaat und Verwaltungsgerichtsbarkeit," in *Der bürgerliche Rechtsstaat,* ed. M. Tohidipur (Frankfurt, 1978), 2:525–47. More generally, see R. J. Ross, "Enforcing the Kulturkampf in the Bismarckian State and the Limits of Coercion in Imperial Germany," *Journal of Modern History* 56 (1984): 456–82.

130. Examples in LASB, E 107, 129, 142–44, 260–63, 265, 382; BAT, B III, 11, 14/4, 27, 42; *Prozess vor dem Zuchtpolizeigericht,* 13–17.

131. See LHAK, 442/10419, 175–77; Kammer, *Trierer Kulturkampfpriester,* 36, 75.

132. LASB, E 107, 104, 279–83.

133. On these frustrations, see Blackbourn, *Marpingen,* chap. 7.

134. J. Schauff, *Die deutschen Katholiken und die Zentrumspartei* (Cologne, 1928), 75.

organized Catholic response to the *Kulturkampf* through these channels is fairly familiar to historians.[135] Less familiar, but no less important, were the countless examples, large and small, of what contemporaries referred to as "passive resistance."[136] These included hiding priests on the run or trying to block their arrest, bringing pressure to bear on those (locksmiths, for example) who "collaborated" with the authorities, and secreting church records or funds before state commissioners could seize them.[137]

Both forms of response can be found in Marpingen. In an area where formal organization was very thin, village notables worked together with prominent outsiders to publicize what had happened in Marpingen and to seek redress. Well-known priest-publicists such as Radziwill and Paul Majunke helped villagers to use all the available channels of public life to make their case: petitions to the authorities, legal action, and press coverage. Both of these men were also members of the Reichstag, and Radziwill in particular used his position as a member to work for the release of the three girls. Further advice was sought from other Center Party figures. In the long run these initiatives enjoyed much success, although it is fair to say that until a relatively late stage, Marpingen did more for the local fortunes of the Center Party than the party did for Marpingen.[138]

Meanwhile, in the village itself, a different kind of everyday resistance was being practiced. Occasionally it was violent;[139] mostly it fell into the category of "passive resistance." Gendarmes were frozen out or mocked; a public prosecutor complained wearily that the population "performed spying duties on every corner and path, in order to bring the activity of the authorities to a standstill"; house searches had to be undertaken with locksmiths from outside the village; and villagers worked with the sexton and members of the parish council to spirit away money donated by pilgrims, just as elsewhere church funds were secreted.[140] When Neureuter was released from jail at the beginning of December 1876, he received a festive welcome home as the

135. Sperber, *Popular Catholicism,* 207–76; Blackbourn, "Progress and Piety."

136. Pius IX, in an encyclical of February 1875, declared the May Laws "null and void" and called on Catholics to practice "passive resistance": see K. Bachem, *Vorgeschichte, Geschichte und Politik der Deutschen Zentrumspartei* (Cologne, 1927–32), 3: 299–300.

137. See examples in Kammer, *Trierer Kulturkampfpriester;* H. Schiffers, *Der Kulturkampf in Stadt und Regierungsbezirk Aachen* (Aachen, 1929); L. Ficker, *Der Kulturkampf in Münster,* ed. O. Hellinghaus (Münster, 1928); W. Jestaedt, *Der Kulturkampf im Fuldaer Land* (Fulda, 1960).

138. See details in Blackbourn, *Marpingen,* chap. 8.

139. LASB, E 107, 18, 38–45, 156–57; LHAK, 442/6442, 157–58; *Kölnische Zeitung,* 24 November 1876; *Nahe-Blies-Zeitung,* 1 February 1877; and *Saarbrücker Zeitung,* 2 February 1877; and *Saar- und Mosel-Zeitung,* 6 February 1877. Klaus-Michael Mallmann ("Volksfröm-migkeit," 218–19) exaggerates the degree of violence.

140. LASB, E 107, 166–69, 224 ff, 431–32; Radziwill, *Ein Besuch,* 4; LHAK, 442/6442, 117 (quotation from public prosecutor Petershof, 20 September 1877).

young men of Marpingen rode out to meet him on the St. Wendel road and provide a guard of honor.[141] The circumstances turned these declarations of faith into implicit acts of defiance. The emblems of the apparition movement—the cross that marked "the place" and the flowers that adorned it, the lighted candles and pictures, the Marian hymns—became potent symbols of noncompliance with the dictates of the state. Again and again, Marpingen Catholics placed the representatives of authority in a vulnerable or laughable position. Officials painted themselves into the position of treating the flowers left at "the place" as evidence of law breaking, just as eleven girls in Schweich were imprisoned for being caught in possession of garlands after celebrating the release of their parish priest.[142] The refusal of villagers to accept the closing of the woods is particularly interesting. It recalls earlier, bitter disputes with Prussian forestry officials over rights to former communal woodland, and it indicates a stubborn reluctance to concede that the state had a right to dictate where Catholics should go and how they should behave.[143] It was, in short, a defense of "public space" and its uses, which had less dramatic counterparts elsewhere during the *Kulturkampf.* In Münster, for example, efforts to open a narrow road near the bishop's palace to wheeled vehicles were resisted, the papal flag was defiantly flown in the woods, and—following a ban on flags during a papal jubilee—a young woman climbed up to place a garland of yellow and white flowers on a prominent statue in the Domplatz.[144]

In Marpingen, as in Münster, we are dealing with a particular kind of social movement, one that generally employed moral rather than physical force and proved very difficult to break. It had its own icons and symbols, in the form of rosaries, candles, and the ubiquitous flowers (the symbolic use of flowers during the *Kulturkampf* warrants a study to itself). In its pattern and texture, this kind of Catholic movement clearly drew on the revived popular piety and devotional forms of previous decades. Yet we should not exaggerate the element of clerical inspiration. The clergy often had to restrain frustrated parishioners, and much of the resistance in Marpingen bypassed a struggling parish priest. Like the enthusiastic popular response to the apparitions themselves, the movements of communal self-defense that I have been describing were hybrids. They owed something to the clergy but could also outrun clerical control. They show a Catholic populace willing to be impressed by rank—by aristocratic pilgrims distributing favors or by a Radziwill taking up their cause—but hardly deferential in the customary sense. They indicate finally, if

141. LASB, E 107, 375; *Germania,* 6 December 1876.

142. On the Schweich incident, see Kammer, *Kulturkampfpriester,* 94.

143. On earlier disputes, see Horch *Der Wandel,* 57–64, 93–98, 145–46, 232–34; O. Beck, *Die Waldschutzfrage in Preussen* (Berlin, 1860); and O. Beck *Land- und volkswirthschaftliche Tagesfragen für den Regierungsbezirk Trier* (Trier, 1866), 48–61, 72–76.

144. Ficker, *Der Kulturkampf in Münster,* 221–26, 234–35, 241–44.

Marpingen is any guide, that we should recognize the roles played both by male notables and by women, children, and youth.

The fact that the German apparitions of the 1870s have received so little attention is itself revealing. There are several reasons why Marpingen, say, is less familiar than Lourdes, Knock, or Fatima, not least the fact that it was never officially recognized by the church and persisted as an unofficial cult. But another reason is that this is simply not what we expect of *German* Catholics. We think of nineteenth-century German Catholicism as somehow more "modern"—as, in many respects (such as theology), it was. When German Catholics faced external pressure and threats, we expect them—like German workers—to form organizations. And this, of course, they did. Formal organizations are not everything, however. Few would now want to argue that the history of the working class in Imperial Germany is synonymous with the history of the Social Democratic Party and the free trade union movement. The point is no less true of German Catholics. Germany was indeed, as Hubert Jedin has said, the "classic land" of Catholic associational life.[145] But there is another history of German Catholics that deserves attention: a history of mentalities, of popular piety, and of the ways that these interlocked with migration and social change, the relations between men, women, and children, and the attempt to reconstruct clerical authority. Redirecting attention to that other history can also, and not least, throw new light on political and legal structures. For it would be as wrong to exclude questions of power and politics as it would be to view them too narrowly. In the brief compass of this essay, I have tried to show that there is no reason at all why this sort of research should lead us to neglect politics. Our histories can, and should, bring together the history of mentalities and organizations, everyday life, and politics.

---

145. Jedin, *Handbuch der Kirchengeschichte,* vol. 6, part 2, 220.

Liberals, Conservatives, and the Modernizing State: The *Kaiserreich* in Regional Perspective

James Retallack

Historians generally agree that the political options open to German liberals in the third quarter of the nineteenth century were limited by the contemporaneity of the industrial revolution, national unification, and the introduction of the universal franchise.[1] These developments gave rise to a powerful socialist movement before liberals had mounted an effective challenge to either the Prusso-German state or the entrenched conservative elites. Most historians also agree that antisocialism, nationalism, and government preferment combined in many ways later in the *Kaiserreich* to preserve the disproportionate influence of those elites. To date, however, electoral politics has been con-

This is a revised version of an essay that originally appeared in *Central European History* 23, no. 4 (December 1990): 271–312; it is included here by kind permission of Emory University. Although the essay was written before I had the opportunity to work in the Sächsisches Hauptstaatsarchiv Dresden and the Saxon Landesbibliothek, I have resisted the temptation to insert new archival material, both because that research confirmed my preliminary findings and because I will soon complete a longer study of political culture in Saxony from 1866 to 1918. Instead I have tried to address the themes of the present volume more directly and to update references to the secondary literature. For financial support I am grateful to the Humboldt Foundation, the Free University Berlin, the German Academic Exchange Service, the Social Sciences and Humanities Research Council of Canada, and the University of Toronto.

1. James J. Sheehan, *German Liberalism in the Nineteenth Century* (Chicago, 1978), 152–58; David Blackbourn and Geoff Eley, *The Peculiarities of German History: Bourgeois Society and Politics in Nineteenth-Century Germany* (Oxford and New York, 1984), 18–19; and Geoff Eley, "Liberalism, Europe, and the Bourgeoisie, 1860–1914," in *The German Bourgeoisie: Essays on the Social History of the German Middle Class from the Late Eighteenth to the Early Twentieth Century*, ed. David Blackbourn and Richard J. Evans (New York and London, 1991), 300–301; cf. other essays in the latter collection, and also those in Konrad Jarausch and Larry Eugene Jones, eds., *In Search of a Liberal Germany: Studies in the History of German Liberalism from 1789 to the Present* (New York, 1990).

sidered only tangentially in debates about how antisocialist strategies were actually formulated and invoked, about how individual state governments within the federal empire confronted the specter of socialism in its different guises, and about how those governments viewed the relative advantages of resisting all reform or offering a more flexible response to the challenge of modernizing the state.

The neglect accorded to local and regional franchises is especially remarkable, not least because of their direct and long-term impact on almost all aspects of German political culture. When the subject has been addressed at all, analysis has concentrated on the German Social Democratic Party (SPD) and its attempts to introduce the universal (manhood) franchise for all national, state, and local elections.[2] Although this research has been salutary, historians have rarely explored what the members of the nonsocialist (bürgerlich) parties themselves thought about franchise questions. The manner in which different levels of government sought to change their electoral systems in meaningful but nonrevolutionary ways remains just as obscure. How, for instance, did the "politics of notables" (*Honoratiorenpolitik*), threatened with extinction as a viable political style nationally, operate at the local and regional levels? In what ways did it continue to reflect identifiably *provincial* political agendas?[3] How did local notables and government ministers construe their

---

2. See esp. Gerhard A. Ritter, ed., *Der Aufstieg der deutschen Arbeiterbewegung: Sozialdemokratie und Freie Gewerkschaften im Parteiensystem und Sozialmilieu des Kaiserreichs* (Munich, 1990); Karl Rohe, ed., *Elections, Parties and Political Traditions: Social Foundations of German Parties and Party Systems, 1867–1987* (New York, 1990); and James Retallack, "Politische Kultur, Wahlkultur, Regionalgeschichte: Methodologische Überlegungen am Beispiel Sachsens und des Reiches," in *Modernisierung und Region*, ed. Simone Lässig, Karl Heinrich Pohl, and James Retallack (Bielefeld, 1995).

3. See James Retallack, "Election Campaigns and Franchise Struggles in Regional Perspective," *German History* 13 (1995): 70–79. Recent work on Saxony reveals the fruitfulness of such questions; for preliminary studies of National Liberal, Social Democratic, and Pan-German organizations, see Karl Heinrich Pohl, "Sachsen, Stresemann und die Nationalliberale Partei: Anmerkungen zur politischen Entwicklung, zum Aufstieg des industriellen Bürgertums und zur frühen Tätigkeit Stresemanns im Königreich Sachsen," *Jahrbuch zur Liberalismus-Forschung* 4 (1992): 197–216; Karl Heinrich Pohl, "Die Nationalliberalen in Sachsen vor 1914: Eine Partei der konservativen Honoratioren auf dem Wege zur Partei der Industrie," in *Liberalismus und Region*, ed. Lothar Gall and Dieter Langewiesche (Munich, 1995), 195–215; Simone Lässig, "Zum militärpolitischen Wirken der Sozialdemokratie in Ostsachsen von der Jahrhundertwende bis zum Ausbruch des ersten Weltkrieges unter besonderer Berücksichtigung der Dresdner Wahlkreisorganisationen," 2 vols. (Ph.D. diss., Pädagogische Hochschule Dresden, 1990); Simone Lässig, "The Red Kingdom of Saxony—Myth or Reality?" (Unpublished paper presented to the Annual Meeting of the American Historical Association, Washington, D.C., December 1992); Gerald Kolditz, "Die Ortsgruppe Dresden des Alldeutschen Verbandes von ihrer Entstehung bis zum Verbandstag 1906" (Diplom-Arbeit, Humboldt University Berlin, 1989); and Christoph Nonn, "Arbeiter, Bürger, und 'Agrarier': Stadt-Land-Gegensatz und Klassenkonflikt im Wilhelminischen Deutschland am Beispiel des Königreichs Sachsen," in *Demokratie und Emanzipation zwischen Saale und Elbe*, ed. Helga Grebing, Hans Mommsen, and Karsten Rudolph (Essen, 1993), 101–13.

long-term chances of overcoming the socialist threat through the ballot box? And under what circumstances did they lose faith in their own ability to mount effective election campaigns, resorting instead to patently unfair voting regulations?

This essay addresses these questions, first by examining the willingness and ability of the nonsocialist parties to implement their antisocialist strategy in the electoral sphere, and second by considering how the government of one state—Germany's third-largest and economically most modern[4]—came to see its own electoral system as an essential (but threatened) binding agent between the state and civil society. In this way it may be possible to supplement and perhaps recast what Geoff Eley in the introduction to this volume has identified as the dissatisfyingly Prussocentric and statist perspectives on political modernization in Germany. This in turn may open up new lines of inquiry into the multiplicity of local and regional identities in a Germany that even by 1900 did not possess a unitary national culture.

During the *Kaiserreich,* the need to stem the "red tide" through electoral politics demanded the attention of liberals and conservatives alike, and not in Saxony alone. To be sure, these groups often enjoyed remarkable agreement among themselves and with government officials as to how to combat the socialist threat. However, in a multitude of political contexts, and particularly after 1900, they found themselves embroiled in highly acrimonious and mutually debilitating debates. Rarely were those debates more strident than when they concerned elections and electoral franchises.[5] Although liberals and conservatives professed still to be able to identify the specter of revolution, the axiomatic antisocialism that they had previously embraced frequently became merely a rhetorical affirmation of bygone political constellations. Gradually other "endorsements" became more compelling, especially as the influence of economic interest groups increased and as the self-confidence of liberal leaders

---

4. Saxony remains the least studied of the large German states, perhaps because it does not fit the south German idiom as neatly as Bavaria, Württemberg, and Baden; still useful among older works is Rudolf Kötzschke and Hellmut Kretzschmar, *Sächsische Geschichte: Werden und Wandlungen eines deutschen Stammes und seiner Heimat im Rahmen der deutschen Geschichte,* 2 vols. (1935; reprint, Frankfurt a.M., 1965); cf. Karl Czok, ed., *Geschichte Sachsens* (Weimar, 1989); and *Der sächsische Landtag: Geschichte und Gegenwart* (Dresden, 1990).

5. See, for example, Walter Gagel, *Die Wahlrechtsfrage in der Geschichte der deutschen liberalen Parteien, 1848–1918* (Düsseldorf, 1958), Merith Niehuss, "Party Configurations in State and Municipal Elections in Southern Germany, 1871–1914," in Rohe, *Elections, Parties and Political Traditions,* 83–105; Hartmut Pogge von Strandmann, "The Liberal Power Monopoly in the Cities of Imperial Germany," in *Elections, Mass Politics, and Social Change in Modern Germany: New Perspectives,* ed. Larry Eugene Jones and James Retallack (New York and Cambridge, 1992), 93–117; and Peter Steinbach, *Die Zähmung des politischen Massenmarktes: Wahlen und Wahlkämpfe im Bismarckreich im Spiegel der Hauptstadt- und Gesinnungspresse,* 3 vols. (Passau, 1990).

grew. At the same time, as the option of an all-out confrontation with socialism faded with the decade of the 1890s, the new century revealed in many different ways the urgent need for some modus vivendi with the SPD, at least in non-Prussian territories.

In the past fifteen years, scholars have documented conflicts between liberals and conservatives at the level of Reich politics with enough evidence to dispel the notion that a nationalist "rallying together," or *Sammlung,* of anti-socialist parties provides a unifying thread running through the history of the *Kaiserreich* from the era of unification to World War I. In some older views, this *Sammlung* extended from the so-called "second founding of the Reich" on a protectionist and antisocialist basis in 1878–79 through the decisive triplet of nationally oriented Reichstag campaigns in 1887, 1898, and 1907 to the debacle of the "red elections" in 1912. Since Eley drew attention in the mid-1970s to the ineffectiveness of the *Sammlung* as a political strategy in 1898, historians have become more skeptical about the successes registered by antisocialist forces before and after 1898 as well.[6] Brett Fairbairn, among others, has studied the Reichstag elections of 1898 and 1903 and drawn some surprising conclusions. He has identified the unwillingness of entrenched elites to set aside their differences at election time, the government's refusal to associate itself with any concrete election manifesto, its disinterest in supporting extreme right-wing factions in the Reichstag, and the inability of Conservatives and National Liberals to deflect attention from such "fairness issues" as food prices, taxation, and electoral franchises.[7] More comprehensively still, both Fairbairn and Stanley Suval have stressed not how terribly wrong things went in the Weimar Republic but how well the system actually functioned during the Wilhelmine era.[8] The sense of "pessimism and gloom, bafflement and indig-

---

6. Geoff Eley, *"Sammlungspolitik,* Social Imperialism, and the Navy Law of 1898," in *From Unification to Nazism: Reinterpreting the German Past,* by Geoff Eley (Boston, 1986), 110–53.

7. Brett Fairbairn, "The German Elections of 1898 and 1903" (D.Phil. diss., Oxford University, 1987), esp. chaps. 3, 4; Brett Fairbairn, "The Limits of Nationalist Politics: Electoral Culture and Mobilization in Germany, 1890–1903," *Journal of the Canadian Historical Association,* n.s., 1 (1990): 145–69; Brett Fairbairn, "Authority vs. Democracy: Prussian Officials in the German Elections of 1898 and 1903," *Historical Journal* 34, no. 4 (1990): 811–38; and Brett Fairbairn, "Interpreting Wilhelmine Elections: National Issues, Fairness Issues, and Electoral Mobilization," in Jones and Retallack, *Elections, Mass Politics, and Social Change,* 17–48.

8. Stanley Suval, *Electoral Politics in Wilhelmine Germany* (Chapel Hill, 1985), 9; and Fairbairn, "The Limits of Nationalist Politics," 167. For three similarly provocative views of the transition from *Kaiserreich* to Weimar, see Richard Bessel, "The Formation and Dissolution of a German National Electorate from Kaiserreich to Third Reich," in Jones and Retallack, *Elections, Mass Politics, and Social Change,* 399–418; Peter Fritzsche, "Breakdown or Breakthrough? Conservatives and the November Revolution," in *Between Reform, Reaction, and Resistance: Studies in the History of German Conservatism from 1789 to 1945,* ed. Larry Eugene Jones and James Retallack (Oxford and Providence, 1993), 299–328; and Karl Rohe, *Wahlen und*

nancy" occasioned by Wilhelmine elections, Fairbairn has written, was real enough—but these terms describe the mood of government ministers and right-wing politicians, *not* socialists, facing the challenge of mass politics around the turn of the century.

Nevertheless, the perspective championed by Suval and Fairbairn, for all its merits, concentrates on the universal Reichstag franchise so exclusively, and stresses the positive or "affirming" habits of voters so vehemently, that it may be skewing our understanding of local and regional political cultures.[9] As a result, Wilhelmine Germany's electoral system may appear structurally more coherent than it was in practice and politically more equitable than it was ever intended to be. This essay, based on a case study of the Kingdom of Saxony, offers a different approach and suggests a number of alternative conclusions. As I have argued elsewhere, the notion that members of the German *Bürgertum* practiced unanimous discrimination against the SPD tends to evaporate when the worlds of local and regional politics are viewed in their full complexity. Having examined the rapid mobilization of the Saxon electorate during the early 1890s, which led to the introduction of a highly reactionary three-class franchise for the Saxon Landtag in March 1896,[10] in this essay I turn to the protracted struggle between 1896 and 1909 to find a new, more workable electoral law for Saxony. By examining the reactions of Saxon ministers and parliamentarians as they were forced to consider a dizzying range of constitutional options, my aim is to penetrate beneath their rhetorical claims to be seeking simply the most "fair" franchise possible in order to examine the inner working—or nonworking—of antisocialist strategies in a regional context.

This perspective also makes it possible to consider the determination of National Liberals in Saxony to break with Conservatives as paradigmatic of a broader resurgence of liberalism in the Reich after 1900. Saxony was just one among a number of federal states in Imperial Germany where liberals, largely frustrated in national politics by the temporizing efforts of Chancellor Bernhard von Bülow (1900–1909), challenged the political hegemony of conservatives in individual state parliaments.[11] To be sure, Saxony represents a

---

Wählertraditionen in Deutschland. Kulturelle Grundlagen deutscher Parteien und Parteiensysteme im 19. und 20. Jahrhundert (Frankfurt a.M., 1992), 121–40.

9. See James Retallack, "Die 'liberalen' Konservativen? Konservatismus und Antisemitismus im industrialisierten Sachsen," in *Sachsen im Umbruch?*, ed. Simone Lässig and Karl Heinrich Pohl (Weimar, forthcoming 1996). Great sensitivity to regional circumstances is displayed in Jürgen Schmädeke's *Wählerbewegung im Wilhelminischen Deutschland. Eine historisch-statistische Untersuchung zu den Reichstagswahlen von 1890 bis 1912*, 2 vols. (Berlin, 1994).

10. See James Retallack, "Antisocialism and Electoral Politics in Regional Perspective: The Kingdom of Saxony," in Jones and Retallack, *Elections, Mass Politics, and Social Change*, 49–91.

11. The reports sent to Berlin by the Prussian envoys in Dresden have never been tapped to illuminate this problem, although similar reports from Munich, Stuttgart, and Karlsruhe have been:

special case: not only was it highly industrialized and the bastion of German socialism; it also had a long history of particularly reactionary ministries. But these circumstances make the liberals' achievement only more remarkable. After 1900, as new men and new ideas entered the liberal caucuses in the Saxon Landtag and as popular pressure mounted in the streets, key policy-makers in the Saxon bureaucracy suddenly (albeit ambivalently) embraced the cause of reform.[12] Eventually, liberal parliamentarians and government leaders recognized their mutual interest in displacing the Conservatives' disproportionate influence on state policy, and they chose to begin by transforming a Landtag that one observer described in 1901 as "the most conservative of German parliaments."[13] Although some liberals were disappointed that the Saxon franchise inaugurated in 1909 was not as progressive as those that had recently passed into law in Bavaria, Württemberg, and Baden, others pointed out that far more was accomplished in Saxony than in Prussia. Because a kind of "middle path" was chosen both in Saxony and in the Reich by governments that refused to endorse either radical liberalism or reactionary conservatism, a study of Saxony's constitutional *Sonderweg* offers insight into the crisis of Conservative hegemony at the national level as well.[14]

see Irmgard von Barton, genannt von Stedmann, *Die preußische Gesandtschaft in München als Instrument der Reichspolitik in Bayern von den Anfängen der Reichsgründung bis zu Bismarcks Entlassung* (Munich, 1967); Konrad Reiser, *Bayerische Gesandte bei deutschen und ausländischen Regierungen, 1871–1918* (Munich, 1968); Hans Philippi, *Das Königreich Württemberg im Spiegel der preußischen Gesandtschaftsberichte, 1871–1914* (Stuttgart, 1972); and Hans-Jürgen Kremer, *Das Großherzogtum Baden in der politischen Berichterstattung der preußischen Gesandten, 1871–1918*, 2 pts. (Stuttgart, 1990–92). See also Hans-Joachim Schreckenbach, "Innerdeutsche Gesandtschaften, 1867–1945," in *Archivar und Historiker: Studien zur Archiv- und Geschichtswissenschaft*, ed. Staatlichen Archivverwaltung im Staatssekretariat für Innere Angelegenheiten (Berlin [East], 1956), 404–28.

    12. Crucial biographical information on Saxon ministers can be found in Karlheinz Blaschke, "Das Königreich Sachsen, 1815–1918," and "Minister des Königreichs Sachsen, 1815–1918," in *Die Regierungen der deutschen Mittel- und Kleinstaaten, 1815–1933*, ed. Klaus Schwabe (Boppard a. R., 1983), 81–102, 285–94; and Gerhard Schmidt, "Die Zentralverwaltung Sachsens, 1831–1918, [pt.] II," *Letopis* 27, no. 2 (1980): 113–34.

    13. Report of the Prussian envoy in Saxony, Count Carl von Dönhoff (1833–1906), to Chancellor Bernhard von Bülow, 17 Oct. 1901, in the Political Archive of the German Foreign Office (hereafter PA AA) Bonn, I A Sachsen (Königreich) (hereafter Sachsen) Nr. 60 ("Parlamentarische Angelegenheiten des Königreichs Sachsen"), Bd. 5. All foreign ministry files were consulted either in the original in PA AA Bonn or on microfilm from the U.S. National Archives, Washington, D.C.; the Center for Research Libraries, Chicago; and the University of Michigan, Ann Arbor.

    14. Cf. inter alia David Blackbourn, "New Legislatures: Germany, 1871–1914," *Historical Research* 65, no. 157 (June 1992): 201–14; Hans-Wilhelm Eckardt, *Privilegium und Parlament: Die Auseinandersetzungen um das allgemeine und gleiche Wahlrecht in Hamburg* (Hamburg, 1980); and Hartwig Brandt, "Politische Partizipation am Beispiel eines deutschen Mittelstaates im 19. Jahrhundert: Wahlrecht und Wahlen in Württemberg," in *Probleme politischer Partizipation im Modernisierungsprozeß*, ed. Peter Steinbach (Stuttgart, 1982), 135–55.

By 1909, after the National Liberals had been vying for a decade to gain the upper hand in the Saxon Landtag, little was left of their electoral cartel with the Conservatives. Both parties—known to contemporaries as the *Ordnungsparteien* (parties of order) in Saxony because they generally supported the government—eventually had to acknowledge that their internal feuding threatened their own political survival as much as did socialism itself. As the final component of this analysis, the significance of these antagonisms is tested in the laboratory of the Saxon Landtag elections of October 1909. The only convincing conclusion here is that disagreements over franchise questions so eroded the common ground between the *Ordnungsparteien* in Saxony that they were rendered incapable of mounting an effective antisocialist campaign.

Although their state had a relatively equitable Landtag franchise until 1896, Saxon Conservatives more thoroughly dominated affairs in both houses of the Landtag than did their party comrades anywhere else in the Reich. Under the Saxon franchise law of 3 December 1868, all male citizens over the age of twenty-five who owned property or who paid at least three Marks in state taxes annually were eligible to cast ballots in direct, equal, and secret elections. Every two years, voters chose new deputies in one-third of the Landtag's eighty-two constituencies.[15] Beginning in the early 1880s this electoral system yielded a permanent Conservative majority (between forty and fifty seats) in the Landtag that seemed unassailable. The Saxon National Liberal Party (NLP), organizationally weaker and ideologically more pliant than most other National Liberal organizations, typically fielded between twenty and twenty-five deputies in association with the two left-liberal groups, the Progressives and the Radicals.

Conservative hegemony eroded from the late 1880s onward as more low-income Saxons became eligible to vote in Landtag elections and as voter turnout increased rapidly.[16] The SPD's caucus in the Landtag grew from five members in 1887 to fifteen in early 1896 while in the same period the Saxon

---

15. These and other details below concerning the Saxon franchise laws of 1868, 1896, and 1909 are taken principally from Victor Camillo Diersch, "Die geschichtliche Entwicklung des Landtagswahlrechts im Königreich Sachsen" (Ph.D. diss., University of Leipzig, 1918); Alfred Pache, *Geschichte des sächsischen Landtagswahlrechts von 1831–1907,* 2d ed. (Leipzig, 1919); and E. Oppe, "Die Reform des Wahlrechts für die II. Kammer der Ständeversammlung im Königreich Sachsen," *Jahrbuch des öffentlichen Rechts der Gegenwart* 4 (1910): 374–409. See also Gerhard A. Ritter with Merith Niehuss, *Wahlgeschichtliches Arbeitsbuch: Materialien zur Statistik des Kaiserreichs, 1871–1918* (Munich, 1980), 163–82; and Gerhard A. Ritter, "Das Wahlrecht und die Wählerschaft der Sozialdemokratie im Königreich Sachsen, 1867–1914," in Ritter, *Der Aufstieg,* 49–101.

16. Dönhoff to Chancellor Leo von Caprivi, 14 and 16 Oct. 1891, PA AA Bonn, Sachsen Nr. 60, Bd. 3; Eugen Würzburger, "Die Wahlen für die Zweite Kammer der Ständeversammlung von 1869 bis 1896," *Zeitschrift des K. Sächsischen Statistischen Landesamtes* 51, no. 1 (1905): 2.

SPD registered steady gains in Reichstag elections. By November 1895 these developments had led Conservatives, National Liberals, and Progressives in Saxony to fear for the future of their parliamentary cartel. They therefore asked the government to prepare a franchise reform bill that would not only preclude the introduction of the universal Reichstag franchise, which the Saxon SPD advocated, but also prevent a further "flood" of SPD deputies into the chamber. Organized by the de facto leader of the Conservative Party, *Geheimer Hofrat* Dr. Paul Mehnert, this campaign achieved its goal when a new three-class franchise was passed into law on 28 March 1896. Immediately labeled "Mehnert's law," the new Landtag franchise was modeled on the Prussian three-class system; only minor attempts were made to diminish the latter's reactionary reputation and plutocratic effects. As a result, with each partial (one-third) election of the Landtag, the fifteen SPD deputies gradually disappeared until none were left in 1901.

Against this patently unfair franchise, the Saxon SPD initially mounted only mute protests. Although contemporaries who belonged to the third class of voters were fully aware of the futility of casting a ballot that hardly mattered in the final outcome, Saxon socialists were hamstrung by deep disagreements over whether Landtag deputies should resign their seats in protest and whether their party should boycott the new system.[17] It was not until 1900 that participation was formally recommended for SPD voters in all states with three-class franchises, and not until Landtag elections in the autumn of 1903 that this policy was fully implemented in Prussia and Saxony. In the meantime, national attention had been focused on Saxony when the Reichstag elections of June 1903 produced socialist victories in twenty-two of twenty-three Saxon constituencies, with 59 percent of the popular vote cast for socialist candidates.[18]

How did the Saxon *Ordnungsparteien* react to the initial disarray in the socialist ranks? Certainly no one could have predicted that it would be the National Liberals, not the SPD, who would begin the process leading to a second revision of the Landtag franchise. Conservatives, National Liberals, and government officials all expressed considerable relief when the Landtag election campaigns of 1897 and 1899 provoked no mass demonstrations against the new franchise. They agreed that the new electoral law was doing exactly what it had been designed to do: prevent the entry of socialists into the lower house and thereby allow Saxon parliamentary life to continue in an "orderly" and "objective" fashion. Indeed, things were going so well that by

---

17. See the articles "Landtagswahlbeteiligung" and "Sächsisches Wahlrecht" in *Handbuch der sozialdemokratischen Parteitage von 1863 bis 1909,* ed. Wilhelm Schröder (Munich, 1910), 257–71, 506–8; Dieter Fricke, *Handbuch zur Geschichte der deutschen Arbeiterbewegung, 1869 bis 1917,* 2 vols. (Berlin, 1987), 2: 765–66; and Eduard Bernstein, "Die Sozialdemokratie und das neue Landtagswahlsystem in Sachsen," *Neue Zeit,* Jg. 14 (1895–96), vol. 2, no. 32: 181–88.

18. These and other percentages in this essay have been rounded.

1899 the Saxon interior minister actually hoped that the SPD would retain "a few" seats in the Landtag, so that the new franchise would not appear too reactionary.[19]

Nonetheless, the Prussian envoy to Saxony, Count Carl von Dönhoff, entertained serious doubts about how well antisocialism would play in individual Saxon constituencies during Reichstag elections. Contributing to his skepticism was the acrimonious Landtag session of 1897–98, when party antagonisms became more strident than at any time in the previous twenty years.[20] Even a month before the Reichstag elections of June 1898, the nonsocialist parties in Saxony—as elsewhere in the Reich—lacked a clear election slogan. Instead, their effort was being undermined by internal bickering, as Dönhoff reported to Chancellor Chlodwig zu Hohenlohe-Schillingsfürst:

> As if there existed no common enemy. . . , the nonsocialist parties are losing precious time in fruitless squabbles. The peculiarity of the German character, perversely insisting on exceptional positions and independent opinions, is coming to the fore here with ultimately dangerous consequences. Groups are breaking away from the cartel . . . in order to represent their special views and to nominate their own candidates.

Thus the National Liberal Reichsverein in Dresden refused to endorse the cartel; it nominated a countercandidate in Dresden-Neustadt, which eventually fell to the SPD. Catholic clerics at the royal court allegedly helped organize the nomination of six Center Party "test candidates." And the National Socials, affiliated with Friedrich Naumann, launched independent candidates of their own, as did the anti-Semites and radical agrarians.

After the elections, the opponents of socialism tried to interpret the results positively. Those who worried about the long-term mobilization of Saxon voters could be pleased that the turnout at the polls dipped significantly from the elections of 1890 and 1893. The proportion of votes cast for German Radicals and anti-Semites also dropped sharply. But the SPD's share of the overall vote rose, and its Saxon contingent in the Reichstag increased from seven to eleven deputies. Moreover, it was clear that the Radicals and the anti-Semites—who were shut out from the cartel—had paved the way for decisive SPD victories in a number of constituencies, even where the *Ordnungsparteien*

---

19. Dönhoff to Chancellor Chlodwig zu Hohenlohe-Schillingsfürst, 25 Oct. 1897, PA AA Bonn, Deutschland Nr. 125 ("Reichstagswahlen"), Nr. 3, Bd. 14, referring to Interior Minister Georg von Metzsch-Reichenbach; see also Dönhoff to Hohenlohe, 10 April, 22 and 30 Sept., 9 and 13 Oct., 8, 11, and 22 Nov. 1897; and Count Georg von Wedel (Kgl. Pr. Legations-Sekretär in Dresden) to Hohenlohe, 28 Sept. 1899, in PA AA Bonn, Sachsen Nr. 60, Bd. 5.

20. Dönhoff to Hohenlohe, 21 March 1898, PA AA Bonn, Sachsen Nr. 60, Bd. 5; Dönhoff to Hohenlohe, 26 May 1898, PA AA Bonn, Deutschland Nr. 125, Nr. 3, Bd. 15.

had been able to agree on a joint candidate. Dönhoff concurred with the Conservatives that "the anti-Semites, with their demagogic intrigues, are ploughing the furrows in which Social Democracy casts its seed."[21]

Perhaps the most noteworthy change of all was the beginning of a National Liberal renaissance. Having polled just 8 percent of the popular vote in 1893, the National Liberals now registered almost 15 percent, and they elected four deputies in place of their previous two. Nonetheless, the NLP was hardly likely to be satisfied with this result. Many of the votes it received were cast for cartel candidates in constituencies where there was little hope of unseating an SPD incumbent, and this probably contributed to the National Liberals' sense of frustration on other issues.[22]

In the half decade between the Reichstag elections of 1898 and 1903, a complex web of factors further splintered the Saxon cartel, partially freeing the National Liberals from their client relationship with the Conservatives and transforming them into serious contenders for power. The worsening economic climate in Saxony was perhaps the most important of these factors. Even though many National Liberal supporters suffered acutely—the financial community was largely discredited in 1901, and small businesses suffered heavy tax burdens[23]—it was their lack of political influence that grated most. When National Liberals complained about the government's financial policy, this reflected their deeper thirst for social acceptance and political power concomitant with their economic achievement. Some National Liberals with ties to small-scale industry ascribed the sharp economic downturn after 1900 to the influence of large industrial cartels. But agrarian Conservatives soon became the principal target. If there was little about the protectionist and fanatically antilabor stance of the Central Association of German Industrialists that elicited admiration from Saxony's National Liberals, they saw nothing at all auspicious in the rise of the agrarian movement. They objected to the Agrarian League (BdL) and its antigovernmental demagoguery—frequently written by

21. See Eugen Würzburger, "Die Wahlen zum Deutschen Reichstag im Königreich Sachsen von 1871 bis 1907," *Zeitschrift des K. Sächsischen Statistischen Landesamtes* 54, no. 2 (1908): 171–80; Dönhoff to Hohenlohe, 10 July 1898, PA AA Bonn, Deutschland Nr. 125, Nr. 3, Bd. 15.

22. On the Saxon NLP, see mainly the work by Pohl cited in note 3 above, and Donald Warren, Jr., *The Red Kingdom of Saxony: Lobbying Grounds for Gustav Stresemann, 1900–1909* (The Hague, 1964). Richard J. Bazillion, *Modernizing Germany: Karl Biedermann's Career in the Kingdom of Saxony, 1835–1901* (New York, 1989), is very thin on the period after 1871.

23. Arthur Schulze, *Die Bankkatastrophen in Sachsen im Jahre 1901* (Tübingen, 1903); Otto Richter, *Geschichte der Stadt Dresden in den Jahren 1871 bis 1902*, 2d ed. (Dresden, 1904); *Mittheilungen für die Vertrauensmänner der Nationalliberale Partei* 14, no. 2 (Sonderbeilage) (n.d. [1902]): "Generalversammlung des Nationalliberalen Vereins für das Königreich Sachsen" (I am grateful to Larry Eugene Jones for providing me with a copy of this report); and Dönhoff's reports to Bülow in 1901–3 in PA AA Bonn, Sachsen Nr. 53 ("Die Finanzen des Königreichs Sachsen"), Bd. 4.

Georg Oertel, editor of the BdL's *Deutsche Tageszeitung* and a close associate of Mehnert's. The National Liberals were also repelled by the BdL's Prussian orientation and its refusal to endorse navalism or imperialism.[24] Compounding this sense of antagonism were five full years of intense public debate about agricultural and industrial tariffs. Most adherents of the Saxon NLP expected no benefit whatsoever from the resolution of this issue by national leaders who supported the so-called Bülow tariffs in December 1902.

Around the same time but for less explicable reasons, Saxon Conservatives also went on the warpath. Certainly the temptation was great to flex their muscle in the Landtag, for with each successive election the Conservative Party moved closer to achieving the two-thirds majority necessary to implement constitutional change. Yet this ascendancy also exposed the gap that had long existed between the agrarian and industrial wings of the Conservative *Landesverein*. Saxon Conservatives became hypersensitive to charges that they represented one-sided economic interests: in 1899, for example, they hurriedly disavowed their Prussian comrades who, under pressure from the Agrarian League, refused to bow to the will of the Kaiser and permit construction of the *Mittelland* canal. Protesting too much, wrote Dönhoff, the Saxon Conservatives were merely trying to paper over deep cleavages within their party; he added that Conservative industrialists might defect if they realized that the NLP better represented their economic interests.[25]

The Conservative leader Mehnert also seemed determined to seek confrontation with the government at every turn. As early as November 1899, shortly after Mehnert was elected president of the Saxon lower house, the Prussian envoy marked a change in his manner. Dönhoff wondered whether "parliamentary success has gone to the head of this relatively young man"; on the other hand, since Mehnert's campaign against the socialists had gone so well since 1896, "perhaps he feels the need to satisfy his lust for battle in other ways." In any case, since the elections of 1901 had brought the Conservatives their constitutionally significant two-thirds majority in the Landtag,[26] when Mehnert focused his attack on the fiscal mismanagement of Saxon railroads in early 1902, he provoked a ministerial crisis and toppled the Saxon finance minister, Werner von Watzdorf. The timing was especially critical, not only

---

24. Warren, *The Red Kingdom;* Dönhoff to Hohenlohe, 31 Jan. 1897, PA AA Bonn, Sachsen Nr. 48 ("Allgemeine Angelegenheiten des Königreichs Sachsen"), Bd. 18; and Wedel to Bülow, 19 Sept. 1902, ibid., Bd. 19.

25. Dönhoff to Bülow, 29 Oct. 1904, in PA AA Bonn, Sachsen Nr. 60, Bd. 7; Hugo Opitz-Treuen, "Soll die Industrie konservativ oder liberal sein?" *Konservative Monatsschrift* 63 (1906): 1125–34; and the Saxon National Liberals' broadside *Die "Industriefreundlichkeit" der Konservativen* (Leipzig, 1914), 3–13.

26. It was at this point that Dönhoff labeled the Saxon Landtag "the most conservative of all German parliaments." See note 13, above.

because King Albert died in June 1902 but also because Mehnert chaired a joint committee to administer the state debt, which immediately inaugurated a discriminatory income tax favorable to landowners. Although meant to pull the state from the brink of bankruptcy, this tax included a highly controversial clause exempting the working capital invested in agricultural enterprises while other forms of property were taxed. This legislation finally convinced the majority of National Liberals that industry, trade, and commerce were being unfairly taxed, which further poisoned their relations with the Conservatives.[27]

It was in this critical conjuncture of 1902–3, then—when the Saxon economy bottomed out, when tariff debates were drawing attention to the political representation of economic interests, and when antisocialist solidarity was about to face the acid test of Reichstag elections—that National Liberals in Saxony first began to consider seriously how they would overcome their traditional political subservience. For a time they were inadvertently aided by Conservatives, who refused to be stirred from their complacent assumptions that socialists would never again invade the lower house and that industrialists would remain underrepresented in the upper. Residues of complacency in both the National Liberal and Conservative camps evaporated briefly in June 1903 when the Saxon SPD scored its stunning Reichstag victory. But now, as the contest grew earnest, the rules of the game became more contentious than ever.

The course of franchise reform in Saxony after June 1903 was in part determined by the very different conclusions that the Conservatives, the National Liberals, and the government drew from the SPD's near sweep of Saxon constituencies.[28] Mehnert and the Conservatives blamed everyone but themselves for the rout. They refused to acknowledge the agitational benefits that the new Landtag franchise had provided the reinvigorated SPD, and they dismissed the impact of other concrete economic and political issues on the election outcome.[29] Too few suitable candidates had agreed to be nominated,

---

27. Warren, *The Red Kingdom,* 35–36; Dönhoff to Bülow, 22 and 31 May 1902, PA AA Bonn, Sachsen Nr. 53, Bd. 4; *Mittheilungen* "Generalversammlung," E-F.

28. Nationally, Bülow had wished to conduct the Reichstag campaign against both the SPD and the Agrarian League, which he described in a secret circular as "the two extreme parties." When Dönhoff explained why a campaign against the BdL in Saxony would destroy the cartel agreement, Bülow concurred that Saxony was a special case. Nonetheless, Saxon ministers operated at cross-purposes with Bülow when they worked behind the scenes to undermine support for BdL candidates. See Bülow's circular ("Ganz geheim!") to Prussian envoys, dated 18 May 1903; Dönhoff's reply ("Geheim!") of 25 May 1903; and Bülow's reply ("Geheim") of 26 May 1903, in PA AA Bonn, Deutschland Nr. 125, Nr. 8, Bd. 16.

29. The following is based on Mehnert to Bülow, 17 June 1903, and reply, n.d. [June 1903], in BA Koblenz, Reichskanzlei-Akten (Rkz), Nr. 1792 (I am grateful to Brett Fairbairn for providing me with notes taken from this correspondence); Dönhoff to Bülow, 1 March, 25 and 31 May, 3, 9, 11, 15, and 18 June 1903, in PA AA Bonn, Deutschland Nr. 125, Nr. 3, Bd. 16; Dönhoff to

Mehnert claimed, because men of education and breeding did not wish to subject themselves to the sort of abuse hurled by SPD Reichstag deputies during the final phase of the 1902 tariff debates. Competing nonsocialist candidacies were dismissed by Mehnert as inconsequential to the result. Instead he pointed to the government's recent cooperation with the Catholic Center Party in the Reichstag; this, he believed, had created much bad feeling in Saxony, because anti-Catholic sentiment had reached a fever pitch in 1902 when the Saxon crown princess eloped under alleged papal involvement. That affair, Mehnert added, had severely damaged the reputation of the monarchy in Saxony. Mehnert claimed, lastly, that the new Saxon finance minister[30] had committed a grievous political error by announcing an unpopular 25 percent surtax on incomes shortly before the elections.

Considered together, these factors helped to assuage the political conscience of a man who wanted to believe that the SPD's victory was merely an expression of the voters' bad temper, and thus could be ascribed to economic, not political, grievances. With this logic Mehnert convinced himself that no change in Conservative Party policy was required—though he also took the prudent step of applying immediately to the Saxon government for funds to establish a new Conservative newspaper in case public opinion shifted further to the left in the future.[31] In this Mehnert was merely anticipating his national party colleagues, who later in the year secretly petitioned Bülow to take the initiative to "stem the tide" of socialism.[32] But the Reichstag debacle in June 1903 convinced Mehnert more firmly than ever that the 1896 Landtag franchise should be retained. Without the three-class franchise, he wrote to Bülow, the Landtag elections scheduled for the autumn of 1903 would yield an SPD majority that could never again be overcome through constitutional means.

Although Mehnert had little trouble finding scapegoats, he did not mention some other important factors that were identified in the postelection analysis of the Prussian envoy. Dönhoff emphasized in his report to Bülow that, as in 1898, the Saxon *Ordnungsparteien* were largely responsible for their own defeat. The outdated practices of *Honoratiorenpolitik* lived on in Saxony, he noted, in the form of an "internally divided [*zerrissene*], loosely organized group of nonsocialist parties that are occasionally brought together for the

---

Bülow, 7 June, 2 July, and 19 Sept. 1903, and Wedel to Bülow, 15 July 1903, in PA AA Bonn, Sachsen Nr. 60, Bd. 6.

30. Konrad Wilhelm von Rüger was hated by the National Liberals during his tenure as finance minister (1902–10) and as nominal chair of the Saxon ministry (1906–10).

31. Wedel to Bülow, 13 Aug. 1903, and other correspondence in PA AA Bonn, Sachsen Nr. 50 ("Die sächsische Presse"), Bd. 4.

32. Count Udo zu Stolberg-Wernigerode to Bülow, 27 Dec. 1903, in BA Koblenz, Nachlaß (NL) Bülow, Nr. 107, Bl. 97; reply, 7 Jan. 1904, in BA Koblenz, Rkz, Nr. 2005 ("Mittellandkanal"), Bl. 127 (excerpt), and ibid, Nr. 1391/5 ("Konservative Parteien"), Bl. 41.

purposes of elections." The inability of local party bosses to forge constitu-ency-level alliances was one important consequence of this. Indeed, the search for candidates became so desperate that the election agreement among the *Ordnungsparteien* had often been abandoned and fresh faces rushed into threatened constituencies, even though recourse to this solution almost invaria-bly elicited mutual recriminations from constituency associations and diminished support for the eventual nominee. And of course, the SPD's deter-mination to highlight the disparities between the Reichstag and Landtag fran-chises produced a supreme effort that could not be matched by the nonsocialist parties. While the SPD had a firm agitational plan, healthy finances, suitable candidates, and efficient organization, Dönhoff reported that among the non-socialist parties "one finds insufficient candidates, indecisiveness, indifference, unwillingness to sacrifice with regard to campaign contributions, [and] in-subordination and obstinacy among small party groups." To this could be added the continued arrogance and lack of popular appeal of cartel candidates themselves and the Conservatives' miscalculation that they could rely on their own newspapers to rebut SPD propaganda.

Whereas Mehnert and the Conservatives were blind to the lessons to be learned from June 1903, the Saxon government reacted quite differently. At this time Saxony's state ministry was firmly under the control of Georg von Metzsch-Reichenbach. Metzsch was already well known for his staunchly conservative views: coming from old Vogtland nobility, he was said to rule Saxony as a large noble estate (*Rittergut*).[33] As minister of the interior after 1891, Metzsch had willingly acceded to the wishes of Mehnert's cartel in implementing the three-class franchise in 1896; and as foreign minister (1891–1906), he rarely opposed Prussian wishes in the Bundesrat. Yet on 10 July 1903, now as chair of the Saxon state ministry (1901–6), Metzsch presided over a meeting that approved franchise reform in principle. Four days later—Metzsch's sixty-seventh birthday and Bastille Day in France—the government made a stunning announcement. The franchise law of March 1896, it declared, had had "the unintended effect of reducing the influence of those delegates elected by the third voting class on the selection of deputies in a manner not in accordance with the principles of fairness."[34] To begin the process of reform, the government declared that it would solicit the views of a forum of "experts," due to convene in late August.

The furor caused by this announcement was entirely predictable. More interesting is the vehemence with which the government claimed that its initia-

---

33. Blaschke, "Das Königreich Sachsen," 98, 289. Saxony did not have a minister-president; the governmental leader was simply designated Vorsitzender des Gesamtministeriums.

34. Dönhoff to Bülow, 2 July and 19 Sept. 1903, and Wedel to Bülow, 15 July 1903, in PA AA Bonn, Sachsen Nr. 60, Bd. 6; see also Oppe, "Die Reform," 378; and Diersch, "Die geschichtliche Entwicklung des Landtagswahlrechts," 213.

tive of 14 July was *not* a consequence of the Reichstag elections barely a month earlier. Metzsch asserted both publicly and privately that the government had begun its preparations in 1902. This point became a bone of contention between the government and the Conservatives for three reasons. First, while the Conservatives continued to believe that the Landtag franchise was an essential bulwark against the socialist threat, the government was now willing to go on record to say that it had *always* regarded the 1896 three-class franchise as neither perfect nor immutable. Although Metzsch had provided few hints that he was contemplating such a dramatic reversal of policy before July 1903, he appears to have recognized the need for reform well before that date. Retrospectively, in recounting to Dönhoff his first audience with King Georg after his ascension to the throne in June 1902, Metzsch provided what is probably the best explanation we have for the government's change of heart on the franchise question:[35]

> After [I] told him that statistics gathered under the present franchise indicated that 80 percent of voters have no influence on the choice of deputies and are therefore unrepresented in the Landtag—which contravenes principles of fairness—also that among this 80 percent are found not only Social Democrats but also many clergy, teachers, lower- and middle-ranking officials, etc., who are embittered because of this disadvantage [*Zurücksetzung*]; and finally, that as a result of these circumstances, the Reichstag has been made into a forum for discussing the domestic political affairs of Saxony, which properly belong only in the Landtag—the king agreed that the government should proceed with electoral reform.

Secondly, Mehnert believed that Metzsch had been politically negligent in not declaring his intentions before the Reichstag vote. On the one hand, the timing of reform made it appear that the SPD victory in June 1903 had been instrumental in initiating change. Thus the Conservative press heaped scorn on the Saxon ministry, which, it claimed, had been moved to action only through "fear" and "weakness." On the other hand, Mehnert believed that the outcome of the elections would have been much more favorable if the Saxon electorate had known beforehand that a revision of the Landtag franchise was already being prepared in government circles. Metzsch discounted this argument, though Chancellor Bülow appears to have been less certain. The third point of conflict was the wish of both Conservatives and the government to be seen as the first to concede the need for franchise reform. Metzsch was very deliberate in refusing to inform Mehnert about the government's plans until just a few

---

35. Dönhoff to Bülow, 19 Sept. 1903, PA AA Bonn, Sachsen Nr. 60, Bd. 6.

days before the announcement of 14 July, fearing that Mehnert would "steal his thunder." He thereby illustrated his determination to undermine the Conservatives' dominant position in the Landtag, in order, as he put it, to address the "galling unfairness" of the Landtag franchise. But then Metzsch told a surprised Dönhoff that he intended to resign, for two reasons. First, the current domestic situation in Saxony evoked what Metzsch referred to as "deep disgust" (*tiefen degout*). Second, he had wearied of doing battle with a man, Mehnert, who was "demagogically inclined," whose tactics were "shrewd and ruthless," and who followed "the dictates of his personal vanity." When Dönhoff conveyed these remarks to Bülow, he predicted sadly but with insight that Mehnert would emerge victorious from this "power struggle" with Metzsch.

What of the National Liberals? Where did they stand in this test of wills between the man whom contemporaries called "Paul I, the uncrowned king of Saxony," and Metzsch, the legitimate first servant of the crown? With some oversimplification one can say that their political reasoning ran remarkably parallel to that of the Saxon government. Just as the Saxon technocrats who were busy drawing up franchise reform proposals in the interior ministry believed that Saxony's future electoral system should facilitate the representation of economic interests, important members of the Saxon NLP now recognized that political power and economic power devolved jointly toward those who could mount effective lobbies at the locus of decision making in the state. Thus 1902 witnessed the first concrete action of a handful of Saxon businessmen, mainly in Dresden and Leipzig, who recruited Gustav Stresemann—the later National Liberal leader and Weimar statesman--to form the Association of Saxon Industrialists (Verband Sächsischer Industrieller, or VSI) in order to press their special economic interests. As another symptom of these men's impatience, the Saxon wing of the NLP disavowed the national party's accommodation with Bülow and the Conservatives over tariffs in late 1902.[36] Within only a couple of years, Stresemann and the four thousand businessmen organized in his new lobby exercised direct influence over the left (and younger) wing of the Saxon National Liberal Party.[37] Concentrating every effort on disengaging the National Liberal Landtag caucus from Mehnert and the Conservatives, they tried to convince their party leaders, first, that a new system of selecting members to both houses of parliament was the conditio sine qua non for the further blossoming of industry in Saxony; and second, that a ruthlessly antilabor and antireform policy was no longer viable in the "red kingdom."

Between 1896 and 1903, National Liberals had discussed franchise reform for the lower house only occasionally. Those deputies interested in the

---

36. Warren, *The Red Kingdom*, 38.
37. See Dönhoff to Bülow, 1 July 1905, PA AA Bonn, Sachsen Nr. 48, Bd. 20; Warren, *The Red Kingdom*, passim.

question at all preferred to snipe away at the inequitable electoral balance between Saxony's thirty-seven urban and forty-five rural constituencies. But immediately after the Reichstag elections of 1903, National Liberal newspapers began to echo the sentiments of Hans Delbrück, who wrote in his influential *Preußische Jahrbücher* that the reentry of Social Democrats into the Saxon Landtag would provide crucial "relief" in future Reichstag elections.[38] In a general assembly of the Saxon National Liberals in early September, the party leadership accepted an anticonservative platform that included demands for a redistribution of rural and urban Landtag seats and for a new franchise based on a system of plural voting (whereby certain privileged voters would be given extra ballots). Metzsch, for one, was not convinced that the National Liberals wanted a genuine reform. Shortly thereafter, however, in the final days of the autumn Landtag campaign, Dönhoff noted "a turning away of liberals of all shades from the Conservatives," adding that they were attacking Conservative candidates in Dresden and Leipzig with "special vehemence." Although Dönhoff's fear that one of these constituencies would go "red" proved unfounded, the political trickery used by the National Liberals to win the Dresden seat from the Conservatives did nothing to ease tensions between them.[39] On the opening day of the new session, the Conservatives excluded liberal deputies from the five standing committees of the lower house.

The forum of "experts" that met to discuss franchise reform did not convene, perhaps wisely, until after the Landtag campaign was completed in October 1903. Among this group the government precirculated a working draft, or *Denkschrift,* that found virtually no support. However, the contradictory views expressed by the participants offered no opportunity for consensus either, so in the end the government simply published its *Denkschrift* in slightly revised form on 31 December 1903.[40]

In the long preamble to this document and in Metzsch's defense of his proposals in the Landtag the following February, the government reiterated its view that the franchise law of 1896 had had many unanticipated and undesirable consequences. The most compelling arguments for reform, it claimed, included the need to address recent changes in Saxony's tax structure, the unfair distribution of rural and urban seats, the devaluation of votes cast in the third voting class, and the invidious system of indirect balloting (first for delegates, then for Landtag candidates themselves). The *Denkschrift* addressed various proposals for reform that had already been put forward, and noted that

---

38. *Preußische Jahrbücher* (hereafter *Pr Jbb*) 113, no. 3 (1903): 374.

39. Dönhoff to Bülow, 19 and 26 Sept., 2, 17, 21, 23, and 30 Oct. 1903, PA AA Bonn, Sachsen Nr. 60, Bd. 6.

40. Dönhoff to Bülow, 30 Oct. 1903, PA AA Bonn, Sachsen Nr. 60, Bd. 6; "Dekret vom 31. Dezember 1903," excerpted in Pache, *Geschichte,* 30–31.

virtually none of these had recommended either the preservation of the old franchise or the introduction of public (that is, nonsecret) balloting. The government rejected the universal, equal franchise because it would surrender the lower house to the SPD. But neither did it favor a franchise wherein the principle of universality was mitigated by an electoral census (*Zensus*): a low tax threshold for enfranchisement, it argued, would not prevent the entry of Social Democrats into parliament, whereas a high one would exclude many Saxons who were currently enfranchised—possibly including a large proportion of the *Mittelstand*. Similar doubts were expressed about raising the age of enfranchisement from twenty-five to thirty.

Mandatory voting was rejected on two grounds: the bureaucracy necessary to enforce it would be unwieldy and costly, and if the government punished all citizens who failed to vote, it would drive many supporters of the state into the arms of the SPD. Proportional representation was rejected with the argument that it served only to augment the negative influence of "party interests" in parliament. So was the selection of deputies exclusively through local councils, in part because municipalities allegedly still retained a "nonpartisan" style of politics, and in part because this would retain the undesirable system of two-tier balloting.[41] Much the same arguments were used against a system whereby all Landtag deputies would be elected on the basis of occupational estates (*Berufsstände*). A similar system had led to difficulties for local elections in Chemnitz, and the government argued that it would be impossible to divide a much larger population fairly or logically into occupational estates. Lastly, a system of plural voting—whereby certain voters would receive extra ballots on the basis of education, military service, ownership of property, age, and other criteria—was rejected. Referring to academic studies and to a similar system recently introduced in Belgium, the *Denkschrift* noted that the provision of only one or two extra votes would not have the desired effect of preventing socialists from dominating the Landtag, while a large number of extra votes would—like a high tax threshold—continue to make the electoral influence of the lower classes "illusory."

In sum, although Metzsch's ministry rejected universal, equal, direct, and secret voting and thereby amply illustrated its continuing opposition to the principle of democracy, its proposals nonetheless made a number of tangible concessions to the cause of electoral fairness. The *Denkschrift* that it had

---

41. Discriminatory franchises introduced in Leipzig (1894), Chemnitz (1898), and Dresden (1905), together with the growing influence of parties and interest groups in municipal elections, showed the hollowness of this first claim. Cf. *Verfassung und Verwaltungsorganisation der Städte,* ed. Verein für Socialpolitik, vol. 4, pt. 1, *Königreich Sachsen* (Leipzig, 1905); and the special supplements to *Kommunale Praxis* entitled *Sächsische Gemeinde-Politik,* which appeared in 1905.

circulated in October actually included other "obeisances (*Verbeugungen*) to the SPD. But these were omitted from the published document when Mehnert intervened and demanded their deletion.[42]

How did the government intend to eliminate the worst features of the 1896 franchise and yet avoid the pitfalls inherent in these alternatives? It proposed a hybrid electoral system, according to which forty-eight deputies would be elected through direct three-class voting (*Abteilungswahlen*) with slight preferment for those possessing a certain level of education and those possessing taxable property; another thirty-five deputies would be elected by voting according to occupational estates (*berufsständige Wahlen*). For the election of the forty-eight deputies through class-based elections, the state would be divided into sixteen constituencies for each of the three voting divisions, eliminating the former distinction between urban and rural constituencies. The estate-bound election, on the other hand, foresaw the selection of fifteen representatives of agriculture, ten representatives of trade and industry, and ten representatives of small business and crafts (*Kleinhandel, Handwerk, Kleingewerb*).

The proposals included in the *Denkschrift* of December 1903 bore so little resemblance to the franchise actually enacted in 1909 that there is no need to chronicle the reactions to them or the parliamentary battle that ensued.[43] The left-liberal *Dresdner Zeitung* was fairly typical in calling this reform "the weakest and worst concoction that the government could possibly have proposed." The Conservative onslaught was led by Hugo Opitz-Treuen, a leading industrialist in the Conservative Landesverein and Mehnert's right-hand man in the Landtag caucus. Opitz complained that the full renewal of the Landtag in each election promised only to heat up, not cool down, passions aroused by "demagogues" and "professionals" in the age of mass politics. Conservatives believed as well that in addition to the Social Democrats who were expected to win all sixteen constituencies allocated to the third voting class, more would be elected either through the occupational elections or in the second voting class, where, Opitz claimed, elements of the *Mittelstand* would not be able to withstand SPD "terrorism." The National Liberals made the same argument, estimating that the government's proposal would result in socialists winning twenty-five seats (roughly one-third of the total) in the new Landtag. Curi-

---

42. Dönhoff to Bülow, 10 Jan. 1904, PA AA Bonn, Sachsen Nr. 60, Bd. 6.

43. See Pache, *Geschichte*, 16–32; Oppe, "Die Reform," 380–82; Diersch, "Die geschichtliche Entwicklung des Landtagswahlrechts," 220–32; on motions for reform of the upper house in December 1903, see Dönhoff to Bülow, 21 Dec. 1903 and attachments; on his discussion with Mehnert, see Dönhoff to Bülow, 10 Jan. 1904; on press reactions to the *Denkschrift,* see Dönhoff to Bülow, 8, 11, 17, 31 Jan. 1904; and on the legislative battle, see Dönhoff to Bülow, 5 Feb. 1904, all in PA AA Bonn, Sachsen Nr. 60, Bd. 6. See also Dönhoff to Bülow, 29 April and 21 May 1904, in ibid., Bd. 7.

ously, neither they nor the Conservatives asked the government directly whether it had made the same calculations itself. The National Liberals were most interested in pushing for plural voting, since they believed that their roots in the elites of property and education would be conducive to electoral victories under such a system. The Radicals preferred either the universal franchise or a return to the franchise of 1868 with a higher tax threshold, and an anti-Semitic deputy spoke in favor of mandatory voting.

From lengthy discussions in committee—described by Metzsch as a "comedy"—consensus emerged on only two points. First, it became clear that an electoral system based on occupational estates would never win majority approval in the Landtag. Second, both the National Liberal minority and the Conservative majority favored plural voting in principle, though the government continued to reject it. The problem was, of course, that each political group wanted a different ranking of the criteria according to which extra ballots would be allocated. Some wanted preferment to be calculated on the basis of taxes paid to the state, while others favored such criteria as age, education, ownership of property, military duty (with distinctions between ranks), other "practical experience," family situation (single, married, widower, number of children), number of employees, and service in public or voluntary office. To complicate matters further, while some foresaw as many as seven supplementary ballots, others insisted on designing the new system on the basis of full, half, one-third, and one-quarter votes. It is not difficult to imagine the fruitless debates to which such proposals gave rise. Partly because so little was accomplished, when the government's *Denkschrift* was rejected by the Landtag on 28 April 1904, Mehnert crowed to Dönhoff that he had carried the day (Metzsch was "not in a rosy mood"). But there was good reason to describe this Conservative victory as Pyrrhic, for two positive signs indicated that the issue of electoral reform was anything but dead. The first was the defection of about twenty Conservatives from their caucus leaders on this and a number of other issues debated during the session. The second was a resolution, passed by a vote of forty-three to thirty and based on the National Liberals' minority committee report, requesting that the government submit new proposals for consideration in the next session. The deputies also charged the government— and for this historians can be thankful—with the task of gathering more comprehensive and reliable statistics to permit the expert consideration of future proposals.

Under Saxony's constitution, new Landtag sessions convened only every second autumn—that is, shortly after each election. Therefore there was a forced hiatus in the discussion of franchise reform between May 1904 and November 1905. Nevertheless, a full year before the Landtag elections scheduled for October 1905, Dönhoff noted that businessmen within the Saxon NLP were more alienated than ever from the Conservatives, despite the continuing efforts of Opitz and other industrialists to solicit their support.[44] Around the same time, the Saxon NLP announced that its electoral cartel with the Conservatives was dead. Thus in March 1905 all the parties had selected most of their candidates—far earlier than usual—and instead of one or two nonsocialist candidates, three, four, and sometimes more were contesting each seat. As Dönhoff followed the campaign, it became clear that the two main antisocialist parties were now bitter rivals in most of the twenty-nine constituencies being contested.

Yet conflicts seething *within* National Liberal ranks continued to confuse the situation through 1905—so much so that one must be careful not to overestimate either the speed or the completeness of the National Liberal rejuvenation. During the Landtag campaign, three astute observers—Dönhoff, Mehnert, and the editor of the *Sächsische Arbeiterzeitung,* Hans Block—all believed that the National Liberals were a long way from being the defenders of political principle to which they laid claim. According to Dönhoff, Stresemann and the youth wing of the Saxon NLP, the Young Liberals, had brought to a halt a fundamental convergence of interests between National Liberals and Conservatives over the previous twenty years. During that time the National Liberals had become more and more inclined to defend their political and economic accomplishments in the Landtag, while the Conservatives had been willing to accommodate liberal interests, especially in the purely economic sphere.[45] Yet the Young Liberals, Dönhoff claimed, were uncertain of their own goals. Even the Association of Saxon Industrialists did not seem to be following an entirely consistent line—for example, in endorsing candidates from all parties as long as they pledged to support business interests. This lack of consistency could be ascribed in part to Mehnert's secret machinations: the Conservative leader confided to Dönhoff that a conservative mole had been infiltrated into the VSI's leadership, managing to attain the position of second vice president.[46] Nonetheless, Dönhoff doubted whether the NLP's election manifesto would succeed in winning over the "old National Liberal" faction within the party, for these men continued to regard cooperation with the Conservatives as preferable to a "general middle-party liberalism."

Exactly the same doubts were voiced a few weeks before the autumn 1905 elections by Block, writing in the socialist *Neue Zeit.*[47] Block claimed that the National Liberals' "pompously announced challenge" to the Conservatives

---

44. For this and the following, see Dönhoff to Bülow, 29 Oct. and 25 Nov. 1904, and 13 March, 23 May, 3 June, 19 Sept., and 3, 4, 26 Oct. 1905, PA AA Bonn, Sachsen Nr. 60, Bd. 7.

45. Cf. "Saxonica. III," von einem sächsischen Konservativen, *Grenzboten* 64, no. 1 (1905): 362–64.

46. Dönhoff to Bülow, 13 March 1905, PA AA Bonn, Sachsen Nr. 60, Bd. 7.

47. Hans Block, "Die 'Wiedergeburt' des Liberalismus in Sachsen," *Neue Zeit,* Jg. 23 (1904–5), vol. 2, no. 48: 693–99, esp. 697; and ibid., no. 49: 730–35.

had so far amounted to nothing, because local NLP associations had been unable to mount independent campaigns. The "murderous slaughter of Saxon agrarianism," Block wrote sarcastically, was nothing more than a "gentle scuffle" for a few Landtag seats; in this contest, he added, liberal principles played no part, only the threatened interests of Saxon industry. Block predicted that economic self-interest and the continued fear of socialism would eventually bring National Liberals back to Mehnert's cartel, even though purely political demands and the issue of franchise reform might detour them for a time. This prediction was in line with Mehnert's assessment of the situation. Mehnert believed that even the Young Liberals in the Landtag would soon see the value of the cartel—once they discovered that their independence served the interests only of Radicals and Social Democrats, once the economic climate improved, and once they learned that "positive work" in the Landtag was possible only in cooperation with the Conservatives.

These assessments were not entirely off the mark. The Landtag elections in October 1905 produced a complete rout of Young Liberal candidates. While the Conservative caucus dropped by four members, to fifty-four, the NLP's caucus increased by only two members, to twenty-four. The anti-Semitic Reform Party and the Radicals each elected two deputies, and a single SPD deputy, Hermann Goldstein, reentered the Landtag. As chair of the Saxon state ministry, Metzsch was happy with this outcome on three counts: Stresemann's group had fallen short of its goal, the Conservative caucus had failed to renew its two-thirds majority, and the election of a Social Democrat (he hoped) would reduce public pressure for franchise reform. Metzsch's hopes for a quieter session were also fueled by a significant improvement in the Saxon economy in 1905. But members of the new Landtag were aware that the SPD's national congress in Jena had recently endorsed the mass strike as a weapon against disfranchisement. And just as the session of 1905–6 opened, they turned one eye to the brewing storm in Russia, where the tsar's October Manifesto had established a four-class franchise.

A number of studies, mainly from a Marxist perspective, have been devoted to the demonstrations by tens of thousands of workers in favor of franchise reform that took place in the streets of Dresden, Leipzig, Chemnitz, and Plauen in November and December 1905.[48] This episode has been discussed in the

---

48. Horst Dörrer, "Die ersten Wahlrechtskämpfe der Dresdner Arbeiter unter dem Einfluß der ersten russischen Revolution von 1905 bis 1907," *Wissenschaftliche Annalen zur Verbreitung neuer Forschungsergebnisse* 5 (1956): 383–400; Ursula Herrmann, "Der Kampf der Sozialdemokratie gegen das Dreiklassenwahlrecht in Sachsen in den Jahren 1905/06," *Zeitschrift für Geschichtswissenschaft* 3 (1955): 856–83; Dieter Fricke, "Der Aufschwung der Massenkämpfe der deutschen Arbeiterklasse unter dem Einfluss der russischen Revolution von 1905," ibid., 5 (1957): 771–90; Richard W. Reichard, "The German Working Class and the Russian

light of franchise struggles in other parts of Germany and Europe at this time—
in Russia, Vienna, Prague, Hamburg, Braunschweig, Lippe, Lübeck, and elsewhere. To date, however, the reasons for the Saxon ministry's dilatory handling
of franchise reform at this critical juncture and its excessive response to the
socialist challenge in the streets have never been adequately explained.

Acrimony from the election campaign carried over to the new session of
the Saxon Landtag, which began in late October 1905. Shortly before parliament opened, Stresemann was warned by one of his like-minded colleagues in
the NLP's Landtag caucus, Wilhelm Vogel, that many old National Liberals
intended to reconcile their differences with Conservatives and abandon franchise reform. The Conservative leaders hoped to speed this process when they
invited NLP deputies back onto the Landtag's standing committees. Conservatives also accused National Liberals of fomenting revolution through their own
reform proposals, and they charged that National Liberals in Bavaria, Württemberg, and Baden—where direct, equal, and secret franchises had been
granted recently—were guilty of forming political alliances with the "party of
revolution."[49]

Although Stresemann's estimate that only half of the twenty-four National Liberal deputies were committed to reform did not promise favorable
results, both the Radicals and the NLP interpellated the government on 25
October 1905, asking whether it planned to introduce franchise legislation in
the current session. A week after the first large socialist demonstrations, on 27
November, Metzsch blandly told the house that he had no new plan. He
claimed that statistical studies had not yet been completed—even though the
director of Saxony's statistical office had actually presented him with scenarios
based on a variety of franchise laws almost eighteen months earlier.[50] Furthermore, Metzsch declared that the government saw no greater merit now than it
had two years earlier in electoral systems based on plural voting, mandatory
voting, or proportional representation. Here, too, he based his remarks on
confidential statistical analysis that indicated that none of these electoral systems would reduce the proportion of votes cast for socialists by more than
about one-fifth or one-sixth over a system based on the universal franchise.
Although National Liberals and Conservatives had fastened on plural voting as

---

Revolution of 1905," *Journal of Central European Affairs* 13, no. 2 (1953): 136–53; Leo Stern,
ed., *Die Auswirkungen der ersten russischen Revolution von 1905–1907 auf Deutschland* (Berlin,
1956), vol. 2, pt. 2, 261–67.

49. Dönhoff to Bülow, 29 Nov. 1905, PA AA Bonn, Sachsen Nr. 60, Bd. 7, also for parts of
the following two paragraphs; Warren, *The Red Kingdom,* 65ff.; and Diersch, "Die geschichtliche
Entwicklung des Landtagswahlrechts," 244–45.

50. Dr. Würzburger to the Saxon interior ministry, 29 Aug. 1904, copy in PA AA Bonn,
Sachsen Nr. 60, Bd. 7. This analysis was based on twelve selected Prussian Landtag constituencies
deemed to bear a close resemblance to Saxon constituencies in terms of social and occupational
structure.

the most feasible basis for franchise reform, Metzsch declared that extra ballots for older voters would not significantly assist the nonsocialist parties at the polls. Neither would a system whereby wealthier voters received one or two extra ballots, while extra ballots awarded on the basis of educational achievement would affect only forty-one thousand voters.

Metzsch confided to Dönhoff after the day's proceedings on 27 November that his speech, though unavoidable, would probably "bring the blood of the German worker to a boil." On the evening of 3 December, he witnessed the truth of his remarks in person as angry mobs marched through the streets of Dresden to the steps of his official residence (prompting a terrified Metzsch to send his wife and young son to a neighbor's house in the middle of the night). Metzsch was sorely tempted to resign, and Dönhoff reported that his nerves were completely shattered. But even resignation evaporated as an option when Bülow sent frantic dispatches urging Metzsch to remain at his post. The Dresden violence, Bülow felt, was not only of local importance; it was "the touchstone for the entire Reich." Therefore Bülow urged Metzsch to repress the demonstrators with all means at his disposal, adding that the Kaiser had suggested that troops, if required, should be instructed to fire on the mob before women and children were pushed to the front lines. Politically it would be an even greater mistake, Bülow added, if the Saxon ministry were to make "even the slightest" concession on franchise reform, at least until complete calm had been restored.[51] Bülow need not have worried. By the time the socialist Goldstein launched another interpellation of the government on 14 December, on the grounds of police brutality against the demonstrators, the National Liberals and other nonsocialist deputies agreed that debate had to be cut short. Subsequently the Saxon police were commended, not censured, for their bloody intervention. By the end of January 1906, thanks in large measure to the calls for calm issued by the Saxon SPD leaders themselves—Metzsch was now recuperating at a retreat outside Dresden—the crisis had passed.

It became apparent during the debates of 27 November and 14 December 1905 that many National Liberals were still uncertain where the real enemy lay: out in the streets or on the Conservative benches in the Landtag? Despite vigorous efforts, Stresemann could not sway the majority of NLP deputies to support franchise reform unreservedly. As a sympathetic editor put it in a note to Stresemann on 7 December, the persistent threat of Social Democracy proved once again that "in Saxony it is not considered fair [*sic*] to be truly liberal."[52] In light of this comment, it is perhaps moot whether the National Liberals or the socialists bear the greatest responsibility for the missed opportunity of 1905–6. But Delbrück, writing in his *Preußische Jahrbücher* in early

---

51. Count Wilhelm von Hohenthal und Bergen to Metzsch, 19 and 22 Dec. 1905, printed in Stern, *Die Auswirkungen,* vol. 2, pt. 2, 261–63.

52. Warren, *The Red Kingdom,* 69–70.

1906, pressed the point. Noting that the National Liberals had lost precious time since 1903 in not pushing harder for franchise reform, Delbrück reported that many Germans from the best circles now believed that neither the Prussian nor the Saxon government could have a clear conscience over the blood that had been spilled because of their dilatory handling of franchise reform. The only solution, Delbrück believed, was the introduction of plural voting for Landtag elections in both states as soon as possible.[53] But the Saxon Landtag session of 1905–6 ended with no positive result. Soon after parliament closed, Metzsch resigned from the Saxon ministry of state. He was replaced as interior and foreign minister and as de facto government leader by Count Wilhelm von Hohenthal und Bergen. Hohenthal sprang from the ranks of Leipzig's upper bourgeoisie and, widely respected personally, had served as Saxon envoy in Berlin for more than twenty years. Around the same time, the Prussian envoy Dönhoff died. He was replaced by a more distinguished but—unfortunately for us—far less diligent or perceptive observer, Prince Hans zu Hohenlohe-Oehringen.[54]

A reinvigoration of the Saxon government coincided with socialist setbacks both in the Reichstag elections of January 1907 and in Landtag elections the following October. In January, special attention was again focused on Saxony as the *Ordnungsparteien* sought to reverse the verdict of June 1903. This time anti-Catholic sentiment was actually whipped up by the nonsocialist parties as a means of exciting Saxon voters against the SPD as well. More importantly, in the middle of the campaign, Saxon newspapers announced "upon reliable authority" that the government had a new franchise reform proposal ready to present to the Landtag. Clearly the government wished to avoid the alleged "mistake" of 1903, when it had failed to provide Saxon voters with any hint that it did not share the Conservatives' do-nothing stance on franchise reform. When the polls closed, the SPD's vote had shrunk from 441,000 in 1903 (59 percent) to just 418,000 (48 percent) in 1907, and they lost fourteen of their twenty-two seats. In the Landtag elections, too, the verdict of 1905 was reversed insofar as no new socialists were elected. National Liberal gains also showed that Conservative hegemony—in the lower house at least—was finally vulnerable. The Conservatives' loss of eight seats, Hohenthal hoped, would compel them not to risk a dissolution of the Landtag by digging in their heels on the franchise question.[55]

The last obstacle to decisive action in 1907 was cleared when reports from

---

53. [Hans Delbrück], "Politische Korrespondenz: Die Reform des Landtagswahlrechts," *Pr Jbb* 123 (1906): 193–95; [Hans Delbrück], "Politische Korrespondenz: Die Wahlrechts-Reform in Preußen und Sachsen," ibid (1906): 402–6.

54. Blaschke, "Das Königreich Sachsen," 99; *Wer ist's*, ed. H. Degener (Leipzig, 1906), 359.

55. See George Crothers, *The German Elections of 1907* (New York, 1968), 147, 176–78; and Hohenlohe to Bülow, 27 Sept. and 18 Oct. 1907, in PA AA Bonn, Sachsen Nr. 60, Bd. 8.

Berlin indicated that Bülow was not opposed in principle to Saxon franchise reform. Despite the worries of Prussian Conservatives that they were being "encircled" by other states with a "radical franchise," and despite Mehnert's own intensive lobbying efforts at Bülow's doorstep, the Saxon ministry knew that Prussian officials were preparing their own reform proposals. Because Bülow had told the Conservatives repeatedly that three-class voting was untenable in the long run—and because "moderate" Conservatives allegedly agreed—Saxon ministers expected the Prussians to look benignly on whatever formula for reform seemed most appropriate to Saxon circumstances. Thus, when a Reich official observed to the Saxon envoy in Berlin that Prussia and Saxony must proceed hand in hand if either state's franchise were not to become merely a provisional arrangement, he was told bluntly that Hohenthal, due to the pressure of public opinion, simply did not have the luxury of waiting for Prussia to act.[56]

Hohenthal's announcement of the government's new plan for franchise reform on 5 July 1907 began a political contest that completely dominated the extraordinarily long Landtag session that stretched from November 1907 to January 1909.[57] This campaign, too complex to chronicle here, can be summarized by concentrating on three of its most important features:

the extreme pressure on all parties to enact reform before the next scheduled elections;

the government's wide-ranging rationale for, and defense of, a unique combination of proportional, communal, and plural voting systems that was clearly intended to undercut Conservative influence in the Landtag; and

the gradual elimination of all viable options for legislating franchise reform except on the exclusive principle of plural voting.

Despite the favorable results of January 1907, nonsocialist deputies did not wish to face their electors again without some tangible achievement on the franchise question. Conservative attacks on the Reichstag franchise published

---

56. On his discussion with Heinrich von Tschirschky und Bögendorff, see the letter of 13 May 1907 to Hohenthal by Count Christoph Vitzthum von Eckstädt, Hohenthal's successor as Saxon envoy to Prussia (1906–9), interior and foreign minister (1909–18), and de facto government leader, printed in Stern, *Die Auswirkungen,* vol. 2, pt. 2, 263–65; on Bülow's alleged preference for plural voting, see Tschirschky to Bülow, 29 Oct. 1908, in PA AA Bonn, Sachsen Nr. 60, Bd. 8.

57. The plan was finally presented to the Landtag in the "Dekret vom 15. Oktober 1907." See Hohenlohe to Bülow, 7 and 20 July 1907, in PA AA Bonn, Sachsen Nr. 60, Bd. 8. The following is based on Diersch, "Die geschichtliche Entwicklung des Landtagswahlrechts," 247–333; Pache, *Geschichte,* 35–120; and Oppe, "Die Reform," 383–409.

during the campaign only made Saxon voters more sensitive on the issue. Parliamentarians from the *Ordnungsparteien* also recognized that the bloc experiment in the Reichstag, labeled by Bülow as a "marriage of liberal and conservative spirits," was at best a marriage of convenience. That the Reichstag voting had created strange bedfellows was even more apparent in Saxony than in many other parts of the Reich. In Meißen, for example, the votes of German Radicals, normally the staunchest defenders of the rights of Jews, were decisive in bringing an anti-Semite to victory. Animosities between Conservatives and National Liberals in other constituencies fueled predictions from national leaders that the coupling of liberals and conservatives would produce only weak offspring or the occasional liaison before both partners sought divorce. No wonder that during the campaign the Saxon socialists had ridiculed bloc candidates as "long-sighed-for, Semitic-anti-Semitic, agrarian-industrial, conservative-radical, bigoted-liberal, mish-mash candidates."[58]

Hohenthal also sought to use public pressure to force compromise upon the Conservative and National Liberal parties. He repeatedly hinted that he would resign and allow the king to appoint a stronger-willed successor, or that he would dissolve the Landtag and call new elections. As Hohenthal told the Prussian envoy, Hohenlohe, at one point, members of the nonsocialist parties feared to undertake an election campaign "with empty hands." On another occasion he declared to the Landtag that a bill passed by a slim margin was not acceptable to the government: a much broader consensus was required.[59] This was more than a simple gesture of political goodwill toward the minority National Liberals; a formal constitutional amendment with the assent of two-thirds of the lower house was required if certain features of the existing franchise were to be revised. Even young King Friedrich August III (1904–18), whose personal quest for popularity among his citizens bordered on the burlesque, was determined not to agree to a franchise reform unless it promised to quell the political unrest among his people.[60]

Pressures of another sort induced members of the *Ordnungsparteien* to shroud their deliberations in secrecy. They were unwilling to let voters learn how seriously they were considering various reactionary options for the new franchise. But when it became known in April 1908, after more than three months of committee deliberations, that no progress had been made, liberals compelled the committee to issue regular reports. Then, when even the committee met an impasse, the leaders of the Conservatives and National Liberals

---

58. Crothers, *The German Elections,* 148, 154–66, and 174.

59. See Hohenlohe to Bülow, 20 July and 27 Sept. 1907; and 13 March, 13 April, 6 June, 19 Nov., and 4 Dec. 1908; in PA AA Bonn, Sachsen Nr. 60, Bd. 8.

60. Friedrich Kracke, *Friedrich August III. Sachsens volkstümlichster König* (Munich, 1964), cited in Blaschke, "Das Königreich Sachsen," 85; cf. Walter Fellmann, *Sachsens letzter König, Friedrich August III.* (Berlin, 1992).

began to meet secretly outside parliament in order to hammer out an agreement. Those deliberations continued through much of the parliamentary recess, from early June until late October 1908. Such backroom politics alienated even nonsocialist observers not privy to the discussions, while the socialists kept up a constant barrage of newspaper articles in favor of the universal franchise. In late 1908 the SPD also began to organize large demonstrations. The most noteworthy of these took place on 1 November in Dresden, Leipzig, and Chemnitz. The rallies were all well organized, the crowds remained calm, and no police action was necessary. However, in the middle of January 1909, on the first Sunday after franchise reform legislation was finally passed, a socialist rally in Dresden demonstrated that the king's wish for a "popular" reform was in vain. This time the throng attempted to reach both Hohenthal's residence and the royal palace, and about twenty demonstrators were injured. It was therefore with deep concern—for their personal careers, for their own party faction, for the integrity of the Saxon Landtag, and for the security of the state—that nonsocialist deputies debated how to transform the Landtag into a "representative" political institution.

Although the government resisted what it regarded as inopportune and extreme National Liberal demands, it was also clearly prepared to endorse franchise proposals that foresaw a permanent end to Conservative domination of the lower house. This was amply demonstrated when a junior diplomatic counselor named Alfred von Nostitz-Wallwitz[61] addressed a meeting of the Dresden Conservative Association on 11 July 1907. In trying to rally support for Hohenthal's reform proposal, Nostitz unofficially but accurately represented government opinion when he warned the Conservatives to face reality and concede some of their overwhelming influence before it was too late. Electoral appeals based on "the struggle against revolution," Nostitz declared to the assembled Conservatives, no longer sufficed to keep the wolf from the door. Instead, law-abiding citizens were being driven to the SPD by the unfair franchise of 1896. Therefore, socialists had to be not only readmitted to the Landtag but also invited onto its committees, for a parliamentary majority that could not cope with "fifteen or twenty" Social Democrats did not deserve to hold power. Moreover, Nostitz continued, the time had come to eliminate the

---

61. Originally I mistook this man to be Hermann von Nostitz-Wallwitz, Saxony's interior minister from 1866 to 1891. In July 1907 Alfred von Nostitz was a highly promising thirty-six-year-old *Legationsrat,* but because of his outspoken critique of the Conservatives, his career went into temporary free fall. After 1907 he was a *Regierungsrat* in the Grand Duchy of Saxe-Weimar, and in 1910 he returned to Saxony to become *Amtshauptmann* of Auerbach and then of Leipzig. By World War I he was again regarded highly by the chairman of the Saxon state ministry; in 1916 he was named Saxon envoy in Vienna, and in October–November 1918 he served as Saxon minister of culture and public education. See Thomas Klein, ed., *Sachsen* (Grundriß zur deutschen Verwaltungsgeschichte, 1815–1918, series B, vol. 14) (Marburg, 1982), 114, 380, 392.

"one-sided, artificial dominance of a single party" in the Landtag. Without mentioning Mehnert's name specifically, Nostitz declared that in Saxony political leaders whose influence was not properly circumscribed by the responsibilities of public office had recently come to prominence. This brought Nostitz to the most celebrated passage in his speech:[62]

> It is known generally that this backstairs government [*Nebenregierung*] has brought to a head the rancor and bitterness felt in the best circles of the people, from the very highest notables to the simplest *Bürger*. . . . The Conservative Party will gain in inner strength in the same measure that it voluntarily relinquishes its artificial and illegitimate dominance [*Übergewicht*].

Nostitz's barely concealed attack on Mehnert, and his use of the word *Nebenregierung* in particular, provoked a storm of controversy in the Saxon political press that lasted for weeks. On the one hand, these remarks again revealed how bad relations were between the Saxon ministry and the Conservatives. More significantly, they linked worries about the outcome of Saxon franchise reform to wider (but no less impassioned) debates about illegitimate influence in the Kaiser's court, since at this time popular attention was being focused on the alleged *Nebenregierung* of Philipp Eulenburg and others implicated in the sensational trials instigated by Maximilian Harden. As the Conservatives' opponents picked up on this theme, the National Liberals took the opportunity to itemize the many abuses of power since 1896 perpetrated in the name of "Paul & Co., G.m.b.H." and under the "System Mehnert—Opitz—Oertel." At last it seemed to Saxon businessmen that their challenge to the Conservatives' hegemony might be supported by a government that acknowledged its own decisive interest in setting Saxon parliamentary affairs on a new footing.

How was the viewpoint expressed by Nostitz reflected in Hohenthal's franchise reform proposal of July 1907? Previously the Saxon government had argued that plural voting was unworkable and unfair, and it had made clear its preference for voting based on occupational estates. Now, however, it reversed itself and proposed the election of forty-two deputies by secret and direct voting, incorporating proportional representation with a moderate system of plural votes, whereby no voter would be accorded more than two votes. It also proposed the election of forty other deputies through the assemblies of local government, namely, the district councils (*Bezirksverbände*) in rural areas and a joint assembly of municipal councillors and senators in the cities. In linking this system with only the most modest increase in the number of urban consti-

---

62. Pache, *Geschichte*, 100, 101–32.

tuencies, the government cited the arguments of Albert Schäffle, a noted sociologist and political observer, who had argued in 1890 that the representation of local interests provided a "counterweight" to other features of an electoral system based on direct and equal voting.[63] It also claimed that its previous criticism of indirect voting was not relevant in this case; although the delegates elected in the first round of balloting under the three-class franchise had been criticized as mere "ballot carriers [*Zettelträger*]" by some, the government noted that local councillors had other functions to fulfill and were sufficiently high-minded not to be overly partisan. Although its motives cannot be determined with certainty, the government appears to have been trying to convince National Liberals that their continued strength in municipal politics might translate into power in the Landtag. The National Liberals, after all, had done very well in local elections since plutocratic franchises had been introduced in Saxony's major cities. Nonetheless, the government chose to ignore the fact that even in 1899, 805 socialists already sat on local councils in Saxony; by 1909 that number had grown to about 1,600, and the SPD's interest in municipal politics showed no signs of waning.[64]

As a gesture to the Conservatives, the government echoed their rather specious argument that the distribution of seats in the reformed Landtag should not be determined solely by population (*Rechte des Menschen*) but should also reflect the geographical expanse of the state (*Rechte der Fläche*). The government rejected the normal system of proportional representation based on party lists as well, for in this instance it conceded that voters would be corrupted by having to vote for a party rather than a particular candidate. Instead it proposed a much more complicated proportional system whereby candidates would run in individual constituencies, and each party would elect only the number of deputies—those with the highest vote totals—accorded it under calculations completed after the voting. Lastly, it was not without irony that the novelty of proportional representation was defended with the argument that under the simple majority formula, a large number of nonsocialist voters had been deprived of representation in the Reichstag in 1903 because the socialists had won twenty-two of twenty-three Saxon seats.

While these features of the government's proposal may have been intended to bring the Conservatives on board, other elements of the plan clearly ran contrary to Conservative wishes. Until the very last moment, the government refused to abandon its hybrid electoral system. Plural voting based on income and property, it continued to insist, would merely retain the worst

---

63. A[lbert] Schäffle, "Die Bekämpfung der Sozialdemokratie ohne Ausnahmegesetz," *Zeitschrift für die gesamte Staatswissenschaft* 46 (1890): 201–87, esp. 255–73. Cf. Albert Schäffle, *Die Aussichtslosigkeit der Sozialdemokratie*, 4th ed. (n.p., 1893).

64. Figures from Fricke, *Handbuch*, 2:777; and Hohenlohe to Chancellor Theobald von Bethmann Hollweg, 22 Aug. 1909, in PA AA Bonn, Sachsen Nr. 60, Bd. 8.

plutocratic features of the three-class franchise. It also refused a Landtag committee proposal whereby permanent residence of not less than two years would be required of enfranchised voters. This stipulation was aimed, of course, not at vagabonds—as the Conservatives claimed—but at the more mobile ranks of younger workers. Under government pressure this residency requirement was reduced to six months. Similarly, the government refused to abandon its proposal that every seat in the Landtag be contested at six-year intervals, even though Conservatives were adamant that general Landtag elections would thereby become as "passionate" and "demagogic" as general Reichstag elections. Lastly, it argued strenuously against two criteria for awarding extra votes: age and economic "independence." The latter criterion was advocated by National Liberals and Conservatives as a means to give greater influence to state officials, clergy, teachers, academics, doctors, and lawyers—though only those with a yearly income of at least eighteen hundred marks. The government, however, believed that neither age nor economic independence provided any guarantee whatsoever that a voter would not cast both his basic and his extra ballot for a socialist. With the same logic, the government forced the *Ordnungsparteien* to abandon plans to introduce a thirty-mark tax threshold for those who wished to stand for election.

Despite this evidence that some aspects of Hohenthal's ideal voting system were less reactionary than either National Liberal or Conservative schemes, it would be a mistake to imagine that the government was consistently high-minded or even sensible with its own proposals. For instance, at a very late date in the reform process—after nothing was left of its original proposals—the government outlined a system of plural voting whereby each voter would have either one or four ballots, but no one would have two or three. This system, Hohenthal claimed, would not only be technically much simpler but would also be fairer to members of the lower bourgeoisie and the *Mittelstand*. To this grossly unfair proposal the government wished to graft a system of proportional representation applying only to the large cities. Presumably this scheme, too, was intended to attract National Liberal support, since a high proportion of National Liberal votes were cast in cities where socialist victories resulted from the simple majority system. As it happened, this proposal found a positive response from neither the Conservatives nor the National Liberals.

Lastly, there were some remarkable agreements, as well as many disagreements, about what the socialists' "legitimate" share of the popular vote should be under a new franchise and—not at all the same question—how many seats should be "conceded" to the SPD in a reformed Landtag. In its proposal of July 1907, the government forecast that socialists would win about fifteen of the forty-two seats to be contested under plural voting and proportional representation. This estimate coincided roughly with its earlier estimate in 1903 that sixteen socialist deputies would probably be elected in the third voting class. To these estimates the Conservatives replied in 1907 that the government's latest plan would actually produce a *majority* of Social Democratic seats. According to their logic, one had to assume that about 30 percent of nonsocialist voters would fail to turn out at the polls in any given election. At other stages of the debate, the government and the National Liberals proved willing to accept plural voting schemes under which socialists would win roughly 38–41 percent of the vote. The vexing thing about these proposals, of course, is the difficulty in distinguishing between disagreements that resulted from differing assessments of the technical or political feasibility of various franchises—including what the Saxon citizenry would tolerate—and those that resulted from rivalries between the antisocialist groups themselves. Though limited sources inevitably evoke frustration on this point, historians can take heart that contemporaries found it just as difficult to disentangle the implications of so many complex and untried franchise schemes.

Conservatives and National Liberals eventually compromised on plural voting with a maximum of four ballots. Under the final agreement worked out in January 1909, the Saxon Landtag franchise became direct, and remained secret, for all males over the age of twenty-five. But it was not equal. In addition to a basic ballot, one, two, or three supplementary ballots were awarded if voters met certain criteria (which can be presented here only in shorthand). Entitled to two, three, or four ballots were those Saxons who had yearly incomes of more than 1,600, 2,200, or 2,800 marks respectively (with lower thresholds for certain professions), as well as those who held property assessed at 100, 150, or 200 tax units or comprising more than 2, 4, or 8 hectares. Extra ballots were also awarded to those voters who qualified for one-year voluntary military service on the basis of education. Upon reaching the age of fifty, a voter automatically received one supplementary ballot, but no voter could have more than four ballots in total. This new franchise became law on 5 May 1909.[65]

None of the parties to this compromise was entirely satisfied. The Saxon government had probably conceded the most. Its proposals of 1903 and 1907 had been swept aside by parties determined to steer their own course, and its wish to calm the public outcry had also been frustrated.[66] To be sure, most Landtag deputies proclaimed the introduction of a law that was vastly fairer to the little man in society than the previous three-class franchise. More than one observer noted that even the most lowly citizen, once he reached the age of fifty and qualified for a second ballot, would have at least half the electoral influence

---

65. "Wahlgesetz für die zweite Kammer der Ständeversammlung vom 5. Mai 1909," reprinted in Oppe, "Die Reform," appendix G.

66. On the continued expansion of the Saxon SPD and its agitation, see Hohenlohe to Bethmann Hollweg, 22 Aug. 1909, in PA AA Bonn, Sachsen Nr. 60, Bd. 8; and also for some of the following details.

of the most privileged member of society. Yet neither the government nor the nonsocialist parties were sanguine as the first test of the new system approached.

With good reason. When elections were held on 21 October 1909 for all ninety-one seats in the reformed legislature, voter turnout approached 83 percent, double that under the old system. Everyone knew that the SPD stood to gain the most from the elimination of three-class voting. But whereas Hohenthal's government apparently expected that the socialists would win no more than thirteen seats, the SPD increased its caucus from one to twenty-five members. One cause of this victory soon became apparent: many more Saxons had cast multiple ballots on behalf of socialist candidates than even the finest calculations of government officials or party experts had anticipated. More than 26 percent of those with three ballots chose socialist candidates, and more than 8 percent of those with four ballots did as well. The Radicals also did very well under the new franchise, increasing their caucus from three to eight members. To no one's surprise, the Conservative caucus shrank dramatically, from forty-six to twenty-nine deputies, while the National Liberals saw their caucus reduced from thirty-one to twenty-nine members also. These losses were all the more galling because the new, plural voting system had provided obvious advantages to the *Ordnungsparteien*. If victory had required only a relative rather than an absolute majority in each constituency, and if the Reichstag franchise had been in effect, the SPD would have won eighty of ninety-one seats.[67] However, since the Social Democrats won almost half of their votes from Saxons entitled to only one ballot, they won only about 39 percent of the popular vote and only 28 percent of seats in the parliament they immediately dubbed the "four-class Landtag." The National Liberals were supported by only 20 percent of Saxon voters; but more than half of those voters were entitled to four ballots, so the NLP won about 26 percent of the total vote and 31 percent of Landtag seats. Conservatives reaped similar benefits from the new system, not least because rural constituencies were still grossly overrepresented.

Each party offered a different interpretation of how the "fairness" of the new franchise had contributed to this outcome. Socialist newspapers conceded that the party's victory had not been entirely its own doing. Just as in 1903, these elections registered the outrage of Saxon citizens—and not only workers—who were still subjected to unfair voting laws. But it was not the franchise alone that was responsible for individual socialist victories, as other observers attested. Immediately after the elections, the Prussian envoy wrote to Chancellor Theobald von Bethmann Hollweg with an analysis that was uncan-

---

67. See Ritter, *Wahlgeschichtliches Arbeitsbuch*, 180.

nily similar to others that he and his predecessor, Dönhoff, had sent over the previous twenty years. Hohenlohe concluded that "many runoff elections could have been avoided if the nonsocialist parties had cooperated more against the socialists and if they had not squandered their votes on rival candidacies." When the Landtag opened, Hohenlohe ascribed the new, pivotal position of the National Liberals to four factors: the new franchise, the Reich finance reform, the disarray among the nonsocialist parties, and the "unbounded demagogy" that the National Liberals had unleashed against Conservatives. A Saxon government official came to the same conclusion. After discussing the bitter disagreements between Conservatives and National Liberals over plural voting and constituency boundaries, he remarked that disunity among the nonsocialist parties had led them to conduct a campaign "more passionate" than any previous one. In fact, he added, Conservative and National Liberal opponents in various constituencies had furthered the socialist cause in a "spectacular" way.[68] Thus although antisocialist solidarity *seemed* to be well maintained in October 1909—in that the SPD participated in fifty-four of fifty-eight runoff elections and won only ten—one must also take seriously the complaints of the Prussian envoy that the nonsocialist parties contributed to their own defeat by refusing to withdraw competing candidates. Moreover, the electoral record indicates that serious competition between Conservatives and National Liberals occurred in no fewer than thirty-eight of ninety-one constituencies, that is, 42 percent of the total.[69] It is difficult to conceive of any more tangible evidence than this to support the hypothesis that antisocialist solidarity in electoral politics had largely evaporated by the time Bethmann Hollweg became chancellor.[70] But if more evidence were required, it was fated not to come from Saxony; the election of 1909 proved the first, and last, test of the new franchise.

An essay of this scope could never hope to cover more than a fraction of the terrain on which questions about antisocialism and electoral politics in Imperial Germany can be addressed. A closer examination of statistics from the Saxon elections of 1909, for example, can reveal a great deal more about the social standing and political preferences of voters with multiple ballots than has been attempted here. Similarly, there is much more to the story of anti-

---

68. Hohenlohe to Bethmann Hollweg, 23 Oct. and 2 Dec. 1909, in PA AA Bonn, Sachsen Nr. 60, Bd. 8; Oppe, "Die Reform," 394.

69. See Eugen Würzburger, "Die Wahlen für die Zweite Kammer der Ständeversammlung vom Oktober und November 1909," *Zeitschrift des K. Sächsischen Statistischen Landesamtes* 55 (1909): 220–43; ibid., 57, no. 1 (1911): 1–168; and ibid., 58, no. 2 (1912): 259–331. I explained the criteria I used to judge when these parties came into serious competition in the original version of this essay (see introductory note), 308–10.

70. See James Retallack, "The Road to Philippi: The Conservative Party and Bethmann Hollweg's 'Politics of the Diagonal,' 1909–14," in Jones and Retallack, *Between Reform, Reaction, and Resistance,* 261–98.

socialism, even in Saxony, than can be conveyed by focusing on election campaigns and "high politics." Considerable research is also needed to integrate the history of franchise struggles elsewhere in the Reich into a broader picture of liberal successes after 1900. Nevertheless, this essay has tried to suggest the range of possible perspectives from which historians can consider these issues and the interrelationships among them.

Questions about the Saxon franchise may appear more problematic—and perhaps also more interesting—than similar questions about the Prussian and Reichstag franchises because the latter were never overturned or even fundamentally revised in the imperial era. Although Conservatives grumbled on about the Reichstag franchise, and although left liberals unsuccessfully railed against three-class voting in Prussia until the last days of the empire, it was in Saxony (and in other states and cities, too) that legislators were compelled to take the bull by the horns and devise new voting laws that could be put into operation immediately. As in Saxony, legislators everywhere operated under circumstances that limited their insight and effectiveness, even though they may have been only dimly aware of such constraints. For this reason, particular attention has been focused not only on the process of franchise reform itself but also on the personal reflections of individuals who determined its outcome. Some of these figures welcomed the opportunity to conceive and implement radically new franchise schemes. But many of them, as we have seen, shrank from such responsibility.

As Suval and Fairbairn have shown so clearly with reference to the Reichstag franchise, it is how individuals understood, defended, and exercised their right to vote that imparted meaning to Wilhelmine Germany's electoral system. Any reasonably educated Saxon who had followed the course of franchise reform in his or her homeland could have made sense of the various voting schemes in place in German cities and states in 1909—whether based on direct or indirect voting, secret or public voting, mandatory voting, plural voting, tax thresholds, class-based franchises, occupational estates, or proportional representation. But as these terms became common currency in Saxony after 1900, supporters of the nonsocialist parties were forced to reexamine their political allegiances and, as part of that process, to reconsider the scope of the socialist threat both in theory and in practice. As has been shown, Conservatives continued to espouse a relatively unproblematic brand of antisocialism, but liberals in Saxony—as elsewhere in the Reich—found the issue much more perplexing and divisive.

This essay has also tried to illustrate why political designations like "liberal" and "conservative" can be misleading when incautiously ascribed to regional political groupings and government bureaucracies. On balance it is clear that the Saxon National Liberals were neither wholly progressive nor wholly reactionary. But were they principled or opportunistic? Were they devoutly antisocialist—or merely "national"? There is no unequivocal answer.

Conversely, Prussian Conservatives have too long been cast as the quintessential *Herrenmenschen* of the *Kaiserreich,* leaving their party comrades in Saxony and other regions in historical obscurity. While it is generally agreed that the leader of the Prussian Conservatives, Ernst von Heydebrand und der Lasa, eminently deserved his reputation as "the uncrowned king of Prussia," perhaps the time has come to find a place in our picture of the *Kaiserreich* for "the uncrowned king of Saxony."[71]

Lastly, it remains difficult to draw conclusions about the general political orientation of a Saxon state ministry whose members have been rightly described as both conservative (Metzsch) and conservative-liberal (Hohenthal).[72] It may be true, as Karlheinz Blaschke has written, that Saxon officials enjoyed relative political autonomy in a land where there was "no court camarilla, no gray eminences, no shadow cabinet behind the scenes, and no company of favorites." But did the *Nebenregierung* of "Paul & Co., G.m.b.H." manage to perpetuate itself in more covert form after 1909? Moreover, when we consider them collectively, did Saxon ministers act as an anchor on the ship of state, as the wartime interior minister claimed? Or did they function instead as a rudder, seeking to avoid dangerous shoals but determined to steer a positive course? Simple answers do not present themselves here, either. Perhaps all that can be said is that the Saxon ministries headed by Metzsch and Hohenthal deserve our attention—if not necessarily our applause—by virtue of their determination to push the cause of franchise reform after 1903, their willingness to implement significant parts of the liberals' political agenda, and their strategic contribution to the demise of Conservative hegemony in the third-largest state of Imperial Germany.[73]

One aim of this essay has been to provide new impetus to those already working on these and related questions through regional studies. By fusing regional history and electoral history, we may be able to penetrate more deeply, and probe more widely, beneath the rhetoric of antisocialism that has for so long confounded our understanding of mass politics in the *Kaiserreich.*

71. Cf. James Retallack, "Dr. jur. Ernst von Heydebrand und der Lasa," in *The Encyclopedic History of Modern Germany,* ed. Dieter K. Buse and Juergen C. Doerr (New York, forthcoming 1996); James Retallack, "Ein glückloser Parteiführer in Bismarcks Diensten—Otto von Helldorff-Bedra (1833–1908)," in *Konservative Politiker in Deutschland,* ed. Hans-Christof Kraus (Berlin, 1995), 185–203; and Retallack, "Die 'liberalen' Konservativen?"

72. For this and the following, see Blaschke, "Das Königreich Sachsen," 97–102, including the citation from the unpublished papers of Interior Minister Dr. Walter Koch, Sächsisches Hauptstaatsarchiv Dresden, Bd. 1, 160–67; cf. Schmidt, "Die Zentralverwaltung."

73. On opportunities for reform at the regional level, see chap. 2 in James Retallack, *Germany in the Age of Kaiser Wilhelm II* (Basingstoke, forthcoming 1996); Lässig, Pohl, and Retallack, *Modernisierung und Region;* Gall and Langewiesche, *Liberalismus und Region;* and Grebing, Mommsen, and Rudolph, *Demokratie und Emanzipation.*

The Myth of an Autonomous State: Industrialists, Junkers, and Social Policy in Imperial Germany

George Steinmetz

The Prussian state and the various historical incarnations of the state in Germany[1] between 1870 and 1945 have played a prominent role in the ideal-typical unconscious of the institutionalist (or "state-centered") tradition of state theory.[2] Theda Skocpol's emphasis on Max Weber and Otto Hintze as central forefathers of the "state-centered" perspective underscores the theoretical centrality of Germany to the statist approach (See Skocpol 1985, 7–8; Hintze 1962–67; Weber 1971; Beetham 1985; Büsch and Erbe 1983; and Kocka 1983). Skocpol represents the Prussian state as archetypically autonomous, calling it an "extraordinarily disciplined and efficient administrative machine" (1979, 106). Although the traditional Prussian landed nobility—the Junkers—

This is a substantially revised version of an article that was originally published in *Comparative Social Research* 12 (1990): 239–93. I am grateful to the editor of that volume for permission to reprint sections of the earlier article. Special thanks are also due to Richard Biernacki, Julia Hell, Bob Jessop, Edward Laumann, Ann Orloff, Adelheid von Saldern, and Daniel Verdier for comments on an earlier draft.

1. I will refer to the Prussian and German states as the "German" state throughout, although a real German state emerged only gradually over the course of the nineteenth century and was finally constructed as a political unit at the end of the 1860s. This shorthand is justifiable, even though the Prussian state continued to exist separately after 1871, since Prussia was intertwined with the German state in terms of competences and personnel until the fall of the Second Empire.

2. By the "institutionalist" (or state-centered) approach to the state, I am referring to the work of contemporary theorists such as Theda Skocpol, Stephen Krasner, Alfred Stepan, and Eric A. Nordlinger, in addition to the earlier writers mentioned in the text. Contemporary sociologists such as Charles Tilly (1975a, 1975b, 1985, 1990) and Fred Block (1977, 1980) seem to stand in an intermediate position between state-centered theory and an opposing set of approaches that explain the state in terms of societal forces. Recent discussions of the statist perspective include Evans et al. 1985; Almond 1988; Brenner 1988; Cammack 1989; Jessop 1990, 278–88; Jürgens 1990; Krasner 1984; and March and Olsen 1984.

were still economically dominant in the early nineteenth century, Skocpol argues that they were "in no institutional position to block concerted policy initiatives" undertaken by the state (1979, 108).[3] This reading of the Prussian/ German state as essentially autonomous from the dominant social class echoes the judgments of German writers over the course of several centuries, reaching back from postwar historiography in East and West Germany to Carl Schmitt, Weber, Hegel, and even the cameralists of the eighteenth century.[4]

The thesis of the autonomous state has coexisted somewhat uneasily with an alternative reading according to which the Prussian and German states are beholden to the Junkers, even after industrial capitalism had become the leading sector of the economy in the *Kaiserreich*. This definition of the state as basically aristocratic is, after all, the political component of the German exceptionalism narrative (Eley 1984). I will discuss the thesis of the "Junker state" and David Blackbourn and Geoff Eley's critiques below. What is crucial to recognize at the outset is that both the autonomous-state and Junker-state interpretations, when applied to the *Kaiserreich,* are compatible with statist theory, since both suggest a rather radical autonomy of the state from society.[5] Both see the *Kaiserreich* as an era in which the German state plied a course independent of industrial capitalism, acting at key moments and in key policy areas against the interests of German industrialists. Even if the two interpretations disagree about who actually controlled the state, they both imply a rather radical disjuncture between political and economic forms, for industrial capitalism was the leading economic sector in the German Empire by the 1880s at the latest (see below). Such noncorrespondence between state policy and class structure is paradoxical from the standpoint of societal theories of the state.

A few historians depart from the prevailing wisdom, describing the German political system from the 1860s onward as expressing the interests or hegemony of the bourgeoisie (Eley 1984, 1986; Machtan and Milles 1980).[6]

---

3. In a significant though perhaps unintentional elision, Skocpol writes that the Prussian state later became the "core of. . . Imperial Germany" (1979, 109), rather than the core of the state in Imperial Germany, thus reducing society to state.

4. East German historians wavered between an interpretation of the Imperial German state as controlled by the Junkers or by industrial capital or as relatively autonomous; indeed, these notions are often combined in a single analysis (e.g., Gutsche 1976, esp. 51). In another study the "system of rule of the empire of 1871" is described as both principally "bourgeois" and as dominated by the Junkers (Canis 1982, 24, 31). On the various strands of cameralism, see Maier 1980; Raeff 1983; and Small 1909.

5. The differences and tensions between the Junker-state and autonomous-state readings are discussed in Bonham 1983, 1984; and Steinmetz 1993.

6. Somewhat surprisingly, this view of the imperial state was not characteristic of the historiography of the former German Democratic Republic, whose historians frequently described the empire as dominated by the Junkers, with industrial capital playing a supporting role. Several contradictory impulses were operative in pulling East German accounts of the imperial state in

These writers acknowledge the German state's unusually active role in directing nineteenth-century economic and social development, yet they insist that
the state promoted capitalist industrialization rather than simply propping up
precapitalist classes or pursuing military goals at the expense of industry. A
central difficulty confronting such interpretations, however, is to explain why
state policy should have been aligned with business interests.

To clarify the questions that need to be asked about the German state, the
first section of this essay will review two of the leading positions in the current
discussions of state theory. These approaches correspond roughly to the historiographical views of the German state mentioned above, which are reviewed
in more detail in the second section.

My goal here is to adjudicate between contending views of the state by
weighing the descriptive evidence about German state policy. To narrow the
analysis down to manageable dimensions, I will focus on poor relief and social
insurance policy in Imperial Germany. Specifically, I will ask whether these
policies were related systematically to industrial capitalist interests, or whether
policy-making deviated regularly from industrial interests. The third section
looks at national policy-making concerning poor relief and related issues,
arguing that these policies were components of a program of industrial growth.
Relief programs were not only favorable to industrialization but were also
formally modern (a term that is used here in a contextual, historicist sense).
The fourth part turns to the imperial welfare state, arguing that industrialists
participated in shaping social insurance and that their interests triumphed over
those of the agrarians. National social insurance was also formally bourgeois,
and more modern than the comparable policies of Germany's economically
more advanced British neighbor.

Having established that German social policy corresponded in various
respects to the requirements of industrialization, in my conclusion I propose a
tentative explanation for this isomorphism between state and society. I argue

---

different directions: (1) a commitment to the basic Marxist theorem of base and superstructure,
which required that states match their economic bases; (2) a dogmatic attachment to almost
anything written by Marx, Engels, or Lenin, whose comments on the German state were notoriously underdeveloped and self-contradictory; (3) the historical legacy of Nazism, which in the
early years of the GDR led to historical interpretations along the lines of the *deutsche Misere,*
emphasizing the survival of prebourgeois values and elites as explaining Germany's profound
deviation from the West (cf. Abusch 1947; and Lukács 1954); (4) the efforts "by the nascent East
German state to define itself as the heir of a progressive, democratic tradition" (Iggers 1988, 16–
17); and (5) the GDR's competition with the West, where in the 1950s the empire was being
evaluated positively and where "reactionary powers" were said to be using "unification and the
Reich as examples and models for impending political decisions" (Seeber and Wolter 1972). The
result of these clashing pressures was a great deal of confusion in most East German writing on the
imperial state. The clearest East German work employed the concept of "Bonapartism" favored by
critical historians in the West.

that public policy was aligned with industrial capitalism due to the ongoing socialization of many of the state's civil servants into modernizing an ethos supportive of industrial capitalism, and due to the state's increasing dependence on resources generated by "private" actors in civil society.

State Theory

Neo-Marxist Theories of the State and the "Class Correspondence Thesis"

At the most general level, Marxist and neo-Marxist writings on the state have in common the claim that states located within capitalist societies tend to reproduce and promote capitalism.[7] Some neo-Marxists make the slightly weaker argument that there are broad but powerful structural limits on dysfunctional state policies.[8]

How do Marxists account for this complementarity between state and economy? The simplest mechanism is the ability of the dominant classes to manipulate the state directly. But the fact that parliamentary systems usually preclude such direct (or "instrumental") control by capitalists, allowing non-propertied groups opportunities to register their will, has provided Marxist state theory with its central puzzle. States are subject to numerous pressures from subordinate groups, and business is often too fragmented to pursue a unified policy. Yet most neo-Marxists have nonetheless insisted that class correspondence (defined as a broad complementarity between public policy and dominant class interests) exists as a sort of boundary condition, regardless of the specific relations between business and the state. Given that business leaders do not generally monopolize political offices in capitalist societies, the central question is, What guarantees that the state will not be used against the interests of the propertied classes?

Marxists have proposed three main accounts of class correspondence other than direct capitalist control of the state. The simplest explanation for an overrepresentation of capitalist interests in policy is that capitalists and their organizations usually possess more resources than other classes (or resources that are more easily mobilized; see Offe and Wiesenthal 1980). The political

---

7. There is no space here for a detailed discussion and comparison of Marxist and neo-Marxist state theories; see the excellent treatments in Jessop 1982, 1985.

8. The claim that public policies in capitalist societies are functionally related to social relations need not be equivalent to arguing that the state is explained functionally. Without repeating the familiar disputes about functionalist explanation in Marxism, suffice it to mention the following clarification (made in Cohen 1978): the state can be functional (i.e., beneficial) for production relations without being functionally explained by those relations. As will become clear, I am inclined toward a nonfunctionalist explanation of German state policy, but I also will suggest that such policies were generally functional for capitalist industrialization.

access of powerful groups may also be enhanced by the state's bureaucratic insulation. But such explanations are weakened in societies like nineteenth-century Germany, where industrial capital faced other powerful and mobilized upper classes with very different interests. As we will see below, German policymakers were frequently forced to choose between these two resource-rich groups.

A second argument is that a range of "structural selectivities"—laws, institutional rules, and norms—are built into the state apparatus itself. The result of these structural biases is that policies are shaped, selected, and censored in ways that systematically benefit a specific class (see, e.g., Offe 1974, 1984b; Offe and Ronge 1984; and Jessop 1983, 1990, 1982, 103–11, 164–65). To avoid functionalism, the original implantation of such selectivities into the state is often traced to active interventions by conflicting social classes, parties, organizations, social movements, and the like (see Esping-Andersen, Friedland, and Wright 1976; and Wright 1978, 181–252). Such biases may be viewed as contingent rather than necessary outcomes, but once they are established, they obviate the need for direct intervention by their beneficiaries.

The third account focuses on the state's supposed exclusion from large-scale engagement in productive activities. Thus prevented from becoming self-supporting, the state is forced into dependence on resources generated in the private economy—taxes, credit, and the like. State policies that overstep certain boundaries of acceptability to business will normally be met by disinvestment or capital flight. In essence, state managers cannot erode business confidence without undermining their own position.[9]

Although this third solution offers an explanation for class correspondence, it still has several problems. First, the state's dependence on funds generated in the private economy can describe only the outer limits, but not the actual content, of policy. Second, it is unclear why state managers may not be led to sabotage the state, either inadvertently or deliberately. The theorists could respond that this would lead inevitably to a business backlash. Yet even in the face of an alienated capitalist class, state officials could attempt to retain power, guide investment, and extract revenues by force. A third problem with this argument is that it relies on the subjective perceptions of class actors and state managers and assumes inappropriately that these perceptions will coincide with objective economic interests. As indicated by the psychological reference in the phrase "business confidence," the intolerability of public pol-

---

9. Block (1977, 1980) suggests that the private economy's ability to censor state managers' initiatives is lowered during economic crises and wars, events that give officials more leeway. A similar argument was proposed by Rudolf Goldscheid and Joseph Schumpeter after World War I, analyzing the limitations imposed on the state's social-policy initiatives through its dependence upon tax revenue. In Hans-Ulrich Wehler's summary of Goldscheid's theory, "the state's fiscal arrangements hold the key to an understanding of its true social constitution" (Wehler 1985, 137; see also Goldscheid 1926; and Schumpeter 1918).

icies is at least partially subjective (at least up to the threshold where the state appropriates the entire surplus). State policy will affect investment behavior only if business perceives it as endangering profits. The theory brackets the ideological construction of politics. Finally, the assumption that states cannot become financially autonomous from society is derived logically rather than demonstrated empirically. Although it has been the historical norm in societies dominated by capitalist property relations for states to be separated from production,[10] no reasons have been adduced for the necessity of such a separation. It seems more reasonable to regard tax dependency and exclusion from production not as universal but as constraints that state officials frequently face.

State-Centered Theory and the Thesis of State Autonomy

The so-called state-centered approach is actually a cluster of perspectives and emphases: a Hintzean view of the state as a personality or actor, embodying the sui generis interests of its political incumbents; an "institutionalist" focus on the ways in which state structures, capacities, and discourses shape the incidence and form of policy outputs (i.e., the state as structural constraint); and finally what Skocpol (1985, 21) calls a "Toquevillian" concern with the ways in which states shape civil society. State-centered theorists vary in terms of the vigor of their rejection of class and societal dynamics as determinants of state action. In this section I will distinguish two main elaborations of the state-centered perspective and examine their treatment of business-state relations.

The first variant is compatible with the argument that states tend to promote industrial capitalism, but the reasons given for that outcome differ from those suggested by neo-Marxists. It is argued that officials pursue their own agendas, although they must rely on class forces in civil society in order to do so. One way of formulating the state's ultimate dependence on business has already been discussed under the rubric of neo-Marxism (again accenting the fluidity of the boundaries between statist and class theories): state elites are driven to promote accumulation in order to pursue their own goals. Other theorists trace the need to promote capitalist industry specifically to the pressures of the international system of competing states. States' intrinsic territoriality pushes rulers to defend or expand their states' geographic boundaries (Mann 1988, 139). At a minimum, state officials must promote industry at levels adequate for national defense. There are divergent understandings of the effects of such interstate pressures. For Charles Tilly (1990), the constraint on absolutist states pursuing their irreducibly military aims lay in their need to

---

10. An exception is cases where external sources of revenue or military weaponry are so generous that political leaders are liberated from reliance on the domestic economy; see Tilly 1990 218–20.

strike bargains with merchant capitalists in order to gain the credit necessary for fighting wars. As warfare became more industrialized, political officials also came to believe that only private industry could provide the weaponry needed to compete militarily (Steinmetz 1993, chap. 4). As a result, states were increasingly tied to industrial producers.

At least two other forms of pressure may have led states to foster industrial capitalism. Rulers' desire for domestic stability, valued as an end in itself, may have wedded them to capital. For example, state managers might accommodate private industry because they fear the destabilizing consequences of unemployment. A final source of pressure could derive from competition for standing in the international states system. This striving for prestige is exemplified by nineteenth-century governments' enthusiastic participation in universal expositions and industrial fairs (Plum 1977). What a nation needs to rise in international rankings of distinction has varied historically, of course, but most of the ingredients since the nineteenth century have presupposed a booming industrial economy.[11]

In sum, states may seek to attain domestic peace or the resources for war or international political competition by overseeing profitable capital accumulation.[12] The underlying logic here is usually understood as more "state centered" than "society centered," since the motor is "internal" to the state. But state elites are forced to accommodate actors in civil society to attain their goals. Like neo-Marxist theories, these attenuated statist views imply that policies will meet the interests of major sectors of business. The distinction between this approach and society-centered theories is really one of emphasis.

A second version of statist theory poses a stronger challenge to societal theories of politics (see Skocpol 1979; Orloff and Skocpol 1984). This approach suggests that officials and bureaucrats often develop policies independently of social interests and pressures, and that their autonomy from dominant classes is potentially complete. States in capitalist societies may reach a "tipping point" (Block 1980), at which they free themselves entirely from the

---

11. In early- to mid-nineteenth-century Europe, the key ingredient may have been a positive trade balance, quality manufactured goods, or a national railroad system; later in the century, overall industrial output was probably more central. Military power was another obvious asset. From 1945 to the 1960s, the emphasis was probably as much on democracy and relative distributional equality, while the current period again emphasizes material rather than normative values.

12. This provides a further twist to Block's argument that war produces the conditions for state autonomization, but it also forces these autonomous states to accommodate industry. Conditions that could loosen this dependency include state takeover of the military industry and a willingness to rely on foreign arms supplies. Yet reliance on arms trade rather than indigenous arms production may create a dangerous situation of dependency and vulnerability to boycott. Where a nation monopolizes some internationally essential product, this danger may be attenuated; the obvious example is oil states, which could be the "exception which proves the rule" (Brenner 1988) of state heteronomy.

moorings and constraints of society and are able to violate the interests of the most powerful socioeconomic actors.

Class-correspondence theories are not weakened by evidence that state managers are elaborating policies in bureaucratic isolation. If it is to be more than a refinement of other approaches, therefore, state-centered theory ultimately requires the demonstration of "class noncorrespondence," that is, instances in which state officials directly and systematically transgress the interests of the economically dominant class(es). Statists need to show that the state can be "captured" by a declining class[13] or that it can be used by state managers to their own benefit, solidifying themselves into a self-reproducing *Beamtenstand* (bureaucratic class).

The German Welfare State as an Example of State Autonomy

The most generous test of state-centered theory would involve examining states with strong administrative capacities and executive leaders, both of which are expected to be conducive to state autonomy (Evans et al. 1985). Much of the state-centered work has focused on Anglo-American states, however, with their relatively weak bureaucracies, or on twentieth-century Scandinavian states, which have been penetrated by social democratic parties that are the ostensible instruments of social interests. The German state in the later nineteenth century seems more likely to fit the statist scenario; it had a rationalized and well-trained Weberian bureaucracy, and its leaders, especially Bismarck, conveyed an intense belief in the notion of raison d'état.

Assessments of state autonomy should also focus on contested policy areas, such as the welfare state.[14] Yet the world's first welfare state, which emerged in Germany in the 1870s and 1880s, has not yet been the object of a self-consciously statist analysis. The central goal of this essay is to explore the relations between social policy and social classes in what can be seen as the Germanic "home territory" of statist theory.[15] The questions that guide the analysis are:

13. Note that Marxists have often claimed that states may represent the interests of ascendant or nascent classes; the clearest example is the traditional Marxist argument about the absolutist state as a transitional but essentially "bourgeois" state (cf. Engels, Poulantzas). Class correspondence is preserved here by extending the time horizon, although the mechanisms by which such a "proactive" correspondence is assured are not explained.

14. See Weir and Skocpol 1985; Skocpol and Ikenberry 1983; Orloff and Skocpol 1984; Orloff 1985; and Weir et al. 1988. It should also be noted that explanations of the welfare state have also been the strength of the class-correspondence theory, in both its more orthodox Marxist versions (e.g., Müller and Neusüss 1975; Booth 1978; Jessop 1982, 78–141) and its neo- or post-Marxist guise (e.g., O'Connor 1973; Offe 1984b).

15. As Karl Erich Born (1972, 180) notes, there are probably fifty different definitions of the term "social policy" (*Sozialpolitik*). In this essay, "social policy" is defined to encompass any intervention into the realm understood by contemporaries as "the social." This definition includes

1. Was state policy related in a systematic way to dominant class interests, or was the state able to detach itself from those interests?
2. If dominant class interests were related systematically to state policy,
   how was such correspondence achieved?

To make sense of the state's relations to dominant class interests and
actions, I will focus first on the content of public policies, and secondly on the
formal and organizational aspects of state interventions. More specifically, I
will evaluate the match between welfare programs and the expressed wishes of
different segments of the industrial bourgeoisie and the agrarian Junker class,
and then examine the policies' fit with an abstract, formal logic of industrial
capitalism. I will examine two different sets of policies: poor relief and social
insurance, exploring both programs at the local and national levels of the
state.[16]

To anticipate my conclusion, I will argue that both poor relief and social
insurance policies coincided with the interests of the leading fractions of the
business elite and corresponded formally to the general structural features of
industrial capitalist society. This match came about through different mechanisms at the national and local levels. Industrial elites directly dominated the
local level of government, especially before 1900, but their impact was only
indirect at the national level. It is therefore possible to discern a "pristine"
model of society-centered politics in the municipal realm, i.e., a politics based
on direct connections between state power and bourgeois agents. Industry and
commerce provided both the personnel and the social base for the urban local
state. Nationally, key industrialists took a positive stance toward various welfare policies. Yet these interventions were not the major reason for class corre-

---

traditional poor relief as well as social insurance and covers the local and regional levels of the
polity. Naturally, there are certain areas of late-nineteenth-century social policy that cannot be
treated here (see Ritter 1986; Steinmetz 1993).

16. It is necessary to challenge the notion of a unified state. The concept of the state must be
disaggregated not only horizontally—looking separately at the military, fiscal, welfare, educational, and other apparatuses (see, e.g., Geyer 1984)—but also vertically—distinguishing the local,
regional, and central levels. My use of the term "local state" does not imply acceptance of a
specific theoretical orientation whereby the local level is seen as performing certain functions in a
hierarchical division of political labor among different parts of a "state system." See Cockburn
1977 for the origin of the term "local state"; see Clark and Dear 1984; Sharpe 1984; Saunders
1979, 1982; and especially Greer 1987 for excellent discussion of different views.

While it is certainly true that the local states in Germany were delegated specific tasks by
central governments, they had a great deal of autonomy in the implementation of such tasks and in
fiscal terms. Nonetheless, local governments were statelike on a number of dimensions: they
exercised legally binding and (generally) legitimate authority backed by violence; their sovereignty operated within a bounded territory; they were institutionally differentiated both internally and externally, i.e., from civil society; and their binding decisions were made in the name of
the general will (see Jessop 1990, 338–69).

spondence of national policy. Instead, state elites' commitment to industrializ-ation was prompted by a dual concern with social order and with international competitiveness. This resulted in an overlap of state and industrial interests, obviating direct business interventions. Nonbourgeois German officials were compelled to promote capitalist industrialization, even while they pursued ultimate goals not fundamentally different from those of classical absolutist states. One result was that even aspects of state policy that were far removed from clashes of economic interest and direct capitalist intervention assumed a "bourgeois" form. The appropriate outcome from a class-correspondence per-spective thus resulted from quasi-statist dynamics, and not from a complete subordination of state to society.

While this essay is primarily structured around discussions of state theory, it is also an appraisal of the dominant view of the imperial state among German specialists. Here I am concerned with the thesis, outlined below, that Imperial Germany was somehow politically backward, exceptional, or premodern in comparison with its neighbors. The demonstration that welfare policy was essentially bourgeois is a partial refutation of the thesis of the German *Kaiser-reich's* "exceptionalism." Indeed, German policies actually foreshadowed many of the prevailing forms of welfare policy in twentieth-century Europe, rather than lagging behind or merely keeping pace. Social policies at the urban and national levels were in the avant-garde in organizational terms—a quality of the programs hereafter referred to in shorthand as their "modernity." This is not a judgment of the programs' value, but rather of the degree to which they anticipated features of an ideal-typical model of later social policy.[17]

State and Social Policy in Imperial Germany and the Exceptionalism Thesis

Studies of the emergence of the world's first welfare state in Germany during the 1880s have been deeply conditioned by the thesis of German exceptional-ism. Eley (1981, 1984, 1986) and Blackbourn (1984) have criticized this view of German development as having followed a unique, "exceptional" path, or *Sonderweg*, profoundly different from the other major capitalist countries. At the core of the exceptionalism thesis is a basic disjuncture between the econ-omy, class, and social structures on the one hand, and political and cultural subsystems on the other. In a typical formulation, "the internal structure of the *Kaiserreich* was riven by a discrepancy between the political and social con-

---

17. "Modernity" refers here to a group of formal dimensions of welfare policy that approxi-mate an ideal-typical twentieth-century model. These dimensions were embraced for reasons of political and administrative efficiency and do not have any evident class logic. While referring to them as indicators of relative modernity, I hope that this periodization avoids any essentialist or teleological insinuations. Modernity is intended here as a historically specific ideal type.

stitution" (Düding 1972, 15).[18] According to authors as different as Thorstein Veblen, Alexander Gerschenkron, Ralf Dahrendorf, and Barrington Moore, Jr., the historical development of Germany was deeply conditioned by the absence of a bourgeois revolution against the precapitalist elite and by the prominent position of the landed nobility in both society and the state throughout the nineteenth and much of the twentieth century.

This image of the neofeudal survivals in recent German history leads historians to invert a number of traditional Marxist views and to recast as atavistic certain elements of German society that were seen as specifically modern by contemporaries. Thus, for example, it is argued that the German social democratic labor movement did not provide other nations with a glimpse of their own future but was instead an indication of the backwardness of the German polity. The highly crystallized class boundaries and class identities in Imperial Germany are understood as a sign of that society's backwardness, and not as an expression of the insistence of class structure. Prussia's efficient bureaucracy and military and Germany's early universal male suffrage for elections to the Reichstag are read as indicators of a profound historical retardation, and not as models of political modernization.

An area that has elicited less discussion is the precocious pre-1914 German welfare state. Unlike many nineteenth-century contemporaries in Germany and abroad, more recent scholarship has often coded Bismarck's social policies as a result of neofeudal paternalism and the weakness of liberalism, or as disqualified by the manipulative motives that inspired it. Hans-Ulrich Wehler (1985, 136) contrasts Bismarck's social insurance with a vaguely specified "modern style of state intervention," one whose "proper effect" would be to redistribute national income. Dahrendorf refers to the German welfare state as "authoritarian" and claims that social policy "immobilized" people rather than promoting capitalism (Dahrendorf 1967, 40, 47, 193, 252). Even studies that acknowledge certain progressive aspects of the early German social interventions discuss them under the aegis of the "defense of traditional authority" (Rimlinger 1971, 112).[19]

Because the *Kaiserreich* was the era in which industrial capitalism became economically dominant in Germany (articulated with a variety of "earlier" modes of production), it is critical for evaluating the exceptionalism

---

18. Mielke speaks of the conservative political opposition to a proper "synchronization of economic and political development" (1976, 17).

19. Another approach is to single out national social insurance as one of Germany's few "positive" deviations from the Western norm—although admitting the modernity of such a key element of German politics would seem to undermine the coherence of the *Sonderweg* thesis. See Puhle 1981, 45, and the more recent opinions of Wehler, which seem to exempt municipal politics and state social policy (as well as scientific research) from the negative balance sheet on the *Kaiserreich* (Wehler 1983, 33).

thesis. Societal theories, including Marxism, expect the rise of industrial capitalism to be accompanied by a series of parallel changes in civil society and the state. But the supposedly distinguishing feature of German development is that the most important of these concomitant effects failed to materialize, even during the height of capitalist industrialization.

Historiography and the German State: *Junkerstaat* or Autonomous State?

There are at least two major interpretations of the Imperial German state that challenge the view that business interests were at the heart of state policy. The first, exemplified by Hegel, Gustav Schmoller, and Hintze, accepts the traditional view of the Prussian bureaucracy as "a neutral force above the competing particular interests of party and class, embodying the universal interest of society as a whole, and endowed with a special political wisdom" (Beetham 1985, 63). According to this reading, the German state stood "above the classes" (Conze 1985, 79). This interpretation provides the closest fit with the strong state-autonomy thesis. Yet it often conflates the attempts by state officials to sail an antibusiness course and their actual successes in doing so.[20]

The second and more common challenge to the economy-centered analysis is what I call the "main" version of the exceptionalism thesis. Rather than arguing for state autonomy, it is claimed here that the state was beholden to Junker interests, which it favored against industry in a number of key policy areas (Bonham 1984, 210).[21] This assertion flies in the face of even the most

---

20. Historians' treatment of the "Hibernia affair" of the early 1900s is an example of a misleading reinforcement of the image of state autonomy. In 1904, the Prussian state challenged industrialists by attempting to nationalize the third-largest coal company in the country, Hibernia. The stakes in the Hibernia affair have typically been assessed in the alternative "Would 'the state' control the economy, or would the economy overwhelm the state?" (Medalen 1978, 93). The Hibernia sale was supported by the Conservative and Center Parties, the leading antimonopolistic employers' association (Bund der Industriellen), and, most importantly, by the agrarians (Mottek 1968, 26). For some contemporaries and historians, the Prussian state's brazenness seems to have overshadowed the fact that it failed in its bid for power: business prevailed, and the Hibernia mine was not nationalized.

21. Those who insist on the German state's autonomy or orientation toward Junker interests often simultaneously describe it as "Bonapartist." But this description of the Imperial German state contrasts sharply with the archetypical Bonapartism of the French Second Empire. The regime of Napoleon III, with its modernizing and proindustry Saint-Simonian advisers, systematically promoted business interests (Plessis 1979, 85–90). As Wolfgang Mommsen writes, Bonapartism refers to a "long-term stabilization of a bourgeois system through plebiscitary means" (1983, 196; see also Draper 1977, 385–463). Bonapartism is the result of a circumstance in which the bourgeoisie is unable to rule alone or to construct viable alliances, and thus "confesses that . . . in order to save its purse it must forfeit the crown" (Marx 1970b, 436). By emphasizing the noncapitalist thrust of imperial state interventions, the standard literature on the *Kaiserreich* thus

flexible class-correspondence theories of the state. Arguments about the privileging of agrarian interests over industrial ones are made with regard to the tariff reforms of 1878–79 and 1902, the finance reform of 1908, the granting of special state subsidies and tax breaks to agrarians, the Stock Exchange Act of 1896, and the fights from 1894 through 1901 on the construction of the Mittellandkanal (a waterway linking the western and eastern parts of Prussia).[22] The Mittellandkanal debate, in which the agrarians gained a series of key victories, "indicated how the administration was ultimately willing to side with the Junkers against heavy industry" (Segre 1980, 334).[23]

The literature on the *Sammlung* between agriculture and heavy industry (the "alliance of iron and rye") often suggests that conflicts of interest between agrarians and industrial capitalists were ultimately amenable to resolution through trade-offs—or else that the two groups' common interest in "keeping the proletariat from gaining control of state power" (Kehr 1973, 276) was sufficient to harness them to one another.[24] The locus classicus of this assessment of the possibility for compromise is the literature on the 1902 tariff reforms and the navy bills, according to which industry granted the reforms in exchange for the bills (Stegmann 1970; Wehler 1985, 97; Barkin 1970, 1987; and Kehr 1973, 276). There was a difference, however, in the relative capacities of the two economic classes to abide by such compromises. Heavy industry could survive and even flourish behind the tariff walls and was therefore ultimately predisposed to accept tariffs for the sake of antisocialist unity.[25]

---

undermines the comparison with the French Second Empire. The use of the term seems more appropriate for writers who view the imperial state as slanted toward capitalist industry.

22. On the battles over these reforms, see Kehr 1973, 283 n. 4; Horn 1958, 1964; Baudis and Nussbaum 1978, 115; Mielke 1976, 22; Barkin 1970; Witt 1970; Born 1957, 164; and Bonham 1985.

23. It is also argued that Junker interests triumphed over conservative-agrarian ideologies in one key area: the Russian question. Whereas conservatives favored an alliance of the monarchies against the democratic Western states, agrarians' interests were threatened most directly by Russian grain. The German-Russian alliance, of course, eventually collapsed, and the key domestic factor contributing to this was the new trade treaty, which was "extorted" from the Russian government under duress following the 1905 revolution. Thus agrarians' economic interests took the upper hand over their political interests. See Kehr 1973, 273–74, especially n. 3.

24. On the *Sammlung*, see Stegmann 1970; and Wehler 1985, 94–99. Recent critical discussions of the model include Pflanze 1983; and Eley 1986, 110–53. Eckart Kehr's uneasy combination of the *Junkerstaat* and *Sammlung* theses is characteristic of later writers. Even "without open public demand," he writes, "Germany was guided according to the desires of capitalistic economy" (1973, 261); elsewhere, however, he throws into question the functionality of the state's interventions for industry (e.g., 1973, 277).

25. This is despite the complaints of organizations such as the heavy-industrial Centralverband Deutscher Industrieller (CDI), whose congresses in the 1890s and thereafter are filled with complaints about agrarians. See CDI, *Verhandlungen, Mitteilungen und Berichte,* no. 100, "Sitzung des Ausschusses" on 5 May 1905, 22–23, 28–29. As the CDI chief Henry Axel Bueck complained, the CDI had inspired the creation of a *wirtschaftlicher Ausschuss* (an advisory council

Agrarians, however, were less able to compromise. The frequent emphasis on the iron-rye alliance notwithstanding, it is clear that in many policy areas a true alliance was impossible. Policies favoring industrialization appeared to threaten the very survival of the eastern agrarian system. Most strongly opposed were programs that loosened the bonds of rural labor or raised the attractiveness or plausibility of migration to the cities and factories. As one analyst puts it,

> To the extent that [the Junkers] were buying fertilizers and agricultural machines they had a vested interest that industry would develop somewhere: preferably not in Germany, however, since the factories would have allured [*sic*] labor into the cities and away from the eastern estates. . . . The manufacturers were of course oriented in the opposite direction: as they envisaged the question, industrial growth should not be discouraged even if it was bound in the long run to undermine the economic and political strength of the landed entrepreneurs. The cherished hope of the latter, that Germany would be a static grain-exporting agricultural nation under their own control, was antithetical to that of the manufacturing class. (Segre 1980, 332)

Sandro Segre voices the orthodoxy of a wide array of historical studies of the empire when he writes that "the administration . . . pursued the alliance of all the conservative forces even at the cost of hampering the country's industrial growth." Although they were allied with heavy industry, the agrarians "had it their own way" when the two interests clashed (332–33). Similarly, Otto Pflanze argues that for Bismarck "the protection of agrarian interests [was] the highest duty of economic policy," and "the course he followed was agrarian or even anticapitalist"; Bismarck attacked one branch of industry after another during the 1870s and 1880s (1983, 158, 192). Earlier in the century, Robert Michels claimed that it was "not the legitimate representatives of the industrial-capitalist economic order, the 'bourgeoisie,' but the legitimate representatives of an essentially antiquated economic system, feudalism, [who] set for the empire its policy abroad, and also and especially its internal direction and goal" (quoted in Kehr 1973, 277).

There are differing views of how this correspondence came about. Some authors emphasize agrarian recruitment into the upper bureaucracy or the aristocratic heritage of the major Prussian and imperial officials, such as Bismarck himself. John Gillis writes that by the 1870s "the civil service was . . . firmly connected to agrarian interests" (1968, 127). According to Hans-

---

similar to the Zollbeirat, or Tariff Advisory Board of the early 1890s), but the government "has stuffed it with the most extreme agrarian interests" (31). In general, however, heavy industry does not seem to have strongly opposed the tariffs (cf. Kehr 1973, 297 ff.).

Peter Ullmann (1976), the Junkers' ability to exercise "passive influence" over German officials was enhanced by values shared by the two groups. Other writers focus on alleged purges of the bureaucracy during the 1880s, which were tied to laws compelling bureaucrats to defend the official positions of the Kaiser and the chancellor.[26] Emphasis is often placed on the powerful agrarian pressure groups, especially the more radical ones that arose in the 1890s. Whatever the mechanisms, this argument differs from those that portray the state elite as autonomous from civil society—although the two theses are often merged in specific analyses.[27]

Marxist Theory and the Critique of German Exceptionalism

The elements of the exceptionalism thesis that have elicited the most critical commentary are the underdeveloped democratization of political relations and the missing "embourgeoisement" (*Verbürgerlichung*) of values and norms in everyday life. The critics of the *Sonderweg* thesis have paid relatively little attention to business-state relations. The exceptionalists' image of the German state is central to my current purposes, however.

Eley's writings have attempted to reformulate the questions about state and society in Imperial Germany. With respect to political liberalism, Eley's interrogation of the *Sonderweg* thesis has involved a quite persuasive critique

---

26. Kehr (1965) made the original argument about the purge of the bureaucracy under Robert von Puttkamer as Prussian minister of the interior. See Anderson and Barkin 1982 for an important critique of this thesis; also Morsey 1957, esp. 186–242.

27. There is a great deal of confusion between these two arguments. Gary Bonham notes that the perception by the "liberal" critics of the Wilhelmine bureaucracy of "an independent administration appears to be contradicted by their contention that it was also dominated by a landed aristocratic social elite" (1984, 207). This conflation is even present in most current writings on the Wilhelmine state, including Wehler (1985). A further dilemma is that the so-called Kehrites (cf. Puhle 1978; Eley 1986) are often considered Marxist because of their emphasis on class control of the state. Yet their assumption that the Junkers controlled the state is deeply at odds with the class-correspondence thesis. Hans-Jürgen Puhle (1978) is thus correct in doubting the unity of the category Kehrite, to the extent that Wehler and Kehr occasionally portray the imperial state as promoting industry.

Both East German historians and some representatives of the Bielefeld school have suggested that industrial, especially monopoly, rather than agrarian interests were served by state policy, even if Junkers held office. Many East Germans stressed a Junker-capitalist entente as opposed to pure capitalist domination (e.g., Klein 1976; and Baudis and Nussbaum 1978). As Eley points out, Jürgen Kocka and Wehler tend to assert a discrepancy between "the state as a system of political domination . . . and its role in the economy (its 'modern' interventionist character)" (1985, 131). But it is precisely the "modernity" of the latter, i.e., the problem of discerning which classes and factions were favored by the state's interventions in the economy, that is in question here. Wehler's writings are particularly enigmatic in this regard, however, even when he endorses the polysemous term "organized capitalism." I would tend to agree with Lothar Gall's assessment of Wehler as viewing the interventionist state as "patriarchal [and] social-conservative, and not as an instrument of new and offensive economic dynamics" (Gall 1978, 558 n. 15).

of the idea that it is possible to identify certain liberal-democratic ideas or institutions as having an essentially bourgeois character, providing a standard by which the German middle class can then be judged. Eley argues (1984, 58, 75–90) that values and ideologies are not associated in an essential, one-to-one way with social classes and modes of production, echoing Ernesto Laclau and other critics of orthodox theories of ideology (Laclau 1977; Laclau and Mouffe 1985). Contrary to both modernization theorists and Marxists such as Nicos Poulantzas (1978), Eley insists that parliamentary structures, liberal ideas, and democratic revolution should not be conflated, nor should they be seen as having an ontological affinity with either capitalism or the bourgeoisie.

How does Eley analyze the German state and its relation to business? Rejecting "instrumentalist" theories, he insists that the bourgeoisie need not occupy the key positions in the state in order to "dominate" society as a whole. Eley suggests that analysts should be less concerned with asking who participates, and focus more on cui bono questions such as how well state policies and political practices met the interests of business. He has rightly stressed that many of the aspects of German "civil society" that had been viewed as precapitalist relics and holdovers were in fact beneficial to industrial capital. The paternalism and repressiveness of German business, for example, have typically been seen as somehow premodern and irrational, yet Eley argues that these strategies represented a "specific form of capitalist rationality" (Eley 1986, 47). By the same token, the nondemocratic political forms of Germany's "revolution from above" may have been "more closely linked to the realization of bourgeois interests than elsewhere"; in Britain and France this realization "was complicated by the unruly interventions of the subordinate classes" (1984, 84).

Eley's point of departure puts him on more solid ground than those who would characterize Imperial Germany by measuring the direct participation of businessmen in government or the degree of illiberalism or paternalism in society at large. Eley argues that "it is by no means clear that the *Kaiserreich* actually was a state dominated by the Junkers" (1986, 51). He suggests that the concept of Bonapartism is probably the "best point of departure" for understanding the German state (1984, 149). Yet his treatment of the state per se is not fully elaborated. Both Eley and Blackbourn have been more persuasive in demonstrating the rationality of bourgeois practices in "civil society" than in explaining the relations between public policies and business interests.

Marxists have sometimes argued that the nineteenth-century German state fulfilled "bourgeois" functions while excluding manufacturing capital from political power. As Marx wrote, "the days when the [German] bourgeoisie wept in Babylonian captivity and drooped their diminished heads were the very days when they became the effective power of the land" (quoted in Elster 1985,

418).[28] Engels argued that even during the early 1870s, "the bourgeoisie was
. . . the economically most powerful class among the population; the state had
to obey its economic interests" (1970a, 417). But, Engels continues, the bourgeoisie "was still far from actual political domination. . . . for the time being,
the executive depended on it, at best, in a very indirect form" (418). German
"Bonapartism" was characterized as ultimately benefiting capital: "The bourgeoisie buys gradual social emancipation at the price of the immediate renunciation of political power" (Engels 1969b, 167). On numerous occasions Engels provided what is now a familiar explanation for this indirect form of rule:
"Our German bourgeoisie is stupid and cowardly; it even failed to understand
how to take hold of and keep the political rule which the working class won for
it in 1848. . . . the German bourgeoisie has never had the ability to lead and
represent the nation as a ruling class (1962, 383–84); "the mass of the bourgeoisie does not want to rule" (Engels 1969a, 160).[29]

Two of the leading postwar Marxist theorists, Poulantzas and Perry Anderson, have offered quite different readings of the Imperial German state.
Anderson interprets the Prussian state as definitive of a specific Eastern European variant of absolutism and as "the classical case in Europe of an uneven
and combined development" (1974, 236). Between the seventeenth and the
mid-nineteenth centuries, such "unevenness" counterposed the more advanced
eastern state structures—"level with the Western States"—against the more
traditional supporting social formations (p. 224). One distinct characteristic of
Prussian absolutism, according to Anderson, was the degree to which it represented a continually renegotiated pact between the Hohenzollern monarchs and
the landed nobility. Social classes whose impress could be felt in the western
variant of absolutism, such as the urban bourgeoisie, were absent from this
compromise. The second distinguishing feature of eastern and especially Prussian absolutism was its particularly violent and warlike nature. This violence
was inherent in the eastern absolutist state, whose function was "to defend the
class position of the feudal nobility against both its rivals abroad and its

---

28. Elsewhere Marx amended this view, calling the Bismarckian state "nothing but a police-
guarded military despotism, embellished with parliamentary forms, alloyed with a feudal admixture, already influenced by the bourgeoisie and bureaucratically carpentered" (Marx 1970a, 27).
As Perry Anderson has pointed out, this is little more than an "agglutination of epithets" (1974,
277), and not a clear conceptualization.

29. Elsewhere Engels seemed to concur with Marx in suggesting that the imperial state
might not even be indirectly capitalist: "in the new German Empire . . . capitalists and workers are
balanced against each other and equally for the benefit of the impoverished Prussian cabbage
junkers" (1970b, 329); "In Germany the state is still to a certain extent a power hovering independently over society, which for that reason represents the collective interests of society and not those
of a single class" (1969c, 348).

peasants at home" (212). War was especially salient within Prussian absolutism, enhanced by the Prussian state's origins as a response to military threats from older powers such as Sweden and by the distinctive character of the eastern "second serfdom."

In the nineteenth century, according to Anderson, there was a shift in the axis of unevenness within Prussian absolutism. Anderson contrasts the powerfully industrializing economy in the western territories with the backward eastern provinces and their agrarian rulers (236). The rising capitalist industry, according to Anderson, gradually led Bismarck to include Rhenish capital along with the Junkers inside the state power structure. Although the state still bore certain precapitalist institutional features (presumably including the exaggerated coercive and military elements and the continuing political presence of the Junkers), in its main lines the state was now "unmistakably *capitalist*" (276):

> The German state was now a capitalist apparatus, over-determined by its feudal ancestry, but fundamentally homologous with a social formation which by the early twentieth century was massively dominated by the capitalist mode of production." (278)

The German state, "*despite its peculiarities,* had now joined the ranks of its English and French rivals" and broken with absolutism (277; my emphasis).

While Anderson stresses the increasing correspondence between state and social structures in Germany, Poulantzas emphasizes their ongoing dislocation. Poulantzas's starting point is the proposition that the state in capitalist society is "relatively autonomous" from the dominant class, rather than controlled directly by it (1978, 47). The state, he argues, is "the official résumé of society," representing in condensed form the entire array of class forces and overlapping modes of production that make up a given social formation. A certain degree of discontinuity between the dominant class in German society and the class background of the state's officials would therefore not seem to pose any immediate problems for Poulantzas.[30]

Complications arise, however, with Poulantzas's contention that the Imperial German state was not fully capitalist, even in structural terms. Treating the German state as an anomaly, Poulantzas seems to reproduce the excep-

---

30. Poulantzas thus argues that "under Bismarck, this state transformed itself from within, as it were, in the direction of a capitalist state" (1978, 180). By the end of the "Bismarckian régime," he suggests, the bourgeoisie was hegemonic (i.e., dominant in political and ideological relations), while the nobility had been reduced to the role of "governing class," or the class charged with running the state (338, 249). The post-Bismarckian state thus secured the interests of capital, even though its form was still somewhat dislocated with respect to capitalist social relations.

tionalism thesis using an alternative vocabulary, as Eley has noted.[31] Poulantzas argues that the Bismarckian period was characterized by "feudal" state structures that were "dislocated relative to the economic level," and that the German state remained partially feudal up to 1914 (1978, 82, 181). Considering Poulantzas's general criteria for distinguishing feudal and capitalist state forms, this description of the German state seems to refer to the strength of the executive branch relative to the legislative and to the fact that elections to all of the parliamentary bodies except the Reichstag were based on a restricted suffrage. These features of the German state would presumably prevent it from accomplishing one of the tasks that for Poulantzas is characteristic of the capitalist state: "maintaining the political disorganization of the dominated classes, by presenting itself as the unity of the people-nation, composed of political-persons/private-individuals" (1978, 189).

Without even challenging the inherent functionalism of these criteria, one could ask how state structures could possibly "lag" so far behind a social formation. If a formally feudal state can serve capitalist interests, does this not undermine the implied importance of the structural analysis of state forms? A state that regularly favored economically nondominant interests (e.g., agrarian ones in the Imperial German case) against dominant (industrial) ones would seem to provide damaging evidence even against neo-Marxist theorists as flexible and "politicist" as Poulantzas. The autonomy of a state that steadily contravenes the interests of the economically dominant class is clearly more than just "relative."

Eley, Anderson, and Poulantzas point to the problem in any class-correspondence approach of specifying the sorts of state activities that would normally be expected (or that would provide confirming evidence for the theory). The first step is to identify the class(es) whose interests should be predominant in state policy. This entails an analysis of the class structure. The second step is to define criteria for recognizing which state policies (or structures) are compatible with dominant-class interests. While this is relatively unproblematic if one uses the criterion of subjective interests—policies then need only be matched against the expressed interests of dominant-class members or representatives—it is much more difficult if one is willing to entertain a notion of objective interests. Third, there is the problem of identifying the specific mechanisms that establish the correspondence between state policy and dominant-class interests. I will discuss only the first issue here and defer treatment of the second and third points to the third and fifth sections below.

---

31. Poulantzas also makes the familiar claim that the German bourgeoisie, traumatized first by the French Revolution and later by the working-class movement, did not break decisively with the nobility and "left to the state the task of establishing its own political domination." Based on these comments, Eley assimilates Poulantzas to Georg Lukács and Isaac Deutscher as a Marxist proponent of the *Sonderweg* thesis (cf. Eley 1984, 46).

One can think of Imperial Germany as a complex social formation characterized by a variety of articulated modes of production.[32] The most significant kinds of production relations were (1) the latifundium-type mode of the great agrarian estates, capitalist agriculture with coerced wage labor;[33] (2) small subsistence peasants; (3) the petty-commodity mode (consisting of artisans, homeworkers, and the commercial farming most common in the southwest); and (4) industrial capitalism. Industrial capitalism was itself integrated with the agrarian modes, which provided it with labor, material, and internal markets.

The industrial capitalist mode of production became economically dominant in Germany during the 1880s and 1890s at the latest (Bade 1983, 121). Even before that time—by the 1860s and 1870s—industrial capitalism was the most dynamic, if not the largest, sector of the economy (Hoffman 1965). This transformation is indicated in table 1, which shows the occupational structure and the national income produced in the agrarian and industrial sectors of the German economy between 1880 and 1913. By the 1880s, the German class structure was perhaps even more dominated by industrial capitalist social relations than in France or the United States (cf. Steinmetz and Wright 1989, table 3). Yet agriculture was still not a negligible factor: a full 26 percent of Germany's net national product derived from agrarian sources in the 1900–1913 period. Again, it should also be kept in mind that agrarian production was itself structured along capitalist lines, even on the eastern estates, as Weber noted in his studies of East Elbian agriculture during the 1890s.[34] But while large agriculture in Imperial Germany was entirely capitalist in terms of market-oriented production, estate laborers were still deprived of certain bourgeois rights and subjected to "precapitalist" forms of coercion.

A neo-Marxist theory clearly does not need to insist that all state structures, policies, or regimes correspond to dominant-class interests. However, a Marxist theory would expect any state that pursued policies unacceptable to the bourgeoisie for a significant length of time to be confronted with economic crisis, capital flight, and the emergence of powerful antistate political forces. It is difficult to specify a priori exactly how long regimes, structures, or policies that are unpalatable to the economic elite can endure without throwing the theory into doubt, but the nearly half-century life span of the *Kaiserreich* would seem to be of adequate duration. Moreover, to the extent that such structural limits are based on capitalist perceptions of state policy, long-term political dysfunctionalism would be especially unlikely in a situation like

32. On these concepts, see Wolpe 1980; and Wright 1985, 11, 109–14.

33. Although this mode was capitalist in economic terms, "this wage labour . . . was itself regulated by a feudal *Gesindeordnung* . . . and imposed a ruthless manorial discipline on agricultural laborers and domestic servants" (Anderson 1974, 274).

34. See especially the results of Weber's main study for the Verein für Sozialpolitik (1892, 1979). See also Moeller 1986; Perkins 1981; and Tribe 1983.

TABLE 1. National Product and Labor Force in the Agrarian and Industrial Sectors (in Percent)

	Agriculture, Forestry, and Fishing		Manufacturing and Extractive Industries	
	National Product	Labor Force	National Product	Labor Force
Five-year average				
1850–54	45.2	54.6*	21.2	25.2*
1880–84	36.2	48.2	32.5	29.8
1885–89	35.3	45.5	34.0	32.3
1890–94	32.2	42.6	36.8	34.2
1895–99	30.8	40.0	38.5	35.7
1900–1904	29.0	38.0	39.8	36.8
1905–9	26.0	35.8	41.9	37.7
1910–13	23.4	35.1	44.6	37.9

*These figures refer to the average of 1849, 1852, 1855, and 1858.
Source: Hoffmann 1965, 33, 35.

Imperial Germany, where even the heavy-industrialists who supported Bismarck complained about the Junkers' overweening claims to social power, and businessmen frequently criticized the state's perilously "agrarian" proclivities. Yet as I will argue in the next section, there is no reason to elaborate an explanation for class noncorrespondence, since there is little evidence that it existed, at least in the realm of social policy.[35]

Industrial and Agrarian Interests in Poor Relief Policy

In this section I will argue that a series of key legislative decisions concerning poor relief favored industry over agriculture and promoted capitalism as the mode of production rather than the quasi-feudal form of agrarian social and property relations typified by the East Elbian estate. Despite continual agrarian attacks, national poor relief legislation persisted in its intrinsically capitalist form throughout the empire, with only a few minor changes. The relief system survived despite only rhetorical allegiance by key German and Prussian officials to the *Agrarstaat* (agrarian state). Not only was poor relief aligned with the long-term interests of the dominant industrial classes;[36] a comparison with

35. For an extension of the case against "class noncorrespondence" into other realms of imperial state policy, see Steinmetz 1993, chap. 4.

36. There have been few studies on the welfare state that have argued explicitly that agrarian interests—as opposed to precapitalist values, which I will discuss below—affected the content of the welfare policy, although it is easy to construct such arguments. In fact, very little effort has been made until recently to understand the relations between elite-class interests and welfare programs in the German Empire.

Britain and a glance at the implementation of poor relief in German municipalities suggest that assistance was bourgeois and "modern" in formal terms.

The National Poor Relief Law and State-Led Industrialization, 1870–1914

No study of the welfare state during the Second Reich can afford to ignore poor relief, although most have done so.[37] The first reason for emphasizing public assistance has to do with its contribution to the creation and reproduction of a mobile, national labor force (see below). Second, more money was probably spent on poor relief than on national social insurance. In 1885, the year of the first reliable national survey, expenditures on poor relief were almost twice as high as social insurance benefits.[38] In 1912, after the Bismarckian system had been operating for almost three decades, poor relief spending still seems to have outstripped social insurance costs. One writer roughly estimated the costs of what he called "indirect unemployment relief" through public assistance as "at least one billion marks annually" (Ostwald 1912, 14); spending for the three major social insurance schemes (health, workmen's compensation, and old-age pensions) totaled less than that in the same year (Hohorst et al. 1978, 154–56).[39]

Last, poor relief provided enormous opportunities for public authorities to intervene directly in poor people's lives (even if more people were enrolled in social insurance funds than were assisted by relief). The number of voluntary and paid guardians working in the administration of poor relief was undoubtedly much larger than the numbers working in the social insurance bureaucracy. And while the labor movement had some impact on the implementation of national social insurance programs (especially sickness insurance; see Tennstedt 1976, 1983b), it was less able to influence the operation of relief. Poor

---

37. The absence of poor relief from most German social histories until recently is all the more perplexing when one considers its centrality in English social history. The relations between the welfare state and poor relief are addressed in Sachße and Tennstedt 1980, 1983, 1988; Tennstedt 1975, 1976, 1981a, 1981b, 1981c, 1983a, 1983b; Leibfried and Tennstedt 1985; and Leibfried et al. 1985. See Schinkel 1964; Volkmann 1968; and Koselleck 1989 for discussions of Prussian poor relief legislation before 1871.

38. More than ninety-two million marks were spent on direct relief costs (Kaiserliches Statistisches Amt 1887, 50); in the same year fifty-nine million marks were spent on goods, services, and transfers in social insurance (Andic and Veverka 1963, 247).

39. The 1912 poor relief estimate is speculative and perhaps exaggerated, since there were no national poor relief surveys after 1892. The order of magnitude of change is greater than what we might expect from a city like Berlin, whose relief spending during the same period (1885–1912) rose by only about 300 percent (Meinerich 1919, 50); in Essen, spending rose by 419 percent (Hagenberg 1914, 154); and in Bremen only 251 percent (Funk 1913, 111). But spending may have grown even faster in smaller cities and the countryside than in larger cities, which would partially account for the discrepancy.

relief was therefore an arena in which the conceptions of economic and political elites could be expressed more directly.

The clash between agrarian and industrial interests was also more immediate and drawn out about poor relief and related issues than about other forms of social policy. The agrarian view was that the national poor relief system favored the western and urban industrial parts of the Reich over the rural east and other agrarian regions that were losing population. Throughout the *Kaiserreich,* agrarians tried to change the relief system through pressure on the chancellor, the Reichstag, and the Prussian Landtag, while industrialists opposed such changes. In the end, industrial interests prevailed.

What were the laws governing poor relief, and why did they find such different degrees of support? Both of the key national-level laws originated during the period of national unification. The Freedom of Movement Law (Gesetz über die Freizügigkeit) was passed on 1 November 1867; and the Law of Settlement, or Relief Residence Law (Gesetz über den Unterstützungswohnsitz) on 6 June 1870. Both laws involved extensions of previously existing Prussian laws[40] to other states in the empire. Both were passed during the years of National Liberal dominance in the Reichstag of the North German Confederation and reflected the economically liberal atmosphere of the years preceding the recession of the mid-1870s.

These laws were probably the most critical contributions by the state to the creation of a capitalist labor market since the *Bauernbefreiung* in the early nineteenth century and had long been demanded by industry (Schissler 1978; Engels 1970a, 379). They made it both legal and financially feasible for rural workers to leave the east and migrate to sites of labor demand. In essence, the new Poor Relief Law was an undeclared form of unemployment relief. It was now more or less guaranteed that all needy German citizens—including the able-bodied—would receive relief at a certain level (unspecified in the laws, and left to the discretion of local authorities).[41]

The Freedom of Movement Law stipulated that "every citizen has the right to . . . stop or settle anywhere within the national territory where he has lodging or is able to obtain a place to stay" (Gesetz über die Freizügigkeit, §1). Local authorities were prohibited from evicting a newly arrived person "unless

---

40. These were the Prussian Freedom of Movement and Poor Relief Laws of 1842 and 1855 (see Köllmann 1966; and Deutscher Landwirtschaftsrat 1881, 257). As explained below, not all states immediately took over the Relief Residence Law, and all had slightly differing regulations governing its implementation.

41. Evidence for the use of traditional public assistance to relieve unemployed able-bodied workers is given in Steinmetz 1993. While social policy contributed to the creation of a nationwide labor market, I do not want to claim that imperial policies were necessary conditions for economic development (cf. Tipton 1981) but merely that the state thereby removed one barrier to migration. Undoubtedly, labor migration would have occurred without the national system of poor relief.

it can be proven that he does not possess the necessary powers to support himself and his dependents," and were admonished that "fears of *future* impoverishment do not authorize local officials to reject such a person" (ibid., §4; emphasis added). Only if the person became impoverished before obtaining a new "relief residence" (*Unterstützungswohnsitz*) for reasons other than temporary inability to work was the town allowed to expel him (Gesetz über die Freizügigkeit, §5).[42]

In the agrarians' view, the 1870 Poor Relief Law installed a system that was disproportionately financed by the rural areas, which were losing population. The law regulated the acquisition and loss of the relief residence, which determined which poor law board was to bear the financial responsibility for relief.[43] These regulations became the primary focus of agrarian discontent. The relief residence of an adult (defined as anyone at least twenty-four years old) was transferred to the town in which he or she had lived uninterruptedly for two years without drawing relief. Two new administrative and fiscal units were created (or rather, extended over the entire empire): the local poor law board (*Ortsarmenverband*), which was usually coterminous with, and financed by, a single municipality, and the regional poor law board (*Landarmenverband*). According to paragraph 28 of the Poor Relief Law, all local boards were legally bound to provide an "adequate level" of relief to anyone who became needy while present in the community, regardless of the place of permanent residence. Implementing statutes in most of the federal states specified that a pauper was to be granted shelter, the basic necessities for living (*Lebensunterhalt*), medical care in case of illness, and an appropriate burial in case of death (Kaiserliches Statistisches Amt 1887, 5–6). Municipalities bore the relief bills of resident paupers, while the costs for aiding a nonresident could be demanded and reimbursed from the city where the outsider had relief residence. The regional poor law board covered the costs of paupers for whom no relief residence could be determined.

---

42. This provision resembled settlement laws in colonial America (Abramovitz 1985, 126).

43. The Relief Residence Law was complemented by a number of implementing statutes (*Ausführungsgesetze*) of the various federal states. See Bätzner 1873; Gugel 1910; and Wohlers 1876. It was taken over by Württemburg and Baden after their entry into the newly founded German Empire but was not adopted by Alsace-Lorraine until 1910 and Bavaria until 1916. Until 1910, laws dating from the French Revolution (1793 and 1796) regulated poor relief in Alsace-Lorraine, where it remained voluntary (*Denkschrift über die Lage des Armenwesens der Stadt Kolmar* 1898, 4–5; Böhmert 1888, 105; Goltz 1896; and Sachße and Tennstedt 1980, 204). See also *Reichsgesetzblatt* 1913, 495; and Zentrales Staatsarchiv I Potsdam (hereafter ZStA I, now Bundesarchiv, Abteilungen Potsdam), Rep. 15.01, Nr. 1266. Bavaria retained the older system (*Heimatrecht*), whereby the place of birth was also the relief residence throughout a person's life, although by 1896 legislation had converged with the national norm to the extent that a new relief residence could be gained within the state of Bavaria if one resided in a town for four uninterrupted (and nonimpoverished) years (Baron 1983, 20).

The significance of this legislation for the agrarians derived from their status as major local taxpayers in the eastern agrarian regions. The agrarians saw themselves as underwriting the creation of a new industrial labor force by paying a disproportionate part of the costs of mass labor migration to the west. In principle, Junker estates and rural communities would retain their responsibility for the relief bills of former residents whom they had not seen for years—until those people lost their original relief residence. Indeed, during the first two decades of the law, rural communities paid several million marks to subsidize what Claus Offe (1984a) calls "active proletarianization."[44] As a commission of the quasi-official agrarian organization Deutscher Landwirtschaftsrat (German Farmers' Council) reported in 1876, rural workers

> go the cities and the industrial areas when they are seventeen or eighteen—the girls at an even younger age. . . . it is a great burden for the countryside that the hometown must bear the risk of everything that happens to this frivolous lot until it reaches the age of twenty-four, and still for two more years in the place where its labor power is exploited. (Deutscher Landwirtschaftsrat 1880, 446)

The East Prussian Agrarian Central Association (Landwirtschaftlicher Centralverein) complained in a petition to the Reichstag of the

> continuous emigration of young male and female workers from the countryside to the big cities, and from the agricultural east to the industrial west. . . . While the countryside bears the costs of these workers' physical and spiritual education and suffers an unremitting loss of potential labor [*Arbeitskapital*] through their steady exodus, they are a gift to the large cities and industrial regions, in the form of trained labor power. . . . They often begin their migration to these areas when they are only sixteen or seventeen, yet the home poor law board . . . retains responsibility for their fates until they reach the age of twenty-six.[45]

---

44. In the two eastern, agrarian provinces of East Prussia and Gumbinnen alone, almost 19,000 marks were paid in 1884 by local and regional relief boards for people who had immigrated to the west and become impoverished there; in 1890 the total was nearly 26,500 marks. Over the total seven-year period (1884–90), 165,557 marks were paid out in reimbursements to western relief boards by these two eastern provinces. If these figures are representative for other agrarian regions losing population, several million marks may have been paid by rural relief boards to boards in areas receiving their rural workers during the first two decades of the Relief Residence Law. See ZStA I, Rep. 15.01, Nr. 1274 (pp. 97 ff.): report of 21 January 1892 on "costs of relief paid by eastern relief boards for persons impoverished in the west."

45. Reichstag, *Verhandlungen, Aktenstücke,* 4th legislature period, 3d session, 1880, no. 183, 944.

Another financial drain was traced to the simple fact that rural districts were "producing more people than they were consuming," as the Conservative parliamentarian Theodor Graf zu Stolberg-Wernigerode put it in a parliamentary debate. He estimated the average costs to a locality of an individual's primary education at three thousand marks.[46]

The agrarians also accused the 1867 and 1870 laws of exacerbating the westward immigration of the rural poor and thus contributing to the rural labor shortage. The eastern agrarian provinces suffered the greatest population losses through overseas migration and were deprived of inexpensive Polish labor replacements through harsh immigration restrictions during the 1880s (Bade 1983; Deutscher Landwirtschaftsrat 1883, 485–86).[47] In Prussia (indeed, throughout Eastern Europe), the primary objective of the landlord class from the seventeenth century onward had been "to arrest the mobility of the villager and to bind him to the estates" (Anderson 1974, 207). This political-economic goal was ideologically articulated with more sweeping warnings against the destructive cultural consequences of *Landflucht* (rural flight), "emigration fever," urbanization, and industrialization (Langewiesche 1977). In 1880 a future Prussian minister of agriculture, Ernst von Hammerstein-Loxten, decried the Poor Relief Law's contribution to "uprootedness" (*Heimatlosigkeit*), a common agrarian complaint. Such "uprooting" was a menace that bore "great moral dangers," he insisted, and was antithetical to the "German soul" (Deutscher Landwirtschaftsrat 1880, 444).

Soon after the founding of the empire, eastern agrarians began pressuring the state to change the Poor Relief Law and restrict workers' freedom of movement (Barkin 1970, 28). One of the main goals of the Junker-dominated Vereinigung der Steuer- und Wirtschaftsreformer (Association of Tax and Economic Reformers) at its first meeting in 1876 was to obtain reductions in rural laborers' freedom of movement, along with changes in the Poor Relief Law (Fricke et al. 1986, 4:360). The more powerful Bund der Landwirte (Farmers' League) also called for revisions of the Freedom of Movement Law at its first meeting in 1893 (Fricke et al. 1983, 1:244). Despite these agrarian pressures, however, the legislation underwent only minor changes. In the 1891–92 legislature, the Conservatives offered a bill that would have limited the freedom of

---

46. Reichstag, *Verhandlungen, Stenographische Berichte,* 4th legislature period, 4th session, 1881, 1300.

47. It is impossible to establish whether the Poor Relief Law actually increased people's willingness to emigrate, or whether freedom of movement regulations, combined with economic and social pressures, provide an adequate account. It is interesting that while a steep rise in overseas immigration characterized the years immediately following 1870, "internal" migration did not become dominant until the first half of the 1890s, when the shortage of industrial jobs abated (Deutscher Landwirtschaftsrat 1883, 485; Langewiesche 1977).

movement of those under twenty-one years; after 1894 the government was somewhat responsive to such measures.[48]

The financial drain introduced by the reimbursement system sharpened agrarian opposition to the Poor Relief Law. Gradually, agrarians came to accept the existence of the relief residence system. Since it was unlikely that workers could be prevented from migrating westward, this system meant that the hometowns would at least not be supporting them forever.[49] The agrarians were now interested in making it easier for migrants to obtain a new residence or to lose their old one. After a lull in agitation against the laws during the 1870s, a petition to the Reichstag from the East Prussian Landwirtschaftlicher Centralverein in 1880 called for changes in the Poor Relief Law. This inaugurated a steady stream of petitions and bills from the conservative parties, rural county representatives (*Kreisvertretungen*), the Deutscher Landwirtschaftsrat, and later the Bund der Landwirte.[50]

Bismarck's views on the Poor Relief Law resembled the system favored by the agrarians and the Conservative Party. In 1877 Bismarck argued that the best arrangement would be one in which the full costs of relief would simply be carried by the town in which a pauper became needy. Bismarck also suggested making the town in which the pauper worked, rather than the town in which he or she resided, liable for the costs of sickness relief. Finally, Bismarck stressed

---

48. Reichstag, *Verhandlungen, Stenographische Berichte,* 8th legislature period, 1st session, 1891, 3363, 4966; Barkin 1970, 65, 216.

49. Many southern German officials—from the Reichspartei, and the Center, Conservative, and National Liberal Parties—preferred the old *Heimatswohnsitz* or *Heimatsgesetz* (hometown relief residence system), in which the *Heimat* (usually the birthplace) remained the relief residence throughout one's life. Cf. the typical argumentation by Karl Gottlob Varnbüler in Reichstag, *Verhandlungen, Stenographische Berichte,* 4th legislature period, 4th session, 1881, 1292; and Reichstag, *Verhandlungen, Aktenstücke,* 4th legislature period, 4th session, 1881, 713–14; also Alfred Franz Rembold in Reichstag, *Verhandlungen, Stenographische Berichte,* 9th legislature period, 2d session, 1894, 977.

50. The Landwirtschaftlicher Centralverein demanded above all lowering the age from twenty-four to twenty; cf. Reichstag, *Verhandlungen, Aktenstücke,* 4th legislature period, 3d session, no. 183, 1880, 944–45. Conservatives called for changes throughout the 1880s and 1890s; see Reichstag, *Verhandlungen, Stenographische Berichte,* 7th legislature period, 1st session, 1887, 61; 7th legislature period, 4th session, 1889, 1995; and 8th legislature period, 2d session, 1891, 3363. On the *Kreisvertretungen,* see Reichstag, *Verhandlungen, Aktenstücke,* 6th legislature period, 2d session, no. 223, 1886, 1045–46. At its 1876 and 1881 meetings, the Deutscher Landwirtschaftsrat called for a lowering of the age at which a new relief residence could be obtained and argued that the regional poor law boards should bear the costs of persons with no relief residence. The problem was discussed again at the twentieth plenary session of the Deutscher Landwirtschaftsrat in 1892; see ZStA I, Rep. 15.01, Nr. 1285, p. 4; and Nr. 1288, pp. 24 ff.; also Deutscher Landwirthschaftsrat 1880, 441–63, 1881, 36, 239–87.

the need for a "workfare" regulation linking benefits to willingness to work.[51] In 1881 Bismarck suggested that the regional poor law boards should assume the costs of all but the able-bodied poor, whose relief would continue to be covered by the local relief boards.[52] This idea was aired simultaneously with his attempts to implement a national social insurance system largely financed by public funds (through indirect taxes). Bismarck was unable to gain the Reichstag's support for any of these recommendations while he was chancellor.[53]

During and after Bismarck's tenure, eastern agrarian groups continued to press for a variety of changes in the law that they hoped would lower their fiscal burden.[54] Above all, they tried to transfer most of the responsibility for assistance costs to the town in which the pauper had been working. The rationale was that industry, which had profited from the pauper's labor, should also bear the burden of his or her care.[55] Yet the agrarians were unable to alter the basic contours of the combined system of free migration and public support for the poor. They were able to relieve their financial burden slightly through two amendments to the 1870 law. A revision in 1894 lowered the age at which relief residence could be gained or lost from twenty-four to eighteen years, and transferred part of the costs to the town in which the pauper had been working.[56] But this alteration probably had little effect, as most of the reimburse-

---

51. Given the unlikelihood of realizing this goal, however, Bismarck supported shortening the length of time necessary for gaining a new relief residence to one year. See ZStA I, Rep. 15.01, Nr. 1272, pp. 38 ff.: Bismarck's vote of 28 March 1877 on reforms in the Poor Law.

52. ZStA I, Rep. 15.01, Nr. 1272, pp. 130 ff..

53. A bill from the Imperial Chancellery that would have made it easier for migrants to gain a new residence was rejected by the Prussian minister of the interior, who opposed placing new burdens on the cities, and it was defeated in the Bundesrat; ZStA I, Rep. 15.01, Nr. 1272, pp. 38 ff. The government responded to attempts to reintroduce the matter in the Reichstag during the 1880s with the claim that the social insurance legislation would remove much of the burden of the Poor Relief Law; see the statements by the state secretary.

54. In 1886, an East Prussian county (*Kreisvertretung*) petitioned to have the relief residence system introduced in Alsace-Lorraine (Reichstag, *Verhandlungen, Aktenstücke*, 6th legislature period, 1st session, 1885–86, no. 223, 1045–46). The law was not taken over by Alsace-Lorraine until 1910; ZStAI, Rep. 15.01, Nr. 1266.

55. ZStA I, Rep. 15.01, Nr. 1275, pp. 192, 292 ff: list of demands sent to the Kaiser by the Prussian Haus der Abgeordneten following the debate on the crisis of rural labor.

56. It stipulated that the costs of aid for the first sixteen weeks of illness were to be paid by the relief board of the town in which the pauper had worked. In addition, §361 of the Criminal Code was altered such that a negligent parent who failed to care for dependents could be jailed or fined up to 150 marks. See *Blätter für das Armenwesen*, 1894, 65; *Reichs-Gesetzblatt* 1894, no. 9, 259–77; Reichstag, *Verhandlungen, Stenographische Berichte*, 8th legislature period, 2d session, 1893, 1677–1743; 9th legislature period, 1st session, 1894, 977–97, 1101–02; and Reichstag, *Verhandlungen, Aktenstücke*, 8th legislature period, 2d session, 1893, no. 130, 751–54; 9th legislature period, 1st session, 1894, nos. 117 and 142, 727–44 and 807–08.

ments paid by rural poor law boards were for paupers over the age of twenty-four, and many migrants were younger than eighteen.[57]

Agrarian agitation against the Poor Relief Law did not abate with the 1894 revision but actually intensified along with the rise of agrarian interest-group politics during the 1890s. However, little changed under the next two chancellors (1894 through 1908), for reasons similar to those that had prevented major revisions during the Bismarck era. The government feared further alienating industry with changes in the Relief Residence Law, especially in the context of battles over the 1902 tariff (see Barkin 1970; Bonham 1985). At a 1900 meeting of the Prussian Staatsministerium, Minister of the Interior Arthur von Posadowsky-Wehner (then chiefly responsible for social policy) insisted that changing the Relief Residence Law was not a timely idea because "industry would see it as directed against its interests." There was already danger of an industrial backlash due to the new tariffs. According to Posadowsky, it would be especially unfortunate to introduce the bill at that moment because the discussion in the Landtag had made the "tactical mistake" of tying Poor Relief Law reforms to limits on freedom of movement (Freizügigkeit)—a change that industry opposed even more strongly. Even the "agrarian" Prussian finance minister Johannes von Miquel agreed that it would be better to delay introduction of a bill, given that industry was becoming "difficult" (*misslich*) due to the "clumsy operations of the Bund der Landwirte."[58] This discussion suggests that the commitments of top officials were the proximate mechanism by which industrial interests were translated into state policy. Why officials had these commitments is a separate matter, however, to which I will return in my conclusion.

A second modest reform in 1908 lowered the age and the number of years for gaining and losing relief residence to sixteen years and one year, respectively.[59] But the overall contours of the system remained in place until 1924, including the seemingly inequitable partial subsidization of the costs of relieving the unemployment and poverty of rural migrants by the areas they had left. Moreover, these limited proagrarian changes in the Poor Relief Law were offset by the overall development of the national relief system. A network of "itinerant unemployed stations" (*Naturalverpflegungsstationen* and *Wanderar-*

---

57. ZStA I, Rep. 15.01, Nr. 1274, pp. 97 ff.

58. ZStA I, Rep. 15.01, Nr. 1275, pp. 257 ff. Miquel had been the strongest Junker ally among the higher Prussian and Reich officials in opposing trade treaty revisions during the early 1890s, seeking "consistently either to prevent a reduction of the agricultural tariff or to undermine the treaties altogether" (Bonham 1985, 178). He was also the leader of the resistance to the Mittelland canal at the turn of the century, another measure strongly opposed by the Junkers (Bonham 1985, 189, 206 n. 51, 211).

59. See *Reichs-Gesetzblatt*, 1908, no. 35, 377–96; and Deutscher Verein für Armenpflege und Wohltätigkeit 1906, (vol. 76).

beitsstätte) had been set up throughout Germany during the 1880s. These were relief stations typically spaced at approximately a day's walk apart. Unemployed laborers could obtain food and shelter, usually in exchange for several hours of work, and then continue along the road. The stations were often coupled with a labor exchange or job office. This network was meant to provide further inducements to migration toward areas of labor demand. The number of these stations declined from 1,957 in 1890 to 1,285 in 1896,[60] but by 1901, Hans von Hammerstein, the Prussian interior minister, was calling upon the provincial prefects (*Oberpräsidenten*) to set up stations in provinces that lacked them.[61] In 1902 the Prussian government decided to increase by ten million marks state subsidies to the provincial authorities for the construction of more stations.[62] Together with the creation of local "labor exchanges," urban emergency public works, public housing, and other municipal social programs (Faust 1981a, 1981b, 1982, 1986), these institutions did nothing to halt the exodus of rural labor.

A Bourgeois Form of Relief?

One possible objection to the foregoing discussion is that regardless of the economic interests that were directly promoted by poor relief, the precise manner in which these policies were implemented by local elites, their form, was eminently traditional. And in the chain of connotations that has become common sense to students of German history, traditional equals neofeudal, which means favorable to the agrarian Junker class. An appropriate response to this critique would involve demonstrating that poor relief was also "bourgeois" in formal terms. This requires that we reject the collapsing of the terms "modern" and "bourgeois" and insist that they refer to separate and irreducible dimensions. The ideal-typical distinction between public assistance as "traditional" and social insurance as "modern" does not speak directly to the issue of social policies' "class" character. Gaston Rimlinger (1971), T. H. Marshall (1970, 1977), and others assume that the welfare state is situated at a developmentally "higher" stage than poor relief, a normative assessment referring to an implicit scale of rights (e.g., "social citizenship"), not to an analytical differentiation among forms.[63]

---

60. *Blätter für das Armenwesen*, 1896, 89.
61. See ZStA I, Rep. 15.01, Nr. 1289.
62. *Blätter für das Armenwesen*, 24 May 1902, no. 21.
63. The distinction in this literature between poor relief and the welfare state is often fairly vague. According to Marshall, "the British Poor Law had the functions, but not the spirit, of a welfare service" (1970, 44); yet elsewhere he writes that the emphasis on the "contractual character of social insurance . . . . led people to exaggerate the distinction between social insurance and social assistance" (1970, 48).

Marshall's dimension can be contrasted with one that makes analytical distinctions among the class logics of different policy forms. Specifically, one can attempt to distinguish bourgeois and less bourgeois forms of welfare policies. In doing so, one faces the complication that social insurance always represents at least a partial infringement on pure capitalist property relations, as recognized by both Marshall and more recent writers such as Gösta Esping-Andersen. When workers have a right to unemployment relief, sick pay, and so forth, there is a concomitant decline in employers' ability to use labor markets as a disciplinary "whip." In an ideal "capitalist world," there would be no social policy above the basic minimum required to produce and reproduce labor power. Most aspects of the welfare state thus result at least partially from motives and forces that are humanitarian, social-democratic, or legitimatory, and not "purely bourgeois." Yet even where the impulse to engage in social reform is unavoidable, elites face choices among various alternatives, some more attractive than others.

We can distinguish three criteria according to which policies can be classified as more or less adapted to the basic structures of capitalist societies. The first is the dimension of commodification and decommodification; policies that encourage actors' orientation to market mechanisms have been described as inherently more bourgeois than policies that bypass or obviate markets (Offe and Ronge 1984; Esping-Andersen 1985a and 1985b).[64] Two sides of the de/commodification of policy actually need to be distinguished, one involving labor power (the degree to which recipients of social benefits are forced insistently back into labor markets), the other involving consumption (the extent to which benefits are given in kind). Less commodified forms of social policy are often seen as more advanced (cf. Marshall 1977, 121; Turner 1986). Although such policies may be rendered compatible with capitalism, they are less bourgeois when measured against an abstract model of capitalist relations. It follows that public assistance systems are generally more bourgeois than social insurance, even though social analysts typically view them as more traditional.

Michel Foucault's (1979) discussions of the inculcation of self-regulating forms of subjectivity during the transition to modernity direct us to a second, separate dimension of social policy.[65] Social programs that require recipients

---

64. But decommodified policies may be more patriarchal; as feminist critics of the American welfare state have pointed out, in-kind relief characterizes the more "feminized" sector of the welfare state (food stamps, AFDC, etc.). Such decommodified relief clearly does not decrease the dependence of women welfare clients (Fraser 1987). Nancy Fraser argues further that means-tested programs "familialize" their clients and treat claimants as unpaid family workers, while social insurance programs "individualize" claimants and treat them as wage workers (Fraser 1987); see also Nelson 1984; and Gordon 1988. I have addressed the complex set of issues around gender and German welfare policy in Steinmetz 1989.

65. My account is different from Foucault's, of course, since he refuses to understand the

to take responsibility for their own care also lead them to "internalize the state," thus fortifying bourgeois society.[66] This dimension of the modern welfare state also recalls Louis Althusser's notion of the "ideological state apparatus," which causes subjects to "'work by themselves' in the vast majority of cases" (1971, 121).

Finally, programs can be evaluated as more or less bourgeois in relation to fields of class formation and conflict. Social policies may inhibit the threats that working-class movements pose to propertied groups. Policies are useful from a bourgeois standpoint if they reinforce distinctions between subordinate individuals who form only an incipient or "theoretical" group, a "class on paper" (Bourdieu) but might otherwise converge as a real social group or class.[67] Pierre Bourdieu's notion of "classification struggles" provides a metaphor for thinking about the effects of social policies on class formation (Bourdieu 1984, 1987).[68] Seen from this perspective, state policies that multiply distinctions among subordinate groups can be considered bourgeois.[69]

To summarize, dimensions of welfare policy that one might consider "bourgeois" include commodification, the creation of self-monitoring subjects, and reclassification through accentuation of differences among the dependent poor. But it is important not to posit necessary, transhistorical relations between policy forms and class interests. Eley's criticisms of the equation of liberal democracy and bourgeois capitalism would apply with equal force to

---

emergence of the modern subject in class terms. Clearly, the technologies of self-discipline, once established historically, can undergird nonbourgeois regimes (e.g., state-socialist ones). What Foucault's analyses reveal, however, is the extent to which these new technologies of subject creation emerged concurrently with capitalism.

66. Fraser 1987 underscores this association, characterizing the American welfare state as a "Juridico-Administrative-Therapeutic Apparatus."

67. As critics of traditional Marxism have recognized, working-class formation is not strictly derivable from class structure (cf. Przeworski 1977; Laclau and Mouffe 1985; and Steinmetz 1992). Pierre Bourdieu writes: "While the probability of assembling a set of agents . . . rises when they are closer in social space . . . alliance between those who are closest is never necessary . . . and alliance between those most distant from each other is never impossible" (1985, 726).

68. The logic of the state's role in "classification struggles" is clearly illustrated in Kocka's analyses of the effects of the post-1900 German social insurance legislation in solidifying distinctions between white-collar and manual workers (e.g., Kocka 1980, 1981); see also Luc Boltanski's (1984) similar treatment of the impact on the solidification of the social category "cadres" by the Vichy administration's granting of legal status to the "cadres" in the 1941 *charte du travail.*

69. Given the formal similarities between this argument and Poulantzas's claims about the "disorganizing effects" of the capitalist form of state and parliamentary democracy (1978, 134, 189–94; 277, 287), it is perhaps necessary to underscore that I am not claiming that all social policies necessarily attempt to splinter subordinate classes, nor that all bourgeoisies attempt to shape welfare policy along these lines. Note also that the creation of male and female "streams" in the welfare state—distinctions between men and women, rather than within a theoretically unified working class—may follow a similar logic.

such an essentialist scheme. One major difference, of course, is that I am not aligning classes with ideologies, values, and worldviews but rather with interests. Yet one can easily imagine circumstances in which bourgeois interests would be better served by decommodified policies or a less differentiated working class. Instead, the argument should be framed in terms of strong affinities between different class interests and policy forms within a given historical conjuncture.[70]

The following questions are thus central for the following part of the analysis: To what extent did the impetus for social reform come from business? Once such an impetus existed, to what extent did the specific policy correspond to either the conscious interests of the bourgeoisie or to the formally bourgeois criteria developed above?

The Elberfeld System: Implementation of Poor Relief at the Local Level

The actual implementation of German poor relief took place at the local level, especially in the municipalities. State and national legislation specified only the broad contours of actual assistance. In the towns, relief took the form of the Elberfeld system, which was decidedly bourgeois, according to the criteria outlined above: it stressed individual responsibility, self-monitoring, and quick reintegration of the poor into labor markets. The structure of local poor relief (and local social policy more generally) illustrates an alternative, more direct relation between businessmen and the state.

The Elberfeld system of poor relief was named after the city where it was first codified, although other cities were using similar systems.[71] Most large German municipalities had adopted the system by 1914. The central tenets of the Elberfeld system, according to the slogans of its proponents, were the "decentralization" and "individualization" of relief (Tennstedt 1981b, 77). Traditionally, each decision to honor or reject an individual's request for aid was made at meetings of the entire staff of poor relief officials. Once aid had been granted, however, there was comparatively little effort to monitor or reform the recipients. "Individualization" signified a huge increase in the number of poor relief guardians in the field and thus in the intensity of "individualized" treat-

---

70. These "bourgeois" criteria could change in other periods. The "bourgeois subject" may be well suited to certain postcapitalist societies or ill suited to contemporary, late capitalism; unified working classes are more stabilizing at certain moments than divided ones; elites often prefer decommodified policies from a political standpoint of social reproduction.

71. There is a vast nineteenth-century literature on the Elberfeld system, beginning with the overview by Georg Berthold (1881) and the excellent study by Victor Böhmert (1888); see also Schlaudraff 1932; Köllmann et al. 1953; Sachße and Tennstedt 1980; and Lube 1984. The *Schriften* of the Deutscher Verein für Armenpflege und Wohltätigkeit also deal frequently with the Elberfeld system, especially volumes 18, 49, and 63.

ment and surveillance. "Decentralization" referred to the devolution of decision-making authority into the hands of the guardians, who could best judge their clients' needs. The Elberfeld system was the cornerstone of an overall strategy of increased discipline of the poor, intended to force an orientation toward the labor market and to combat welfare dependency.

Other dimensions of poor relief that were "bourgeois" in character included the increased use of cash relief rather than in-kind aid and the greater reliance on short-term rather than ongoing grants of assistance. In 1913 a Bremen municipal official justified the commodification of relief in an altogether typical manner, writing that "it is preferred nowadays to provide the pauper with cash . . . in order to help him learn to employ it more economically and to thereby exercise a pedagogical influence on him (Funk 1913, 116). A new poor relief regulation (*Armenordnung*) introduced in Hamburg in 1903 replaced an older guideline whereby 25 percent of aid should be provided as "soup coupons" with the stipulation that cash relief should be the rule, "so that the pauper remains economically independent and is able to satisfy his needs, which he himself knows best" (Buehl 1903, 272). The new 1901 *Armenordnung* in Kassel also called for more reliance on cash and stressed the "pedagogic moment, that the pauper should retain his independence and the feeling of his own responsibility." Berlin used virtually no in-kind relief; in 1911, 86 percent of its non-poorhouse relief was provided in cash (Grieken 1927, 23).

The stress on reforming behavior and encouraging self-monitoring, through techniques such as requiring the poor to keep budgets of their expenditures, corresponds to the Foucauldian image of the creation of the modern (bourgeois) subject. Beside bringing the lives of the poor in line with the core principles of the capitalist market economy, the goal of reliance on cash relief was to instill a more general sense of self-discipline.

The growing reliance upon what was called "temporary" (as opposed to "ongoing") relief awards was also geared toward encouraging self-reliance and "recommodifying" impoverished workers.[72] Temporary grants of aid were used as a form of relief for the conjuncturally unemployed. The director of one Berlin public assistance district noted already in 1878 that during the period of seasonal unemployment, nearly one-fifth of all relief in his district was provided in small grants, while another in 1880 complained that the guardians tended to give higher monthly awards to people who received short-term aid

---

72. "Ongoing" relief referred to cases in which a specific termination of the relief period was not foreseen or established from the beginning. It was generally distributed in monthly portions. See *Die Ergebnisse der am 1.12.1900 erfolgten statistischen Erhebung über die im Gebiete der Stadt Hamburg in offener Armenpflege unterstützten Personen unter besonderer Berücksichtigung der Wohnungsverhältnisse,* 5.

than to the "truly miserable and needy . . . relief recipient."[73] By 1901, nearly as much was spent for short-term as for ongoing relief in some Berlin districts.[74] The economically useful, able-bodied, jobless workers seem to have generally received more generous relief. This market principle of selection was foreign to the public poor relief of the eighteenth and early nineteenth centuries.

Bourgeois social interventions were especially visible at the municipal level, particularly in southern Germany (White 1976, 100). It is not difficult to explain why local policies such as poor relief were attuned to bourgeois interests. This convergence was overdetermined by a variety of powerful tools at the disposal of local middle classes. The most important of these was the "plutocratic" electoral franchise operative in some form in the majority of the German states, which usually weighted individuals' votes according to their income and frequently required them to pay a fee. This system excluded many workers from voting altogether (Hirsch and Lindemann 1905).[75] The most grotesque results of this system were revealed in cities such as Essen and Elbing, where during certain years one individual—the highest taxpayer— elected 33 percent of the city councillors with his single vote. Businessmen often had other political privileges. In Ludwigshafen, the firms paying the highest taxes had a full voice in votes on the city budget, equivalent to that of a city councillor (Breunig 1976, 402–3). Local government was the part of the state in which the bourgeoisie came closest to ruling directly, through the medium of progressive liberal or National Liberal parties (Sheehan 1971).[76] It should therefore not be surprising, except in light of assertions about the

---

73. Stadtarchiv Berlin (StadtA Berlin), Rep. 03, Nr. 54, p. 208: report by Seeger, 10 April 1880.

74. Report to Berlin poor relief commissions from Director Emil Münsterberg, Sept. 1901 in StadtA Berlin, Rep. 03, Nr. 352, p. 54.

75. An average of 13 percent of the population in the cities with more than fifty thousand inhabitants was eligible to vote in the years 1900–1910. The maximum was 20 percent, the minimum 1 percent. These calculations are from a variety of sources, listed in Steinmetz 1987, appendix 2.

76. Before the turn of the century, the majority of Liberal councillors in many cities were bankers, industrialists, or businessmen of some kind. In Mülhausen, for example, Liberals held a majority of town council seats before 1900; in 1886, almost half of the councillors were members of the "bourgeoisie" by this broad definition (calculated from Mühlhausen 1887–88, 200–201). Participation in local government by the traditional urban elite began declining at the end of the century, perhaps due to increased demands on their time, as Helmut Croon has suggested in his studies of the cities in Rheinland and Westphalia (1960, 38). In Krefeld in 1890, for example, ten of the twenty councillors elected in the top two classes were silk manufacturers and dealers; in 1918, they were represented by only one official (Jaeger 1967, 87). But the restrictive municipal franchise and the tradition of middle-class *Honoratioren* self-government meant that these economic elites were succeeded not by workers but by a "new, middle-class" majority composed of home owners, professionals, and scientists.

"feudalization" of the middle classes, that German urban social politics resembled or even foreshadowed those in Britain and France.[77]

A Modern Form of Relief?

While it is difficult to determine how "bourgeois" a given policy is, it is even harder to assess the degree to which it approximates an ideal-typical model of twentieth-century welfare (or what we are calling its modernity). Yet it is important to grapple with this issue, given the alleged traditionalism of German policy. An acceptable alternative to essentialist definitions of "modernity" would be strictly historicist: policies can be considered modern if they provided other states with a glimpse of their own future.

To address this issue, there is no better starting point for comparison than Germany's supposedly more modern English rival.[78] Reversing the familiar contrast, however, the central dimensions of the evolving poor relief system in the *Kaiserreich* appear to have been more "modern" than their English counterparts. As Marshall wrote, "Nowhere else [but in England] could you find quite the same combination of harsh deterrent principles, centralized policy control, and administration by an isolated authority" (1970, 34). Paupers in England were a broad, undifferentiated category, unified only in negative terms. Georg Simmel noted in 1906 that the English system "completely neglect[ed] the criterion of personal worthiness" and relied instead on the work-house test, at least in principle (18).[79] In Germany, by contrast, poor relief was directed "at the individual and his condition" (Simmel 1906, 6). German relief officials enthusiastically multiplied distinctions among categories of paupers. The German goal of thorough, individualized assessment of each relief case and the guardians' penetration into the private dwellings of the poor signaled a much higher level of (local) state "infrastructural" power, to use Michael Mann's terms.[80]

---

77. These local social policies are discussed in detail in Faust 1981a, 1981b, 1982, 1986; Krabbe 1979, 1981, 1985; and Saldern 1973, 1984.

78. On the English Poor Law, see Fraser 1976, 1981; Hay 1981; Rose 1972, 1981; and Williams 1981.

79. Under the new poor law of 1834, a pauper could theoretically receive relief only if shut off in a poorhouse (Polanyi 1957). It was assumed that only those who were genuinely needy would be willing to undergo the humiliations of the poorhouse. There is an enormous literature arguing that out-relief continued after the passage of the 1834 Poor Relief Law, and that the poorhouse system was only incompletely implemented. Karel Williams 1981 argues, however, that out-relief was in fact curtailed after 1834. The crucial point is not whether the poorhouse system was in fact implemented but that the Elberfeld ideology of individualized out-relief did not take root in England.

80. "Infrastructural power" is Mann's term for "the capacity of the state actually to penetrate civil society, and to implement logistically political decisions throughout the realm" (Mann

A final indicator of the "modernity" of the German assistance system is its popularity among reforming and business circles in Britain. During the nineteenth century, British businessmen and poor law officials favored the Elberfeld system (Reulecke 1986; Rose 1981, 66–67; Hay 1981, 115). The head of the Berlin poor relief board, Emil Münsterberg, was called on to testify before hearings on the reform of the Poor Law in 1908 (cf. Great Britain 1910). Although the poorhouse had been designed as a deterrent, many reformers had come to see it as encouraging long-term dependency. The English Poor Law also lacked the elements of behavioral reform and state penetration that figured prominently in the German system.

The National Welfare State and Industrial Interests

The preceding section showed that the regulations, legislation, and local implementation of poor relief in the German Empire were oriented toward industrial rather than agrarian interests, and that they were formally "bourgeois" in terms of commodification, individualization, and self-discipline. In this section I will explore a more familiar area, the national social insurance laws that were codified during the 1880s. Because more has been written on this segment of the German welfare state than on local relief policies, my discussion will be brief.

Recent writings on the imperial welfare state by sociologists and historians have created a greater diversity of opinion than one finds in most other areas of research on the empire. Yet there is still a strong tendency to see welfare policy in Imperial Germany as somehow prebourgeois, corporatist, and traditional, as an expression of neofeudal paternalism and of the weakness of liberalism (see Esping-Andersen 1990, 59–61). Dahrendorf (1967) refers to the welfare state as "authoritarian" and claims that social policy "immobilized" people rather than promoting capitalism (40, 47, 193, 252). Rimlinger (1971) speaks of German social policy in terms of "welfare monarchy" (100), the "mixing of feudal and socialist elements" (106), and the "defense of traditional authority" (112). Wehler disqualifies Bismarck's social insurance because of the manipulative motives that inspired it, contrasting it with a vaguely specified "modern style of state intervention," one whose "proper effect" would be to redistribute national income (1985, 136). Bismarck pursued a variety of political motives through state social insurance: bypassing the Reichstag, splitting the liberals, and binding workers directly to the state. The split between left- and right-wing liberals was indeed partially provoked by disagreements over Bismarck's plans. Bismarck dreamed of replacing the Reichstag with a parallel but nonelected set of corporate institutions, including the administrative bodies

---

1986a, 113). In *The Sources of Social Power,* Mann uses slightly different terms, distinguishing "intensive" vs. "extensive" and "authoritative" vs. "diffused" types of power (1986b, 7–10).

for social insurance (Paur 1981). Workers were to be tethered to the state through public pensions, as Napoleon III—closely observed by Bismarck— had attempted in the French Second Empire.

One problem with this is that Bismarck was only partially successful. Moreover, if one focuses on the relations between bourgeois agency, business interests, and the welfare state, a very different picture emerges. According to the criteria for identifying "bourgeois" forms of policy used in the earlier discussion of poor relief, the aims of social insurance were by no means clearly prebourgeois. This point will be developed in more detail below.

The Imperial German welfare state also appears to be strikingly modern in terms of the historicist definition used above, i.e., it expressed *in nuce* most of the typical characteristics of a European welfare state in the twentieth century. It has often been recognized that the Bismarckian social insurance laws of the 1880s were international models.[81] Yet the empire's social innovations are sometimes offered as further evidence of its antimodern exceptionalism.

Only a model of modern social insurance will permit a less arbitrary assessment of the claim that the Imperial German welfare state was backward. The features of a mid-twentieth-century "modern" welfare state would include the following:

1. Compulsion (i.e., compulsory participation, and often compulsory contributions by employers)[82]
2. Benefits whose levels are income-related or -graded and tend toward wage-replacement levels
3. Administrative centralization and unification
4. Universal (albeit differentiated) coverage
5. Eligibility for benefits based on entitlement, not on means tests
6. Macroeconomic demand management, generalization of mass consumption norms, and the coordination of capital and consumer goods through social policies

---

81. Interpretations coming from administrative-science circles rather than historians do tend to depict the early German welfare state in more favorable terms as "modern," flexible, adaptable, and even genuinely pathbreaking. Cf. Zöllner 1982; Köhler and Zacher 1983; and Zacher 1979. These writings are useful for descriptive detail, even if they are hesitant to speculate about the causes of social policies or the meaning of specific policy forms.

82. Although compulsion looked traditional and authoritarian to some German Liberals and to British observers, it was actually the more "traditional" Catholic countries that continued to adhere to the voluntary principle (Ritter 1986, 6). Not surprisingly, the German government viewed the conviction that "only the greatest measure of freedom for the individual can develop the best and most efficient resources of the nation" as traditional rather than modern (Ritter 1986, 7–8).

Not all of these features were typical of the pre-1914 German system, a point I will refer to below.

Industry, Agrarians, and the Creation of the German Welfare State

Research on Bismarck's social insurance laws of the 1880s has often focused on explaining the precocity of Germany's welfare state. Yet until recently little attention was paid to the stance of the dominant social classes and groups vis-à-vis social insurance. Was social policy favorable to German industry, both before and after Bismarck's fall in 1890? Which sectors of industry were favored? Were industrialists in favor of the major social insurance legislation?[83]

Social insurance was one of the many national policy arenas in which agrarians clashed with industrialists. The Junkers and their organizations argued that the Bismarckian social insurance programs made industrial labor more attractive than the rural laborer's life.[84] The agrarian interest organizations were also excluded from the crucial critical stages of policy-making. Against the energetic protests of the German Agricultural Council (Deutscher Landwirtschaftsrat), the original accident and sickness insurance laws excluded agricultural workers. Only in 1914 were rural laborers finally included in the sickness law (the extension was part of the 1911 law, but not implemented until 1914; cf. Deutscher Landwirtschaftsrat 1883, 54 ff.; Ritter 1986, 46).

By contrast, industrialists not only favored the national social insurance reforms of the 1880s but also played a decisive role in their creation (Machtan 1985; Baron 1979; Ullmann 1979; White 1976, 99). Some of the earliest plans for compulsory accident insurance were proposed by industry, and the government discussions preceding the 1884 accident insurance bill were largely based on a memorandum written by the Bochum industrialist Louis Baare (Vogel 1951, 98; Baare 1881). The Saarland industrialist and Reichstag deputy Carl-Ferdinand von Stumm agitated for national pension and disability insurance (Vogel 1951, 39–40; Rothfels 1938, 298). Imperial Germany's leading association of heavy industry, the Centralverband Deutscher Industrieller (CDI), vigorously supported the sickness, accident, and old-age pension insurance laws of the 1880s (Deutscher Handelstag, *Verhandlungen,* vol. 16, 1889, 1;

---

83. Space constraints preclude a narrative account of the enactment of the major national social policy laws during the *Kaiserreich,* or even a list. The best accounts, aside from the massive oeuvre of Florian Tennstedt, include Born 1957; Hentschel 1983; Ritter 1986; Rothfels 1927, 1970; Vogel 1951; and Zöllner 1982.

84. According to Stegmann (1970, 103), the agrarians called for an end to social policy to put a halt to "rural flight" (*Landflucht*). See also Richthofen 1901, 43, 52.

Bueck 1905). After the 1880s, however, prominent manufacturers and heavy-industry associations opposed the elaboration of new social programs, such as unemployment insurance and worker protection, and the expansion of existing programs. Industry was still influential, but its impact on policy-making was mainly negative.[85]

As heavy manufacturing abandoned social reform after 1890, light and export industry took up the call for new welfare legislation. These branches were represented by organizations such as the Federation of Industrialists (Bund der Industriellen; see Ullmann 1976), the allied Association of German Employers' Associations (Verein deutscher Arbeitgeber-Verbände), and later the Hanseatic Federation for Business, Commerce, and Industry, or Hansa-Bund (Mielke 1976). In 1901 the Federation of Industrialists promoted the idea of a national labor bureau (*Reichsarbeitsamt*), calling it "a social reform that would equally promote the interests of employers and employees" (the CDI rejected the idea; cf. Fricke et al. 1983, 1:223). The original purpose of the Association of German Employers' Associations was to provide financial support to struck firms. At the same time, the association supported negotiations with labor unions, in contrast to the repressive strategy of the heavy-industrial strike-relief organization (the Hauptstelle Deutscher Arbeitgeberverbände). Similarly, the Hansa-Bund committed itself in its 1909 founding program to social policies "aimed at securing the future of all workers and the preservation of their eagerness to work" (Mielke 1976, 202). The umbrella organization of the German Chambers of Commerce, the Deutscher Handelstag, representing mainly small industry and merchants, also backed a more activist social policy after the 1890s.[86]

Several researchers have explored the economic motives behind heavy industry's support for the initial social insurance schemes. Rüdiger Baron (1979) argues that Bismarck's social legislation was not a "carrot" to conciliate the working class for the "stick" of the concurrent Antisocialist Law. Instead, he argues, big employers hoped that social insurance would create the more skilled, healthy, and disciplined labor force that they needed to compete inter-

---

85. There is ample documentation of the swing in heavy industry's attitude toward social policy after the late 1880s in the pages of the *Deutsche Industrie-Zeitung* (organ of the CDI), *Der Arbeitgeber* (organ of the Hauptstelle Deutscher Arbeitgeberverbände), and the *Deutsche Arbeitgeberzeitung* (representing the Verein Deutscher Arbeitgeber-Verbände).

86. This is shown in the minutes of both the Handelstag's annual meetings and its "permanent commission" (*bleibender Ausschuß*); see Deutscher Handelstag *Verhandlungen*, 1881, appendix 1, p. 2 (10th meeting of the permanent commission, discussion of the accident insurance bill). See also various issues of the Handelstag's *Deutsche Wirtschafts-Zeitung*, e.g., 1906, 870 ff., 919 ff. ("Die Belastung der Betriebe durch die Arbeiterversicherung"); and 1907, 163, praising the recommencement of social policy under Wilhelm II ("Die deutsche Sozialpolitik im Jahre 1906"). After 1909 most of the chambers of commerce urged their members to join the liberal Hansa-Bund (Fricke et al. 1984, 2:142).

nationally. Ullmann (1979) challenges parts of this analysis while agreeing on the importance of industrial patronage of social insurance. He demonstrates that the initial support for the accident insurance legislation emanated from the sector of large firms characterized by steady and continuous production processes, recruitment problems, higher accident rates, and an orientation toward domestic rather than international markets. In a careful study of the social-political stances of chambers of commerce and industrial organizations, Monika Breger (1984) confirms that industry generally supported the welfare state measures of the 1880s; she also corroborates Ullmann's finding that sectors oriented toward the domestic market tended to be more supportive of social insurance.

Various liberal parties also supported national social insurance, especially after 1890. This is important because the liberals (especially the National Liberals) were closely tied to various factions of industry.[87] The left-liberals were unfriendly or openly hostile to national welfare legislation during the 1880s, while the "governmental" National Liberal Party backed Bismarck's social policy in its 1884 Heidelberg program and in the Reichstag (Röhl 1967, 62; White 1976, 121, 169). The final decade of the century witnessed a growing acceptance of social policy and state intervention among the other liberal political parties (Blackbourn 1985, 267–68). Indeed, the roles were now reversed, and the left-liberal parties became the more resolute supporters of social reform.[88] During the 1890s, even the Liberal Association (Freisinnige Vereinigung) moved away from the "Manchesterist" self-help doctrine that had dictated its opposition to social insurance during the 1880s to energetic support for social policy (Wegner 1968, 14–16; Düding 1972, 163).[89] The association was heavily backed by banks and finance capital (Düding 1972, 160 ff.).

The welfare state was thus not introduced against the interests of industrial capital but rather was backed by leading sectors of German industry during the *Kaiserreich*. Businessmen in heavy industry played an active and public role in the elaboration of the major social insurance laws. The expansion

---

87. The ties between the National Liberal Party and industry are most readily documented; the Liberal Association (Freisinnige Vereinigung) was close to financial and commercial interests (see Sheehan 1983). Many heavy-industrialists were closer to the Imperial Conservative Party (Reichs- und freikonservative Partei), whose social-policy views paralleled those of the CDI. A helpful visual overview of the complicated splits among German liberal parties from 1871 to 1914 can be found in Elm 1969; see also Sheehan 1978; and Fricke et al. 1983–86.

88. Although the National Liberal Party leader Ernst Basserman called for new reforms and increased social spending between 1898 and 1909, his position in the party was increasingly tenuous; see Basserman 1919; Düding 1972, 175; Eschenburg 1929; and Heckart 1974.

89. The Liberal Association leader Theodor Barth called for tactical alliances with the Social Democrats and cultivated relations with the right wing of the SPD beginning in 1890 (Wegner 1968, 112; Elm 1969, 40, 117). The notion of "social liberalism" was propagated by the Liberal Association; its Berlin section started calling itself the "Social Liberal" Association.

of the welfare state after 1890 was less directly the result of business pressure, if one ignores the rise of policies intended to shore up the independent middle classes (so-called *Mittelstandspolitik*). But the government was never running completely at cross-purposes to industry. Policies introduced after 1890 generally had broad backing in the export, light manufacturing, and finance sectors of capital and among the liberal parties. These policies included the introduction of limits on the length of women's workdays; the requirement that all factories have a set of labor regulations (*Arbeitsordnung*); the introduction of *paritätische*, municipal *Gewerbegerichte*, or industrial courts (at first voluntary, later obligatory in cities with more than twenty thousand inhabitants); the Prussian mine policy reforms; the legalization of unions; and various extensions of the 1880s social insurance laws (Born 1957). Significantly, policy areas in which Germany lagged behind Britain, such as national unemployment insurance, were broadly opposed by most sectors of industry.[90] German social policy offended only part of the business community and was always supported by major sectors of it.

The German Welfare State as Modern and Bourgeois

The German welfare state was also distinctly "bourgeois" in terms of the formal criteria set out above. For reasons suggested in my conclusion, this correspondence between the welfare state and bourgeois interests was not entirely due to the direct involvement of capitalists in social policy-making.

First, most social insurance benefits were given in cash.[91] To qualify for accident and sickness insurance, workers had to be steadily employed in industry, which provided an incentive to the "commodification" of one's labor power.[92] There were only minimal state contributions: fifty marks per year to worker pensions and none to the other insurance forms, meaning that "state-socialist" principles (as they were called at the time) were minimized.

That the welfare state could have encouraged a "bourgeois" form of subjectivity may sound paradoxical in the current political context, where conservatives rail against the deleterious psychological effects of welfare "de-

90. Heavy industry's vehement opposition to unemployment insurance was repeatedly expressed by the CDI; see Bueck 1905, 3:414–18, 559. The influential newspaper *Der Arbeitgeber* (until 1910 the *Mitteilungen der Hauptstelle Deutscher Arbeitgeberverbände*) came out repeatedly against unemployment insurance (e.g., 1908, no. 27; 1909, no. 14 [esp. 163]; 1910, no. 15; 1911, nos. 19–20; 1912, nos. 12, 15, 19; 1913, nos. 21–24 [esp. no. 22, 274–77]); see also *Deutsche Industrie-Zeitung* (1911, no. 22, 393–95). Some chambers of commerce opposed it as well; see Handelskammer für den Kreis Heidelberg, 1909. Only scattered groups of German industry appear to have supported unemployment insurance; cf. Varlez 1909, 415.

91. Some sickness insurance benefits were given in kind: free medical treatment was general, and hospital treatment could be substituted for sick pay (Zöllner 1982, 29).

92. But see Quataert 1984 on limits on pension rights for unpaid family workers.

pendency." Nonetheless, the German social state attempted to promote thrift, regularity, and self-responsibility among the insured. To participate in pension and disability funds, the worker was required at periodic intervals to stick special stamps into a membership booklet, indicating payment. After social reformers had attempted for decades to inculcate a "Protestant" savings ethic in the working class through popular savings banks, a nearly irresistible method for drawing workers into this kind of behavior had finally been found. The evolution of sickness insurance legislation gradually undermined genuine worker self-management, first by undercutting trade union mutual funds and then, in 1911, by limiting worker representation in the administration of the public funds. But the legislation vastly expanded the number of workers who were required regularly to contribute to such funds. Finally, the "insurance" metaphor strengthened the idea that workers—like their employers—were "investing" in their own future (see Quadagno 1988 for a similar argument in the context of contemporary U.S. social security policy).

Finally, the German welfare state engaged in social reclassification via the accentuation of differences among the poor. The manual workers were not only differentiated from white-collar employees through the creation of separate funds with different rules and benefits (Kocka 1981); manual workers also tended to be differentiated in an "exclusionary" way from the poor below (Parkin 1979; Simmel 1906, 27). By limiting eligibility to the stably employed workers in mainly industrial occupations, social insurance undergirded ideas of a "respectable" and primarily male working class. As Heide Gerstenberger writes, "Social insurance did not destroy 'solidarity among the working class'"; rather, what it did was to organize the desire to be different" (1981, 58).

The form of the German welfare state was also distinctly "modern" in terms of the criteria set out above. There are four main aspects of this modernity.

1. Compulsory social insurance plans. Despite opposition from certain liberal groups, German social insurance plans were compulsory; the state required and enforced the involvement of specified groups of wage earners and employers. Although it was precisely this aspect that led British observers initially to reject the German approach, by 1911 Lloyd George and Winston Churchill were converts to compulsory insurance (Hennock 1987), and compulsion is a standard feature of contemporary social insurance.

2. Income-related benefits. These were accepted with the 1889 old-age and disablement pension law, and variable benefits were also the de facto result of the decentralized sickness insurance system instituted in 1883 (Ritter 1986, 55, 76). Although socialists have often opposed

stratified benefit levels (though not in Germany), flat rates have been the exception rather than the rule in twentieth-century social insurance systems.

3. Administrative unification. Another modern element of the prewar German welfare state was the administrative unification of the various types of insurance in the painstakingly thorough 1911 Imperial Insurance Regulation (*Reichsversicherungsordnung*). The social insurance system in the United States remains much less unified even today than the German system of 1911.

4. Legal entitlement to benefits. None of the German insurance systems were means-tested; instead, contributors had a legal right to their pensions or benefits. This stands in contrast to the British old-age pension system introduced in 1908, for example. Germans could also contest decisions on their sickness or workman's compensation benefits or their old-age and disability pensions (Zöllner 1982, 30). Following a revision in 1899, workers could be represented in local pension offices and have some voice in deciding the level of individual pensions (Born 1957, 177).[93]

Conclusion: State Elites and the Promotion of Bourgeois Interests

I have argued that in key respects the poor relief and social insurance systems of the German Empire served industry rather than agriculture, and that agrarians were unable fundamentally to change the poor relief system in their favor. I have also argued that poor relief and social insurance were both modern and bourgeois. They were also more modern and more bourgeois than contemporaneous programs in Britain. While England may have provided Germany and other nations with a glimpse of their own economic futures, the German welfare system played the same role vis-à-vis Britain.

I have provided descriptive support for the class-correspondence perspective. What is missing is an explanation for the form and content of policy. (I am only able to outline an argument within the limits of this essay; a more complete account is developed in Steinmetz 1993.) The paradox is that the social insurance reforms of the 1880s were bourgeois, even though their ultimate authors were not businessmen but upper-level imperial and Prussian ministers, the chancellor, and the Kaiser. Why would imperial state elites put a consis-

---

93. The major missing dimensions here are universal coverage and a macroeconomic regulation of demand through social policy. I have explained the "class" reasons for nonuniversal coverage above; full-scale demand management had to await the development of Keynesianism (see Weir and Skocpol 1985).

tently bourgeois-industrial stamp on social policy despite their own largely aristocratic backgrounds and the presence of strong agrarian pressure groups? Three factors seem best able to account for this industrial orientation of state managers and thus ultimately to explain the class correspondence of social policy: (1) the state's dependence on the private economy for financial resources (required for the state's general operations as well as its specific military needs); (2) the state's dependence on private development and production for its military needs; and (3) the socialization of the state's civil servants into an ethos and habitus supportive of capitalist industrialization. These three factors—fiscal dependence, military dependence, and socialization—forced state officials to attend to industrial capitalist voices and to internalize an industrial capitalist logic when making policy. State-centered dynamics must be invoked to explain an ostensibly society-centered outcome.

First, the Prussian and German states were increasingly dependent on the private economy for fiscal resources. Most public revenues were raised through taxes, fees, tariffs, and loans from private sources. Although the Prussian state had traditionally tried to liberate itself from these constraints through ownership of demesne lands, mines, and other state property, it depended increasingly on revenues raised through taxes. By 1901, the net revenue from the Prussian state's own properties made up only 17.8 percent of total revenues; and by 1913 it had declined to 9.7 percent of the total.[94] The leading source of revenues was the Prussian railroads; the second largest source was the general income tax; and revenues were also culled from a property tax (*Ergänzungssteuer*).[95] The national state faced similar constraints. The empire had few productive assets of its own and depended mainly on indirect taxes, duties, and fees until 1914. The biggest source of central government revenues during the 1872–1914 period was tariffs.[96] As a result, the Prussian-German state was structurally dependent on capitalist prosperity and was obligated to the economic bourgeoisie as a "state-bearing" social class. Direct taxes required the compliance of property owners; credits required the goodwill of banks; and indirect taxes, fees, and tariffs could not exist without economic

---

94. All figures are from the *Statistisches Jahrbuch für den preußischen Staat,* vol. 1 (1903) through vol. 13 (1913), section "Finanzen." All of these are final rather than projected budget figures.

95. In 1913 income taxes brought in 392 million marks, while the railroads' net earnings were 590 million. See *Statistisches Jahrbuch für den preußischen Staat* 13 (1915): 318.

96. The imperial government did, of course, make some money on its railroads, but these brought in less than the Prussian rails—only 143 million marks in 1911, for example, as compared to 520 million marks for the Prussian railroads in the same year. Figures from *Statistisches Jahrbuch für das deutsche Reich* 34 (1913): 334; and *Statistisches Jahrbuch für den preußischen Staat* 14 (1916): 274. The other large source of imperial revenue was the yearly transfers (*Matrikularbeiträge*) from the federal states.

growth and a prospering capitalist economy. A politically induced slump could lower imports, railroad traffic, consumption levels, and business in general, thus emptying the state's coffers.

The second factor driving the state into a condominium with industry was its dependence on private development and production for its military needs. The state's dependence in military matters went beyond its need for private credit and increasingly encompassed industrial production and technical developments in the private sector as well. Most of the key innovations in armaments during the nineteenth century had emerged in the private sector— the breech-loading needle gun, widely credited with Prussian victory against Austria in 1866; Krupp's cannons; smokeless gunpowder and explosives; and even the Prussian railroads, which proved militarily indispensable (Showalter 1975, 161–90, 213; Messerschmidt 1975, 358; Osten-Sacken 1913, 67–91). Research and development played an increasingly important role as the arms race heated up in the decades before World War I. Moreover, although some military production could be carried out by state-owned firms, private industry was crucial for emergency resource mobilization and for large-scale production, including the navy's battleships and heavy cruisers and military airplanes, which were produced entirely by private enterprises before 1914 (Morrow 1976). Private companies supplied 72 percent of the weaponry for the artillery units in the late Wilhelmine era, and by 1914 they received 60 percent of total matériel spending (Schmidt-Richberg 1968, 119; Messerschmidt 1975, 370). The Imperial German state thus needed industry in order to continue building upon its peculiar advantage.[97]

How did these fiscal and national-military considerations influence the form of social policy? The main connection was an overarching determination by state officials to preserve the economic health and the loyalty of capital, especially its heavy-industrial faction. As a result, most national policies were propelled in the direction of support for a modernizing industrial capitalist economy. In future research it will be important to identify the specific characteristics of the ideological discourses within the state, as well as the more mundane features, such as sanctions and criteria for bureaucratic promotion, that produced these systematic effects.

The third factor moves from external constraints on policy to the "produc-

---

97. The issue of military motives and class correspondence is slightly more complex than is suggested here, since the state could sometimes be led by military considerations to engage in social policies against industrial interests. This is illustrated by the 1905 miners' strike and the government's response to the mine employers' plans to import strikebreakers from abroad. The Prussian government's response actually met certain of the striking miners' key demands, culminating in a revision of the Prussian mining code. The state's liberalism and flexibility in this case probably reflected the strategic military importance of mine production (Born 1957, 184–85).

tion" of German officials, their education and career-long ideological "interpellation" (Althusser 1971). Administrative elites within the imperial state offices and Prussian ministries were deeply imbued with an ethos of promoting industrialization. This commitment derived from the meritocratic form of their careers, the nature of their university education, and a specific political culture within the state apparatus. The system of civil-service qualifying examinations, which started as early as the 1730s (Geib 1955–56, 320; Delbrück 1917, 4), forced even aristocratic boys to operate according to bourgeois meritocratic standards. Administrative careers required an internship period as *Referendar,* and there were further examinations after service began (Armstrong 1973, 202–3). Upper-level bureaucrats were required to have an academic degree in Prussia after 1770, and the university degree became progressively more important (Bleek 1972, 47, 54, 80–81; Mueller 1984, 68). Although sons of the nobility were still overrepresented in the bureaucracy, selection from this pool was based on mastery of bourgeois skills.

The core of future officials' studies from 1743 until the nineteenth century was cameralistic science. During the eighteenth century, cameralism developed into the science of governing with respect to the maintenance and improvement of the economy. Although the ultimate goal of this "new" cameralism was to strengthen the state and its coffers, this was seen as depending on the economic welfare of society. Both the new cameralism and the German field of "national economy," which supplanted it in the nineteenth century, put a positive value on industry and development, and unlike laissez-faire approaches, both assumed that the state should be deeply involved in promoting economic modernization (Tribe 1988). After 1817 legal studies and practice in the law courts and urban and rural administration began to replace cameralistics and internships in agriculture or industry in the training of administrative officials, although "cameralistic schooling continued to influence the criteria of admission" (Koselleck 1989, 245). The general belief persisted, however, that state officials had the "explicit duty to function predominately as a dynamic and formative element" (Geib 1955–56, 322; see also Gillis 1972, 17). Moreover, in many respects the legal focus actually intensified the capitalist orientation of training. The task of the state was now to eliminate obstacles to the expansion of capitalism.

The ongoing (re)socialization of noble civil servants into a bourgeois outlook continued after they entered the administration. As Gary Bonham (1985) has shown in a detailed biographical analysis, the stance of Imperial German and Prussian officials on specific policy issues was largely determined by career experiences and location within the administration. Apprenticeship in the civil service had a "modernizing" effect on most Prussian and Reich ministers; only in a few specific branches of the Prussian state was there an enhancement of anti-industrial attitudes.[98] Further research will probably also show that an ideological or discursive structure within the state apparatus constantly referred officials back to the bourgeoisie.[99] Whatever their initial impulses, many state managers who rose in the bureaucratic hierarchy came to embrace a modernizing industrial ideology.

Perhaps the Prussian state was not autonomous after all; but this was its official myth (Medalen 1978, 93). Indeed the German state of the late nineteenth and early twentieth centuries was highly dependent on private industry to carry out its projects. Nonetheless, the motives that forced the state into an alliance with industry were the state's "own" interests, and not the result of some sort of mysterious economic "determination in the last instance." Skocpol is correct in arguing that the state, in its search for internal order and international competition, may provoke conflicts of interest with the dominant class (1979, 30). Yet the nineteenth-century German state, which in so many respects seems to be located at the core of the state-centered perspective, rarely obstructed the interests of the industrial bourgeoisie. By bringing the entire range of government activities within our field of vision, including the state's local projections, we only strengthen this conclusion. In order to pursue its specific goals, the state had no choice but to ally with modern business.

References

Abramovitz, Mimi. 1985. "The Family Ethic: The Female Pauper and Public Aid, Pre-1900." *Social Service Review* 59, no. 1: 121–35.
Abusch, Alexander. 1947. *Der Irrweg einer Nation*. Berlin: Aufbau Verlag.
Almond, Gabriel A. 1988. "The Return to the State." *American Political Science Review* 82, no. 3: 853–74.
Althusser, Louis. 1971. "Ideology and Ideological State Apparatuses." In *Lenin and Philosophy,* by Louis Althusser, 121–72. London: NLB.
Anderson, M. L., and K. Barkin. 1982. "The Myth of the Puttkamer Purge and the Reality of the Kulturkampf." *Journal of Modern History* 54:647–86.
Anderson, Perry. 1974. *Lineages of the Absolutist State*. London: Verso.
Andic, Suphan, and Jindrich Veverka. 1963. "The Growth of Government Expenditure in Germany since the Unification." *Finanzarchiv,* n.s., 23, no. 2: 169–273.

---

98. This antimodern effect was observed among ministers who made a career in the Prussian departments of agriculture, finance, and the interior rather than in the Reich administration (Bonham 1985, 375).

99. The way this worked is illustrated by the dismissal of the Prussian minister Miquel when he transgressed a political-cultural boundary within the administration: supporting the Junkers once too often against the Kaiser and industry. Indeed, Bismarck's dismissal has also been traced to a comparable sin; see Draper 1977, 425.

Armstrong, John A. 1973. *The European Administrative Elite.* Princeton: Princeton University Press.

Baare, Louis. 1881. "Gesetz-Entwurf betreffend die Errichtung einer Arbeiter-Unfall-Versicherungs-Kasse nebst Motiven." *Annalen des Deutschen Reiches* 14:69–90.

Bade, Klaus J. 1983. " 'Kulturkampf' auf dem Arbeitsmarkt: Bismarcks 'Polenpolitik,' 1885–1890." In *Innenpolitische Probleme des Bismarck-Reiches,* edited by Otto Pflanze, 121–42. Munich: R. Oldenbourg Verlag.

Baron, Rüdiger. 1979. "Weder Zuckerbrot noch Peitsche: Historische Konstitutionsbedingungen des Sozialstaates in Deutschland." In *Gesellschaft: Beiträge zur Marxschen Theorie,* 12:13–55. Frankfurt a.M.: Suhrkamp.

———. 1983. "Die Entwicklung der Armenpflege in Deutschland vom Beginn des 19. Jahrhunderts bis zum 1. Weltkrieg." In *Geschichte der Sozialarbeit: Hauptlinien ihrer Entwicklung im 19. und 20. Jahrhundert,* edited by Rüdiger Baron and Rolf Landwehr, 11–71 Weinheim: Beltz Verlag.

Barkin, Kenneth D. 1970. *The Controversy over German Industrialization, 1890–1902.* Chicago: University of Chicago Press.

———. 1987. "1878–1879: The Second Founding of the Reich: A Perspective." *German Studies Review* 10, no. 2: 219–35.

Basserman, Karola. 1919. *Ernst Basserman: Das Lebensbild eines Parlamentariers aus Deutschlands glücklicher Zeit.* Mannheim: Verlag der Druckerei Dr. Haas.

Bätzner, W. 1873. *Handbuch der neuen Armengesetzgebung über die öffentliche Armenpflege nach deutschem und württembergischem Recht.* Stuttgart.

Baudis, Dieter, and Helga Nussbaum. 1978. *Wirtschaft und Staat in Deutschland vom Ende des 19. Jahrhunderts bis 1918/19.* Vol. 1. Berlin: Akademie Verlag.

Beetham, David. 1985. *Max Weber and the Theory of Modern Politics.* Cambridge: Polity Press.

Berthold, Georg. 1881. *Die offene Armenpflege der Stadt Elberfeld im Juni 1881.* Elberfeld: S. Lucas.

Blackbourn, David. 1984. "The Discreet Charm of the Bourgeoisie: Reappraising German History in the Nineteenth Century." In *The Peculiarities of German History: Bourgeois Society and Politics in Nineteenth-Century Germany,* edited by David Blackbourn and Geoff Eley, 159–292. Oxford and New York: Oxford University Press.

Blätter für das Armenwesen. Various issues. Stuttgart: G. Hasselbrink'sche Buckdruckerei.

Bleek, Wilhelm. 1972. *Von der Kameralausbildung bis zum Juristenprivileg: Studium, Prüfung und Ausbildung der höheren Beamten des allgemeinen Verwaltungsdienstes in Deutschland im 18. und 19. Jahrhundert.* Berlin: Colloquium.

Block, Fred. 1977. "The Ruling Class Does Not Rule." *Socialist Revolution* 33:6–28.

———. 1980. "Beyond Relative Autonomy: State Managers as Historical Subjects." In *The Socialist Register, 1980,* edited by R. Miliband and J. Saville, 227–42. London: Merlin Press.

Böhmert, Victor. 1888. *Das Armenwesen in 77 deutschen Städten und einigen Landarmenverbänden.* Dresden: Armenstatistisches Bureau des Deutschen Vereins für Armenpflege und Wohltätigkeit.

Boltanski, Luc. 1984. "How a Social Group Objectified Itself: 'Cadres' in France, 1936–45." *Social Science Information* 23, no. 3: 469–91.

Bonham, Gary. 1983. "State Autonomy or Class Domination: Approaches to Administrative Politics in Wilhelmine Germany." *World Politics* 35:631–51.

———. 1984. "Beyond Hegel and Marx: An Alternative Approach to the Political Role of the Wilhelmine State." *German Studies Review* 7:199–225.

———. 1985. "Bureaucratic Modernizers and Traditional Constraints: Higher Officials and the Landed Nobility in Wilhelmine Germany, 1890–1914." Ph.D. diss., University of California-Berkeley.

Booth, Douglas A. 1978. "Karl Marx on State Regulation of the Labor Process: The English Factory Laws." *Review of Social Economy* 36:137–57.

Born, Karl Erich. 1957. *Staat und Sozialpolitik seit Bismarcks Sturz.* Wiesbaden: Franz Steiner Verlag.

———. 1972. "Staat und Sozialpolitik im Deutschen Kaiserreich." In *Geschichte in der Gegenwart: Festschrift für Kurt Kluxen,* edited by Ernst Heined, 179–97. Paderborn: Schöningh.

Bourdieu, Pierre. 1984. *Distinction.* Cambridge, Mass.: Harvard University Press.

———. 1985. "Social Space and the Genesis of Groups." *Theory and Society* 14, no. 6: 723–44.

———. 1987. "What Makes a Class? On the Theoretical and Practical Existence of Groups." *Berkeley Journal of Sociology* 32:1–18.

Breger, Monika. 1984. *Die Haltung der industriellen Unternehmer zur staatlichen Sozialpolitik im Deutschen Kaiserreich.* Frankfurt a.M.: Haag und Herchen.

Brenner, Robert. 1988. "The Autonomy of the State?" Unpublished paper, Center for Social Theory and Comparative History, University of California-Los Angeles.

Breunig, Willi. 1976. *Soziale Verhältnisse der Arbeiterschaft und der sozialistischen Arbeiterbewegung in Ludwigshafen am Rhein, 1869–1919.* Ludwigshafen a. R.: Stadtarchiv.

Bueck, H. A. 1905. *Der Centralverband Deutscher Industrieller, 1876–1901.* 3 vols. Berlin: J. Guttentag.

Buehl, A. 1903. "Die Reorganisation des Hamburger Armenwesens und ihre Erfolge." *Blätter für das Hamburgische Armenwesen.*

Büsch, Otto, and Michael Erbe, eds. 1983. *Otto Hintze und die moderne Geschichtswissenschaft: Ein Tagungsbericht.* Berlin: Colloquium Verlag.

Cammack, Paul. 1989. "Bringing the State Back In: A Polemic." *British Journal of Political Science* 19, no. 2: 261–90.

Canis, Konrad. 1982. "Kontinuität und Diskontinuität im junkerlich-bourgeoisen Klassenkompromiß, 1890–1897." *Zeitschrift für Geschichtswissenschaft* 30, no. 1: 23–38.

Centralverband Deutscher Industrieller. 1905. *Verhandlungen, Mitteilungen und Berichte.* No. 100. Berlin: Centralverband Deutscher Industrieller.

Clark, Gordon L., and Michael Dear. 1984. *State Apparatus: Structures and Language of Legitimacy.* Boston: Allen and Unwin.

Cockburn, Cynthia. 1977. *The Local State.* London: Pluto Press.

Cohen, G. A. 1978. *Karl Marx's Theory of History: A Defence.* Princeton: Princeton University Press.

Conze, Werner. 1985. "From 'Pöbel' to 'Proletariat': The Socio-Historical Preconditions of Socialism in Germany." In *The Social History of Politics: Critical Perspectives in West German Historical Writing since 1945,* edited by Georg Iggers, 49–80. Leamington Spa, Warwickshire: Berg.

Croon, Helmut. 1960. *Die gesellschaftliche Auswirkungen des Gemeindewahlrechts in den Gemeinden und Kreisen des Rheinlandes und Westfalens im 19. Jh.* Cologne: Westdeutscher Verlag.

Dahrendorf, Ralf. 1967. *Society and Democracy in Germany.* New York: Norton.

Delbrück, Clemens von. 1917. *Die Ausbildung für den höheren Verwaltungsdienst in Preußen.* Jena: Gustav Fischer.

Denkschrift über die Lage des Armenwesens der Stadt Kolmar. Colmar, 1898.

Deutscher Handelstag. Various years. *Deutsche Wirtschafts-Zeitung: Zentralblatt für Handel, Industrie und Verkehr.* Berlin: R. v. Decker's Verlag.

———. Various years. *Verhandlungen des Deutschen Handelstages: Stenographischer Bericht.* Berlin: L. Simon.

Deutscher Landwirtschaftsrat. Various years. *Archiv des Deutschen Landwirthschaftsraths.* Berlin: Paul Paren Verlag.

Deutscher Verein für Armenpflege und Wohltätigkeit. Various years. *Schriften.* Leipzig: Duncker und Humblot.

Draper, Hal. 1977. *Karl Marx's Theory of Revolution.* Vol. 1, *State and Bureaucracy.* New York: Monthly Review Press.

Düding, Dieter. 1972. *Der Nationalsoziale Verein, 1896–1903.* Munich: R. Oldenbourg Verlag.

Eley, Geoff. 1981. "James Sheehan and the German Liberals." *Central European History* 14:273–88.

———. 1984. "The British Model and the German Road." In *The Peculiarities of German History: Bourgeois Society and Politics in Nineteenth-Century Germany,* edited by David Blackbourn and Geoff Eley, 39–155. London and New York: Oxford University Press.

———. 1986. *From Unification to Nazism: Reinterpreting the German Past.* Boston: Allen and Unwin.

Elm, Ludwig. 1969. *Zwischen Fortschritt und Reaktion: Geschichte der Parteien der liberalen Bourgeoisie in Deutschland, 1893–1918.* Berlin: Akademie-Verlag.

Elster, Jon. 1985. *Making Sense of Marx.* Cambridge: Cambridge University Press.

Engels, Friedrich. [1889] 1962. "Die Abdankung der Bourgeoisie." In *Werke,* by Karl Marx and Friedrich Engels, 21: 383–88. Berlin: Dietz Verlag.

———. [1870] 1969a. "Preface to the Second Ed. of *The Peasant War in Germany.*" In *Selected Works,* by Karl Marx and Friedrich Engels, 2:158–65. Moscow: Progress.

———. [1875] 1969b. "Supplement to the Preface for the Third Ed. of *The Peasant War in Germany.*" In *Selected Works,* by Karl Marx and Friedrich Engels, 2:165–71. Moscow: Progress.

———. [1872–73] 1969c. "The Housing Question." In *Selected Works,* by Karl Marx and Friedrich Engels, 2:305–75. Moscow: Progress.

————. [1895–96] 1970a. "The Role of Force in History." In *Selected Works*, by Karl Marx and Friedrich Engels, 3:377–428. Moscow: Progress.

————. [1884] 1970b. "The Origin of the Family, Private Property and the State." In *Selected Works*, by Karl Marx and Friedrich Engels, 3:204–334. Moscow: Progress.

Die Ergebnisse der am 1.12.1900 erfolgten statistischen Erhebung über die im Gebiete der Stadt Hamburg in offener Armenpflege unterstützten Personen unter besonderer Berücksichtigung der Wohnungsverhältnisse. 1902. Hamburg: Lütcke und Wulff.

Eschenburg, Theodor. 1929. *Das Kaiserreich am Scheideweg: Bassermann, Bülow und der Block.* Berlin: Verlag für Kulturpolitik.

Esping-Andersen, Gösta. 1985a. "Power and Distributional Regimes." *Politics and Society* 14, no. 2: 223–56.

————. 1985b. *Politics against Markets: The Social Democratic Road to Power.* Princeton: Princeton University Press.

————. 1990. *The Three Worlds of Welfare Capitalism.* Princeton: Princeton University Press.

Esping-Andersen, Gösta, Roger Friedland, and Erik Olin Wright. 1976. "Modes of Class Struggle and the Capitalist State." *Capitalistate*, nos. 4–5: 186–220.

Evans, Peter B., Theda Skocpol, and Dietrich Rueschemayer. 1985. "On the Road toward a More Adequate Understanding of the State." In *Bringing the State Back In*, edited by Peter B. Evans, Dietrich Rueschemayer, and Theda Skocpol, 347–66. New York: Cambridge University Press.

Faust, Anselm. 1981a. "Konjunktur, Arbeitsmarktstruktur und sozialpolitische Reaktion: Arbeitsnachweis, Arbeitsbeschaffung und Arbeitslosenversicherung im Deutschen Kaiserreich." In *Wachstumsschwankungen: Wirtschaftliche und soziale Auswirkungen,* edited by Hermann Kellenbenz, 235–55. Stuttgart: Klett-Cotta.

————. 1981b. "State and Unemployment in Germany, 1890–1918 (Labour Exchanges, Job Creation and Unemployment Insurance)." In *The Emergence of the Welfare State in Britain and Germany, 1850–1950,* edited by W. J. Mommsen, 150–63. London: Croon Helm.

————. 1982. "Arbeitsmarkt in Deutschland: Die Entstehung der öffentlichen Arbeitsvermittlung, 1890–1927." In *Historische Arbeitsmarktforschung: Entstehung, Entwicklung und Probleme der Vermarktung von Arbeitskraft,* edited by Toni Pierenkemper and Richard Tilly, 253–72. Göttingen: Vandenhoeck und Ruprecht.

————. 1986. *Arbeitsmarktpolitik im Deutschen Kaiserreich: Arbeitsvermittlung, Arbeitsbeschaffung und Arbeitslosenunterstützung, 1890–1918.* Supplement 79 to *Vierteljahrsschrift für Sozial- und Wirtschaftsgeschichte.* Stuttgart: Franz Steiner Verlag.

Foucault, Michel. 1979. *Discipline and Punish: The Birth of the Prison.* New York: Vintage Books.

Fraser, Derek. 1981. "The English Poor Law and the Origins of the British Welfare State." In *The Emergence of the Welfare State in Britain and Germany, 1850–1950,* edited by W. J. Mommsen. London: Croon Helm.

Fraser, Derek, ed. 1976. *The New Poor Law in the Nineteenth Century.* London: St. Martin's Press.

Fraser, Nancy. 1987. "Women, Welfare and the Politics of Need Interpretation." *Hypatia: A Journal of Feminist Philosophy* 2, no. 1: 103–21.

Fricke, Dieter, et al., eds. 1983–86. *Lexikon zur Parteiengeschichte: Die bürgerlichen und kleinbürgerlichen Parteien und Verbände in Deutschland (1789–1945).* 4 vols. Leipzig: VEB Bibliographisches Institut.

Funk, M. J. 1913. *Geschichte und Statistik des bremischen Armenwesens.* Bremen: Kommissionsverlag von F. Leuwer.

Gall, Lothar. 1978. "Zu Ausbildung und Charakter des Interventionsstaats." *Historische Zeitschrift* 227:552–70.

Geib, Ekkehard. 1955–56. "Ausbildung des Nachwuchses für den höheren Verwaltungsdienst unter besonderer Berücksichtigung der Geschichte der Justiz- und Verwaltungsausbildung in Preußen." *Archiv des öffentlichen Rechts* 80:307–45.

Gerstenberger, Heide. 1981. "Von der Armenpflege zur Sozialpolitik oder: Plädoyer für eine materialistische Fragestellung." *Leviathan* 9, no. 1: 39–61.

"Gesetz über die Freizügigkeit." 1867. In *Bundes-Gesetzblatt des Norddeutschen Bundes,* 55–56. Berlin.

Geyer, Michael. 1984. "The State in National Socialist Germany." In *Statemaking and Social Movements: Essays in History and Theory,* edited by Charles Bright and Susan Harding, 193–232. Ann Arbor:: University of Michigan Press.

Gillis, John. 1968. "Aristocracy and Bureaucracy in Nineteenth Century Prussia." *Past and Present* 41:105–29.

———. 1972. *The Prussian Bureaucracy in Crisis, 1840–1860: Origins of an Administrative Ethos.* Stanford: Stanford University Press.

Goldscheid, Rudolf. 1926. "Staat, offentlicher Haushalt und Gesellschaft." In *Handbuch der Finanzwissenschaft,* edited by Wilhelm Gerloff and Franz Meisel, 1:146–84. Tübingen: Mohr.

Goltz, Theodor von der. 1896. *Straßburgs Armenpflege.* Strasbourg.

Gordon, Linda. 1988. "What Does Welfare Regulate?" *Social Research* 55, no. 4: 609–47.

Great Britain. 1910. "Report by Dr. Emil Münsterberg." In *Parliamentary Papers. Royal Commission on the Poor Law,* 49:480–98. Berlin: HMSO.

Greer, James L. 1987. "The Political Economy of the Local State." *Politics and Society* 15, no. 4: 513–38.

Grieken, Friedrich Wilhelm van. 1927. "Die offene Armenpflege der Stadt Berlin." Ph.D. diss., University of Giessen.

Gugel, H. 1910. *Die Reichsgesetze über den Unterstützungswohnsitz (in der Fassung durch Reichsges. v. 30. Mai 1908).* Mannheim: J. Bensheimer.

Gutsche, Willibald. 1976. "Probleme des Verhältnisses zwischen Monopolkapital und Staat in Deutschland vom Ende des 19. Jahrhunderts bis zum Vorabend des ersten Weltkriegs." *In Studien zum deutschen Imperialismus vor 1914,* edited by Fritz Klein, 33–84. Berlin: Akademie Verlag.

Hagenberg, Wilhelm. 1914. "Das Armen- und Fürsorgewesen der Stadt Essen von 1800–1913." Ph.D. diss., University of Tübingen.

Handelskammer für den Kreis Heidelberg. 1909. *Gutachtliche Äußerung der Handelskammer für den Kreis Heidelberg nebst die Stadt Eberbach zu der von dem Großherzoglichen Badischen Ministerium des Innern herausgegebenen Denkschrift über die Frage der Arbeitslosigkeit.* Heidelberg.

Hay, J. R. 1981. "The British Business Community, Social Insurance, and the German Example." In *The Emergence of the Welfare State in Britain and Germany, 1850–1950,* edited by W. J. Mommsen, 107–32. London: Croon Helm.

Heckart, Beverly. 1974. *From Basserman to Bebel: The Grand Bloc's Quest for Reform in the Kaiserreich, 1900–1914.* New Haven: Yale University Press.

Hennock, E. P. 1987. *British Social Reform and German Precedents.* Oxford: Oxford University Press.

Hentschel, Volker. 1983. *Geschichte der deutschen Sozialpolitik, 1880–1980.* Frankfurt a.M.: Suhrkamp.

Hintze, Otto. 1962–67. *Gesammelte Abhandlungen.* 2 ed., edited by Gerhard Oestreich. Göttingen: Vandenhoeck und Ruprecht.

Hirsch, Paul, and Hugo Lindemann. 1905. *Das kommunale Wahlrecht.* Berlin: Vorwärts.

Hoffmann, Walther. 1965. *Das Wachstum der deutschen Wirtschaft seit der Mitte des 19. Jahrhundert.* Berlin: Springer.

Hohorst, Gerd, Jürgen Kocka, and Gerhard A. Ritter. 1978. *Sozialgeschichtliches Arbeitsbuch: Materialien zur Statistik des Kaiserreichs, 1870–1914.* 2d ed. Vol. 2. Munich: Verlag C. H. Beck.

Horn, Hannelore. 1958. "Die Rolle des Bundes der Landwirte im Kampf um den Bau des Mittellandkanals." *Jahrbuch für die Geschichte Mittel- und Ostdeutschlands* 7:273–358.

———. 1964. *Der Kampf um den Bau des Mittelland-Kanals.* Cologne: Westdeutscher Verlag.

Iggers, Georg. 1988. Introduction to *German History in Marxist Perspective: The East German Approach,* by Andreas Dorpulen. Detroit: Wayne State University Press.

Jaeger, Hans. 1967. *Unternehmer in der deutschen Politik (1890–1918).* Bonn: Ludwig Röhrscheid Verlag.

Jessop, Bob. 1982. *The Capitalist State.* New York: New York University Press.

———. 1983. "Accumulation, State, and Hegemonic Projects." *Kapitalistate* 10–11:89–112.

———. 1985. *Nicos Poulantzas: Marxist Theory and Political Strategy.* New York: St. Martin's Press.

———. 1990. *State Theory: Putting States in Their Place.* University Park: Pennsylvania State University Press.

John, Michael. 1988. "The Peculiarities of the German State: Bourgeois Law and Society in the Imperial Era." *Past and Present* 119:105–31.

Jürgens, Ulrich. 1990. "Entwicklungslinien der staatstheoretischen Diskussion seit den 70er Jahren." *Aus Politik und Zeitgeschichte,* 23 Feb.: 14–22.

Kaiserliches Statistisches Amt. 1887. "Statistik der öffentlichen Armenpflege im Jahre 1885." *Statistik des deutschen Reiches,* n.s., vol. 29. Berlin: Verlag von Puttkammer und Mühlbrecht.

Kehr, Eckart. 1965. "Das soziale System der Reaktion in Preußen." In *Das Primat der Innenpolitik,* edited by Hans-Ulrich Wehler, 64–86. Berlin: W. de Gruyter.

———. 1973. *Battleship Building and Party Politics in Germany, 1894–1901.* Chicago: University of Chicago Press.

Klein, Fritz. 1976. *Deutschland, 1897–1917.* 4th ed. Berlin: VEB Deutscher Verlag der Wissenschaft.

Kocka, Jürgen. 1980. *White Collar Workers in America, 1890–1914: A Social-Political History in International Perspective.* London and Beverly Hills: Sage.

———. 1981. "Class Formation, Interest Articulation, and Public Policy: The Origins of the German White-Collar Class in the Late Nineteenth and Twentieth Centuries." In *Organizing Interests in Western Europe,* ed. Suzanne Berger, 63–82. Cambridge: Cambridge University Press.

———. 1983. "Otto Hintze, Max Weber und das Problem der Bürokratie." In *Otto Hintze und die moderne Geschichtswissenschaft: Ein Tagungsbericht,* edited by Otto Büsch and Michael Erbe, 150–88. Berlin: Colloquium Verlag.

Kocka, Jürgen, ed. 1987. *Bürger und Bürgerlichkeit im 19. Jahrhundert.* Göttingen: Vandenhoeck and Ruprecht.

Köhler, P. A. and H. F. Zacher, eds. 1983. *Beiträge zu Geschichte und aktueller Situation der Sozialversicherung.* Berlin: Duncker und Humblot.

Köllmann, Wolfgang. 1966. "Die Anfänge staatlicher Sozialpolitik in Preußen bis 1869." *Vierteljahresschrift für Sozial- und Wirtschaftsgeschichte* 53:28–52.

Köllmann, Wolfgang, et al., ed. 1953. *Hilfe von Mensch zu Mensch: Hundert Jahre Elberfelder Armenpflege-System.* Wuppertal: Presse- und Werbeamt.

Koselleck, Reinhart. 1989. *Preußen zwischen Reform und Revolution: Allgemeines Landrecht, Verwaltung und soziale Bewegung von 1791 bis 1848.* Munich: Deutscher Taschenbuch Verlag/Klett.

Krabbe, Wolfgang. 1979. "Munizipalsozialismus und Interventionsstaat." *Geschichte in Wissenschaft und Unterricht* 5:265–83.

———. 1981. "Die Gründung Städtischer Arbeiterschutz-Anstalten in Deutschland: Arbeitsnachweis, Arbeitslosenfürsorge, Gewerbegericht und Rechtsauskunftstelle." In *Arbeiterexistenz im 19. Jahrhundert,* edited by Werner Conze and Ulrich Engelhardt, 425–45. Stuttgart: Klett-Cotta.

———. 1985. *Kommunalpolitik und Industrialisierung.* Berlin: Kohlhammer.

Krasner, Stephen. 1984. "Approaches to the State: Alternative Conceptions and Historical Dynamics." *Comparative Politics* 16, no. 3: 223–46.

Laclau, Ernesto. 1977. *Politics and Ideology in Marxist Theory.* London: Verso.

Laclau, Ernesto, and Chantal Mouffe. 1985. *Hegemony and Socialist Strategy: Towards a Radical Democratic Politics.* London: Verso.

Langewiesche, Dieter. 1977. "Wanderungsbewegungen in der Hochindustrialisierungsperiode: Regionale, interstädtische und innerstädtische Mobilität in Deutschland, 1880–1914." *Vierteljahresschrift für Sozial- und Wirtschaftsgeschichte,* 64 no. 1: 1–40.

Leibfried, Stephan, and Florian Tennstedt, eds. 1985. *Politik der Armut und die Spaltung des Sozialstaates.* Frankfurt a.M. Suhrkamp.

Leibfried, Stephan, et al., eds. 1985. *Sozialpolitik und Sozialstaat: Bericht zum 10.10.1985.* 3 vols. Bremen: Zentraldruckerei der Universität Bremen.

Lube, Barbara. 1984. "Mythos und Wirklichkeit des Elberfelder Systems." In *Gründerzeit,* edited by Karl-Hermann Beeck, 158–84. Cologne: Rheinland-Verlag.

Lukács, Georg. [1954]. 1973. *Die Zerstörung der Vernunft.* Vol. 1. Darmstadt: Luchterhand.

Machtan, Lothar. 1985. "Risikoversicherung statt Gesundheitsschutz für Arbeiter: Zur Entstehung der Unfallversicherungsgesetzgebung im Bismarck-Reich." *Leviathan* 13, no. 3: 420–41.

Machtan, Lothar, and Dietrich Milles. 1980. *Die Klassensymbiose von Junkertum und Bourgeoisie: Zum Verhältnis von gesellschaftlicher und politischer Herrschaft in Preußen-Deutschland, 1850–1878/79.* Frankfurt a.M.: Ullstein.

Maier, Hans. 1980. *Die ältere deutsche Staats- und Verwaltungslehre.* 2d ed. Munich: C. H. Beck'sche Verlagsbuchhandlung.

Mann, Michael. 1986a. "The Autonomous Power of the State: Its Origins, Mechanisms, and Results." In *States in History,* edited by John A. Hall, 109–36. Oxford: Basil Blackwell.

———. 1986b. *The Sources of Social Power.* New York: Cambridge University Press.

———. 1988. "Capitalism and Militarism." In *States, War, and Capitalism,* by Michael Mann, 124–45. Oxford: Basil Blackwell.

March, James, and Joann Olsen. 1984. "The New Institutionalism: Organizational Factors in Political Life." *American Political Science Review* 78:734–48.

Marshall, T. H. 1970. *Social Policy in the Twentieth Century.* Hutchinson University Library. London: Hutchinson.

———. 1977. *Class, Citizenship, and Social Development.* Chicago: University of Chicago Press.

Marx, Karl. 1970a. "Critique of the Gotha Program." In *Selected Works,* by Karl Marx and Friedrich Engels, 3:13–30 Moscow: Progress.

———. 1970b. "The Eighteenth Brumaire of Louis Bonaparte." In *Selected Works,* by Karl Marx and Friedrich Engels, 1:394–487. Moscow: Progress.

Medalen, C. 1978. "State Monopoly Capitalism in Germany: The Hibernia Affair." *Past and Present* 78:82–112.

Meinerich, Theodor. 1919. "Die Leistungen der Stadt Berlin für die Armen- und Krankenpflege seit dem Anfange des 19. Jahrhunderts: Eine statistische Untersuchung." Vol 1. Ph. D. diss., University of Greifswald.

Messerschmidt, Manfred. 1975. *Die politische Geschichte der preußisch-deutschen Armee.* Vol. 4, part 1 of *Handbuch zur deutschen Militärgeschichte, 1648–1939.* Munich: Bernard und Graefe Verlag für Wehrwesen.

Mielke, S. 1976. *Der Hansa-Bund für Gewerbe, Handel und Industrie, 1909–1914.* Göttingen: Vandenhoeck und Ruprecht.

Moeller, Robert G., ed. 1986. *Peasants and Lords in Modern Germany: Recent Studies in Agricultural History.* Boston: Allen and Unwin.

Mommsen, Wolfgang. 1983. "Die Verfassung des Deutschen Reiches von 1871 als dilatorischer Herrschaftskompromiß." In *Innenpolitische Probleme des Bismarck-Reiches,* edited by Otto Pflanze, 195–216. Munich: R. Oldenbourg Verlag.

Morrow, John Howard, Jr. 1976. *Building German Airpower, 1909–1914*. Knoxville: University of Tennessee Press.

Morsey, Rudolf. 1957. *Die oberste Reichsverwaltung unter Bismarck, 1867–1890*. Münster: Verlag Aschendorff.

Mottek, Hans. 1968. "Zur Verstaatlichung im Kapitalismus: Der Fall Hibernia." *Jahrbuch für Wirtschaftsgeschichte*, no. 4:11–39.

Mueller, Hans-Eberhard. 1984. *Bureaucracy, Education, and Monopoly: Civil Service Reforms in Prussia and England*. Berkeley: University of California Press.

Mülhausen [city]. 1887–88. *Verwaltungsbericht der Stadt Mühlhausen in Elsaß für das Rechnungsjahr 1887–1888*. Mühlhausen.

Müller, Wolfgang, and Christel Neusüss. 1975. "The Social State Illusion and the Contradiction between Wage Labour and Capital." *Telos* 25:13–90.

Nelson, Barbara. 1984. "Women's Poverty and Women's Citizenship: Some Political Consequences of Economic Marginality." *Signs: Journal of Women in Culture and Society* 10:209–31.

O'Connor, J. 1973. *The Fiscal Crisis of the State*. New York: St. Martin's Press.

Offe, Claus. 1974. "Structural Problems of the Capitalist State: Class Rule and the Political System: On the Selectiveness of Political Institutions." In *German Political Studies*, edited by Klaus von Beyme, 1:31–58. London: Sage.

———. 1984a. "Social Policy and the Theory of the State." In *Contradictions of the Welfare State*, 88–118.

———. 1984b. *Contradictions of the Welfare State*, edited by John Keane. Cambridge, Mass.: MIT Press.

Offe, Claus, and Volker Ronge. 1984. "Theses on the Theory of the State." In *Contradictions of the Welfare State*, edited by John Keane, 119–29. Cambridge, Mass.: MIT Press.

Offe, Claus, and Helmut Wiesenthal. 1980. "Two Logics of Collective Action." In *Political Power and Social Theory*, edited by Maurice Zeitlin, 1:67–115. Greenwich, Conn.: JAI Press.

Orloff, Ann Shola. 1985. "The Politics of Pensions: A Comparative Analysis of the Origins of Pensions and Old Age Insurance in Canada, Great Britain, and the United States." Ph.D. diss., Princeton University.

Orloff, Ann Shola, and Theda Skocpol. 1984. "Why Not Equal Protection? Explaining the Politics of Public Social Spending in Britain, 1900–1911, and the United States, 1880s-1920." *American Sociological Review* 49: 726–50.

Osten-Sacken und von Rhein, Ottomar Frhr. von der. 1913. *Kaiser Wilhelm II. und sein Heer, 1888–1913*. Berlin: E. S. Mittler und Sohn.

Ostwald, Hans. 1912. "Armenpflege-Arbeitsbeschaffung." *Blätter für die Berliner Armen- und Waisenpflege*, February, 13 ff.

Panitch, Leo. 1986. "Theories of Corporatism: Reflections on a Growth Industry." In *Working Class Politics in Crisis*, edited by Leo Panitch, 160–86. London: Verso.

Parkin, Frank. 1979. *Marxism and Class Theory: A Bourgeois Critique*. New York: Columbia University Press.

Paur, Philip. 1981. "The Corporatist Character of Bismarck's Social Policy." *European Studies Review* 11, no. 4: 427–60.

Perkins, J. A. 1981. "The Agricultural Revolution in Germany, 1850–1914. *Journal of European Economic History* 10, no. 1: 71–118.

Pflanze, Otto. 1983. "'Sammlungspolitik,' 1875–1886: Kritische Bemerkungen zu einem Modell." In *Innenpolitische Probleme des Bismarck-Reiches*, edited by Otto Pflanze, 156–93. Munich: R. Oldenbourg Verlag.

Plessis, Alain. 1979. *De la fête impériale au mur des fédérés, 1852–1871.* Paris: Éditions du Seuil.

Plum, Werner. 1977. *Les expositions universelles au 19e siècle: Spéctacles du changement socio-culturel.* Bonn-Bad Godesberg: Friedrich-Ebert-Stiftung.

Polanyi, Karl. [1944] 1957. *The Great Transformation.* Boston: Beacon Press.

Poulantzas, Nicos. 1978. *Political Power and Social Classes.* London and New York: Verso.

Przeworksi, Adam. 1977. "Proletariat into a Class: The Process of Class Formation from Karl Kautsky's *The Class Struggle to Recent Controversies.*" *Politics and Society* 7, no. 4: 343–401.

Puhle, Hans-Jürgen. 1978. "Zur Legende von der 'Kehrschen Schule.'" *Geschichte und Gesellschaft* 4:108–19.

———. 1981. "Deutscher Sonderweg." *Journal für Geschichte* 4:44–45.

Quadagno, Jill. 1988. "Generational Equity and the Politics of Class." Paper presented at the Annual Meeting of the American Sociological Association.

Quataert, Jean H. 1984. "Workers' Reactions to Social Insurance: The Case of Homeweavers in the Saxon Oberlausitz in the Late Nineteenth Century." *Internationale Wissenschaftliche Korrespondenz* 20, no. 1:17–35.

Raeff, Marc. 1983. *The Well-Ordered Police State: Social and Institutional Change through Law in the Germanies and Russia, 1600–1800.* New Haven: Yale University Press.

Reulecke, Jürgen. 1986. "Formen bürgerlich-sozialen Engagements in Deutschland und England im 19. Jahrhundert." In *Arbeiter und Bürger im 19. Jahrhundert: Varianten ihres Verhältnisses im europäischen Vergleich*, edited by Jürgen Kocka (with Elisabeth Müller-Luckner), 261–85. Munich: R. Oldenbourg Verlag.

Richthofen, Elisabeth von. 1901. "Über die historischen Wandlungen in der Stellung der autoritären Parteien zur Arbeiterschutzgesetzgebung." Ph.D. diss., University of Heidelberg.

Rimlinger, Gaston. 1971. *Welfare Policy and Industrialization in Europe, America, and Russia.* New York: Wiley.

Ritter, Gerhart. 1986. *Social Welfare in Germany and Britain: Origins and Development.* Leamington Spa, Warwickshire: Berg. Originally published as *Sozialversicherung in Deutschland und England: Entstehung und Grundzüge im Vergleich.* Munich: Beck, 1983.

Röhl, John C. G. 1967. *Germany without Bismarck: The Crisis of Government in the Second Reich, 1890–1900.* London: B. T. Batsford.

Rose, M. E. 1972. *The Relief of Poverty, 1834–1914.* London: Macmillan.

———. 1981. "The Crisis of Poor Relief in England, 1860–1890." In *The Emergence of the Welfare State in Britain and Germany, 1850–1950*, edited by W. J. Mommsen, 50–70. London: Croon Helm.

Rothfels, Hans. 1927. *Theodor Lohmann und die Kampfjahre der staatlichen Sozialpolitik (1871–1905): Nach ungedruckten Quellen.* Berlin: E. S. Mittler und Sohn.

———. 1938. "Bismarck's Social Policy and the Problem of State Socialism in Germany." *Sociological Review* 30:81–94, 288–302.

———. 1970. "Prinzipienfragen der Bismarckschen Sozialpolitik." In *Bismarck: Vorträge und Abhandlungen,* 166–81. Stuttgart: W. Kohlhammer.

Sachße, Christoph, and Florian Tennstedt. 1980. *Geschichte der Armenfürsorge in Deutschland.* Stuttgart: Kohlhammer.

———. 1988. *Geschichte der Armenfürsorge in Deutschland. Vol. 2, Fürsorge und Wohlfahrtspflege, 1871–1929.* Stuttgart: Kohlhammer.

Sachße, Christoph and Florian Tennstedt, eds. 1983. *Bettler, Gauner und Proleten: Armut und Armenfürsorge in der deutschen Geschichte.* Reinbek: Rowohlt.

Saldern, Adelheid von. 1973. *Vom Einwohner zum Bürger: Zur Emanzipation der städtischen Unterschicht Göttingens, 1890–1920: Eine sozial- und kommunalhistorische Untersuchung.* Berlin: Duncker und Humblot.

———. 1984. *Auf dem Weg zum Arbeiter-Reformismus: Parteialltag in sozialdemokratischer Provinz Göttingen (1870–1920).* Frankfurt: Materialis Verlag.

Saunders, Peter. 1979. *Urban Politics: A Sociological Interpretation.* London: Hutchinson.

———. 1982. "Why Study Central-Local Relations?" *Local Government Studies* 8:2.

Schinkel, Harald. 1964. "Armenpflege und Freizügigkeit in der preußischen Gesetzgebung im Jahre 1842." *Vierteljahresschrift für Sozial- und Wirtschaftsgeschichte* 51, no. 4: 459–79.

Schissler, Hanna. 1978. *Preussische Agrargesellschaft im Wandel.* Göttingen: Vandenhoeck.

Schlaudraff, Elsa. 1932. "Ein Vergleich zwischen dem Elberfelder, dem Straßburger und dem Frankfurter System in der Armenpflege." Ph. D. diss., University of Erlangen.

Schmidt-Richberg, Wiegand. 1968. "Die Regierungszeit Wilhelms II." In *Von der Entlassung Bismarcks bis zum Ende des Ersten Weltkrieges (1890–1918).* Vol. 5 of *Handbuch zur deutschen Militärgeschichte 1648–1939,* edited by Hans Meier-Welcker and Wolfgang von Groote, 9–155. Frankfurt a.M.: Bernard und Graefe Verlag für Wehrwesen.

Schmitter, Phillipe. 1979. "Still the Century of Corporatism?" *In Trends toward Corporatist Intermediation,* edited by Phillipe Schmitter and Gerhard Lehmbruch, 7–52. Beverly Hills: Sage.

Schumpeter, Joseph. 1918. *Die Krise des Steuerstaates.* Graz: Leuschner und Lubensky.

Seeber, Gustav, and Heinz Wolter. 1972. "Neue Tendenzen im bürgerlichen Geschichtsbild der BRD über die Reichsgründung von 1871." *Zeitschrift für Geschichtswissenschaft* 20, no. 9: 1073–75.

Segre, Sandro. 1980. "The State and Society in Imperial Germany (1870–1914)." *Cahiers internationaux d'histoire économique et sociale* 12:322–43.

Sharpe, L. J. 1984. "Functional Allocation in the Welfare State." *Local Government Studies* 10, no. 1.

Sheehan, James. 1971. "Liberalism and the City." *Past and Present* 51:116–37.

———. 1978. "Deutscher Liberalismus im postliberalen Zeitalter." *Geschichte und Gesellschaft* 4:29–48.

———. 1983. *German Liberalism in the Nineteenth Century.* Chicago: University of Chicago Press.

Showalter, Dennis E. 1975. *Railroads and Rifles: Soldiers, Technology and the Unification of Germany.* Hamden, Conn.: Archon Books.

Simmel, Georg. 1906. "Zur Soziologie der Armut." *Archiv für Sozialwissenschaft und Sozialpolitik* 22:1–30.

Skocpol, Theda. 1979. *States and Social Revolutions.* Cambridge, Mass.: Harvard University Press.

———. 1985. "Bringing the State Back In: Strategies of Analysis in Current Research." In *Bringing the State Back In,* edited by Peter B. Evans, Dietrich Rueschmayer, and Theda Skocpol. New York: Cambridge University Press.

Skocpol, Theda, and John Ikenberry. 1983. "The Political Formation of the American Welfare State in Historical and Comparative Perspective." *Comparative Social Research* 6:87–147.

Skowronek, Stephen. 1982. *Building a New American State: The Expansion of National Administrative Capacities, 1877–1920.* New York: Cambridge University Press.

Small, Albion. 1909. *The Cameralists: The Pioneers of German Social Polity.* Chicago: University of Chicago Press.

Stegmann, Dirk. 1970. *Die Erben Bismarcks: Parteien und Verbände in der Spätphase des Wilhelminischen Deutschlands.* Cologne: Kiepenheuer und Witsch.

Steinmetz, George. 1987. "Social Policy and the Local State: A Study of Municipal Public Assistance, Unemployment Relief, and Social Democracy in Germany, 1871–1914." Ph.D. diss., University of Wisconsin-Madison.

———. 1989. "Women as Agents and Objects of Social Policy: Gender and Welfare in the German Empire." Paper presented to the 1989 German Studies Association, Milwaukee, 1989.

———. 1992. "Reflections on the Role of Social Narratives in Working-Class Formation: Narrative Theory in the Social Sciences." *Social Science History* 16, no. 3 (Fall): 489–516.

———. 1993. *Regulating the Social: The Welfare State and Local Social Politics in Imperial Germany.* Princeton: Princeton University Press.

Steinmetz, George, and Erik Olin Wright. 1989. "The Fall and Rise of the Petty Bourgeoisie." *American Journal of Sociology* 94, no. 5: 973–1018.

Tennstedt, Florian. 1975. "Quellen zur Geschichte der Sozialversicherung." *Zeitschrift für Sozialreform* 29:225–33, 358–65, 422–27.

———. 1976. "Sozialgeschichte der Sozialversicherung." *Sozialmedizin in der Praxis.* Vol. 3 of *Handbuch der Sozialmedizin,* edited by Maria Blohmke, et al. Stuttgart: Enke.

———. 1981a. "Vorgeschichte und Entstehung der Kaiserlichen Botschaft vom 17. November 1881." *Zeitschrift für Sozialreform* 27:663–736.

————. 1981b. "Fürsorgegeschichte und Vereinsgeschichte: 100 Jahre Deutscher Verein." *Zeitschrift für Sozialreform* 27:72–100.

————. 1981c. *Sozialgeschichte der Sozialpolitik in Deutschland: Vom 18. Jahrhundert bis zum Weltkrieg.* Göttingen: Vandenhoeck und Ruprecht.

————. 1983a. "Anfänge sozial-politischer Intervention in Deutschland und England—einige Hinweise zu wechselseitigen Beziehungen." *Zeitschrift für Sozialreform* 29:631–48.

————. 1983b. *Vom Proleten zum Industriearbeiter.* Cologne: Bund Verlag.

Tilly, Charles. 1975a. "Reflections on the History of European State-Making." In *The Formation of National States in Western Europe,* edited by Charles Tilly, 3–83. Princeton: Princeton University Press.

————. 1975b. "Western State-Making and Theories of Political Transformation." In *The Formation of National States in Western Europe,* edited by Charles Tilly, 601–38. Princeton: Princeton University Press.

————. 1985. "War Making and State Making as Organized Crime." In *Bringing the State Back In,* edited by Peter B. Evans, Dietrich Rueschmayer, and Theda Skocpol, 167–91. New York: Cambridge University Press.

————. 1990. *Coercion, Capital, and European States, A.D. 990–1990.* Cambridge, Mass., and Oxford: Basil Blackwell.

Tipton, Frank B. 1981. "Government Policy and Economic Development in Germany and Japan: A Skeptical Reevaluation." *Journal of Economic History* 41, no. 1: 139–50.

Tribe, Keith. 1983. "Prussian Agriculture—German Politics: Max Weber, 1892–1897." *Economy and Society* 12:181–226.

————. 1988. *Governing Economy: The Reformation of German Economic Discourse, 1750–1840.* Cambridge: Cambridge University Press.

Turner, Bryan. 1986. *Citizenship and Capitalism.* London: Allen and Unwin.

Ullmann, Hans-Peter. 1976. *Der Bund der Industriellen.* Göttingen: Vandenhoeck und Ruprecht.

————. 1979. "Industrielle Interessen und die Entstehung der deutschen Sozialversicherung." *Historische Zeitschrift* 229:574–610.

Varlez, Louis. 1909. "Die Bekämpfung der unfreiwilligen Arbeitslosigkeit, 1907–1909." *Soziale Kultur* 29 (July).

Vogel, Walter. 1951. *Bismarcks Arbeiterversicherung: Ihre Entstehung im Kräftespiel der Zeit.* Braunschweig: Georg Westermann Verlag.

Volkmann, Heinrich. 1968. *Die Arbeiterfrage im preußischen Abgeordnetenhaus, 1848–1869.* Berlin: Duncker und Humblot.

Weber, Max. 1971. *Gesammelte politische Schriften,* edited by Johannes Winckelmann. Tübingen: Mohr [Siebeck].

Weber, Max. 1892. *Die Verhältnisse der Landarbeiter im ostelbischen Deutschland: Dargestellt aufgrund der vom Verein für Sozialpolitik veranstalteten Erhebungen.* 3 vols. Schriften des Vereins für Sozialpolitik, vol. 55: Leipzig: Duncker und Humblot.

Weber, Max. [1894] 1979. "Developmental Tendencies in the Situation of East Elbian Rural Labourers." *Economy and Society* 8:172–205.

Wegner, Konstanze. 1968. *Theodor Barth und die freisinnige Vereinigung: Studien zur Geschichte des Linksliberalismus im wilhelminischen Deutschland (1893–1910)*. Tübingen: Mohr [Siebeck].

Wehler, Hans-Ulrich. 1985. *The German Empire, 1871–1918*. Leamington Spa, Warwickshire: Berg.

Wehler, Hans-Ulrich. 1983. "Vorzüge und Nachteile des deutschen Sonderwegs." In *Preußen ist wieder chic . . . Politik und Polemik in zwanzig Essays*, by Hans-Ulrich Wehler, 33–36. Frankfurt a.M.: Suhrkamp.

Weir, Margaret, and Theda Skocpol. 1985. "State Structures and the Possibilities of 'Keynesian' Responses to the Great Depression in Sweden, Britain and the United States." In *Bringing the State Back In*, edited by Peter B. Evans, Dietrich Rueschmayer, and Theda Skocpol, 107–63. New York: Cambridge University Press.

Weir, Margaret, Ann Shola Orloff, and Theda Skocpol, eds. 1988. *The Politics of Social Policy in the United States*. Princeton: Princeton University Press.

White, Dan S. 1976. *The Splintered Party: National Liberalism in Hessen and the Reich, 1867–1918*. Cambridge, Mass.: Harvard University Press.

Williams, Karel. 1981. *From Pauperism to Poverty*. London: Routledge and Kegan Paul.

Witt, Peter-Christian. 1970. *Die Finanzpolitik des Deutschen Reiches von 1903–1913: Eine Studie zur Innenpolitik des Wilhelminischen Deutschland*. Lübeck: Matthiesen Verlag.

Wohlers, Wilhelm. 1876. *Das Reichsgesetz über den Unterstützungswohnsitz vom 6. Juni 1870, erläutert nach den Entscheidungen des Bundesamtes für das Heimatwesen*. 1st ed. Berlin: Vahlen.

Wolpe, Harold. 1980. Introduction to *The Articulation of Modes of Production*, edited by Harold Wolpe, 1–43. London: Routledge and Kegan Paul.

Wright, Erik Olin. 1978. *Class, Crisis and the State*. London: New Left Books.

———. 1985. *Classes*. London: Verso.

Zacher, H. F., ed. 1979. *Bedingungen für die Entstehung und Entwicklung von Sozialversicherungen: Colloquium der Projektgruppe für Internationales und Vergleichendes Sozialrecht der Max-Planck-Gesellschaft*. Berlin: Duncker und Humblot.

Zöllner, Detlev. 1982. "Germany." In *The Evolution of Social Insurance, 1881–1981: Studies of Germany, France, Great Britain, Austria and Switzerland*, edited by P. A. Köhler, H. F. Zacher, and M. Partington, 1–92. New York: St. Martin's Press.

The Ambiguities of Modernity: Welfare and the German State from Wilhelm to Hitler

David Crew

The search for the origins of Nazism has dominated German historians' discussions of both the Wilhelmine Empire (1890–1918) and the Weimar Republic (1919–33). In the late 1960s and early 1970s, Hans-Ulrich Wehler, Jürgen Kocka and other members of the Bielefeld school of West German historians proposed a view of recent German history that rapidly attained the status of a new orthodoxy. This interpretation saw Nazism as the inevitable end product of Germany's political and social "misdevelopment" in the Wilhelmine and Weimar periods. Unlike other Western European nations (especially Britain), Germany failed to establish a stable, liberal parliamentary system of government, a democratic political culture, or an egalitarian civil society. Rather than following the "British road" to democracy, the new German industrial nation traveled a quite different path, that of "Prussianism." The old preindustrial elite, the aristocratic Prussian Junker class, refused to give way to the rising German middle classes. The middle classes, in turn, increasingly frightened by the emergence of a socialist working class, forsook their "historic mission." Renouncing their earlier liberal goals, they allied, albeit as junior partners, with the reactionary Prussian aristocracy and the authoritarian German state to resist the forces of democracy in Germany. By 1933, this conspiracy of preindustrial Junker and "feudalized" bourgeoisie could turn only to Hitler in a last, desperate, and ultimately disastrous gamble to fight further democratization and the threat of Bolshevism in Germany.

In the past decade, this interpretation of recent German history has attracted considerable criticism. In *The Peculiarities of German History,* David Blackbourn and Geoff Eley argued that the discussion of the Wilhelmine period must be shifted away from the "failed bourgeois revolution" and "preindustrial" continuities to a consideration of Germany's specific forms of "bourgeois society" and "modernity." The "peculiarities of German history," so Blackbourn and Eley argue, are to be found in the contradictions of the distinctively "bourgeois" and "modern" features of twentieth-century German society rather than in the persistence of preindustrial remnants per se. In a similar vein, moreover, Detlev Peukert has recently argued that Nazism was the pathological outcome of a "crisis of classical modernity." He suggests that the *Kaiserreich* introduced a period of classical modernity that experienced its crisis years during the Weimar Republic (*Krisenjahre der klassischen Moderne*).[1] Combining radical Weberian with Habermasian and Foucauldian perspectives, Peukert suggests that classical modernity is characterized not only by advanced capitalist forms of production and economic organization but also by bureaucratization, the growing rationalization of society and culture, and the "social disciplining" or "normalization" of the everyday lives of the masses. Instrumental reason and the spirit of science now assumed hegemonic roles in the ordering of German society. But the "dream of reason" (*Traum der Vernunft*) was experimental, plagued with contradictions, and consequently crisis-ridden. The "project of modernity" could lead in very different directions; the Third Reich was one extreme and pathological form of this modernity.

Like Blackbourn and Eley, Peukert argues for a "normalization" of modern German history; yet he wishes neither to downplay the significance of Nazism nor to suggest that the "normal" modernity of other countries is innocent of contradiction or pathology:

> Positing the relative normality of German society as it modernized should trivialize neither National Socialism nor its prehistory. Rather it stands as a warning against the fallacious notion that the normality of industrial society is harmless.[2]

In the Bielefeld school's discussion of the German *Sonderweg*, the British model was taken as the measure of German "misdevelopment." But Peukert argues that by the 1920s Germany provided the most advanced contemporary model of modernity:

> the era of the "golden twenties" defined itself as the high point of rationalization—not just of technology and the economy but of all the ways of life and societal structures. The ersatz religion of social and

---

1. Detlev J. K. Peukert, *Die Weimarer Republik: Krisenjahre der Klassischen moderne* (Frankfurt: Suhrkamp, 1987).

2. Detlev J. K. Peukert, "The Weimar Republic—Old and New Perspectives," *German History* 6 (1988): 137.

technical utilitarianism, the euphoria with regard to "progress," reached a peak with "Americanism."[3]

Yet at the same time, the crises and contradictions of "modernity," which Weimar shared with other modern industrial nations, *still led Germany down a "special path" to fascism:*

> Each individual symptom of the crisis in Germany can also be found in other modern industrial countries. To that extent the German crisis is paradigmatic. However, in Germany the modernization process prevailed during the 1920s in a more brutal and direct manner than in other countries. . . . What was "special" in Germany between 1918 and 1932 was the abrupt and unadorned breakthrough of modernization on the one hand and the conjuncture of all too many crisis factors on the other. This special situation, however, points precisely to the vulnerability to crisis of those modernization processes which we are accustomed to regard as normal.[4]

Peukert thus sees Weimar as neither an isolated and doomed "democratic interlude" in German history nor an unproblematic "model" for the post-1945 democratic project of the Federal Republic or for the recently united Germany.

Social Policy and the German State, 1890–1933

Germany was the Continental home of the modern "welfare state" but remarkably, the history of welfare in Germany is still poorly developed in comparison with Great Britain. Existing research has been selective; historians have focused on Bismarck's social insurance policies while neglecting the history of poor relief and the Poor Law. This is no accident. Concentrating on Bismarck's social insurance policies has allowed supporters of the *Sonderweg* thesis to argue that it was the political interests of the preindustrial ruling elites and not those of the bourgeoisie that both produced and profited from the precocious development of the modern welfare state. As George Steinmetz puts it in an excellent discussion of these issues,

> scholars have typically not seen Bismarck's social policies as appropriate to a market-based economy and modern bourgeois society, but as expressions of a neo-feudal paternalism.[5]

---

3. Ibid., 140.

4. Ibid., 142–43.

5. George Steinmetz, "The Myth and the Reality of an Autonomous State: Industrialists, Junkers and Social Policy in Imperial Germany," *Comparative Social Research* 12(1990):239–93.

Counter to these views, Steinmetz sees the German social insurance system as unmistakably "modern" and "bourgeois"; it had much stronger support from industrial than from agrarian interests, and the practical ideologies according to which it functioned were quintessentially bourgeois.[6]

In comparison with social insurance, poor relief appears to have been a "traditional" form of social provision. But in reality it, too, was emphatically "bourgeois." Before World War I, systems of poor relief were largely constructed and implemented at the level of the local state by the liberal middle classes, who still dominated local government and administration. The major nineteenth-century model of poor relief—the Elberfeld system—came from Germany's Manchester.[7] According to Steinmetz, the Elberfeld system was

> the cornerstone of an overall strategy of increased discipline of the poor, intended to force an orientation toward the labor market and to combat welfare dependency.[8]

The specifically "bourgeois" aspects of the Elberfeld system included "commodification; the creation of self-monitoring subjects; and the reclassification through accentuation of differences among the dependent poor."[9] The Elberfeld system's emphasis on regular visiting to achieve the intense "individualized" treatment and surveillance of the poor anticipated the central practices of twentieth-century social work. It achieved the transformation of

> questions of political rights and social organization into issues of personal conduct and morality, [which] is a continuing feature of social politics in the twentieth century.[10]

German poor relief was in fact decidedly more "modern" than the British new poor law of 1834. Indeed, British social reformers in the 1880s encouraged imitation of the Elberfeld system, and many of its principles did become central elements in the practice of the influential British Charity Organization Society.[11]

By the late nineteenth century, however, bourgeois social reformers were beginning to insist that the German state would have to do more to promote the

---

6. Ibid.

7. Bernd Weisbrod, "Wohltätigkeit und 'symbolische Gewalt' in der Frühindustrialisierung: Städtische Armut und Armenpolitik im Wuppertal," in *Vom Elend der Handarbeit,* ed. Hans Mommsen and Winfried Schulze (Stuttgart, 1981), 334–57.

8. Steinmetz, "The Myth and the Reality," 30.

9. Ibid., 29.

10. David Garland, *Punishment and Welfare: A History of Penal Strategies* (Brookfield, Vt., 1986), 120.

11. Gareth Stedman Jones, *Outcast London: A Study in the Relationship between Classes in Victorian Society* (Oxford, 1971).

health and welfare of the German people as a whole than the existing framework of the poor law allowed. If Germany was to become a world power, and if its political order were not to be undermined by the spread of socialism among the poor and underprivileged, welfare activities must be removed from the shadow of the old poor law. Only by eliminating the political stigma attached to poor relief, it was argued, could the welfare system reach a constituency that was larger than the "deserving poor." Alongside the old poor relief system, there now emerged maternal and infant welfare centers, public-health agencies that campaigned against tuberculosis, youth-welfare officers, and housing inspectors.[12]

By the end of the nineteenth century, "welfare" had become an ambitious project for the "reorganisation of German social life," which depended on a new program of "popular enlightenment" (*Volkserziehung* or *Sozialpädagogik*).[13] As Christoph Sachße and Florian Tennstedt put it, "The social problem was reformulated as a problem of information and guidance."[14] In contrast with the poor law, the Wilhelmine reform program would provide a system of "preventive care," that reached into people's daily lives before things started to "go wrong." Advice and information would be dispensed, even to "healthy" families and individuals, to educate them in rational and scientific methods of reproducing and raising children, caring for the body and the home and managing family economies. The welfare system was to function, in Althusserian terms, as a new component of the "ideological state apparatus," promoting popular "enlightenment":[15]

> Welfare was . . . increasingly understood as education in the methodical, rational conduct of life, as conformity of the everyday existence of the lower orders to the demands of scientific rationality.[16]

Peukert argues that the growth of the modern welfare state in Germany was inspired, and in turn nourished, by a "utopian" view of social policy. Drawing on the "knowledge" constructed by the newly emerging "human sciences" (Foucault)—preeminently sociology, psychology, and criminol-

---

12. See for example, Adelheid Gräfin zu Castell Rudenhausen, "Die Erhaltung und Mehrung der Volkskraft: Die Anfänge der sozialhygienischen Gesundheitsfürsorge im Regierungsbezirk Düsseldorf," in *Stadtgesellschaft und Kindheit im Prozess der Zivilisation: Konfigurationen städtischer Lebensweise zu Beginn des 20. Jahrhunderts,* ed. Imbke Behnken (Opladen, 1990), 26–42.

13. Garland, *Punishment and Welfare,* 112.

14. Christoph Sachße and Florian Tennstedt, *Geschichte der Armenfürsorge in Deutschland,* vol. 2, *Fürsorge und Wohlfahrtspflege, 1871–1929* (Stuttgart, 1988), 30.

15. Louis Althusser, "Ideology and Ideological State Apparatuses," in *Lenin and Philosophy and Other Essays,* by Louis Althusser (London, 1971).

16. Sachße and Tennstedt, *Fürsorge und Wohlfahrtspflege,* 12.

ogy—welfare professionals maintained that just as medical science had learned to cure diseases previously thought to be hopelessly fatal, so too modern social welfare would be able to heal the body social. This *Fortschritts-optimismus* seduced social policy experts into believing that they could soon achieve a "final solution" of the social problem:

> From the 1890s . . . the conviction that social reform was necessary was increasingly outflanked and overtaken by the belief that all social problems could find their rational solution through state intervention and scientific endeavor . . . The dream of a final solution of the social problem resonated in the plans of modern "social engineers," regardless of whether they were active as youth-welfare workers, social hygienists, or city planners. Just as medicine had dealt a death blow to bacteria, so would the union of science and social technology in public interventions make all remaining social problems disappear.[17]

Weimar represented the high point of this enterprise, when social policy became firmly anchored in the state:

> Weimar installed the new principle of the social state, in which, on the one hand, the citizen could now claim public assistance in [his/her] social and personal life, while on the other, the state also set up the institutional and normative framework [defining how] a "normal" life of a citizen of the state should progress.[18]

But it was also during the Weimar Republic that the "limits of the welfare state" were revealed for the first time. In social policy, as in other areas of social, political, and economic life, Weimar was the crisis period of classical modernity:

> This process, which had already begun before the turn of the century, reached its apex in the Weimar Republic and was also thrown into crisis, as the limits of what social technology could achieve were reached in every direction.[19]

German society proved to be a very sickly patient, especially after 1929, when the Great Depression, mass unemployment, and state welfare cutbacks created previously unimaginable material deprivation and social dislocation. But rather than accepting the fact that history had frustrated their ambitions,

---

17. Peukert, *Die Weimarer Republik,* 137, 138.
18. Ibid., 351.
19. Ibid., 139.

welfare experts began to redefine their utopia. If German society as a whole could not be cured of its social problems, then healthy individuals must be protected from the influence of the "incurables." The "scientization" of the social and the "medicalization" of social problems had, so Peukert argues, opened the door to a new and distinctly modern "pathology," which found its ultimate expression in the Nazi program of separation of the "healthy" German *Volk* from its "degenerate" racial and biological enemies (*Ausgrenzung*), followed by their sterilization or extermination.[20]

Racism also offered a way out of the normative crisis produced by the triumph of science and reason over religion. Although nineteenth-century medical science had been able to prolong life, it could not overcome death; and, unlike religion, it offered no spiritual consolation for this failure. Peukert argues that racism solved these problems by shifting attention from the individual body to the *Volkskörper* (the "eternal," eugenic "body" of the *Volk*). Although each individual must eventually die, the "healthy" race could survive. But while racism promised immortality for each individual's "healthy" genes, it also made the "elimination" of the "unfit" carriers of "deficient genes" a duty owed by the current generation to its posterity. This prescription had murderous results during the Third Reich. But Peukert insists that "social racism" was not a uniquely Nazi deformation; it had, in fact, already been produced by the "human sciences" themselves:

> National Socialism provides a special case, a particularly fatal form of the tense relationship that runs through the entire history of social policy between . . . the "normality" that is to be fostered and required and . . . the "nonconformity" that is to be segregated or eliminated.[21]

Critique

Peukert has drawn attention to themes in the history of modern social policy that are generally ignored. Yet his discussion of the "pathologies of modernity" in its German context oversimplifies a complex, conflict-ridden history.[22] The Weimar welfare state drew its inspiration less from the confident faith in social progress described by Peukert than from Germany's desperate need for "social

20. Detlev J. K. Peukert, "Die Genesis der 'Endlösung' aus dem Geist der Wissenschaft," in *Max Webers Diagnose der Moderne,* by Detlev J. K. Peukert (Göttingen, 1989), 102–21. See also the official justification for the Community Aliens Law, quoted in Jeremy Noakes, "Social Outcasts in the Third Reich," in *Life in the Third Reich,* ed. R. Bessel (Oxford, 1987), 95.

21. Detlev Peukert, "Zur Erforschung der Sozialpolitik im Dritten Reich," in *Soziale Arbeit und Faschismus,* ed. Hans-Uwe Otto and Heinz Sünker (Bielefeld, 1986), 129.

22. This criticism can be applied more generally to Michel Foucault and Foucauldian approaches. See especially Jürgen Habermas, *The Philosophical Discourse of Modernity: Twelve Lectures* (Cambridge, Mass., 1987), 238–93.

reconstruction" following war, defeat, revolution, and inflation. The Weimar welfare state was seen by contemporaries more as a form of "damage control" than as the culmination of a utopian project initiated in the 1890s. Yet World War I and its aftermath find no significant place in Peukert's discussion.

During and immediately after World War I, Germany faced a massive "social reproduction crisis." The fundamental institution of civil society—the German family—seemed no longer able to ensure cultural or even biological reproduction of the healthy and productive postwar generations that Germany would require to overcome the devastation of "total war." But although comprehensive state intervention into "social reproduction" seemed to be a social, economic, and political necessity, there was no agreement among welfare experts and interests about the ideological and political assumptions of the welfare project. The Weimar state welfare system was, at best, a compromise—the result of intense political conflicts among a complex variety of welfare interests:

> Despite its pretensions to rational efficiency and social planning, the welfare state was a chaos of competing authorities, under-funded agencies, and a mixture of voluntary and public bodies. Its diversity reflected its origins as a product of diverse political forces. Socialists, liberals inspired by the "one nation" ideology of Friedrich Naumann, and the Catholic Centre Party combined to support its formation.[23]

Moreover, the ideological vantage points of most of the major welfare interests immunized them against exaggerated expectations. Representatives of the religious welfare organizations thought state welfare was an unrealizable Social Democratic illusion:

> The socialist belief that the extensive building up of preventive welfare will reduce the actual work of healing to a diminishing minimum remains utopian. It ignores the fact that in many cases conditions of poverty are to be traced back to causes deep within the individual . . . [that] cannot be altogether eliminated, even under the very best imaginable circumstances.[24]

But in reality even the most reformist Social Democrats did not believe that welfare alone could solve the social problem. Indeed, they insisted that it was far more a "bourgeois" than a Social Democratic illusion

---

23. Paul Weindling, "Eugenics and the Welfare State during the Weimar Republic," in *The State and Social Change in Germany, 1880–1980,* ed. W. R. Lee and Eve Rosenhaft (New York, 1990), 133.

24. Dr. Karl Bopp, *Die Wohlfahrtspflege des modernen deutschen Sozialismus* (Freiburg i. Br., 1930), 77.

to exhibit ideals for whose . . . achievement every single precondition is lacking in a capitalistically organized society . . . [We] must continually encourage recognition and understanding of the fact that every effort [of the welfare system], even if it has some success in individual cases, will be completely wasted . . . if everything simply remains the same in the overall condition of the proletariat . . . [I]n itself the significance of welfare is much more modest in our eyes than in the opinions of our fellow bourgeois social workers, who want to heal the wounds of this society with welfare alone.[25]

Far from establishing a depoliticized "regime of experts," the Weimar welfare system created a new terrain of social and political power where the socialist welfare organization (Arbeiterwohlfahrt) and the Christian welfare organizations (the Catholic Caritas and the Protestant Innere Mission) fought one another for state funds and for religious and ideological control over welfare clients. Social Democrats insisted that German workers be allowed to participate directly in the administration of the welfare system rather than remaining its passive "objects."[26] But both the Caritas and the Innere Mission were intent on blocking this "godless," secular, socialist influence on welfare work.[27]

Socialists and nonsocialists also disagreed about state intervention into German family life. Weimar socialists were less troubled than nonsocialists by state intervention into what they regarded as an already weakened family structure.[28] Religious spokesmen and women found the intrusions of state welfare agencies more problematic; in 1929, for example, a report of the annual meeting of the Catholic *Caritas* warned

against a development of the youth offices, which . . . to an ever increasing degree places decisions about the welfare . . . of minor children in the hands of "political" agencies, among which, unfortunately, the youth offices must often be counted, while at the same time weakening the

25. Paula Kurgass, "Die sozialistische Fürsorgerin: Gegen die Isolierung der Wohlfahrtspflege," *Arbeiterwohlfahrt* 1, no. 5 (1 Dec. 1926): 133–36.

26. Hedwig Wachenheim, "Ausbildung zur Wohlfahrtspflege," *Die Neue Zeit* 39, no. 2 (1921): 303; Landesrat Hans Wingender, "'Modernisierung'" der Fürsorgeerziehung," *Die Gemeinde*, 1924, 187–90.

27. See for example, "Sitzung der Stadtverordneten," *Beilage der Volkszeitung*, Düsseldorf, 35, no. 256 (Thursday, 30 October 1924); "Kinderfürsorge und Arbeiterwohlfahrt," *Rheinische Volkswacht*, 14 June 1925; Walter Friedländer, "Die Neuwahlen der Jugendamter," *Arbeiterwohlfahrt* 3, no. 12 (15 June 1928): 363–72; and Martin Breuer, "Von den Schutzaufsichten" *Arbeiterwohlfahrt* 7 (April 1929): 319–21.

28. Irma Fechenbach, "Schulfürsorge: Wie sie ist und wie sie sein soll," *Arbeiterwohlfahrt* 2, no. 23 (1 Dec. 1927): 724.

influence of the parental home. . . . [This] will also increasingly reduce the parents' sense of responsibility toward their children.[29]

Catholic and Protestant welfare organizations also doubted that the specifically "educational" character of welfare would be compatible with the institutional forms provided by state agencies. The religious charities viewed welfare work as a "charismatic," not a "functional-rational," relationship. The youth-welfare worker would "save" the endangered child by the force of his or her personal example and influence. In the process, the gap between the classes, produced by industrialization, urbanization, and, not least, Marxism, could be bridged; the practice of welfare would contribute to the construction of a *Volksgemeinschaft*.[30] As one expert put it in 1929,

> Social welfare [is] . . . a means of restoring the often lost collectivity; . . . a new way of binding together not only individual human beings but also classes and estates. . . . [I]t is not only a question of forming healthy, productive, and intelligent human beings but also . . . [of producing] the collective human beings [*Gemeinschaftsmenschen*] [who are] prepared to fit into the community, to serve the whole. . . . [H]ere, social welfare goes . . . to the roots, precisely because it searches people out where they are in danger, when they run the risk of becoming "antisocial" [*asozial*].[31]

For many who shared these views, the state form of welfare (promoted by the Social Democrats) too often threatened to degenerate into merely formal "bureaucratism"—the orderly, anonymous, rational disposition of cases according to abstract, impersonal criteria . . . dispensing material benefits but providing no real "educational care."

The Weimar welfare establishment also included local government officials and tens of thousands of volunteer workers (*ehrenamtliche Organe*), who were often more concerned with reducing the costs of welfare administration than with extending its panopticon gaze. Welfare "experts" and professional social workers might claim a scientific "knowledge" of social problems, derived from the human sciences, but their desire for a hegemonic role in welfare theory and practice did not go undisputed. Jeanne Bauer, a professional social worker in the Social Democratic Prenzlauer Berg district of Berlin, explained that there was always an "old guard" in the administration:

---

29. Direktor K. Joerger, "Der 29. Deutsche Caritastag vom 28. August bis 4. September 1929 zu Freiburg i. Br.," *Caritas*, 1929, 455.

30. Hans Windelkinde Jannasch, *Alarm des Herzens: Aus den Papieren eines Helfers* (Stuttgart, 1928).

31. Dr. Else Wex, *Die Entwicklung der sozialen Fürsorge in Deutschland (1914 bis 1927)* (Berlin, 1929), 77.

You can imagine—when the Nazis came, these officials said thank God, common sense at last—and the first thing they got rid of was therapeutic casework. The case histories were passed round the office as common reading. . . . The men in the administration had always opposed such methods, really. And the new ideas on psychology that had played a role in social work before 1933—the people who had introduced them were thrown out.[32]

Despite the promises of the Weimar Constitution and the guarantees of the 1924 *Reichs-Fürsorge-Verordnung,* the ghost of the old poor law stalked the corridors of even the most up-to-date Weimar welfare offices. Like the Wilhelmine poor law, the Weimar public welfare system applied a means test to its potential clients. It is tempting to dismiss means-tested relief as merely an outdated holdover from the Wilhelmine era that would steadily be replaced by the more "modern" and "progressive" principles of social insurance. But there are two reasons why this is inaccurate: first, means-tested forms of relief actually expanded during the Weimar years. Rather than being consigned to a residual status, means-testing even invaded the administration of unemployment insurance benefits in the early 1930s.[33] Second, there is little to suggest that social insurance was inherently a more "modern" form of social provision than means-tested relief. Indeed, there are good reasons for seeing these apparently opposed forms as complementary tactics in a larger welfare strategy. Social insurance was meant to preserve or restore the physical capacity to labor of mainly male, skilled workers during periods of unemployment, sickness, or disability. But unemployment benefits had a limited duration. Means-tested relief would deter insured workers from extending their vacations from the labor market. In addition, means-tested relief "recommodified" unskilled and irregularly employed workers who were not insured, although at a lower material level than the social insurance system. Means-tested relief also had a unique task: the enforcement of "domestic labor discipline" among women on

---

32. Quoted in Elisabeth Harvey, *Youth Welfare and Social Democracy in Weimar Germany: The Work of Walter Friedländer* (Oak Villa, New Alyth, Perthshire, 1987), 79

33. Bürgermeister Friedrich Kleeis, "Die 'Individualisierung' der öffentlichen Fürsorge," *Arbeiterwohlfahrt* 6, no. 8 (15 April 1931): 225–28. Repeated insistence upon the need to treat each individual case on its merits, rather than awarding support on a more schematic basis, can be found in Staatsarchiv Hamburg (hereafter StAHbg), Sozialbehorde, I VG.24: 21–32, Niederschriften über die Leitersitzungen, especially 9 Sept. 1921, 21 Nov. 1921, 2 Jan. 1922, 17 July 1922, 31 July 1922, 20 Nov. 1922, 5 Feb. 1923, 7 May 1923, 25 Feb. 1931, and 22 October 1932. It should be pointed out that before 1927 the administration of unemployment relief also incorporated a means test; see Karl Christian Führer, *Arbeitslosigkeit und die Entstehung der Arbeitslosenversicherung in Deutschland, 1902–1927* (Berlin, 1990), 386–97; and Karl Christian Führer, "Unterstützung und Lebensstandard der Arbeitslosen, 1918–1927," in *Arbeiter im 20. Jahrhundert,* ed. Klaus Tenfelde (Stuttgart, 1991), 277–79.

welfare. In sharp contrast to both the Weimar social insurance system and the Wilhelmine poor law, means-tested welfare in the Weimar Republic had a heavily female "clientele," whereas those who had a right to social insurance were more commonly male, skilled workers. Welfare state interventions into women's lives were generally not intended to force them back into the labor market but rather to rehabituate them to a life of assiduous, disciplined labor in the household.

Local welfare authorities carefully policed the boundaries between these two welfare streams to prevent social insurance principles from seeping into the practices of means-tested relief, but they were quite prepared to tolerate, even encourage, a reverse flow. Perhaps the single largest group of women whose lives were touched by the Weimar welfare system were pregnant and nursing mothers.[34] Before the War, only pregnant women who were insured with a *Krankenkasse* (sickness insurance fund) received any financial support in the period just before and immediately after the birth of their children. During the war, however, this coverage was extended. The 1924 decree regulating the operation of the Weimar welfare system allowed women who had no claim to the *Wochenhilfe* (maternity benefit) paid through the *Krankenkassen* to receive a rough equivalent, called *Wochenfürsorge*.[35] But under the mounting pressures of the fiscal crisis of the local state, *Wochenfürsorge* was increasingly administered as a form of public relief, subject to a means test. As the news service of the German Association for Private and Public Welfare reported in 1925, this confounded pronatalist efforts:

> Handing over the maternal welfare services to the local authorities has by no means been greeted uniformly with enthusiasm. Some fear that the local authorities will . . . not pay enough attention to the role that these services are meant to play in support of our population policies but will instead simply look at them as another form of poor relief.[36]

Advocates of the Weimar welfare project argued that it was a more effective way of treating social problems than the coercive technologies of power

---

34. Sachße and Tennstedt, *Fürsorge und Wohlfahrtspflege*, 124. Before the war, maternal and infant welfare programs had already begun to lead the way in the "social reformation" (*soziale Ausgestaltung*) of the old Wilhelmine poor law. During the Weimar Republic, these maternal and infant welfare activities were greatly expanded; see Sachße and Tennstedt, ibid., 122–124; and Ute Frevert, "The Civilizing Tendency of Hygiene: Working-Class Women under Medical Control in Imperial Germany," in *German Women in the Nineteenth-Century: A Social History*, ed. John C. Fout (New York and London, 1984), 320–43.

35. See for example, Louise Schroeder, "Mutterschutz in der Deutschen Republik," *Arbeiterwohlfahrt*, 15 October 1932, 618, who claimed that 66–70 percent of all pregnant women had some claim to *Wochenhilfe*, while the remainder could apply for *Wochenfürsorge*.

36. StAHbg, Sozialbehörde I, Bd. II 1925–32, "Aus der Praxis der Wochenfürsorge," Nachrichtendienst, 67, Nov. 1925.

employed by the Wilhelmine poor law. As a new practice, social welfare would rely not upon compulsion but upon consent; this was the justification for seeing it as the provision of "protection" and "care" rather than the exercise of force. Weimar Social Democrats claimed that it was their achievement to have removed "the police character of the poor law."[37] Women's organizations and female social workers insisted that Weimar social work was sharply differentiated from police work by the gender of its practitioners: "Men use fear and force against individuals to insure public order and health." Women, on the other hand, use "preventive, protective, and healing approaches to helping individuals and thereby serve the welfare of all."[38] Yet the break with the practices of the nineteenth-century poor law and with contemporary "male" police work was not as complete as welfare reformers, Social Democrats, and feminists liked to think. Eckart Pankoke points out that

> this area . . . always had its roots in the tradition of thinking about the policing of state order—even when the transition from "repressive" to "preventive" forms of intervention dissolved the "police" concept, heavily loaded with repressive connotations, by formulas oriented more toward prevention, such as "protection," "care," and "welfare." It is in this sense that preventive administrative tasks, such as "welfare," "social welfare," "protection of youth," "youth welfare," and "family aid" developed out of the older state-policing complex.[39]

Consequently, the attempts to give welfare work a new popular legitimacy did not remove the taint of repression. As late as 1927, for example, the director of the Hamburg Youth Office admitted:

> The Youth Office is still . . . a bogeyman. The justifiable distaste for the "Discipline School" (which, as is well known, was done away with in 1905) . . . still has an effect . . . [Our] reformatories . . . are run in a pure spirit of education and welfare, . . . but we must continuously plead for

---

37. Clara Henriques, "Psychologische Schwierigkeiten und Möglichkeiten sozialistischer Wohlfahrtsarbeit," *Arbeiterwohlfahrt* 2, no. 15 (1 August 1927): 456.

38. Erika S. Fairchild, "Women Police in Weimar: Professionalism, Politics, and Innovation in Police Organizations," *Law and Society Review* 21, no. 3 (1987): 387. See also Ursula Nienhaus, "Einsatz für die 'Sittlichkeit': Die Anfänge der weiblichen Polizei im Wilhelminischen Kaiserreich und in der Weimarer Republik," in *'Sicherheit' und 'Wohlfahrt': Polizei, Gesellschaft und Herrschaft im 19 und 20. Jahrhundert,* ed. Alf Lüdtke (Frankfurt a.M., 1992), 243–66.

39. Eckart Pankoke, "Von 'guter Policey' zu 'socialer Politik': 'Wohlfahrt,' 'Glückseligkeit' und 'Freiheit' als Wertbindung aktiver Sozialstaatlichkeit," in *Soziale Sicherheit und soziale Disziplinierung: Beiträge zu einer historischen Theorie der Sozialpolitik,* ed. Christoph Sachße and Florian Tennstedt (Frankfurt, 1986), 171.

the trust of the parents, without which our educational task is very difficult, even hopeless.[40]

Compulsion and consent were inextricably combined in welfare practices. Once the welfare gaze was fastened upon a family and its children, there could indeed be no guarantee that intervention would not escalate from the "softer," more advisory, to the "harder," more coercive forms:

> Through personal visits and individual participation, the helper attempts to have an educational effect on the parents, so that any disorders or dangers to the child can be reduced or eliminated within the family; any resistance or restraints put up by the parents are to be overcome with the help of the guardianship court; but as a last resort, to rescue the physically, spiritually, or morally endangered child, there is always *Fürsorgeerziehung* [correctional education].[41]

The policing of the family carried out by Weimar youth offices was even more intrusive than normal police practices because it was triggered by amorphous, arbitrarily defined threats of "endangerment" (*Verwahrlosung*). Modern "case work" in Weimar Germany also disenfranchised the new "client" from the outset. Parents might themselves seek help and advice from welfare agencies. Yet even without their consent or knowledge, many parents and children were reported to the welfare authorities by private charities, by local "moral authorities" (such as pastors), and by concerned or vengeful neighbors.[42]

Moreover, the welfare system seldom gave its "clients" precisely what they wanted or felt they needed. Indeed, social workers assumed that "clients" were incapable of correctly assessing their own problems and needs:

> The person seeking help comes to the welfare agency without any real knowledge of his condition of need but rather as a result of certain symptoms, which are signs of a social illness, but which do not permit him to

---

40. StAHbg, Staatl. Pressestelle I–IV, 3125, "Gutachten, Auskünfte, Berichte der offentlichen Jugendfürsorge, 1922–1929 (no official date, 18 January 1927 in margin).

41. Karl Seidel, "Die kommunale Wohlfahrtspflege: Ihr Begriff und ihre Bedeutung, unter Berücksichtigung der kommunalen Wohlfahrtspflege der Stadt Cassel" (Ph. D. diss., University of Marburg, 1922), 181.

42. These procedures sometimes embroiled the welfare agencies in family conflicts and tenement feuds. In 1930, for example, a Hamburg newspaper reported: "A considerable number of the charges lodged with the criminal police are unfounded, produced by nothing more than the desire for revenge on the part of relatives and neighbors" ("Die weibliche Kriminalpolizei berichtet," *Hamburger Anzeiger,* 9 May 1930). See also David Crew, "'Eine Elternschaft zu Dritt'—staatliche Eltern? Jugendwohlfahrt und Kontrolle der Familie in der Weimarer Republik, 1919–1933," in *'Sicherheit' und 'Wohlfahrt': Polize:, Gesellschaft und Herrschaft im 19. und 20. Jahrhundert,* ed. Alf Lüdtke (Frankfurt a.M., 1992), 267–96.

recognize the essence of this disorder. The person in need . . . turns to the welfare agency for money, not for treatment.[43]

It was up to the social worker to provide the appropriate "social diagnosis" and prescribe the necessary "treatment."[44] Only compliance, or a convincing simulation of cooperation with the "therapy" prescribed by the social worker, might eventually free "endangered" children and their families from the welfare "gaze."

Gender, Welfare, and the State

Facing the effects of what Ute Daniel calls the "social reproduction crisis" of World War I, Weimar welfare experts insisted on the urgency of restoring and reconstructing the dominant gender regime of the Wilhelmine era and imposed upon women welfare clients a very limited official identity as actual or prospective mothers. Diligent application to the task of reproductive labor was the obligation of all German mothers. Intense overcrowding, clearly inadequate cooking, cleaning, washing, and sanitary facilities, the refusal of landlords to undertake even the most necessary repairs, together with the effects of food shortages, inflation, and increasing unemployment, all made it difficult, sometimes impossible, for many women to secure the physical survival of their families. If Weimar women faltered, failed, or refused to continue, even to intensify their household labor under what were at best adverse conditions, social workers would intervene to "rehabilitate" them.

This "gender project" prescribed comprehensive state intervention into family life. In 1919, for example, one socialist spokesperson insisted:

> The activity of the Youth Welfare Office should begin, at the very latest, with the fifth month of the mother's pregnancy and only end when the young person has reached legal maturity.[45]

And in 1922, a south German welfare officer suggested that it "would be the ideal situation if the Youth Office . . . could provide a helper for every mother and child."[46] Christopher Lasch, Jacques Donzelot, and Philippe Meyer all argue that the twentieth-century welfare state has invaded and colonized the

---

43. Siddy Wronsky and Prof. Dr. Kronfeld, *Sozialtherapie und Psychotherapie in den Methoden der Fürsorge* (Berlin, 1932), 32.

44. Siddy Wronsky, "Behandlungsmethoden in der Fürsorge," *Jugend und Volkswohl* (Hamburg), vol. 6, nos. 10–11 (Jan.–Feb. 1931): 202–3.

45. Rudolf Wissel, "Jugendfürsorge," *Die Neue Zeit* 37, no. 1 (1918–19): 206.

46. Hauptstaatsarchiv Stuttgart, E 151 i II, Jugendamt-Göppingen 1919–39, Zeitungsausschnitt aus *Der Hohenstaufen,* Göppingen, Nr. 181, 5 August 1922, "Die Aufgaben des Jugendamts von E. Krauss beim JA. Göppingen."

family, replacing its private powers with a "patriarchy of the state."[47] They lament the passing of private patriarchal powers into public hands. But some feminist historians argue that women benefited from this state-sponsored dissolution of unrestrained patriarchy within the family. Sonya Michel and Seth Koven have shown that middle-class women played an important, yet neglected part in the formation of the welfare state in France, Germany, Britain, and the United States.[48] In her study of family violence in America, Linda Gordon argues that campaigns against child abuse provided immigrant and working-class women with support in their attempts to resist oppressive patriarchy.[49] However, other feminist historians have presented a less positive view. British research indicates that state social policy and welfare practice in the twentieth century reinforced or reimposed female subordination to, and dependence on, males.[50] I would argue that the construction of the Weimar welfare state had profoundly ambiguous effects on German women that cannot be understood simply in terms of "losses" or "gains"; as Jürgen Habermas puts it, "From the start, the ambivalence of guaranteeing freedom and taking it away has attached to the policies of the welfare state."[51] Female clients of the welfare state might receive material benefits or escape patriarchal oppression only by accepting a new dependent status as subjects of an official "tutelary complex."[52]

The relationships of women clients to the Weimar welfare system was complicated by the fact that the authorities with whom they had to deal most directly and frequently were usually other women, the female social workers who examined their individual cases. Social workers clearly viewed the breakdown of the "reproductive labor discipline" of women as a major threat to the continued existence of many of the families who ended up on the welfare rolls. As a Hamburg social worker put it in 1928, she and her colleagues had the job of "ferreting out the weak spots, plugging the holes, and holding back the decline of individual families."[53] The social worker's visits might be welcomed if they brought concrete improvements to the welfare of the family. But

---

47. Christopher Lasch, *Haven in a Heartless World* (New York, 1977); Jacques Donzelot, *The Policing of Families* (New York, 1979); and Philippe Meyer, *The Child and the State* (Cambridge, 1983).

48. Sonya Michel and Seth Koven, "Womanly Duties: Maternalist Politics and the Origins of Welfare States in France, Germany, Great Britain, and the United States, 1880–1920," *American Historical Review* 95, no. 4 (October 1990): 1076–1108.

49. Linda Gordon, *Heroes of Their Own Lives: The Politics and History of Family Violence, Boston, 1880–1960* (New York, 1988).

50. See especially Elizabeth Wilson, *Women and the Welfare State* (London, 1977).

51. Jürgen Habermas, *The Theory of Communicative Action*, vol. 2, *Lifeworld and System: A Critique of Functionalist Reason* (Boston, 1987), 362.

52. Donzelot, *The Policing of Families*, 96–168.

53. StAHbg, Sozialbehörde, I VG.24.2

when women welfare clients received no obvious material benefit from the social worker's attentions, they began to question these invasions of their family lives. In 1931, for example, a south German newspaper carried the following story about the grandmother of an illegitimate child in Zuffenhausen (northern Württemberg):

> from time to time a sister from the youth-welfare office came to the house and always had something to bleat about [*meckern*]. The grandmother was naturally incensed and finally ordered the sister out of the house with these words: "So long as I do not get any money for the child, then you have no reason to come snooping around in my house."[54]

In the early 1930s, a left-wing social policy journal tried to play on these resentments:

> The snooping around about the most intimate family matters appears to be going even further; it has been proposed that the social workers will instruct families in the making of their own clothes, give them tips on economical shopping, pressure them to sublet rooms, encourage women to bring in more income by washing their lodgers' clothes or preparing their meals and God knows what else. After the social worker has established the household needs of each of the families in her care, she will figure out the amount of support they should receive. . . . The old poor law guardians of earlier times did snoop around in the clothes closets, . . . but it is the particular achievement of the [present system] that it seeks to dictate how the proletarian wife will run her household.[55]

But conflicts between women welfare clients and women social workers involved more than material grievances. Female social workers attempted to present motherhood as a profession that no ordinary and certainly no working-class woman could fully learn and practice by herself without the help of a trained social worker.[56] This gendered variant of the "scientization of the social" was not accepted unquestioningly by the women who were its targets. Indeed, the idea of "social motherhood," which was meant to legitimize the role of the professional social worker, could in fact intensify conflicts between women welfare clients and women social workers. To the battles over material

54. "Das Ideale Jugendamt Feuerbach" (Arbeiter-Korrespondenz), *Süddeutsche-Arbeiter-Zeitung,* 20 Feb. 1931, 42.

55. Frieda Rosenthal, "Die anerkannten Spitzenverbände der privaten Wohlfahrt—Die Arbeiterwohlfahrt," *Proletarische Sozialpolitik* 5 (1928): 139.

56. See Christoph Sachße, *Mütterlichkeit als Beruf: Sozialarbeit, Sozialreform und Frauenbewegung, 1871–1929* (Frankfurt, 1986); and Henny Schumacher, *Die proletarische Frau und ihre Erziehungsaufgabe* (Berlin, 1929).

benefits were added conflicts about less tangible but equally important issues, such as the autonomy and reputation of women welfare clients as wives and mothers.

Ironically, the official ideology of "social motherhood" gave women welfare clients a linguistic and symbolic purchase in their skirmishes with social workers and the welfare authorities. Women welfare clients could, for example, dispute the (usually single) woman social worker's competence to judge them as mothers and to offer advice that was not based on everyday experience and common sense. In 1928, a Hamburg welfare official claimed that women welfare clients were "quite disinclined to accept the advice of a social worker, whose merely theoretical knowledge . . . provokes feelings of resistance."[57] And in 1932, a welfare mother in Cologne wrote to the local Communist newspaper complaining:

> A few days ago I went to the social worker, Frl. Z., to get a milk coupon for my fourteen-month-old child. In an uppity tone she told me that my child was too old for milk . . . and she had the indecency to inform me that I had probably neglected my child and not looked after it properly, . . . Isn't it a scandal that we have to be spied upon and harassed by such ladies, who themselves have not the least idea of life and who are paid a good salary? And the people in charge are puzzled when we sometimes lose our patience in the [welfare] office!!![58]

Rejection of the social worker's competence as a "social mother" was, however, not anchored in any single language of formal politics. Although the complaint quoted above appeared in a Communist newspaper, similar strains of argument appeared in a letter sent to the Cologne lord mayor, Dr. Konrad Adenauer, by Frau Alexander H., a Catholic "female academic and daughter of the now dead, but well-known Viennese trial lawyer, Landesgerichtsrat a.D. Dr. Hermann P."[59] Her husband, the scion of "a very old, very rich Duisburg family," had left her to live with his mistress in an expensive pension on the Ringstrasse. While he bought jewelery for his mistress and entertained her with luxurious trips to Hamburg, his wife had to get used to the unfamiliar taste of poverty and homelessness. Frau H. complained bitterly about the social worker in charge of her case, who had refused her all financial help:

> Do we now live in such barbaric times, does the state really pay such women to give advice, so that they can indeed say to a poor, starving mother that no one can help them . . . I do not want to burden you with my

---

57. StAHbg., I VG 24.28, 19 November 1928.
58. *Sozialistische Republik* (Cologne), 5 July 1932.
59. Stadtarchiv Köln, 902, Nr. 198, Fasz. 3: 501–1052, Köln am 24 Sept. 1930.

sad case alone; rather, I write in the name of every mother who might find herself in my position . . . if my husband had been a poor worker, he would long since have been sitting in the local workhouse; but the welfare office appears to have a colossal respect for "distinguished" gentlemen wearing monocles who let their families starve on the streets. . . . Otherwise the welfare office in Deutz would have long since found some way to make my husband live up to his responsibilities to his wife and child.[60]

Popular Politics and Welfare

The new ideology of social welfare gave social policy and public health experts the responsibility for structuring the German welfare system according to the imperatives of the emerging human sciences. This "scientization of the social" was meant to achieve a broad political consensus on social reform and remove social-policy decisions from the realm of political debate and social conflict.[61] But this project failed. The institutions of the Weimar welfare state became arenas where official and popular constructions of identities and interests confronted and challenged one another.

Indeed, the Weimar Republic produced an unprecedented politicization of the public discourse on welfare, evident above all at the level of local government, which bore the greatest administrative and financial responsibility for the Weimar welfare system.[62] The democratization of local government after 1918 allowed Social Democrats, Communists, and German women to penetrate this once exclusively middle-class, male, liberal preserve. The Social Democrats, in particular, insisted on the right of the labor movement to participate fully in the administration of the new welfare agencies. Writing after the German Revolution, Hedwig Wachenheim suggested, for example, that

It is not enough to have a socialist running a youth office; this person must also have under him people who are in close, daily contact with working-class youths and their parents, in other words, people who are "class comrades." . . . [A]ll of [the welfare system's] work serves the welfare of the working masses, their material well-being, but also their spiritual march forward, the raising up of their consciousness and self-confidence, and their will to social action.[63]

---

60. Ibid.
61. Sachße and Tennstedt, *Fürsorge und Wohlfahrtsptlege,* 18–22.
62. Jeremy Leaman, "The Gemeinden as Agents of Fiscal and Social Policy in the Twentieth Century: Local Government and State-Form Crises in Germany," in *The State and Social Change in Germany, 1880–1980,* ed. W. R. Lee and Eve Rosenhaft (New York, 1990), 260–69.
63. Hedwig Wachenheim, "Ausbildung zur Wohlfahrtspflege," *Die Neue Zeit* 39, no. 2 (1921): 303.

Social Democrats expected to profit at the polls from their support of municipal welfare programs.[64] In 1929, for example, Emma Woytinsky, a female activist in the Düsseldorf Social Democratic Party, attempted to persuade her female readers just before an important municipal election that

> The working-class woman is energetically supported by a local government that is sympathetic to the working class, not only in her most material worries but also in her family life. If a needy woman is ill and requires help in the household, then the community health visitor comes into her house. The municipality, acting as the guardian for an illegitimate child, presses its claims for support and carries through the necessary . . . proceedings [against the father]. Nursery schools, day-care centers, and kindergartens are set up by the municipality to relieve the mothers of some of their burden.[65]

But the fundamental political and economic contradictions of the "local state" in the Weimar Republic put the SPD in an unenviable political position. For although

> The year 1918 marked the end of the period of relatively successful bourgeois manipulation of communal politics . . . it did not mark the beginning of a corresponding manipulation of local government by working-class parties within a bourgeois state under the new conditions of universal franchise—there was no real municipal socialism to follow the bogus municipal socialism of the Kaiserreich.[66]

Weimar local governments were, in addition, squeezed between their extensive responsibilities for the implementation of nationally decreed welfare policies and their dwindling capacity to finance these social programs. Consequently, the SPD became the target of simultaneous attacks from both the Left and the Right. While the Communists viciously ridiculed Social Democratic claims that the "the social institutions of the republic are already a piece of socialism," the bourgeois parties savaged the Social Democrats for "reckless" welfare spending.[67]

---

64. See, for example, Emma Woytinsky, "Arbeiterin und Gemeinde: Was jede Frau wissen sollte," *Rheinische Zeitung* 314 (15 November 1929).

65. Ibid.

66. Leaman, "The Gemeinden as Agents of Fiscal and Social Policy," 260.

67. Senator Paul Neumann, *Russland ein Vorbild? Eine vergleichende Darstellung russischer und hamburgischer Sozialpolitik* (Hamburg, n.d.); and Reichstagsabgeordneter Otto Thiel, "Sozialpolitik und kommunale Wohlfahrtspflege," in *Kommunalpolitik und Deutsche Volkspartei,* ed. Gustav Wittig (Berlin, 1929), 92. Critics of the SPD charged that under its influence local per

"In the Weimar Constitution of 11 August 1919," Peukert observes, "the 'social state' received legal guarantees."[68] But he does not explore the political effects of the new constitutional language. Weimar "republicanism" proclaimed welfare clients' rights and assured them that the "odium of the poor law" would no longer taint public assistance and stigmatize those who received it.[69] But the Weimar discourse of democratic republicanism could also draw attention to the welfare system's shortcomings and contradictions. For example, Albert N. had been a merchant in Hamburg. But the depression made him one of millions of "welfare unemployed" who had to turn to local welfare systems for support. Describing himself as a "social spokesman for nationalist workers,"[70] Alfred N. nevertheless disputed the Hamburg welfare office's right to pay the unemployed who worked on city building projects at a lower rate than the prevailing standard wage for the building and construction trades:[71]

Where . . . are the [unemployed] workers' legally guaranteed rights, e.g., the Works Councils Law and the constitution? Or are we now experimenting with [new forms of] social slavery [that will make] . . . Farmsen [a public works site] another Siberia? . . . [F]or years we have been assured that we live in the freest, most democratic state in the world, . . . but the fact that a state system whose basis has been propagandized for more than two generations as the highest remuneration of labor power . . . should itself abrogate [this principle] and demolish the institutions that protect it is either an indication that the otherwise normal wage scales are simply no longer feasible in the current economic situation or it is an admission of the unfeasibility of Marxist demagogy.[72]

---

capita welfare costs had increased from 6.85 marks in 1913–14 to 30.79 marks in 1927–28; by 1929, welfare expenditure accounted for at least one-third of the total budget of most municipalities. See Dr. F. D. von Hansemann, "Wir und die Sozialdemokraten," in *Kommunalpolitik und Deutsche Volkspartei,* ed. Gustav Wittig (Berlin, 1929), 102.

68. Detlev J. K. Peukert, "Wohlfahrtsstaat und Lebenswelt," in *Bürgerliche Gesellschaft in Deutschland: Historische Einblicke, Fragen, Perspektiven,* ed. Lutz Niethammer et al. (Frankfurt a.M., 1990), 348.

69. Senator Paul Neumann, "Von Armenpflege zur sozialen Fürsorge," *Hamburger Echo* 32 (1 February 1928).

70. StAHbg, Sozialbehörde, I Aw 00.54, Arbeitsfürsorge, Angriffe und Beschwerde, 1928–31.

71. Ibid., Albert N. speaking at meeting of shop stewards and delegates from several public building sites in Hamburg, 2 February 1930.

72. StAHbg, Sozialbehörde, I AW 00.54, a petition signed by thirty-four workers, 11 November 1929: An die Wohlfahrtsbehörde, Abteilung Arbeitsfürsorge.

When a social worker came to inspect Kurt A.'s newborn infant in Düsseldorf in 1932, the latter also appealed to the constitution in support of rather different objections to welfare practices:

> Raising children to the proper state of physical and social fitness is the highest duty and the natural right of parents. If it appears that this responsibility is in danger of being improperly performed . . . then the state has the right to intervene. . . . But I find it quite unjustified that without any real reason and without having previously checked our reliability, an examination of the child was undertaken. . . . Such a form of examination and investigation cannot be reconciled with the spirit of freedom with which the constitution of our nation breathes.[73]

Weimar Social Democrats were unable to deflect such attacks by constructing a broadly based popular "politics of welfare" for several reasons. First, they thought that the slow but steady work of "practical socialism" was the only realistic working-class political option. This led them to dismiss Communist criticisms as nothing more than "demagogic propaganda" but also to ignore the popular experiences and grievances that the Communists were attempting, albeit in their own limited fashion, to reflect and express. Second, the Social Democrats were trapped inside a political language that allowed them only to criticize the failure of the Weimar welfare state to do more of what it was already doing—supplemented by tirades against short-sighted, backward-looking, archconservative foes of the "welfare state," who used all means to halt the "forward march of progress"—and were consequently unable to subject the idea of "progress" itself to closer scrutiny and critique. Finally, the Marxist language of "class" inherited by the Social Democrats from the era of the Second International made it difficult for them to represent social interests newly constructed as official identities by the welfare state. Neither pensioners nor illegitimate children nor single mothers and juvenile "delinquents" fit readily or easily into a class analysis, and their interests could not properly be expressed by a language of class conflict. The absence from the Social Democratic political imagination of a specifically feminist critique of the welfare state was a particularly severe weakness. Hampered by the limitations of their political imagination, Social Democrats were unable to provide welfare clients with a collective political identity that could bridge the characteristic divisions among welfare clients created by the welfare state's tendency to differentiate, label, and categorize increasing numbers of subgroups receiving different forms of welfare treatment.

---

73. Stadtarchiv Düsseldorf, III, 4052, 19 February 1932.

The history of the welfare state between Wilhelm and Hitler demonstrates the importance of an essential aspect of "modernity," the "public sphere,"[74] about which Peukert says very little in his analysis of the history of German social policy. The crisis of the welfare state in Weimar Germany was intimately connected with the fiscal and political crisis of the local state.[75] The nineteenth-century German local state grew out of the very restricted bourgeois, male, liberal "public sphere"—that is, one organized around voluntary associations. The Weimar invasion of this previously restricted "public sphere" by workers, women, and other former "outsiders," including even the welfare clients themselves, engendered a prolonged crisis of political representation in local government. Nazism provided a simple, violent resolution of this impasse by physically destroying the republican, democratic "public sphere" and brutally terminating the intensely politicized Weimar discourse on welfare.

A Hidden *Sonderweg?* Welfare and the State from Weimar to Hitler

The "pathological" turn in the direction of German social policy after 1933 was by no means already inscribed in its Weimar prehistory. Eugenic interpretations of social problems did gain greater prominence and respectability after 1929, when the depression forced social-policy makers to confront the "limits of the welfare state."[76] Some welfare professionals preferred to blame the genetic deficiencies of the welfare system's more intractable clients rather than admit the failure of their own welfare schemes. Extreme "therapies," including "custodial care" (*Bewahrung*) for adults as well as forced sterilization, were prescribed to contain or eliminate the "genetic threat" carried in the bodies of the "incorrigibles." Yet until 1933 the attempts to legalize such repressive measures were successfully resisted in the Reichstag. It was only after 1933, when the parliamentary-democratic restraints on a full-blown racist resolution of the social problem were brutally swept away by the Nazis, that negative eugenic measures were integrated into everyday welfare practices.

The discourse on welfare at the end of Weimar was dominated by a

---

74. See, for example, Jürgen Habermas, *Strukturwandel der Öffentlichkeit* (Neuwied, 1962); see also Geoff Eley, "Nations, Publics, and Political Cultures: Placing Habermas in the Nineteenth Century," in *Habermas and the Public Sphere,* ed. Craig Calhoun (Cambridge, Mass., 1992), 289–339.

75. See for example, Harold James, "Municipal Finance in the Weimar Republic," in *The State and Social Change in Germany, 1880–1980,* ed. W. R. Lee and Eve Rosenhaft (New York, 1990), 228–54.

76. See especially Paul Weindling, "Eugenics and the Welfare State during the Weimar Republic," in *The State and Social Change in Germany, 1880–1980,* ed. W. R. Lee and Eve Rosenhaft (New York, 1990), 131–60.

mounting ideological backlash against the utopian ambitions of the welfare state, not, as Peukert suggests, by eugenic reformulations of this utopia.[77] After 1929, the depression tore apart the fragile, always contested political compromise that had produced the Weimar welfare system. The religious welfare organizations demanded the "reprivatization" of welfare activities to free the charitable energies necessary for Germany's recovery from the "mechanistic" and "bureaucratic" straitjacket imposed by the state welfare system:

> Our Caritas work has been virtually forced to adopt the methods of the public sector in our joint work with the public welfare system, and even in the organization of our charitable activity we have been compelled to imitate the model of a bureaucratic agency. . . . [The result has been] that we have to a certain extent neglected our most essential tasks and have lost much of our real connection with the people. We are now seen only as an extension of public welfare, and the person in need of help sees us as an alienated institution rather than as a part of the "community" in which we are all members, helpers as much as those in need of help.[78]

The call for reprivatization was coupled with criticism of the effects on German families of long years of depending upon welfare: "traditional feelings of responsibility, even toward close relatives, are in the process of disappearing. 'The city or the state must look after them,' that is what is now heard all over."[79] Critics also pointed to the contradictions of state social policies that attempted to protect the family by constructing individual subjects and identities:

> Article 119 of the Weimar Constitution gave this goal a programmatic formulation: "It is the task of the state to keep the family pure and healthy; the social promotion of the family is likewise the task of the state and the community." But at the very same time, the constitution provided for a whole range of social welfare measures that applied, above all, to the individual, and especially to the mother and the child and that intervened

---

77. See Peukert, "Die Genesis der 'Endlösung' aus dem Geist der Wissenschaft."

78. Dr. Kurt Lucken, "Grundsätzliches und Kritisches zur Caritasarbeit der Gegenwart, III (Schluss)," *Caritas,* 1932, 58–59. See also "Mensch und Amt in der Fürsorge: Von einer in der kommunalen Fürsorge tätigen Diakonisse," *Innere Mission,* 1932, 112–16; Dr. Karl Bopp," Lebenshaltung aus Fürsorge und aus Erwerbstätigkeit," *Caritas,* 1932, 103–7; StAHbg, Staatliche Pressestelle I–IV, 3202, Bd. 1, Winterhilfswerk 1929–33, 42. *Hamburger Echo,* 59, 28 February 1929.

79. Jannasch, *Alarm des Herzens,* 6. See also Staatsarchiv Ludwigsburg, E191/4698, Tätigkeitsbericht des Bezirkswohlfahrtsamts Ehingen für das Rechnungsjahr 1929: "In the past, people exhausted all other possibilities of assistance, only turning to the state welfare as an absolute last resort. Today, people often go right away to the state. The war, state economic controls and the inflation increasingly have all forced the state and other public bodies to assume the primary responsibility in cases of emergency and distress."

into the family to undertake corrections or to supplement its role. . . . So the question can well remain an open one, whether this whole system has not, perhaps . . . contributed to a weakening of family responsibility. . . . Against the atomizing tendency of public assistance aimed at the individual, one can pose another "organic" way of thinking oriented [more] toward the people and the family.[80]

Local authorities exploited this ideological backlash to pass state spending cuts along to individual families, claiming this would reinforce family bonds.[81] Women shouldered the main burden.[82] But welfare authorities' attempts to enforce "reproductive labor discipline" were not accepted passively. In 1932, for example, two women's committees in Hammerbrook, a district of Hamburg, warned an official that they would leave their children in the welfare office if they did not receive the clothing, potatoes, and fuel they needed.[83] Women also participated in welfare office demonstrations, rent strikes, and collective actions against evictions.[84] Angry clients directed verbal abuse, even physical violence, against welfare officials, some of whom demanded weapons for their own protection:[85]

excited confrontations are often accompanied by writing tables being knocked over, [and] objects being thrown. . . . [T]he spitting and hysterical screaming of agitated women . . . deeply disturb the normal business of the welfare office for hours at a time.[86]

---

80. Dr. Adolf Stahl, "Sorge um die deutsche Familie: Eine nachdenkliche Wanderung durch die neue Fachliteratur," *Innere Mission*, 1932, 76–80.

81. Heidrun Homburg, "Vom Arbeitslosen zum Zwangsarbeiter: Arbeitslosenpolitik und Franktionierung [sic] der Arbeiterschaft in Deutschland, 1930–1933, am Beispiel der Wohlfahrtserwerbslosen und der kommunalen Wohlfahrtshilfe," *Archiv für Sozialgeschichte* 25 (1985): 251–98; and "Die Berücksichtigung des Arbeitseinkommens in der Familiengemeinschaft bei Bemessung der Fürsorgeleistungen," *Nachrichtendienst des Deutschen Vereins für öffentliche und private Fürsorge*, 1931, 354–58.

82. Wilhelm Polligkeit, "Not und Existenzminimum," (Die Familie in Sozialpolitik und Fürsorge. Zweite Internationale Konferenz für Soziale Arbeit vom 10.–14. Juli 1932 in Frankfurt am Main), in *Soziale Praxis: Zentralblatt für Sozialpolitik und Wohlfahrtspflege*, vol. 41, no. 27 (7 July 1932): 818–22; "Wie leben unsere Wohlfahrtserwerbslosen? 73 Fürsorgerinnen-Berichte aus der Stadt Hannover," *Sonderdruck aus der "Wohlfahrts-Woche," Schriften des Wohlfahrtsamtes der Stadt Hannover* 4 (1932): 4.

83. StAHbg, Sozialbehörde I VG.24.32, 14 December 1932: 201.

84. *Der Arbeitslose: Organ der revolutionären Gewerkschafts-opposition der Bezirk Wasserkante, Nordwest Niedersachsen und Mecklenburg,* 1 Beilage, 49 Wochen-Ausgabe 1931.

85. Stadtarchiv Köln, 902/198/4, Seite 501–956, Auszug aus der Niederschrift über die Verwaltungskonferenz am 9.8.32

86. StAHbg, Sozialbehörde I VG. 74.12, Bd.1, Schreiben an Amtsgerichtspräsidenten Dr. Blunk.

Nazism and Welfare

Hitler's seizure of power brutally silenced fractious clients along with the Social Democratic supporters of the Weimar welfare state. But Nazism offered Weimar's critics the appealing prospect of a social policy that promised to serve the *Volksgemeinschaft*. This specifically Nazi resolution of the political crisis of the Weimar welfare state, not the crisis itself, created the conditions for a radical, racist redefinition of the welfare project. The Nazis themselves were well aware of the relationship between their racist social policies and the changed political context after 1933:

> The governments of the period of the System (Weimar) . . . did not utilize the findings of genetics and criminal biology as a basis for a sound welfare and penal policy. As a result of their liberal attitude, they constantly perceived only the "rights of the individual" and were more concerned with his protection from state intervention than with the general good. In National Socialism the individual counts for nothing when the community is at stake.[87]

The Nazis reduced complex social problems to simplistic biological formulas. In the Third Reich, the German family was again a central focus of social policy; but now biological explanations of "family failure" obliterated economic and psychological viewpoints. Nazi "racial hygiene" promoted the reproduction of "healthy" Aryan families and made "antisocial" families the targets of negative "eugenic" measures.[88] The *Volksgenossen/innen* could expect to pay a high price for cultural nonconformity or the "pleasures of refusal";[89] a spell in a concentration camp, forced sterilization, even extermination. And women were made the special victims of Nazi "social racism."[90]

---

87. Official justification for the Community Aliens Law, quoted in Noakes, "Social Outcasts in the Third Reich," 95.

88. See Klaus Scherer, *"Asozial" im Dritten Reich: Die vergessenen Verfolgten* (Münster, 1990).

89. See Dick Hebdige, *Hiding in the Light: On Images and Things* (London and New York, 1988), esp. 17–36.

90. See especially Gisela Bock, "Racism and Sexism in Nazi Germany: Compulsory Sterilization, and the State," in *When Biology Became Destiny: Women in Weimar and Nazi Germany,* ed. Renate Bridenthal, Atina Grossmann, and Marion Kaplan (New York, 1984), 271–96; David Kramer, "Volkspflegerische Aspekte eines weiblichen Berufes im Dritten Reich," in *Soziale Arbeit und Faschismus: Volkspflege und Pädagogik im Nationalsozialismus,* ed. Hans-Uwe Otto and Heinz Sünker (Bielefeld, 1986), 419–30; Detlev J. K. Peukert, *Inside Nazi Germany: Conformity, Opposition and Racism in Everyday Life* (New Haven, 1987), 208–35.

World War I and the German Welfare State: Gender, Religion, and the Paradoxes of Modernity

Young-Sun Hong

The German government hoped to win World War I in order to secure hegemonic global power. However, by the summer of 1916, this war, which had originally been expected to last only a few months, had become a total war, bogged down in a new form of muddy trench warfare which appeared to ensure that the war would be anything but brief and economically fought. The nature of war in modern industrial society seriously endangered the civic truce (*Burgfriede*) in whose name the German government hoped to bring about a suspension of class, religious, gender, and regional conflict for the duration of the war in order to assure a united home front. One of the great paradoxes—or ironies—is that the massive death and social dislocation caused by the war contributed decidedly to undermining those traditional patterns of social deference and political authority that the war was presumably being fought to protect.

World War I transformed the heroic figure of the father-breadwinner-soldier into an emasculated worker who, as Ernst Jünger put it, "exchanged heroism's iridescent mantle for the dirty smock of the day-laborer" working in the trenches.[1] This "apocalypic" war, Sandra Gilbert has argued, "virtually completed the Industrial Revolution's construction of anonymous dehumanized man, that impotent cipher who is frequently thought to be the twentieth century's most characteristic citizen."[2] A sense of exploitation, alien-

---

First appeared as "The Contradictions of Modernisation in the German Welfare State," *Social History* 17, no. 2 (May 1992). Reprinted with permission.

1. Cited in Eric J. Leed, *No Man's Land* (Cambridge, 1981), 91.

2. Sandra M. Gilbert, "Soldier's Heart: Literary Men, Literary Woman, and the Great War," in *Behind the Lines: Gender and the Two World Wars,* ed. Margaret R. Higonnet et al. (New Haven, 1987), 198.

ation, and often sexual impotence was a direct product of this "militarized proletarianization," which haunted their memories long after the war's end.[3]

On the home front, industrial workers and the lower middle classes experienced especially severely the inequalities of sacrifice and suffering caused by wartime shortages. The unprecedented growth of state intervention into the economy to regulate war-related production and ensure the adequate distribution of consumer goods—especially food—highlighted the extent to which access to these commodities was determined by the existing unequal relations of power and money. The general populace was increasingly forced to turn to the family unit to secure the means of subsistence, which neither wage labor nor state redistributive activities were capable of guaranteeing. As the purchasing power of wage labor declined, the strategic importance of nonmarket means of securing adequate food supplies steadily increased.[4] The majority of the populace was forced to rely on various survival strategies that often crossed the boundary between legality and criminality. As early as 1915, spontaneous popular rebellions against wartime shortages emerged in the form of food riots, hunger marches, shop plundering, and theft, in which women played an important role.[5] By the winter of 1916–17, intensified war efforts had led to the radicalization of these popular movements, which was first expressed in anti-war sentiment and, eventually, in mass strikes protesting against government policies.

World War I precipitated a fundamental contradiction in the conditions necessary for maintaining and reproducing existing social relations in Germany. The total mobilization of society and the massive social dislocation caused by the war itself undermined precisely those existing political, social, and economic relations of domination and subordination that the war was ostensibly being fought to preserve. This contradiction was further aggravated by the government's inability to transform the "ideas of 1914" into an ideological construct that would be capable of resolving, at an ideal level, the legitima-

---

3. Leed, *No Man's Land,* 73–114.

4. Ute Daniel, "Women's Work in Industry and Family: Germany, 1914–1918," in *The Upheaval of War,* ed. Richard Wall and Jay Winter (Cambridge, 1988), 275–76. Although wage workers in war-related industry were better compensated than those in consumer-goods industries, only highly skilled workers were able to maintain a relatively adequate standard of living.

5. Volker Ullrich, "Everyday Life and the German Working Class, 1914–1918," and U. Daniel, "The Politics of Rationing versus the Politics of Subsistence: Working-Class Women in Germany, 1914–1918," in *Bernstein to Brandt: A Short History of German Social Democracy,* ed. Roger Fletcher (London, 1987), 55–64 and 89–95, respectively. See also Robert W. Whalen, *Bitter Wounds* (Ithaca, 1984). Statistics show an increase in the crime rate—especially of property crimes—among women from 1916 onward. Almost 99 percent of women arrested in 1917 had no previous criminal record; see Ludwig Preller, *Sozialpolitik in der Weimarer Republik* (Düsseldorf, 1978), 11.

tion crisis of the late Wilhelmine state caused by unprecedented mass distress and the gradual polarization of social relations.

Scholars working on the development of the German welfare system have properly characterized World War I as the turning point in the development of a *social*-welfare state.[6] However, they tend to view wartime social-welfare ideas and activities as being determined and implemented primarily by the state without investigating either the exact nature of this interventionist state or the way that different social groups responded to this intervention. The development of the social-welfare system cannot be understood exclusively or even primarily from such a perspective. The modern social-welfare system, as it emerged during the volatile period of war, revolution, and hyperinflation, was not the end product of a unilinear process of state-centered modernization. Rather, the rise of a welfare state was the result of a multitude of essentially contested social, ideological, and political responses to the problems raised by the rapid but thoroughgoing transformation of liberal civil society and the market economy.

This essay will examine the contradictions or paradoxes of the modernization of the German social-welfare sector during World War I. I would like to put forth three closely interrelated arguments. First, the fundamental politicization of both social reproduction and the welfare sector during the war irreparably blurred the traditional distiction—held by liberals and conservatives alike—between the state and society. This inaugurated the definitive transformation of the Wilhelmine *Rechtsstaat* into a welfare state whose precise contours necessarily reflected the changing balance of social forces in society at large. Second, the political struggle to reshape the social welfare sector during the latter years of the war and the immediate postwar period was itself an integral aspect of the general process of state formation. Consequently, the formation of the Weimar welfare system was itself an essentially contested political struggle that revealed many of the contradictions and asynchronicities of modernity, not the end product of a smooth, teleological modernization process. Third, it is important to recognize the extent to which questions of gender and family served as a prism that focused and refracted these political struggles, whose outcome determined the nature of the Weimar state. These struggles to redefine the relation of state and society were waged in and through a gendered language that forced the participants to formulate their

---

6. Christoph Sachße and Florian Tennstedt, eds., *Geschichte der Armenfürsorge in Deutschland*, vol. 2, *Fürsorge und Wohlfahrtspflege, 1871 bis 1929* (Stuttgart, 1988); Rolf Landwehr, "Funktionswandel der Fürsorge vom Ersten Weltkrieg bis zum Ende der Weimarer Republik," in *Geschichte der Sozialarbeit: Hauptlinien ihrer Entwicklung im 19. und 20. Jahrhundert*, ed. Rüdiger Baron and R. Landwehr (Weinheim, 1983), 73–138; Richard Münchmeier, *Zugänge zur Geschichte der Sozialarbeit* (Munich, 1981); and C. Sachße, *Mütterlichkeit als Beruf* (Frankfurt, 1986).

competing programs for welfare reform in terms of a widely perceived "crisis of the family." In turn, the organizational structure and practical welfare policies of the emergent Weimar social-welfare system gave legal and institutional expression to the dominant conceptions of the role of women and the family in society, thereby lending the Weimar state an indelibly gendered dimension.

The Politicization of Social Reproduction and Welfare in "Total War"

World War I was the catalyst for the transformation of those political, economic, and legal relations that played the central role in the social construction of gender in prewar Germany. By permitting and even compelling women to perform those activities that had traditionally been reserved for men, the war demystified the presumed naturalness of prevailing bourgeois conceptions of gender and family and revealed how they were inscribed within the legal-political infrastructure of the Wilhelmine state. To a large extent, this change marked an acceleration of prewar trends conditioned by the concentration of capital and the rise of global economy. During the war, however, the massive death of enlisted men, the entrance of women into previously male-dominated sectors of the labor market, and the growing self-consciousness among working-class women and youth during the war precipitated a widely perceived "crisis of the family."

The dominant public discourse on the collapse or failure of the family crystallized on the fear that the mother-child bond—which was viewed as the best and most natural basis for child rearing—was breaking up. This perception both reflects the actual wartime changes in gender roles and family structure and mirrors the public perception of the "emancipation" of women in the immediate postwar years. Such new social categories as "war widows," "soldiers' wives," and "war orphans" underlined the public fear that the working wives of soldiers were vulnerable and in danger of neglecting their motherly, nurturing task.[7] At a preparatory meeting for the creation of the German Committee for the Welfare of Small Children (Deutscher Ausschuß für Kleinkinderfürsorge) in 1915, Wilhelm Polligkeit, a leading welfare reformer, expressed the widely shared belief that the family was becoming increasingly inadequate as the primary site of social reproduction and, in response, called for the active intervention of such public authorities as the juvenile courts and youth-welfare offices to meet these new needs: "The collapse of the family has

---

7. The image of young children left unattended while their fathers served at the front and their mothers labored in the factory was one of the most vivid contemporary expressions of this perceived crisis of the family. On the public prejudice against soldiers' wives, see U. Daniel, *Arbeiterfrauen in der Kriegsgesellschaft* (Göttingen, 1989), chap. 3.

determined the direction and the course for the new association. . . . In the coming years, social policy must become a social policy for the family. We must step in and help everywhere where the family has collapsed."[8]

This perceived crisis of social reproduction led to what Jane Jenson has called "moments of efflorescence in the universe of political discourse, when competing actors, bearing a variety of collective identities, may successfully struggle to extend the reach of their world views."[9] The vociferous public debate on the proper course of welfare reform and the political mobilization of various social groups—bourgeois social reformers, feminists, socialists, and religious groups—were propelled by competing and often contradictory conceptions of family and motherhood and their role in state and society. The discourse surrounding the development of the modern welfare system both reflected and generated bitter religious, cultural, and social-political conflicts and, in so doing, played a central role in shaping and, ultimately, undermining the Wilhelmine and Weimar states.

The most decisive factor in the unprecedented politicization of the sphere of personal-familial life and the subsequent political mobilization of social groups was the necessity of politically mobilizing and organizing national resources for total war.[10] In the perception of the head of the War Office, General Wilhelm Groener, the 1916 Battle of the Somme was "an event unheard-of in the history of mankind, an event whose violence will perhaps be exceeded by events yet to come."[11] The introduction of the Hindenburg program and the Auxiliary Service Law in December 1916 marked the beginning of the massive mobilization of society and economy, under the overall direction of the Supreme Military Command, with the sole aim of "increasing production at any price."[12] As Groener argued,

our troops stand deep in the enemy's land, an iron wall. . . . This steel wall, forged from human bodies, must hold, and in order that it hold, there

---

8. Archiv des Deutschen Caritasverbandes Freiburg (ADCV), 319.4: E VIII 6, "Besprechung über den Zusammenschluß zwecks Organisation der Kleinkinder-Fürsorge" (30 June 1915).

9. Jane Jenson, "The Play of Light and Shadow: Paradigms and Political Discourse" (paper given at the 1988 American Political Science Association Conference in Washington, D.C.), 5.

10. Michael Geyer, "German Strategy in the Age of Machine Warfare, 1914–1945," in *Makers of Modern Strategy from Machiavelli to the Nuclear Age,* ed. Peter Paret (Princeton, 1986), 527–97.

11. Wilhelm Groener, "Niederschrift über die 1. Sitzung des Nationalen Ausschuß für Frauenarbeit im Kriege," 29 January 1917 at the Kriegsamt, Stab, ADCV, CA XIX 15.

12. Marie-Elisabeth Lüders, *Das unbekannte Heer: Frauen kämpfen für Deutschland, 1914–1918* (Berlin, 1937), 125. See also Gerald Feldman, *Army, Industry, and Labor in Germany, 1914–1918* (Princeton, 1966).

must be a *Volk* that stands united behind this wall with an absolute will to persevere and to win.[13]

World War I contributed in decisive ways to dissolving the traditional boundary between the state and civil society and to repoliticizing definitively not only the spheres of the economic and the social but also that of the personal-familial.[14] The dissolution of this boundary was most evident in the unprecedented extension of governmental planning and regulation into the sexual and familial spheres in order to mobilize all available resources for war production. As Marie-Elisabeth Lüders, a leading organizer of women's wartime labor service, noted, in the age of total war (*Volkskrieg*), "the entire sphere of women's private life became a matter of concern for war politics. . . . Military policy and social policy entered the battlefield hand in hand."[15]

The year 1917 marked a turning point. As Lüders pointed out, war itself now became the single, all-consuming end, to which everything else— including human beings—was subordinated as a means: "People and things are transformed by the pressure of war. Right and wrong, good and evil are dislocated by its force. Everything appears twisted and distorted. Death and life, everything is the same."[16] One essential aspect of this collapse of the boundary between the public and the private was the militarization of both the national economy and family life. Women—both the symbolic guardian of the home front and the largest reserve army of the labor force—had to be mobilized and organized for war:

> Women manned the fortress whose walls and trenches were defended by their husbands and brothers. If the fortress raised the white flag, then the trenches and walls would be stormed. For this reason, no aspect of garrisoning and the provision of armaments for the defense of the fortress could be left to chance. Even though the weapons needed by women might be different from those used at the military front, they were no less important than canons and guns.[17]

In an effort to drive able-bodied women out of the domestic sphere to fill jobs vacated by men called to the front, the government called on women for their

---

13. Minutes of the Nationaler Ausschuß für Frauenarbeit im Kriege (NAfFiK) meeting of 29 January 1917, ADCV, CA XIX 15.

14. Elisabeth Domansky, "World War I as Gender Conflict in Germany" (unpublished paper, 1988); M. Geyer, "Professionals and Junkers: German Rearmament and Politics in the Weimar Republic," in *Social Change and Political Development in Weimar Germany,* ed. Richard Bessel and E.J. Feuchtwanger (London, 1981), 77–133.

15. Lüders, *Das unbekannte Heer,* 180, 183.

16. Ibid., 125, 179.

17. Ibid., 181.

service for the fatherland. In order to ensure the most efficient mobilization of female workers and increase the "willingness, capability, and perseverance" to work, the military authority created the National Commission for Wartime Female Labor (Nationaler Ausschuß für Frauenarbeit im Kriege, NAfFiK) and the Female Labor Center (Frauenarbeitszentrale, FAZ) at the War Office.

At the first meeting of the NAfFiK on 29 January 1917, Groener emphasized the urgent need to rethink the nature of social welfare under the conditions of modern industrial warfare. Welfare services, he argued, should not be undertaken "for the sake of social welfare, but for the sake of enhancing production," and he maintained that all existing private welfare organizations should be willing to coordinate their activities toward this end.[18] In so doing, Groener, a champion of modern technology and efficiency-oriented management, played a decisive role in transforming the older, primarily religious conception of voluntary charitable activity into an explicitly political issue that was directly related to both the structure of, and tensions within, a modern industrial society. Social welfare for children of women working in war industries and agriculture should be no longer guided by religious or humanitarian considerations but by the criteria of efficiency and economy aimed at maximizing total national productivity. To this end, private, voluntary charitable activities should be replaced, Groener argued, by a rationalized and unified national welfare system. It was at the same meeting, in January 1917, of the NAfFiK that he stated that "women's work and men's work cannot be forced into the same mold; they must be approached individually. With regard to women's work, we must take account of family, bodily strength, and all possible such things, which are of no account in considering men's work."[19]

By the second half of the war, the growing national-political concern for pronatalism and public health called for the marked expansion of public welfare aimed at promoting a population capable of sustaining a modern industrial war.[20] The decree of 25 October 1916 by the provincial president of Potsdam represented one of the first concrete government attempts to centralize and bureaucratize infant-, child-, and youth-welfare activities, which the government viewed as "the most important task of the present" for the goal of "preserving and increasing the *Volk*."[21] In order to achieve the maximal result

18. Minutes of the NAfFiK meeting of 29 January 1917, ADCV, CA XIX 15.

19. Minutes of the NAfFiK meeting of 29 January 1917, ADCV, CA XIX 15.

20. For more, see Cornelie Usborne, "'Pregnancy Is the Woman's Active Service': Pronatalism in Germany during the First World War," in *The Upheaval of War,* ed. Richard Watt and Jay Winter, 389–416. The *Reichswochenhilfe für schwangere Frauen*—first introduced in December 1914 for wives of the military servicemen who had been insured by social insurance and then expanded in April 1915 to include women whose husbands had not been covered by social insurance—was one of the first few "welfare" measures whose main purpose was to maintain population growth.

21. Bundesarchiv Koblenz, R 86: 2316.

with "minimal use of manpower and finance," local authorities were strongly urged to centralize all the branches of social hygiene services by creating a network of public welfare offices throughout Prussia and to employ trained female social workers (*Kreisfürsorgerinnen*).[22] The establishment of public welfare offices became the most powerful and visible symbol of the state's intention not only to undertake more extensive welfare activities itself but also to use its financial and regulatory powers to control the activities and underlying values of voluntary welfare organizations as well.

This change dramatically accelerated the extension of bureaucratic rationality—which had long governed economy and politics—into the reproductive sphere of sexuality and family. The intense and rapid intrusion of state authority in these areas led to the repoliticization of those conceptions of gender and family that had been relegated to the presumed "private," "prepolitical" sphere in the process of the *political-ideological* construction of the bourgeois family and civil society in the nineteenth century. The interventionist welfare state created the potential for sharp cultural and religious conflict among the various competing social groups often holding diametrically opposed views of the relation of family and state. The major participants in this struggle were the state bureaucracy, whose primary goal was to assert its control over the multitude of social-welfare activities in order to make optimal use of their resources; confessional charity organizations, which had traditionally predominated in the welfare sector; bourgeois feminists, who hoped to use welfare activities as an instrument to carve a niche in public life; socialist welfare reformers, who advocated the transformation of the traditional disciplinary poor relief system into a democratic, *social*-welfare system; and male Progressives, whose main concern was to promote national efficiency and productivity. Throughout the later war years and the Weimar Republic, the social-welfare sector was increasingly politicized and polarized by a number of conflicts among these groups in matters of fundamental principles.

The attempt to restructure the welfare system under the direction of the governmental authorities raised the fundamental political question of the relationship of the state to social organizations. Most traditional private welfare agencies, which had heretofore enjoyed a high degree of autonomy, began to chafe at the increasingly aggressive regulatory activities of the state and sought to guard their autonomy from state encroachment. The confessional welfare organizations, in particular the Catholic Caritasverband, were the most vocal opponents of the growing influence of secular voluntary welfare groups and the "mechanical state bureaucracy" in the welfare sector. The tension between the

---

22. The growing demand for *Kreisfürsorgerinnen* accelerated the creation of social work institutions and short-term programs, many of which were now financed and supervised by public authorities. Municipal authorities in Charlottenburg, Cologne, and Düsseldorf were the first to create such training institutions during the war.

specific Christian-moral values underlying their activity and the external guidance and coercion by the leveling, uniform policies of the sovereign state was the fundamental issue against which all other conflicts and issues paled in comparison.

The confessional views on the problem of welfare reform were shaped by the belief that the highest aim of Christian charitable activity was not so much the immediate improvement of the material standard of living of the indigent as their moral and religious betterment, to which material help was a secondary means. State coercion and regulation therefore appeared as an unnatural force that violated the quintessentially religious nature of voluntary charitable activity. Most of all, the bureaucratization of the children-, youth-, and family-welfare system was considered as a direct threat to the charitable organizations' identity and moral authority. Consequently, they regarded the defense of their traditional prerogatives in these areas as ultimate ends that had to be defended at all costs. The Caritasverband, for instance, refused to submit to the guidance of public welfare offices, arguing that this would "degrade" private welfare to a mere "acquiescent helpmate to powerful governmental welfare."[23]

There was a similar tension within societal, voluntary welfare organizations. Most of all, the Social Democrats, with their outspoken anti-Christianity and the proselytizing activity encompassing all aspects of life, emerged as a potentially powerful enemy of the confessional welfare groups. Most immediately, the socialists castigated the moralizing approach to charitable activity of the confessional organizations for intentionally obscuring the real cause of poverty in modern society. It was not, however, until the 1918–19 revolution that the creation of the Social Democratic Organization Workers' Welfare (Arbeiterwohlfahrt) posed a genuine threat to the confessional organizations. The latter attacked the legitimacy of socialist welfare activity, regarding the focus on material interests as incompatible with the true spiritual nature of charitable activity. The socialists, in turn, argued that their materialist worldview and their ideas for remedying the ills of capitalist society did, in fact, belong to the sphere of ultimate ends.

During the war itself, the confessional groups were much more concerned with the challenges presented by secular bourgeois welfare organizations, which they viewed as potential competitors for the allegiance of both Protestants and Catholics. The major nonconfessional welfare societies—led by the German Association of Public and Private Welfare (Deutscher Verein für Armenpflege und Wohltätigkeit, DVfAW) and the Central Societies of Private Welfare in Berlin (directed by Albert Levy) and in Frankfurt (directed by Polligkeit)—had long advocated the creation of an interventionist welfare state

---

23. "Denkschrift des Caritasverbands betr. den Ausbau der kath. Caritasorganisation in Deutschland," prepared by Konstantin Noppel in 1915, ADCV, R2.

based on the rational division of labor among public and private welfare organizations according to the principles of professionalized administration and training.[24] They all shared the belief that welfare work in modern society should be based on methods and goals fundamentally different from those underlying traditional confessional charity. Christian J. Klumker, a youth-welfare reform activist and close colleague of Polligkeit, insisted that the autonomy and independence of welfare activity lay in its exclusive emphasis on efficiency and national productivity. On this ground, Klumker harshly criticized the confessional charitable activity for confusing and distorting the nature of modern welfare by conflating questions of economy with questions of Christian morality.[25] Also a number of bourgeois feminists believed that the traditional charity activities were predominantly guided by "purely private," often "emotional" or "irrational" motivations and therefore stood in constant conflict with the interest of the national community. Modern *social* work was clearly distinguishable from *charitable,* religious activity, they argued, by its exclusive devotion to increasing the productive and reproductive capacities of welfare recipients for the benefit of society in general.[26]

Polligkeit, one of the most energetic leaders of progressive welfare-reform movement, was very critical of the traditional child- and youth-welfare system because he believed that its irrational, minimalist principles aimed only at the "poorest, weakest, and delinquents." Instead, he argued, the most efficient and effective form of welfare activity should aim at systematically promoting the right frame of mind and attitudes among the indigent and not limit

---

24. These reform advocates had worked together with the leading members of the Federation of German Women's Associations (Bund Deutscher Frauenvereine, BDF) to raise the level of training of professional welfare workers. For example, Alice Salomon's professional social-work school for women cooperated most closely with the Central Society of Private Welfare in Berlin. Rosa Kempf directed a women's professional social-work school in Frankfurt, in whose foundation the Institut für Gemeinwohl (owned by Wilhelm Merton) and its daughter organization, the Central Society of Private Welfare, had played an important role.

25. Christian J. Klumker, "Das Wesen der Fürsorgetätigkeit," *Zeitschrift für das Armenwesen* 18 (1917): 37–51.

26. Gertrud Bäumer, "Die Ziele der sozialen Frauenschule und des sozialpädagogischen Instituts in Hamburg," *Die Frau* 24, no. 6 (March 1917): 338–48; Alice Salomon, "Die Ausbildung zur sozialen Berufsarbeit," *Die Frau* 24, no. 5 (Feb. 1917): 263–76. Marie Bernays, another bourgeois feminist social-work educator, argued that because the fundamental goal of social work was to "preserve, awaken, strengthen, and increase" Germany's productive forces, "in peace and war, the modern world cannot survive without social work, and cannot progress without the social work of women"; Marie Bernays, *Ein Jahr soziale Kriegsarbeit* (Karlsruhe, 1915), 4–6. Leading bourgeois feminists believed that this activity of promoting the economic value of human capital (*Menschenökonomie*) could best be accomplished by women, thanks to their innate caring, creating, nurturing power (*Frauenkräfte*). On the notion of the "social" and its inseparable relationship to the bourgeois women's movement and the development of social work as a profession, see A. Salomon, "Fünfundzwanzig Jahre Mädchen- und Frauengruppen für soziale Hilfsarbeit," *Blätter für Soziale Arbeit* 10, nos. 11–12 (1918): 41–44.

itself to merely ministering to the physical needs of the young. The rationalization of welfare activity would finally make it possible to realize the Fichtean ideal of a program of "national education": "What remained an unrealizable ideal at that time does not seem unattainable today. . . . Complete success requires only a generously conceived plan and a clear division of forces."[27] Contemporary social policy ought, Polligkeit argued, to reach beyond the regulation of capital-labor relations to include "the promotion of cultural values" in familial and personal life:

> In view of the dependence of our entire social life on the functioning of the family as the fundamental unity of our state, there can be no doubt that this cultural policy will primarily extend to the strengthening and preservation of family life.[28]

Finally, arguing that "we must capitalize on wartime conditions in order to perfect our organization in its parts and total structure,"[29] he proposed creating a national youth-welfare parliament in which different associations representing diverse interests and ideals could meet and reach a consensus regarding the most rational and efficient way of coordinating youth-welfare services.

In September 1917, the issue was addressed at the national level at a conference sponsored by the DVfAW, "Welfare in Transition from War to Peace."[30] At this conference, it became clear that the majority of the participants were deeply convinced of the need for voluntary cooperation, not only between public and private welfare but also among the private welfare organizations themselves. However, they also recognized both the limits of voluntary cooperation within Polligkeit's "association of associations" and the fact that the autonomy and the specific nature of voluntary private welfare was at stake. While the discussion initially appeared to focus on the question of possible organizational restructuring, in reality the debate centered on the question of the nature of the state.

At the conference, there was a clear division of opinion into two opposing camps: those who called for voluntary self-regulation "from below" among leading welfare organizations and those who called for the regulation of the activities of the private welfare sector under the leadership of the state as a

---

27. ADCV, 319.4: E VIII, 6, Agenda for the *Kriegstagung der deutschen Jugendfürsorgevereine* (no date but probably summer 1915).

28. Speech delivered to the conference of the German Center for Youth Welfare (Deutsche Zentrale für Jugendfürsorge) in 1915, cited in "Familienpolitik und Frauenstimmrecht," *Zeitschrift für Frauenstimmrecht* 19 (1 November 1915).

29. Circular, signed by Polligkeit, from the Kinderschutzverband (22 July 1915), ADCV, 319.4: E VIII 6.

30. The participants in the conference included representatives from a wide range of governmental and social organizations and agencies.

"supervising, educating, and leading authority." Polligkeit's argument that "organization"—the catchword used since the turn of the century among welfare reformers—did not necessarily mean centralization went right to the heart of the matter:

> An organization must be created in such a way that both the national-political ends of public social welfare for the purpose of assuring the common good and the ideal ends of private social welfare for the purpose of assuring the welfare of the individual are fulfilled. We only have an organization in the full sense when justice is done to both parts.[31]

The idea of a mixed economy in the welfare sector in the form of an *Arbeitsgemeinschaft* seemed to Polligkeit to offer the possibility for a cooperative integration of members that would not impair the autonomy of each. While the formation of corporatist institutions to facilitate cooperation between the state, organized labor, and organized capital had previously been motivated by the goal of increased efficiency, for those welfare organizers who understood their activities as manifestations of ethical and religious values, cooperation could take place only on the basis of a "community of values" (*Gesinnungsgemeinschaft*), which appeared to offer a way of overcoming both divisions within the private sector as well as the increasingly important public/private distinction. The ultimate possibility of overcoming conflict depended, Polligkeit argued, on "bringing about in a right manner and fully developing the inner spirit of social welfare."[32] He noted, however, that the realization of this idea depended upon a leader who would "point out the goals and indicate the paths by which his [sic] coworkers could arrive at this goal."[33] Undoubtedly, Polligkeit sought to cast himself in this leading role.

The question was whether or not the leading confessional welfare groups would bend to the necessities of modern society and recognize the equal right of the humanitarian and socialist organizations, as well as the state welfare bureaucracy, to welfare activity and cooperate with them. At stake was the willingness of various competing groups to compromise their ultimate convictions and enter the sphere of public, political life; otherwise public life would become a battlefield where the clash of incompatible ultimate values—expressed through the institutional egoism and self-interest of the various welfare organizations—would defeat the idea of a common good. Catholic mistrust of the state control of welfare activity was deeply ingrained in the historical memory of the *Kulturkampf.* More fundamentally, the Catholics

---

31. Wilhelm Polligkeit, "Das Zusammenarbeiten der Wohlfahrtsvereine," *Schriften der Zentralstelle für Volkswohlfahrt,* n.s., 14 (1918): 50–51.

32. Ibid., 52.

33. Ibid., 51.

regarded the well-being of children of Catholic parents in primarily religious and spiritual terms and consequently regarded the care of these children as an indisputable prerogative of the Catholic church and its welfare organization. The Inner Mission made similar claims for Protestant children, as Workers' Welfare later did for all working-class children irrespective of confession. This was the most important reason why the confessional welfare organizations tended to view the politics of youth-welfare reform in terms of the clash of conflicting worldviews.

As the best way of counteracting this clash, leaders of the Caritasverband recommended the centralization and rationalization of the Catholic charity efforts as a whole. In the summer of 1916, the bishops' conference officially recognized the Caritasverband as the legitimate representative of the German Catholic church in the sphere of welfare activity, thus allowing the Caritasverband to consolidate all Catholic welfare activity under its authority.[34] They felt that the best way for organized Catholicism to respond to the manifold crises of German society was to adhere more firmly than ever to their own convictions. During the last several months before the revolution, Lorenz Werthmann, the head of the Caritasverband, had organized a Catholic boycott of the German youth-welfare conference (*Deutscher Jugendfürsorgetag*) scheduled for September 1918. The conference had been organized by Polligkeit, Klumker, and the DVfAW in order to discuss the urgent issue of state control of private youth-welfare associations through public welfare offices and laws, an issue that was all the more pressing due to the impending passage of the Prussian youth-welfare law. Werthmann was furious that neither the Caritasverband nor the Inner Mission had been asked to play a role in organizing the conference and setting the agenda. He interpreted this exclusion as characteristic of the prejudice of the DVfAW and the Klumker/Polligkeit clique against confessional welfare groups, especially the Caritasverband. In spite of intense efforts by leaders of the DVfAW to persuade Werthmann of their unbiased intentions and the need for cooperation and trust among the different organizations, he viewed the entire incident as an illustration of the way the deepest concerns of Catholic charitable activity were endangered by even the most minor organizational and administrative problems.[35]

The crucial period of war and revolution provided a powerful impetus for the Catholic welfare groups to centralize and rationalize their organizations in order to be able to compete more effectively with other welfare organizations. The great paradox in the activity of the Caritasverband and the other confes-

---

34. *Zeitschrift für die Werke der Nächstenliebe im Kath. Deutschland* 8, cited in "Vertrauliche Mitteilungen" of the Inner Mission, 4 (4 July 1917), Archiv des Diakonischen Werkes in Rheinland (ADWR), 10/1–2, 2.

35. The correspondence surrounding this incident can be found in ADCV, 319.4: A II, 5e.

sional welfare organizations lies in the fact that the fundamental politicization of the social-welfare sector since the 1890s—which had been rapidly accelerated by the unprecedented growth of the interventionist state during the war—forced these organizations to adopt highly rationalized, instrumental, organizational, and political means in order to achieve their traditional, value-oriented ends under the changed political and economic situation of the decade after 1914. A distinctly modern clash of worldviews and the fundamental politicization of traditional society led to the secularization of traditional worldviews and revealed the ambiguities and contradictions inherent in all attempts to establish a "postliberal" social order. In the following two sections, I will examine two fundamental conflicts in the emergent rationalized and bureaucratic welfare state: first, that between bourgeois feminists and the state bureaucracy and second, that between the Catholic Women's Association (Katholischer Frauenbund Deutschlands, KFD) and the male-dominated Caritasverband.

From the Modern "Social Woman" to the "Social Family"

During the war bourgeois feminists advanced more forcefully their prewar belief that "spiritual motherhood" should serve as the basis for the modern welfare state. While the antifeminist conservatives tended to channel the idea of motherhood into women's biological capacity to "supply the state with children, children, and more children,"[36] bourgeois feminists emphasized the social and cultural character of *Volksmütter,* in and through which the public-political and the personal-familial were mediated. Claiming that women's specific power (*Frauenkräfte*) constituted the foundation of national power (*Volkskraft*), female social reformers advocated the creation of a comprehensive public welfare program, ranging from labor protection to compulsory maternity insurance, designed to protect women.[37] The postwar welfare state, they agreed, should provide services to meet the needs of women's multiple roles in the productive and reproductive spheres.[38] Most bourgeois feminists envisioned a form of the state that would recognize a modern *public* role of women as autonomous participants in the national community. The emergent

---

36. Minna Cauer, "Zur Dienstpflicht der Frau," *Die Frauenbewegung* 22, no. 5 (1 March 1916).

37. Maternalist welfarism provided reform-minded bourgeois and socialist women with a common platform and a basis for cooperation, though not without tension, in a number of important social-reform organizations. Especially Josephine Levy-Rathenau, Helene Simon, and Käthe Gabel gained deep respect from both sides.

38. This issue was discussed intensively during the BDF *Kriegstagung* in Weimar in 1916. Most participants projected an acceleration of the Taylor system in which the female labor force would play an indispensable role. See the anonymous report on the conference in Stadtarchiv Köln, 1067: 262.

public welfare system and the rapid development of social work as a paid occupation for women in wartime Germany at first seemed to put into practice their desire to institutionalize "separate but equal" female roles in the national-political sphere.

During the war, women's organizations played an indispensable role in national and local welfare administration, especially in organizing welfare services for working women, war survivors, and children and in mobilizing women's labor under the FAZ and NAfFiK. Since women in the FAZ and the NAfFiK were granted a certain bureaucratic authority because of their connections to the War Office, they hoped that war-induced changes would further promote their conception of the sexual division of labor in public life and ultimately lead to the full recognition of women's rights to participation and self-determination. The Catholic Women's Association was very enthusiastic about these activities, which appeared to have opened the way for greater women's participation in public life:

Since the war, women's participation has proven itself in all branches of German wartime welfare services and has been recognized. For this reason, women can legitimately expect to participate and be represented in all local or provincial welfare offices, commissions, and committees.[39]

In spite of the obstacles erected in opposition to the seemingly growing prominence and authority of women in the state bureaucracy, the leading members of the Federal Association of Women's Organizations (Bund Deutscher Frauenvereine, BDF) hoped that those welfare services and administrative channels that had been established especially for women for the duration of the war would be maintained after the war.[40]

This led to the creation of additional female social-work schools directed by leading members of bourgeois feminist organizations. Marie Baum and Gertrud Bäumer, the president of the BDF, created a school in Hamburg, which had the reputation for having the most advanced, theoretical curriculum. Other leading BDF members, such as Marie Bernays and Elisabeth Altmann-Gottheiner, founded the Social Women's School in Mannheim. And Kempf, who had been the director of a women's social-work school in Frankfurt, moved to a newly created school in Düsseldorf (which was later taken over by Lüders). These schools all shared the desire to realize the ideal of a modern female personality as a social woman by providing students with a broad

---

39. "Wichtiges für unsere Mitglieder und die Zweigvereine zur Mitarbeit bei der soz. Kriegsfürsorge" (no date, probably 1917), ADCV, 319.4: BII 3.
40. Lüders, *Das unbekannte Heer,* 179–87.

theoretical education in law, politics, and national economy, as well as in social ethics and pedagogy.[41]

The modernization and rationalization of the social-welfare system in World War I Germany appeared to create the opportunity for women to play a broader role in public life. However, the paradox of this modernization was that it also provided a pretext for limiting the role of women in the welfare field by undermining the belief that social work was a uniquely feminine calling, a belief that these women had originally relied upon to justify their new public roles. The increasingly legalistic and bureaucratic structure of the welfare system tended to reinforce the emergent two-tiered structure of the welfare system. On the one hand, men were placed in positions of administrative authority by virtue of their presumed rationality and capacity for "universalistic," bureaucratic thought. On the other hand, women were relegated to those less important, practical tasks—such as house visits—for which their peculiarly feminine nature was supposedly better suited. This view of women as subordinate assistants to male administrators and physicians began to alienate many of those women who had entered the field of social work to achieve their own political and cultural aims. Furthermore, male administrators went on the offensive to limit the role of women within the welfare sector by creating their own social-work training schools to compete with those under the direction of bourgeois feminists. As early as 1916, the Prussian government attempted to marginalize women in the field by requiring state licensing of female social workers.[42]

Following the same logic that motivated the original bourgeois feminists, those men who opposed the growing influence of women and their prominence in positions of administrative authority could appeal to the traditional patterns of paternal authority to justify their own monopolization of higher administrative positions. As much as women were mothers, one leading administrator of the Caritasverband argued, men were also fathers:

Precisely for this reason, men's paternal qualities must be made useful for social life, and everywhere where these qualities are necessary we must also have men for welfare activities.[43]

---

41. Ilse Behrens, "Ueber einige Unterrichtsfächer an sozialen Frauenschulen," Blätter für soziale Arbeit 10, no. 3 (March 1918).

42. See Young-Sun Hong, "Femininity as a Vocation: Gender and Class Conflict in the Professionalization of German Social Work," in German Professions, 1800–1950, ed. Geoffrey Cocks and Konrad Jarausch (Oxford, 1990), 232–51.

43. Constantin Noppel at the 1918 conference of the Zentralstelle für Volkswohlfahrt over the issue of the future shape of social work, Schriften der Zentralstelle für Volkswohlfahrt, n.s., 14 (1918): 158.

Similarly, Heinz Marr, a welfare administrator in Frankfurt, argued that certain aspects of women's nature, such as intuition and a nurturing instinct, made women better suited for assisting men than for executing administrative tasks, for which men's rationality and sense of objectivity was better suited. To train women as administrative organizers would, he continued, weaken the "subconscious" of women:

> For this reason, women don't fit without inner compulsion into the specifically male type which reveals itself even in the authority structure of our central welfare agencies and offices.[44]

Conservative male welfare politicians feared that giving bureaucratic authority to women would be nothing less than catastrophic.

Here Salomon found herself in the awkward position of having to defend the gender specificity of social work against these attacks:

> For us women, social welfare as a calling is one of the very few into which we can in fact pour the innermost of our essence, in which we can find a way to express our entire essence, our uniqueness. And, for this reason, I believe that precisely in this area women have a special mission to fulfill.[45]

Salomon repeatedly emphasized that social work was the "royal property of women." Gender competition was unthinkable, she argued, because men did not possess the "natural" aptitude essential for welfare work—that is, femininity and the capacity for motherhood.[46] However, her energetic efforts to defend the gender specificity of the profession remained without resonance.

The wartime transformation of the social-welfare system seriously undermined the viability of the highly idealized conception of social work as a gender-specific activity—a *soziale Frauenberuf*—to which the bourgeois feminist social workers had originally appealed to legitimate their demand for political roles. The increasing bureaucratization of the profession provided the opportunity for male bureaucrats and welfare administrators to turn this rhetoric of the gender specificity of social work against its authors. By appealing to the traditional view of the role of men in the patriarchal family and to the presumed superior capacities of men for rational, legal thought, these men attempted to relegate women social workers to menial tasks associated with child care and hygiene and remove them from positions of public-political

---

44. *Schriften der Zentralstelle für Volkswohlfahrt*, n.s., 14 (1918): 147.
45. Ibid., 106.
46. Ibid., 105.

responsibility. Most important, the emergence of the rationalized, corporatist social-welfare system in response to the increasing politicization of the spheres of social reproduction and welfare during the war gave the final blow to the hopes of the bourgeois feminist social workers. In the following section, we will examine one vital aspect of this challenge to organized women's aspiration for, and claims to, their prerogatives of determining, representing, and organizing "interests" of women and family. The clash between the KFD and the male-dominated Caritasverband provides a revealing example of this paradox of the modernization of the social-welfare sector.

The Gendered Politics of the Rationalization of the Social-Welfare System

The increasingly intense competition within the welfare sector after 1917 can be clearly studied in the politics surrounding the FAZ and the NAfFiK. Though Groener insisted on subordinating particular values and interests to the needs of administrative efficiency, Werthmann and the church hierarchy were unwilling to compromise on their understanding of welfare as *Seelsorge* with either the state bureaucracy or other welfare organizations.[47] After being rebuffed initially by Groener, the Catholics began to lobby to ensure that Catholic women were given greater representation in the agencies overseeing welfare services for women workers. Cardinal Felix von Hartmann of Cologne protested to Groener that Protestant women, but no Catholics, were being appointed in the Rhineland.[48] Werthmann also complained to Groener about "anti-Catholic machinations" at the War Office, which, he believed, were resulting in the underrepresentation of Catholic women.[49]

Despite the resistance of such organizations as the BDF, which viewed the NAfFiK and especially the FAZ as a kind of "feminized" sphere free from the domination of men, Werthmann succeeded in persuading Groener to force them to admit the Caritasverband and other such male-dominated organizations as the German Union for Infant Protection and the German Committee for the Welfare of Small Children.[50] These hegemonic aspirations of the Caritasverband aroused the resentment and opposition of the KFD. Maria Hessberger, the director of the KFD's Berlin branch, argued that since the FAZ dealt with "women's issues," the women of the KFD ought to

---

47. See the letter of 21 February 1917 from Groener to Cardinal Felix von Hartmann, ADCV, CA XIX 15.

48. Minutes of the meeting of the central committee of the KFD (31 January 1917), ADCV, 319.4: F I, 1a.

49. Letter from Werthmann to Groener (5 February 1917), ADCV, CA XIX 15.

50. Letter from Werthmann to Hessberger (5 March 1917), Archiv des Katholischen Frauenbundes Deutschlands (AKFD), Mappe: Caritasverband II.

have full autonomy and responsibility in dealing with matters related to the FAZ:

> Now, should we give up the position that we have only won through much effort, abandon it either wholly or in part to the Caritasverband, the only mixed organization in which the leadership lies almost exclusively in the hands of men? After calm, objective reflection it is perfectly clear to us that the position that the KFD has attained in the women's movement would be shaken to its foundations [by such an action]. In all areas we would lose that ground that has cost us so much effort to conquer.[51]

Matthias Erzberger, a leading member of the Center Party, shared the KFD's concerns and argued that this "would make an [independent] Catholic women's movement practically impossible and open it up to public ridicule."[52]

The basic issue at stake in this conflict was whether charitable activity was something temporal and aimed at the material betterment of welfare recipients and the political position of the women welfare workers themselves, or whether it was an essentially spiritual act of charity to which the recipient had no right and for which the donor should expect no reward. Werthmann insisted on the charitable nature of welfare service. Since the Caritasverband had long been recognized as the official representative of the church in the sphere of welfare and charitable activity, Werthmann had the support of the church hierarchy on this issue. The Caritasverband believed that the KFD's main task was to represent "particular interests of women from a Catholic viewpoint" and to mobilize the Catholic *Frauenkräfte*.[53] Furthermore, in Werthmann's view,

> many representatives of the KFD commit a fundamental error when they assume that every affair that deals with women falls within the purview of the KFD, which should assume representation and leadership in the matter. We cannot recognize this position. Just as the Catholic Church cannot place the care of women's souls in the hands of women, so we cannot place charitable activity for women, especially spiritual charity or the religious influencing of women . . . [through charitable organizations] under the authority of women.[54]

---

51. Letter from Hessberger to Werthmann (2 March 1917), AKFD, Mappe: Caritasverband II.

52. Quoted in a letter from Hessberger to Hedwig Dransfeld (8 March 1917), AKFD, Mappe: Caritasverband II.

53. Letter to Weihbischof (probably in Cologne), 23 February 1917, ADCV, R2.

54. Letter from Werthmann to Hessberger (5 March 1917), AKFD, Mappe: Caritasverband II.

In fact, Werthmann harbored an ambitious plan to subordinate the KFD and its affiliated Catholic women's organizations to the authority of the Caritasverband.[55]

Once Werthmann had secured his influence over the NAfFiK and the FAZ, he began to work to oust Lüders from her post as the first head of the FAZ. Through the authority of the War Office, the Commission for Child Welfare at the FAZ provided bourgeois feminists with a potentially important institutional basis to administer the maternal- and child-welfare system in accordance with their notion of motherhood. Anna von Gierke served as the chair of the Commission for Child Welfare and worked closely with Lüders. In May 1917 the FAZ issued the *Guiding Principles for Child Welfare* and attempted to enforce specific standards governing such issues as space use in child-care facilities and the specific educational programs to be used in these facilities. Also, a plan was being considered that would institutionalize a nationwide basis for public child-welfare commissions, which would be administered by a woman and staffed by well-trained women social workers.

The male-dominated child-welfare organizations—including the German Union for Infant Protection (whose president was the well-known antifeminist von Behr-Pinnow)—resisted this effort to centralize and feminize the sphere of child and youth welfare because they saw these activities as a challenge to their authority not only in the welfare sector but in society at large. To stem the expansion of this women's "domination couched in dangerous forms," these organizations submitted a petition to the government requesting that Lüders be removed from her position because, they argued, neither Lüders nor Gierke were qualified for their positions, since they had no training in medicine or hygiene.[56] Since child and maternity welfare focused primarily on health and hygiene, they argued, the absence of male physicians at the top was unacceptable.[57] In addition they accused Lüders of being too assertive and judgmental, despite her lack of knowledge of the medical science; they felt that this was all the more dangerous, since she had been attempting to build a broad coalition of women who agreed with her approach to child welfare. These charges were obviously rationalizations of deeper religious and political differences.

To protect Catholic ideals and interests from the dangers of "interconfessionalization," Werthmann argued that the particular interests of all Catholic organizations must be put aside in order to provide for a unified, rationalized internal organization and to present a unified front toward the outside world so that they could best respond to the growing competition from both the govern-

---

55. Letter from Hessberger to Dransfeld (8 March 1917), AKFD, Mappe: Caritasverband II.

56. The organizations that cosigned the petition also included the Caritasverband, the conservative aristocratic Patriotic Women's Associations, and the Krippenverband, as well as the *German Committee for the Welfare of Small Children*.

57. (No date, presumably 1917), ADCV, CA XIX 15.

ment and other confessional organizations.[58] While Werthmann proposed forming an *Arbeitsgemeinschaft* that would unite all Catholic social services under his direction, the leaders of the KFD strongly opposed Werthmann's plan to "merge" Catholic women's organizations into the Caritasverband. Despite their opposition, Werthmann intimidated the KFD by directing the local Caritasverband offices to assume the administration of the women's auxiliary labor service. Supported by the bishops' council and the church hierarchy, Werthmann eventually succeeded in forcing the KFD to capitulate to his demands.

There is an interesting paradox in this conflict between the male-dominated Caritasverband and the KFD that reveals a great deal about the fortunes of traditional institutions and the nature of modernity in the increasingly secular and pluralistic world of late Wilhelmine Germany. On the one hand, the Caritasverband found itself increasingly constrained to justify its traditional, religious values and ends by appealing to the standards of national welfare rather than revealed truth. The Caritasverband had always been extremely obstinate in resisting all challenges to its traditional prerogatives, no matter whether they came from the state, the socialists, or even liberal or feminist reformers within the church. It was precisely these challenges to the Caritasverband, which followed in the wake of the fundamental politicization of the welfare sector during the war, that forced the Caritasverband to reassert with increasing vehemence the absoluteness of its spiritual prerogatives and obligations and to resist all the more strongly all compromises with this increasingly pluralistic world. Werthmann's stern warning to Hessberger that all Catholic social work was not "social" work but charitable, spiritual activity that, precisely because of its spiritual nature, must be subordinated to the authority of the church hierarchy was the clearest and most radical statement of this rationalized, "modernized" restatement of traditional values.

On the other hand, the very vehemence with which Werthmann and the Caritasverband asserted the absoluteness of their own traditional position forced the other participants in this political process to define their own aims in opposition to those of the Caritasverband and to assert the superiority of their own criteria—such as national efficiency or social justice. Werthmann insisted that the KFD be subordinated to the Caritasverband precisely because its activities were charitable, spiritual activities requiring the guidance of church authorities. Such an argument virtually forced the leaders of the KFD to define their own goals in increasingly "unspiritual"—in fact, un-Catholic—terms in order to find a viable, independent basis to justify those cultural and political aspirations that the church, with its old-fashioned views on the role of women and the family in society, refused to recognize. Hedwig Dransfeld, the presi-

---

58. Letter to Weihbischof (probably in Cologne), 23 February 1917, ADCV, R 2.

dent of the KFD, refused to accept Werthmann's characterization of women's auxiliary labor service as "charitable" activity in the sense that Werthmann had used the term because this would have meant accepting Werthmann's conclusions.[59] Instead, she sought to justify the autonomy of the KFD in terms that were non-Catholic without being explicitly anti-Catholic. She argued that the welfare services that had grown out of the Auxiliary Service Law reflected issues that primarily concerned women *as women*, rather than women as Catholics, and pointed out that the original authorization and legitimacy of their activities had come not from the Caritasverband but from the state.[60] Dransfeld's seemingly innocuous insistence that "work for women should primarily be performed by women," in fact, harbored the seed of a deep and fundamental conflict between the Catholic Church and the Catholic women's movement, a seed that blossomed during the last years of the war.[61] This is why Werthmann felt it necessary to assert his authority over the KFD. And the fact that he succeeded attests to the continued appeal of traditional values in World War I Germany and the power of entrenched interests in the institutional structure of the church.

Conclusion

In this essay I have suggested that state intervention into the spheres of charitable activity and reproductive life during World War I played a central role in bringing about the fundamental politicization of social reproduction and consequently the mobilization of social groups into the domain of power politics. Although intended to preserve traditional structures of political and social domination, the unprecedented subjection of the reproductive sphere to state power revealed unintentionally the heretofore unstated political, economic, cultural, and religious values that underlay both the bourgeois family and the voluntary charitable activities devoted to its preservation. This "consciousness of the contingency, not only of the contents of tradition, but also of the techniques of tradition, that is, of socialization,"[62] to borrow Jürgen Habermas's words, made the fundamental principles of the modern family and charitable activities the object of political contention among a variety of social groups. These groups sought to shape the emergent social-welfare system in accordance with their own, often incompatible conceptions of the nature and purpose of welfare activity.

---

59. Minutes of the meeting of the central committee (14 March 1917), ADCV, 319.4: FI, 1a.
60. Dransfeld. ADCV. 319.4: F I, 1d, meeting of the central committee of the KFD (1917).
61. Letter from Dransfeld to Werthmann, 6 March 1917, AKFD, Mappe: Caritasverband II.
62. Jürgen Habermas, *Legitimation Crisis,* trans. Thomas McCarthy (Boston, 1975), 71–72.

The politicization of the central issues of welfare and the role of the state in social reproduction reached its peak during the 1918–19 revolution. The radical socialists advocated replacing poor relief and charity with a democratized national welfare system. By demanding that welfare be taken out of the realm of "bourgeois" religious and ethical values, they linked the politics of welfare reform to the legitimacy of the state itself. The major confessional welfare organizations, in contrast, firmly believed that social welfare must stand in the services of transcendent values, which alone enabled it to affect not only the material circumstances but also the personality and spiritual needs of the indigent. In particular, the Caritasverband continued to assert forcefully the primacy of the church over the state in this important area of social relations and viewed both the state welfare bureaucracy and the socialists as representing worldviews inimical to their own understanding of the nature and purpose of charitable activity.

The inability of the confessional welfare organizations and the Social Democratic Arbeiterwohlfahrt to reach an agreement among themselves was a chronic problem in Weimar Germany. The difficulty in reaching a consensus raised the problem of the role that the state should play in mediating the political conflicts among the different private welfare organizations. In particular, the active entry of the socialists into national political affairs made the state appear as a magnet for political conflict rather than allowing it to serve as the guardian of a universalizable common good. The major confessional welfare organizations questioned seriously the nature of the Weimar welfare state. They feared that the Weimar state could turn into a political weapon in the hands of the socialists and become a purely compulsory institution. Faced with such a possibility, those groups that intransigently insisted on the absolute validity of one's own religious worldview tended to see the state as a demonic force whose every action represented a senseless violation of their own individuality. This unresolved conflict between church, society, and state threatened to undermine the legitimacy of the state and its claim to represent the common interest of society as a whole.

The fundamental politicization of social reproduction and the decisive undermining of the presumed naturalness of family structure, gender roles, and charitable activity have two important implications for understanding the development of the Weimar social-welfare system. First, the necessity of politically reconstructing the spheres of familial and reproductive life, which formed a central component of the Weimar state, blurred the separation of state and society, while the specific form of the Weimar welfare system came to reflect both the increasingly conservative balance of social forces and conservative conceptions of family and gender. Second, although the necessity of competing with each other in the public-political domain forced the different social groups to articulate their worldviews in increasingly rational, secular terms, the very severity of this clash of worldviews prevented them from cooperating effectively. As a result, their differences were translated directly to the level of fundamental, constitutional conflicts and played an important role in the crises of the later Weimar Republic.

By 1930 the domain of the Weimar social-welfare system turned into the battlefields of a *Weltanschauungskampf:*

Social welfare is the great, decisive sphere of cultural struggle, a gigantic struggle for self-assertion and domination between the Christian confessions and atheistic worldviews that are enemies of the church. The public authorities—the Reich, the states, and the communal administrations— stand in the middle of this struggle, which is waged with increasing bitterness from year to year. We must admit, with deep disturbance, that precisely in this area, in which the entire *Volk* is called into the community of help and service, that the most bitter battles are fought out. What can be the cause of this? It can only lie in the fact that here it is a question of *truly ultimate values* [*wirklich entscheidende Dinge*], that are in conflict with one another, upon which the being or nonbeing, life or death, of the community depends.[63]

In the end, unable to reconcile their absolute and religious claims within the existing state, the major welfare associations began searching for the so-called ideal commonality, such as *Volkstum,* that could serve as the spiritual basis for the cooperation of various *ideological* associations.

This organicist vision represented an entirely new form of the state: the state as the "becoming conscious of *Volkstum,*" as the embodiment of the transcendent ideal of a community based on mutual trust and recognition that was capable of performing the pedagogical mission so dear to the private organizations without resorting to mere force or degenerating into a particular, absolute interest of its own. According to leading representatives of the Caritasverband, "a new conception of the state and a new will to the state would grow among the *Volk.* In such a state there would also be the necessary freedom of movement for confessional charity, since in such a state mutual relationships would be based on trust."[64]

This conception of the state as *"Volkstum* that has become conscious of itself" was extremely influential because it incorporated into the idea of the state the belief that the state, too, could be a transcendent goal and a

---

63. Joachim Beckmann, "Wohlfahrtspflege und Kirche im Weltanschauungskampf der Gegenwart," *Gesundheitspflege* 5, no. 10 (Oct. 1931): 255.

64. Joseph Beeking, the representative of the Caritasverband, in minutes of the Kommission zur Vorbereitung einer Konferenz über das Zusammenarbeiten der öffentlichen und der freien Wohlfahrtspflege (22 April 1925), ADCV, discussion section, 25, 460.055.

Weltanschauung. The increasing willingness to invoke an organic conception of the relation of state and individual was symptomatic of the inability of welfare associations to respond to the problems raised by the politicization of the social-welfare sector. It represented an attempt to find a way of politically representing their own absolute, transcendent worldviews by sublimating them to an organic vision of social life. This permitted them to avoid the dangers that parliamentary debate and cooperation with the socialists posed to their own conception of the essentially moral purpose of welfare activity.

"She Is the Victor": Bourgeois Women, Nationalist Identities, and the Ideal of the Independent Woman Farmer in German Southwest Africa

Lora Wildenthal

In 1907, Clara Brockmann declared her intention first to live a colonial novel and then to write it (Hintrager 1955, 78). She left Germany for Southwest Africa (Namibia) and worked there as a secretarial civil servant for four years. As it turned out, Brockmann wrote no novels but rather two travel books intended to attract German settlers to Southwest Africa: *The German Woman in Southwest Africa: A Contribution to the Woman Question in Our Colonies* (1910) and *Letters from a German Girl in Southwest* (1912). The books received favorable press notice, and colonial organizations recommended them to male and female prospective settlers. Brockmann particularly encouraged women to settle in Southwest Africa; the woman settler, she asserted, made a unique and necessary contribution to the German nation. The woman farmer or farmer's wife (*Farmersfrau*) and the female agricultural intern (*weibliche Farmvolontär*) were especially prominent among her descriptions of women's possible occupations in the colony. In her descriptions of the kind of woman Southwest Africa needed, Brockmann evoked an ideal of the independent woman farmer.

Brockmann's open enthusiasm for the life of an unmarried, economically independent woman in Southwest Africa was unusual among women authors who wrote about the German colonies. She embedded her surprising visions of

This essay was previously published in *Social Analysis*, no. 33 (September 1993). Reprinted with permission.

feminine independence within widely held views on the importance of social divisions based on "race" and on the virtues of bourgeois womanhood. While Brockmann was not necessarily "typical," her books reveal underlying tensions within bourgeois nationalist German society.[1]

This essay will suggest two contexts for Brockmann's ideas, contexts that helped shape German politics and society in the decade preceding World War I: the formation of German national identity and the bourgeois (*bürgerlich*) women's movement.[2] Although the background of World War I and *Weltpolitik* (Germany's assertion of a new, international role in diplomacy and politics) are among the most researched themes in modern German history, relatively little is known about the formation of national identity in those years with respect to Germany's colonies.[3] The fact that the Allies conquered Germany's colonies soon after World War I broke out ought not to obscure from the historian's view the colonies' significance in forming German identities before 1914. As contemporary literature shows, Germans believed that status as a colonizing power helped make Germany the political and cultural equal of the other European great powers.

The anticolonial war of 1904–7 in Southwest Africa, hailed at the time as the "first war of Wilhelmine Germany," unleashed both a nationalist and a parliamentary crisis in Germany. The brutal military repression in Southwest Africa, as well as in Cameroon and German East Africa in the same years, shook Germans' confidence in their "cultural achievements" as colonizers. After domestic political battles over colonial policy culminated in the dissolution of the Reichstag in December 1906, the government pronounced a new era of reform. Brockmann's books are two examples of the hundreds of essays and books that appeared between 1907 and 1914 offering suggestions for rebuilding the colonial order in the aftermath of war. Such "reform era" prescriptive literature can reveal much about currents in nationalist German thought.

The second context—the bourgeois women's movement—is important in terms of personal as well as ideological connections with nationalist and col-

---

1. In this essay, I draw upon Brockmann's writings to support many of my statements. However, my theses are based on a wide reading of material on all the German colonies. A fully referenced analysis of the issues presented here is available in my dissertation, "Colonizers and Citizens: Bourgeois Women and the Woman Question in the German Colonial Movement, 1886–1914."

2. Among thought-provoking scholarship on these two areas, see Allen 1991; Kaufmann 1988; Stoehr 1983; Janssen-Jurreit 1979; Prokop 1979; and for the Weimar and Nazi periods, Koonz 1987.

3. Gründer 1991 has an excellent bibliography on German colonialism. There is a growing body of literature on German women, gender, and colonialism: see Kratzer 1993; Warmbold 1989; Chickering 1988; and Theweleit 1987. The literature on the British case is more extensive: see Chaudhuri and Strobel 1992; Strobel 1991; and the references there. For Dutch colonial and comparative analyses, see Stoler 1989a, 1989b, 1991, 1992.

onialist activism. Tensions between conservative views of women's social place and the contemporary movement for middle-class women's political and social emancipation helped shape women's colonialist activities in Germany. Women of various political persuasions defined their public involvement in colonialism by means of middle-class feminist issues: improving educated women's career opportunities, citizenship and family status, and emphasis on the benefits to society of emancipating cultured, patriotic women. Women colonialists were often, but not necessarily, more conservative than organized feminists, nor did they necessarily stand to the left of men colonialists; their activism marked out a new political space with respect to women's issues and male-dominated nationalist thought.

By analyzing women colonialists' travel writing, fiction, and journalism, we can discern ways in which men and women constructed patriotic Germanness differently. Each attached gendered qualities to true Germanness and citizenship, but not always in the same way.[4] In the four sections that follow, the issue of white German women's settlement in Southwest Africa serves to throw into relief conflicting views within bourgeois society of what it meant to be German. First, I address the question, Why were white German women thought necessary for Southwest Africa, and what role were they to play there? This was the "woman question in our colonies" to which Brockmann's 1910 title referred. In the second section, I situate the German woman settler within ideas about the qualities of Germanness, and suggest how the colonial context helped shape those ideas. In the third section, I describe how internal contradictions plagued an apparently straightforward attempt to sponsor unmarried women's emigration from Germany to Southwest Africa by the colonial administration and the German Colonial Society (Deutsche Kolonialgesellschaft, a colonialist organization with mostly male membership). Disagreements arose when bourgeois women attempted to take their place alongside men of their own class in addressing "the woman question in the colonies." In the fourth and final section, we will see how Brockmann's version of women's emancipation implicitly responded to the issues of the first three sections. Hers was a vision of highly personal, yet also impeccably patriotic, emancipation for a few unmarried German women. She placed her vision in a colonial landscape of complete freedom, where not only modern industrial Germany's social ills but also German men were absent.

---

4. Here I use "colonialist" to refer to persons who lived and worked in Germany and actively promoted the colonies' development in the German public sphere. Some colonialists, like Brockmann, traveled to the colonies and even lived there; many never did. The term "colonialist" is meant to distinguish such organizers and activists from an overlapping group of "colonists," i.e., those Germans who settled permanently in the colonies and may or may not have been active politically.

Scholars have frequently noted Brockmann's obvious and virulent racism but have not considered it in relation to the independent role for women she evoked.[5] Powerful divisions based on racial categories were integral to her notion of bourgeois German women's independence as well as necessary to colonialists' definitions of Germanness. As Brockmann situated the ideology of national identity within the racially defined colonial setting, she reworked existing notions of the German woman citizen.

"The Woman Question in the Colonies"

In its earliest and simplest form, the "woman question in the colonies" was a matter of numbers of German women, and "woman" was synonymous with wife and mother. There were not enough German women in Southwest Africa to marry each German male settler. As early as 1896, men colonialists proclaimed the need for German women in the colonies. They referred to the "scandalous" number of German men cohabiting with African women and to the (considerably fewer) men who had married African women (Schulte-Althoff 1985, 62).[6] In 1901, for example, there were about eighteen unmarried white men for each unmarried white woman in Southwest Africa (there were one hundred such women living there) ("Die weiße Bevölkerung" 1902). Although great disparities also existed in other German colonies, Southwest Africa's "woman question" was considered the most pressing case. In contrast to the trade colonies, where no lasting settlement was anticipated, colonialists wanted Southwest Africa to absorb German emigration and become "our new Germany on African soil" (Brockmann 1910, iv).

If the transplanted German society of Southwest Africa was to be "volks-tümlich" (Brockmann 1912, v), that is, a colony truly of the (German) people, then colonial Germans had to successfully prevail "racially," politically, and economically over the other inhabitants. In the view of many colonialists, the German nation was fighting a two-front war for genuine mastery in Southwest

---

5. Among scholarship analyzing Brockmann's books, see Sadji 1985 and 1986; and Benninghoff-Lühl 1983.

6. The missionary Pater Kassiepe estimated that more than 90 percent of European men in the German colonies had conducted extramarital sexual relations with native women (Kassiepe 1912, 305). There are no exact statistics on the number of mixed marriages between Germans and colonial subjects, since a considerable number were concluded outside colonial borders and since the race and citizenship status of the spouses (generally wives)—and thus the mixed element of a given marriage—remained controversial through 1914. Clearly, however, there were very few such marriages. When mixed marriages were declared retroactively invalid in Southwest Africa in 1907, only thirty marriages were affected, from a white population of 7,110 that same year (*DKH* 1913, 1). In 1912, the next year with available statistics on the nonwhite population, there were 87,769 native, mixed and nonnative colored persons (DKH 1913, 2).

Africa: against colonized Africans and against other white colonizers. German women were useful, even necessary, for fighting on both fronts.

On one front, the presence of white German women was thought necessary to counteract marriages and sexual relations between German men and African women. Such familial relations posed a threat to political categories of rule in the colonies, constituting an important aspect of the so-called race question (*Rassenfrage*), that is, the question of which form legal and other relations between colonizers and the colonized ought to take. Children of Afro-German descent represented a "danger" that had to be eradicated by reducing their legal and social status to that of "pure" Africans (Schulte-Althoff 1985, 62). Because the children might occasionally claim or receive support from a German father, property and prosperity that were once purely "German" might be "lost" to a person of African ancestry. If German men married their African partners, the "loss" was even further reaching: those women became German citizens and technically enjoyed the rights accorded to white German women citizens (Fuchs 1909, 40). White German women, whose rights and property were likewise mediated through German husbands (Gerhard 1988), found that possibility profoundly disturbing.

The debate in Germany over mixed marriage had two outcomes that are important for the discussion here. Women colonialists reinforced their ties with the bourgeois women's movement when they pressed for the prohibition of mixed marriages on the basis of the white German women citizens' rights. Furthermore, all parties in Germany who joined the debate about the colonial sexual order consciously drew upon the notion of a racial basis of German citizenship, making a usually implicit concept explicit (Fuchs 1909, 40; Schulte-Althoff 1985, 67–68). Both men and women agreed on the "solution" of sending a larger supply of German women to Southwest Africa. Their presence, it was believed, would make German men's sexual relationships with African women "unnecessary" and would restore color as an unquestioned category of colonial rule.

On the second front of the struggle for German colonial mastery, Germans faced competition from the other colonizers of European descent in Southwest Africa. Most of these were Boer and British settlers who had emigrated from neighboring South Africa. As Brockmann described it, each Boer- or British-owned farm or business that prospered in Southwest Africa made inroads into German culture and economic life, threatening the colony's very "German" nature (Brockmann 1910, 63–64). In particular, German colonialists fretted over the influence of the Boers, whose language, customs, and poverty, it was asserted, had a degrading effect on the cultural level of the German colonizers.[7]

---

7. This in spite of the well-documented German sympathy for the Boers (for a contemporary's account of the German-Boer friendship, see Hintrager 1955, 180–86; see also, e.g., Ander-

The permanent settlement of German women and, by implication, of German families was suggested as an antidote to prolific Boer families. Although opposition to British and Boer influence obviously sought different ends than did opposition to Africans, the categories used to define the situation were the same: people of another culture (or race or nation—the terms were often used interchangeably) threatened the integrity of the productive, colonizing German.

The German wife's purported ability to preserve and strengthen the German race along with its language, customs, and prosperity meant that she was uniquely placed to keep Southwest Africa and its property German. Brockmann called on German women to advocate

> the prevention of mixed marriages, which spell the spiritual and economic ruin of the settler, the attainment of a profitable farming operation, which cannot reach full flourishing development without the cooperation of the housewife, and in general the incorporation [*Heimischwerden*] of German ways and customs, of German family life. (Brockmann 1910, 3)

However, not only wives and mothers were called for. Even before she married, the German woman could fill another proclaimed need in Southwest Africa, namely, for servants of like race who could relieve German wives from the domestic grind:

> [O]n isolated farms, it is undesirable that the housewife, who is needed everywhere, be hobbled to the nursery. . . . [That would lead to] a one-dimensional overburdening and narrow her horizons at the expense of the whole family's spiritual-intellectual [*geistige*] life. Here the dependable white female servant must assume a role. (Niessen-Deiters 1913, 61–62)

The assistance of the "white female servant," it was argued, helped protect the German domestic sphere from "racial" or "cultural" contamination (Brockmann 1910, 23). Women colonialists argued that where possible, Africans, and above all African women, ought not to work in the household. They persisted in this view even in the face of resistance from German colonists,

---

son 1939). Nevertheless, some Germans—particularly within Southwest Africa—*also* viewed the Boers as a political and cultural threat to German colonization. During the Boer War, for example, the German Colonial Society worried about future Boer expansionism at German expense in case of a Boer victory, or, in case of defeat, a wave of Boer refugee immigration into Southwest Africa (Pierard 1964, 194). After the Boer War, the colony's governor, Theodor Leutwein, registered his resentment that the second possibility had materialized before the Reichstag and stated that Boer settlers were in the majority in the colony's southern region, and that the children of German-Boer marriages grew up as Boers and were therefore "lost" to the German community ("Die Buren" 1903).

who were unwilling to renounce the services of their African servants (Brockmann 1910, 21–31 and below).

It seems that two classes of white German woman were needed to establish permanent settler families: the middle-class *Farmersfrau* and the working-class or peasant white domestic servant, who was to care for children and cook. African servants were then to carry out heavy housework and field labor, excluded from the intimate family circle. Brockmann and other women colonialist authors enthusiastically welcomed both groups of German women settlers, insisting that patriotism ought to know no class bounds. The merging of the German woman-as-farmer-and-owner with the German woman-as-waged-worker remained unproblematic for women colonialists until practical steps were taken to supply Southwest Africa with "the" German woman.

The class distinctions that were built into colonial "women's tasks" (marriage and motherhood on the one hand, paid domestic work on the other) existed in Germany, too, of course. Class lines likewise divided the organized women's movement. Sometimes in alliance with the Social Democratic working-class women's movement, more often in opposition to it, middle-class women activists fought for the social and political rights that corresponded to their class (Frevert 1989; Greven-Aschoff 1981).[8] The relationship between the "woman question" in Germany and the "woman question in the colonies" with respect to class is complex and cannot be explored fully here. It appears, however, that as middle-class women in Germany became active in the colonial movement, they reshaped men colonialists' conceptions of the "woman question in the colonies" to develop a kind of emancipating, if reactionary, vision for German women. Women authors and activists widened the scope of the "woman question in the colonies" from maternity to a cultural, social, and national mission.

The way in which women colonialists envisioned such emancipation drew upon notions of gender difference current in the bourgeois women's movement. German feminists transposed their own "domestic" realm onto the "social" realm, then claimed a special ability in fields that seemed suitable to feminine empathy, such as social work, the teaching of girls, and medical care for women. The exact nature of women's special qualities was apparently difficult to define. Summing up texts from the bourgeois women's movement, one historian has concluded:

---

8. Typical of the efforts of bourgeois women to distinguish their emancipatory struggle from that of "unpatriotic" Social Democratic women was the claim made by the procolonial journalist Leonore Niessen-Deiters: if women who were fighting for rights also demonstrated their nationalism by supporting the colonies, they could shield themselves from the common "suspicion of undermining the state [*Staatsfeindlichkeit*]" (Niessen-Deiters 1913, 295). *Staatsfeindlichkeit* was the standard accusation used against Social Democrats.

The concept of feminine culture was not defined in terms of ends that were fundamentally different from men's. It was not what was done that was decisive, but rather how something was done. The feminine principle was realized in a unique attitude toward things (Greven-Aschoff 1981, 42).

The same could be said for colonialists' efforts to define the essence of Germanness. Brockmann and other colonialist authors insisted that true Germans embodied certain qualities or attitudes, which permeated all realms of activity, however mundane. Women colonialist authors made use of both femininity and Germanness as they defined their own unique niche in strengthening *Deutschtum* (a word signifying both the quality of being German and the German community in any region of multiple nationalities). Life in Southwest Africa, away from the petty class and party enmities of Germany, permitted that essence of Germanness to be lived to the fullest.

Nationalist Identities and Southwest Africa: Pure Germanness in Pure Colonial Space

When Brockmann returned to Germany after four years in the colony, she felt "a deep longing for Southwest Africa, *for the land of purity, peace, and strength*" (Brockmann 1910, 65). In her view, even Southwest Africa's reputation as a gathering place for swindlers and other unsavory types could never taint its purity: "*The land is not at fault. It is only the people who go there who bring their sin and guilt with them*" (Brockmann 1910, 53). What difference did the setting of a "pure" Southwest Africa make to definitions of German nationalist identity?

References to the purity and freedom of Southwest Africa supported a number of colonialist claims: that economic performance was a direct measure of one's labor and virtue; that social ills and conflicts had no place in the colony; and that a strong community of purpose among true Germans occurred naturally in the colonies. The colonial German community was supposedly able to develop in clear contradistinction to others, whose "natural" differences were described as racial and moral. The pure and free colonial landscape was a perfect ideological backdrop for elaborating upon specifically "German" virtues of hard work and thoroughness.

The principle that prosperity and success evinced true Germanness worked not only as a positive colonial dream but also as an exclusive strategy that defined failure as occurring only outside the true German community. Colonialists constantly reiterated distinctions of class and race not only with respect to the colonized Africans but also with respect to German colonizers. For example, the imperial and colonial governments as well as private colonialist groups wished to prevent the formation of a colonial white proletariat. To this end, the state discriminated among potential German settlers on the basis of personal wealth: Togo, Cameroon, Samoa, and Southwest Africa required proof of a job contract or cash in escrow from Germans entering those colonies. Destitute Germans risked expulsion back to Germany (*DKH* 1913, 10–11, 18–19, 34, 39).[9] In contemporary Germany, labor and class injustices had become such highly charged issues that Europe's largest Marxist working-class movement had formed there. Yet in the faraway context of Southwest Africa, colonialists were able to argue that class discrimination among Germans was <u>necessary</u>, both to preserve Africans' "respect" for the colonizers and to ensure the colony's economic future.

Colonialists frequently used the racial expressions "verburen" and "verkaffern" to describe German farmers who failed in various ways to embody the ideal colonizer and culture bearer. The expressions may be translated as "to degenerate into a Boer" or "into an African" and are analogous to the English phrase "go native." The "degeneration" could reveal itself through social choices, for example if a German neglected to socialize with other Germans or lived with an African woman. Some fell prey to economic "degeneration," for example by adopting extensive, low capital intensive cattle ranching (as carried out by Boer and, before that, African cattle holders). Such cattle operations offended colonialists' notions of a properly bounded, neatly kept, and bustling German farm. The expressions "verburen" and "verkaffern" typify colonialists' attempts to align economic characteristics with a person's color, culture, race, or nation—the categories through which colonialists defined the individual. In contrast to such "degenerate" Germans, those farmers who combined economic prosperity and cultural self-consciousness could be defined as truer or purer Germans.

Just as the colonial setting threw into relief "true" German virtues, so did it also emphasize "true" German feminine virtues in women colonialists' writings. Given the history of German women's scarcity in Southwest Africa, women authors were able to depict the impact of German women's arrival in dramatic fashion. A ubiquitous anecdote was the transformation of a bachelor farmer's messy house into a thrifty, spotless home at the hands of his newly arrived German bride (e.g., Brockmann 1910, 5–6). "Natural" differences between German men and women, such as housekeeping ability, emerged sharply in the women's writings. Women colonialist authors assigned the German woman settler a key role in the creation of colonial prosperity and success after the 1904–7 war.

---

9. On the question of a white proletariat in Southwest Africa, see Bley 1971, 76. Stoler 1989a, 1989b offers a discussion of race and class boundaries in other European colonial empires.

In characterizing German women's work as irreplaceable, the women authors created a new colonial niche for unmarried as well as married German women. "Pure" colonial space focused attention on the essential qualities of German women's work, whether it was done for a husband or for an employer. The attention to both groups of women qua women and not as potential wives or mothers lay the basis for a redefinition of the "woman question in the colonies." By placing such high value on women's work, women authors assigned cultural and national, rather than just sexual or maternal, importance to women's presence in Southwest Africa.

The praise that women colonialists lavished on women's colonial work contrasted sharply with their descriptions of African women's work. Indeed, the German woman's arrival meant the exclusion of the African woman from the household's most intimate spheres—a basic part of putting the bachelor's house "in order." Both German women and men attempted to exclude African women from familial and near-familial positions. The psychological process behind those attempts was a far knottier problem for German women than for German men, however. German women settlers confronted colonial house-holds in which African women were already performing German women's usual productive and reproductive tasks, as servants, concubines, and (rarely) wives. Women colonists had constantly to justify their presence in the colony, to a much greater degree than German men. The women justified themselves in part by opposing their own domestic and feminine qualities to those of "the native woman." This took extreme and caricatured forms: where German women were presented as cultured, thorough at work, and as raising healthy families, African women were depicted as barbaric, careless, and the mothers of flawed children. Although the African women whom Brockmann encountered came from a wide variety of class and cultural backgrounds, she represented them all as uniformly undependable and ineducable (Brockmann 1910, 25–27, 1912, 102–14).

Once women colonialists had "proven" that African women could not be "real" housewives or mothers for German men or "dependable" servants for German households, they had created a niche for both classes of German woman settler: the unmarried servant and the married *Farmersfrau*. By claim-ing that African women lacked true feelings and culture, German women lent their own work, paid or unpaid, new cultural and patriotic importance.

The unmarried German woman nevertheless occupied an odd place in the colonial hierarchy of property and authority, especially given the contempo-rary bourgeois ideology, which defined women in terms of their relations to men. Yet the category of race and an unimpeachable nationalist mission smoothed over the awkwardness. In the following example, the reader can see what a difference the colonial setting made in defining German women's paid work:

the position [of the women servants] is more privileged in every way over the one they held in Germany; due to having the same race, the employer holds the German girl above the native servants. Indeed, tact and skill is necessary to place oneself at the proper level, one that signifies on the one hand dependence on the family and on the other superiority over the colored subordinates. (Brockmann 1910, 30)

Difference from, and superiority to, the other working women in the household, defined in terms of race, elevated the German woman servant's status. At the same time, "having the same [German] race" helped resolve the white female servant's ambivalent position into one of friendship and a kind of equality with her middle-class employers:

If a maid or housekeeper comes to a farm . . . it is her responsibility to make herself indispensable to the young farmer's wife and to move from the status of paid worker to that of a friend and companion. (Brockmann 1910, 30–31)

In the colonial setting, the idea of a common German race (or culture or nation) served to blur class boundaries between women workers and women employers—both were colonizers. By presenting the running of a household and child care as matters of an exclusive German women's culture, Brockmann merged paid with unpaid "women's work." In a quite subtle way, such writings by German women moved German men off the nationalist center stage; German women performed invaluable cultural tasks, regardless of the position they held with respect to German men.

Women colonialists combined their claims to racial and class superiority with current notions of women's especially close bonds to culture. It was German women who were necessary for the building of truly German families, "German" not only in color but also in the supposed marks of thrift and energy (Brockmann 1910, 3–6). In so describing the irreplaceable cultural role of women, colonialist authors such as Brockmann cast women as the saviors of *Deutschtum*. In their writings, German women became self-sufficient cultural actors, uniquely able to embody and to perpetuate Germanness.

The set of feminine national virtues outlined above had both repressive and emancipatory aspects. In Brockmann's hands, feminine cultural self-sufficiency was the key to complete personal emancipation. She did not reach that conclusion by a direct path, however. The ideal of a patriotic woman colonist bore elements of bourgeois ideology, which simultaneously attracted and constricted women colonialists: for example, the premises of economic independence and sexual virtue. If a woman was not financially secure, she was sexually vulnerable. The German woman's sexual virtue constituted her racial and therefore national value in a quite gender-specific manner. A German woman who "betrayed" her race was useless to her nation, to the colony, and to German men. The colonial woman was held to a standard of "race purity" (Niessen-Deiters 1912, 1) which, as everyone knew, German men had failed to meet from the beginning.

Lurking beneath the discussion's surface was the knowledge—troubling for German women—that it was actually German men's sexual behavior that constituted the "woman question in the colonies." Women colonialist authors, including Brockmann, negotiated the emancipatory and repressive aspects of the woman colonist's situation by evading the issue of German men and their sexual behavior. Instead, they focused on the economic and patriotic (not just sexual) importance of German women in Southwest Africa and placed women at the center of the "woman question in the colonies." Women colonialist authors used the colonial context to reformulate women's place in German society at one remove from reality, just as colonialist authors in general constructed fables of a truer Germanness against the backdrop of putative colonial freedom. The figure of the productive nationalist woman colonist was capable of negotiating the contradictions between the bourgeois woman and work, marriage and independence, private family life and public patriotic citizen. Let us see how the conceptions outlined so far were first put into practice.

A Practical "Solution" to the "Woman Question in the Colonies"

Alone among the German colonies, Southwest Africa was the object of a program to send single German women to marry German settlers. The German Colonial Society and Southwest Africa's governor, Theodor Leutwein, organized the program in 1897 and sent the first sixteen sponsored women in 1898 (VR 1899, 1471, 1473). The women received free passage to Southwest Africa, where they took arranged jobs as domestic servants. The program's organizers assumed that soon thereafter the women would find husbands and marry.

When the German Colonial Society requested a state subsidy for the program in 1899, the undertaking came under the scrutiny of the Reichstag. In plenary debate, objections focused on the job contracts' draconian provisions: a woman had to perform whatever tasks her employer assigned, whether or not normally considered servant's duties, and if she were able to convince the colonial governor to terminate her position with her employer, she was then obliged to accept whatever work the governor saw fit to offer her (RKA 1907–30, 6). Reichstag members were especially disturbed that no arrangements had been made for a paid return trip to Germany if she decided not to stay. As the leading Social Democrat August Bebel exclaimed, even contracts for "coolie" labor required money to be placed in escrow for the worker's return trip (VR 1899, 1475). The Reichstag refused the subsidy.

The Colonial Society, which had drafted the contract, saw things quite differently. The premises underlying their effort to solve the "woman question in the colonies" emerged clearly in the Reichstag debate. One defender of the scheme, Count Hermann von Arnim-Muskau, retorted: "The guarantee of a return trip was left out of the contract on purpose, in order to avoid abetting the fickleness [*Wankelmuth*] of the women" (VR 1899, 1473). Another, Prince Franz von Arenberg, protested against taking the contract too seriously:

> Gentlemen, the point of the whole matter is not to send servant girls to Southwest Africa, but rather to found German families there, and this whole contractual relationship is just a transitional stage. (VR 1899, 1476)[10]

Clearly, the women were to be kept under pressure to marry. The Colonial Society and Governor Leutwein were not interested in improving the conditions of women's employment.

In fact, they had firmly opposed the suggestions of certain educated, middle-class Berlin women who had also shown interest in solving the "woman question in the colonies" (VR 1899, 1471, 1473). These women, including Minna Cauer, Anna Pappritz, and others from the women's organization Frauenwohl, had drafted an alternative contract.[11] Their draft provided more protection of the sponsored servants' rights and requested that job opportunities other than domestic service be developed. Female teachers, nurses, and agriculturalists (*Landwirtinnen*), they claimed, were surely also needed for the colony's growth (RKA 1907–30, 5). The mutual interest of members of the German women's movement and the male-dominated colonialist movement in sending women to Southwest Africa led to the first confrontation between men and women over how to put into practice the "solution" of sending German women to Southwest Africa.

The Colonial Society flatly dismissed the suggestions and continued to

---

10. Arnim-Muskau (1839–1919), Conservative Party delegate, and Arenberg (1849–1907), Catholic Center Party delegate, were prominent politicians and had both served as vice president of the German Colonial Society. Arenberg was the key mediating figure between the government and the Catholic Center Party regarding colonial matters.

11. Cauer (1841–1922), a leading radical-bourgeois feminist in Berlin, was known inter alia for her work for women's suffrage and improvement of women's employment. Cauer founded the organization Frauenwohl in 1888 in order to pursue a wide variety of feminist goals. Although Cauer is one of the most studied German feminists, I know of no published scholarship that mentions her interest in colonial matters. Pappritz (1861–1939) was a Berlin feminist active in campaigns against the state regulation of prostitution and other public-morality issues.

send women using the exploitative contract. Yet the women had wedged their foot in the door. The issues they raised concerning better working conditions and career possibilities for educated (*gebildete*) women reappeared a few years later and laid the basis for the ideal of the independent woman farmer.

Within a decade much had changed in the German colonial empire. Scandals and costly wars, above all the Southwest African war of 1904–7, had exposed and shaken German colonialism. These events caused a deadlock in the Reichstag over colonial budget appropriations, whereupon Chancellor Bernhard von Bülow dissolved parliament and called for new elections in 1907. In the election campaign, the colonial issue symbolized "patriotic" opposition to the Social Democrats and their allies. Although the "patriotic" parties and the colonialists emerged victorious, popular support for colonialism now depended on conspicuous reform efforts. The domestication of Germany's settlement colony was in order, and in this context the "woman question" arose again. Both men and women in the colonialist movement believed that the presence of women in Southwest Africa would promote the peaceful long-term development that was to follow the era of adventure and war. Between 1907 and 1914, as in 1898, German men's "need" for German wives justified women's participation in colonial activities (insofar as the women were not missionaries or nurses). Likewise, middle-class women again questioned a colonial role that limited them to marriage and motherhood.

In 1906 and 1907, a group of aristocratic army officers' wives based in Berlin convinced the German Colonial Society that women ought to be in charge of choosing suitable wives for colonists. The women referred to prevailing notions of difference to insist that women were best suited to choose and guide other women. The result was the Women's Association of the German Colonial Society (Frauenbund der Deutschen Kolonialgesellschaft), which officially took over the task of organizing single German women's immigration to Southwest Africa (Pierard 1971; Chickering 1988, 175–77). The goal of the Frauenbund was "above all to preserve and strengthen the spiritual and intellectual [*geistigen*] bonds between the women in the motherland and the women struggling for their culture [*Kulturkämpferinnen*] in the colonies" (Brockmann 1910, 29). The new organization worked to mobilize and educate women in Germany about the colonies as well as to assist German women settlers. The Frauenbund attracted a variety of women and men: people who had lived in the colonies and were interested in all aspects of colonial policy; the women from Frauenwohl mentioned above, who advocated suffrage and an increased public role for women; conservative middle-class women who opposed women's political emancipation but saw here a feminine patriotic duty; and eugenicists, who were attracted by an organization that counteracted "race mixing" with its own selection procedures.

The issue of which German women ought to be sent to the colonies was central to the whole undertaking of the Frauenbund. In trying to define the right combination of gender and class attributes, women colonialists reflected their own social dilemmas and class origins. The applicants tended to be working-class, petite-bourgeoise, and peasant women. Yet the Frauenbund wished to sponsor women in its own bourgeois image, and collided with the existing selection practices of the German Colonial Society. The Colonial Society thought that country women and seasoned servants were best suited to the physical trials of colonial life. It had gladly sponsored peasant and working-class women, who in fact were willing to emigrate, marry promptly, and start families. But for the middle-class women colonialists in the Frauenbund, being white and eager to emigrate and marry was not sufficient to ensure that a woman was fit to represent the German nation and save the colonies. Looking back at the German Colonial Society's program, Brockmann reproached the men for their superficial selection criteria:

Due to the need for rapid settlement and the scarcity of candidates, young women were sent over who turned out not to be equal to the challenges of their new surroundings. Since they had come with the best recommendations, no one had any cause to doubt that characters that had proven themselves in Germany could not also stand a trial by fire across the ocean in Africa. Nor could the German Colonial Society read the human heart. (Brockmann 1910, 21–22)

The problem, it seems, was that these women enjoyed too much upward mobility and became selfish. Brockmann continued:

The awareness of being joyfully awaited in the colony, where at that time [German] women were quite rare, inflated their sense of self-worth from the beginning. . . . simple country girls tried to play the lady; in the shortest time many became soldiers' brides and in no way served their original purpose, namely, to be skillful and industrious domestic help. Some married very quickly and played the parvenu's spouse in a pushy manner, others let themselves go and worked as barmaids and in doubtful trades. (Brockmann 1910, 22)

According to Brockmann, the Colonial Society had created a class of nouveau riche women in the colony who did not know their place. She and the women colonialists of the Frauenbund asserted that the "good woman material" (Brockmann 1910, 30) that Southwest Africa so badly needed was better found among women of some education who already led a middle-class life. In order to attract such women, job opportunities such as teaching, secretarial work, nursing, and certified housekeeping ought to be promoted in Southwest Africa. Even if women with certified training cost more to hire, they would repay their employers with higher-quality work and provide cultured company for wives on lonely farms. Brockmann conceded that the qualities of an educated [gebildet] woman did not always find ready takers: "With a servant girl, one pays for physical work, as opposed to talent or intellectual and social skills; the latter are more difficult to turn into money" (Brockmann 1910, 32).

Of course, no man colonialist would have objected to sponsoring well-trained, conscientious German women as future wives for German settlers. After all, colonialists did not want "low-class" Germans in the colony, since that might call into question European cultural superiority. Yet to be the wife of a simple German settler seemed respectable enough to the men; they were blind to any finer class distinctions among German women. In the men's view, the "woman question in the colonies" was confined to the need for German women to marry in Southwest Africa and have children. The women colonialists' emphasis on the need to send educated women frustrated the men, and this issue as well as other rivalries strained the relationship between the two organizations (Chickering 1988, 181–83).

In part, the disagreements between the men and women derived from divergent conceptions of the colonial woman: as bourgeois individual and as bourgeois wife and mother. In the colonial setting, the individual was the free and independent settler, and he—or she, as Brockmann would have it—was one of the most powerfully attractive images of colonialism in Germany and other European states. By contrast, a wife and mother derived her status merely from assisting her husband. The women of the Frauenbund envisaged a colonial woman with her own skills and education.

One reason for the men's refusal to consider the Frauenbund's suggestion may well have been the fact that in any dispute between colonialist women and men, an uncomfortable truth remained: German women were officially desirable in Southwest Africa not for their talents or intellect but for their ability to supply the German settlers with white German babies. The patriotic and ambitious plans of a Brockmann or Cauer to carve out a heroic national role for women in Southwest Africa always threatened to collapse into men's ungracious version of the situation. The humor of the following passage from the (all-male) Reichstag debates was typical (Conservative Party delegate Georg Oertel speaking):

> [The German woman] is the best export item we could possibly have (Laughter.)—not that I would want to do without the women here (Laughter.) but rather because I heartily welcome the men out there to share the pleasure. (Laughter.) I believe that it is a duty of the Reichstag to thank the

private men's and women's organizations in Germany that have done so much for this great task. (Hear, hear!) (VR 1913, 4358)

Women colonialists were vulnerable to such humor precisely because they did share the men's assumptions. They, too, believed that sexual relationships between African women and German men constituted a problem, and that the opportunity to marry German women would satisfy the male settlers' sexual desires. When women colonialists accepted such a supply-and-demand view of sexual unions in Southwest Africa, they in fact conceded that their bodies were their key contribution to the colony and that they were interchangeable with, and therefore in some sense equivalent to, African women. It was difficult to reconcile the acceptance of the "woman question in the colonies" as a matter of supplying German women to male settlers with the ideal of the educated woman patriot that Brockmann and other women in the Frauenbund put forth. One woman at a public rally in Germany put her finger on the difficulty when she asked why a German woman of the finest patriotic and moral type should be sent off into the desert to be a "broodmare" (Niessen-Deiters 1913, 24–25).

Nevertheless, putting middle-class women in charge of the emigration program did result in a shift in emphasis from women settlers' sexual function to their qualities as citizens, patriots, and cultural and economic actors in their own right. The actual realization of the independent type of colonial woman was fraught with difficulties, above all the lack of appropriately middle-class "women's work" in Southwest Africa. Typical of the obstacles that faced the Frauenbund was German settlers' hasty withdrawal of employment offers after they had heard that the sponsored women held certification and were therefore entitled to higher wages (RKA 1907–30, 27). The colonial government rebuked the Frauenbund for driving up labor prices in the colony. Another example of the Frauenbund's difficulties was settlers' lack of interest in a kindergarten cosponsored by the Frauenbund and the Protestant church. It languished for years because German settlers preferred to leave their children with their African servants, "refusing to recognize the danger of constant contact between the children and natives" ("Mitteilungen" 1911–12). The ideals of the middle-class women in Germany did not necessarily correspond to the realities of settler life in Southwest Africa.

Given the complications of fitting German women into the colonizing enterprise, certain aspects of Brockmann's writings may be read as roundabout answers to those complications. We have already seen how she blurred class boundaries between the unmarried working woman and the married, landowning *Farmersfrau*. The next and final section shows how Brockmann took the Frauenbund's idea about sending women able to support themselves to its logical conclusion. In so doing, Brockmann implicitly contradicted the original justification for sending women: to supply German men with brides and mothers.

Brockmann and the Ideal of the Independent Woman Farmer

The image of the self-sufficient farm (*Scholle*) held a certain mystique in colonialist politics and ideology. The farm was thought to be a bastion of native German virtue, free of modern industrial society's conflicts, and symbolized nationalist German cultural renewal (Smith 1986, 21–29). One material result of the fascination with the farm was the Colonial Office's practice of subsidizing settlers who wanted to establish small farms of their own. Brockmann drew upon the farm's ideological mystique as she interpreted its meaning from the vantage point of the nationalist German woman: as a site that united economic production with family reproduction. Conventional boundaries between women's domestic reproduction and men's public production were thereby set aside; classical bourgeois-liberal values of freedom, prosperity, and patriotism could enter the domestic and reproductive spheres, where German women were ideologically located. Brockmann's interpretation of the farm as the site of these possibilities for nationalist women emerged particularly clearly when she recounted the experiences of two women friends. These two women were living out the colonial dream of becoming independent farmers. As Brockmann told of their hopes and successes, she blurred the boundary between women doing "men's" work as their husband's partners—the more usual presentation of the *Farmersfrau* in colonialist women's literature—and women who did "men's" work and thereby rendered German men superfluous to their lives as colonists in Southwest Africa.

One way Brockmann moved men off the colonial center stage was by insisting that the rigors of colonial life meant that women could and indeed had to be able to do all the farming tasks a man did. By virtue of necessity, then, the traditional spheres of men's and women's activity became parallel rather than separate. For example, Brockmann had this praise for a farmer's wife:

> I recall a *Farmersfrau* of whom it was said that she rode with the others into the fields like a man to oversee her workers. We need such women for Southwest. (Brockmann 1910, 8)

The story of a female farm worker who befriended Brockmann served as Brockmann's fable of success in Southwest Africa. Brockmann assured her audience that this woman "certainly performed as well as her [male] predecessor" at her job (Brockmann 1910, 37). Brockmann observed her at work, firing clay tiles with her own hands, and nailing corrugated tin sheets securely onto the roof of a stable she had built herself. . . . in time she developed considerable facility in building corrals, driving cattle, and building dams. (Brockmann 1910, 36–37)

Given such female self-sufficiency, it was a short step to a farming career without a man. Brockmann declared:

We live in the age of progress. A few years ago it was a great and astonishing enterprise if a girl decided to follow the man of her choice to Africa. . . . today it hardly seems daring when a lady of mature character and some experience undertakes on her own initiative to create a position for herself there. (Brockmann 1910, 36)

Brockmann's own anecdotes reveal, however, that women doing farm work did astonish many people. Brockmann herself was astonished when she first discovered that her friend was a farm worker:

I made her acquaintance at a ball given by the governor and remembered her as a tender, shy creature in a white cotton dress. How surprised I was when someone later told me he had come across her wearing short riding pants and a floppy hat, smoking tobacco out of a short pipe while driving her cattle from one station to the next. (Brockmann 1910, 38)[12]

The friend confided to Brockmann that her choice of farm work did not find ready acceptance. She said:

"I know that my relatives think I am an oddball. If I wrote home for ribbons, clothes, and expensive soaps, they would send me all of it immediately. But if I ask for shovels, scales, and mechanical implements, I meet resistance and prejudice." (Brockmann 1910, 40)

The goal of the woman's "step toward independence" was to own her own self-sufficient farm (Brockmann 1910, 37). She even insisted that the state help her to achieve her dream, applying to the Colonial Office for a farm subsidy. Brockmann described the woman's reasoning:

every man who applied was sold land; often he was from the city and had no experience with agriculture. Why shouldn't the government give a

---

12. Sibylle Benninghoff-Lühl's interpretation of this passage misses the mark: "The price for [women farmers'] self-confident behavior was the loss of classically feminine attractiveness" (Benninghoff-Lühl 1983, 278 n. 93).

woman a farm or a cottage if she could prove that she knew rationalized agricultural methods? (Brockmann 1910, 37)

She apparently hoped that in Southwest Africa, her education and ability would prevail over prejudice against single women as farmers. When Brockmann asked her why she came to Africa, she answered: "I just don't fit into the narrow ways of Germany, where people treat every deviation from the norm like a crazy idea. My motto is to struggle and work in Southwest, the land of freedom" (Brockmann 1910, 40).

This woman fully expected to make a place for herself as a farmer without a husband and shared her plans with another woman who had the same ambitions. Brockmann thought their dream was certain to be realized:

> After some time she met her better self, her other half. It was a lady, roughly the same age as she, who had come to Africa with the same plan. . . . The two were united in their favorite idea: the wish to own a farm. I believe the time is not far off when the two, peacefully united, will stand on their very own jointly owned land. (Brockmann 1910, 40)

The two women were in fact well-educated, middle-class women. They used their middle-class status and skills to pursue farm life. Brockmann and the two friends held well-paid white-collar jobs in Windhuk, the capital of Southwest Africa. The two friends had only taken those positions in order to attain the goal of owning a farm; they preferred to work as hired farm hands, but such work was a luxury they could not always afford. Positions for educated women were very rare in the colonies, yet these women dreamed constantly of leaving their jobs to live on their own farm and produce for all their own needs.

Brockmann's independent-minded friend had been a teacher back in Germany (Brockmann 1910, 36). When she first arrived in Southwest Africa, she worked as an agricultural overseer in order to gain experience, and she bought livestock and farm equipment on the side. However, she was unable to save money for her farm quickly enough that way, so she reverted to teaching. After she had purchased some acreage with a house and added a barn herself, she still needed a "steady income" (Brockmann 1910, 38) to run it, so she took a position with the colonial government. After each day at the office, her African driver took her back to her farm in her American car. Her companion had also taken a paid agricultural position upon arriving in Southwest Africa and started buying cattle. She had likewise switched to the higher salary of an office job and augmented her income by managing the household of a high-level civil servant. All the while, she boarded her growing livestock herd at various farms.

Brockmann appears to have been the wealthiest of the three. She worked at the governor's office in Windhuk and lived on a "homestead" outside of town. She was proud of her little farm's capability to produce for almost all its own needs. She paid more than 1,200 marks for a year's rent alone—as much as a housekeeper's or nanny's entire annual salary (Brockmann 1910, 31, 42, 44). In her most treasured moments in Africa, she and her friends watched the sun set from the veranda and rode horses across the moonlit plains (Brockmann 1912, 45–46). Through such scenes, Brockmann suggested that she appreciated her wealth above all for the freedom that it brought her. One anecdote demonstrates especially strongly her refusal of conventional feminine dependency in marriage: she found diamonds in the sand and proudly cast them down with the comment: "[Diamonds] leave me cold . . . but my poor foolish sisters . . . hurl themselves into misery and unhappiness—all for [diamonds'] sake!" (Brockmann 1912, 178).[13]

The dream of farm ownership in Southwest Africa became a reality for only very few women. The first real-life independent women farmers were widows whose husbands had been killed in the colonial war of 1904–7. Brockmann cited their achievements as proof that women were capable of running farms alone (Brockmann 1912, 66–67, 88). In fact, widows remained virtually the only unmarried women farmers before World War I.[14] While colonial widows did make their own choice to carry on farming after their husbands' deaths, such a choice must be seen at least in part as a matter of following in their husbands' footsteps rather than as the creation of a new way of life in Brockmann's sense.

The independent woman farmer, then, was certainly unusual. In fact, most women in Germany who joined the Frauenbund and read Brockmann's books apparently did not even consider going to Africa themselves, much less becoming women farmers. Theirs was a vicarious experience of empire. They found not only fantasies of independence and power in Brockmann's passionate descriptions but also confirmation of ideas that were quite conventional. Patriotism legitimized a woman's independent colonial undertaking while financial security protected her sexual and moral integrity.

Hierarchy in terms of race was central to Brockmann's and other versions of the independent woman farmer. One of the German woman settler's tasks was to "raise" (*erziehen*) Africans to accept orders from Europeans. Whether as *Farmersfrau* or as a female agricultural intern (*weiblichen Farmvolontärin*), German women supervised African women and men at work; Brockmann listed "ability and experience in the handling of their natives" among the

---

13. Diamonds were discovered in Southwest Africa in 1908, leading to a prospectors' rush. The controversy over how to distribute the sudden wealth led to the downfall two years later of Colonial Secretary Bernhard Dernburg, the initiator of colonial reform (Schiefel 1974, 101–8).

14. Their number was few; in one 1913 colonial directory, only thirteen single women listed themselves as *Farmbesitzerin* or *Farmerin*. Twelve of the thirteen were widows (Schulze 1913, 65–209).

qualifications of her two friends (Brockmann 1912, 87). Brockmann's repeated harsh remarks concerning Africans' "need" to be controlled helped to situate German women in the colony's top social position: successful German farm owner and employer with wide powers over her African employees.

Brockmann focused on control over African women and men workers to the exclusion of another issue: German men's marital and sexual relations with African women. The subject raised an issue difficult for colonialist women to discuss directly: German men's and women's asymmetrical power relations in sexuality, marriage, and family. Brockmann implicitly raised questions concerning women's emancipation, then offered an imaginary solution to women in Germany—to leave Germany and its internecine political battles, and to reenact in the colonies the hierarchical power relations between German men and women in terms of the "natural" divisions of "race."

Southwest Africa and the other German colonies were, in fact, no less problematic settings for social relations between the sexes than Germany itself. Yet the political and professedly unpolitical organizations that advocated German colonization afforded to both conservative and progressive men and women an ideological space onto which social conflicts and reforms could be displaced and, if only temporarily, common interests found. Once a unified national purpose and profound "racial" differences between the "civilizing" Germans and Africans "needing" to be "civilized" had been posited, vexing domestic issues, such as the "woman question," appeared in a new, "constructive" light. Brockmann claimed that German feminists' energies spent on agitation for political rights and career opportunities ought to be redirected toward women's work supporting the colonies. Without that "higher" purpose, such struggles were merely "petty party bickering that some women push into, trying to force their way into illegitimate influence" (Brockmann 1910, 63–66; 1912, 94). There was fulfilling and important work to be done, she insisted, for women in both Germany and in the colonies.

The unusual aspirations of Brockmann and her two friends led them not only to support colonialism from Germany but also to experiment with settler life and indicate that they made a conscious break from social convention. Apparently speaking from experience, Brockmann noted the pain and loneliness that accompanied such a break, but she insisted that the unconventional woman colonist's personal isolation was outweighed by "the love for her fatherland, which never disappoints" (Brockmann 1912, 93–94).

To be a fighter for Germany's greatness—is there anything more brilliant [*Lichtvolleres*] than this consolation? And once she has prevailed, a new life full of beauty, work, and gratitude will lie before her. She is the victor! (Brockmann 1912, 94)

Brockmann indicated a path of public and personal fulfillment via colonialist activism and settlement for German middle-class women that did not necessarily rest on the mediation of a husband. In that respect, she went well beyond other activists in the women's movement, who often defended the centrality of marriage and family. Moreover, although Brockmann, like other men and women colonialists, described at length the feminine qualities of the bourgeois wife and mother as defining women's contributions to colonial life, her most detailed accounts of settler women portray them as bourgeois individuals, that is, masculine. Her two friends aspired to ownership, authority over African laborers, and personal autonomy.

The national identities of Brockmann and her friends were formed at the edges of powerful ideologies of gender and family roles, colonialism, and that nationalism—more usually encountered in studies of the *Kaiserreich*—which was elaborated and lived out by men. In the colonies, where one's race proved one's membership in the nation, Brockman saw the possibility of reconciling the tensions arising from the position of the independent-minded colonialist women. In the colonies, at the cost of other people's political and personal autonomy, a German woman could serve herself and her nation.

References

Allen, Ann Taylor. 1991. *Feminism and Motherhood in Germany, 1800–1914.* New Brunswick, N.J.: Rutgers University Press.

Anderson, Pauline R. 1939. *The Background of Anti-English Feeling in Germany, 1890–1902.* Washington, D.C.: American University Press.

Benninghoff-Lühl, Sibylle. 1983. *Deutsche Kolonialromane 1884–1914 in ihrem Entstehungs- und Wirkungszusammenhang.* Bremen: Übersee-Museum.

Bley, Helmut. 1971. *South-West Africa under German Rule, 1894–1914.* Evanston: Northwestern University Press.

Brockmann, Clara. 1910. *Die deutsche Frau in Südwestafrika: Ein Beitrag zur Frauenfrage in unseren Kolonien.* Berlin: E. S. Mittler und Sohn.

———. 1912. *Briefe eines deutschen Mädchens aus Südwest.* Berlin: E. S. Mittler und Sohn.

"Die Buren und Südwestafrika," 1903. *Koloniale Zeitschrift* 4, no. 16: 307.

Chaudhuri, Nupur, and Margaret Strobel, eds. 1992. *Western Women and Imperialism: Complicity and Resistance.* Bloomington: Indiana University Press.

Chickering, Roger. 1988. "'Casting Their Gaze More Broadly': Women's Patriotic Activism in Imperial Germany." *Past and Present* 118 (February): 156–85.

DKH (*Deutsches Kolonial-Handbuch*). 1913. Berlin: Hermann Paetel.

Frevert, Ute. 1989. *Women in German History: From Bourgeois Emancipation to Sexual Liberation.* Oxford: Berg.

Fuchs, V. 1909. "Zur Frage der Mischehe zwischen Reichsangehörigen und Eingeborenen in Deutsch-Südwestafrika." *Deutsche Kolonialzeitung* 26, no. 3 (16 January): 40.

Gerhard, Ute. 1988. "Die Rechtsstellung der Frau in der bürgerlichen Gesellschaft des 19. Jahrhunderts." In *Bürgertum im 19. Jahrhundert: Deutschland im europäischen Vergleich,* ed. Jürgen Kocka, 1:439–68. Munich: Deutscher Taschenbuch Verlag.

Greven-Aschoff, Barbara. 1981. *Die bürgerliche Frauenbewegung in Deutschland, 1894–1933.* Göttingen: Vandenhoeck und Ruprecht.

Gründer, Horst. 1991. *Geschichte der deutschen Kolonien.* 2d ed. Paderborn: Schöningh.

Hintrager, Oskar. 1955. *Südwestafrika in der deutschen Zeit.* Munich: R. Oldenbourg.

Janssen-Jurreit, Marielouise. 1979. "Nationalbiologie, Sexualreform und Geburtenrückgang—über die Zusammenhänge von Bevölkerungspolitik und Frauenbewegung um die Jahrhundertwende." In *Die Überwindung der Sprachlosigkeit: Texte aus der neuen Frauenbewegung,* ed. Gabriele Dietze, 139–75. Darmstadt and Neuwied: Luchterhand.

Kassiepe, Pater. 1912. "Die Stellung der katholischen Missionen zur Rassenmischehe." In *Zeitschrift für Missionswissenschaft* 2:293–306.

Kaufmann, Doris. 1988. *Frauen zwischen Aufbruch und Reaktion: Protestantische Frauenbewegung in der ersten Hälfte des 20. Jahrhunderts.* Munich: Piper.

Koonz, Claudia. 1987. *Mothers in the Fatherland: Women, the Family and Nazi Politics.* New York: St. Martin's.

Kratzer, Barbara. 1993. "Ambivalente Stimmen aus einer Kolonie: Deutsche Frauen in Südwestafrika (1893–1914): Ein Vergleich mit amerikanischen Frauen der westlichen Frontier und des Antebellumsüdens." Ph.D. diss., University of Oregon.

———. 1911–12. "Mitteilungen." *Kolonie und Heimat* 5, no. 24: 8.

Niessen-Deiters, Leonore. 1912. "Rassenreinheit! Eine deutsche Frau über die Mischehen in den Kolonien." *Kolonie und Heimat* (Nachrichtenbeilage) 5, no. 36: 1.

———. 1913. *Die deutsche Frau in den Schutzgebieten und im Auslande.* Berlin: Egon Fleischel.

Pierard, Richard Victor. 1964. "The German Colonial Society, 1882–1914." Ph.D. diss., Iowa State University.

———. 1971. "The Transportation of White Women to German Southwest Africa, 1898–1914." *Race* 12, no. 3: 317–22.

Prokop, Ulrike. 1979. "Die Sehnsucht nach Volkseinheit: Zum Konservatismus der bürgerlichen Frauenbewegung." In *Die Überwindung der Sprachlosigkeit: Texte aus der neuen Frauenbewegung,* ed. Gabriele Dietze, 176–202. Darmstadt and Neuwied: Luchterhand.

RKA (Reichs-Kolonialamt Akten). 1907–30. Betreffend den Frauenbund der Deutschen Kolonialgesellschaft. No. 6693. January 1907-August 1930. Bundesarchiv, Abteilung Potsdam, Germany.

Sadji, Amadou Booker. 1985. *Das Bild des Negro-Afrikaners in der deutschen Kolonialliteratur: Ein Beitrag zur literarischen Imagologie Schwarzafrikas.* Berlin: Reimer.

————. 1986. "African Nature and German Culture: Colonial Women Writers on Africa." In *Blacks and German Culture,* ed. Reinhold Grimm and Jost Hermand, 22–34. Madison: University of Wisconsin Press.

Schiefel, Werner. 1974. *Bernhard Dernburg, 1865–1937: Kolonialpolitiker und Bankier im wilhelminischen Deutschland.* Zurich: Atlantis.

Schulte-Althoff, Franz-Josef. 1985. "Rassenmischung im kolonialen System: Zur deutschen Kolonialpolitik im letzten Jahrzehnt vor dem Ersten Weltkrieg." *Historisches Jahrbuch* 105: 52–94.

Schulze, A., ed. 1913. *Deutsch-Südwestafrikanisches Adreßbuch.* Swakopmund: Schulze.

Smith, Woodruff. 1986. *The Ideological Origins of Nazi Imperialism.* New York: Oxford University Press.

Stoehr, Irene. 1983. "'Organisierte Mütterlichkeit.' Zur Politik der deutschen Frauenbewegung um 1900." In *Frauen suchen ihre Geschichte,* ed. Karin Hausen, 221–49. Munich: Beck.

Stoler, Ann. 1989a. "Rethinking Colonial Categories." *Comparative Studies in Society and History* 13, no. 1: 134–61.

————. 1989b. "Making Empire Respectable: The Politics of Race and Sexual Morality in Twentieth-Century Colonial Cultures." *American Ethnologist* 16, no. 4: 634–60.

————. 1991. "Carnal Knowledge and Imperial Power: Gender, Race and Morality in Colonial Asia." In *Gender at the Crossroads: Feminist Anthropology in the Postmodern Era,* ed. Micaela di Leonardo, 51–101. Berkeley: University of California Press.

————. 1992. "Sexual Affronts and Racial Frontiers: European Identities and the Cultural Politics of Exclusion in Colonial Southeast Asia." *Comparative Studies in Society and History* 34, no. 3: 514–51.

Strobel, Margaret. 1991. *European Women and the Second British Empire.* Bloomington: Indiana University Press.

Theweleit, Klaus. 1987. *Male Fantasies.* Vol. 1, *Women, Floods, Bodies, History.* Minneapolis: University of Minnesota Press.

VR (Verhandlungen des Deutschen Reichstages). 1899. 10th legislative period, 1st session, 54th assembly. Vol. 166. 11 March.

————. 1913. 13th legislative period, 1st session, 128th assembly. Vol. 288. 7 March.

Warmbold, Joachim. 1989. *Germania in Africa: Germany's Colonial Literature.* New York: Peter Lang.

————. 1902. "Die weiße Bevölkerung in Deutsch-Südwestafrika." *Deutsches Kolonialblatt* 13, no. 6 (15 March): 143.

Reconsidering Habermas, Gender, and the Public Sphere: The Case of Wilhelmine Germany

Belinda Davis

What purpose does Jürgen Habermas's notion of the "public sphere" serve for contemporary historical analysis, particularly as it pertains to questions of gender, women, and politics? The public sphere, specifically as Habermas defined it in his 1962 *Strukturwandel der Öffentlichkeit* (The Transformation of the Public Sphere), has had until recently relatively little currency in the English-speaking world, although its purchase is still enormous in Germany.[1]

Thanks to Tim Burke, Victoria de Grazia, Geoff Eley, Jennifer Jones, Alf Lüdtke, and members of the German Women's History Study Group, particularly Renate Bridenthal, for their helpful comments; and to the Rutgers Center for Historical Analysis for providing the time to complete this essay. An earlier version of this essay appeared in *Michigan Feminist Studies* 6 (1991).

1. This seminal work has only recently been translated into English (J. Habermas, *The Transformation of the Public Sphere* [Cambridge, Mass.: MIT Press, 1989]). It has been re-released in Germany with an important new introduction addressing Habermas's critics (J. Habermas, *Strukturwandel der Öffentlichkeit,* Frankfurt: Suhrkamp, 1990). The two volumes of Habermas's subsequent study on the public sphere, *The Theory of Communicative Action,* were released in English in 1984 and 1987. New work in English is now beginning to accrue: see, e.g., C. Calhoun, ed., *Habermas and the Public Sphere* (Cambridge, Mass.: MIT Press, 1992); and, more broadly, A. Honneth et al., eds., *Cultural-Political Interventions in the Unfinished Project of Enlightenment* (Cambridge, Mass.: MIT Press, 1992). While English-language feminist scholarship has long employed the notion within the schema of "separate spheres," the term "public sphere" in such instances often lacks specific theoretical import or draws its meaning from traditions outside of Habermas's critical theory. The notion has likewise long been under scrutiny in the feminist context (e.g., the classic critique by M. Rosaldo, "The Use and Abuse of Anthropology: Reflections on Feminism and Cross Cultural Understanding," *Signs* 5 [1980]: 389–417) and remains actively under debate. Examples are too numerous to name; but see the discussion in S. M. Reverby and D. O. Helly, "Introduction: Converging on History," *Gendered Domains: Rethinking Public and Private in Women's History,* ed. S. M. Reverby and D. O. Helly (Ithaca: Cornell University Press, 1992). It is only quite recently that specific reference to Habermas has entered

In the last few years, a number of American and British scholars have employed the public sphere in powerful fashion to demonstrate that the liberal bourgeois system that Habermas idealized necessarily prohibited women's participation in political public life, both in its ideological formulation and historically. But these findings may be founded on what are perhaps unnecessary restrictions that Habermas himself attaches to his well-developed elaboration of the concept. In an examination of the relations between the state and civil society in World War I Berlin, I will try to show that Habermas's notion of the public sphere, useful in investigating both how society constructs and transforms gendered identities, can help to reveal how women have historically participated politically in public life, negotiating and reworking legal and ideological constraints to create political voices for themselves. This in turn enables us to call into question some of the standard assumptions regarding "politics from above" in Wilhelmine Germany.

Habermas's Public Sphere and Its Critics

Habermas defines the public sphere broadly as the place in which the state and an autonomous civil society interact. The modern public sphere is historically located with the growth of both industrial capitalist society and urban culture, providing a space for a "commerce" or "traffic" in ideas among private citizens. Thus it acts as the locus for the development of "public opinion," a space for debate and a place of political influence. Although Habermas at times narrowly locates the political public sphere in parliamentary halls, he also notes that "a portion of the public sphere comes into being in every conversation in which private individuals assemble to form a public body."[2] The political public sphere is interdependent with a literary public sphere, which aids in the trafficking of ideas among members of the public, as well as in providing a tool for influencing state action.

The concept of the public sphere, defined as such, provides a very useful, and usefully broad, tool with which to discuss political efficacy in the modern era. We might employ it most meaningfully, I submit, as a sort of sensitizing device, particularly on four issues:

1. It leads historians to question where politics takes place, opening up the complexity of such a question.

---

this discussion. See, as a sampling, N. Fraser, "What's Critical about Critical Theory?" and I. M. Young, "Impartiality and the Civic Public," both in *Feminism as Critique: On the Politics of Gender,* ed. S. Benhabib and D. Cornell (Minneapolis: University of Minnesota Press, 1986), 31–56; 57–76; and J. Landes, *Women and the Public Sphere in the Age of the French Revolution* (Ithaca: Cornell University Press, 1988). Such work by anglophone historians, as opposed to political philosophers, is still rare. But see Mary Ryan, *Women in Public* (Baltimore: Johns Hopkins University Press, 1990).

2. J. Habermas, "The Public Sphere," *New German Critique* 3 (1974): 49.

2. It helps us to examine which public identities individuals act through politically, and how these identities are formed.
3. It challenges historical linearity in the development of politics in the modern era, as well as the notion of an ideal type of politics against which a historical case might be measured.
4. It calls into question the differentiation between a "good" and "bad" politics, based on rationality versus emotion, and the pursuit of perceived general goals versus absolute, individual needs. Used as such, the concept of the public sphere is problematized rather than naturalized, and is "fuzzy" precisely where Habermas has been rigid and totalizing (though often contradictory) in the concept's application.

These four issues encompass areas in which Habermas himself has been taken to task, by critics and acolytes alike.[3] A number of scholars have sought to revise the notion of the public sphere (along with that of "the public" and, to some degree, "the political") in a fashion potentially revealing for historians of the *Kaiserreich*. Some criticisms of the model stem from tensions among Habermas's multiple applications of the concept: as an analytical category, as an ideal type, and as a particular historical moment.[4] Habermas makes the move to equate his ideal vision of the modern public sphere with a particular historical moment in order to compare its prevailing incarnation unfavorably.[5] Other critics of *Strukturwandel* have questioned the impermeability and inelasticity of the public sphere when applied as an analytical category. Along related lines, revisionists have asserted that Habermas is unnecessarily restric-

---

3. For a more extended discussion of critiques of Habermas, see the essays in Calhoun, *Habermas and the Public Sphere*, especially Calhoun's introduction and G. Eley's very useful piece, "Nations, Publics, and Political Cultures: Placing Habermas in the Nineteenth Century"; see also Habermas's own new introduction to his work in the 1990 release of *Strukturwandel*.

4. See, e.g., P. U. Hohendahl, "Critical Theory, Public Sphere and Culture: Jürgen Habermas and His Critics," *New German Critique* 16 (1979): 89–118; G. Eley, "Nations, Publics, and Political Cultures"; and M. Hansen, *Babel and Babylon: Spectatorship in American Silent Film* (Cambridge, Mass.: Harvard University Press, 1991). Habermas acknowledges the potential contradictions in applications of the public sphere in his new introduction to *Strukturwandel*, 12.

5. Writing in West Germany in the Adenauer ascendancy, Habermas looks particularly to France, England, and Germany of the eighteenth and early nineteenth centuries, in contrast to advanced capitalist society and, by implication, particularly to twentieth-century Germany. But it is unclear how and why these historical examples, chosen as most closely approximating democratic society in Habermas's view, might be meaningfully used to judge another society's democratic potential. These examples also fail to provide a political agenda for democracy, as, by Habermas's own admission, the circumstances of the earlier period are irreproducible. From the perspective of 1968, see the alternative vision of Oskar Negt and Alexander Kluge in *Öffentlichkeit und Erfahrung: Zur Organisationsanalyse von bürgerlicher und proletarischer Öffentlichkeit* (Frankfurt: Suhrkamp, 1972), now translated as *Public Sphere and Experience* (Minneapolis: University of Minnesota Press, 1993).

tive in ascribing political voice exclusively on the basis of citizenship and franchise.[6]

This leads in turn to detractors' differences with Habermas regarding what may constitute the public sphere, and where public opinion may fruitfully develop. Students of Habermas, including Oskar Negt, Alexander Kluge, and Günther Lottes, have employed the concept of the public sphere to talk about working-class arenas of sociability that, they argued, have permitted even this historically disenfranchised class to debate issues and exercise notable political influence. Finally, commentators have noted, there are problems inherent in Habermas's idealization of a public that acts with a single voice, according to a kind of "general will."[7] In the varied sites for the formation and articulation of public opinion, such as in pubs and on the streets, scholars have found evidence of counter- and subhegemonic "publics": competing publics that vie for legitimacy with one another and make contradictory demands on the state.[8]

These are very useful correctives to Habermas's theory of the public sphere, correctives that retain the basic components of the theory while relaxing the problematic framework in which Habermas couched his 1962 work. Yet a number of American and British feminist scholars have challenged such flexible use of Habermas's theory in a compelling fashion. These scholars have variously offered many of the same criticisms as earlier revisionists. But they maintain that employing the concept of the public sphere demonstrates women's necessary place outside it, or indeed that the concept is too mired in the trappings of the modernist mode to be useful. In *Strukturwandel,* Habermas

---

6. This criticism is acknowledged by Habermas, *Strukturwandel,* 15; he recognizes here the power that individuals wielded from the literary public sphere. Habermas notes in his original work that the populations of the literary and political public sphere are not necessarily distinct, as in his comments on the role of women in the former; see *The Transformation of the Public Sphere,* 56. J. Landes, C. Hall, and L. Davidoff discuss women's power in the literary public sphere relative to the political public sphere. See Landes, *Women and the Public Sphere;* C. Hall, "Private Persons versus Public Someones," in *Language, Gender and Childhood,* ed. C. Steedman et al. (London: Routledge, 1985), 10–33; and L. Davidoff and C. Hall, *Family Fortunes* (Chicago: University of Chicago Press, 1987), especially 416–49. I want to challenge here Habermas's restriction from *within* the "political" public sphere.

7. It seems, moreover, that this Rousseauan ideal is not consistent in Habermas, who invokes alternately John Locke and the Philosophes, in sometimes contradictory fashion, in his discussions of the founding Enlightenment principles.

8. See, e.g., A. Kluge and O. Negt, *Öffentlichkeit und Erfahrung;* Negt and Kluge, *Geschichte und Eigensinn* (Frankfurt: Zweitausendeins, 1981); and G. Lottes, *Politische Aufklärung und plebejisches Publikum* (Munich: Oldenbourg, 1979). I propose to take off in part from this suggestive work to look at gender as well as class. However, I find the notion of multiple publics actually less useful than that of a single (necessarily amorphous) public composed of infinite, overlapping, and constantly transforming constituent groups, or subpublics. I elaborate on this below.

casts as his ideal type the "liberal bourgeois" public sphere, which would institutionally guarantee the unrestricted assembly of educated private individuals, acting through a public identity, in the rational, critical, open discussion of matters of general interest. Feminist scholars in particular have disputed the virtue of the "liberal bourgeois" paradigm itself, arguing that its philosophical roots always already marginalize women. According to such political philosophers as Carole Pateman, women are thus preemptorily shut out of the public in modern western society by virtue of the originary patriarchal "social contract," which fixed gender relations.[9] Habermas implies a belief that, *ceteris paribus,* the political inequities of his historical prototype might have been remedied through truly universal franchise and citizenship. But at the same time, he describes the political public sphere as dependent on the coexistence of the private realm of the bourgeois family, which appears to circumscribe women's roles within it. Recent work examining actual historical cases might seem to confirm these limitations. In an important study of France 1750–1850, the *locus classicus* of Habermas's liberal bourgeois public sphere, political scientist Joan Landes uses Habermas's analytical tool to test the possibilities for women's public participation in the modern order.[10] She concludes indeed that the emergence of the modern public sphere cut off even previously existing avenues to public life, and to politics, for women. Despite her attention to Negt and Kluge, Landes engages completely Habermas on his own terms: thus she carefully limits her definition of what constitutes politics, of how women might act politically and through what kind of identities they might act. It is such an analytic use of the public sphere, even as critique, that convinces some feminist scholars that the notion should be jettisoned altogether, that it is tied inescapably to a vision of politics that should be transcended.[11]

This forceful rejection of Habermas's ideal vision of the liberal bourgeois political public sphere requires of us great care in any application of the notion in a specific historical case. It should not, however, entirely deprive us of the

---

9. See C. Pateman, "Feminist Critiques of the Public/Private Dichotomy, in *Feminism and Equality,* ed. Anne Phillips (New York: New York University Press, 1987), 103–26; C. Pateman, *The Sexual Contract* (Cambridge, Mass.: Polity, 1988); see also S. M. Okin, "Women and the Making of the Sentimental Family," *Philosophy and Public Affairs* 11, no. 1 (1981): 65–88; and S. M. Okin, *Women in Western Political Thought* (Princeton: Princeton University Press, 1981).

10. Landes, *Women and the Public Sphere.*

11. Political scientist and therapist Jane Flax has suggested it would be difficult to disengage Habermas's conceptual tools from presuppositions such as, for example, "rational discussion" as the basis for true democracy. See J. Flax, "Responsibility without Grounds," unpublished manuscript; J. Flax, "The End of Innocence," in *Feminists Theorize the Political,* ed. J. Butler and J. Scott (New York: Routledge, 1992), 445–63; and J. Flax, "Is Enlightenment Emancipatory?" in *Disputed Subjects: Essays on Psychoanalysis, Politics, and Philosophy* (New York: Routledge 1993), 75–91.

conceptual tools provided by Habermas, which, I would argue, do not ineluctably bear a particular political worldview but rather may be used as a critique of that worldview.[12] To repudiate the broader usefulness of Habermas's concept is perhaps to be trapped by his own effective merging of the notion as analytical tool and as historical example.[13] If we attempt to unearth and reconsider the binary categories entrenched in Habermas's description, particularly that of public versus private, we can indeed examine in specific historical contexts the intimation of some of these critics: that is, that gender is a category of inviolable primacy and exclusion in any Enlightenment-based Western society.[14] We may employ the concept of the "public sphere" to reveal precisely how societies continually reconstruct gender and gendered identities, to question the fixed nature of political interests, and to discover the variety of ways in which

---

12. Of course, the notion of the public is not exclusively a modernist one, as Habermas's own historical discussion demonstrates. Moreover, as Judith Butler and Joan Scott assert, "To perform a feminist deconstruction of some of the primary terms of political discourse is in no sense to censor their usage, negate them, or to announce their anachronicity. On the contrary, this kind of analysis *requires* that these terms be reused and rethought, exposed as strategic instruments and effects, and subjected to a critical reinscription and redeployment" (Butler and Scott, *Feminists Theorize the Political,* xiv).

13. As Landes, Hall, and Sally Alexander make clear in their own work, hegemonic political relations inscribing gender endured as they did from the Enlightenment through much of the nineteenth century because they functioned well for those in power, who were able to prevent serious incursions into that power. These historians' use of "culture," as well as their sensitivity to contemporary perceptions of "public" and "private," can be seen to contribute to the revitalization of Habermas's notion. See Hall, "Private Persons versus Public Someones"; L. Davidoff and C. Hall, *Family Fortunes;* and S. Alexander, "Women, Class and Sexual Differences," *History Workshop Journal* 17 (Spring 1984): 125–49. See also V. de Grazia's very useful "The Gendering of Consumption: How It Has Constructed and Destructed Private and Public" (unpublished manuscript), which historicizes Habermas's public and private in the twentieth century, taking issue with Habermas's flat dismissal of the positive political potential for the sphere of mass consumption.

14. In a related vein, we might mention, although not develop here, Habermas's relegation of the political to the public sphere—a notion which was first widely challenged by the second wave of the women's movement. On politics in the private sphere, see the work of the *Alltagshistoriker* in Germany, e.g., A. Lüdtke, "Cash, Coffee-Breaks, Horseplay: *Eigensinn* and Politics among Factory Workers in Germany circa 1900," in *Confrontation, Class Consciousness and the Labor Process,* ed. M. Hanagan and C. Stephenson (New York: Greenwood, 1986): 65–95. On the politics of the "intimate sphere," see J. Weeks, "Rethinking Private Life" (unpublished manuscript). In "What's Critical about Critical Theory?" Nancy Fraser notes, moreover, that Habermas gives unnecessary primacy to the political as opposed to the economic—which he relegates to the private and therefore implicitly less effective sphere, though one in which women have consistently demonstrated certain kinds of power. See also in this vein J. Jones, "Coquettes and Grisettes," in *The Sex of Things: Gender and Consumption in Historical Perspective,* ed. V. de Grazia (Berkeley: University of California Press, forthcoming 1996). To push the argument further, the discrete and even oppositional use of "economic" and "political" forms yet another binary relation that must be reconsidered.

women did participate meaningfully in public life, despite legal and ideological restraints.[15]

Habermas's own assumptions may appear incompatible with the terms of recent feminist discourse on politics and the public. But it would seem that notions of "identity politics" and recent discussions of the relation between politics and experience, and the concepts of gender, rights, and citizenship are all usefully tested through the tool of Habermas's public sphere, even insofar as they strengthen the critique against the term as used by "modernist" political philosophers and historians.[16] I would make the case further for the importance

---

15. It should be noted that many German feminist scholars still find the concept useful, as opened up by the revisions discussed above. German feminist historians have introduced their own debates, which have ultimately served to transform and thereby preserve the usefulness of the "public sphere" for feminist scholars. Parallel to the trend in American historiography, German historians have in the last two decades utilized the public/private distinction to discuss women's roles; see, e.g., K. Hausen, "Family and Role Division: The Polarisation of Sexual Stereotypes in the Nineteenth Century," in *The German Family*, ed. R. Evans and W. Lee (London: Croom Helm, 1981): 51–83; and essays in K. Hausen, ed., *Frauen suchen ihre Geschichte* (Munich: C. H. Beck, 1983). But Carola Lipp has recently argued that the strict division of public/private along gender lines was neither perceived nor acted upon by the men and women of mid-nineteenth-century Germany; see C. Lipp, "Frauen auf der Strasse: Strukturen weiblicher Öffentlichkeit im Unterschichtsmilieu," in *Schimpfende Weiber und patriotische Jungfrauen im Vormärz und in der Revolution 1848/49*, ed. C. Lipp (Moos: Elster Verlag, 1986), 16–24; see also G. Bock, *Zwangssterilisation im Nationalsozialismus* (Opladen: Westdeutscher Verlag, 1986). In her argument, Lipp implicitly supports the enduring utility of Habermas's public sphere, as qualified by her revision. This debate has continued more expansively, for example at the 1989 conference on the public sphere and the private, organized by Hausen at the Technische Universität, Berlin; in the articles in "Gegen-Öffentlichkeit," the theme of *Feministische Studien* 1 (1989); and in the ongoing discussions in *New German Critique* (see, e.g., H. Schlüpmann, "Feminism as Productive Force: Kluge and Critical Theory," *New German Critique* 49 [Winter 1990]: 69–78). See also V. Schmidt-Linsenhoff, ed., *Sklavin oder Bürgerin? Französische Revolution und neue Weiblichkeit, 1760–1830* (Frankfurt: Jonas, 1989).

16. On the construction of identity and subjectivity, see, for a sampling, J. Scott, *Gender and the Politics of History* (New York: Columbia University Press, 1988); B. Martin and C. Mohanty, "What's Home Got to Do With It?" in *Feminist Studies/Critical Studies*, ed. T. de Lauretis (Bloomington: Indiana University Press, 1986), 191–212; J. Butler, *Gender Trouble: Feminism and the Subversion of Identity* (New York: Routledge, 1990); S. Hall, "Cultural Identity and Diaspora," in *Identity, Community, Culture, Difference*, ed. J. Rutherford (London: Lawrence and Wishart, 1990), 222–37; K. A. Appiah, *In My Father's House: Africa in the Philosophy of Culture* (New York: Oxford University Press, 1992); and H. Bhabha, "Interrogating Identity," in *The Location of Culture*, by H. Bhabha (New York: Routledge, 1994), 40–65. On rights and citizenship, see I. M. Young, "Polity and Group Difference," *Ethics* 99 (January 1989): 250–74; C. Mouffe, "Feminism and Radical Politics," in *Feminists Theorize the Political*, 369–84; and Fraser, "What's Critical about Critical Theory?" On experience, see inter alia J. Scott, "Experience," in Butler and Scott, *Feminists Theorize the Political;* William Sewell, Jr., "How Classes Are Made," in *E. P. Thompson: Critical Perspectives*, ed. H. Kaye and K. McClelland (Philadelphia: Temple University Press, 1990), 50–77; and Butler, *Gender Trouble*. Negt and Kluge, *Öffentlichkeit und Erfahrung* and Landes, *Women in the Public Sphere* work explicitly to mesh the category of experience with Habermas's public sphere.

of *Alltagsgeschichte* in drawing out the contradictory and complicated functioning of the public sphere, in actual practice, demonstrating the practice of politics at a given historical moment.[17]

Wilhelmine Germany and the Political Public Sphere

I am not calling for the complete divorce of Habermas's notion from its modernist groundings; indeed, for the historian, it is vital to understand the role that such a concept has played contemporaneously in the periods s/he examines. This contemporary currency of the public sphere is another persuasive ground for the historian's conscious use of the concept. Moreover, as the literary critic Rey Chow notes, the modernist mode still governs mainstream political life and culture, even if feminists and postmodernists seek to challenge its sway.[18] The point is precisely to historicize the term. Habermas himself drew on an already existing concept, of course, with a broad and mutable set of meanings in place.[19] In early twentieth-century Germany, the prevailing understanding of *Öffentlichkeit,* or the public sphere, directly informed how contemporaries perceived politics—with implications specifically for women's political power.[20] No shibboleth of academic rhetoric in early twentieth-century Germany, the concept was actively employed, for example, by denizens of the Prussian ministry of the interior and of the Berlin police presidium in World War I Berlin, as civil servants explicitly discussed the best methods for protecting the state against the pressures of those inhabiting this space.

Application of the concept by politicians and civil servants was flexible and protean as may be traced particularly well over the course of World War I. But the term consistently bore the attributes named above: that is, a set of sites at which a relatively autonomous public was created, in which a traffic in ideas and opinions might flow, and from which this public might influence others

---

17. For overviews of this literature, see, e.g., H. Medick, "Missionaries in the Rowboat? Ethnological Ways of Knowing as a Challenge to Social History," *Comparative Studies in Society and History* 29 (January 1987): 76–98; E. Rosenhaft, "History, Anthropology, and the Study of Everyday Life: A Review Article," ibid. 99–105; and D. Crew, *"Alltagsgeschichte:* A New Social History 'From Below'?" *Central European History* 22 (September 1989): 394–407.

18. R. Chow, "Postmodern Automatons," in Butler and Scott, *Feminists Theorize the Political,* 102. Landes makes much the same point in *Women and The Public Sphere,* 7–8.

19. Habermas traces the history of the term in *Strukturwandel.* He himself draws from a Hegelian Formulation, building on Hegel's divison of society between the state, civil society, and the family.

20. Habermas himself talks about the importance of prevailing ideological concepts on politics of the moment, just as he notes, rightfully, that such concepts at the same time reflect contemporary politics.

and, ultimately, press its interests on the state. Reading off contemporary documents, one finds the perception of a wide variety of sites from which many different segments of the public interacted to influence one another and officials. While officials might draw a distinction between "public opinion" and "popular sentiment," as does Habermas, the lines of division were blurred and were not attached isomorphically to particular populations (of bourgeois versus workers or of men versus women).[21] Finally, while a notion of "general will" is evident in contemporary documents of all types (translated as the "good of the people" or "good of Germans"), becoming ubiquitous during World War I, it is attached by officials, by the press, and in other public documents to a range of different identities that are seen to act for the moment as leading components of the larger public.

If contemporary officials distinguished flexibly between the "public" and the "popular" as identities shifted, likewise they did not establish a necessary opposition between the public and private spheres. Habermas would claim that this was evidence of the limitations of the prevailing public sphere. Yet I submit that it would not only be unnecessarily limiting but also a poor practice of history to assume the location of the private sphere as counterpart to the public when this assumption was belied ipso facto by contemporaries. It is worth noting that the word "Öffentlichkeit" does not necessarily imply the private as its opposite or complement. It is Habermas himself who fixed this binary relation in his interpretation of particular historical circumstances, based on his (selective) use of Enlightenment philosophers;[22] and it appears to be, in many cases, feminist scholars who have reinscribed it as a constant of the modern era. I would suggest that the opposition of public and private was historically contingent and that the place of gender across this opposition was likewise malleable. Correspondingly, there was no fixed historical opposition between the categories of citizen/noncitizen and thinker/feeler, or even between bourgeois/worker and man/woman; nor were there consistent relations between these sets of terms (worker or woman as "feeler," not "thinker"). None of these terms should be assumed to be arrayed along a fault line of public and private, particularly where the former term is used to envelop the political.

The example of Wilhelmine Berlin suggests, moreover, that the public sphere may represent a powerful tool of the public, even in less-than-ideal

---

21. This is notable in view of our standard understanding of Wilhelmine political culture as divided, from the perspective of the politics in power, between "bourgeois politics" and the politics of the "inner enemy," the Social Democrats.

22. See Lucian Hölscher, *Öffentlichkeit und Geheimnis* (Stuttgart: Klett-Cotta, 1979), who casts "public" in opposition to "secret," which characterizes the less open practices of German governance in various periods. See also *A History of Private Life: Passions of the Renaissance*, ed. Roger Chartier (Cambridge, Mass.: Belknap Press, 1989), for dicussions of the constitution of the public sphere from within the realm of the private.

incarnations. As the seat of a constitutional monarchy forged, in the now standard conceit, by "revolution from above," and the hub of Prussia, with its "three-class" vote, early twentieth-century Berlin hardly boasted the paradigmatic public sphere as described by Habermas. The onset of World War I brought to Berlin and to Germany still greater repression of public life and violation of civil liberties, culminating in virtual military dictatorship in August 1916.[23] Finally, the corporatist tendencies of German politics were accelerated by the war, leaving what would have been a public sphere of little efficacy in Habermas's view. Yet for all that, the German state was vulnerable to the demands of its public, and particularly the public of its turbulent, high-profile capital, Berlin. Indeed, it was precisely at a moment when the German state attempted most forcefully to restrict civil rights, and to assert its authority to do so, that the signs of an emergent German sovereignty shone through most clearly. That is, there was clearest evidence of the newly widespread public belief that "the German people," and not the state, were the site of the nation and the culture.[24] Deliberate examination of the German public sphere can lead us to a somewhat revised view of the political culture of the *Kaiserreich*.

Such circumstances permit us already to challenge Habermas's more rigid, linear model of the public sphere's historical development, and the relation of his ideal to particular political forms. The notion of the modern public sphere was tied to the emergence of a "traffic" in ideas, linked to certain forms of capitalism, to urbanization, and to the expansion of both literacy and literary markets; this historical setting sets some parameters around, and marks the comparability between, the various historical moments of the modern era. However, to impose a linearity or teleology on the historical process limits rather than opens up what we may find using these analytical tools. Indeed, if we match up Habermas's curious "progress then regression" model of politics, crudely stated, with his own ideal constitutional forms, we find that democratic politics has in many instances operated most "ideally" when the state has attempted somehow to foreclose on existing civil rights, or even when these

---

23. Invoking the Prussian Law of Siege, officials declared a state of emergency on 4 August 1914. Press censorship, a ban on political assembly, and close police monitoring of public spaces were some of the measures instituted. The "dictatorship" of August 1916 was realized in part through public demand. See Thierry Bonzon and Belinda Davis, "Feeding the Cities," in *Capital Cities at War,* ed. J. M. Winter and J.-L. Robert (Cambridge: Cambridge University Press, forthcoming). This popular quest ostensibly to further abrogate public political rights would seem to be a vindication of Habermas's argument for the disintegration of the public sphere and of political rationality in the impending era of mass culture. However, the demand for "dictatorship" seems in this instance to have signified rather desire for better enforcement of perceived "general interests," as publicly promulgated, in contrast with what many saw as the laissez-faire attitude of the civilian government toward (or even its active collusion with) the pursuit of private interests.

24. The role of sovereignty is further developed in B. Davis, "Bread and Democracy in World War I Berlin" (unpublished manuscript).

rights have not been guaranteed; while, in Habermas's own view, the Basic Law of the Federal Republic, written to maximally guarantee civil rights, seems to have bred complacency and withdrawal from politics for two decades.[25]

German officials and the broader public at the fin de siècle had no trouble envisioning "Social Democratic pubs" or the street as important sites of the political public sphere (if not of the "liberal bourgeois public sphere") in which individuals could gather, in which a traffic of opinions might flow, and from which segments of "the public" could exert considerable influence on other individuals and on the state.[26] The street in particular was considered contemporaneously as a foremost "public" site. From at least the *Vormärz* period, the street was also a site of regular unrest in Berlin, one which moreover drew widespread attention: domestically, internationally, and, in turn, from officials.[27] Thus in 1910 Berlin Police Commissioner Traugott von Jagow attempted in vain to reappropriate this site in the name of the state, issuing posters to be hung on kiosks that stated, "Rights on the street are hereby proclaimed. The street serves only for traffic. Countermanding state authority on this issue will result in the use of weapons. I warn the curious."[28]

The concern of the authorities reveals a number of contemporary so-

---

25. To be sure, the Basic Law emphasizes representative rather than participatory democracy. This example could certainly be extended to the contemporary United States, where, despite the relative stability of a certain core of civil rights, a majority of the citizens refuse to routinely exercise even the right to franchise. Conversely, civil disobedience across the West, as in the sixties, was widely condemned and repressed by the state, which in West Germany elicited response in the form of the terrorism of the seventies: that is, activity entirely outside of the accepted public political framework. Obviously, I do not mean to suggest the syllogism that repressive governments are most conducive to political freedoms but rather merely to challenge the spectrum of political freedoms as it is cast by Habermas. See also Eve Rosenhaft's take on the limits of women and politics in the Weimar public sphere, in her "Women, Gender, and the Limits of Political History in the Age of 'Mass' Politics," in *Elections, Mass Politics, and Social Change in Modern Germany,* ed. Larry Eugene Jones and James Retallack (Cambridge: Cambridge University Press, 1992), especially pp. 170–72.

26. On police observation of pubs, see Richard Evans, ed., *Kneipengespräche im Kaiserreich: Stimmungsberichte der Hamburger politischen Polizei, 1892–1914* (Reinbek: Rowohlt, 1989); on police and activity in the streets, see V. Ullrich, *Kriegsalltag: Hamburg im Ersten Weltkrieg* (Cologne: Prometh, 1982); as well as C. Lipp, "Frauen auf der Strasse"; and K. Hagemann, "Men's Demonstrations and Women's Protests," *Gender and History* 5, no. 1 (Spring 1993): 101–19. For the case of eighteenth-century France, Arlette Farge emphasizes the attentiveness with which police listened to voices in the streets and like "public sites," and communicated the sense of these voices to high-level authorities. See her *Subversive Words* (University Park, Penn.: The Pennsylvania State University Press, 1995).

27. See the essays in M. Gailus, ed., *Pöbelexzesse und Volkstumulte in Berlin* (Berlin: Europäische Perspektiven, 1984); as well as M. Gailus, *Strasse und Brot* (Göttingen: Vandenhoeck und Ruprecht, 1990); and T. Lindenberger, "Strassenpolitik: Zur Sozialgeschichte der öffentlichen Ordnung in Berlin, 1900–1914" (Ph.D. diss., Technische Universität, Berlin, 1992).

28. Cited inter alia in M. Gailus's introduction to Gailus, ed., *Pöbelexzesse,* iii.

ciological beliefs revolving around the public sphere. One axiom was, it appears, that the mere fact of collective presence constituted *Ansammlung,* or "assembly," by those present.[29] Thus policemen and journalists both consistently described the long wartime queues for food as assemblies, constituted by one identifiable population or another. A second truism was that the experience of "assembly" created in turn a sense of common identity, interest, and purpose among the implicated. Political policeman Dittmann suggested, for example, that the sight of those in line for scarce food supplies "elicit[ed] almost the impression that many women had found community in standing together before the shops."[30] A third belief was that the image itself of such "assemblies" attracted outside attention, disrupting public order and moreover providing a forum for the views expressed by participants.[31] Fourth, officials put much store in the notion of a propensity of assemblies to become "riots" (*Aufläufe*)[32] as a result of the natural "unreason" of the crowd.[33] Thus officials demonstrated an almost paranoid fear of any populous presence in the street, including even the demonstrations of "patriotic support for the war" that arose in the first weeks of World War I.[34] In light of the danger to Germany's image abroad that authorities believed was posed by such events, Prussian authorities proclaimed in October 1915 that any participants in a crowd of people on the street *"threatening* to become a demonstration" would be subject to punishment as traitors to the state. It is notable that, through these beliefs, whatever their basis in the experience of the day, officials and others had invested in the crowd in the street a power to influence public sentiment and opinion that was belied by the limited official franchise. And, finally, observers asserted that assemblies in the street were *de facto* political.

---

29. The issue of the particular site was distinct but related to the concern about "assembly." It would be worth attempting to play out the terms with still greater specificity regarding what constituted assembly, and what was thereby politically threatening; but for the moment it is important to note that these lines were indeed not fixed.

30. Landesarchiv Potsdam Provinz Brandenburg, Repositur 30, Berlin C, Titel 95 (hereafter LAP, Pr Br Rep 30 Bln C Tit 95), Nr. 15820, Report on Morale, Diercks, April 1917. Note also the reference specifically to women, though there were very likely not exclusively women in the queue. The implications of this identification are discussed below.

31. Political police were to keep officials informed of any disturbance in the making, through *Stimmungsberichte* (reports on morale) that specifically depicted the *Strassenbild,* that is, the "picture of the street," or the tableau created for the eyes of both participants and observers in any activity.

32. This also translates as "unlawful assembly," suggesting that the act was actually in violation of legal rights, in this state-controlled sphere. Once again, the very ambiguity and soft-edged nature of the concept play an important role that must be accounted for.

33. This "unreason" was, however, not opposed to "public" comportment.

34. See, e.g., LAP Pr Br Rep 30, Bln C Tit 95, Nr. 15806, p. 46, Report on Morale, 22 August 1914. Notably, in terms of the notion of *Strassenbild,* officials also worried even about the hanging of flags (German or Prussian), though a symbol of support for the war effort.

Habermas's own hesitance in validating "street politics" stems in part from his concern to distinguish between institutionalized autonomous political forums, in which educated citizens may debate, and the uncontrolled settings of popular, plebiscitary activity, which command no obligatory hearing by authorities, and, especially, which may be vulnerable to demagogic manipulation. Yet here too it is not clear that this distinction consistently holds true in historical examples. The lines between these categories were surprisingly easily blurred for Wilhelmine authorities. The Prussian three-class vote could be said to demonstrate the graded nature of legally inscribed political participation: one was not either "in" or "out" by the litmus test of this central civic power. Moreover, the right of franchise at the state level cut through the Prussian lower *Mittelstand,* but it is not clear how cleanly this cut promoted divergent political tactics within this group—or how the voting segment of the class was better able to make its interests heard. Officials in World War I Berlin differentiated in internal reports between criticisms expressed by the "public" (or "citizenry") and demands asserted by the "populace." Yet as the war progressed, this distinction was dissolved in practice: the "public" and the "populace" were used virtually interchangeably, as were the terms "public opinion" and "popular sentiment."[35] While this may be evidence for Habermas of the limits of the democratic potential of the Wilhelmine public sphere, it also points up the question of how useful citizenship is as a measure of political power, certainly as an exclusive measure, in any real historical instance.

Finally, while contemporary officials referred frequently to "the public" (itself a mutable term in everyday use with respect to such features as class and gender), they indicated as often particular identities that comprised—and that were forged within—this larger category. In the classic example of Wilhelmine Germany, heavy industrialists and Junkers fought light industrialists, merchants, and one another through appeal to the state, each lobby attempting to make its case for better serving the good of the nation. Habermas would find such circumstances evidence of society's dissolution into private, economically oriented interest groups, of the "mutual infiltration of the public and private spheres."[36] But implicit in Habermas's original notion is potentially a kind of totalitarianism directly at odds with his own professed political ideal of a truly democratic society. Invoking his Enlightenment paradigm, Habermas seems to assert unproblematically the possibility of a common political public will. Despite his own professed pluralism, he dismisses the political validity of a plurality of visions, proposing axiomatically that the political participation of

---

35. See particularly the reports of the Berlin political police. Early reports actually began with the juxtaposition of the "opinion of the citizenry (or bourgeoisie)" (*bürgerliche Meinung*) and the "sentiment of the populace" (*Stimmung der Bevölkerung*).
36. Habermas, *The Transformation of the Public Sphere,* 141.

individuals acting within social subgroups or categories obviates the possibility of democratic practice. Moreover, it would be difficult to find a historical example of a democratic society in which a single "general will" transcended the range of particular interests over some extended period of time.

These identities were not extrapublic or extrapolitical, as Habermas asserts, but rather attained and lost status as legitimate political subgroups of the public. Indeed, such subgroups effectively lobbied for the legitimacy of their interests on the implied basis both of publicly perceived "rights" (which did not always correspond to legal rights)[37] and of the greater good for Germany (or the general will). The wider public, as defined by those with some form of access to public communications, adjudicated, along with the state.[38] Thus, for example, as will be discussed below in the example of World War I, "soldiers' wives" lost status as a legitimate subgroup of the public in the particular circumstances of the war; while "women of little means" gained status, thereby winning the right to influence the wider public and to pressure the state. Notably, these public identities were both explicitly gendered female. And while the Wilhelmine state denied women the vote and, until 1907, even the right to "associate politically,"[39] the women who filled these roles won or lost their political voices largely on the basis of public determination. The power that particularly poor women were able to amass in these circumstances speaks to the limits of state control over participation in the public sphere; it suggests that the autonomy of the public is related to, but not restricted by, specific legal rights and guarantees.

In the instance of both identities, that of "soldier's wife" and "woman of little means," the category of gender was a primary component. However, the meaning invested in the category at that time worked variously to diminish and augment access to public power. Where did this meaning come from? I identify three sites at which and from which (gendered) public identities were construed interactively by the state and civil society: the *juridical,* including laws, public orders, and policy, whether applying specifically to women or differentiating by gender in their application; the *institutional,* corresponding largely to "the public" in Habermas's original sense as opinion debated in the press,

---

37. The firm distinction between "natural" and "civil" rights might also be usefully challenged in this context.

38. I see this relationship as one of sparring forces wherein the amalgam of interests comprising the state and the public forged these determinations together, sometimes in open conflict, most often not clearly so. The role of intentionality and agency is also relevant here. See W. Sewell, "Ideologies and Social Revolutions: Reflections on the French Case," *Journal of Modern History* 57, no. 1 (1985): 57–85.

39. This serves to demonstrate the contemporary belief that "political association," even by the disenfranchised, could exert influence against the interests of the state. In the war period, *all* political assembly was prohibited—including any "congregation in the street."

parliamentary halls, and associational literature; and the *performative*,[40] meaning people acting, and constructed, as women, and in other roles as modified by their femaleness, in the streets, or *Strassenbild*. Sources reveal in turn the dynamic of the identification process among a number of contenders. These include the bloc of interests called "the state"; that bloc comprising "the greater public"; and the bloc (or subbloc) comprising, in this instance, broadly, "poorer women," to which the two identities we have named were potentially applied.[41] None of these sites or agents was more germane than the others to the construction of political subjectivities; rather, interaction among these blocs was key in establishing the identities and maintaining their legitimacy.

World War I Berlin and the Case of the "Soldier's Wife"

Let us look at the "transformation of the public sphere" specifically in a case study of World War I Berlin. How did gender figure into political identities constructed in this sphere? And what did these identities mean for the ability of women to negotiate politically? To respond to these questions, we will examine these two identities, forged within the public sphere, that were of particularly high profile in World War I Berlin: the "soldier's wife" (*Kriegerfrau*) and the "woman of lesser means" (*minderbemittelte Frau*).[42] These labels were commonplace in the war period, revealing a centrality of "woman"—and women—in German political life still insufficiently recognized in this period, and perhaps with implications for the preceding decades as well.[43] This

---

40. I use "performative" in the sense asserted by Butler, as in *Gender Trouble;* see also Jean-François Lyotard, *The Post-Modern Condition* (Minneapolis: The University of Minnesota Press, 1984), 41–53. Butler characterizes a process by which acts and gestures serve to order attributes into gendered identities, which in turn tends to reinforce, but can also transform, the terms of the identities as they have already been constituted. See also I. M. Young, "Impartiality."

41. In this sense, the term "public" delimits not by virtue of *who* acts, but rather *when* and *how* one acts. It is important to note that those to whom an identity was ascribed were also actively engaged in constructing the identity.

42. On the broader picture of women in World War I Germany, see Ute Daniel's excellent *Arbeiterfrauen in der Kriegsgesellschaft* (Göttingen: Vandenhoeck und Ruprecht, 1989). While her own questions are cast differently, she, too, attends to the significance of certain female identities, such as soldiers' wives, that became prominent in the war.

43. I want to distinguish, however, between the forging of gendered identities and "women" *an sich*. That is, unlike Temma Kaplan, I do not find that the women I have studied took on a cohesive identity and acted collectively as "women," though the identities that groups of women may have taken on were often explicitly gendered female, particularly by outsiders, and this was not without importance. This distinction is elaborated further in B. Davis, "Food Scarcity and the Empowerment of the Female Consumer in World War One Germany," in de Grazia, *The Sex of Things*. See T. Kaplan, "Female Consciousness and Collective Action," *Signs* 7, no. 3 (Spring 1982): 545–66; and T. Kaplan, *Red City, Blue Period: Social Movements in Picasso's Barcelona* (Berkeley: University of California Press, 1992), 105–26.

centrality was not only objective, in the sense that these "types" and the persons that filled them were subject to rapt scrutiny and discussion. It was also subjective; operating within such roles, groups of women plied their resources for public power and political responsiveness, with significant results. Indeed, it is clear that, while accounting for the importance of the use of language in the establishment of these public identities, we must be equally attentive to what real people were doing as they acted through these identities. In this way, the methods of discursive analysis and *Alltagsgeschichte* together provide a means for examining the question of agency in the public sphere.

The results of these women's actions are in turn instructive in understanding the functioning of the public sphere. They point to a powerful role played by "legitimacy," a Weberian notion here extended to apply not only to political leadership but also to a wide range of political "players."[44] The public continuously reworked active political identities within its ranks and reassessed their legitimacy. This reassessment was based on the perceived "rights" of that group, as well as on its believed commitment to, and implications for, a general (German) good, often defined in the war years as "patriotism."[45] Thus in World War I Berlin, official concessions to soldiers' wives rested on the state's perception of this group's publicly established "rights," which were based on the soldiers' sacrifices in the name of the state. But in light of soldiers' wives' loss of public legitimacy, these concessions were revoked or diminished. "Women of lesser means," however, though legally doubly disenfranchised by gender and class, pled their case to a more sympathetic general public in the context of the wartime circumstances; this sympathy was based both on these women's own putative commitment to the war effort and on their right to a basic "German" diet for themselves and their families. The state had unwittingly played a role in forging the image of this patriotic commitment in the public sphere;[46] and now, in consequence of this legitimation, officials were held responsible for responding to the demands of this population.

---

44. This apposite Weberian concept is not invoked in *Strukturwandel*, despite the volume's reliance on other Weberian categories. Cf. Habermas's own later attention to legitimacy, as in his *Legitimation Crisis* (Boston: Beacon Press, 1975). See also Wolfgang J. Mommsen, *Max Weber and German Politics 1890–1920* (Chicago: University of Chicago Press, 1984), 448–53 and passim, for a very engaged discussion of Weber's use of the term. See also B. Davis, "L'État Contre La Société? Nourrir La Cité," in *Guerres Mondiales et Conflits Contemporains* (forthcoming 1996) for greater development of the notion of legitimacy in the context of World War I Germany. Suzanne Desan discusses the historian's use of legitimacy, in a somewhat similar fashion, in the context of community, the "moral economy," and crowd activity in her useful essay "Crowds, Community, and Ritual in the Work of E. P. Thompson and Natalie Davis," in *The New Cultural History*, ed. L. Hunt (Berkeley: University of California Press, 1989), 56–60 and passim.

45. I believe this move from discussion of patriotism to the good of Germans, or the good of the people, was related to the rising sense of sovereignty, which was perceived broadly to rest indeed with women of little means.

46. For more on officials' role in creating this image, see Davis, "Food Scarcity and the Empowerment of the Female Consumer."

Despite state recognition of this shift in viable political identities, officials were never able to meet the immediate needs (particularly regarding food supplies) of "women of lesser means," as these needs were defined by the latter, with public sanction. Ultimately, the credibility of the state itself was seriously damaged when the public deemed the state's response irremediably inadequate. Indeed, the state's pattern of minimal reactions served to further legitimate popular demands and brought disappointment and scorn for officials' measures in response. This example challenges Habermas's view that public political power rests narrowly with the rights of citizenship—or even that it ought to—for it is unclear what more or "better" political power "women of little means" might have won under such circumstances. It also questions the critique of some scholars who adopt this view of Habermas, and who thereby see European women of this era as effectively and necessarily restricted from public political life.

The earliest of any subgroups or identities highlighted in the wartime police reports was that of "soldiers' wives." This attention reflected anticipation on the part of the authorities that this identity would be an object of public discourse and concern. It represented as well the authorities' belief that this collectivity was capable of invoking and influencing public opinion. The wife of the active soldier was an already existing identity, but one that had had no physical incarnation since the rapid and successful war of 1870–71. In recognition of the earlier legitimacy of this population, which elicited specific state obligations, authorities released propaganda at the onset of hostilities assuring official support for soldiers' wives. One of the first acts of wartime Germany was to broaden and increase subsidies to this group, which, it was feared, might provoke sentiment against the war if the circumstances of its members became too visibly distressed. But the state had assumed that this identity would retain its earlier meaning for the broader public. In fact, the public experienced the "soldier's wife" as something very different under these different historical circumstances.

This disparity between the projected and actual public response to the "soldier's wife" was driven home to officials in the wake of the Battle of the Marne, which was fought in the first half of September 1914, a painful symbol that the war would not be won in the *Blitzkrieg* that propaganda had promised. From this point on, a shift in public opinion may be observed. By 21 September, police reports begin to note "public concern" that soldiers' wives as a group had been negligent in paying rent, in the apparent belief that such obligations were suspended while the so-called primary provider served his fatherland.[47] This negligence raised the ire of some landlords, who did not

---

47. No doubt, soldiers' wives offered this justification as a strategy of their own, coping with their new circumstances through aspects of their newly acquired identity and its concomitant status.

believe that sacrifice of their profit accreted to the benefit of the Fatherland, or the common good, particularly in the event of a long war. These landlords aroused the sympathy of other property owners, who observed that they themselves had not been relieved of mortgage payments.[48]

In the early months of the war, however, property owners did not want to risk potential criticism from the wider public by antagonizing soldiers' wives, and thus directed their concerns, via the press and associational communication, to local and state authorities for resolution. But police reports also recorded the "public" claims of soldiers' wives, who argued that current subsidy levels prohibited payment of rent. In this way, police reports served as a conduit for the communication of these women's concern as it was expressed in the street, no less than the press or parliamentary representation, the elements on which Habermas focuses. This also shows how officials' preexisting concern for what might take place in the street informed the nature of their response to the populations that gathered there. In the event, acknowledging the dual obligation to both war dependents and property owners, which authorities believed had been sanctioned by public opinion, *Reich*-level officials responded immediately to allay tensions between the two public identities (or subblocs), arranging for additional rent allowances for soldiers' wives.[49]

But the "soldier's wife" had lost legitimacy as a public identity in the eyes of other groups besides landlords, and the raising of subsidies served only to intensify the grievances of these other groups. Broad segments of the public discredited the notion that soldiers' wives were needy as a result of the loss of the family "head" and "breadwinner," for the latter's public—or performative—image was of a population faring particularly well under the circumstances.[50] The old, and especially the new, *Mittelstand* protested that the state had disturbed the natural order of class by legislating particular subsidies, for, they claimed, wives of working-class soldiers now lived better than their social superiors.[51] This publicly expressed sentiment was recorded poignantly by policemen, who felt moreover that the state was indebted to them as well as to

---

48. See, for example, reported comments in LAP Pr Br Rep 30 Bln C Tit 95, Nr. 15808, Reports on Morale, October 1914.

49. This rent supplement applied only to Berlin and was paid through the city at the command of the central government.

50. While, as Ute Daniel confirms, Berlin soldiers' wives were not becoming wealthy on their subsidies, there is some evidence that the loss of the "male breadwinner" was not necessarily in itself disastrous, in light of the percentage of income he himself consumed when present. There seems, however, to be little evidence that the physical counterpart of the rhetorical soldier's wife spent her days in cafés, enjoying cake.

51. Cf. LAP Pr Br Rep 30 Bln C Tit 95, Nr. 15808, p. 229, Report on Morale; and Nr. 15819, p. 281, Report on Morale.

soldiers' wives.[52] The vast number of working families left unemployed in the first months of the war used the streets to voice their own sharp resentment of aid offered only to soldiers' wives and families.[53] Recording the image that such protests created, Police Sargeant Schwarz noted that

> it must be a painful fact that, among the poorer population, dependents of soldiers are often considerably better off than those even temporarily unemployed. The wives of active soldiers are well taken care of: the city covers the rent for a small apartment, room, or room with a kitchen. The others, the city lets drop. Food is also mostly taken care of, because of the famous state support, to which the city also contributes its share. In addition, the[se] workers' wives keep up their former occupations. . . . It's something else entirely for families with many children, or with unemployed. There, there is no adequate support: thus the reigning bitter despair at home.[54]

Observing the various resentments of different populations and the generalized effects of the protest, police averred that "it is asserted from all sides that war dependents from the working class are doing considerably better than before the war."[55] Police claimed that, according to "broad public opinion," such particularized subvention was not a right but rather an unfair privilege offered to an exclusive collectivity fashioned "artificially" by the state, that is, without the affirmation of the public.[56] This ill will led to the characterization of soldiers' wives as work-shy and spendthrift.[57] But it was understood that,

---

52. The stature of policemen and other civil servants had always derived more from "honor" and status than from income level (see J. Caplan, "'The Imaginary Universality of Particular Interests': The 'Tradition' of the Civil Service in German History," *Social History* 4, no. 2 (1979): 299–317). To some degree, status itself provided one means to obtain what was perceived to be necessary goods. However, by the end of 1915, neither status nor income sufficed to acquire such goods. Because of this the primacy of policemen's self-identification as civil servants, with all that that signified, was open to revision in this period, and policemen threatened to cease performing through this role. Agents of "the state" constituted a no more monolithic entity than "the public."

53. More than 22 percent of unionized workers were unemployed in August 1914. The percentage of employment was much higher for nonunionized workers.

54. LAP Pr Br Rep 30 Bln C Tit 95, Nr. 15808, p. 199, Report on Morale, Schwarz, 11 December 1914.

55. LAP Pr Br Rep 30 Bln C Tit 95, Nr. 15808, p. 141, Report on Morale, Jagow, 30 November 1914. Jagow actually uses the unusual term *Arbeiterstand*, "workers' estate," to describe the aggrieved, perhaps telegraphing some of the new confusion in the social hierarchy.

56. The term "artificial" was used frequently in popular parlance to denote that which did not ring true or just to the common ear—or, in the terminology used here, that which was not legitimate. Soon this description would be applied particularly to the rise in food prices.

57. At the same time, soldiers' wives were also accused of stealing jobs away from others who were not so fortunate as to receive a separation allowance.

naturally, soldiers' wives would accept money offered to them honorably. Widening segments of the public therefore vented their fury on the state, which had deemed this support appropriate, apparently flouting public opinion on the subject.

The state was concerned by this transformation in perception on the home front. Separation allowances were an issue not only of civilian public demand. Officials worried that frontline soldiers might express severe reservations at fighting a war that state propaganda had figured as defensive—literally for the protection of Germany's women and children—only to leave their own families vulnerable to the "economic war" at home. But more intense pressure was exerted by the domestic furor by virtue of its perceived greater potential to thwart state ends, because of the widening segments of the public engaged on the issue, and because of the greater autonomy and thus uncontrollability of this population. Remarkably diverse populations had come to express coincident interests on the issue of soldiers' wives; and altogether this translated into a compelling, if not overwhelming, voice among the broader public.

In the context of such strong public opinion, the response of the Prussian and imperial authorities was motivated by fear for the ramifications of not taking rapid action. For property owners denounced the distinction and privileging of this group, and lower middle-class and working-class Berliners asserted that their own sacrifice and their need[58] were as great as those of the soldiers' wives; thus, these diverse populations claimed, the state elevated the good of the few over the well-being of a much wider population, which defined itself increasingly as "the people" and "Germans." Indeed, in this atmosphere public demand developed in the fall of 1914 for a far more generalized subsidy, and one that, like separation allowances, would not bear the stigma associated with poor relief. In the eyes of state officials, this demand clearly had to be quelled. In response, in one of its few acts of the era that defied military considerations, the civilian administration chose finally to retreat (at least temporarily) from support of war dependents altogether.[59]

---

58. Protesters couched their demands both in terms of their own services to the state and in terms of need. Barbara J. Nelson notes a similar dual basis, in both "rights" and "needs," for the developing U.S. welfare state early in this century. See Nelson, "The Origins of the Two-Channel Welfare State: Workmen's Compensation and Mothers' Aid," in *Women, The State, and Welfare,* ed. Linda Gordon (Madison: University of Wisconsin Press, 1990), 123–51. For evidence of this transformation emphasizing need as a legitimate basis for subvention, see Paul Hirsch, *Die Versorgung der Kriegsteilnehmer, ihrer Familien und Hinterbliebenen* (Berlin: Singer, 1915)—though, ironically in terms of widespread opinion, this social Democratic pamphlet employs the case of soldiers' families to argue precisely for their support on the basis of need.

59. This occurred on 3 January 1915. It must be added that this subsidy was soon reinstated—along with subventions for the unemployed and other broader groups, just as the state had hoped to avoid. The act to rescind separation allowances was not taken without conference with military authorities. But civilian officials convinced the military authorities that domestic

The story of the soldier's wife illustrates the historically contingent validity of particular identities to vie publicly for their interests. But it also calls into question presumptions regarding the relation between public and private in the modern era and regarding the role of women, both as subjects of discourse and as actors, within this schema. For it seems that, in the case of soldiers' wives, their identity lost its political validity in part by virtue of its inscription exclusively in the private sphere, both within the bourgeois family unit and within the realm of privilege.[60] Rather, in the changing terrain of image and experience brought by the war, the public legitimated those identities gendered female that operated primarily in the public sphere, those which were "open" to the public (in which gender did not operate as a closed category), and those through which one acted in "public" fashion.

As rising numbers of men went off to war, and as other prevailing circumstances changed with whom one lived and what roles one played, the nuclear family temporarily lost a certain amount of validity as a meaningful place through which to establish one's identity. Moreover, the patriarchal family lost some significance as an economic unit; likewise, absence of the male family head called into the question the role of the family as the appropriate political unit through which women must—or even might—act. Public opinion condemned separation allowances, intimating that it was not the family unit but the soldier alone who had entered relations of reciprocal obligation with the state. Thus women might not press for support from the state on the basis of their husband's "patriotism"; this support was an unfair privilege, closed off to others regardless of their sacrifice to the fatherland and to the German people. There is in this scenario an opposition played out between the public and the private; but public opinion suggested that women were able to operate in either sphere easily enough.

---

peace was seriously at risk, which threatened the successful prosecution of war. Herein lay another way in which the population wielded political power via extraparliamentary means.

60. The phenomenon of this jaundiced view of women's traditional "bourgeois" roles within the family during the war years may be related to the linguistic and historical link between the notions of "private" and "privilege." This association follows in German as well. For it was the notion of an unjust privilege associated exclusively with these female identities that provoked protest. "Public" is, conversely, historically associated with that which is open and fair (see R. Williams, *Keywords: A Vocabulary of Culture and Society* [Oxford: Oxford University Press, 1976], 242–43; R. Sennett, *The Fall of Public Man* [New York: Random House, 1974], 89–106; and Landes, *Women and the Public Sphere*). The discourse set in motion by protest against separation allowances and the articulation of a state obligation to the entire population reinforced this dual repudiation of the private sphere and a particular notion of privilege, both associated with the dominant bourgeois ideology. See for comparison Paula Hyman, "Immigrant Women and Consumer Protest: The New York City Kosher Meat Boycott of 1902," *American Jewish History* 70 (September 1980): 91–105, who argues that much of women's actual everyday activity at the turn of the century, far from being limited to the private, was at the very least "semipublic."

In 1915 Berlin, talk on the street suggested indeed a generalized, if temporary, disapprobation for female identities that were grounded in the bourgeois family structure and its system of interdependency—and that "benefited" thereby from the circumstances of war. Thus, for example, the "mother of many children" (*kinderreiche Frau*) became, as did the soldier's wife, a term of abuse, at least as it was heard in the street, referring to a figure who received some form of aid from the state on the basis of her private role, without contemporary public validation of that role in serving general interests.[61] Police reported the widespread belief that such women lived high on the extra rations received for their children, spending the money on personal luxuries while their children ran hungry and cold.

This view of soldiers' wives and mothers of many children is quite striking in contrast to what we might expect in the war years. These transformations in the terms of "legitimate" female identities seem to have been related in part to the fact that, by virtue of a variety of circumstances related to the war, women spent significantly more time in public, relative both to their own prewar experience and to the proportion of men, whose presence had dominated the street before the onset of hostilities. Their daily lives were played out in the streets, lined up for ration coupons, at newspaper kiosks, and, above all, before understocked food shops. Perhaps because of women's actual enhanced public presence as hostilities continued—coupled with the diminution of a male presence—new public mores seemed to frown upon efforts of women to mediate relations with the state and greater public through their husbands, or at least with reference to the latter's contribution to the state.

Rise of the "Woman of Lesser Means"

It was in this context that the "woman of lesser means" became a prominent identity and earned public legitimacy, even as other female identities lost validity. The prevailing experience worked to transmute the hard lines of gender, as well as of class, across new public identities. This case challenges the notion of an essential division by gender among publicly constructed identities. How did these transformations take place? A central experience informing public identities in the war years was the "economic war" that ravaged Germany, specifically in the form of shortages of basic foods, from the

---

61. These mothers were contrasted with those with grown children, who worked all day away from home (in prewar conditions, a very favorable situation), and therefore could not spend the time and effort necessary to procure food. Wives of well-paid munitions workers were also derided as a category (though not their husbands) for their "undeserved" good fortune. Notably, these three categories together covered a large population of working-class and lower middle-class women.

beginning of the war on, and the rapidly rising price of foodstuffs.[62] By the winter of 1914–15, the burning issue of food shortages began to occupy virtually the entire public. And although the pricing and distribution patterns of food at the time provides evidence for great economic and social polarization, ironically the issue worked to level the kinds of barriers, such as exclusivity, that had prevented the public from sympathizing with soldiers' wives. Shared interest in acquiring food razed important traditional social ramparts between classes, as a perceived common lack of access—and common lack of privilege—among consumers cut across social strata.[63] And though women continued to increase in public prominence, it might be argued that "woman" figured at this moment as the kind of absolute, primary, and impermeable category less than some historians and political scientists have asserted.

In the absence of sufficient food available at affordable prices, the questions of consumption and of means became central and overshadowed common emphases on production and income. Police reports and the press reveal a riveting attention as early as the spring of 1915 to the resources that one might use to procure necessities, including connections (e.g., to rural family members) and goods or services to barter. Broad social strata coalesced under the banner of "the consumer" in a shared sense of injustice regarding the inaccessibility of basic foods. The state's own notion of an economic war waged against the consumer acted as a powerful rhetorical filter through which the public experienced the circumstances of scarcity. The collectivity was formed internally from the physical, performative manifestation of interminable lines for food, which were ubiquitous particularly in poorer areas of the city. The length of time that shoppers were forced to spend in these lines; the anxiety, frustration, and sense of injustice that shoppers felt; and the tension created by interaction between shoppers and putatively profiteering shopkeepers served to forge an identity and sense of shared experience among these consumers— much as contemporary officials had feared.

Likewise, officials appear to have accurately anticipated the effect of such assemblies before bakeries and dairies on outside observers. By early 1916, the economic war was arguably of more constant concern—in "public" and "popular" opinion—than events on the front;[64] and the broad public had cast its

---

62. The notion of an "economic war" was first used in the hostilities in reference to Britain's economic blockade of Germany though it came to refer also to the battle among Germans for access to blockaded goods. It was used to refer almost exclusively to conflicts surrounding food.

63. At the same time, interclass resentments continued to be expressed, as can be often read in the remarks of police on fixed incomes.

64. Cf. the concerns expressed in "Wird die Lebensmittelteuerung Anhalten?" *Berliner Börsen Zeitung,* 15 September 1915. This conservative paper noted that "winning the economic war" was of the highest priority—precisely to forestall ominous popular threats, which might wreak havoc on military efforts as well as on the domestic status quo. In this way, too, poorer women in the streets had effectively brought their interests to center stage.

support on the side of the highly visible yet nebulously defined "women of lesser means." Police reports, newspapers, and other communications increasingly applied the description "minderbemittelt," of lesser means, to this new collectivity, bridging the gulf between the working class and lower levels of the *Mittelstand*.[65] Berliners who were not so severely affected by the economic war also recognized the collectivity by virtue of its physical representation before shops and legitimized it through their shared concern regarding the availability of food and the causes of its shortage. Those better off demonstrated strong empathy for this newly formed population in public—or at least published—opinion, in part because of the loose and inclusive nature of the terms "consumer" and "of lesser means." This sympathetic response was exhibited in the press from interest groups on the Left to, remarkably, the far Right.[66]

This new openness, or the nonexclusivity of this public identity, and the currency of the economic war had an impact on the functioning of gender as well as of class. Just as the universal "worker" was customarily cast as a man, so the "consumer" was envisioned as a woman. Thus, first of all, a more favorable image of "woman" emerged than was evident in earlier war-era identities, arousing sympathy across the wider public, including the police spies who reported to the government.[67] But second, with this prominent female role, gender appeared not as an absolute and limiting identity but rather as a place in the societal schema in which, under prevailing conditions, a much broader population could "assemble."[68] The "consumer," and even the "woman of lesser means," differed in this way from the "soldier's wife," or even the "wife/mother," which were closed categories on juridical or physical grounds. These latter identities left no space for rhetorical play within the public sphere; their closed nature was related to their perception as positions of unjustified privilege.

---

65. This new terminology simultaneously drove a wedge between shopkeepers and other segments of the *Mittelstand*. Use of epithets such as "the profiteer" and "the Jew" (often in abstract form) were used to impose alternate categories of distinction.

66. This response is evident in the consistently surprising remarks of such conservative newspapers as *Die Deutsche Tageszeitung, Die Berliner Börsen Zeitung,* and *Der Reichsbote,* which served Berlin and even populations outside the city.

67. To mitigate this rising sympathy and the concomitant resentment against the state, political police were categorized by 1916 as "heavy laborers"—a category notably assigned in practice only to men—and given extra subsidies.

68. For discussion of cultures that historically have explicitly distinguished between gender and the sexed body, see work on Berdache Native Americans (e.g., W. Williams, *The Spirit and the Flesh: Sexual Diversity in American Indian Culture* [Boston: Beacon, 1986]), and on the Mahu of Hawaii (C. Robertson, *Musical Repercussions of 1492: Encounters in Text and Performance* [Washington, D.C.: Smithsonian Institution Press, 1992]).

This is not to say that men now thought they were women, any more than women now working for the first time in munitions factories thought they had become men. Nor is it to imply that the category of gender had lost all significance; rather, it had gained new significance. Indeed, it could be said that qualities understood contemporaneously as feminine, such as vulnerability, came to signify a generalized, deeply felt sentiment, representing a part of each person.[69] Thus contemporary documents freely merged descriptions of "the consumer," "women," "the population," and "the public," beginning a sentence with its subject designated as one of these terms and changing it for another by the end. By the beginning of 1916, police, the press, and associational literature employed these identities as identical with "the Germans" and "we, the people," with notable implications for the political power gained by those women in the streets widely perceived to embody this role. This merging suggests further the growth of a notion of German sovereignty in this period, as heated public debate over the availability and distribution of food transformed into discussions of what the state owed "the people," broadly speaking, in return for their sacrifices to the war effort.[70]

Positionality, or relations with other social identities, was a key element in the construction of these subjectivities. In turn, positionality played a crucial role in the everyday politics of the era. While the "soldier's wife" had been, surprisingly, cast in opposition ultimately to the people, the "woman of lesser means" found her enemy in the universally despised profiteer, or black marketeer. The notion of a raging economic war grew ever stronger as an organizing rhetoric under which identities arrayed themselves. In consequence, officials aimed to transform the already sinister black marketeer into a scapegoat for the government's failed policies and negligence. Yet once more their efforts failed to have the desired effect, as they were unable to control the reception and transformation of the image of the speculator. As in the case of soldiers' wives, Berliners expressed little surprise that individuals would attempt to exploit available means to satisfy personal needs. But within the terms of this war on the home front, public opinion now held that the state was fully responsible for protection of its subjects, citizens or not, against such "en-

---

69. This "vulnerability" was, moreover, less associated with a mentality of "blaming the victim" than it had been earlier in the war. Propaganda had from the onset of war justified hostilities by the need to defend the weaker, more vulnerable elements of the population, that is, women and children. Such propaganda worked in tandem with other rhetoric early in the war to reinforce sentiment which was directed against the women who seemed to represent an exposed area for incursion into the German nation.

70. It is no coincidence that the slogan "*Dem deutschen Volke*" (both to and of the German people) was inscribed on the pediment of the Reichstag in 1916. My thanks to Fred Bode for noting this.

emies," in view of these subjects' own commitment, as Germans, to the war effort.[71]

This belief was only reinforced by the generalized sense of vulnerability. Indeed, the state would rue its own war propaganda which proclaimed its obligation to defend Germany's "weaker" population. For the expectations of generalized state protection that had been aroused in the rage over the "soldier's wife" took on ever greater cogency in its application to the "woman of little means." Dissatisfied consumers in the streets demanded increasingly interventionist measures of Prussian and imperial authorities, from rationing and price controls to state confiscation and distribution of all foodstuffs. The broad spectrum of the press and other public literature came quickly to support the range of demands. The combined effect from these sites of public opinion put enormous pressure on the state. Frightened by the recurrent and increasingly violent unrest in the streets, and cognizant of waxing public support for the protesting population, top officials responded to these demands—though always too little too late, in the public eye.

It was not only this imagined "woman of little means" whose increased prominence figured centrally in the growing domestic turbulence. The outstanding public position of *women* is also notable. Poorer women assumed leadership in promoting the notion of a generalized state obligation to the civilian population as they stood in line for food, ration booklets, and related essentials.[72] These women thus assembled publicly, constructed effective rhetorical strategies (recorded both by police and by the press), established the

---

71. For greater discussion of how this reciprocal obligation was established, largely through the government's own misfired propaganda, see Davis, "Food Scarcity and the Empowerment of the Female Consumer."

72. The prominence of women was related to that of the dominant gendered identity but does not correspond directly, as I have tried to show. This high profile was due both to the traditional (although not exclusive) role of women as procurers of food and to the more general "feminization" of the population as a result of the conscription. Of course, it is not always simple to distinguish in sources between the generalized female-gendered subject that I have tried to establish and biological women. I think it is possible to do this through careful attention to general populations and particular individuals who are named in the same reports, as well as by comparing written depictions and the plentiful photographs of the phenomenon. A policeman might describe a bread line as composed of "women of lesser means" and then note particular men in the line, singled out, for example, for drunkenness. For that matter, police might describe queues for coal (hauling coal was a "man's task," by virtue of tradition and practicality) as occupied by the "population of lesser means"; but this identity still retained its contemporary gender specificity. In any case, details make it reasonably clear that lines for food and most other articles were constituted primarily, though not exclusively, by women; and, most important, that it was predominantly women who initiated acts of oral and physical force, asserting their demands for a "fair" food policy. But it is also notable that police reporters distinguish between the "legitimate" demands of the women who constituted food "assemblies" and the merely "rabble-rousing" tendencies of "drunken men" and "boys," who also formed part of the crowd.

legitimacy of their demands in the wider public,[73] and exerted on the whole an influence unfettered by the long-term official restraints on women's public political participation and by the more generalized severe civil restrictions that obtained in the war years.[74] They accomplished this largely through negotiation of their identity as it had become established in the public sphere. Officials registered no great surprise at these women's ability to assemble as a public body and stake their claims. It was the memory of earlier demonstrations— also of an "economic" nature—that informed the resolve of state agents to send police spies out to the streets and shops, even before the bread lines and subsequent unrest had begun. By November 1915, Police Commissioner Jagow noted that extraparliamentary means were now believed to be the best means to successfully elicit official action—and " 'extraparliamentary means' meant none other than demonstrations in the street."[75] Most important, under the existing circumstances, officials recognized the need to respond positively to demands made in this forum.

Indeed, despite their recognition of the dangers, police knew that they could not prevent the populace from assembling for food. This is why food lines in particular were the central focus of police attention, even before they began, as evidenced by reports of August and September 1914, which noted that food prices and scarcity had "not yet" been a problem.[76] In turn, the resultant disturbances, created by the scarcity and especially by the perceived deception of merchants and growers, were in this period very difficult for police to control through socially acceptable means. The unrest arose out of the simple circumstance of many people trying to procure for themselves some of the inadequate supply of potatoes; the scarcity itself stopped up the flow of pedestrian traffic and created an "assembly" of the masses. While police could often dissipate the crowds who remained to protest once a shopkeeper had declared his or her supply exhausted, the potato protests of February 1915

---

73. This was accomplished despite the lack of "reason" that official propaganda attributed to the female consumer. Indeed women of little means turned the question of reason and rationality around in the course of 1915–16 and used it against the state. These consumers transformed this "inability to understand" into an admitted "lack of comprehension" of the state's apparently "irrational" policies regarding food.

74. We might compare this relative success to the contortionist efforts of the (Majority) Social Democratic Party, members of which were largely tongue-tied by the party's commitment to the civil truce and by efforts to prove its patriotism.

75. Jagow cites from the left Social Democratic daily *Volksfreund Braunschweig,* 2 November 1915, in LAP Pr Br Rep 30 Bln C Tit 95 Nr. 15814, p. 298, Report on Morale, 5 November 1915.

76. See LAP Pr Br Rep 30 Bln C Tit 95 Nr. 15806, p. 44, Report on Morale, 22 August 1914. Naturally, the "planned lack of official planning" for the domestic food supply played a role in anticipating the streets and marketplaces as a site of potential unrest.

proved early the limits of such power. Jagow ruminated on the inability of police to maintain quiet and "order" on the streets:

> Above all in Andreas Street, this has led to circumstances that police were unable to control. I am therefore in contact with the local authorities there. But their suggestion that a more open space be created to sell such goods is impossible from a security point of view, as there would likely be upwards of ten thousand excited people, especially women and children, gathered together.[77]

These beliefs provide insight into the upheaval of this period. Moreover, they constituted a series of self-fulfilling prophecies, for the state's own concern served to focus attention on the masses in the street, though this concern never translated into adequate official action—unfortunately for the status of the existing powers.

Such popular politics by acclamation or its inverse as this example represents are denounced by Habermas in favor of a politics carried out by an educated, reasoning public that is schooled in parliamentary political practices. Yet we cannot say that women were not involved in the political process because they did not boast this formal education, nor can we say with certainty that they could have asserted their interests more effectively had they had use of this asset. I do not even think that we can say that the form of politics practiced by these women on the streets was necessarily less democratic for its irregularity; and it is democratic politics about which Habermas is most concerned. To make this case is, obviously, not to defend limited franchise or authoritarian rule; nor is it to ignore the dangers of demagoguery as it has historically been associated with "mass politics." Most important, I am not trying to suggest that women as a rule were able to exert political influence as easily as men—there are many reasons why this was not the case. But the politics idealized by Habermas would not in this case necessarily have guaranteed more democratic—or effective—political participation than these women had already achieved, albeit for a circumscribed place and time. Indeed, for all their spontaneous "activism" in this period, poorer women remained relatively cool to the campaigns for universal suffrage led in the war years by bourgeois women's groups and the Social Democratic Party.[78]

---

77. LAP Provinz Brandenburg, Repositur 30, Berlin C, Titel 95, Nr. 15809, p. 20, memorandum Jagow to von Loebell, 18 February 1915.

78. Habermas would probably respond that the corporatist politics of this era had indeed rendered the franchise less meaningful and therefore less worthy of pursuit. But the actual political dividends of franchise might perhaps be questioned in his own historical examples. Once more, I am not disputing the virtues of democratic rule. I am merely challenging the practicable nature of Habermas's own political ideal, which has been assumed as the starting point for some of his critics.

It is difficult, moreover, to deny the broad political ramifications of the activity of "women of little means," though they developed out of apparently meager demands.[79] Women who protested in the streets were not consciously radical in their demands for "fair" food policy, a policy that would guarantee the accessibility of sufficient basic foods. Nor did they claim to have an understanding of public policy or the economics of food supply beyond their daily contact with the results of such policy. But when the institution of limited state and municipal ordinances failed to alleviate the desperation of the population of lesser means, shoppers waiting before stores called for increasingly drastic state measures. Women of lesser means turned to a rhetoric of customary right and to a moral economy founded on the attack on unfair privilege that was inscribed in their new identity, and informed by expectations of state protection aroused in the "soldier's wife" uproar. Thus by the end of 1915, this population of poorer women came to demand state confiscation of all foodstuffs (as well as fuel and clothing) from private entrepreneurs and the equal distribution of the same at cost or even at subsidized prices for the poor. Though these demands appeared to these women perfectly justified under prevailing conditions, they were revolutionary. They implied no less than an enormous transformation of the economic, social, and political structures of Germany, a transformation that ultimately superseded the special circumstances of the war.[80]

These circumstances ought to be incorporated into our assessment of the German Revolution of November 1918 and its prospects to be both authentic and successful. It is vital to acknowledge the popular and widespread nature of demands regarding the obligations of the state, which directly fed the revolutionary rhetoric of 1918, as well as the officials' fear of the power of these demands. And the public sphere was the terrain in which this transformed vision of relations between state and society were debated and legitimized. I am not arguing that the revolution was inevitable as early as 1915–16. The state had not lost all legitimacy for a large portion of the citizenry, certainly not until military defeat was announced. Indeed it can be argued that the authorities' continued, if inadequate, attentiveness to consumer needs throughout the war was crucial to preventing revolutionary protest earlier in the war.[81] But it was in this domestic failure that the seeds of revolution were planted.[82] The

---

79. These women's demands and their expectations of the state did not remain meager, however; they soon caught on to the fact of their new social and political power and became all the more aggressive in pressing their claims on authorities at all levels. See B. Davis, "Bread and Democracy."

80. The casting of these demands opened potential for both radical Left and radical Right resolution, a conflict that became generally apparent only after the revolution of November 1918.

81. See Thierry Bonzon and Belinda Davis, "Feeding the Cities."

82. Jürgen Kocka observed already in 1973 the role of civilian dissatisfaction early in the

events of 1918 make clear the way in which the rising level of protest and violence, and the state's falling legitimacy, can be traced directly from the circumstances that I have outlined for the first years of the war. These circumstances must be related to mass strikes that occurred and the assessment of officials that they had to "allow" revolution, at least in some form, to take place.[83] While women of little means were not ultimately able to elicit a satisfactory response to their demands, the state certainly paid a heavy price for its inadequacy. It would be difficult to dispute the power of these women over the state gained through their activity in the public sphere.

---

war in promoting the November 1918 revolution (see J. Kocka, *Facing Total War: German Society, 1914–1918* [Leamington Spa, Warwickshire: Berg, 1984], 7). Ute Daniel first suggested the prominence of women in voicing this dissatisfaction.

83. See chapter 8 of B. Davis, "Home Fires Burning: Politics, Identity, and Food in World War I Berlin" (Ph.D. diss., University of Michigan 1992), for an elaborated account of the relation between food riots, "women of little means," and the revolution.

Militarization and Reproduction in World War I Germany

Elisabeth Domansky

World War I completed the transition from the nineteenth to the twentieth century. Not only did millions of soldiers lose their lives on battlefields all across the world; a whole century met its death: the global political order of the nineteenth century was destroyed, the territorial map of Europe changed beyond recognition, political systems collapsed, and the social organization of all European nations was radically restructured. The militarization of the twentieth-century world, which grew out of the ravages of total war, was based on a fundamentally new relationship between "the military and civil society, between war and peace, production and destruction."[1] It was also grounded, as I want to show in this essay, in a fundamentally new relationship between military destruction, industrial production, and the organization of the social and biological reproduction of society.

Earlier versions of this essay were presented to the History Departments at Columbia University and the University of Washington, to the Five-College Faculty Seminar in German Studies at Mount Holyoke College, at the 1990 meeting of the American Historical Association, and to the conference "The Kaiserreich in the 1990s: New Research, New Dimensions, New Agendas," held at the University of Pennsylvania in 1990. I would like to thank Renate Bridenthal, Michael Geyer, and Christine Ruane for their valuable comments on earlier drafts of this article. Lorraine Berry Andrews, Mott Greene, Norman Naimark, Thomas Lekan, Margaret Ries, Jay Winter, and Glennys Young have commented extensively on this version. I would like to thank all of them for supportive criticism, helpful suggestions, and stimulating discussions. I am especially indebted to Geoff Eley for his inexhaustible patience.

1. Michael Geyer, "The Militarization of Europe, 1914–1945," in *The Militarization of the Western World, 1870 to the Present,* ed. John R. Gillis (New Brunswick, N.J., 1989), 72. I follow Michael Geyer's definition of militarization as "the contradictory and tense social process in which civil society organizes itself for the production of violence" (79). But I depart from his interpretation by emphasizing the key role of reproduction in the militarization of the Western world. See Geyer's and other authors' contributions to Gillis's volume for further references on the topics of militarization and militarism.

The process of recasting the triad of [production, reproduction, and destruction] during World War I led to the collapse of the existing political order and of the class and ethnic structures of major belligerent nations. It also shook the foundations of the nineteenth century's system of gender relations in the industrialized countries of Europe. But while France and Great Britain seem to have emerged from the "gender crisis" of total war with their patriarchal systems still intact, patriarchy, as I will argue in this essay, was destroyed in Germany.[2] By this, I do not mean that male domination over women came to an end. It did not. Male supremacy, however, was no longer rooted in men's/ fathers' role in the family.[3] [The family ceased to exist for the duration of the war as a unit of economic and social power and, beyond the war's end, as the site of society's social and biological reproduction.] Neither the war nor the "militarized peace"[4] that followed it were organized on the basis of the traditional family unit.[5]

The dissolution of the bourgeois family, which had been a prominent

---

2. On France and Great Britain, see Michelle Perrot, "The New Eve and the Old Adam: French Women's Condition at the Turn of the Century," in *Behind the Lines: Gender and the Two World Wars,* ed. Margaret Randolph Higonnet et al. (New Haven, 1987), 51–60; and Elaine Showalter, "Rivers and Sassoon: The Inscription of Male Gender Anxieties," in Higonnet et al., *Behind the Lines,* 61–69. See also the contributions to Richard Wall and Jay Winter, *The Upheaval of War: Family, Work and Welfare in Europe, 1914–1918* (Cambridge, 1988); and Susan Pedersen, *Family, Dependence, and the Origins of the Welfare State: Britain and France, 1914–1945* (Cambridge, 1993). A majority of French families even pressured the French state into supporting a campaign of "bringing the dead back home" so that the fallen soldiers could be buried in their family plots and home parishes. This reclaiming of the dead from the nation and the dead's reunion with their families had no parallel in either Great Britain or Germany after the war. See Jay M. Winter, *Sites of Memory, Sites of Mourning: The Great War in European Culture History* (forthcoming: Cambridge University Press, 1995).

3. In considering patriarchy to be one—historically contingent—form of male supremacy, I follow Linda Gordon, *Heroes of Their Own Lives: The Politics and History of Family Violence, Boston, 1880–1960* (New York, 1988), vi.

4. Cynthia Enloe, "Beyond Steve Canyon and Rambo: Feminist Histories of Militarized Masculinity," in Gillis, *The Militarization of the Western World,* 121.

5. In this assessment I differ from a number of studies claiming that after the war the old gender and family systems were reconstituted. See, for example, Renate Bridenthal and Claudia Koonz: "Beyond *Kinder, Küche, Kirche:* Weimar Women in Politics and Work," in *When Biology Became Destiny: Women in Weimar and Nazi Germany,* ed. Renate Bridenthal, Atina Grossmann, and Marion Kaplan (New York, 1984), 33–65. Ute Daniel coined the term "a lease on emancipation" ("Emanzipation auf Leihbasis") in Daniel, *Arbeiterfrauen in der Kriegsgesellschaft: Beruf, Familie und Politik im Ersten Weltkrieg* (Göttingen, 1989), 259–65. See also Sabine Hering, *Die Kriegsgewinnlerinnen: Praxis und Ideologie der deutschen Frauenbewegung im Ersten Weltkrieg* (Pfaffenweiler, 1990), esp. 142–47. A curious example is Wall and Winter, *The Upheaval of War.* The essays in this volume by Reinhard Sieder, "Behind the Lines: Working-Class Family Life in Wartime Vienna," 109–38, and by Jürgen Reulecke, "Männerbund versus the Family: Middle-Class Youth Movements and the Family in Germany in the Period of the First World War," 439– 52, show, in my opinion, that the postwar family was no longer the same as the prewar one. In his introduction to the volume, however, Richard Wall arrives at the conclusion that the war "first . . .

feature of the organization of nineteenth-century European societies, went hand in hand with those societies' rethinking of the state and of the relationship between the state and society.[6] The cultural war over the reconstruction of societies and their new system of gender relations formed one of the many battlefields of total war. In Germany, this struggle ended neither in 1918 with the cessation of armed conflict nor in 1924 with the conclusion of the cataclysmic period of revolution and counterrevolution. It ended only with the implementation of the new social order of National Socialism. This order owes its existence to World War I in a much more fundamental way than is commonly assumed. Neither the "trauma of defeat"—if it ever existed—nor the economic legacies of World War I nor, as I believe, the "brutalization of German politics" can explain Germany's commitment to the National Socialist project unless these factors are seen in the context of the wartime restructuring of the relations among production, reproduction, and destruction on the one hand and the related need for a new system of gender relations on the other.[7]

The central role of war for the organization of German society—and of the Western world at large—in the twentieth century cannot be denied. It would be wrong, however, to see the new configuration of the spheres of production, destruction, and reproduction in European societies, and the ensuing battle over a new system of gender relations, simply as results of the subordination of all sectors of state and society to the exigencies of total warfare. The mobilization of whole societies against whole societies was cer-

---

disturbed family life by military and industrial mobilisation; but, secondly, . . . released social and political forces which helped restore family life in its older forms" (Wall, introduction, 3). But see Mary Louise Roberts, *Civilization without Sexes: Reconstructing Gender in Postwar France, 1917–1927* (Chicago, 1994) who shows for France that there was not simply a "return" to prewar gender systems.

    6. The only author who—so far—also argues that the German family was dissolved as a result of Germany's social reorganization during World War I is Young Sun Hong. See "The Contradictions of Modernization in the German Welfare State: Gender and the Politics of Welfare Reform in First World War Germany," *Social History* 17, no. 2 (May 1992): 251–70, reprinted here in this volume.

    7. Ulrich Heinemann and Geyer both have convincingly—albeit to no avail—argued that the "trauma of defeat" and the related issue of a perceived mood of "revenge for Versailles" belong more in the realm of historical legends than in that of facts. See Ulrich Heinemann, *Die verdrängte Niederlage: Politische Öffentlichkeit und Kriegsschuldfrage in der Weimarer Republik* (Göttingen, 1983); and Michael Geyer, "Nation, Klasse und Macht: Zur Organisation von Herrschaft in der Weimarer Republik," *Archiv für Sozialgeschichte* 26 (1986): 44 n. 44. See also Cynthia Enloe's reflections on perceptions of "lost" wars and "national humiliation" in "Beyond Steve Canyon," esp. 123–24. On the controversy about the economic collapse of the Weimar Republic, see Ian Kershaw, *Weimar: Why Did German Democracy Fail?* (London, 1990). On the "brutalization of German politics," see George Mosse, *Fallen Soldiers: Reshaping the Memory of the World Wars* (New York, 1990), esp. 159–81. But see also Robert Weldon Whalen, *Bitter Wounds: German Victims of the Great War, 1914–1939* (Ithaca, 1984), who shows that the war experience did not necessarily lead to a general and all-encompassing "brutalization."

tainly *necessary* because of the requirements of total war; total war was in turn *possible,* however, because a rearrangement of the spheres of production and reproduction and, consequently, of the social organization of violence had been under way since the late nineteenth century.

War, as military historians have argued, is at the center of the organization of society in the twentieth century, but it neither occupies this center alone, nor has it moved there solely because of the complex set of factors commonly described as the "industrialization of war."[8] Rather, war moved toward the center of society because the positioning of production and reproduction in the structure of society changed. In the late nineteenth century, reproduction moved progressively from the periphery to the center of the social organization of society, not exactly replacing production but rearranging the relationship between production and reproduction and redefining their role for the social and cultural construction of society and the global political order. This new constellation of production, reproduction, and destruction emerged as part of the discursive shift toward the "culture of scientism," which transformed the project of modernity in the Western world in the late nineteenth century. This discursive shift consisted of an attempt to reorganize all economic, cultural, social, and political relations on the basis of "applied science."

While the "scientific" organization of social and cultural relations in the sphere of production had gained ground steadily throughout the nineteenth century, it was not until the late 1880s that societies discovered that science could be applied to the realm of the biological reproduction of society. This discovery changed the relationship between the spheres of production and reproduction fundamentally. If reproduction were no longer connected to the uncontrollable forces of nature but instead could be subjected to the controlling forces of science, as eugenicists, racial hygienists, and bourgeois feminists argued, then it could—or, rather, had to—be removed from its assigned place in the "private" (female) sphere and transferred to the "public" (male) sphere instead. European nations no longer linked concepts of national identity, strength, and international competitiveness—now often termed "survival"— primarily or exclusively to their productive capacity but rather to their quantitative and qualitative reproductive capacity. Under the influence of sociobiological concepts in general and Darwinist concepts—or pseudo-Darwinist ones, as the case may be—in particular, the biological reproduction of society gradually moved from the periphery to the center of the social organization of society, of imagining the nation and of rethinking the global order. Most Western states began to develop concerns about the "health" of their respective national "bodies," and international competition no longer

---

8. On the "industrialization of war," see Geyer, "The Militarization of Europe." See also Michael Geyer, *Deutsche Rüstungspolitik, 1860–1980* (Frankfort a.M., 1984).

centered solely on efforts to out-produce other nations but increasingly on efforts to out-reproduce other nations.[9]

This shift in thinking and organizing society changed European societies' perceptions about the means and goals of national and international competition quite radically. Imagining competition as competition about market shares did not necessarily require the complete physical and spiritual destruction of a competitor. Defining competition in connection with the concept of the "survival of the fittest," however, entailed the subjugation or ultimate extinction of the "other." Without the "scientization" of reproduction and reproduction's subsequent new role in the social and cultural construction of societies and of the imagined global order, total war and the militarization of the twentieth-century world cannot fully be understood. By this I do not mean to say that competition for racial hegemony ranked high among the causes of World War I, although imperialist discourses had become increasingly racist. Racist discursive strategies, which linked the biological reproduction of society to the "survival" of the nation, did, however, contribute to the organization and protraction of a war that, originally intended to last a few short weeks, dragged on for four nightmarish years.[10]

---

9. During the past twenty years, historians in the history of science and of medicine have produced an impressive body of work on social Darwinism, eugenics, neo-Lamarckism, and the concepts of evolution and race. Although some of these studies explicitly link the "scientization" of human reproduction to the development of National Socialism, they stop short of pursuing the consequences of their findings for our understanding of the changing roles of production and reproduction in the social and cultural organization of Western societies at the end of the nineteenth century and the beginning of the twentieth. The same is true for those studies that have explored the Third Reich's "therapeutic state." Scientism, professionalism, and racism—and violence, for that matter—are usually explored without examining their shared foundation: reproduction's new and central role in thinking and organizing society. On the scientization of human reproduction, see Daniel Gasman, *The Scientific Origins of National Socialism: Social Darwinism in Ernst Haeckel and the Monist League* (New York, 1971); Daniel Kevles, *In the Name of Eugenics: Genetics and the Uses of Human Heredity* (New York, 1985); Stephen J. Gould, *Ontogeny and Phylogeny* (Cambridge, Mass., 1977); Peter Weingart, "The Rationalization of Sexual Behavior: The Institutionalization of Eugenic Thought in Germany," *Journal of the History of Biology* 20, no. 2 (Summer 1987): 159–93; Peter J. Bowler, *Evolution: The History of an Idea*, 2d. ed. (Berkeley, 1989), esp. chap. 10; and Paul Weindling, *Health, Race and German Politics between National Unification and Nazism, 1870–1945* (Cambridge, 1989). But see as an exception David G. Horn's study, *Social Bodies: Science, Reproduction and Italian Modernity* (Princeton, N.J. 1994), which appeared after this essay was submitted to the publisher. On the therapeutic state—the state envisioned as a gigantic hospital to cure the "ills" of society—and the participation of scientific elites in this new construction of the state, see, for example, Robert Proctor, *Racial Hygiene: Medicine under the Nazis* (Cambridge, Mass., 1988).

10. I want to emphasize that this was by no means a specifically—let alone "peculiarly"—German development. On the scientization of race and the subsequent new racism, see, in addition to the titles in note 9, Bernard Semmel, *Imperialism and Social Reform: English Social-Imperial Thought, 1895–1914* (London, 1960); Leon Poliakov, *The Aryan Myth: A History of Racist and*

These years both allowed and forced German society to restructure itself and to experiment with a new social order more thoroughly than other Western nations. This stemmed, on the one hand, from Germany's lack of colonies as resources for the organization of war and, on the other hand, from Germany's deep commitment to the project of modernity. In order to wage and sustain total war, Germany had to pursue a path of radical self-exploitation of its national resources and therefore endured the militarization and mobilization necessary for war to a much greater degree than either France or Great Britain. A large sector of German society also greeted the war as a chance to reconstruct society on a new basis.[11]

Although the new social order, defined as the community of the *Volk* (*Volksgemeinschaft*), met with growing resistance during the war and was temporarily defeated in the revolution of 1918–19, key elements remained in place and became part of the social organization of the Weimar Republic. While military historians have argued this point regarding the new relationship between production and destruction most cogently, they have paid little attention to the principal factor of militarized societies' new approach to organizing *reproduction*.[12] Most social historians, on the other hand, who have produced an impressive body of work on the social and biological reproduction of society during World War I, do not see the fundamental changes that occurred in European society during the war in the context of this all-encompassing process of militarization of twentieth-century Europe. They consequently

Nationalist Ideas in Europe (New York, 1974); John S. Haller, *Outcasts from Evolution: Scientific Attitudes of Racial Inferiority, 1859–1900* (Urbana, 1975); George L. Mosse, *Toward the Final Solution: A History of European Racism* (New York, 1978); and Michael Banton, *Racial Theories* (Cambridge, 1987). On reproduction, racism, and imperialism, see Hans-Günther Zmarzlik, "Social Darwinism in Germany," in *From Republic to Reich: The Making of the Nazi Revolution*, ed. Hajo Holborn (New York, 1972), 435–74; and Anna Davin, "Imperialism and Motherhood," *History Workshop* 5 (Spring 1978): 9–65.

11. On the role of the English and French colonies in the war, see Ernest A. Benians et al., eds., *The Cambridge History of the British Empire*, vols. 5–8 (New York and Cambridge, 1932–36); and Christopher M. Andrew and A. S. Kanya-Forstner, *France Overseas: The Great War and the Climax of French Imperial Expansion* (London, 1981). On Germany's organization for war, see Gerald D. Feldman, *Army, Industry and Labor in Germany, 1914–1918* (Princeton, 1966); Ludwig Preller, *Sozialpolitik in der Weimarer Republik* (Düsseldorf, 1978), 3–85; and Jürgen Kocka, *Facing Total War: German Society, 1914–1918* (Leamington Spa, Warwickshire, 1984). A comparative project on Paris, London, and Berlin during World War I shows that the wartime restructuring of the respective societies had graver consequences for the German population's economic and social well-being than for that of the French or the British populations. See J. M. Winter, "Paris, London, Berlin: Capital Cities at War, 1914–1920," *International Labor and Working-Class History*, no. 44 (Fall 1993): 106–18; and Jay Winter and Joshua Cole, "Fluctuations in Infant Mortality Rates in Berlin during and after the First World War," *European Journal of Population* 9 (1993); 235–63. See also Jay M. Winter and Jean-Louis Robert, *Paris, London, Berlin: Capital Cities at War, 1914–1919* (forthcoming: Cambridge University Press, 1996).

12. See note 1.

overlook the role of war in the social organization of postwar societies, as well as militarized societies' new ways of gendering the relations among production, reproduction, and destruction. They also overlook what I consider to be one of the key links between World War I and the rise of fascism and National Socialism: the militarization of the sphere of reproduction and of gender relations.[13]

The National Socialist project of recreating German society and the global order on the basis of racist reproductive politics is, in the final analysis, grounded in the Western world's project of modernity in general and in the German Empire's passionate pursuit of that project specifically. However, those groups in Germany that had begun to envision a new social order based on a new role of reproductive politics and on a reorganization of society on the basis of "applied science" gained through World War I an unforeseen and unrivaled chance for experimenting with their social vision. During World War I Germany sought to create a national community of the *Volk,* devoted to the survival of the nation. Later, National Socialism managed to capitalize on the new discursive strategies developed during the Great War and also exploited the fears and anxieties that this experiment had engendered. National Socialism reorganized German society on the basis of racist reproductive politics while at the same time ending the gender conflict that had resulted from the thorough militarization of reproductive politics and gender relations in World War I—without, however, reinstituting patriarchy.[14]

National Socialism grew out of World War I, and while it is true, as I have argued above, that the war had in a way grown out of the German Empire, it had also outgrown it. World War I, in my opinion, therefore constitutes not a "link" between the Second and the Third Reich but a radical rupture in German

---

13. See note 5.

14. The question whether or not the Third Reich was grounded in the project of modernity has been—and still is—as hotly debated as the question of how to define the project of modernity. I consider the "rationalization" and "scientization" of *all* spheres of society and *all* aspects of human interaction and the subsequent rearrangement of the spheres of production, reproduction, and destruction to be at the core of that project, as well as of the Third Reich's therapeutic state. To argue this does not mean, as Michael Burleigh and Wolfgang Wippermann claim in their polemical refutation of modernization theories that "all our societies are latently like Nazi Germany" (Michael Burleigh and Wolfgang Wippermann, *The Racial State: Germany, 1933–1945* [Cambridge, 1991], 304). It does mean, however, that Nazi Germany and contemporary and current Western nations share the same foundations. National Socialist racist reproductive politics were a straightforward application of late-nineteenth-century science to the organization of society and to the structure of a new global order. This, of course, is hard to swallow if we want to continue "otherizing" the Third Reich. See Christopher Browning's critique of this position in his review "Barbarous Utopia," *Times Literary Supplement,* 20 March 1992, 5. On the role of eugenicist discursive strategies for the acceptability of National Socialist racist politics, see Claudia Koonz, "Genocide and Eugenics: The Language of Power," in *Lessons and Legacies: The Meaning of the Holocaust in a Changing World,* ed. Peter Hayes (Evanston, Ill., 1991), 155–77.

history. It is this rupture more than any kind of perceived continuity between pre- and postwar German society that produced National Socialism in Germany—and fascism in other countries. In the following pages, I will describe what I see as the beginnings of a new social and cultural construction of German society by examining the militarization of reproduction and gender relations and the simultaneous gendering of the militarization of German society in World War I.

Militarizing Reproduction—Gendering Total War

Within a few weeks after the beginning of World War I, it became clear that those few observers who had predicted that the next international conflict would be of an entirely new character had been right. Expectations of yet another short war that would complement Germany's successful wars of unification by securing for the newly unified empire its "deserved" status as a world power proved to be illusory. Instead of welcoming its troops back by Christmas, German society began to prepare for a prolonged war that would alter its political, social, economic, and cultural fabric beyond recognition. The difference between the old prewar society and the new one that emerged out of the bloodbath of World War I was so fundamental that contemporary witnesses of this violent transformation repeatedly used the metaphor of "the death of the nineteenth century" to describe their experience. A whole era had ended, a whole world disappeared.[15]

The sense of irretrievable loss, melancholy, but also anger that permeates much of the wartime and postwar reflections on the war is inextricably linked to the carnage of the "war of machines," which dealt a death blow to the nineteenth century's hopes regarding technological, scientific, and cultural progress.[16] The "forces" of industrialization and modernization that had been expected to simultaneously eliminate poverty, disease, and social strife did not lead to a better life for the majority of Germans but instead produced death and destruction on a theretofore unimagined scale. Moreover, war did not, as politicians had promised and a plethora of intellectuals had not tired of asserting, produce the transition from a civilization based on conflict to a community of the *Volk* based on harmony; rather, it deepened or created new divisions between classes, between shopkeepers and consumers, between city and countryside, between bureaucrats and citizens, between veterans and civilians, and, above all, between women and men. The radical restructuring of gender

---

15. In order to keep the number of footnotes to this essay within a reasonable limit, I shall refrain from referring to easily accessible general histories of World War I.

16. On feelings of loss and melancholy and the development of the "defensive personality" and its neuroses, see, in addition to Whalen, *Bitter Wounds,* Eric J. Leed, *No Man's Land: Combat and Identity in World War I* (Cambridge, 1979), esp. 105–14, 163–92.

relations that constituted one of the key factors of German society's organization for total war did not affect everybody in the same way. Different social classes experienced the militarization of gender and the gendering of war differently; so did different age groups, and so did men and women. There was no one in German society, however, who was not affected by the collapse of the old system of gender relations and the battle over what was to replace it. How did this process work, and what were its main elements?

Total mobilization for war encompassed every woman, every man and every child in German society. This was a result of the "industrialization of warfare" and the ensuing subordination of all spheres of German society to the demands of war. The creation of a front that consisted of two parts, a "front" and a "home front," was an essential element of total war. The interdependency of these two fronts destroyed the barriers that had separated the military and civil society throughout the nineteenth century in Europe. When everyone became part of the "war machine," civil society ceased to exist. The front was everywhere, and everyone was at the front. The complete militarization of German society and the dissolution of the separation between the military and civil society were processes of the simultaneous deconstruction and reconstruction of gender roles and gender relations. This becomes clear when we try to understand how the home front and the front and their relationship toward each other were constructed.

Fighting on the home front did not simply mean that the simultaneously increasing demands for human "cannon fodder" and for arms production were met by turning more and more male workers into soldiers to be sent to the front and by channeling more and more women workers into armaments and armaments-related industries. It also meant converting the predominantly female home industries into war-related industries. The restructuring of the labor force had profound consequences for existing concepts of gender roles and for men's and women's roles in the family. Not only were traditional perceptions of "male" and "female" occupations and the related gendered wage system challenged; women also increasingly replaced men as the only or the primary breadwinner in the family. Moreover, "housework" assumed an entirely new role during the war. This was a result of the war's long duration, the Allied blockade of Germany, and the miserable failure of German war bureaucracies to manage ever scarcer resources.[17] Cooking, sewing, the home manufacture of goods that were previously bought, and, above all, the saving of precious resources and energy through the production of "substitutes" of all kinds—foods, soap, fuel, wax, to name a few—suddenly became important

---

17. On the chaotic organization of Germany's economy during World War I, see, in addition to Feldman, *Army, Industry and Labor,* Jay M. Winter, "Some Paradoxes of the First World War," in Wall and Winter, *The Upheaval of War,* 9–49.

aspects of the national war economy. Managing a household was no longer a "private" matter connected only to the more or less well functioning family economy; rather, it became an officially recognized and required contribution to the war effort. This deprivatization and nationalization of women's reproductive work gradually came to include their biological reproductive work. The longer the war lasted, the louder grew the din of those often shrill voices that demanded that government and public attention be turned to Germany's demographic survival. The machine-god of war seemed to swallow human lives with a greed that threatened the survival of the nation, or so it was argued. Women's biological reproductive work therefore could no longer remain a family affair; instead, it became a contribution to the war effort and, thereby, a national duty.[18]

The recruitment of women into formerly "male" occupations and the deprivatization and simultaneous nationalization of all aspects of women's reproductive work resulted from the collapse of the barrier between the military and civil society. They, in turn, brought about the collapse of the barrier that had previously been constructed as separating the "private" (female) and the "public" (male) spheres. The militarization of German society thus destroyed the principal foundation of the system of gender inequality that had characterized bourgeois society in the nineteenth century. It also destroyed the family model that had developed together with the perceived system of separate spheres. By removing men from their families, by moving women into the position of the principal familial breadwinner, and by separating women's reproductive work from the context of the family, militarization dissolved both the family as the institution that guaranteed the reproduction of bourgeois society and the power basis for the role of the family patriarch.

Although the institutional power of the family and the system of patriarchy were destroyed, male supremacy did not come to an end. Rather, male domination over women was reconstituted on different grounds in a tense and often bitter struggle—a struggle, moreover, in which women actively participated as both promoters and opponents of the new social order. The main foundation of the new system of gender inequality consisted of the generally

---

18. On the war's effects on women's role in the labor force and on private households, see Daniel, *Arbeiterfrauen;* see also Ute Daniel, "Women's Work in Industry and Family: Germany, 1914–18," in Wall and Winter, *The Upheaval of War,* 267–96; Winter, "Some Paradoxes"; and Richard Wall, "English and German Families and the First World War, 1914–18," in Wall and Winter, *The Upheaval of War,* 43–106. On women's reproductive work, see, in addition to Daniel, *Arbeiterfrauen,* Christoph Sachße, *Mütterlichkeit als Beruf: Sozialarbeit, Sozialreform und Frauenbewegung, 1871–1929* (Frankfurt a.M., 1986), 151–56; 162–73. Sachße describes the wartime development as the " 'socialization' of reproduction" (151). See also Cornelie Usborne, "Pregnancy Is the Woman's Active Service," in Wall and Winter, *The Upheaval of War,* 389–416.

accepted gendered division of the "killing fields"[19] into a male front and a female home front. Total mobilization destroyed the divisions between the military and civil society and between the "public" and the "private" spheres, only to replace them with the separation between the male combat zone of the battlefield and the female noncombat zone of producing and reproducing the means of destruction. The process of militarizing German society deprived men of their family-related foundations of power over women. It concomitantly endowed men, however, with a new foundation of power over women: the exclusive power to kill. Women's exclusion from the right—or duty, as it were—to use the arms that they produced became the new foundation for male supremacy. Beginning with World War I, male supremacy was no longer grounded in men's role in the family as an institution but in their relationships to the military as an institution. Men's dominance over women derived no longer from their role as *fathers* but from their role as *soldiers*.

In order to better understand the complexities of the new militarized system of male supremacy, it is first necessary to realize that the process of gendering the production and reproduction of the means of destruction into a female sphere and that of gendering the consumption of the means of destruction into a male sphere were neither self-evident nor "natural." By this, I mean to say that these two interrelated processes cannot be explained by simply referring to existing gender stereotypes, which characterized men as violent and women as pacifist. Rather, those stereotypes became increasingly blurred at the time of World War I. If we compare the gendered division of the killing fields among some of the belligerent nations, we find different approaches to the drawing of lines between women's and men's roles on the front or home front. There were, for example, women truck drivers and messengers in the British army, but not in the German army. There were even protracted conflicts in Germany over whether or not nurses could serve in field hospitals. As a result, German nurses often joined the Austrian army, which pursued less restrictive gender politics than the German army. Austria-Hungary also accepted women physicians as members of the army. The German military considered this practice unacceptable for its soldiers because, as doctors, women would have been of higher military rank than most soldiers. In addition, it was well known at the time that women served in the Russian revolutionary forces, and that there was a long-standing tradition of *soldaderas* fighting in Mexican armies, especially in the 1910 Mexican Revolution.[20] These examples help us

---

19. I use this term in order to emphasize that both front *and* home front participated in the process of killing and that front and home front were parts of a complex discursive and nondiscursive field of differentiated functions.

20. On different approaches to women in the armed forces, see Arthur Marwick, *Women at War, 1914–1918* (London, 1977); Jean Bethke Elshtain, *Women and War* (New York, 1987); Anne Summers, *Angels and Citizens: British Women as Military Nurses, 1854–1914* (London and New

to understand that the creation of an exclusively male combat zone and the resulting system of gender inequality in Germany need further exploration.

Second, it is important to remember that basing male supremacy on men's role in combat did not reflect any superiority of the front over the home front in the organization of total war. Rather, as I have argued above, the "industrialization of warfare," with its demands on armaments production and on the nationalization of the sphere of reproduction, had rendered obsolete notions that the production of death and the consumption of the means of death were of greater importance for the maintenance and outcome of the war than the home front production of the means to administer death. If we cannot relate the gendering of war and the consequent recasting of the power basis of male supremacy either to existing inflexible gender stereotypes or to the actual relationship between front and home front, what, then, informed the way in which war was gendered?

If we examine more closely the new role of women's reproductive work in organizing total war, it becomes evident that it was precisely the newly gained national importance of women's reproductive work that provided society with a new rationale and new tools for disempowering women rather than endowing them with new power, as some nineteenth-century bourgeois feminists had hoped. While the war's enormous demand for soldiers' lives could still be met by only sending *men* to the front, it nevertheless seriously depleted Germany's resources of male "cannon fodder" and thus threatened its future military strength or "fighting power" (*Wehrkraft*). Women's exclusion from combat, therefore, did not result from men trying to defend their right to kill as the last bastion of male power. Rather, women *had to be* confined to the home front because they had become one of society's most valuable resources, not just for the production of the means of destruction but also for the reproduction of the users of the means of destruction. It was precisely when and because militarization made German society more dependent on women's reproductive work than ever before that society's need to control that work, and thereby control women, took a quantum leap; women's subordination to men no longer derived from their role as wives and mothers of *families* but from their role as "mothers of the *nation*."[21]

York, 1988); and Elizabeth Salas, *Soldaderas in the Mexican Military: Myth and History* (Austin, 1990). See also—as a few examples out of many—the memoirs of the physician Käte Frankenthal, *Der dreifache Fluch, Jüdin, Intellektuelle, Sozialistin: Lebenserinnerungem einer Ärztin in Deutschland und im Exil* (Frankfurt a.M. and New York, 1981); and of the nurses Anne-Marie Wenzel, *Deutsche Kraft in Fesseln: Fünf Jahre deutscher Schwesterndienst in Sibirien (1916–1921)* (Potsdam, 1931); Helene Mierisch, *Kamerad Schwester, 1914–1918* (Leipzig, 1934); and Henriette Riemann, *Schwester der Vierten Armee: Ein Kriegstagebuch* (Berlin, 1930).

21. This issue had been debated for quite a while among eugenicists and racial hygienists. Ernst Haeckel's Monist League, for example, had favored women's emancipation, while at the

This connection forms an important part of the new configuration of reproduction and destruction. It is not, however, the whole picture. The thorough militarization of the sphere of reproduction, while guaranteeing men's domination over women on the one hand, also entailed, on the other, men's loss of freedom. Since biological reproduction requires the active or passive cooperation of both women and men, the reproductive rights of both sexes were curtailed when reproduction became subordinated to the perceived needs of a militarized nation. Militarized society, as I will show below, was interested not only in controlling women's reproductive work—and therefore, women's sexuality—but men's as well.

Why did women accept their continued subordination to men, although the perceived "value" of their lives for a militarized nation had surpassed that of men's? And why did men accept society's ruthless expenditure of their lives? There is no one answer to these questions. Women and men go to war and participate in the construction of male supremacy for a variety of reasons.[22] One of the principal factors of German women's and men's acceptance of the gendered organization of total war, however, was a public discursive strategy that developed simultaneously with the gendered reconstruction of militarized society. This discursive strategy reinscribed men's lives with a new and heightened value precisely at that historical moment when their lives became expendable, thereby turning total war's creation of a value imbalance between women's and men's lives upside down. Ironically, this novel value of male life was grounded on men's new closeness to death.

Men's contribution to the war effort was constructed as a "sacrifice of blood and lives"—their own as well as society's of its men—and this sacrifice was considered to be a more important contribution to the war than women's.[23]

---

same time redefining emancipation as a biological process, not a social one. Women, or so it was argued, could reach emancipation best by accepting their reproductive obligation to the nation, whereas "the full emancipation of women, ... based upon exact equality of the sexes, could lead to 'racial death'" (Gasman, *The Scientific Origins*, 99).

22. See Enloe, "Beyond Steve Canyon." On the analytical category "gender" and the difference between "feminine/masculine" and "female/male," see Joan Wallach Scott, "Gender: A Useful Category of Historical Analysis," and "On Language, Gender, and Working-Class History," in *Gender and the Politics of History,* by Joan Wallach Scott (New York, 1988), 28–50, 53–67.

23. "It needs," Oberst Bauer wrote in 1922, "in my opinion no further elaboration to explain that the main burden of war at the front—and this burden was indeed a bitter one—rested on men; so did the main part, quantitatively and, furthermore, qualitatively, of work at the home front" (Oberst Bauer, *Der große Krieg in Feld und Heimat: Erinnerungen und Betrachtungen,* 3d ed. [Tübingen, 1922], xv). Not only men but also women participated in this construction of a gendered imbalance between men's and women's contributions to the war effort. See, for example, "Wochenbericht einer tapferen Hausfrau," in which a woman continuously compared—and thus relativized—her suffering and that of the men at the front, in Ernst Johann, ed., *Innenansicht eines Krieges: Deutsche Dokumente, 1914–1918* (Munich, 1973), 232. See also Ulrich Linse,

This construction distorted the picture of the new gender hierarchy that the militarization of German society had created; it constituted, in fact, a substantial strategy of repression. This repression made it possible for German society to forget that men went to the front not to die but to injure and to kill other soldiers;[24] and that total war claimed women's lives and wounded women's bodies as much as it did men's.

While women directly experienced neither the machine war's new and horrifying ways of inflicting wounds on human bodies nor the new faces of death that men saw on the battlefields, total war did consume women's bodies in its own way. This process affected women of different social classes in different manners. Women of the working class and lower middle class paid a higher toll than affluent women. At work, women in certain sectors of armaments production found themselves exposed to chemicals that entered and changed their bodies as projectiles did men's. Women ammunition workers whose hair had turned a greenish color, for example, were a familiar sight in wartime Hamburg. The number of work accidents increased as a result of the wartime strain on women workers. Malnutrition and the concomitant weight loss and chronic fatigue made women more susceptible to diseases like influenza, pneumonia, and tuberculosis and raised pregnancy-related health risks.[25] Of the estimated 300,000 so-called civilian deaths that were directly related to the war, two thirds were women—an estimation that in my opinion is certainly

---

"'Saatfrüchte sollen nicht vermahlen werden!' Zur Resymbolisierung des Soldatentodes," *Kriegserlebnis: Der Erste Weltkrieg in der literarischen Gestaltung und symbolischen Deutung der Nationen*, ed. Klaus Vondung (Göttingen, 1980), 262–74; Hering, *Die Kriegsgewinnlerinnen*, 126; Karin Hausen, "The German Nation's Obligations to the Heroes' Widows of World War I," in Higonnet et al., *Behind the Lines*, 126–40; and Whalen, *Bitter Wounds*, 23–35, 79.

24. Elaine Scarry has recently recalled this to our consciousness; see her "Injury and the Structure of War," *Representations* 10 (Spring 1985): 1–51.

25. Avner Offer has recently questioned some of the standard assumptions about war-related starvation in Germany, without, however, denying the effects of an unbalanced and unsteady diet on the German population; Avner Offer, *The First World War: An Agrarian Interpretation* (Oxford, 1989), esp. 45–78. But see Jürgen Reulecke, "Der Erste Weltkrieg und die Arbeiterbewegung im Rheinisch-Westfälischen Industriegebiet," in *Arbeiterbewegung an Rhein und Ruhr*, ed. Jürgen Reulecke (Wuppertal, 1974), 222; and Volker Ullrich, *Kriegsalltag: Hamburg im Ersten Weltkrieg* (Cologne, 1982), 73–75, 93–96. See also Käte Kestien's antiwar novel *Als die Männer im Graben lagen* (Frankfurt a.M., 1935). This novel, as well as the letters that women wrote to the front, shows that many women experienced the war's effects on their bodies as damage not only to their health but also to their beauty. Women felt prematurely old and, much like the soldiers at the front, feared that their mutilated and scarred bodies would no longer be attractive and lovable. On men's fears, see Leed, *No Man's Land;* and Whalen, *Bitter Wounds*, esp. 49–57. An as yet completely ignored and unexplored facet of the war's consumption of women's bodies is the Red Cross's collections of women's hair; see the title page of Johann, *Innenansicht*. On the complex issue of "the body at war" see Jane Marcus, "Afterword: Corpus/Corps/Corpse: Writing the Body in/at War," in Helen Zenna Smith, *Not So Quiet . . . Stepdaughters of War* (2d ed.: New York, 1989), 241–300.

much too low.[26] War wounded not only women's bodies, however, but their souls as well. Constant worries about the lives of their loved ones at the front, as well as those of their children or elderly relatives at the home front, exacted their price. Many women consequently characterized the years of war as years that they had "lost" and experienced the death of a husband as the end of their own lives.[27]

Neither women's physical and psychological suffering nor their casualties were acknowledged in the public discourse about the war. Through war monuments, memorial days, and literature and films, this discourse created an image of the war according to which men sacrificed their lives for the "idle" and "helpless" women and children at home, whereas in reality men, women, and children had been drafted for active duty in total war. This construction served the dual purpose of reconciling men to the death sentence that society had imposed on them and of justifying the state's rejection of women's demands for greater political and social equality. This was clearly expressed in Wilhelm II's famous speech on Easter of 1917 (*Osterbotschaft*), in which he promised German workers electoral reforms. In this speech, women were never mentioned. Since women's active contribution to the war effort was not acknowledged, it did not seem necessary to grant voting rights to women.[28]

The discursive gendering of the killing fields into an arena of sacrificial death and a separate sphere of trivial life owed its acceptance not least to feelings of shame and guilt among those whose lives were spared toward the war dead.[29] These feelings guaranteed that the many-layered discursive veil that covered society's militarized form of male supremacy was not lifted. It successfully concealed men's loss of reproductive freedom. It hid the fact that the longer the war lasted, the more important women's reproductive work became for the current organization of war, as well as for the future organization of the militarized peace: women were to reproduce the new generation of soldiers. This discursive veil also prevented insight into the terrible truth that while the reproduction of a new generation of soldiers became increasingly important, individual men's lives grew increasingly cheap. Their lives became an accepted expenditure that was calculated in relation to the new weapons

---

26. The estimates are quoted from Winter, "Some Paradoxes," 30. I consider these estimates to be too low because they do not take into consideration the war's long-term effects on women's—and other "civilians'"—health and life span. A number of presumably "normal" deaths in the Weimar Republic are certainly war-related.

27. See Whalen, *Bitter Wounds,* esp. 69–77; and Hausen, "The German Nation's Obligations."

28. On the public discourse about the war, see Linse, "'Saatfrüchte'"; and Whalen, *Bitter Wounds,* 32–35, 181–92. On the *Osterbotschaft's* exclusion of women, see Hering, *Die Kriegsgewinnlerinnen,* 128.

29. On the cult of the fallen soldier, see Mosse, *Fallen Soldiers,* 70–106; and Linse, "'Saatfrüchte.'"

systems' firepower. Last, but not least, the veil covered the wounds that war inflicted on women. It shrouded their dead bodies and rendered invisible the fact that war claimed women's lives in massive numbers.

The veil was also intended to conceal the fact that, as in the German patriarchal system, where the domination of the "public" over the "private" sphere had not rendered either all men or all women equal, the new system of male supremacy did not eliminate but rather reconstituted other sources of power inequality between men and men, women and women, and women and men. Among them were ethnicity, age, and, above all, class. While most layers of the discursive veil were so tightly woven that it is still difficult for the historian's gaze to penetrate them, the layer that covered class relations was thoroughly torn asunder early in the war.[30] This occurred because the militarization of reproduction and the gendering of war destroyed the basis of the German working class's survival, that is, the family. Recovering the family as a unit of economic and social power was the issue that allowed for the formation of a discursive counterstrategy against the militarization of society and of an opposition movement against the war that would, finally, end the war.

This opposition, however, would not be able to win the battle over the postwar reconstruction of Germany, as I will argue. In order to explore these complex issues further, I will examine more closely the dissolution of the family and the ramifications it had on men and women. I will then explore the politics of two groups of women, those involved in the bourgeois women's movement and those of the working class, which developed competing discursive strategies about the organization of society during the war and which influenced the course of the war in decisive and, as I believe, as yet unrecognized ways. From there, I will return to the questions of continuity and discontinuity between wartime and postwar German society that I raised at the beginning of this essay.

The Dissolution of the Family during World War I

One of the most immediate, drastic, and enduring results of German society's gendered mobilization for total war was the disappearance of men—of fathers, husbands, brothers, and sons—from their families. By 1918 almost half of all German men between the ages of fifteen and sixty had been drafted. About two million of them never returned. Of those two million, one-third had been married.[31] While it is true that not every man went to the front, men did leave in sufficient numbers to make the home front seem to be women's territory and to

---

30. On the wartime deepening of class divisions, see especially Kocka, *Facing Total War.*

31. Sachße, *Mütterlichkeit,* 152; Winter, "Some Paradoxes," 27; and Hausen, "The Nation's Obligations," 128.

exchange the traditional family picture for one portraying only women and children.

The temporary or permanent absence of men from their families had immediate consequences for these families' ability to function as an economic unit. Families lost either their principal breadwinner or a family member who had contributed to the family income. The women, young adults, and children who remained, particularly those of the lower middle class and the working class, could not bridge the financial gap on their own. This was due to a continued gender and age bias in financial remuneration. Total war had destroyed the basis of the prewar system of gendering the labor market but not the imbalance between women's and men's, adults' and adolescents' wages, salaries, or pensions. While wage differentials between skilled and unskilled workers as well as between women and men did decrease during the war, women's average daily wages did not even reach 50 percent of the figure for men.[32] The separation of men from their families meant, therefore, that these families experienced an immediate drop in their standard of living and, with the increasing crisis in the supply of staples, an eventual slide into poverty. The strategies that remaining family members pursued in order to cope with their desperate economic situation contributed to the further erosion of the family unit. Families that depended on women's and/or young adults' employment in factories experienced this situation in different ways from families that tried to subsist by supplementing compensations for soldiers' families or pensions for soldiers' widows with income from work in the expanding home industries. Both types of family, however, endured changes that profoundly altered their character.

If we examine the situation of women workers during the war, we find that their percentage in the workforce did not rise as sharply as one might expect but remained within the prewar growth rate of female industrial employment. Thus the quantitative changes of women's participation in the labor market were rather insignificant; the qualitative changes, however, were quite dramatic. The number of women in military industries—in the iron and steel, metal and chemical industries and in coal mining—rose to between 100 and 800 percent of prewar figures. Most of the women who moved into these "male" industries did not enter the workforce for the first time in their lives but had worked either in other industries, especially in the textile, leather, and rubber industries, in agriculture, in domestic service, or in clerical jobs.[33] While many of them had experience with factory labor, all of these women had to get used to new and unfamiliar kinds of work, which often required more physical

---

32. Daniel, *Arbeiterfrauen,* 111–17; and Kocka, *Facing Total War,* 21–24.

33. See especially Daniel, *Arbeiterfrauen,* 35–50; Kocka, *Facing Total War,* 16–19; and Preller, *Sozialpolitik,* 7–8.

strength than the work that they had previously performed. Moreover, with the beginning of the war, workers' protection laws were revoked, which then enabled employers to stipulate longer working hours, to remove limitations on women's shift work, and to abolish provisions protecting women from exposure to hazardous substances.[34] In order to comprehend fully the consequences of this new work situation for women, we need to view these changes in the context of the overall economic situation in Germany. Food shortages and the authorities' inability to organize and enforce an efficient system of distributing the food that was available led to famine as early as 1915 and culminated in the notorious "turnip winter" (*Steckrübenwinter*) of 1916–17. By 1916, food rations had sunk below the minimal nutritional requirements for adults.[35] Women therefore not only found themselves exposed to harsher working conditions but were simultaneously unable to sustain their bodies and maintain their health.

While the overall immiseration of the working class affected women *and* men, only women suffered from a worsening of the conditions under which they performed their reproductive work. The shortage and rationing of food, fuels, and other supplies meant an increase in the hours that they had to spend on housework. Not only did they need more time to produce substitutes for the food that they had previously bought; they also spent hours waiting in line for those necessities that could be bought or scavenging both town and countryside in daytrips for those that could not. Since sixteen-hour workdays were not infrequent for women factory workers, women who lived alone with their children often chose to work night shifts in order to perform the increasingly difficult task of providing for their children and other family members during the day.[36] They could not spend the time that they had thus gained with their children, however, but had to invest these hours into securing the means to feed and clothe them.

The situation of working-class and lower middle-class women who did not work outside of their homes was not much better than that of those who did. State compensation for soldiers' wives and pensions for soldiers' widows were too low to allow the recipients and their families to get by, much less to maintain their prewar standard of living. The system of compensation payments for soldiers' families was structured so that it would not interfere with the existing military hierarchy, while concomitantly addressing the different economic needs of families. Thus, payments were not based on a man's last

34. Preller, *Sozialpolitik*, 9–11, 34–35, 37, 40–41, 43, 55–58.

35. Preller, *Sozialpolitik*, 9–11, 48; Kocka, *Facing Total War*, 21–26; Daniel, *Arbeiterfrauen*, esp. 183–232; and Armin Triebel, "Variations in Patterns of Consumption in Germany in the Period of the First World War," in Wall and Winter, *The Upheaval of War*, 159–95. But see Offer, *The First World War*.

36. See especially Daniel, *Arbeiterfrauen*, 212–32.

civilian income but rather on his military rank and the size of his family. Wives of common soldiers—the most common rank of lower middle-class and working-class men—were in the lowest compensation category. Payments consisted of a basic sum, to which an additional subsidy for every child in a soldier's family was added. Women could also apply for rent allowances and other subsidies, thus augmenting the overall amount of money they received. In most cases, however, payments were much lower than men's last prewar wages or salaries, and consequently most lower middle-class and working-class families of women who stayed home also experienced a sharp decline in their standard of living.[37]

In order to make ends meet, such women sublet rooms that had been vacated by men at the front, worked in part-time or temporary jobs, or took in homework or increased the amount they were already doing. This meant that women who stayed home also had much less time to spend with their children than before the war, especially since these women, too, had to spend a substantial amount of their time hunting for supplies or producing the goods that they had previously purchased. The gendered mobilization of German society for total war thus separated not only men but also women—whether they worked outside the home or not—from their families.

The erosion of the family was further exacerbated by the fact that children and young adults were also mobilized for total war. They were recruited into public works such as harvesting, selling war bonds, collecting money and material goods for welfare organizations, knitting socks for soldiers, preparing materials for the production of surgical dressing, helping in soup kitchens, and delivering mail. Many of these activities were organized on the basis of children's membership not in families but in peer groups, in most cases their classes at school. This form of mobilizing children for war further weakened existing family ties. This process was propelled further by the fact that families increasingly depended on children's and young adults' help to make ends meet. They would shop—that is, stand in line to get the family's staples—collect firewood, participate in the homework that their mothers took in, or, if all else failed, steal the much-needed food and supplies. In addition, teenagers of both sexes began to work in factories earlier than their counterparts had before the war. They also worked longer hours than their prewar predecessors.[38] While

---

37. On the compensation system and its failure to support women and children, see Daniel, *Arbeiterfrauen*, 29–34, 169–83; Sachße, *Mütterlichkeit*, 152–61; and Whalen, *Bitter Wounds*, esp. chaps. 5–8.

38. There is still no comprehensive study on young adults and children during World War I. On the mobilization of women students, see Daniel, *Arbeiterfrauen*, 97–98. On young adults in the labor force, see Preller, *Sozialpolitik*, 9. See also Whalen, *Bitter Wounds*, 78–81; Young Sun Hong, "The Contradictions"; and Elisabeth Domansky, "Politische Dimensionen von Jugendprotest und Generationenkonflikt in der Zwischenkriegszeit in Deutschland," in *Jugendprotest und Genera-*

children's and young adults' contributions to the subsistence of families helped individual family members survive, this could only be achieved by spending less time in the family and with other family members.

As I have shown, total war and the gendered militarization of German society destroyed the material basis of the family as an economic unit in manifold ways. Mobilizing men, women, and children as distinct and separate groups in different ways and for different purposes was the first step in dissolving actual family units. The gendered income structure and the supply crisis further contributed to the collapse of the family as a unit of economic power. Despite their efforts, most lower middle-class and working-class families could not make it by simply tapping the combined resources of remaining family members. The strategies that these families used to find needed resources constituted additional components of the process by which the prewar German family was dissolved. Two such tactics, the formation of new self-help groups and the use of the growing welfare system, were particularly important in this regard.

One of the principal strategies that lower middle-class and working-class women pursued in order to sustain themselves and their families was to cross the boundaries of the prewar nuclear family in order to pool resources. Women created informal networks among neighbors and relatives to share shopping, cooking, and care for children or elderly relatives. These new institutions for organizing and sharing reproductive work were often formed along kinship lines, including, for example, a grandmother, mother, aunt, children, and cousins, and were meant to last only for the duration of the war. These networks nevertheless contributed to the further dismantling of the nineteenth-century bourgeois family, especially since some of them continued to exist beyond the war's end.[39]

These new support networks not only dissolved actual families but the *model* of the family as an institution of economic and social power as well. Nothing, however, equaled the wartime state and private welfare system's contribution to the destruction of the nineteenth-century bourgeois family.[40] Because the men, women, and children who had been mobilized for total war

---

tionenkonflikt in Europa im 20. Jahrhundert: Deutschland, England, Frankreich und Italien im Vergleich, ed. Dieter Dowe (Bonn, 1986), esp. 116–26. This essay contains numerous bibliographical references.

39. On women's networks, see Daniel, *Arbeiterfrauen,* 125–139, esp. 138; and Whalen, *Bitter Wounds,* 110. See also Kestien, *Als die Männer im Graben lagen.*

40. There is an impressive body of literature on the emergence of the Western welfare state and its gendered nature. For a recent survey of the literature, see Seth Koven and Sonya Michel, "Womanly Duties: Maternalist Politics and the Origins of the Welfare States in France, Germany, Great Britain and the United States, 1880–1920," *American Historical Review* 95, no. 4 (Oct. 1990): 1076–1108. See especially Young Sun Hong, "The Contradictions," who also argues that the wartime welfare system dissolved the nineteenth-century bourgeois family.

were serving their country, and because the women and children who served at the home front could not survive on their own, the state and a number of public and private welfare organizations stepped in as substitutes for the absent men. Compensation payments for soldiers' wives, pensions for soldiers' widows and children, and a plethora of other social-welfare offerings were meant to ward off the worst hardships that split families had to endure. But because their compensation payments, pensions, and other provisions were not sufficient to replace the absent men economically, the state and numerous welfare organizations only contributed enough to enable these families to subsist, not to flourish. They did manage, however, through their financial assistance, to usurp men's and women's control over their families, thus playing an important part not in the protection but in the institutional erosion of the family.

The sharp fall in family income that most lower middle-class and working-class families experienced could be cushioned to some degree by supplementing state compensation payments, pensions, or wages and salaries with aid from welfare organizations. These agencies set up soup kitchens, collected and distributed food and clothing, offered medical care, organized classes in wartime household management, provided day-care facilities, and helped women find work. Thus, with the beginning of the war, large numbers of women and children began to profit for the first time from a social-welfare system that until then had been tailored to match the needs of industrial (male) workers. Their dependency on state and private welfare, however, also opened new ways for the administering organizations to gain control over the family. As mentioned, state bureaucracies and social reformers calculated compensation payments by granting a family a fixed sum of money, to which they added additional subsidies according to the number of children and the specific needs of a family. In doing so, they helped many women and children cope with growing poverty. Simultaneously, however, this compensatory procedure enabled these bureaucracies to impose their opinions on needy families about how much money they should spend and on what, thereby reducing families' autonomy in budgeting their income. The dream of nineteenth-century social reformers, who had tried to fight a war against poverty not by redistributing social wealth but by teaching lower middle-class and working-class women the "efficient" management of low-budget households thus came true in the early twentieth century, when World War I produced both the opportunity, in the theretofore unknown level of poverty, and the means, in state and welfare organizations, to control families through their pocketbooks. One of the most blatant, if ultimately unsuccessful, attempts of state authorities to interfere with families' budgets were the so-called forced-savings decrees (*Sparzwangerlasse*). These decrees allowed employers to freeze a portion of young women's and men's wages in savings accounts to which they and their families had no access during the course of the war, in order to prevent young people from spending their money on "superfluous" items. Most young people worked, however, not because they wanted to spend money on leisure-time activities or "luxuries" but because their families were dependent on their additional income. The forced-savings decrees, therefore, led to massive protests and strikes by young men and women and eventually were abolished.[41]

In addition to a loss of autonomy regarding the family budget, women and men also lost control over the reproductive functions of the family. The militarization of German society and the gendering of war dissolved the family not only as an economic unit but also as the institution that contained and controlled women's and men's sexuality, their biological reproduction, and the raising of children. Drafting men to the front and mobilizing women and children for the home front separated not only families from their principal breadwinners but also women and men from their sexual partners and children from their primary caretakers. Since, as I have argued above, with the duration of the war, concerns about Germany's demographic survival gained ground in German society, the state stepped in to secure the biological reproduction and the spiritual and physical well-being of the future generation. In order to guarantee not just the quantitative but also the qualitative reproduction of a "healthy" nation, the state increasingly diminished parental autonomy regarding children's spiritual and physical health, women's and men's reproductive freedom, and women's and men's sexual autonomy.[42]

German society's wartime sexual politics was based on the assumption that heterosexuality was the norm of sexual orientation. The dominant concept of heterosexuality assumed that men were sexually aggressive and needed to be sexually active in order to maintain their physical and emotional health. Their sexuality and their reproductive function were thus constructed as separate entities.[43] Women, by contrast, were considered to be sexually passive, and their sexuality and reproductive function were considered to be inseparable. Moreover, because of their assumed innate weakness of character, women were thought to require male control of both their sexuality and their reproduc-

---

41. On state allowances for soldiers' families and widows, see Whalen, *Bitter Wounds,* 75–77; 88–91; Daniel, *Arbeiterfrauen,* 169–83. On the forced-savings decrees, see Daniel, *Arbeiterfrauen,* 163–67.

42. Magnus Hirschfeld, Andreas Gaspar, et al., *Sittengeschichte des Ersten Weltkrieges,* 2d ed. (Hanau a.M.; 1966), contains a wealth of information regarding the wartime discourse about sexuality, although it presents its findings as an accurate reflection of a perceived "reality." On the state's interference in sexuality and reproduction, see Daniel, *Arbeiterfrauen,* 139–47; Usborne, "Pregnancy"; and Weindling, *Health,* esp. 282–85; see also Paul Weindling, "The Medical Profession, Social Hygiene and the Birth Rate in Germany, 1914–18," in Wall and Winter, *The Upheaval of War,* 417–37.

43. Weingart, "The Rationalization of Sexual Behavior."

tive work. During World War I, the state and military authorities therefore stepped in to meet soldiers' perceived sexual needs, as well as to control women's sexuality in lieu of the absent men.

Military authorities procured front brothels and organized soldiers' visits to prostitutes. The same state that had deprived its soldiers of their sexual partners at home thus provided them with new sexual partners and opportunities for sexual activity. This occurred, however, not because military authorities were interested in the individual soldier's happiness but because they wanted to maintain troop morale and, thereby, Germany's military fighting power (*Wehrkraft*). Thus men's sexuality was deprivatized and "nationalized," that is, subordinated to the needs of a nation at war. This functionalization of male sexuality for the purpose of war deprived men of their autonomy in choosing sexual partners and the circumstances of sexual encounters. Moreover, the state, through its military authorities, even tried to interfere with the kind of sex that soldiers practiced. In order to prevent the spread of venereal diseases, war authorities distributed condoms and promoted their use. Again, this happened not in the interest of the individual soldier's health but because such diseases, like other epidemic diseases, were considered to be a serious threat to Germany's *Wehrkraft*. While at the beginning of the war, men's sexuality and reproductive function were treated as distinct entities, they became increasingly linked when concerns about Germany's demographic survival caught the attention of military authorities. Venereal diseases were no longer primarily linked to Germany's current fighting power but to that of its future. These diseases were now perceived as impairing men's fertility and creating a serious hazard for their wives' and, therefore, the future generation's health. Men's sexual practices thus had to be controlled in order to guarantee the biological reproduction of a "healthy" nation.

As we have seen, the state—in this instance, military authorities—stepped in for the absent women and provided men with sexual partners. This process not only affirmed existing gender stereotypes about men's sexual drives but simultaneously separated men's sexuality from the context of the family. Men's sexuality became subordinated first to the nation's need of sexually satisfied and thus highly motivated soldiers and second to its need of healthy soldier-fathers, that is, soldiers as future fathers and as fathers of future soldiers. While double moral standards about men's and women's sexuality were maintained and contributed to the continued subordination of women to men, men nevertheless lost their sexual and reproductive autonomy when their sexuality was separated from the family and connected to the nation.

Women's sexual and reproductive autonomy, which had been restricted by the prewar system of gender relations, was even further diminished by society's wartime effort to nationalize their sexuality and their biological reproductive work. In order to maintain troop morale, as well as the moral double standards of German society, the state felt called upon not only to provide its soldiers with opportunities for sexual activity but also to safeguard their sexual "property" at home. Women's sexual activity thus came under close surveillance in order to prevent them from having extramarital sexual relations. State control of prostitution was tightened, and it became legally admissible to report women who had several male visitors in a month's time to the police as suspected prostitutes. In cases where such denunciations occurred repeatedly, women could be forced to register as prostitutes. Such regulations should not be read as a reflection of the state's attempt to keep women sexually within the confines of the family. Rather, since the state's control of women's sexuality occurred in the context of maintaining troop morale, women's sexuality, like men's, was deprivatized and nationalized in the context of German society's reorganization for total war. Women no longer possessed the opportunity of negotiating their sexual activity with their husbands—or with their fathers and brothers, for that matter—but were now forced to confront extrafamilial, public authorities—that is, the state.

Women lost not only their sexual but also their reproductive freedom. In order to understand the complexities of this process, we have to bear in mind that the mobilization for war and the gendering of war reduced women's reproductive autonomy in two ways. First, men's absence and women's poverty, exhaustion, malnutrition, and illness reduced women's chances of conceiving and giving birth to and of breastfeeding and maintaining children. Due to physical and emotional stress, many women suffered from the so-called famine or war amenorrhea, that is, the cessation of menstruation. Many women who did give birth to children were, for the same reasons, unable to breastfeed them, thus severely impairing their chances of survival. Second, we must remember that this situation alarmed the wartime state and society, but not because women were deprived of reproductive choices. Rather, Germany's health professionals—physicians, racial hygienists, and eugenicists—and other groups, such as demographers, politicians, and members of the bourgeois women's movement, joined the military in developing discursive strategies concerning Germany's demographic survival. The military, German health professionals, and the numerous and varied specialists of reproduction, while vying for power with each other, increasingly gained influence over state policies and legislation. During the course of the war, labor protection laws for women workers were reintroduced, and women who bore and then breastfed children were granted higher food rations. Such positive pronatalist politics were complemented by negative ones. In order to secure a high birth rate, the same state that provided its soldiers at the front with condoms in order to maintain their health banned the advertisement of contraceptives at the home front and attempted to pass new laws that were meant to tighten the existing abortion laws.[44]

These laws were introduced in parliament so shortly before the revolution and the subsequent end of the war that they could not be passed. The parliamentary and public debates about those laws and about reproductive politics show, however, that the state and broad strata in German society had abandoned the concept of the family as the nucleus of German society. Women and men were no longer considered to be responsible for reproducing bourgeois society through the institution of the family but rather, through the surrender of their reproductive capacity to the nation. In this context, the traditional concept of the state was replaced by a new one. Once seen as consisting of a myriad of nuclear families, the state was now reconstituted as a militarized national family (*Wehrfamilie*) consisting of men, women, and children in their respective—and separate—gender and age camps.

The new concept of the state had direct ramifications for mainstream moral standards and assumptions about parental authority. The state and several parts of German society were willing to abolish the legal inequality of legitimate and illegitimate children. During the war, efforts were made to eradicate legal discrimination against children born out of wedlock, because this discrimination was seen as contributing to these children's disproportionately high mortality rate. Moreover, the wartime state began to interfere directly with parental authority regarding children's health. Regular physical checkups for children, conducted by physicians in schools, were organized. If it was deemed necessary, children could be temporarily removed from their families and sent to the countryside to improve their health (*Kinderlandverschickung*).[45] The attempts to end the legal discrimination of illegitimate children and the usurpation of parental authority over children's health by state and public health authorities did not occur in the interest of those individual children but in the interest of the nation's "health." Both processes completed the wartime dissolution of the family as a reproductive unit.

While the new reproductive politics led to a loss of women's and men's sexual and reproductive freedom, the increasing emphasis on the production of "healthy" offspring and the concomitant link between the health of individual bodies and that of the imagined "national body" simultaneously introduced and

---

44. On pronatalism and attempts to control women's sexuality and biological reproductive work, see especially Usborne, "Pregnancy." On famine amenorrhea, see Emmanuel Le Roy Ladurie, "Die Hungeramenorrhoe (17.–20. Jahrhundert)," in *Biologie des Menschen in der Geschichte: Beiträge zur Sozialgeschichte der Nenzeit aus Frankreich und Skandinavien,* ed. Arthur E. Imhof, Kultur und Gesellschaft: Neue historische Forschungen, vol. 3 (Stuttgart, 1978), 147–66.

45. On the state's medical intervention in families', especially children's, health, see Weindling, "The Medical Profession"; and Young Sun Hong, "The Contradictions."

legitimized racist concepts into the public discourse about reproductive politics. I use the term "racist" to refer to all reproductive policies and politics that differentiate between degrees of desirability of human lives, whether such judgments are based on health, beauty, ethnicity, race, or other such culturally constructed criteria, and that assume a "right"—or a "necessity," as it were—to include or exclude individuals from existing or future collectives. The implicit or explicit racism of reproductive politics that were pursued by different groups in World War I Germany, in my opinion, sheds new light on other racist wartime politics. During World War I, anti-Semitism was on the rise. Jews were discriminated against because of their perceived avoidance of military service, that is, their assumed unwillingness to surrender to the nation.[46] The extremist Fatherland Party (Vaterlandspartei), which was founded in 1917 as the political channel of Germany's strong prowar movement, was, not coincidentally, also anti-Semitic.[47] In addition, war aims promoted by numerous groups in German society, such as the Pan-German League or German intellectuals, clearly expressed the notion of German superiority over ethnic populations in Eastern Europe. Moreover, the concept of Germany's cultural mission in World War I—that is, to liberate the world from the dangerous "ideas of 1789" and to replace those French and British values with the German "ideas of 1914"—reflected assumptions about Germany's ethnically grounded cultural superiority.[48] All of these developments—the increasing anti-Semitism, the fantasies of the subordination of Eastern Europe, and the project of Germany's cultural mission—cannot be fully understood unless we see them in the context of wartime reproductive politics. Those politics simultaneously emphasized both the need for reproductive competition with groups within and outside of Germany, because of Germany's wartime loss of population, and the possibility of engaging successfully in such re-

---

46. See Egmont Zechlin, *Die deutsche Politik und die Juden im Ersten Weltkrieg* (Göttingen, 1969).

47. On the Vaterlandspartei, see Dirk Stegmann, "Zwischen Repression und Manipulation: Konservative Machteliten und Arbeiter- und Angestelltenbewegung, 1910–1918: Ein Beitrag zur Vorgeschichte der DAP/NSDAP," *Archiv für Sozialgeschichte* 12 (1972): 351–432; Dirk Stegmann, "Vom Neokonservatismus zum Proto-Faschismus: Konservative Partei, Vereine und Verbände, 1893–1920," in *Deutscher Konservatismus im 19. und 20. Jahrhundert: Festschrift für Fritz Fischer*, ed. Dirk Stegmann, Bernd-Jürgen Wendt, and Peter-Christian Witt (Bonn, 1983), 218–33.

48. On Germany's war aims, see Fritz Fischer's classic study *Griff nach der Weltmacht: Die Kriegszielpolitik des kaiserlichen Deutschland, 1914/18* (Düsseldorf, 1961). See also Roger Chickering, *We Men Who Feel Most German: A Cultural Study of the Pan-German League, 1886–1914* (Boston, 1984). On war aims and the "ideas of 1914," see Reinhard Rürup, "Der 'Geist von 1914' in Deutschland: Kriegsbegeisterung und Ideologisierung des Krieges im Ersten Weltkrieg," in *Ansichten vom Krieg: Vergleichende Studien zum Ersten Weltkrieg in Literatur und Gesellschaft*, ed. Bernd Hüppauf (Königstein/Ts., 1984), 1–30. See also Klaus Vondung, "Geschichte als Weltgericht: Genesis und Degradation einer Symbolik," in Vondung, *Kriegserlebnis*, 62–84.

productive competition, because of the state's and professional bureaucracies' gain of power over the social and biological reproduction of German society.[49] The war's racist reproductive strategies thus tied together and endowed with future potential the various racist projects that were developed in World War I Germany.

The processes of militarizing reproduction and gendering total war and the subsequent dissolution of the system of patriarchy and the nineteenth-century bourgeois family did not proceed smoothly. Even among those who actively promoted these processes, there were debates about how to do so most efficiently and, above all, who should be in control of the wartime reorganization of the social and biological reproduction of society. Moreover, among those groups that felt the consequences of German society's reorganization for war most drastically, resentment and, later, open protest developed because of the state's and society's rampant mismanagement in the reorganization of the spheres of production and reproduction. In order to cast light on different groups' interests and politics in wartime Germany, I will now explore the politics of two groups of women, those involved in the German bourgeois women's movement and those of the working class.

Reproducing Class or Nation?

The process of militarizing the sphere of production in World War I Germany was neither centralized nor exclusively state-controlled. Rather, the reorganization of German armaments production was negotiated between German industry and the military, thus fundamentally changing the character of what is usually called the "military-industrial complex"—that is, the relationship among state, military, and industry.[50] The process of militarizing the sphere of reproduction in World War I Germany occurred in a similar fashion. Numerous state bureaucracies, religious, and professional organizations, and semiprivate and private organizations participated in the nationalization of society's sphere of reproduction, vying with each other and with the state for control over this process.[51] The German bourgeois women's movement played a key role in mobilizing German society for war. This resulted from its "truce" with the German state, which was forged in August 1914, mirroring the so-called *Burg-*

---

49. On the Monist League's racist expectations of the war's effects, see, for example, Gasman, *The Scientific Origins,* 126–29. For readers less familiar with the history of eugenicism and racial hygiene, I would like to mention that the Monist League and other eugenicist groups were by no means marginal right-wing fringe groups in German society. Rather, they belonged to the mainstream of Germany's cultural elite. Haeckel's public standing, for example, was comparable to that of Charles Darwin in England or Albert Einstein in the United States.

50. See Feldman, *Army.*

51. This further supports the argument of the German state's weakness. See Geyer, "Nation, Klasse und Macht."

frieden between the state and the working class.[52] Much more important than its wartime contribution, however, was the bourgeois women's movement's prewar contribution to "thinking the war," that is, to developing discursive strategies that aimed at the nationalization of women's reproductive work. While the bourgeois women's movement was only one of a plethora of groups—which included natural scientists, racial hygienists, and health professionals—that were devoted to developing such strategies, it deserves closer attention because its reconceptualization of the gendered organization of society and of the relationship between state and society was further advanced than most other groups'.

The majority of the members of the bourgeois women's movement supported Germany's entrance into war wholeheartedly. Together with religious and nationalistic women's organizations, the Federation of German Women's Associations (Bund Deutscher Frauenvereine, BDF) founded the so-called National Women's Service (Nationaler Frauendienst), which organized welfare measures, a labor exchange for women, collections of food and clothing, care for the wounded, and propaganda campaigns that aimed at mobilizing women for total war. The bourgeois women's movement's enthusiasm for the war was inextricably linked to its prewar definition of "emancipation" and its reconceptualization of the relationship between state and society. Before the war, the majority of the bourgeois women's organizations had not conceived of women's emancipation as a process in which women would enter the male domain but rather as one in which they would create a separate female domain that would be acknowledged as being of equal importance as the male sphere for the construction of society. No matter how many different ideological factions there were in the bourgeois women's movement, most of them were convinced that women and men were fundamentally different. These factions did not believe, however, that this difference should continue to be used to justify women's subordination to men, for, as they saw it, many female qualities were actually superior to those of men.

Around the turn of the century, these ideas were articulated into a comprehensive theory, under the leitmotiv of "organized motherliness."[53] This theory rested on the assumption that women possessed as "natural" charac-

---

52. On the bourgeois women's movement's contribution to the war effort, see Ute Frevert, *Women in German History: From Bourgeois Emancipation to Sexual Liberation* (Oxford and New York, 1989), 151–67; Richard J. Evans, *The Feminist Movement in Germany, 1894–1933* (London, 1976); and Hering, *Die Kriegsgewinnlerinnen.*

53. See Sachße, *"Mütterlichkeit,"* 105–16; Frevert, *Women,* 104–6; and especially Ann Taylor Allen, "Spiritual Motherhood: German Feminists and the Kindergarten Movement, 1848–1911," *History of Education Quarterly* 22, no. 3 (Fall, 1982): 319–39; Ann Taylor Allen, "Mothers of the New Generation: Adele Schreiber, Helene Stöcker, and the Evolution of a German Idea of Motherhood, 1900–1914," *Signs* 10, no. 3 (1985): 418–38; and Ann Taylor Allen, *Feminism and Motherhood in Germany, 1800–1914* (New Brunswick, N.J., 1991).

teristics the faculties of caring, sharing, and nurturing. While these qualities were considered to be specifically female, they were not seen as dependent on women's biological motherhood. Women could therefore apply their specific talents not only within the confines of their families but also in the public professions of healing, education, and social welfare, thus contributing to society's general improvement. This line of reasoning not only separated women's reproductive work from the family but, in addition, linked it in new ways to the maintenance of the nation. Women's potential contribution to the organization of society was compared to men's military service, and many women consequently championed the introduction of a compulsory year of "women's service." While the insistence on gender-specific qualities maintained the concept of separate spheres, the boundaries of these spheres were completely redrawn as compared to the beginning of the nineteenth century. The expansion of women's work from the confines of the family dissolved the female sphere as a "private" sphere and turned it into a "public" sphere. The concept of organized motherliness not only dissolved the traditional boundary between the "public" (male) and the "private" (female) spheres but reconceptualized the organization of society within the framework of an all-encompassing militarization. Bourgeois women systematically constructed the male role as that of defending the nation against an outer enemy, while the female role was to consist in protecting the "national body" from internal enemies, that is, disease, physical weakness, and immorality.[54] The dissolution of the boundaries between the "public" and the "private" spheres redefined the relationship between state and society. Within the bourgeois women's movement's theory of organized motherliness, the family was no longer seen as the nucleus and basis of the state that guaranteed the reproduction of the state's citizenry; rather, the state was depicted as a national militarized family, the reproduction of which was guaranteed by men and women in their respective public realms.

The conceptual deprivatization and nationalization of women's reproductive work went hand in hand with the professionalization and rationalization of that work. While "motherliness" was still considered to be a specific female quality, it was, as it was claimed, in need of "training." Household manage-

54. See Allen, "Mothers of the New Generation"; and Ann Taylor Allen, "German Radical Feminism and Eugenics, 1900–1908," *German Studies Review* 11, no. 1 (1988): 31–56, where Allen argues against linking all feminist eugenicists to racism because eugenicist politics were pursued by left-wing as well as by right-wing groups and were used to support conservative as well as progressive politics (32). In my opinion, however, racist politics are racist politics, no matter who pursues them (see my definition of racism). The racism of even left-wing bourgeois feminists, shocking though it is, testifies to the fact that around the turn of the century, scientific racism had become a staple of the mainstream. On the widespread acceptance of "racial science," see John M. Efron, *Defenders of the Race: Jewish Doctors and Race Science in Fin-de-Siècle Europe* (New Haven and London, 1994).

ment and the raising and early education of children could no longer be based on "natural talents" but required "skills," because women's reproductive work was no longer linked to the well-being of families but to that of the nation. Germany's declining birth rate demanded, as bourgeois feminists and male eugenicists did not tire of insisting, that women realize their responsibility for the quantitative as well as the qualitative biological reproduction of society. Eugenics and racial hygiene therefore had to become the guiding principles of women's reproductive work. Women thus had to become "reproduction specialists"—some specializing in quality reproduction and some in teaching the required "know-how." In order to help women enter the public sphere, the bourgeois women's movement relied not on competition of women and men in that sphere as it was traditionally viewed but on adding a new female sector to it. Women's emancipation was thus defined not so much within the discursive framework of the liberal construction of power relations in representative parliamentary systems as within that of the late-nineteenth-century bourgeois project's construction of power relations in the political culture of scientism.[55] Bourgeois women joined their male counterparts in the project of depoliticizing interest conflicts and organizing power relations on the basis of a system of professional knowledge and expertise. This system—which served to undermine parliamentary politics because professional expertise and not voting rights became the basis on which political decisions, disguised as "technical" ones, were made—promised bourgeois women who moved into it access to social control and participation in political power rather than the attainment of voting rights.

The close affinity between the concept of organized motherliness and the structure of German society's mobilization for total war helps us understand why the German bourgeois women's movement welcomed the war so enthusiastically.[56] The war seemed to provide the bourgeois women's movement with a golden opportunity for experimenting with its social vision. Total mobilization, as I have argued above, destroyed the separation between the public and the private spheres and nationalized women's reproductive work. Moreover, bourgeois women did gain institutional power during the war. At the war's end, approximately one thousand bourgeois women worked in the various war offices for women's affairs. Many more participated in the numerous church-related, semiprivate, and private welfare organizations. Through their new institutional power, bourgeois women not only gained control over other women in the process of mobilizing them for war; they also gained power vis-

---

55. See Allen, "German Radical Feminism," who points this out very perceptively, though without linking this development to the general bourgeois project of developing a culture of scientism (32).

56. See Allen, "German Radical Feminism," 47–49. Regarding the similarity between this and other eugenicists' response to war, see note 49.

à-vis the state. One of the primary examples of such power is bourgeois women's role in the debates regarding the introduction of the famous Auxiliary Service Law (Vaterländisches Hilfsdienstgesetz) in 1916. Originally, German industry and the military had wanted to establish a compulsory national service for all men between the ages of sixteen and sixty, as well as for all women. Along with other groups, the National Women's Service fought these plans and argued instead for a continuation of women's voluntary mobilization for war. The failure of industry and military to win enough support for the compulsory service of women constituted a victory for the National Women's Service, since it secured its own role in mobilizing women for war and thus its control over a sector of society's wartime organization. One cannot argue with the fact that the bourgeois women's movement mobilized for a war that, because women were not represented in the Reichstag, it had no voice in choosing. The bourgeois women's movement did not however simply become a pawn of the state in German society's mobilization but, at certain junctures, also sought— and managed—to restrict the state's control over the organization of the war. This represented a decisive contribution of the bourgeois women's movement to the reconstruction of the relationship between state and society in wartime Germany.[57]

It is as tempting as it is futile to speculate about the course German history might have taken in the twentieth century if Germany's decentralized organization of the war effort had been as successful as, for example, Great Britain's centralized and state-controlled one. As it was, German society's self-organization for war proved to be a miserable failure. This homemade chaos, which was exacerbated by the Allied blockade, led to the immediate collapse of the "truce" between the classes as well as that between the sexes in German society—if, in fact, these truces ever existed. The continued gendered division of Germany's wage and compensation system and the new gendered division of the killing fields resulted, as I have shown above, in a theretofore unknown immiseration not only of the German working class but, specifically, of women and children of the working class and of the lower middle class. This immiseration was caused by the dissolution of the family as an economic unit, because women's and children's material existence was gravely affected by men's leaving for the front.

It is therefore neither strange nor an expression of "traditional thinking" on their part that working-class and lower middle-class women made the maintenance or the reconstitution of their families a key issue in their antiwar

---

57. In assessing the women's movement's gain of power, I am revising an earlier position of mine; see Elisabeth Domansky, "Der Erste Weltkrieg," in *Bürgerliche Gesellschaft in Deutschland: Historische Einblicke, Fragen, Perspektiven,* ed. Lutz Niethammer et al. (Frankfurt a.M., 1990), 312–13. As a result of the above-mentioned context, state power became increasingly diffuse; see Young Sun Hong, "The Contradictions"; and Geyer, "Nation, Klasse und Macht."

protests. Women of these classes led famine revolts, demonstrations against the chaotic supply system, and strikes for higher wages and against the forced-savings decrees. Since the dissolution of the family as an institution was the indispensable cornerstone of Germany's mobilization for total war, we should see all these actions, which started as early as 1915, as political protest.[58] Working-class and lower middle-class women's efforts at maintaining or re-constituting their families represented an attack on the very core of Germany's militarized social structure, and thus on the war itself. In this attack, the family and its survival was not only the protesters' main goal; indeed, the family became one of the principal units for organizing antiwar protests. Women would, for example, send their children to shopkeepers who were suspected of hoarding bread in order to sell it on the black market. If the children's pleas were ignored, women would storm the stores, using their children's lives as the justification for transgressing the property laws of civil society. In my opinion, these women's goals and tactics were more than rhetorical strategies or protest tactics used to justify violations of the law. Rather, they resulted from the fact that women and children realized that their lives depended on the existence of an intact family unit.[59]

This perception was not limited to working-class and lower middle-class women. There is, on the contrary, abundant evidence that men's growing unwillingness to continue fighting was a result of their families' immiseration. The concern that women and men shared about their families' survival was the link that connected the famine revolts, demonstrations, and strikes of the home front and the antimilitary and antiwar strike of the front, which eventually grew into the revolution of 1918–19.[60] Opposition against the nationalization of the social and biological reproduction of society and the concomitant dissolution of the family, which had been one of the pillars of the working class's exis-tence, was one of the main, if mostly overlooked, goals of the revolution. This revolution—which ended the war, but not German society's militarization— was profoundly defined and carried out by working-class women. Thereby, they not only gained the right to vote but also the restoration of workers' families and thus the basis of their and their children's survival—at least, if

---

58. On the German working class and the mass movements against the war, see the collec-tively edited *Deutschland im Ersten Weltkrieg,* 3 vols. (Berlin [East], 1968–69); Feldman, *Army;* Friedhelm Boll, *Massenbewegungen in Niedersachsen, 1906–1920: Eine sozialgeschichtliche Untersuchung zu den unterschiedlichen Entwicklungstypen Braunschweig und Hannover* (Bonn, 1981); and Daniel, *Arbeiterfrauen.*

59. But see Daniel, *Arbeiterfrauen,* for example, 274; and Frevert, *Women,* 166–67, who both, implicitly following the tenets of modernization theories, characterize women's wartime protests as the return of "older," "traditional," and "anachronistic" types of protest.

60. On the communication between front and home front, see Daniel, *Arbeiterfrauen,* 148–51, 233–41; F. L. Carsten, *War against War: British and German Radical Movements in the First World War* (London, 1982), 78, 183–88.

their men had survived the war. The removal of women from men's jobs in the context of demobilization should therefore not be read as a defeat but as a victory of working-class women. Because of the continued existence of a gendered compensation system, women's support of men's reintegration into the labor force was not an expression of "traditional" thinking—or "false consciousness," for that matter—but of their accurate assessment of their economic situation.[61]

Conclusion

Did the end of the war and the subsequent demobilization reconstitute, as many historians argue, Germany's return to its prewar system of gender relations? Such a conclusion would be premature. At the end of the war, women did leave "male jobs," and the surviving women, men, and children returned to their families. These families, however, were no longer the same as those of the prewar era. On the one hand, there was a large number of fatherless families; and on the other, fatherly authority seems to have changed in those families to which men returned. This resulted from women's and children's experience with self-sufficiency and from the neuroses that men brought home from the front. Because many fathers felt weakened, there were apparently numerous families in which one of the father's front comrades was in some way incorporated into the family structure as a substitute—or backup, as it were—authority for the father.[62]

In addition, many men, whether they were married or not, preferred the comfort of the numerous "comrade leagues" (*Kameradschaftsbünde*) to that of their family or else used this institution in addition to the family. The family no longer functioned as an emotional, recreational sphere. Nor did it provide the legitimacy for male supremacy. Many men thus continued to define themselves not through their role in their families but through their role in the military. Even many young men who had not actively participated in the war retreated into male leagues (*Bünde*). The bourgeois German youth movement, for example, reconstituted itself after the war as exclusively male and thus excluded

---

61. But see Daniel and Frevert (as cited in note 59) and also Richard Bessel, " 'Eine nicht allzu große Beunruhigung des Arbeitsmarktes' Frauenarbeit und Demobilmachung in Deutschland nach dem ersten Weltkrieg," *Geschichte und Gesellschaft* 9, no. 2 (1983): 211–29.

62. On fatherless families, see Hausen, "The German Nation's Obligation"; and Whalen, *Bitter Wounds*. Whalen shows that men's wartime replacement by women did not always and necessarily lead to men's loss of authority in their families (78–81). Rather, soldiers were often idealized by their wives and children, especially their sons, and subsequently endowed with new authority. This authority was based on men's role as soldiers. See also Sieder, "Behind the Lines," esp. 115–16, 128–38.

women from membership.[63] In church-related youth organizations, we find a telling change in symbolism. The veneration of the virgin-mother Mary by young men who were called "Sons of Mary the Immaculate" or "Mary's Knights" was replaced by a new cult of Christ. In addition, the figure of Aloysius of Gonzaga, who was constructed as the exemplary model of a "Knight of Mary," lost its appeal to young men after World War I. They now embraced the heroic fighter figure of the archangel Michael as their new role model. Young Catholic women also chose martial forms of organization. The new "Grail movement" (*Gralbewegung*), which had originated in the Netherlands, gained ground in Germany in 1932. This movement considered itself to be an "army of the church" (*eine Wehrmacht der Kirche*).[64] Moreover, the retreat into same-sex groups occurred not only among men but also among women. Young women who had been members of the German youth movement, for example, developed the concept of the "holy island" of femininity. This "holy island" was not simply an imagined space of inner retreat but referred to actual communes that women founded—often in the countryside and often linked to some kind of school-reform project.[65] Not only did many women and men retreat into same-sex spheres; society continued to organize young adults and children outside of the family unit. The Weimar Republic is characterized, among other things, by an all-encompassing effort of political parties, trade unions, and the churches to mobilize ever younger children into children's organizations.[66]

---

63. The English word "comrade" translates into two distinctly different words in German. The term "Genosse" is used as the socialist address "comrade"—a use that the Nazis usurped, usually adding the prefix "Partei" ("Parteigenosse"). The term "Kamerad" refers to a wartime comrade. The term was also used in the prewar German youth movement around the turn of the century in order to describe asexual relationships between young women and men. On the origins and uses of the term in the youth movement, see Hans Heinrich Muchow, *Sexualreife und Sozialstruktur der Jugend* (Reinbek bei Hamburg, 1959), 115–19. On the youth movement, see ·Walter Laqueur, *Young Germany: A History of the German Youth Movement*, 2d ed. (New Brunswick, N.J., and London, 1984); on the Weimar youth movement's retreat into male leagues, see Reulecke, "Männerbund." On some men's retreat into male comrade leagues and on veterans' constructions of their identities, see James M. Diehl, *The Thanks of the Fatherland: German Veterans after the Second World War* (Chapel Hill, 1993), 6–30; and Klaus Theweleit's study of free-corps fighters, *Male Fantasies*, vol. 1, *Women, Floods, Bodies, History* (Minneapolis, 1987); and vol. 2, *Male Bodies: Psychoanalyzing the White Terror* (Minneapolis, 1989).

64. Irmtraud Götz von Olenhusen, *Jugendreich, Gottesreich, Deutsches Reich: Junge Generation, Religion und Politik, 1928–1933*, Edition Archiv der deutschen Jugendbewegung, vol. 2 (Cologne, 1987), 80–83 (Mary vs. Christ), 83–85 (Aloysius of Gonzaga vs. Michael), 97–99 (Grail Movement).

65. Marion de Ras, "Die Heilige Insel—Neue Weiblichkeit zwischen Natur und Kultur," *Jahrbuch des Archivs der deutschen Jugendbewegung* 15 (1984–85): 87–108.

66. On the mobilization of youth in Weimar, see Hermann Giesecke, *Vom Wandervogel zur Hitlerjugend: Jugendarbeit zwischen Politik und Pädagogik* (Munich, 1981). According to this study, in 1927 about 54 percent of all young men and about 26 percent of all young women

The continued self-organization and mobilization of society into non-family-based groups went hand in hand with a continued increase in societal and state control over existing families. These families did not regain the autonomy they had lost during World War I, because the social interventionist welfare state that had emerged during the war was developed even further in the Weimar Republic. As a result of Weimar's laws for the protection of youth and children, the state could supersede parental authority regarding the objectives of children's health and ethical education, even forcibly removing children from their families and placing them in foster homes if their parents failed to function according to the standards defined by society and the state. In addition, welfare offerings to needy families, be they families of war widows or low-income families, continued to allow social workers to interfere with those families' autonomy in budgeting their family income.[67]

Even those groups that seemed to promote the continuity of the family as an institution did not attempt to reconstitute patriarchy. Groups on the political Right continued to link women's and men's reproductive work not to the family but to the survival of the nation, thus accepting the collapse of the distinction between the "private" and the "public" spheres.[68] The numerous sexual reformers on the Left, on the other hand, developed distinctly different concepts of marriage and the family from those characteristic of patriarchy. The new concept of the *Kameradschaftsehe* ("marriage of comradeship") broadened the definition of comradeship to include women. This definition expressed these reformers' positive response to the collapse of patriarchy, which was seen as a chance to create a greater equality between women and men. The concept of "comradeship" included the—in my opinion—highly ambiguous concept of "rationalized" sexuality and gender relations.[69] More important, however, was the discursive shift in defining marital loyalty. Marital

---

belonged to at least one of the numerous youth organizations. See also Domansky, "Politische Dimensionen," 126–35.

67. See David F. Crew, "German Socialism: The State and Family Policy, 1913–33," *Continuity and Change* 1, no. 2 (1986): 235–63. See also Elisabeth Harvey, *Youth and the Welfare State in the Weimar Republic* (Oxford and New York, 1993); and Susanne Zeller, *Volksmütter: Frauen im Wohlfahrtswesen der zwanziger Jahre* (Düsseldorf, 1987).

68. On the political Right's monopolization of the eugenicist discourse in Weimar, see especially Weindling, "The Medical Profession"; and Weindling, *Health*. See also Anna A. Bergmann, "Von der 'Unbefleckten Empfängnis' zur 'Rationalisierung des Geschlechtslebens': Gedanken zur Debatte um den Geburtenrückgang vor dem Ersten Weltkrieg," in *Frauenkörper, Medizin, Sexualität: Auf dem Wege zu einer neuen Sexualmoral,* ed. Johanna Geyer-Kordesch and Annette Kuhn (Düsseldorf, 1986), 127–58.

69. See Weingart, "Rationalization of Sexual Behavior"; and Atina Grossmann, "The New Woman and the Rationalization of Sexuality in Weimar Germany," in *Powers of Desire: The Politics of Sexuality,* ed. Ann Snitow, Christine Stansell and Sharon Thompson (New York, 1983), 153–71.

loyalty was defined within the linguistic framework of a shared combat experience, thus redefining the family as a unit of combatants. Thus right-wing and left-wing reconstructions of gender relations were firmly grounded in the militarization of German society during the war and its continuation in the Weimar Republic. The collapse of the barrier between the military and civil society and the concomitant collapse of patriarchy and its family model proved to be irreversible. Thus the "family romance" in Germany was over.[70] Not coincidentally, at the end of the Weimar Republic, a broad sector of German society supported as its future leader—and symbolic representation of its social structure—a man who was not a father figure or a brother. Adolf Hitler was a war veteran, a comrade.

This link to the rise of National Socialism needs to be explored further. As we have seen, in the wartime battle between discursive strategies that linked class and reproduction on the one hand and reproduction and the nation on the other, the former won for the brief period of the German Revolution. Weimar society, however, reconstituted itself not simply as a society at peace but as a militarized society at peace. The wartime restructuring of the spheres of reproduction, production, and destruction did not come to an end therefore but continued to form the basis for Germany's postwar reconstruction. This reconstruction did not "automatically" or "naturally" lead to the rise of National Socialism. It provided, however, the political Right in Weimar with the opportunity to capitalize on a discursive strategy that could successfully compete with liberal and socialist strategies. Liberals and socialists still clung to the mid-nineteenth-century idea that placed production in the center of the social organization of society. Such concepts—imaginative though they had been at the outset—had, however, become completely anachronistic during the war. The political Right in Weimar realized its chance and began to monopolize the discourse about society's social and biological reproduction as the constitutive element of nation formation.[71] This, I believe, explains women's electoral support of parties of the Right much more conclusively than references to their forced retreat into domesticity or their "false consciousness."[72] There were women, as the war had conclusively shown, who were interested in, and derived power from, society's reconstruction on the basis not of production's but reproduction's central role.

Not all concepts of moving reproduction to the center of society's organization and of defining the nation are fascist, prefascist, or racist. The concepts that were developed in Germany, however, were, since they linked reproduc-

---

70. This is a reference to Lynn Hunt's book *The Family Romance of the French Revolution* (Berkeley, 1991).
71. See note 68.
72. But see Bridenthal and Koonz, "Beyond *Kinder, Küche, Kirche.*"

tion not simply to the nation but to a "healthy" nation, thus creating an exclusive, not inclusive, definition of the nation and a national community. These concepts made National Socialist racist reproductive politics seem not outlandish but familiar to many Germans.[73] Moreover, World War I and the thorough militarization of wartime and postwar German society provided the structures within which the Third Reich could pursue its racist reproductive politics. Such politics depended on the dissolution of the patriarchal family.

The late nineteenth century's culture—and cult—of scientism provided the discursive framework within which, as I have argued, the relationship between the spheres of reproduction, production, and destruction began to change. World War I provided German society with an unforeseen opportunity to restructure itself based on the new role of reproductive politics that had become possible when reproduction became open to "scientific" biological engineering. These structures were the same as those used by the Third Reich's therapeutic state.[74] National Socialism's addition to these existing concepts and structures was their thorough impregnation with "scientific racism," thus creating a deathly fusion of elements that late-nineteenth-century bourgeois society had developed for its own creation of man after the death of God. This fusion was, as I have hoped to show, relatively easy, although not inevitable. As to the reason *why* it actually took place, however, I have no better answer than anyone else.

---

73. See Koonz, "Genocide and Eugenics." See also the literature on the history of eugenicism and racism cited in notes 9 and 10.
74. See the literature cited in notes 9 and 10.

The Creation of a Culture
of *Sachlichkeit*

Frank Trommler

One of the more entertaining approaches to the odd relationship between politics and culture in Wilhelmine Germany has been devised from the juxtaposition of official culture and artistic innovation. Students of the period take delight in contrasting the pronouncements of Emperor Wilhelm II on the miserable state of the arts with the actual flourishing of a German avant-garde before 1914. They point to the Kaiser's decision not to send modern art objects as part of the official German contribution to the 1904 Saint Louis World's Fair as symptomatic of this cultural chasm. It has not gone unnoticed, however, that the emperor's interventionist policy "clashed with the views of senior bureaucrats, who believed that the state should stand above the battle between traditional and modern art."[1]

One obvious question is whether in Wilhelmine Germany the mutual interference of avant-garde, public culture, and politics, which assumed such prominence in the Weimar Republic, manifested itself in different ways or was really negligible. Judging by the mutual isolation in which academic disciplines have articulated their overall view of this period, exchange and understanding between these spheres would seem to have been minimal. Historians of art and literature have generally taken the cue for their narrative from expressionism and later from the 1920s, while projecting a rather autonomous expansion of artistic modernity against the aesthetic and political agenda of the Wilhelmine state. Corresponding with the understanding of modernism in other countries, particularly France and the United States, this interpretation held sway without much challenge, since it provided a useful tale of the heroic origins of modern art and literature. The German version of the tale was enhanced by the fact that a first manifestation of *völkisch* concepts of art

---

1. Peter Paret, "The Artist as *Staatsbürger:* Aspects of the Fine Arts and the Prussian State before and during the First World War," *German Studies Review* 6 (1983): 430.

entered the public debate, foreshadowing the brutal attack on modern art in Nazi Germany. Regressive aesthetic developments in the *Kaiserreich* were labeled prefascist, and it was in this definition of continuities where cultural and political historiography came in contact with one another or even overlapped.[2] Generally, the far-reaching reorientation of the historiography on Wilhelmine Germany toward social and economic structures that Hans-Ulrich Wehler and his colleagues at Bielefeld initiated was achieved without benefit of arguments from the cultural and aesthetic spheres. Wehler's critics, in particular Thomas Nipperdey, Geoff Eley, and David Blackbourn[3] have anchored their stance in a more comprehensive conceptualization that draws less upon the continuities with later events between 1933 and 1945.

The fact that cultural factors were little studied in conjunction with the social changes before World War I seems to account for the long-standing notion that cultural pessimism—reflecting the feeling of a deep crisis of *Kultur*—brought about much of the irrational self-affliction of the twentieth-century German bourgeoisie. Pointing to the dialectic between the exhaustion of bourgeois culture and the *völkisch* rejuvenation that culminated in George L. Mosse's *Nazi Culture*,[4] this perception was instrumental in highlighting continuities between the Germany of the Kaiser and that of the Führer. Fritz Stern's *Politics of Cultural Despair*, a study of the influential *Kulturpessimisten* Paul de Lagarde, Julius Langbehn, and Arthur Moeller van den Bruck, who laid the ideological groundwork for the *völkisch* renewal of German culture and society, provided the most prominent reference. In his analysis of the German *Kulturideologie*, Stern exploited the link between the idealism of *Kultur* and the idealization of power as a pillar of Wilhelmine Germany, referring to Max Weber's verdict that the bourgeoisie was politically too immature to rule, too prone to yearn for a new Caesar, too willing to substitute "ethical" for political ideals. "Others could not see Weber's vision of political truth," Stern added, "but were oppressed by vague and formless premonitions of disaster."[5]

What Stern did not acknowledge in his book is the fact that Weber himself maintained a concept of aesthetic culture that was as status-oriented, highbrow, and exclusive as that of the imperial elites in general. In his attempt to preserve a sphere of individual autonomy above the iron cage of rational necessities,

---

2. A particularly influential example is George L. Mosse's *The Crisis of German Ideology: Intellectual Origins of the Third Reich* (New York, 1964).

3. Thomas Nipperdey, *Deutsche Geschichte 1866–1918*, vol. 1, *Arbeitswelt und Bürgergeist* (Munich, 1990); David Blackbourn and Geoff Eley, *The Peculiarities of Germany History: Bourgeois Society and Politics in Nineteenth-Century Germany* (Oxford and New York, 1984).

4. George L. Mosse, *Nazi Culture: Intellectual, Cultural and Social Life in the Third Reich* (New York, 1966).

5. Fritz Stern, *The Politics of Cultural Despair: A Study in the Rise of the Germanic Ideology* (New York, 1965), 21.

Weber expressed a similar cultural pessimism, although as a social historian he took the definition of culture much beyond the realm of artistic production and bourgeois identity. Recent debates about Weber's debt to Friedrich Nietzsche have illuminated the extent to which his projection of the charismatic leader is intertwined with the redemptive notions of art and science that prevailed among German mandarins.[6] While Weber was unique as a critic of the illiberalism and political dilettantism of the imperial elites, he very much reflected their bourgeois superego in his confirmation of tragic high-mindedness above the cultural submission of the masses, protracting the notion for subsequent generations of mandarins that *Kultur* in Wilhelmine Germany primarily meant compensation for the ever increasing rationalization of the world (*Entzauberung*).

Well acquainted with the idiosyncrasies of German academics (*The Sea Change*), H. Stuart Hughes has already pointed to their peculiar nationalist and cultural conformity within the Wilhelmine state and concluded that in order to account for the cultural mobilization in this period, one might better turn to different agents. Hughes detected "two complimentary and contradictory processes—a cultural revival and the beginnings of a 'secession of the intellectuals.'"[7] Yet while the secession of the intellectuals from the dominant discourse of academics has received the appropriate attention—Heinrich Mann, Maximilian Harden, and the writers of the Weimar Left and Right have become part of an intellectual canon—the cultural revival, which took shape outside of the confines of the university, was too easily subsumed under the heading of expressionism and separated from the political and social history of that period. References to culture usually meant highlighting the voices of a cultural crisis. This allowed conclusions concerning the insecurity of the German bourgeoisie, although it found its most urgent expression mainly among academics and *Bildungsbürger* who feared the loss of their status and influence.[8] In a curious way, Nietzsche's much quoted verdict of the failed cultural renewal of the united Germany after 1871—"the defeat, even extirpation of the German spirit in favor of the German Reich" in the first of his *Untimely Meditations*—has been maintained much beyond the period it was meant for

---

6. Wilhelm Hennis, "Max Webers Fragestellung," *Zeitschrift für Politik* 29 (1982): 241–81; Wolf Lepenies, *Die drei Kulturen: Soziologie zwischen Literatur und Wissenschaft* (Munich, 1985); Detlev J. K. Peukert, "Die 'letzten Menschen': Beobachtungen zur Kulturpolitik im Geschichtsbild Max Webers," *Geschichte und Gesellschaft* 12 (1986): 425–42.

7. H. Stuart Hughes, *Consciousness and Society: The Reorientation of European Social Thought, 1890–1930* (New York, 1961), 51.

8. Dieter Langewiesche, "German Liberalism in the Second Empire, 1871–1914," in *In Search of a Liberal Germany: Studies in the History of German Liberalism from 1789 to the Present*, ed. Konrad H. Jarausch and Larry Eugene Jones (New York, 1991), 233.

because it provided a convenient critique of the reckless style of the German politics that led to World War I.

A product of German universities, the sociology of knowledge still provides particular insights into their idiosyncrasies. The use of cultural pessimism as a device for maintaining a narrative of high and low—the presupposition of tragic tensions—is one of the more self-serving features of the mandarin culture, passed on less in the form of particular concepts than through mental and professional attitudes.[9] Similarly, the notion of the *Krise des Bürgertums*[10] continues to be extremely successful as a catalyst for historical narratives; Thomas Mann's novels—complete with the critique of the "machtgeschützte Innerlichkeit" (the turn to inner self protected by authority) in Wilhelmine Germany—are as useful as any other textual document to indicate the anxieties of a privileged class. It is hardly surprising that the retrospective dynamics of this notion of crisis still hold the key to the pre-1914 period, despite an increasing awareness that its culture was at least as much shaped by optimism as by pessimism toward modernization.[11] Fritz Ringer's distinction between an "orthodox" majority and a "modernist" minority was a first step toward a differentiation of the ambiguities, but his model remains inside the mandarin culture. In order to determine the agents of the cultural mobilization, one has to look outside of the universities and beyond the *Bildungsbürgertum,* and in order to understand these agents in their relationship to social and technological modernization, one has to include the study of their attitudes toward everyday social reality.[12]

---

9. Fritz Ringer, *The Decline of the German Mandarins* (Cambridge, Mass., 1969). On the attitudinal aspects of this study see the debate among Fritz Ringer, Charles Lemert, and Martin Jay in *Theory and Society* 19, no. 3 (1990). For a characteristic assessment in the 1920s, see Georg Steinhausen's essay "Verfallstimmung im kaiserlichen Deutschland," *Preussische Jahrbücher* 194 (1923): 153–85, and his book *Deutsche Geistes- und Kulturgeschichte von 1880 bis zur Gegenwart* (Halle, 1931). A more recent overview is Walter Wiora, "Die Kultur kann sterben: Reflexionen zwischen 1880 und 1914," in *Fin de Siècle: Zu Literatur und Kunst der Jahrhundertwende,* ed. Roger Bauer et al. (Frankfurt, 1977), 50–72.

10. See the historical assessment in Konrad H. Jarausch, "Die Krise des deutschen Bildungsbürgertums im ersten Drittel des 20. Jahrhunderts," in *Bildungsbürgertum im 19. Jahrhundert,* vol. 4, *Politischer Einfluß und gesellschaftliche Formation,* by Konrad H. Jarausch (Stuttgart, 1989), 180–205.

11. Blackbourn and Eley, *The Peculiarities of German History,* 211–21.

12. Such a study presupposes a critique of Ringer's reductionism in defining modernity (which is based, in part, on Weber's reductionism). See my response to Ringer, "Rethinking Modernity in Germany," in *Culture and Politics in Nineteenth- and Twentieth-Century Germany,* ed. Hartmut Lehmann, German Historical Institute Occasional Paper, no. 8 (Washington, D.C.: German Historical Institute, 1992), 39–45. After completion of this essay, I learned of the project of "rewriting the history of modern architecture in Germany," which the Deutsches Architektur-Museum at Frankfurt initiated with the exhibition *Moderne Architektur in Deutschland, 1900–1950: Reform and Tradition* in 1992. Its goal, well presented in the catalogue—Vittorio Magnago

Literary and art historians usually have extracted the challenges to the elitist idealism of high culture from the pamphlets of futurists, expressionists, and dadaists.[13] Yet in their secession, the artists and intellectuals hardly relinquished their own elite status. In their polemics, German expressionists pursued their own glory as young prophets at least as much as the destruction of the self-satisfied habitus of the fathers. In contrast to their rhetorical recycling of high-art concepts—to which the dadaists claimed to take exception—the German Werkbund, which was founded in 1907 by designers, architects, and entrepreneurs, did not compete in the rescue of art from the lower depths of materialism. The practitioners of the Werkbund program linked the definition of culture to its application within the pragmatic pursuits of modern life, to the reconciliation of aesthetic form and the usefulness of its products. After historicism and *Jugendstil,* after the failed revitalization of German cultural life through elaborately invented historical traditions and the decorative staging of contemporary bourgeois life, this program meant a rapprochement with materialism, as well as a corruption of the traditional idealist privileges of high art and its audience. The projected harmonizing of production, product, and consumption was conceived as a step into a new era, not just into a new style. Its centers lay outside of the universities and were connected with industry, craft firms, and state-sponsored institutions such as craft schools and academies. In the understanding of industrialization as the manifest destiny of the German nation, this modernism was as much a pattern of behavior, the expression of a modern attitude (*Haltung*), as it was an aesthetic structuring of political and economic pursuits. The fact that the increasingly widespread notion of *Sachlichkeit* (matter-of-factness, sobriety, objectivity) was used at least since 1904 in order to expound the characteristics of the reform movement also attests to its attitudinal dynamics: *Sachlichkeit* as a new, sober attitude toward reality from which a new stylistic pattern could emerge.

The Political Dimension

Before expanding on the aesthetic aspects of this cultural revival, I should outline what is meant by the aesthetic structuring of political and economic

---

Lampugnani, ed., *Moderne Architektur in Deutschland, 1900 bis 1950: Reform und Tradition* (Stuttgart, 1992)—corresponds to the gist of my argument. A broadly based reinterpretation of the cultural developments has been presented in the series Kunst, Kultur und Politik im Deutschen Kaiserreich, published under the direction of Stephan Waetzoldt. See especially volume 3, Ekkehard Mai et al., eds., *Ideengeschichte und Kunstwissenschaft: Philosophie und bildende Kunst im Kaiserreich* (Berlin, 1983). A similarly comprehensive perspective is presented in Francesco Dal Co, *Figures of Architecture and Thought: German Architectural Culture, 1880–1920* (New York, 1990).

13. See Peter Bürger, *Theory of the Avantgarde* (Minneapolis, 1984).

pursuits in this period. Many contemporaries expressed misgivings about the confrontational practices of political parties and interest groups that had taken shape in the 1890s. These practices were considered inadequate to the increasing cultural needs of the middle class—cultural in the sense of the much debated notion of *Lebensgestaltung* (shaping patterns of living).[14] As politicians neglected to address the changes inherent in the modernization of everyday life, public debates were increasingly reformulated under such headings as *Lebenskultur* (everyday culture), *Ausstattungskultur* (design for living), *Rationalisierung* (rationalization), and *Publikumsgeschmack* (public taste). While liberalism, as Friedrich Naumann maintained, lacked "ideas" concerning the democratization of German society,[15] the debate transforming traditional patterns of building, producing, consuming, living, and enjoying became a key enterprise in shaping public concerns and participation. Naumann himself, who drafted some of the crucial culturalist treatises, had to learn that the advancement of modernity under national auspices attracted much interest among middle-class Germans but did not translate into the organization of party politics. His Nationalsozialer Verein never really took off and failed as a political party.

Although the new dynamic synthesis of imperialism and social reform before World War I has been interpreted as an invigoration of liberalism,[16] the discontent with its political practices is at the roots of the culturalist turn. This discontent overlaps with the dissatisfaction concerning the inability of the Wilhelmine state to provide a form of guidance that was able to reach beyond the paternal pattern of dominance above and the alternatives of submission or subversive analysis below. Structuring social politics (*Gesellschaftspolitik*) through rethinking its aesthetic and technological dimensions challenged not only the idealist notion of *Kultur* but also the prevailing concept of politics as party and interest politics. The challenge was successful mainly because it projected an overcoming of politics in general—doubtless an ominous self-deception in a society without firm democratic traditions. This did not escape the liberal commentator Samuel Saenger who followed this mobilization with much sympathy in the journal *Die Neue Rundschau* but insisted that modern society did not tolerate public pursuits without politics. The demise of liberalism, Saenger pointed out in 1908, had left Germany bereft of a concept of

---

14. See Klaus Vondung, ed., *Das wilhelminische Bildungsbürgertum: Zur Sozialgeschichte seiner Ideen* (Göttingen, 1976).

15. There is a particularly blunt assessment in his "Die gebildete Jugend und der Liberalismus," *Die Zeit* 2 (1902–3): 744–48.

16. Geoff Eley, "Liberalism, Europe, and the Bourgeoisie, 1860–1914," in *The German Bourgeoisie: Essays on the Social History of the German Middle Class from the Late Eighteenth to the Early Twentieth Century*, ed. David Blackbourn and Richard J. Evans (London and New York, 1991), 310.

politics that would enable the country to articulate a coherent stance in foreign affairs and develop a new collective spirit at home. Saenger shared with Weber the complaint that Germany had no competent leaders, yet he did not adopt Weber's notion of charismatic leadership. For Saenger, the culturalist turn was an indispensable ingredient of democratization:

> The armies of undifferentiated slaves in antiquity or of Christians in the Dark Ages let themselves at best be ruled by heroic supermen or re-strained by the iron bars of tamers of animals (à la Hobbes), but the strongly differentiated millions who breathe in an atmosphere of light and enlightenment, who have successfully fought for the right of hygiene, education, work, nursing, accident insurance, and ballot, let themselves be directed only through cultural means and cultural methods [Kulturmittel und Kulturmethoden].[17]

Saenger's continuous comment on German affairs gives witness to the political dimension of the culturalist reshaping of social politics. He illuminated why the pessimism about the state of liberalism, *Geist,* and politics did not neces-sarily translate into cultural pessimism. Unlike in Austria, for which Carl Schorske has diagnosed an equation between "the high cultural productivity" and "a revolution of falling expectations in the class which produced the culture,"[18] the self-invigoration through an attitude of *Sachlichkeit* provided a strong basis for rising expectations in prewar Germany.

As a scholar whose early years were shaped by Edmund Husserl's phe-nomenological call "zu den Sachen," Helmut Plessner has demonstrated in his magnum opus, *Die verspätete Nation* (1935), and in the essay "Die Legende von den zwanziger Jahren" (1962) that the national agenda behind this cultural mobilization should not be mixed up with the foreign and domestic power play of the Wilhelmine state. Tracing the German alienation from the Western concept of politics back through history, Plessner argued that the Germans compensated for the lack of political belief in progress with a belief in scien-tific and industrial progress.[19] His assessment relied heavily on the middle-class reformers: "Estate and caste, property regulations, and class antagonism could not be overcome. What remained was only the path of a social reform through a reform of culture and its sensually comprehensible expression in arts, crafts, and architecture, in a renewal of life through the reform of its forms and

---

17. Samuel Saenger, "Kulturpolitik: Gedanken, Ziele, Wege," *Die Neue Rundschau* 19 (1908): 163.

18. I quote Carl Schorske in the discussion "New Trends in History," *Daedalus* 98 (1969): 731.

19. Helmuth Plessner, *Die verspätete Nation,* in *Gesammelte Schriften,* by Helmuth Plessner, vol. 6, ed. Günter Dux et al. (Frankfurt, 1982), 101.

vessels."[20] Plessner placed the "ethical-aesthetic revolution of 1900"[21] in the context of the pathos of *Sachlichkeit*. Another of Husserl's students, Max Scheler, interpreted the abrupt turn with which the Germans had embraced materialism and modernity as a vanguard move among nations. In his widely read defense of Germany in World War I, "Der Genius des Krieges und der Deutsche Krieg," Scheler endowed this turn with the nimbus of the timely exodus from the paradise of the good life, a turn that caused hatred among those nations that had to follow suit.[22]

The fact that English contemporaries had propagated efficiency as a national goal by pointing to Germany as a model[23] had indeed not gone unnoticed in Germany. Yet such a confrontation was considered only one element in the increasing international competition. Much of the refurbished feudal representation of the Wilhelmine state manifested a rather different commitment, in which the imperial insignia of dominance—including the Kaiser's theatrical appearances—were destined to counterbalance the upsetting effects of materialism and modernity. Wilhelm II, who cherished his friendship with Albert Ballin, the Hamburg businessman, showed himself committed to supporting the technical and scientific advancement of the nation and joined the effort to elevate the technical universities to the level of the traditional universities. When Naumann articulated his version of a *"soziales Kaisertum,"* whereby the emperor would lead a modern German industrial state, he testified to the effectiveness of Wilhelm's contemporary interests. Naumann's idea, however, did not survive the *Daily Telegraph* affair. In turn, the alarm rang on the Right as soon as efficiency was elevated to a social and aesthetic legitimacy without imperial representation, refuting the invention of feudal traditions. Through denouncing the nineteenth century as an age of historicist self-indulgence, allegorical pseudoreality, and unrestrained capitalist exploitation, efficiency's champions reclaimed it from the hierarchical stratification. While a reconciliation between the Werkbund artists and the Hohenzollern throne was not beyond imagination,[24] the break with idealist aesthetics remained a provocation for a large part of the ruling elites.

The emperor's public posturing as an advocate of idealism—a completely reified notion of a high-minded habitus without the palpitations of human existence—was in keeping with the attempts of conservative groups to create

---

20. "Die Legende von den zwanziger Jahren," ibid., 270.
21. Ibid., 278.
22. Max Scheler, "Der Genius des Krieges und der Deutsche Krieg," in *Gesammelte Werke,* by Max Scheler (Bern, 1982), 4:322.
23. G. R. Searle, *The Quest for National Efficiency: A Study in British Politics and Political Thought, 1899–1914* (Berkeley, 1971), 54–67.
24. Tilmann Buddensieg, "Aesthetic Opposition and International Style," in *Berlin 1900–1933: Architecture and Design,* ed. Tilmann Buddensieg (Berlin, 1987), 27.

Kulturpolitik as a weapon against the materialism of the proletariat and the advancing middle classes. In the pioneering treatise of 1901, *Kulturpolitik,* Robert Scheu castigated the "*Vulgärpolitik*" of the parties. *Kultur,* in this view, was to represent a counterstrategy from above against an increasingly pragmatic and *sachorientiert* public discourse. Reactionary critics did not condemn technology and industry—after all, these phenomena were vivid manifestations of German power—but rather their use for a cultural democratization. Alfred von Tirpitz's widely acclaimed big navy remained above the contaminating waters of *Sachlichkeit,* useless for the coming battles of attrition in World War I yet impressive as a floating allegory of Germany's "Griff nach der Weltmacht."

The Aesthetic Dimension

The break with the nineteenth-century juxtaposition of art and industry marks the central contribution of the German reform movement to the development of what has been labeled "Modernism" or "International Style." At its core stands the compromise with which artistic elites reclaimed important segments of society's material life for an aesthetic approach: the compromise with the pragmatics of capitalist production and consumption.[25] While designers, architects, and artists expanded their productive terrain to the extent that one spoke of a reconciliation of art and industrial society through applied arts, craft firms and, following the pioneering efforts of Peter Behrens at the Allgemeine Elektricitats-Gesellschaft, manufacturing industries[26] won new markets both in and outside of Germany thanks to the innovative aesthetic qualities of their products.

Due to this compromise with profit-making materialism, the aesthetics of reform failed to win the same attention that the projection of revolt and rupture in the realm of high art received, on which the concept of the avant-garde has been built and maintained. Later categorizations of the German reform movement as an avant-garde only underline the misconceptions about its specific departure from the traditional view of high art. The notion of avant-garde was imported in Germany as it was in the United States. The practice according to which the aesthetic innovation has to legitimize itself as a rebuff to the real or

---

25. For a more detailed assessment, see my essays "Vom Bauhausstuhl zur Kulturpolitik: Die Auseinandersetzung um die moderne Produktkultur" in *Kultur: Bestimmungen im 20. Jahrhundert,* ed. Helmut Brackert and Fritz Wefalmeyer (Frankfurt, 1990), 86–110, especially pp. 92–99; and "Technik, Avantgarde, Sachlichkeit," in *Literatur in einer industriellen Kultur,* ed. Götz Grossklaus and Eberhard Lämmert (Stuttgart, 1989), 46–71.

26. On the specifics of the manufacturing industry and modernization, see Hartmut Pogge von Strandmann, "Widersprüche im Modernisierungprozess Deutschlands: Der Kampf der verarbeitenden Industrie gegen die Schwerindustrie," in *Industrielle Gesellschaft und politisches System,* ed. Dirk Stegmann et al. (Bonn, 1978), 225–40.

perceived *academie,* constantly stylized into a reincarnation of the great revolution, represents a French phenomenon. It has its equivalent in the way that technology was integrated into the culture; the official promotion of the *culture technique,*[27] especially in the world exhibition of 1900 in Paris, focused much more on the celebration of the avant-garde status of French technology than on the needs of industrial production and organization.

A characteristic assessment of the transformations that took place in German arts and crafts and in the craft industry between 1904 and 1909 was presented by S. Tschierschky in *Technik und Wirtschaft,* the journal of the Verein Deutscher Ingenieure. Tschierschky highlighted the exhibitions in Dresden and Munich as important steps for the ascent of the culture of *Sachlichkeit* and explained:

> We still encounter in recent publications and articles the opinion that art and machine, crafts and machine work, represent completely *opposing* perceptions and procedures of production. In particular everything artistic is supposed to perish as soon as it analyzes, copies, and proletarianizes for mass production the industrial machinery with iron arms. Fortunately this thought has now been completely given up. Fritz Schumacher formulated this sentence in his critical talk about the third German crafts exhibition in Dresden: "We know nowadays that the taste-defining [geschmacksbestimmend] triumphal march of the machine product cannot be stopped, or even influenced on its route by the small circle of the consumers of precious but costly crafts; therefore we make the second step by calling not for the battle *against* the machine but rather for the battle *allied with* the machine . . ." This slogan alone can lead to "mass" victory.[28]

Tschierschky's assessment is characteristic in explaining the innovative momentum as a consequence of a specific conjunction of forces, above all as the irresistible advance of mechanization. Moreover, it points to the fact that innovation results from a realistic insight into the state of modernization, that is, from a *sachlich* attitude toward reality. The aim is no longer a harmonizing stylistic ambition, as in *art nouveau* or *Jugendstil. Sachlichkeit* as a formula takes its cue from the mode of production in the broadest sense, encompassing the return to "natural" materials in the design of a chair as well as the elevation of the design of a factory as an expression of social responsibility.

---

27. Neve Gesellschaft für Bildende Kunst, ed. *"Absolut modern sein": Culture technique in Frankreich, 1889–1937* (Berlin, 1986).

28. S. Tschierschky, "Kunst, Kunstgewerbe, und Kunstindustrie," *Technik und Wirtschaft* 2 (1909): 101.

Hermann Muthesius, who as an attaché to the German embassy in London had studied the English Arts and Crafts movement, raised the notion of *Sachlichkeit* to a productive attitude through which the Germans would be able to overcome "the ornament and style gadgets" of the nineteenth century. He elaborated his incantation of *Sachlichkeit,* which first appeared in the essay "Stilarchitektur und Baukunst" of 1902, as follows:

> The more our arts and crafts movement converts to this *Sachlichkeit,* the more it will be truly modern, i.e., appropriate to the general trends of our time, and will produce from the spirit of this time. Our endeavors toward *Sachlichkeit,* which can clearly be observed in the design variations of the past hundred or hundred fifty years, cannot be banned permanently from the world by a general sentiment anymore. Our machines and vehicles, our bridges and train stations, will remain faithful to the *Sachlichkeit,* which will also continue to dominate our clothes. Should the difference be maintained between these formations, which hitherto were maligned as "inartistic," and those in crafts and architecture, which were praised as "artistic"?[29]

Formulating his opinion as a question, Muthesius asserted that the distinction between high and low (applied) art, from which painters and writers continued to draw legitimacy, could not be maintained. It became obvious that his fellow architects and designers in the Werkbund, especially Henry van de Velde, were less enthusiastic about giving up the aura of artistic freedom in favor of the mechanical standards (*Typisierung*) required by industrial production,[30] but this did not diminish their commitment to the practices of aesthetic reform. Peter Behrens, Walter Gropius, and others made special efforts in their publications to stress that the agenda of such a reform evoked a similar spirit of high-mindedness in its devotion to national progress.

Gropius was among the most influential advocates of the moral and national legitimacy of the new aesthetic-industrial synthesis. In 1910 he began to develop plans of prefabricated houses for low-income families. Impressed by his encounter with the American functional architecture,[31] he illustrated the speech "Monumentale Kunst und Industriebau," which he gave in 1911—the year of his acclaimed design for the Fagus factory—with illustrations of concrete silos in Baltimore (Ohio), Buffalo, and Minneapolis. In the same speech,

---

29. Hermann Muthesius, *Kultur und Kunst: Gesammelte Aufsätze über künstlerische Fragen der Gegenwart* (Jena and Leipzig, 1904), 74–75.

30. On the debates that culminated at the Werkbund convention in 1914, see Wend Fischer, ed., *Zwischen Kunst und Industrie: Der Deutsche Werkbund* (Munich, 1975), 56–115.

31. Thomas P. Hughes, *American Genesis: A Century of Invention and Technological Enthusiasm, 1870–1970* (New York, 1989), 311–19.

he expressed the high-minded aspirations in terms of a national and social reconciliation:

Devoted to work, palaces have to be erected that will not only provide light, air, and cleanliness to the factory worker, the slave of modern industrial work, but which also will give him the feeling of the dignity of the common great idea that moves the whole. Not until then will the individual be able to subsume the personal to the impersonal thinking without losing the joy in the joint work toward great common values, which formerly could not be achieved from the orbit of the individual. This awareness, awakened in the individual worker, could perhaps prevent a social catastrophe that, due to the unrest in today's economic life, threatens every day.[32]

Gropius put Naumann's national-social agenda to good use for advancing his projects in housing and industrial architecture. He highlighted the yearning toward a collecting point (*Sammelpunkt*) for the centrifugal forces and interest groups whose reconciliation seemed to fail in the political process. In his article of 1914, "Der stilbildende Wert industrieller Bauformen," Gropius stressed the principle of the integration of diverse forces into a functional whole, correlating the work of architects and engineers with the need of modern society for integration. He did not promote aesthetic production as the actual synthesis but rather delineated it as a paradigm for the envisioned national synthesis.

The rhetoric of social confrontation began to be affected by this aesthetic conceptualization of a national production effort, now fully designed with "light, air, and cleanliness" for the workers. New arguments were created for a public discourse that subsumed the concern with the class struggle under the promise of a new ethics of the producers. Such a promise struck a chord among middle-class citizens, who learned social responsibility through the first consumer-oriented campaigns for a more accountable culture of taste (*Geschmackskultur*) in Germany. Although Ferdinand Avenarius's journal *Kunstwart*—and, after 1902, the *Dürerbund,* which was intended to be a "*Partei der Sachlichen*"—never mustered more than several thousand devotees, these journals were instrumental in creating this language of social responsibility without engaging in an overtly political discourse.[33]

It is hardly surprising that such aesthetic "strategies" became the target of the polemics that Karl Kautsky directed against the "ethical-aesthetic" faction

---

32. Quoted from Helmut Weber, *Walter Gropius und das Faguswerk* (Munich, 1961), 27.

33. See Gerhard Kratzsch, "'Der Kunstwart' und die bürgerlich-soziale Bewegung," and Rüdiger vom Bruch, "Kunst und Kulturkritik in führenden bildungsbürgerlichen Zeitschriften des Kaiserreichs," in Mai et al., *Ideengeschichte und Kunstwissenschaft,* 371–96, 313–48.

inside the Social Democratic Party. These polemics, which in 1905 led to the dismissal of Kurt Eisner as the editor of *Vorwärts*, the party's main newspaper, and to a growing alienation of the revisionist group around the journal *Sozialistische Monatshefte*, reconfirmed the resolve of the party authorities not to sacrifice Marxist positions to culturalist thinking. Although the SPD continued to claim the legacy of German classical literature and philosophy, calling itself a *Kulturbewegung*, it left the discourse on the reforms of society's material life, including the physical experience of work and the workplace, to bourgeois activists.[34] It developed no counterstrategy against the increasing interest in the Werkbund debates on a "cultural reform of work," which expanded into a public discussion about the notion of joy in work (*Arbeitsfreude*).[35] Similarly neglected were the efforts of elevating work to a national icon (*deutsche Arbeit*). These efforts were designed to reverse the perception of work as the crucial factor of alienation in favor of a view in which *Arbeit*, associated with the notions of *Werk* and *das arbeitende Volk*, accommodated the antimodernist longing for an authentic experience—of course, among the middle classes, not in the working class. Only under such ascetic auspices could the alienating reality of work, its markings of pain and endurance, be turned into a manifestation of authenticity that was to restore a sense of personal wholeness, allowing a spiritual divorce from capitalist profit-making.

For the reformers, the term "Sachlichkeit" was also useful because it denounced the succession of styles as a camouflage for the constant need of the capitalist market for variation. Dismantling the ornaments—the spiritual as well as the visual ones—became an intellectual and an architectural goal in itself. It expressed freedom from commercialism. By refuting fashions and styles, the new tectonic functionalism synthesized the anticapitalist currents among professional elites. It played into their misgivings concerning the "evasive banality" and the spiritual "weightlessness" (Nietzsche) of industrial life and its attendant liberal, positivistic philosophy. Its extension toward the national whole corresponded to various forms of anti-semitism that projected the problematic features of modern life, the capitalist profit-making, onto the Jews and kept the constructive phenomena, *Arbeit, Werk,* and *Technik* for the Germans.

Correlating the search for a new *Gestalt* of the self and its *Lebenskultur* above the class struggle with the search for a new *Gestalt* of the nation gave the reform movement a powerful momentum. The specifically German dimension

---

34. See my *Sozialistische Literatur in Deutschland: Ein historischer Überblick* (Stuttgart, 1976), 247–82, 325–38.

35. Joan Campbell, *Joy in Work, German Work: The National Debate, 1800–1945* (Princeton, 1989), 25–27, 69–72, and passim. See also Gerd Selle, *Die Geschichte des Design in Deutschland: Entwicklung der industriellen Produktkultur* (Cologne, 1978), 62–77.

was, on the whole, characterized by the rejection of the allegories of Wilhelmine power and history and the pursuit of a function-oriented design of buildings, appliances, machines, and luxury and everyday objects. A tradition of a German crafts practice was invented that never existed in this elaborate formation. Yet extracting the *Gestalt* of contemporaneity from the projection of efficiency was not necessarily a very national enterprise. Gropius did not have to repeal the formal assumptions of his design when he legitimized the Bauhaus program in the Weimar Republic through its social commitment and international applicability.

In addition to its capacity for organization—the constructive compromise with manufacturers and the crafts—it was the Werkbund's presentist symbolism of the national agenda that made its international success possible. Recent studies have shown that the shortcomings of the French decorative arts at the beginning of the century were to a considerable extent caused by a much stronger national agenda that forced designers and decorators to return to specifically French traditions in order to make their objects recognizably French. When contemporaries summed up the essence of Frenchness as "sensibility, grace, charm, elegance, spirit, facility," they could count on complete consent. A reputation could be destroyed by describing design as "un-French" or, more provocatively, as "German." Given the elitist bent of the crafts in which the French had excelled—such as marquetry and lacquerwork—the German movement appeared as an intrusion from the street. In 1912, in the climate of increasing tensions between the two neighbors, critics denounced modernist art as "anti-French and a threat to the central cultural integrity of the nation."[36] According to the critics, the government was to be prohibited from officially supporting the Salon d'automne (which they described as an organization dominated by foreigners) by excluding its annual exhibition from the Grand Palais. André Breton argued in the chamber of deputies: "Gentlemen, it is in fact absolutely unacceptable that our national palaces are permitted to be used for exhibitions of a character that is so clearly antiartistic and antinational."[37]

As Peter Paret has documented in *The Berlin Secession,* while the national arguments in the debate about modern art reached grotesque proportions at the turn of the century in Germany, the French invested no less energy in an equivalent debate a decade later. Characteristically, however, these debates differed in their focus on fine and applied arts appropriate to the innovative potential in the two countries. While France lost its international position as arbiter of taste in the applied arts, it maintained leadership in the fine arts, not

36. Pierre Lampué as quoted in Nancy Troy, *Modernism and the Decorative Arts in France: Art Nouveau to Le Corbusier* (New Haven, 1991), 101.

37. Ibid.

least through a more aggressively pursued concept of the avant-garde, which resulted in the ever more rigid distinctions between fine and applied arts in galleries and in critical writing. In contrast, the German reform movement, by blurring the boundaries between art and industrial production, expanded the aesthetic understanding and structuring of the material realities of the modern world. While France maintained the aura of the arbiter in the area of fine arts, Germany reaped the economic benefit of the collaboration of designers and manufacturers. In 1916, Marius Vachon, in *La guerre artistique avec l'Allemagne,* lamented about the trade in decorative arts:

> If one examines in particular the figures for French commerce with Germany in the last three years before the war, [one discovers that] these are hardly to our advantage. The importation of German-made objects rose by 100 million between 1911 and 1913, while French exports rose by only 50 million. And, analyzing the nature of the objects in question, one finds that this rise in French exports has less to do with the products of the art industries than with minerals, chemicals, and other such materials.[38]

According to Nancy Troy, French decorative artists were fully aware of the economic benefits resulting from the German pattern of cooperative production. Nonetheless, "their ideologically motivated commitment to the French craft tradition made it virtually impossible for them to assimilate any really substantive aspect of what the Germans had to offer."[39]

The Historical Dimension

In German literary and art history, the term "Neue Sachlichkeit" has been used to define the modernist currents of the twenties with the help of an expression of the period. The difficulty of finding an adequate translation into English— "New Objectivity," "New Sobriety," "New Matter-of-Factness"—confirms the peculiar nature of the concept, even illustrates its peculiar Germanness. For cultural historians of the twenties, who generally prefer to stress the uniqueness of "Weimar culture" in order to enhance the drama before its demise in 1933, such a term displays more historical flair than would the general notion of modernism. Of most importance for its broad academic application, however, is the fact that it can be traced to a specific origin: a circular of 18 May 1923 in which the art historian Gustav Friedrich Hartlaub announced his plan to stage an exhibition in the Mannheim art gallery. Giving the exhibition the title *Neue Sachlichkeit,* Hartlaub wanted to feature paintings that were neither "impres-

---

38. Marius Vachan, *La guerre artistique avec l'Allemagne: L'organisation pour la victoire* (Paris, 1916), 21, quoted in ibid., 102.

39. Ibid., 102.

sionistically dissolved" nor "expressionistically abstract" but rather "in an almost proclamatory way remain loyal or rediscover their loyalty to a positively tangible reality."[40] After careful preparation, the event took place in 1925 and established the term for a wider public.

Neue Sachlichkeit became synonymous with a kind of aesthetic mid-course correction of "Weimar culture" after the political excesses of war and revolution, the economic excesses of hyperinflation, and the artistic excesses of expressionism. At last, artists and writers realized that they had to adjust to the realities of a defeated country. In retrospect, Bauhaus, Bertolt Brecht, and Georg Grosz are contextualized as the sobering medicine for a public that had an unrealistic sense of what art should be and for artists who had gone astray in their expressionistic perception of the redemptive power of their aesthetic mission. Beyond a confirmation of this call for a sober and sobering attitude, however, the scholarly definition has made little progress, as expressed in the title of an essay: " 'Neue Sachlichkeit': Stilbegriff, Epochenbezeichnung oder Gruppenphänomen?"[41] It is in response to this kind of ambiguity that I will discuss the historical dimension of the culture of *Sachlichkeit* in Germany in the concluding section.

Most evident is the question why the debate about *Neue Sachlichkeit* has prospered without much reference to the prewar manifestations of this phenomenon. In the twenties now and then referred to as *Alte Sachlichkeit* and later mentioned as the origin of the artistic productivity of the period—as, for instance, in Peter Gray's *Weimar Culture* of 1968—these prewar manifestations were not unknown. Yet they were understood primarily as a prelude to the full show of creative talent, giving credence to Karl Mannheim's celebrated comparison of Weimar with Periclean Athens, which, after all, had not suddenly leaped out of Athena's head. When Henry Pachter, at the commemorative conference on Weimar in New York in 1971, took issue with this form of Weimar-centricity, he emphasized the derivative strain in this culture but did not speculate on whether the previous period had generated the crucial creative momentum. ("We were not great innovators, we were innovators on a small scale.")[42]

Another obvious question concerns the negligence toward the attitudinal connotations of the term "Sachlichkeit": Why were these aspects recognized in

40. Jost Hermand, "Unity within Diversity? The History of the Concept 'Neue Sachlichkeit,' " in *Culture and Society in the Weimar Republic,* ed. Keith Bullivant (Manchester, 1977), 166.

41. Klaus Petersen, " 'Neue Sachlichkeit:' Stilbegriff, Epochenbezeichnung oder Gruppenphänomen?" *Deutsche Vierteljahrsschrift für Literaturwissenschaft und Geistesgeschichte* 56 (1982): 463–77.

42. Henry Pachter, "The Intellectuals and the State," in *Weimar Etudes,* ed. Henry Pachter (New York, 1982), 130.

the change of social and aesthetic temper, even style, after the end of the hyperinflation, but not traced beyond the confrontations with the visionary aesthetic attitude of such expressionists as Franz Werfel and Georg Kaiser, Oskar Kokoschka and Emil Nolde, Wassili Kandinsky and Alban Berg? As a result, the definition of *Sachlichkeit* as an aesthetic attitude or state of mind was tied to its juxtaposition with expressionism as the manifestation of eccentric, yet high-minded modernism. To be sure, in the period of relative stabilization after 1924, the term "Sachlichkeit" gained credibility through the reference to the United States, where the orientation toward mass production and consumption seemed to bolster the democratic organization of society. Yet this kind of advantage from a positive Americanism—there existed a negative Americanism, too—translated into an attitude: one organized things in an "American way, and art and culture were reconceptualized according to an "American" attitude toward the popular taste. Meanwhile, established traditions of high culture were defended with an eye on the dignified behavior that they demanded and due to which they had survived.

Little needs to be said about the fact that crediting the Weimar Republic with a lively interaction of aesthetic innovation, public culture, and politics has strengthened the course of democracy in Germany. Of course, the intention to stress Weimar's uniqueness was considerably less pronounced in the Federal Republic than among émigré intellectuals, who transformed this republic into a piece of living history. Nonetheless, most cultural historians have adhered to the political periodization, presupposing expressionism as the aesthetic convulsion that accompanied Germany's transition from the *Kaiserreich* to the republic. In recent years, this interpretation has started to give way to a more comprehensive perspective with which both questions can be addressed, thus recognizing the historical continuities. The awareness that the notion of *Sachlichkeit* began to be used as a catalyst for an aesthetic reform movement around 1904 helps to situate the developments of the 1920s within the rocky history of the democratization of culture in Germany. In turn, the reforms through which modernity was invented or, more precisely, designed in imperial Germany can be better categorized vis-à-vis the reified notion of the avantgarde, which has dominated the other—international—narrative on the culture of the period.

Most intriguing is the study of the extent to which modernity was not just an invention but a venture in which commercial and aesthetic interests merged. This would not have upset the French inventor of the term "avant-garde" almost a century before, as long as the artists remained a crucial force in furthering social progress. What Henri de Saint-Simon had prescribed for the avant-garde in the 1820s found a more congenial echo in the English, German, and Austrian reform movements than among the French artistic elites in the late nineteenth and early twentieth centuries, which shielded the avant-garde from functional pursuits. Saint-Simon saw the *artiste* and the *industriel* as equals in leading a better society. Addressing the scientist and the *industriel,* he had stated: "Let us unite. In order to reach the same goal each of us has a different task to fulfill. We—the artists—will be your vanguard [avant-garde]. The power of the arts is in effect the most immediate and most rapid of all powers. We have all kinds of weapons. . . . We address ourselves to man's imagination and sentiments; consequently we are always bound to have the sharpest and most decisive effect."[43] To be sure, designers and architects such as Van de Velde, Behrens, and Gropius, who could claim to fulfill the role of Saint-Simon's *artiste* vis-à-vis the *industriel,* felt uneasy in this collaboration and aired their misgivings about Muthesius's call for *Typisierung.* Nevertheless, their agenda encompassed more of Saint-Simon's original notion of the avant-garde than that of the contemporary French artists. When Marcel Duchamp offered a highly successful about-face of their position on the involvement with material reality and its trivial objects, he found new and promising ways of confirming the high status of the avant-garde artist. German artists and writers who accepted the label of expressionism for their style of excitement held on to a comparable distinction of their movement.

While this self-stylization yielded exciting formal innovations and attracted broad attention, with its revitalizing of the image of the oppositional genius, it held by no means the only key to the temper of the time. Karl Scheffler's analysis of the young generation's behavior in 1912 gives little or no indication of the often assumed expressionist flair. It could have been written in 1926:

Youth tends, also in other professions, to make the ideal practical, unromantic, and *sachlich.* Therefore the progress of technology becomes an ideal in itself. Ideal perceptions that amount to extended notions of culture are being linked to everything technical. The utopian idea is being tied to scientific calculation, the fantastic vision of endless possibilities emanates from the idea of the work. In this sense, art is not the most aristocratic organ of enthusiasm anymore; the idea of culture [Kulturidee] has taken its place. Which means: a political-economical and logically expedient idea of perfection that cannot be separated anymore from world-power instincts. Hence the new youth, not at all romantically sentimental, does not despise the business sense; rather, it understands that its cultural ideal can be realized only commercially and technically, only politically and

---

43. "The Artist, the Scientist, and the Industrial: Dialogue," in *Henri Saint-Simon (1760–1828): Selected Writings on Science, Industry and Social Organization,* ed. Keith Taylor (London, 1975), 281.

concretely. . . . One does not lose oneself in and at the things but rather attempts to control them.[44]

Such an assessment, which is corroborated by numerous texts of this period, primarily describes an attitude or a state of mind, an attitude toward reality. Scheffler's assertion that the idea of culture takes the place of art is his way of expressing the shift from high to applied art. As a consequence, the wide range of manifestations of a culture of *Sachlichkeit* allow the critical repositioning of expressionism with its antirealistic and antimaterialistic momentum; it was a movement against *Sachlichkeit,* rather than vice versa.[45] More to the point, the style of excitement with which expressionists were able to conquer theater, dance, poetry, and other genres in the framework of great art had all the trappings of a—highly self-involved—swan song of the belief that high art can redeem society and that the charismatic artist can lead the way, through *Untergang* (fall), to a *Verwandlung* (rebirth) of humankind. While propagated mostly by middle-class sons (seldom daughters), the redeeming mission of abstraction found its most receptive audience in the period of World War I, when the disenchantment with capitalist materialism and the destructive power of technology was particularly strong. These were the years when the fortunes of the Werkbund and related organizations subsided and its representatives resorted to a romantic revival of the crafts.

Nevertheless, there can be little doubt that the war became a more powerful agent for expanding the relevance of *Sachlichkeit* than that of the expressionist projection of defiance and prophecy. One of the leading oppositional journals, *Das Forum,* offered this conclusion already a few months after the excitement of August 1914. Appalled by the noisy surrender of German academics, intellectuals, and artists to the war fever, Wilhelm Herzog, a close associate of Heinrich Mann's, juxtaposed their hysterical rhetoric with the need for *Sachlichkeit* to win the war. As an appendix to his article with the suggestive title "The Overestimation of Art," Herzog quoted the letter of an officer from the front: "I am disgusted when I read in newspapers invectives against our enemies or exuberant jingoism. We will not win on this basis but rather on that of calm [Ruhe] and *Sachlichkeit* and tenacious energy. We need no hatred: we modern people can do without it."[46] The art historian Wilhelm Hausenstein

---

44. Karl Scheffler, "Die Jugend," in *Gesammelte Essays,* by Karl Scheffler (Leipzig, 1912), 231–32.

45. Despite new insights into elements of *Sachlichkeit* in early expressionism, Peter Sprengel confirms the basic antagonism of expressionism and *Sachlichkeit.* ("Von der Baukunst zur Wortkunst: Sachlichkeit und Expressionimus im *Sturm*," *Deutsche Vierteljahrsschrift für Literaturwissenschaft und Geistesgeschichte* 64 [1990]: 680–706.)

46. Wilhelm Herzog, "Die Überschätzung der Kunst," *Das Forum* 1, no. 2 (1914–15): 455–56.

added an illuminating footnote to the German-French confrontation: "Until now, we have considered the always excited, insultingly excited subjectivity of the French as a nuisance that is even disastrous for France and have, not without reason, praised our greater objectivity. But it seems that we produce the nuisance . . . to a large extent ourselves."[47] Others lauded the "*sachlich* seriousness, the calm without rhetoric" of the professional officers in contrast to the jumpy excitement of intellectuals and artists.[48]

It did not take long for the war to assume the characteristics of a heroic exercise in applied *Sachlichkeit*, embellished with the most horrifying markings of rationalized slaughter and death. Herzog's hope that the war would generate "men of a new spirit who want to be *sachlich* and just"[49] materialized in the genesis of the figure of the worker-soldier, whom Ernst Jünger endowed with the mission to bring about the total mobilization of society, and whom Joseph Goebbels conjured as the carrier of the steely *Sachlichkeit* of the new Germany.

This aspect appears to open more issues than it puts to rest. I place it at the center of my concluding remarks in order to signal the open state of the reflections on the German culture of *Sachlichkeit*. As World War I turned *Sachlichkeit* from an attitudinal and aesthetic conceptualization of social reality into an attitude vis-à-vis battle, death, and destruction, it carried the seeds for a highly explosive design of society and its political formation. Once morality is transformed into *Sachlichkeit*,[50] politics deteriorates into the worst form of ideology. This means that since the experience of World War I the definition of *Sachlichkeit* also entails the ultimate *Versachlichung* of humans into things. It also means that the *Neue Sachlichkeit* of the twenties has to be seen not only as a continuation of the prewar culture of *Sachlichkeit* but also as an attempt to regain this concept from its usage by those, especially on the Right, whose agenda is to constitute a permanent state of war. To link *Sachlichkeit* with the democratic message from America is part of the aesthetic politics of the Weimar Republic. Under these auspices, *Neue Sachlichkeit* appears artistically less, and politically more, propitious than usually assumed.

In view of this powerful and ambiguous mobilization of modernity, tracing the potential of the *völkisch* ideologies back to the manifestations of cultural despair in Wilhelmine Germany seems to address a rather limited source of Nazi strength. While Marxist critics of this mobilization, from Karl Kautsky to Georg Lukács, Herbert Marcuse and Theodor Adorno, who saw it as a combination of capitalism and irrationalism, were at least aware of its energies,

---

47. Wilhelm Hausenstein, "Sache oder Floskel," ibid., 437.
48. Hortense von Beaulieu, "Waren wir vor dem Kriege zu ästhetisch?" ibid., 139.
49. Wilhelm Herzog, "Der neue Geist," ibid., 465.
50. See Hermann Lübbe, *Politische Philosophie in Deutschland: Studien zu ihrer Geschichte* (Munich, 1974), 165.

the more recent projections of the continuities between bourgeois disenchantment and precapitalist *völkisch* ideology have not even addressed the dynamics of this phenomenon. A more comprehensive study of these dynamics is imperative if one wants to clarify the strength that Germany under Hitler drew from a particular German approach to modernity. Such a study would help us to understand how the Nazis could tap a source of physical, mental, creative, and destructive energies that in German culture to this day is considered a virtue: *Sachlichkeit.*

The *Kaiserreich's* Ruins: Hope, Memory, and Political Culture in Imperial Germany

Rudy Koshar

"Redemptive" Historiography

This is a time for archaeological metaphors in the study of history. Frank Trommler has recently written of German history as an "artifact" with reference to Anselm Kiefer's paintings, and Keith Michael Baker has likened French political culture to a "living archaeological site."[1] Michel Foucault's discussion of the "space of knowledge" and of the "archaeology of the human sciences" had, of course, already set the tone for such language,[2] but it is not difficult to trace the origins of this terminology back somewhat farther, to Walter Benjamin's visualizations of nineteenth-century consumer goods from the Paris Arcades as "fossils" and "ruins."[3] One could extend the genealogy. From my point of view, the issue is that such metaphorical language stresses the materiality of historical research, its operation in "a field of entangled and confused parchments,"[4] and thus places the historian in the context of an object world in which images and things circulate far afield from their origins in time and (often) place. This language is part of the self-historicization of the historian that has come with continuing debates over epistemology in the human

---

1. Frank Trommler, "Germany's Past as an Artifact," *Journal of Modern History* 61 (December 1989): 724–35; Keith Michael Baker, ed., *The French Revolution and the Creation of Modern Political Culture,* vol. 1, *The Political Culture of the Old Regime* (Oxford, 1987), xii.

2. Michel Foucault, *The Order of Things: An Archaeology of the Human Sciences* (New York, 1970).

3. Susan Buck-Morss, *The Dialectics of Seeing: Walter Benjamin and the Arcades Project* (Cambridge, Mass., 1989).

4. Michel Foucault, "Nietzsche, Genealogy, History," in *Language, Counter-Memory, Practice,* by Michel Foucault (Ithaca, 1977), 139.

sciences, and it is with such language in mind that I want to reflect on the political culture of Imperial Germany.

When West German historians of the 1950s wrote a German past in the aftermath of the destruction of the National Socialist dictatorship, they configured Imperial Germany in a particular way. Assuming that the roots of Nazism could be found in World War I and the Weimar Republic, they stressed discontinuity between *Kaiserreich* (in some narratives qualified to mean the *Kaiserreich* before 1890) and "Third Reich." This enabled them to retain a key feature of German historiography, the *Sonderweg* thesis, or Germany's exemplary divergence from the history of the West. If memory of the distant, positive uniqueness of the *Kaiserreich* (or at least of the early *Kaiserreich*) could be maintained, then German divergence from the West could be defended against what was characterized as a militarism inspired ultimately by the French Revolution, class conflict, mass politics, and the evolution of a basically Western (rather than specifically German) totalitarianism.[5] Critics of this discontinuity thesis (who are by no means a homogeneous group in methodological or political terms) put forward a much different version of German history but still added to the "chain of supplements" that the *Sonderweg* argument had become.[6] Fritz Fischer, Hans-Ulrich Wehler, Jürgen Kocka, and many others constructed Imperial Germany as a seedbed of authoritarianism, anti-Semitism, militarism, and hypernationalism—a political culture permeated with the kind of antimodern, antidemocratic traditions that Nazi propagandists would later mobilize.[7] In this view, another discontinuity emerged, namely, that between the *Kaiserreich* and the Federal Republic (or the later, more democratic Federal Republic), which now painfully disengaged itself from its authoritarian heritage. Yet German divergence from a generic West was still assumed, even though the West was now idealized. Both versions began with Nazism as the key problem of modern German history. Both attempted to keep the traces of the twelve-year *Reich* from contaminating those of other, valued historical epochs, whether of the early *Kaiserreich* or later Bonn republic.

---

5. See Georg G. Iggers, *The German Conception of History: The National Tradition of Historical Thought from Herder to the Present*, rev. ed. (Middletown, Conn., 1983), 245–68; for a discussion of the *Sonderweg* thesis and Weimar, see Bernd Faulenbach, *Ideologie des deutschen Weges: Die deutsche Geschichte in der Historiographie zwischen Kaiserreich und Nationalsozialismus* (Munich, 1980).

6. For the notion of a chain of supplements (here with reference to Jean-Jacques Rousseau), see Jacques Derrida, *Of Grammatology* (Baltimore, 1976), 156–57.

7. Still the best single example of this genre is Hans-Ulrich Wehler, *Das deutsche Kaiserreich, 1871–1918* (Göttingen, 1973); see also Iggers, *The German Conception of History*, 275–84, for a discussion of this and other works in this group.

The last two decades have seen numerous challenges to such views.[8] These challenges have been organized around an interdisciplinary project of redemption that is not unrelated to that carried out by the historians of the first two decades of the post–World War II era. The *Kaiserreich* has been redeemed in a triple sense: first, from a historiography that constructed it as an unproblematically reactionary fundament of Nazism; second, from the status of being an idealized golden age before the fall; and third, from the imagery of an elite-centered monolith in which workers, women, and social and sexual outsiders played no substantial role. Redemption has thus had the effect of promoting study of the *Kaiserreich* in its own right—rather than only with respect to its origins or its failure—and simultaneously folding Imperial Germany into a longer historical narrative whereby the more than five decades of German history after 1945 could be brought into some positive relationship with the era that produced what Hajo Holborn called "the greatest European industrial nation."[9] Sociopolitical history, comparative history, and women's history are instrumental in this redemptive historiography, having created—or having the potential to create—new ways of writing about a political culture whose relationship to the present has become a matter of direct political import now that there is once again a formally unified German entity in Central Europe.

By using the notion of redemptive historiography, one cannot avoid reference to Benjamin's work or, more accurately, of recent receptions of his work.[10] For Benjamin, there was a messianic component to redemptive criticism, a notion that he used to refer to the process of illuminating the present in a moment of danger by remembering certain moments of the past as they could be read in works of art, architecture, commerce, and literature. His goal was that "all of the past" could be "brought into the present," an idea that was analogous to Georg Simmel's notion from 1911 that contemplation of architectural ruins (in the literal sense) allowed the observer to take in the whole of

---

8. A large literature (which need not be recapitulated here) has grown up around this debate, with David Blackbourn and Geoff Eley, *The Peculiarities of German History: Bourgeois Society and Politics in Nineteenth-Century Germany* (Oxford, 1984) at its center. Recently, the debate has somewhat indirectly crystallized around discussions over the place of the *Bürgertum* in German history. See above all Jürgen Kocka, ed., *Bürgertum im 19. Jahrhundert: Deutschland im europäischen Vergleich*, 3 vols. (Munich, 1988); and David Blackbourn and Richard Evans, eds., *The German Bourgeoisie: Essays on the Social History of the German Middle Class from the Late Eighteenth to the Early Twentieth Century* (London and New York, 1991).

9. Hajo Holborn, *A History of Modern Germany, 1840–1945* (New York, 1969), 233.

10. The most accessible primary sources for Anglo-American readers of Benjamin remain the two essay collections *Walter Benjamin, Illuminations: Essays and Reflections*, ed. Hannah Arendt (New York, 1969); and *Reflections: Essays, Aphorisms, Autobiographical Writings*, ed. Peter Demetz (New York, 1986).

human history in a single instant.[11] But one can also use the term to refer to a process of reclamation or retrieval that stops short of positing some "extra-historical" moment. One can use Benjamin's idea that there is a "double nature" to some kinds of history writing consisting of "positivity and negativity at once," which means that the historian (or critic or philosopher) first breaks down or destroys the subject under study before reconstructing it to create a new relationship with the past. Redemption proceeded from the initial destruction of the object (Benjamin spoke of "mortification").[12] This is the connotation I want to emphasize, and this is something like what has happened in the redemptive historiography mentioned above. By borrowing Benjamin's idea to argue that some historians have destroyed the old *Kaiserreich* in order to reclaim it for a new version of Imperial Germany, and by disengaging Benjamin's notion of a redemptive criticism from his historically specific religious-political interests, I am "mortifying" Benjamin's work itself, a process that the philosopher would have understood,[13] though it is more than likely that he would have criticized my adherence to professional standards of "historicist" research and argumentation.

But then how does one write the political culture of the *Kaiserreich*? If the *Kaiserreich* has been destroyed and made available for reclamation, what is its future? How does one construct the *Kaiserreich,* now that its previously determinate or predictable relationship to Weimar, the rise of Nazism, and the Federal Republic has been so effectively questioned? More to the point, does one simply reconfigure tried-and-true tropes of continuity/discontinuity or the *Sonderweg* in its exemplary or critical modes? Or does one walk away from them, following Richard Rorty's claim that the most creative method is not to contest preexisting analytical vocabularies but to create new vocabularies that "redescribe lots and lots of things in new ways"?[14]

It would be impossible to address these questions in a short, speculative, and experimental essay such as this, but I must say I find Rorty's notion of redescription useful.[15] The point of the following brief remarks is to suggest that the deconstructing of the *Kaiserreich*'s relationship to subsequent periods

---

11. Taken from Benjamin's unpublished *Das Passagen-Werk*, as reprinted in *Gesammelte Schriften,* ed. Rolf Tiedemann and Hermann Schweppenhauser (Frankfurt a.M., 1972–85), vol. 5, part 1 (1982), 573, and cited in Michael W. Jennings, *Dialectical Images: Walter Benjamin's Theory of Literary Criticism* (Ithaca, 1987), 38. Georg Simmel's "The Ruin" is reprinted in Kurt H. Wolff, ed., *Georg Simmel, 1858–1918: A Collection of Essays with Translations and a Bibliography* (Columbus, Ohio, 1959).

12. I refer to Jennings's discussion in *Dialectical Images,* 38, 39, 40, 62.

13. Jennings, *Dialectical Images,* 212–13, has pointed this out with reference to literary scholars' use of Benjamin.

14. Richard Rorty, *Contingency, Irony, and Solidarity* (Cambridge, 1989), 9.

15. See Rudy Koshar, "Playing the Cerebral Savage: Writing German History before the Linguistic Turn," *Central European History* 22, nos. 3–4 (September–December 1989): 343–59.

of German history (to say nothing of previous periods) should now be followed by creative and provisional rethinking. The goal should be to produce a battery of narratives that point out broad correspondences and differences between specialized research areas—new emplotments for a historical period for which there are still many topics that have not been explored, despite the outpouring of monographic research over the past quarter century. Specifically, I want to use Benjamin's image of the ruin, or rather Susan Buck-Morss's reading of it, as a metaphor for reflecting on such questions. The formation of ruins will be used as an analogy for thinking about the development of certain processes within the *Kaiserreich*'s political culture, a term I specify with reference to Gramscian notions of hegemony and Reinhard Koselleck's work on hope and memory. I argue that recent historiography leads to a potential new emplotment of the history of Imperial Germany, and by using several brief examples from my current research on national memory and the preservation of historical landmarks, I suggest how this emplotment might be developed further.

Political Culture

Historians use the term "political culture" with increasing frequency, but they rarely try to define it systematically. It is, of course, a notoriously difficult term to specify, and the following remarks offer no exhaustive answer to the irresolution of previous work on the subject. I want to highlight two features.

First, Baker has argued that "if politics, broadly construed, is the activity through which individuals and groups in any society articulate, negotiate, implement, and enforce the competing claims they make one upon another, then political culture may be understood as the set of discourses and practices characterizing that activity in any given community."[16] The notion of a set of discourses and practices is troublesome because it suggests completeness. It is analogous to saying that at any moment in time, a society has a more or less coherent, bounded cultural repertoire that is available for interpretation once one has deciphered the relations of social life and the representations by which they are given meaning. Such assumptions are questionable, and the notion of political culture requires an especially sensitive treatment of the volatility, open-endedness, and instability of those discourses and practices that hardly constitute anything like a coherent set. Nonetheless, Baker's interpretation does have the advantage of referring to a multiplicity of social actions. It also allows us to think of political culture as directly and constitutively involved in social conflict but simultaneously imbricated in discourses and practices that have little direct relationship to the political sphere in the narrower sense of the term.

---

16. Baker, *The Political Culture of the Old Regime,* xii.

Baker refers to political culture as "a historical creation." I will take this to mean that it must be defined in relation to patterns of domination, subordination, negotiation, noncompliance, and resistance. It may be useful to theorize political culture in terms of the complex relationships between consent, or cultural direction, and coercion in the manner that Antonio Gramsci's discussions of hegemony suggest.[17] In Gramsci's view, dominant class-based coalitions can rule safely only under conditions in which their authority assumes a naturalness that leaves the coercive fundament of authority unquestioned. But this natural state is in fact a "moving equilibrium" in which no particular class gains permanent control over other classes. Conflict is always possible, although not always visible or developed. Social leadership—as opposed to open coercion—has to be forged and constantly renegotiated in political parties, educational institutions, voluntary associations, and many other public spaces, which in some cases have little direct connection to politics. Using such notions, we can define political culture as the discourses and practices that reflexively give meaning to these relationships of consent and coercion within and between the state and social life.

The second main dimension of political culture that I want to refer to is "anthropological" or "metahistorical."[18] Reinhart Koselleck has argued that "concrete history [is] produced within the medium of particular experiences and particular expectations." Hope and memory, or what Koselleck refers to as the horizon of expectation and the space of experience, are the conditions of possible histories. (I use the term "memory" broadly to include both "history," as the "objectivizing" study of the past for its own sake, and memory proper, which by comparison is more "subjective," adaptive, practical, and unreflective.)[19] Experience is "present past, whose events have been incorporated and can be remembered," whereas expectation is "the future made present," which "directs itself to the not-yet."[20] Koselleck argues that tension between experience and expectation generates historical time. More specifically, he argues that the modern period is characterized by a growing asymmetry between hope and memory, expectation and experience. His discussion suggests that the relationship of the present to either past or future is asymptotic: experience as well as expectation constantly recede as they are approached in the present.

---

17. I rely here on Antonio Gramsci, *Selections from the Prison Notebooks,* ed. Quintin Hoare and Geoffrey Nowell Smith (New York, 1971), in which the author's discussions of hegemony, civil society, and other terms are diffuse but always evocative.

18. I rely here on Reinhart Koselleck, "'Space of Experience' and 'Horizon of Expectation': Two Historical Categories," in *Futures Past: On the Semantics of Historical Time,* by Reinhart Koselleck (Cambridge, Mass., 1985), 267–88.

19. See David Carr, *Time, Narrative, and History* (Bloomington, 1986), 168.

20. Koselleck, "'Space of Experience,'" 271, 272.

Political action in the late modern age, in Koselleck's view, has the task of bridging the great difference between space of experience and horizon of expectation. Just as "republicanism" was "a concept of expectation developed out of a concept filled with experience" at the time of the French Revolution, subsequent concepts of "movement"—democracy, liberalism, socialism, communism, and fascism—anticipated a political future that was to be realized through practical work based on experience and remembrance, albeit a remembrance that may have had little to do with the origins of the concepts in question.[21] Within this context, political culture as I have defined it, shaped within changing relations of consent and coercion, refers to the multiple discourses and practices that political activity uses to bridge memory and hope, experience and expectation. In the following pages, I devote more attention to these discourses and practices—the cultural and social raw materials of politics—than to the specific political movements that made use of them.

The Image of the Ruin

According to Buck-Morss's philosophical picture book of Benjamin's Paris Arcades project—a book about a book that was never written—Benjamin thought of physical objects in the arcades as significant fragments whose "meanings" could be constructed allegorically.[22] On the one hand, these objects were anticipatory in that they suggested "wish-images" of the future, yet on the other hand they were profoundly devalued by the very processes of production and consumption that had produced them, making them outmoded before they were used up. Their original moral-political meaning, which Benjamin was sure could be deciphered, had been hollowed out, leaving them as bare shells. These "ruins" were objects that bore traces of previous eras but that had lost their "soul." In Benjamin's opinion, once they were blasted from the wreckage of the past, they could be made to function as emblems, structures of word and image, for the transitoriness and destructiveness of nineteenth-century capitalist culture. It is important to note, as Buck-Morss does, that Benjamin's status as culture hero of much poststructuralist theory is somewhat inappropriate, for he thought that ruins, and material objects in general, had something "objective" about them once they were exposed to the critic's destructive gaze, something that could be discerned in a way that allowed the philosopher or historian to do more than see her/his reflection.[23] He was no advocate of semiotic free-fall, and thus his attraction for deconstructionists is problematic. But he was also a rather idiosyncratic materialist, since his belief

---

21. Ibid., 286.
22. For the following, see Buck-Morss, *The Dialectics of Seeing,* esp. chap. 6.
23. Ibid., 13, 338–39.

in knowledge about the object world had a mystical quality that has perplexed, provoked, and annoyed numerous interpreters. Finally, he was convinced of the need for political action. "The crumbling of the monuments that were built to signify the immortality of civilization becomes proof, rather, of its transiency," writes Buck-Morss of Benjamin's perspective. But this did not justify resignation, for "the fleetingness of temporal power does not cause sadness; it informs political practice."[24] In this sense Benjamin, though deeply nostalgic, stands very much to the side of a long tradition of melancholy in the political culture of the German *Bürgertum,* a melancholy that has been read as both symptom and cause of political impotence.[25]

One use of the image of the ruin is to call attention to the fact that historical evidence amounts to a world of material objects "accessed" in particular institutional spaces. This is an unsurprising observation, but it is in fact a useful one because it makes the historian think about what s/he is actually doing when research in an archive or library is undertaken. Just as Benjamin could use the object world to reflect on larger moral-political meanings, historians should think of the *Kaiserreich,* or any historical period, as a field of objects—written texts, documents, photographs, works of art, buildings, consumer goods—that they use to imagine pasts. This may be no problem at all for scholars of ancient history, to take an obvious example, since the materiality of historical research in this field is vividly expressed in the use of a limited supply of sources, such as coins and other archaeological artifacts. (Although historians of the ancient past may be no more willing to recognize the implications of such a statement than their counterparts in more modern fields are.) For later periods of history, such observations have a less obvious or a secondary importance, at least to professional historians, who are accustomed to overlook the material nature of research that uses primarily books and archival documents in circumscribed institutional settings.

Nonetheless, even if the materiality of research is stressed, the creative process of constructing the past from what is always material culture is problematic, because the field it engages is subject to numerous contradictions and ambiguities. The artifacts of the *Kaiserreich* coexist with the physical remains of many historical eras that came before and after Imperial Germany, seemingly lessening distances between them and flattening differences. They are images and things interwoven with a world of commodities, in which every object has real or potential exchange value, academic or commercial. Their "truths" are lost to us, not merely because of changes in their physical integrity but also because of the absence of those individuals and groups that gave them

---

24. Ibid., 170.
25. I am thinking here of Wolf Lepenies, *Melancholy and Society* (Cambridge, Mass., 1992), chap. 4.

meaning in their specific historical contexts. The objects have been displaced; they have no home except that of the academic or commercial marketplace. Because they belong to these marketplaces, they cannot escape that "etherealization" and "abstraction" of production and consumption of late-twentieth-century "hypercapitalism" that Dick Hebdige argues are the characteristic features of the age of the "withering signified."[26] Archivists, museum directors, librarians, preservationists, collectors, and historians may try to remedy this by "reconstructing" the past (through writing particular kinds of history books or creating museum displays, for instance) or by trying to keep these remains from being contaminated by the remains of other eras or by the commodity world in general, but they fight against insurmountable odds. They deal with ruins.

We are left with a sense of the futility of studying the *Kaiserreich* or any other historical period—as a field of extant "things"—in its own right, of redeeming it in any historicist sense of recreating a past world after scientific study of its discursive or nondiscursive artifacts, of returning the signified to its proper place. Indeed, the physical objects with which historians have tried to read and write the past reveal that transitoriness, that same hollowing out of their original meaning, that Benjamin found so powerfully emblematized in the consumer goods of the nineteenth-century arcades.

Yet the objects remain with us, inviting reflection on them even when we know they cannot tell an authentic story. Moreover, even if the hermeneutic project of reconstructing authorial intention and original meaning faces extraordinary obstacles, it is not very interesting to act as if the ruins were not once the products of human beings who thought of themselves as intending "authors" and knowing "readers."[27] Indeed, the notion of the ruin suggests there may have been past meanings, which, although no longer fully present, may be evoked—rather than explained—in historical narratives. To say the least, evocation is a powerful and, in my opinion, necessary cultural activity.

Benjamin's image of the ruin, couched in elusive prose that defies easy characterization, is useful in the present context because of its emphasis on the transience of anticipations of the future in capitalist modernity. I want to argue that a central characteristic of political culture in advanced capitalist states is the evolution of discourses and practices that try to map out the social conditions, practical consequences, cultural forms, and moral obligations of present and future relations of coercion and consent. These discourses and practices point to collective "wishes" about how political claims will be defined, pre-

---

26. See Dick Hebdige, *Hiding in the Light: On Images and Things* (London and New York, 1988), esp. 161–67.

27. See Joyce Appleby, "One Good Turn Deserves Another: Moving beyond the Linguistic: A Response to David Harlan," *American Historical Review* 94, no. 5 (December 1989): 1326–32.

sented, and adjudicated. These futures operate dialectically, reaching back to mythic, distant, or recent pasts at the moment they emerge. At the same time, however, they contain their own failure, as the destructiveness and dynamism of the modern political marketplace sweep away the possibility of their fulfillment. The literal ruins of political culture—texts, buildings, consumer goods—thus point to the "ruinlike" quality of the interactions that produced them. But it is perhaps inappropriate to refer to these ruins as bare shells, as Benjaminian discourse does. For they become "filled" with new uses and meanings by successive political generations, who rely on new pasts to envision possible futures. It is this conflictive flow of meanings through such objects and processes that makes the ruin metaphor so compelling.

Emplotments

The redemptive historiography mentioned in the introduction to my essay has effectively demonstrated that the *Kaiserreich* was more capable of reform, more pluralistic, and more like "the West," to which it has been so often negatively compared, than had previously been thought. At the same time, it has not overlooked the peculiarities of the *Kaiserreich,* such as the frustrations of parliamentary power there when compared to other advanced capitalist states. The still-unrealized potential of this research is that it can effectively challenge "comic" emplotments of German history, in which "hope is held out for the temporary triumph of man over his world by the prospect of occasional reconciliations of the forces at play in the social and natural worlds."[28] This comedic element—despite being supplemented by satiric and tragic elements in the works of individual historians—seems to have been present in the historiography of the 1950s as well as in the West German social-historical and social-scientific work of the 1970s and early 1980s, for although each tradition had a different view of the *Kaiserreich,* both looked to a secular epiphany, of varying content and timing, that would finally "come to terms" with the German past. Some version of social harmony would eventually be established, conflicts would be resolved, if only imperfectly, goals would be met—if not by conservative nationalism then by social liberalism or social democracy.

I would argue that the current redemptive historiography (and perhaps a part of the historiography against which the redemptive work was first directed) is moving toward a satirically tragic emplotment, one that emphasizes reconciliations more somber than those of comedy, more skeptical about the abilities of human beings to alter the conditions in which they live—although still not without an emphasis on human agency—and more doubtful

---

28. Hayden White, *Metahistory: The Historical Imagination in Nineteenth-Century Europe* (Baltimore, 1973), 9.

about the adequacy of our visions of social and political life.[29] The imagery of the ruin meshes well with this view of the past.

The tragic element of the *Kaiserreich*—and of the larger narrative of German history, in which it is presently being reintegrated—stems from the transitoriness of its anticipated political futures. We can see this in many areas of social, cultural, and political life. Challenging European and global power relationships, at the very moment that Germany became Holborn's great industrial nation, the *Kaiserreich* generated those physical remains—factories, monuments, social infrastructures—that now leave us with an image of the fleeting nature of power. At the moment when industrialization gave Germany the power to redraw the geopolitical map of Europe, domestic conflict and increased international resistance to the rise of Germany fortunately subverted its governments' ability to realize a violent, expansionist *Weltpolitik* in two world wars. At the moment that Germany laid the institutional framework for "making Germans," for constructing a notionally stable national identity, its political culture produced an array of multiple identities (parties, social movements, electorates based on class and religion, new constructions of gender). At the moment that a space in Central Europe named modern Germany appeared, it disappeared in world war, revolution, dictatorship, and division. It may be unpopular but necessary to stress this transience in the context of contemporary politics, as certain people within a new post–cold war Germany claim a lineage with previous versions of the German nation.

My perspective is an imposition on the history of the *Kaiserreich* as men and women lived it, as all historical narratives are. But there is lots of evidence to suggest that it is a useful story about the historical *Kaiserreich* because it illuminates important features of the contemporary political culture. Moreover, there is abundant evidence that the *Kaiserreich* was able to "process" the profound destruction of its political futures across a range of cultural endeavors. Taking only one example from the early empire, one could read the elegiac quality of German realist literature in the two decades after 1870 as part of a worrisome but hopeful discourse on the rapidity with which larger social and political changes, such as those described above, hollowed out all previous forms of authority.[30] But such examples multiply for the later *Kaiserreich*. By the turn of the century and beyond, there was an anxious attempt to step out of the nineteenth century in architecture (abstracted historicism), in literature (from naturalism to a new Nietzschean subjectivity that included both optimism and visions of future disaster), in industrial design (the cultural agenda of *Sachlichkeit*), in social science (most notably in the work of Max Weber, who

---

29. Ibid., 9–10.
30. See Thomas Nipperdey, *Deutsche Geschichte, 1866–1918,* vol. 1, *Arbeitswelt und Bürgergeist* (Munich, 1990), 758–60.

regretted the loss of past community even as he pinpointed and accepted the rationalization of society), as well as in politics (the search for new, more activist forms of nationalist politics, which were often based on mythic inflections of the German past).[31] These processes were motivated in part by a sense that an epoch of German and Western history had ended, and that new ways of relating to the past and future, of organizing memory and hope, were needed. Yet at the same time, such new initiatives had a sense of futility that was different from the cultural pessimism of Paul de Lagarde or Julius Langbehn but was also critical of an earlier liberal belief in progress.[32] Instead of trying to give more undeveloped examples of this anxious hopefulness—this political-cultural discourse on ruins—I will try to pinpoint its manifestation in the subsequent discussion of historic preservation, a small though significant site in the political culture.

Cities, Towns, Monuments, Memory

Since I have stressed the materiality of historical research and the actual physical placement of the historian in an object world, it would be useful to use some specific examples from the built environment to develop such points further. It is obvious from the previous discussion that the metaphor of the ruin is not applicable only to the built environment, but it would be unfair not to mention that I began thinking about such metaphorical uses as I became interested in the political content of architecture and the physical fabric of urban and small-town life. The built environment is a subject area rich in evidence about political culture but inconsistently used by historians other than those who have specific interests in architectural or art history.[33] It is also an

---

31. For examples from architecture, see Barbara Miller Lane, *Architecture and Politics in Germany, 1918–1945* (Cambridge, Mass., 1968), 11–27; for literature, besides Nipperdey, *Deutsche Geschichte,* 1: 775–76, see the examples of a sense of catastrophe in Klaus Vondung, "Träume von Tod und Untergang: Präludien zur Apokalypse in der deutschen Literatur und Kunst vor dem Ersten Weltkrieg," in *Von kommenden Zeiten: Geschichtsprophetien im 19. und 20. Jahrhundert,* ed. Joachim H. Knoll and Julius H. Schoeps (Stuttgart, 1984), 143–68; on pre–World War I *Sachlichkeit,* see the essay in this volume by Frank Trommler; on Weber, see the comments on Weber's simultaneous championing of rationalization and nostalgia for "decisionist" vitalism by Charles Maier, *The Unmasterable Past: History, Holocaust, and German National Identity* (Cambridge, Mass., 1988), 156; and on a newly activist nationalist politics, see Roger Chickering, *We Men Who Feel Most German: A Cultural Study of the Pan-German League, 1886–1914* (Boston, 1984); and Geoff Eley, *Reshaping the German Right: Radical Nationalism and Political Change after Bismarck* (New Haven, 1980).

32. On cultural pessimism, see Fritz Stern, *The Politics of Cultural Despair: A Study in the Rise of the Germanic Ideology* (New York, 1961); and Stephan Popov, *Am Ende aller Illusionen: Der Europäische Kulturpessimismus* (Cologne, 1981).

33. A notable exception is Thomas Nipperdey. See his "Der Kölner Dom als Nationaldenkmal," in *Nachdenken über die deutsche Geschichte,* by Thomas Nipperdey (Munich, 1986), 156–

area of substantial complexity, since it involves discussing specific architectural objects, or photographic or other evidence of those objects, as well as discourse about the objects and their relationships to politics, culture, and society. It is a social realm in which a distinctive kind of double imaging takes place.

The urban and architectural history of the *Kaiserreich* lends itself well to such double imaging. Although much of the nineteenth-century German city has been destroyed or rebuilt, enough of it remains, and enough of it has been "preserved" in photographs and drawings, to offer a rich field of material evidence. Indeed, one could say that a substantial part of the nineteenth-century city was reinstated in the past three decades, when historic preservationists, art historians, architects, planners, museum directors, tourists, home buyers, and professionals generally began to pay much more attention to nineteenth-century architecture in Germany, much of it from the previously scorned period of the *Kaiserreich*.[34] Using the written artifacts generated by the historical city of the *Kaiserreich,* social and political historians have been no less active in the repositioning of the historical city. Much of this work has concentrated on working-class history. By comparison, the middle-class characters of the narrative are much more unevenly developed. It is surprising to find how much remains to be done in areas such as the local history of German liberalism, urban planning, administration, bourgeois perceptions of urban life, and broader interrelationships of middle-class local politics and social structure during the *Kaiserreich*.[35] But whether we focus on working-

---

71; and "Nationalidee und Nationaldenkmal in Deutschland im 19. Jahrhundert," in *Gesellschaft, Kultur, Theorie: Gesammelte Aufsätze zur neueren Geschichte,* by Thomas Nipperdey (Göttingen, 1976), 133–73.

34. This tendency is critically discussed as an aspect of the 1970s nostalgia wave in West Germany by Reinhard Bentmann, "Der Kampf um die Erinnerung: Ideologische und methodische Konzepte des modernen Denkmalkultus," in *Denkmalräume, Lebensräume,* ed. Ina-Maria Greverus, Hessische Blätter für Volks- und Kulturforschung, vol. 2/3 (Giessen, 1976), 213–46, esp. 218–22. See also Willibald Sauerländer, "Erweiterung des Denkmalbegriffs?" *Deutsche Kunst und Denkmalpflege* 33, nos. 1–2 (1975): 117–30, esp. 126–28.

35. See, for example, the substantial literature cited in Jürgen Reulecke, *Geschichte der Urbanisierung in Deutschland* (Frankfurt a.M., 1985), which deals mainly with the period from the middle of the nineteenth century to World War I and reveals considerable gaps in current knowledge about the nineteenth-century city. The argument could also be made with respect to current debates on the *Bürgertum* (for example, Kocka, *Bürgertum im 19. Jahrhundert*), which have left large parts of the urban middle-class experience unexplored. See, in this regard, Friedrich Lenger, "Bürgertum und Stadtverwaltung in rheinischen Grossstädten des 19. Jahrhunderts: Zu einem vernachlässigten Aspekt bürgerlicher Herrschaft," in *Stadt und Bürgertum im 19. Jahrhundert,* ed. Lothar Gall (Munich, 1990), 97–170. Brian Ladd, *Urban Planning and Civic Order in Germany, 1860–1914* (Cambridge, Mass., 1990) suggests again how little is known about specific communities' experiences in the *Kaiserreich* in seemingly well-researched areas such as the history of urban planning.

class or middle-class history, the condition for reconsidering the urban history of Imperial Germany is the reconstitution and repositioning of written and nonwritten artifacts in the present. To put it another way more directly relevant to the present discussion, new emplotments for urban history's relationship to the political culture of the *Kaiserreich* are based not only on discovery of new evidence but also on the creative production of preserved, restored, and re-designed evidence. The historian who studies the city of the *Kaiserreich* must begin with the assumption that s/he studies a re-presented (and still to be presented) *Kaiserreich.*

The Benjaminian metaphor leads one to view the German urban experience in a particular way. For example, "civic pride" was one of the primary features of German city-building, a specific aspect of bourgeois reformers' and officials' attempts to organize a rapidly expanding urban environment.[36] Beyond this, civic pride gave the bourgeoisie a sense of solidarity and legitimization for action. Sewers, road systems, social-welfare offices, bathhouses, monuments, and grand public buildings all had an aura, a quality of "psychological inapproachability—an authority"[37] based on a developing bourgeois tradition of urban reform. The "auratic" quality of the German city was recognized by contemporary observers, such as the Cleveland civic activist C. Frederick Howe, who in 1915 praised the accomplishments of German municipal government: "Apparently nothing is left to chance. Everything is under control. The city suggests a conscious directing intelligence that looks out from the *Rathaus* as a group of architects might plan a world's fair; as engineers might design a war-ship; as an individual erects a great office-building. Everything suggests intelligence, oversight, and the application of art and science to the city's building."[38]

But everything was not under control. The "conscious directing intelligence" looking out from the *Rathaus* was in fact peering out at a rapidly changing city. At the time that Howe was writing, the German city had already experienced a deep fragmentation along political lines, a fragmentation that would worsen under conditions of universal suffrage and rising Social Democratic influence in the Weimar Republic. Urban planning during the *Kaiserreich* mirrored not a single, cohesive program but an array of conflicts revolving around bourgeois attempts to maintain public and private distinctions. These distinctions were increasingly difficult to uphold in an economic and political system that made them irrelevant. At the same time, bitter disputes over the place of urban life in the German nation punctured the forward-looking boosterism of municipal officials and entrepreneurs, suggest-

---

36. See Ladd, *Urban Planning and Civic Order.*
37. I take the phrase from Jennings, *Dialectical Images,* 168.
38. Quoted in Ladd, *Urban Planning and Civic Order,* 9. Jennings, *Dialectical Images,* 168–69, uses the term *auratic.*

ing visions of a more coherent past that shamed the chaotic present.[39] The German city was deprived of its triumph just when it seemed to have gained its greatest success. Its physical shape bore the marks of contending visions of hope and memory. The cities of the *Kaiserreich* generated those physical remains—factories, public and residential buildings, monuments, social infrastructures, and mountains of documents—that now leave us with an image of the fleeting nature of contending political pasts and futures.[40]

The ruinous qualities of such conflicts can be seen with reference to individual works of architecture and monuments as well. The last three decades of the nineteenth century saw an extraordinary surge in the building of what in 1903 the Viennese art historian Alois Riegl called "intentional monuments"—statues, plaques, busts, and other commemorative objects "erected for the specific purpose of keeping single human deeds or events (or a combination thereof) alive in the minds of future generations." Many of these were part of a larger attempt to legitimize the rule of national political regimes by creating a sense of national memory.[41] But "unintentional monuments" became even more important to this process of memory creation. These were buildings, ensembles of buildings, and even whole townscapes, whose commemorative value stemmed not from their original purpose but from the historical importance ascribed to them by later generations. They were artifacts whose original uses were lost and whose lease on life depended on their gaining historical significance in the present and future. Following the process of how commemorative meanings congeal around such monuments offers a richer and perhaps more revealing picture of the play of hope and memory than does the

---

39. On party conflict at the urban level, see Reulecke, *Geschichte der Urbanisierung,* 133–39; on urban planning and public and private distinctions, see Ladd, *Urban Planning and Civic Order,* 249–50; on criticism of urban life, see Klaus Bergmann, *Agrarromantik und Großstadtfeindschaft* (Meisenheim am Glan, 1970); Reulecke, *Geschichte der Urbanisierung,* 139–46; and Andrew Lees, *Cities Perceived: Urban Society in European and American Thought, 1820–1940* (New York, 1985), 142–48.

40. A comparable argument may be found in Michael Brix, *Lübeck: Die Altstadt als Denkmal* (Munich, 1975), 5, which makes the case for seeing the architectural and urban fabric as an expression not only of "beauty" but also of "class conflicts, interest conflicts, and suffering."

41. For the political context and examples from the built environment as well as other areas, see Eric Hobsbawm, "Mass-Producing Traditions: Europe, 1870–1914," in *The Invention of Tradition,* ed. Eric Hobsbawm and Terence Ranger (Cambridge, 1983), 263–307; see also Nipperdey, "Nationalidee und Nationaldenkmal"; for types of intentional national monuments in Imperial Germany, see Helmut Scharf, *Kleine Kunstgeschichte des deutschen Denkmals* (Darmstadt, 1984), 207–66; for Alois Riegl, see Alois Riegl, "The Modern Cult of Monuments: Its Character and Its Origin," *Oppositions* 25 (Fall 1982): 20–57; originally published as "Der moderne Denkmalkultus: Sein Wesen und seine Entstehung," in *Gesammelte Aufsätze,* by Alois Riegl (Augsburg and Vienna, 1928); 1 quote from "The Modern Cult," 21. More broadly, on the scope of referents for national memory, see Pierre Nora, ed., *Les lieux de mémoire,* vol. 2, *La nation* (Paris, 1986), which deals only with France but is suggestive for any such discussion.

study of monuments that were begun with singular commemorative purposes in mind, although even in the case of intentional monuments, one can see new commemorative meanings arise and old ones fall away. In German-identified Central Europe, unintentional monuments had come to play an important role, having given rise to what Riegl said was a "cult of [unintentional] monuments."[42] Scholars of German and European political culture have devoted much less attention to these kinds of objects than to intentional monuments, perhaps because they mistakenly assume that studying the latter type substitutes for studying the greater variety and more complex diffusion of the former.

Unintentional monuments often owed their continued existence to the practice of historic preservation, which before the past two decades or so in western modernity, was conducted largely by middle-class males in the professions.[43] In Germany for the past century, city and state governments have played a big role in protecting a widening range of key landmarks. Although historic preservation in its modern form appeared first in the early nineteenth century as a response to the sense of rupture fostered by the French Revolution, the turn of the century was a key formative moment in the history of this mode of public memory. The appointment of the first provincial conservator of monuments by Prussia in the Rhineland in 1891 (Prussia as a whole had a conservator since 1843); the appearance in 1899 of *Die Denkmalpflege,* published by the Prussian state as Germany's first journal devoted entirely to historic preservation; and the holding of the first preservationist congress, the *Tag für Denkmalpflege,* in Dresden in 1900—all signaled the rise of new, more

---

42. For Riegl's definition of unintentional monuments, see "The Modern Cult," 23.

43. For historic preservation in the Anglo-American world, see David Lowenthal, *The Past Is a Foreign Country* (Cambridge, 1985), esp. chap. 7; Patrick Wright, *On Living in an Old Country: The National Past in Contemporary Britain* (London, 1985); and Charles Delheim, *The Face of the Past: The Preservation of the Medieval Inheritance in Victorian England* (Cambridge, 1982). The history of historic preservation in Germany has generated much literature but remains fragmentary and impressionistic. For information on its origins and development, see Peter Findeisen, *Geschichte der Denkmalpflege Sachsen-Anhalt: Von den Anfängen bis in das Erste Drittel des 20. Jahrhunderts* (Berlin-East, 1990); Norbert Huse, ed., *Denkmalpflege: Deutsche Texte aus drei Jahrhunderten* (Munich, 1984); Heinrich Magirius, *Geschichte der Denkmalpflege Sachsen: Von den Anfängen bis zum Neubeginn 1945* (Berlin-East, 1989); Ekkehard Mai and Stephan Wätzoldt, eds., *Kunstverwaltung, Bau- und Denkmalpolitik im Kaiserreich* (Berlin, 1981); Cord Meckseper and Harald Siebenmorgen, eds., *Die alte Stadt: Denkmal oder Lebensraum? Die Sicht der mittelalterlichen Stadtarchitektur im 19. und 20. Jahrhundert* (Göttingen, 1985); Stefan Muthesius, "The Origins of the German Conservation Movement," in *Planning for Conservation,* ed. Roger Kain (New York, 1980), 37–48; Uwe K. Paschke, *Die Idee des Stadtdenkmals* (Nuremberg, 1972); Rheinischer Verein für Denkmalpflege und Landschaftsschutz, ed., *Erhalten und Gestalten: 75 Jahre Rheinischer Verein für Denkmalpflege und Landschaftsschutz* (Neuss, 1981); and Michael Siegel, *Denkmalpflege als öffentliche Aufgabe: Eine ökonomische, institutionelle, und historische Untersuchung* (Göttingen, 1985).

organized efforts to protect architectural monuments.[44] The appearance in 1906 of regional associations, such as the Rheinischer Verein für Denkmalpflege und Heimatschutz, which was patronized by the Rhenish Bürgetum, furthered preservation's cause at the local level, where historical societies and beautification clubs added to the number of preexisting and newly formed voices advocating the protection of unintentional monuments.[45] The rise of nature preservation societies, some of which had close contacts to historic preservation groups, the mobilization of the *Heimatschutz* movement, and growing concern for aesthetic matters in urban planning also furthered the emphasis on saving such cultural resources. This activity found substantial support from the Kaiser, who praised lovingly preserved cities, such as Hildesheim, and who had close personal friends in preservationist circles.[46] But beyond the evidence for the importance of preservation to the *Kaiserreich* and the fact that it is a rarely studied phenomenon by students of political culture is an additional reason for discussing it: preservation is one of the activities that has redeemed the built environment of the *Kaiserreich,* in the sense that I used the term above, since roughly the late 1960s, when a new "cult of monuments" emerged in West Germany.[47]

I want to focus for a moment on two aspects of preservationist discourse: its attempt to make a contribution to a larger attempt to right the imbalance between hope and memory—in short, its placement in, and response to, a ruinous social and political environment—and its sense that this project ran the danger of becoming a ruin.

Historic preservation had a deeply political aspect. *Die Denkmalpflege* claimed that it promoted the saving of "documents of stone," with which the nation read its own history and took its place among "cultural nations," which protected heritage and tradition in the modern world. The Strasbourg art historian Georg Dehio, editor of the famous and still-used but now heavily edited

---

44. For a statement of *Die Denkmalpflege's* mission, see Otto Sarrazin and Oskar Hoßfeld, "Zur Einführung," *Die Denkmalpflege* 1 (4 Jan. 1899): 1–2. For the preservation congresses before World War I, aside from the full published stenographic reports themselves, see Adolf von Oechelhaeuser, ed., *Auszug aus den stenographischen Berichten des Tages für Denkmalpflege* (Leipzig, 1910–13).

45. On the founding and evolution of the Rhenish association before World War I, see Josef Ruland, "Kleine Chronik des Rheinischen Vereins für Denkmalpflege und Landschaftsschutz," in Rheinischer Verein, *Erhalten und Gestalten,* 13–19. The last word of the association's name, "Heimatschutz," was changed to "Landschaftsschutz" after a reorganization in 1970.

46. On Wilhelm II's praise of Hildesheim's preservation efforts, see the short notice under "Vermischtes," *Die Denkmalpflege* 2, no. 14 (7 Nov. 1900): 111. A close associate of the Kaiser was Bodo Ebhardt, architect, restorer of the Hohkönigsburg in Alsace in 1899–1908, and head of the Vereinigung zur Erhaltung Deutscher Burgen. See "Bodo Ebhardt," in *Neue deutsche Biographie* 4 (1957), 260–61.

47. See Bentmann, "Der Kampf um die Erinnerung."

Dehio handbooks of historic monuments begun before World War I, had stressed the nationalist functions of preservation in a speech before the Kaiser and other dignitaries in 1905, suggesting its importance as a way of tracing the German people's continuity through time.[48] This was a "historiographic politics" that tried to give the nation-state of the *Kaiserreich* deep roots in a cultural-national past that extended into the future.[49] At one level, it was a very superficial politics because it sought aesthetic solutions for deep social and political divisions. Yet various statements by preservationists suggest that there was a realization of the need for (if not a willingness to consider) thorough changes in the social and political texture of the age if documents of stone were to have an effect on national memory. Dehio's statement in the above-mentioned 1905 address is perhaps the most notable remark in this genre: he argued that the protection of landmarks led to "socialism" in the sense that it necessitated significant limits on economic liberalism.[50] Dehio was, of course, not the first *bürgerlich* thinker to endorse a socialism whose ideological referents were those of German nationalism rather than of Marxian internationalism. The point here, however, is that preservationists stated publicly their adherence to a national political agenda, in the broadest, cultural-national sense of the term. But in their published work, most preservationists avoided discussion of direct state-political issues, other than those directly affecting legislation pertinent to preservation interests; which is to say that they replicated a practice, associated with the identity of the German *Bürgertum*, of rhetorically disavowing political concerns. This absence was often eloquently present in the histories that preservationists told about the landmarks they protected; such narratives were usually stripped of the specific political and social conflicts of which they were a part.

Preservationist narratives favored preindustrial times. This emphasis was not a pure invention, since there were plenty of structures around that could make the distant past appear to be alive and well in the present. The pages of *Die Denkmalpflege* were filled with articles, photographs (almost always without human figures), and sketches on cathedrals, castles, city halls, and other

---

48. For the comment on "documents of stone" and the cultural nation, see Sarrazin and Hoßfeld, "Zur Einführung," 1. Dehio made the remarks before a royal audience in a speech at Strassbourg University on the occasion of Wilhelm II's birthday on 27 January 1905. See Georg Dehio, "Denkmalschutz und Denkmalpflege im neunzehnten Jahrhundert," reprinted in *Konservieren nicht restaurieren: Streitschriften zur Denkmalpflege um 1900,* ed. Marion Wohlleben (Braunschweig, 1988, 88–103). I refer to this reprint in the following.

49. I take the notion of historiographic politics from Jürgen Habermas, who uses it to critique West German neo-conservatism's narratives of continuity in the 1980s. See his "Historical Consciousness and Post-Traditional Identity: The Federal Republic's Orientation to the West," in *The New Conservatism: Cultural Criticism and the Historians' Debate,* by Jürgen Habermas (Cambridge, Mass., 1989), 249–67.

50. Dehio, "Denkmalschutz und Denkmalpflege," 92.

artifacts of premodern or early modern history. In the first decade of the twentieth century, groups like the Rheinischer Verein subsidized a limited range of preservation projects, most of them dealing with structures built before the nineteenth century and usually much before it.[51] But this distant past was in danger. Preservationists argued that historic landmarks were daily being chopped away by industrialization (although the worst period had been the fifteen years or so after national unification), the expansion of cities, and the inept cultural policy of the cities and states. Awareness of this destruction is one of the reasons why definitions of the monument began to take in more and more structures. Not only castles and cathedrals but also peasant and *Bürger* houses became worthy of preservation. Like the grander past of the great monuments, this more vernacular past reached deeply into the present, although it was said to have very ancient roots.

One of the leading representatives of historic preservation before World War I was the Bonn art historian Paul Clemen, the first conservator of monuments for the Prussian Rhine Province in 1891 and one of the leading advocates of preservation right up to his death in 1946.[52] Clemen was unusual in historic preservation because he combined in his career the practical work of the conservator, the historical research of the art historian, and (to a more limited extent) the literary-journalistic work of the cultural critic. He is best known outside the ranks of specialists for his 1933 publication, *Die Deutsche Kunst und die Denkmalpflege: Ein Bekenntis,* a collection of essays that combined remarks on preservation technologies with a mythic nationalism inspired in part by Stefan George and prefaced with praise of Hitler's publicly stated love for German heritage.[53]

Clemen was one of the forerunners in the preservation of Rhenish vernacular architecture as well as in the use of that architecture to inspire contemporary building design. To use Kevin Lynch's distinction, he had begun to make the move from simple preservation to conservation, "that is, toward an

---

51. For the period from 1906 to 1916, the Rheinischer Verein subsidized or directly undertook the restoration or preservation of 23 castles and medieval urban fortifications; 30 churches and other religious monuments; 54 city halls and Bürger houses; 60 "rural" monuments (mainly half-timber houses), and 43 miscellaneous items, including garden houses, fountains, and the like. See E. zur Nedden, "Geschäftsbericht für die Jahre 1906–1916," *Mitteilungen des Rheinischen Vereins für Denkmalpflege und Heimatschutz* (hereafter *MRVDH*) 10, no. 3 (November 1916): 275–322, esp. 293–98.

52. For Clemen, see Johannes Horion, "Paul Clemen und die Rheinlande," *Festschrift zum Sechzigsten Geburtstag von Paul Clemen* (Düsseldorf, 1926), 11–16; Albert Verbeek, "Paul Clemen (1866–1947)," *Rheinische Lebensbilder,* vol. 7, ed. Bernard Poll (Cologne, 1977), 181–201; and Hans Peter Hilger, "Paul Clemen und die Denkmäler-Inventarisation in den Rheinlanden," in Mai and Wätzoldt, *Kunstverwaltung, Bau- und Denkmalpolitik,* 383–98.

53. For Clemen's comments on Hitler, see the foreword to *Die Deutsche Kunst und die Denkmalpflege* (Berlin, 1933), vii.

attempt to manage change so as to maintain links with the past and to conserve resources which still have present value"[54]—although he emphasized the importance of conservation to primarily national goals. Like so many *bürgerlich* thinkers, he argued that local traditions of vernacular architecture fed into a larger narrative of national continuity. But both the local tradition and the national narrative were threatened. He argued in 1908 that medieval building styles had persisted in the Rhineland until some time into the late eighteenth and early nineteenth centuries, when industrialization and the decline of traditional artisanal skills cut off modern history from its medieval heritage. This brought the living tradition of such styles into Clemen's grandparents' lifetime. But the styles themselves were distinguished by their antiquity.[55]

In Clemen's view, the rupture of the lineage resulted in a situation in which the nineteenth century had no style at all but only styles. Even worse was the fact that the buildings of the nineteenth century lacked authenticity, the quality that John Ruskin (whom Clemen admired and studied) had said was essential to all good architecture.[56] This lack of authenticity revealed itself in a presumptuousness and ambition that suppressed the easy simplicity and dignity of earlier ages. "The main difference between the *bürgerlich*-small town and rural architecture of today and that of the past," Clemen said, "is precisely that the architecture of recent decades wanted to be more than it was; that it wanted to be refined was the most unrefined thing about it."[57] There was an implicit narrative of class in such discussions, as the small-town and rural building styles metaphorically referred to the rise of presumptuous social groups that failed to recognize their proper place, an issue that it is impossible to discuss in the present context. There was also a connection between preservationist discourse and Werkbund ideology, which likewise stressed the need for a new, dignified, and streamlined authenticity in all aspects of public-design culture.[58] But the main point here is that this kind of memory work could identify traces of a more authentic and unrefined past, one that was not contaminated by the ambitiousness and striving of the new age of capitalist growth and mobility or (and this I can only refer to in passing here) by the overblown monumentality of Wilhelmine public culture. The future suggested by this past was thus one of simplicity, a return to authenticity, and an overcoming of

---

54. Kevin Lynch, *Good City Form* (Cambridge, Mass., 1981), 452.

55. See the protocol of Clemen's address "Die überlieferte heimische Bauweise und ihr Wert für die heutige Architektur" at the 17 December 1908 Bonn conference "Herbeiführung einer besseren Bauweise in Stadt und Land," printed in *MRVDH* 3, no. 1 (1 March 1909): 26–29 (with the main points of Clemen's address printed on 11–13).

56. See Paul Clemen, *John Ruskin* (Leipzig, 1900).

57. Clemen, "Die überlieferte heimische Bauweise," 26.

58. See Joan Campbell, *The German Werkbund: The Politics of Reform in the Applied Arts* (Princeton, 1978); and G. B. von Hartmann and Wend Fischer, eds., *Zwischen Kunst und Industrie: Der Deutsche Werkbund* (Munich, 1975).

exaggerated expectations. And since the artifacts produced by such traditions worked as "documents of stone" for the nation, their endangered status signaled a national crisis.

Clemen's perspective was neither unique nor particularly well crafted in comparison with cognate statements of cultural crisis in Germany in this period. Many German intellectuals bemoaned the loss of tradition and authenticity in the *Kaiserreich,* and many of them mourned more compellingly than Clemen did. Early-nineteenth-century cultural critics as well as Friedrich Nietzsche had prepared the way for this kind of mourning, although Nietzsche in particular offered radical, all-encompassing, and bitterly ironic responses to the sense of loss that more cautious minds were unable or unwilling to comprehend. For many thinkers, awareness of what the *Kaiserreich* had lost resulted in nostalgia, as I argued above. But it is worth reemphasizing that scholars who have pinpointed this elegiac strand in *Kaiserreich* political culture have too often stressed its pessimistic side. Like many other cultural commentators of the period—and unlike some of the better-known cultural critics of the age—Clemen was not desperate; he felt the situation could be changed. He advocated careful preservation of buildings that typified the four main Rhenish architectural styles for "petit-bourgeois [kleinbürgerlich] and rural forms of building," the lower Rhenish brick house, the black-white-green "Bergisch" house, the stone house of the Aachen-Limburg region, and the various versions of the Rhein-Mosel half-timber house. Preservation of such structures would provide models for contemporary architects, artists, building foremen and construction workers, and skilled artisans, giving them the chance of a "resumption" (Wiederanknüpfung) of local traditions.[59] The link between local and national narratives would thus be reclaimed.

But using these models would not mean simple copying. Taking his cue from the emerging discourse of modernism, Clemen argued that the form and spirit of the old styles was what architects and builders should aim for, not the actual content. There should be no attempt at "the galvanization of a cadaver."[60] For Clemen, protecting historic landmarks as never-to-be-duplicated models for the present and future was a way of attacking the imbalance between hope and memory that shaped the modern age and threatened the sense of continuous national time. The built environment of the national political future would be molded according to the form or morphology of the built environment of distant, local pasts, such as those exhibited in the Rhenish houses. The loss of tradition in the present would be counterbalanced with a new but always adaptive reliance on the localized micromemories that some-

---

59. Clemen, "Die überlieferte heimische Bauweise," 28.

60. Ibid., 27. For a discussion of this approach to the past among modernist architects in Germany in the period before World War I, see Lane, *Architecture and Politics,* 11–27.

how added up to the nation. The extravagance of hope in the contemporary age would be tempered in an ongoing adoration and adaptation of remembered futures. Preservation would not produce ruins for the political culture, at least not in the sense that monuments of national and regional memory would become bare shells of hollowed-out meaning. Instead, favored monuments would avoid such destructiveness by being preserved carefully and engaged constructively in the flow of historical time. Their past futures would not be eviscerated by a ruinous present.

I noted before that the attempt to offer aesthetic solutions to social problems was superficial. But there was a harder, more self-critical side to preservation that recognized the limitations of such activity and called for broader solutions; we are reminded again of Dehio's remark on preservationist "socialism." But if preservation had a limited but important role to play in such endeavors, Clemen himself would admit that it had not played even this limited role satisfactorily. Clemen's views on where preservation had been and where it was going right before World War I suggest that he felt that historic preservation as a discourse was in danger of becoming (or had already become) a ruin. At his 1911 address in Salzburg at the annual preservation congress—the first congress to bring together preservationists and representatives of the developing *Heimatschutz* movement—Clemen pinpointed preservation's shortcomings by giving what he called a *"Gewissensprüfung,"* a critical self-examination.[61] This was necessary because, Clemen argued, the movement to protect historic buildings had entered a crucial period, and it was time to take stock of the previous decade before moving ahead to consolidate past gains and prepare for future victories.

Clemen said that much had been accomplished. Preservationism had continued Germany's tradition of regional memories by avoiding what Clemen saw as the potential disaster of all-encompassing national preservation legislation, relying instead on the variety of individual states' laws. Historic preservation had an increasing popularity and widened vision, thanks in part to its alliance with *Heimatschutz*. It emphasized more than ever before the protection of vernacular architecture. It was determined to be open to the influence of "living art," partly because of the influence of people such as Clemen himself within the movement. It had made a substantial assault on the practice of prettying the past by stressing the importance of conserving historic buildings more or less as they had been handed down to the present rather than restoring them to a point of presumed stylistic purity.

---

61. Clemen made his comments in a session entitled "Entwickelung und Ziele der Denkmalpflege in Deutschland und Österreich." The cospeaker was the Viennese conservator Max Dvorak. See *Gemeinsame Tagung für Denkmalpflege und Heimatschutz in Salzburg 1911: Stenographischer Bericht* (Berlin, 1911), 51–64. All page references are to this publication. A revised version of this talk was published in Clemen, *Die Deutsche Kunst und die Denkmalpflege,* 64–72.

Yet Clemen warned against undue optimism. He said that large parts of the population remained immune or hostile to the preservation message, furthering a well-established *bildungsbürgerlich* trope in which the German people appeared to be incapable of appreciating the past that intellectuals such as Clemen were trying to give them. Legislation had not yet assured that local communities would act to protect as many historic buildings as they should. Indeed, Prussian legislation of 1907 had proved to rest on what Clemen called a "heroic error" that allowed cities too much autonomy in protecting monuments. They had used this autonomy not to bring more historic buildings under protection but to avoid more aggressive and therefore more costly preservation laws and strategies.[62] The traces of purist historicism remained, and conservation had not yet won out over restoration, as the numerous articles on the rebuilding and reconstruction of castles and other historic landmarks in *Die Denkmalpflege* suggested. This led to the possibility that historic monuments became not the sites of political futures based on memory but rather dead, restored monuments, unconnected to the vital "life" swirling around them and thus unable to negotiate the difficult path between experience and expectation. The implication was that preservationism was threatened by the very ghoulishness that had led Nietzsche to criticize the work of "antiquarians and gravediggers" who too slavishly worshiped the past.[63]

Commenting further on the issue of restoration, Clemen recalled that Dehio had said in 1905 that restorationism would "be put back to bed" once a vigorous contemporary artistic language was found. Clemen saw this language in the nascent architectural modernism of the *Kaiserreich:* "May we not say that we have this clear and coherent architectural vision, if only we will acknowledge it?"[64] This seemed especially evident in the Kingdom of Saxony, Clemen's birthplace, where renovators of the Freiberg cathedral had invited four important contemporary architects, Bruno Schmitz, Julius Wilhelm Graebner, Wilhelm Kreis, and Theodor Fischer, to submit plans. This risky but necessary move made it possible to restore monuments by using current artistic forms rather than strictly historic ones, which were impossible to reproduce in the present. Clemen congratulated such efforts: was this not exactly the kind of thing that German historic preservation should be doing, to think of itself as "a branch of a coherent and indivisible contemporary artistic culture"?[65] If this does not happen, if the artist or architect does not have a way of being creative with historic buildings while also respecting "that which has become [das

---

62. Clemen, "Entwickelung und Ziele," 56.

63. Clemen's warnings appear in ibid., 61–64; for Nietzsche, see his 1874 essay "On the Uses and Disadvantages of History for Life," in *Untimely Meditations,* ed. Friedrich Nietzsche (Cambridge, 1983), 104.

64. Clemen, "Entwickelung und Ziele," 63.

65. Ibid., 64.

Gewordene]," then preservationism will be in danger of "being thrown from the onrushing wagon of contemporary art and run over."[66] Clemen said he had faith that this would not happen. But the metaphor of being thrown from the wagon revealed a deep anxiety about falling out of step with contemporary culture. Clemen feared that preservationism, like the historicism from which it sprang, would be a living ruin. It would not disappear, but it would, again like historicism, become a prospering artifact with little relevance to the difficult project of bringing hope and memory in line. It would, in short, be stripped of its original intentions before its full potential had been realized, suddenly made impotent at the moment that it crystallized as a cultural-political force, suddenly made a ruin as it endeavored to protect monuments from becoming ruins.

The subsequent history of preservation demonstrates that Clemen's fears were well founded. The protection of historic buildings had become a ruin in later periods if it was not already one when Clemen spoke at Salzburg in 1911. Historic preservation gained much from the Weimar Republic's grounding of heritage conservation in the Weimar Constitution and even more from Hitler's public adoration of historic landmarks. Nonetheless, in both regimes, historic preservationists never gained the systematic purchase on contemporary public culture that they hoped to have, relying instead on a position of what might be called privileged marginality. This privileged marginality was used for quite different political purposes in each period; arguments of continuity in historic preservation must be heavily qualified with reference to such changing political contexts. In addition, there is much evidence that in the Nazi dictatorship preservationists used their marginality to defend themselves against the regime's total occupation of the field of historic landmarks; organizing a discursive ruin could have advantages.[67] In the decades of rebuilding after World War II, historic preservation retained a circumscribed voice in the cultural policy of the Federal Republic, allowing an array of restored, fictionalized, and conserved monuments to withstand the unprecedented destruction of the economic miracle. But it was only in the 1970s that preservation achieved some of the goals that people such as Clemen envisioned—wide popularity, systematic concern for vernacular architecture, coordination of preservation with urban and economic planning. But it did so only under conditions in which national memory had become—depending on one's perspective—more dependent on restoration and copying of monuments, more abstract, more oriented to social rather than national concerns, more commercialized, more forgetful of tradition as such, and more challenged due to the mobilization of alternative projects, such as citizens' initiatives and history workshops. It is part of the

---

66. Ibid.

67. Rudy Koshar, "Altar, Stage, and City: Historic Preservation and Urban Meaning in Nazi Germany," *History & Memory* 3, no. 1 (Spring 1991): 30–59.

logic of the ruin that things and processes are hollowed out only to acquire uses and meanings that they were never intended to have. By the 1970s, some conservators argued that not too little but too much historic architecture was being saved.

Provisional Conclusions

These brief remarks need much more substantiation and development. But they have enough meat on them to lead to a provisional conclusion about the implications of the metaphor of the ruin for studying the political culture of the *Kaiserreich*. The metaphor presupposes that ruins, as things and processes, emerge because continuities are eviscerated. The devaluation of wish images of the future by the present results in the rapid formation of new meanings, new wish images dependent on pasts to envision a future. The play of hope and memory within political culture thus has a kind of circularity when it is discussed with reference to ruins; whatever repeats itself does so in rapidly altered contexts in which new futures generate new pasts. How rapidly such contexts may change—that is, what the particular chronology of the making of ruins might be, and whether this chronology is altered according to the rapidity of historical change in any given time period—has not been specified here.

Following this logic, emplotments of the *Kaiserreich*'s history that depend on the imagery of the ruin work most evocatively when they emphasize discontinuity. The already mentioned emplotment of Imperial Germany as a satirical tragedy has precisely this emphasis. This emplotment—based on a vision of somber reconciliation of historical conflicts, a skeptical championing of human agency, and a doubt-filled epistemology—has an ambience of thwarted possibility. This ambience relies on narratives in which the intentions of historical actors, whether those of dominant or subordinate classes, are subverted, suppressed, or realized under conditions that are entirely unexpected. There are many such narratives for Imperial Germany, whose historical specificity, from my point of view, is that its political culture generated more ruins, more objects and processes with rapidly eviscerated futures and pasts, than any previous or subsequent period of German history.

In this sense, the *Kaiserreich*'s hopefully skeptical adjudications between hope and memory—illustrated here with an abbreviated example from the discourse of historic preservation—appear not to point forward in any direct way to World War I, the Weimar Republic, or the National Socialist dictatorship. Instead, they suggest the unpredictable uses to which they were put in subsequent periods. Even if it is shown that German speakers and audiences of later eras used a language of transience similar to that of the *Kaiserreich,* it would be crucial to point out that this language was always deployed in novel and unanticipated political contexts. In World War I the *Kaiserreich*'s imagined futures were constricted by militarist expansion and unprecedented war, in the Weimar Republic by political polarization, in the Nazi dictatorship by the repression and annihilation of all wish images that did not suit the regime, and in the now concluded postwar era by the division of German pasts and futures into irreconcilable political systems. Benjaminian imagery of the ruin leaves the continuity/discontinuity trope shattered, leaving only the discontinuity of contending hopes and memories as the most compelling provisional narrative of the *Kaiserreich*'s placement in German history.

I began this essay with a critique of two historiographical approaches to discontinuity, one associated with the narrative of an exemplary *Sonderweg*, which pinpointed differences between the National Socialist era and the *Kaiserreich*, the other with an argument of the Federal Republic's achieved distance from Nazism. My argument is that the theme of discontinuity should be generalized to all German histories of the nineteenth and twentieth centuries. Nonetheless, my account potentially instantiates another continuity, one that rests on the fact that Germany's "heritage is not one of solutions, but ultimately one of open questions."[68] Modern German political cultures have rejected, embraced, or ignored this "historical continuity of disjunctures," to use Walter Grasskamp's phrase, but they have also searched for counterbalancing tendencies in culture, society, or politics that denied the possibility of leaving open questions open. If a narrative of continuity bleeds back into my story, then it is this collective denial, this political-cultural inability to walk away from the broken promise of a clearly resolved past and future, that constitutes its main theme. No more barbarous denial could be found than the National Socialist regime, which steeled itself against the instabilities of German history by proclaiming a thousand-year prohibition on all unresolved questions of political identity. Drawn through the provisional filter of recent theoretical debates, my discussion thus reconnects, eventually and unavoidably, to the problem of the origins of Nazism and its relationship with German history as a whole.

---

68. Walter Grasskamp, "A Historical Continuity of Disjunctures," in *The Divided Heritage: Themes and Problems in German Modernism,* ed. Irit Rogoff (Cambridge and New York, 1991), 23.

Contributors

David Blackbourn is Professor of History and Senior Associate of the Center for European Studies, Harvard University.

Kathleen Canning is Associate Professor of History, University of Michigan.

David Crew is Associate Professor of History, University of Texas at Austin.

Belinda Davis is Assistant Professor of History, Rutgers University.

Elisabeth Domansky is Assistant Professor of History, Indiana University.

Geoff Eley is Professor of History, University of Michigan.

Young-Sun Hong is Assistant Professor of History, State University of New York at Stony Brook.

Rudy Koshar is Professor of History, University of Wisconsin-Madison.

M. J. Maynes is Professor of History, University of Minnesota.

Jean H. Quataert is Professor of History and Vice-Chair for Graduate Studies, State University of New York at Binghamton.

James Retallack is Associate Professor of History, University of Toronto.

Willfried Spohn is Adjunct Professor at the Institute of Sociology, Free University of Berlin, and Lecturer in the Department of Sociology, University of Pennsylvania.

George Steinmetz is Associate Professor of Sociology, University of Chicago.

Frank Trommler is Professor of German and Comparative Literature, University of Pennsylvania.

Lora Wildenthal is Assistant Professor of History, Pitzer College.

Index

515